THE GREAT VINTAGE WINE BOOK

by Michael Broadbent

ALFRED A. KNOPF NEW YORK 1981

This book is dedicated to the growers and wine makers who take all the risks and produce fine wines for us to enjoy.

P R E F A C E

This book is about vintages: what they are, how they vary and why. It is also about time: what happens to wine as it ages, whether the wine of recent vintages is ready for drinking and how long it will last. Older wines are evaluated — are they nicely mature or over the hill? For the curious and for those lucky enough to possess a few rarities, I have outlined what the great classic vintages of old were like and if and why they have survived.

Vintage appraisals are supported by tasting notes selected to illustrate the style and quality of the wines made in a particular district in a given year. As far as mere words will allow, I have tried to describe what a wine was like and what it actually tastes like now. These notes will, I hope, give the reader an indication of the nature and comparative quality of individual wines and, cumulatively, the style and standing of certain châteaux, domaines, shippers and merchants. But the book is not a gazetteer, it cannot claim to be comprehensive, and my purpose is not merely to criticize but to stimulate interest. Moreover, it is quite definitely not a guide to run-of-the-mill wines, which are best drunk quickly and as quickly best forgotten. Indeed, my first considered title — *In Praise of Fine Wine* — might be taken as its text.

Tasting wine is highly subjective. In the end it is simply what you and I like that matters. If I have the temerity to inflict my own personal assessments and opinions on the reader, it is not to lay down the law but to share nearly 30 years' experience of tasting, discussing and, of course, drinking wine. Wine stimulates conversation; what better subject for good conversation than good wine. All are at liberty to argue and disagree. At least we can enjoy comparing notes.

Editor Rachel Grenfell
Art Editor Rozelle Bentheim
Assistant Editor Gillian Abrahams
Production Peter Phillips
Executive Editor Alexandra Towle

Index Naomi Good
Illustrations Philip Thompson
Photographs Geoff Smith

Edited and designed by
Mitchell Beazley Publishers,
87–89 Shaftesbury Avenue,
London W1V 7AD

Filmsetting and color printing by
Jolly & Barber Limited
Rugby, England

Text printed and the book bound
by Morrison & Gibb Ltd.,
Edinburgh, Scotland
2 3 4 5 6 7 8 9 10

Library of Congress Cataloging in
Publication Data

Broadbent, Michael
The Great Vintage Wine Book
1. Wine and wine making. I. Title.
TP548.B85 1980 641.2'22 80–7622
ISBN 0–394–51099–2

CONTENTS

INTRODUCTION

I am an inveterate note maker and cuttings collector. For the whole of the time I have been in the trade I have systematically noted and indexed every wine I have tasted and drunk; and over roughly the same period I have extracted reports of weather and market conditions from a variety of sources.

Then, starting with the first edition of *Christie's Wine Review* in 1972, under the somewhat ponderous heading "Chronology and Vintage Notes", I compiled a series of tables summarizing briefly the quality and quantity of wine made each year over a period of a century or so, dealing with different wine areas and wine types in successive issues. I began to assemble this material in one volume, extending the time scale to include the earliest recorded vintages, adding more detail and bringing the tables up to date. As I frequently referred to my own tasting notes to see if old vintages were still enjoyable — and saleable — it seemed a logical progression to include them.

But it was not until the indexed notes in my tasting books had passed the 30,000 level that I seriously wondered whether there was some way in which they could be used: to see if I could convey in words some of the fascination of fine wines, to provide a basis of comparison, and to give others the benefit, if it were possible, of using the information so laboriously built up.

To put my notes in perspective, I cannot remotely claim to have tasted more wines than anyone else. There are *négociants* in Bordeaux, merchants in Beaune, tasters in Vila Nova de Gaia and specialist shippers of German wines who have tasted infinitely more claret, burgundy, port and hock. Nor do I imagine that I am a better taster, for I have a healthy respect for the real professionals in the trade and know amateurs whose refinement of palate and memory — those two supreme factors — are vastly superior to my own. What I *can* say is that I have been exposed to the widest range of wines and vintages that it is possible to imagine, from the most ordinary to the finest and rarest, from the youngest just tastable to the oldest just drinkable; and that the consistency with which they have been noted might allow me to present and others to draw some valid conclusions.

As this book is rather personal, I feel I owe it to the reader to explain something of the background against which I learned and have practised my craft.

I had no family wine-trade connections and we were not a particularly wine-minded family. My first introduction to fine wine was in the late 1940s and early 1950s through a family friend and neighbour in Cheshire, Dr Thomas Kerfoot — a man of means and of great taste. I remember drinking Yquem, I think it was a '37, with ripe nectarines, on his terrace after dinner one warm summer evening; and I would dine with the doctor and his wife in London from time to time. I recall first drinking Lafite with them. I also remember buying a bottle of Ausone '37 at John Marks, then the Fortnum & Mason of Manchester, and taking it home for a special dinner one night. Of course it was thoroughly shaken up and I was a little disappointed. But these were the beginnings.

Entering the wine trade was quite fortuitous. I have now reached the age when I can openly admit that the reason I gave up architecture was that I failed too many exams. In fact, I can think of no one who enjoyed a longer period of education to less effect. I attended various boarding schools from the age of six and a half and later spent five years at university broken only by a two and a half year spell in the army immediately after the war. At the age of 25 I had to pull myself together.

My mother, who was an avid reader of André Simon, John Fothergill, T. A. Layton and others, one day saw an advertisement in *The Times* for a wine trainee. I applied. It was some years later that I learned that Tommy Layton had taken me on purely on the strength of my handwriting, which was then of an Italianate architectural style. I would not be taken on for that reason today.

Tommy Layton was more or less a one-man band. In 1952, when I joined him, he had a flourishing restaurant, a wine bar and a retail business. He edited *Wine* magazine and ran the Circle of Wine Tasters, which his cheeky staff nicknamed Circle of Wine Wasters. It was a change to get down to work and I enjoyed everything, from literally sweeping the cellars to taking and typing orders and driving the delivery van. I met many keen amateurs and wine shippers and learned a lot. Starting from scratch in a business then quite liberally sprinkled with young men born into the trade, and with the new post-war professionals well dug in by the early 1950s, I had a lot of catching up to do. Like many a convert I was keen and I did what I advise all newcomers to do: to read as much about the subject as possible and not to miss any opportunity to taste.

From the outset I started to make tasting notes in a particular sort of book in a particular sort of way. The first entry, a Graacher of Deinhard, was made on 17 September, 1952. It took 12 years to reach volume 10. (I am now halfway through book 43.)

If not exactly an amiable eccentric, Tommy Layton was certainly an imaginative and brilliant one. With him I tasted shippers' samples, selected wines for his list and the Wine Circle tastings and became familiar with his stock-in-trade.

After a year, in September 1953, I left on a busman's holiday with a sheaf of introductions, travelling in a way no longer possible, with empty port pipes by boat to Oporto. I sailed on the *Seamew* down one river, the Thames, and up another, the Douro. The British community in Vila Nova de Gaia were hospitable and I did a lot of tasting in various firms' lodges, travelling a month later by train and bus to Jerez to do the same in sherry bodegas.

My next major move was also fortuitous. In Gibraltar, waiting for a ship to bring me home, I was introduced to the chairman of Saccone & Speed, who in turn gave me a letter to the head of his London office. I started work in Sackville Street, learning the carriage-trade business from Peter Lyons and tasting regularly with Sir Guy Fison, the buyer. Guy has one of the finest palates in the English trade and we still taste regularly at meetings of the III Form Club.

Saccone's were traditional suppliers to officers' messes, but they had absorbed the old West End wine merchants Hankey Bannister and had a remarkably fine list of mature wines, all of which I got round to tasting. I also helped to select more youthful follow-ons. Around this time I started a tasting club for young contemporaries which included Colin Fenton, then at Harvey's, Dick Bridgeman and Freddie Price, both juniors and now both directors respectively of Justerini & Brooks and Dolamore's. Our after-hours tastings were what are now known as "vertical" and "horizontal": the first type being different vintages of the same wine and the second, wines from different vineyards but of the same vintage. Quite the best way to learn.

In 1955 an opportunity arose to join Harvey's of Bristol. After an induction period in the Denmark Street offices and cellars I returned to London, where I found myself under the wing of Harry Waugh. Harry's kindness and enthusiasm is legendary. He is also a great taster with that rare ability to spot a winner, whether it is a youthful beaujolais in the vat, an obscure Pomerol or a raw young médoc in cask. I was fortunate enough to go on one or two tasting trips with him, including an unforgettable tour of Champagne, Alsace, Burgundy and Bordeaux.

"Set a thief to catch a thief": presumably Harvey's had this in mind when in 1956 they posted me to a newly acquired firm in Manchester. As it happens, I rather enjoyed re-creating the Harvey St James's Square image in Cross Street (it was the first time I actually employed my architectural talents) and selling fine wine to fellow northerners.

I passed the Master of Wine examinations in 1960 and from that period started lecturing regularly and writing monthly articles on wine for *Cheshire Life*. Holidays were all spent in wine districts. In 1961 I was transferred to Bristol for a central administration and marketing job. I joined the table-wine buying committee and was put in charge of the weekly tastings for Head Office staff. It was for the latter that I wrote, more or less at one sitting (I find writing infinitely more laborious now), a pamphlet entitled "Guidance in the Technique of Tasting", which was subsequently published by a wine trade journal and then expanded into *Wine Tasting*.

Perhaps the most enjoyably creative period of my Harvey days was a rather specialized sort of retailing. Starting in 1962 with two Harvey shops in department stores, I was given the responsibility of negotiating sites, organizing licence applications (difficult in those days), planning and manning these small, high quality wine outlets. I had an excellent team, with Jimmie Duggan as sales manager and Bruce Wilson in charge of administration. In three years we built up over 20 Harvey's of Bristol "shops within shops", from the West Country to Wales and even in Scotland.

It was a period of much committee work: the Wine Merchants' Union, the Multiple Wine Merchants' Association, the Supermarket Association (Harvey's were the only firm in the wine trade to be represented — very far-sighted), the M.W. education committee and several others. But the further I moved up the Harvey ladder the more remote wine seemed to become.

I heard a rumour that Christie's were thinking of restarting wine auctions and I wrote to the chairman. At the time I was in charge of Harvey's United Kingdom sales force and had been a director of the main trading company for some years. To cut a long story short, the summer of 1966 saw me sitting in an empty office in charge of a non-existent department planning my first season of sales. Out of the blue came Alan Taylor-Restell, who decided that it was better to join forces than compete. He brought with him the solid technical background of a third-generation City wine auctioneer and left me free to develop hitherto parochial sales into the present international operation.

I was where I wanted to be, dealing with clients, from dukes to dustmen, and with wine, from pre-phylloxera claret to bin ends. It has involved much travel, dinners, tastings and dirty work in old cellars — and has been fun, if exhausting.

Above all, I have had the opportunity to explore and write about the world of wine, and to taste the finest and rarest of wines in fascinating company.

How to use this book
The book is divided into sections, the major types of wine being arranged in this order: red bordeaux (claret), white bordeaux, red burgundy, white burgundy, German wines (hock and moselle), champagne, vintage port, madeira, tokay, sherry and other fortified wines, California and Australian wines. Within each major section the vintages are arranged in double columns pre-1945, and in larger type and expanded format from 1945 to the present day. Every vintage has been given a star rating, the weather variations have been noted and the overall quality summarized. The individual wines are arranged in alphabetical order within vintages, first-growth claret and Yquem taking precedence in the case of red and white Bordeaux. The name of the wine is followed by the district or grower, as appropriate.

To find out whether a note appears on a particular wine, look it up in the index. Alongside will be a list of the vintages tasted and the page on which the note appears.

Tasting notes
The tasting notes are generally divided into three parts: the appearance of the wine,

its nose and its taste (each separated by a semicolon). These notes are followed by the tasting date, the individual star rating and, in respect of younger wines, when these wines are likely to be at their best.

Star ratings

However carefully and impartially applied, any system of classification is likely to be contentious. After considering numerical ratings such as the 0–7 scale on the International Wine & Food Society vintage chart, 0–10, 0–20 (quite commonly used at comparative tastings), a straight percentage, or perhaps even a Michelin-type three rosette grading for just the finer wines, I decided on a simple five-star system.

The reasons for not using a broad numerical scale are manifold: it is possible to give 18/20, for example, to a fourth-growth claret tasted in the context of other wines of the same class, yet only 14/20 if tasted with first growths; also, a good wine might be marked 17/20 on one occasion, and one of similar class and age only 15/20 a year or so later. It is not only unfair, it is really quite impossible to work to a hypothetically pure standard of quality. In any case it would be impertinent of me to set myself up as the supreme arbiter. What I seek to do is to give broad guidance and an approximation of overall quality, and for this I think a five-star rating is the most helpful and the least misleading. Thus:

*****	Outstanding quality
****	Very good
***	Good
**	Quite good
*	Fair, average, acceptable
No stars	Poor

The values apply equally to the quality of a vintage or of an individual wine. However, in the case of each vintage the rating refers to its pristine quality, which in turn was determined by the weather conditions leading up to that year's harvest and the general success and reputation of the wine made. In the case of the wines, the stars generally refer to the quality and condition of the wine when last tasted.

For those wines that are still immature I have given some indication of what they are like to drink now, and their potential.

For example:

*(***)	Very immature, a bit of a raw mouthful but considerable potential: probably very good when mature, i.e. * for drinking now, **** in due course.
***(**)	Not fully mature but good to drink now. Possibly outstanding when fully developed.

When to drink?

It can be reasonably assumed that wines of vintages prior to 1945 are now fully mature. The likely or actual state of development of old vintages and specific wines are referred to in the text.

In the case of more recent vintages, the optimum time to drink has been indicated. For example, "Drink 1990 — 2000" means immature now (in the year of publication), but by inference a quality wine, probably reaching its plateau of maturity in 1990 and starting to decline ten years later. This does not mean that the wine cannot be drunk with enjoyment before 1990, or that it will be undrinkably over the hill immediately after the year 2000. Some people like red wines young, fruity and robust; others prefer them older, softer and more delicate. It is a matter of taste. "Drink now — 1985" indicates that the wine is already mature but has probably another five years at its peak before it starts to fade.

Finally, please note that these are not hard and fast assessments; they are a rough guide based on the general quality of the vintage and its pedigree, the particular vineyard and the known standard of wine making.

Sources and acknowledgements

I have adapted vintage ratings from the charts I prepared for various editions of *Christie's Wine Review* and these in turn were based on miscellaneous cuttings, old wine-trade journals and material supplied at one time or another by friends in the trade, acknowledged at the time of publication.

Weather reports relating to the past 20 years have been culled from cuttings, in particular from *Harpers Wine and Spirit Gazette, Wine & Spirit*, and *Revue du Vin de France*, for which I have to thank publishers, editors and their correspondents. Prior to 1930, notes of weather conditions have mainly been extracted from a complete run of *Ridley's Circular* from 1846 to 1929. Summaries were most kindly vetted by Michael Symington in Oporto and Geoffroy de Luze in Bordeaux, with some gaps in the burgundy section filled by Claude Bouchard and Louis Latour.

The tasting notes are first hand and have been extracted from my own detailed records dating from 1952, with the exception of a brief quotation or two in the nineteenth-century sections and some examples of Harry Waugh's particular flair in the mid-1950s. All opinions, assessments and conclusions are my own.

I owe an enormous debt of gratitude to many people. Though some individuals and firms are mentioned in the main text it is simply not possible to name every grower who has let me taste his wine, every wine shipper and merchant who has invited me to lunches and tastings, every private collector who has shared a treasure. I have in fact listed a large number of generous friends in the last three editions of my book *Wine Tasting*, and I refer to the principal tasting clubs and some really outstanding tasting events at the end of this book. To the rest I say thank you. Although hospitality has not all been one way, I know I have been on the receiving end more than somewhat. I just hope that I have ploughed back, through the written word and educational activities, a little of what I have gained from the hospitable cellars and tables of others.

In the preparation of this book I particularly want to thank Patrick Matthews for patiently researching more than 40 volumes of hand-written notes, indexing those not already in vintage order, and for extracting weather reports from my cuttings and reference books; Rachel Grenfell and Gilly Abrahams of Mitchell Beazley for meticulous editing; Rozelle Bentheim for coping with tricky layouts and design and for help with the impossible task of trying to turn a glass of wine into a two-dimensional blob of colour on a piece of white paper; and my secretary Rosemary Ward for some last-minute patching and retyping. Last but not least I should like to thank my wife Daphne, not only for putting up with my obsession with wine for over 25 years and sharing wine holidays (in varying degrees of comfort, including more than 1,000 miles on the pillion of a motor scooter to the Moselle and back, one wet and dismal fortnight in June 1956), but also for helping to pack old wines in cold, dank and dirty cellars and lastly, for typing and endlessly retyping all my manuscripts for this book. She has earned a seaside holiday this year.

ON TASTING

The most important duty of wine is to be pleasant. The highest aspiration of most wines is to be tolerably agreeable and moderately drinkable.

Good wines are made from sound grapes by competent wine makers. They have flavour and character derived from the grape variety and soil type. Climate is important, but therein lies a great variable. Louis Latour wrote recently in *Wine World*: "I must remind all Burgundy drinkers that *the vintage* [his italics] is the most important factor for our business." And I would add that the greatest single influence on the character and quality of a vintage is the weather. This is the variable. This is what makes vintage wines endlessly fascinating.

Paul de Cassagnac wrote: "A perfect wine should be tasted sympathetically not analytically." But there are few perfect wines and few people with Cassagnac's sensitivity and understanding. However, most of us are blessed with sight, a sense of smell and taste, and it is just a matter of applying these senses to wine. There is a natural sequence; observe the wine, "nose" it, then taste it.

What to look for

It was also Cassagnac who said, somewhat ambiguously: "There is nothing like beauty to quicken the senses." He was doubtless referring to the rich ruby *robe* of a fine young burgundy, the gleaming topaz shot with gold of a mature Sauternes. There is no doubt about it, the colour of a fine wine craves attention, demands that the glass should be raised and the wine appreciated.

But there is more to it than that. The appearance of wine, its depth and its hue, varies enormously and significantly. The colour plates give some idea, as do my notes. Basically, red wine is deep and purple when young and gradually loses colour as it matures, the stage of maturity being indicated by the actual colour or hue at the rim: first ruby then red, brick red, mahogany tinged, finally old amber.

Dry white wines have a much more limited spectrum, ranging from almost colourlessness, through pale shades of straw yellow, sometimes green tinged, to a rather bright, positive, almost buttery yellow. The finest dry whites attain a golden hue with age. As white wine almost inevitably shades off to a watery rim, the colour, or lack of it, at the meniscus has no significance.

Sweet, natural dessert wines start off a deeper yellow, soon become a golden colour and with age deepen to what I describe as old gold — the colour of tarnished brass buttons. Eventually they become dull and brown.

Fortified wines have their own colour range. Sherry, a white wine, is basically pale yellow; most of the darkening is due to the addition of "color" wine.

Vintage port is essentially a red wine and follows red wine colour changes. For madeira refer to the colour pages.

The light source is important. As all artists know, a north light is the least distorting. Failing this, a high level of ordinary tungsten lighting is, I think, best for a tasting room. Blue fluorescent light deadens the colour of red; candles make all colours more appealing, but candlelight alone makes it difficult to judge the actual hue and maturity; and, of course, coloured wine glasses make this impossible. Tasting benches or tables should be white — alternatively use a cloth or paper to give the glass a white background.

To observe the depth of colour leave the glass standing on the table and look directly down on it or across, at roughly a 45° angle. For the hue, pick up the glass by the stem and tilt it over a white background, noting the gradation of the wine from the bowl to the rim. It is towards the edge that the vital shade of maturity can be seen. If you hold a glass of a different wine in the other hand and compare the two, the colour values will be that much more apparent.

Next, with its base on the table, rotate the glass and note the way the beads, tears or legs (no matter what they are called) form and ease down the sides of the glass. Light wines just wash down; rich wines, fine wines with high extract (see glossary for this and other tasting terms) form distinctly heavy globules, which take time to sink down to join the body of the wine.

Lastly clarity. Hold the glass up to any light source: the wine should be clear and bright. Really fine white wines seem to have a greater sheen, an extra dimension. Cloudiness in white wines usually signifies a fault; in red it might just indicate that the wine needs decanting.

If I tend to stress — some might say over-stress — the appearance and nose of wine, it is because these, in my experience, are the least appreciated elements of tasting.

Nose or bouquet
The sense of smell is the most primitive and evocative of our senses. In relation to wine it is immensely important yet the most difficult to understand and to communicate.

The word "smell" is somewhat redolent of drains and bad cabbages, so wine men generally refer to the nose of, or nosing, a wine. Bouquet is also sweepingly applied but, as with aroma, has special connotations (see glossary). Bouquet is in fact a charmingly appropriate expression: it evokes a posy of tiny individual scents and fragrances.

The mechanics first. I always recommend repeating the action described in reference to "legs": keep the base on the table, lightly grip the stem and rotate so that the whole of the inside of the glass is coated with wine. Just as a stem is practical for handling, so a tulip-shaped bowl is the most suitable for swirling, for it not only prevents the wine from shooting out but retains the released esters.

Raise the glass to the nose and lightly inhale, concentrating all your attention on that vital, fleeting, first impression. Is it clean and wholesome, forthcoming or dumb, fruity or peppery? Is there a distinct grape smell? An ordinary wine will just have — hopefully — a plain wine smell; a better wine will be vinous, and one from an individual or predominant grape variety will have a varietal character.

Our senses tend to be quicker than our conclusions. It is often difficult to sort out the various components of smell at the first whiff, so give the glass another gentle twirl and take a deeper sniff. In particular, try and identify and isolate the grape; major varieties have quite a distinct aroma. You can read about them, but the best way to learn is to open good bottles. (Incidentally, if, in a blind tasting, you can spot the grape you are part way to identifying the district.)

Various forms of acidity can be detected on the nose; so can a high alcoholic content (pepperiness). Freshness and fruitiness is sought in young wines; mellowness, calm fragrance, a honeyed quality in mature wines.

When I come across a rather "dumb" and undeveloped wine, or if I suspect its condition, I give the wine a good shaking and inhale deeply. If there is underlying fruit, or a fault, it is generally revealed in this way.

To sum up: with young wines use your nose to detect fruit, the individual grape variety, refreshing acidity and balance of elements. Nose becomes more important as the wine ages; look out for harmony, a sort of aggregate of fragrances, bottle-age, a mellow honeyed quality, intensity, and sheer beauty.

On the palate — taste
The eye leads in by indicating weight and maturity; the nose leads on, noting the elements of aroma and bouquet, confirming maturity and general quality. But it is the palate which, in effect, finally reaches conclusions and sums up.

Take a reasonable mouthful. Try drawing air in through pursed lips — "chew" the wine, roll it round the tongue. This is not affectation, it ensures that the wine has access to all the sensitive areas of the palate.

I always look for the touch of softness, the fractional sweetness, on entry: the sign of a fine wine made from ripe grapes. Sweetness, an important factor in white wines, is noted mainly on the tip of the tongue. Next, I judge the weight of the wine in the mouth — the measure of alcohol and extract, the intensity and persistence of flavour, its acidity and, with reds, the tannin content. (These terms are explained in the glossary.)

The weight and style depends on the grape, district and wine type. There are vintage variations, mainly due to the amount of sun in a given year. (Sun creates sugar, which converts into alcohol. Lack of sun equals sugar deficiency equals low alcoholic content.) The acidity also depends on the grape variety, soil and style, but with considerable variations due mainly to the balance of sun and rain during the crucial month or two before the harvest.

Alcohol gives the wine body and backbone and acts as a preservative; tannin is essential to the life and evolution of red wines; acidity gives wine zest, helps its balance. Without acidity, wine is like a body without its nervous system. And the tiny amount of residual sugar in a wine made from ripe grapes is, with other minuscule elements, responsible for its evolution.

In poor years, deficiencies can be remedied — up to a point, like plastering over cracked brickwork. Chaptalization, the process of adding sugar, masks the lack of fruit but soon wears off; it also temporarily conceals the raw acidity of unripe grapes. Time, in respect of poor wine, is not the great healer, it is the eventual revealer.

Really fine wines have a length of flavour that is measurable in seconds; great wines have an intensity and fragrance that continues into the aftertaste.

Making notes
I believe that some form of note is desirable, if only the name of the wine and whether you like it or not. The point is, memory tends to be unreliable; it is often difficult to remember salient features only a matter of an hour or so after the wine has been drunk. If you taste a large and varied range, as I do, an adequate note with a retrieval system is essential. Not that one needs to refer back all that often — the act of note making is an *aide mémoire*, making one familiar with wines, vintages and the spelling of strange wine names.

This is the method I use: I keep a series of small day-books, in which I jot down the date, the occasion, host and guests if appropriate, and the wines in order of tasting. I have columns for the name of the wine, the vintage, the grower, estate, merchant and price, and for appearance, nose and taste. Each book has a cut-away index by type of wine, major areas being subdivided into districts, such as Rheingau, or communes, such as St-Julien or Gevrey-Chambertin. Under these sub-headings I write the name of the wine, the vintage and page number.

Whenever I have a moment to spare, my red and white Bordeaux and vintage port notes are extracted and written up in larger loose-leaf books, the pages arranged in vintage order, with an alphabetical index of châteaux (shippers/quintas in the case of port), with the vintage and page number alongside — rather like the index at the back of this book. Incidentally, I have never bothered to extract and list burgundy in this way because of the endless variations between growers' and merchants' wines. One man's Nuits St-Georges is not the same as another's.

The advantages of the system are obvious: I can refer to a date to see what I have tasted, where and with whom; I can look up a château or port shipper to see at a glance what vintages I have tasted, and, turning to the entry, read the precise notes and the month and year they were made — again, a system followed in this book. The disadvantages are the labour and time involved, and a certain duplication of effort. For the less obsessive I would recommend a card index system kept only for the better and most interesting wines.

Alas, there is no universal system of signs, symbols or notations to record the taste of wine. Numerical ratings are of limited value, particularly in relation to fine wines. For noting and communicating there is no substitute for words, but they must be as clear and as unambiguous as possible. If they are to be understood by others, words should be chosen carefully. Unfortunately, despite some half-hearted attempts, there is still no officially recognized wine vocabulary. As a result of some 20 years of teaching I have compiled a fairly comprehensive glossary, which appears in my book *Wine Tasting* (Cassell/Christie's Wine Publications).

The tasting notes reproduced in this book demonstrate fairly well my own word usage, which, it will be seen, relates more to style, general quality and condition than to a precise description of the actual smell or taste — well-nigh an impossibility anyway. If you doubt this, try putting into words the taste of garlic or the smell of wild thyme. *Pinot* smells like *Pinot*. Those descriptive terms which might need explaining are defined in the following glossary.

But there is no substitute for the glass in your hand.

GLOSSARY

Acetic. Vinegary smell, tart on the palate. An irremediable fault.

Acid, acidity. Sound healthy grapes contain natural acidity, which gives the wine its crisp, refreshing quality. Too much acidity will make the tongue curl; a flabby finish results from too little. *See also* Malic acid, Volatile acidity.

Aftertaste. The taste that remains after a particularly fine rich wine has been swallowed; a fragrant internal bouquet.

Alcohol. One of the essential components of wine, giving it body and backbone. No smell or taste as such, but "peppery" on the nose of a young wine, a feeling of weight in the mouth, and warmth as it is swallowed. Alcohol content of "light" wines varies from around 11 to 14 per cent by volume depending on the sugar content of the grape, which in turn depends mainly on the ripening sun. Of the European classic wines, moselles and Châteauneuf-du-Pape represent the extremes, and red burgundy tends to be higher than red Bordeaux. Alcohol has an effect on the central nervous system, which is why there is an anti-drink lobby. *See also* Chaptalized and Fortified wine.

Aroma. The element of smell that derives from the grape. Descriptions of particular grape smells appear in the tasting notes in the main text. *See also* Bouquet, Nose and Varietal.

Astringent. A bitter, mouth-puckering effect due to excess tannin and acidity, mainly the former, noticeable in young red wines. Unless very pronounced, it usually wears off as the wine matures.

Austere. Mainly in relation to taste: hard, somewhat severe. Not a fault, possibly undeveloped and certainly indicating a lack of obvious flesh and charm.

Balance. The combination and vital relationship of component parts. *See* Well balanced.

Beads at the rim. This is how I describe the string of little tell-tale bubbles clinging to the meniscus which, in my experience, is often a warning that an old wine is cracking up. Not to be confused with *spritzig* (q.v.).

Beefy. An evocative description: a full-bodied wine with high extract (q.v.), a sort of chewable quality and texture.

Beery. The beery, yeasty end taste of a faulty wine.

Beeswing. A traditional and apt description of the filmy pieces of sediment floating in very old port.

Beetroot. Or boiled beetroot: an analogous description of the root-like, mature *Pinot* aroma.

Bite. An acid grip in the end taste, more than a zestful tang and tolerable only in a rich, full-bodied wine.

Bitter. Either a fault or due to too much tannin. Normally no fine mature wine should be bitter on the palate, though bitterness is considered a normal and desirable feature of some Italian reds.

Bitter almonds. An almond kernel, acetate smell usually due to bad fining. A fault.

Blackcurrants. An evocative smell and taste generally associated with *Cabernet-Sauvignon* and *Sauvignon-Blanc*.

Bland. Implies lack of character, too mild.

Body. A physical component: weight of wine, alcohol, extract. Varies according to wine type and vintage. *See* Full bodied.

Bottle-age. Hard to describe but easily recognizable once you know what to look for: the ameliorating, softening effect of a wine aged in bottle, detected on the nose; a mellow sweetness; on white wines a honey smell.

Bouquet. The element of smell that is a result of the wine-making process and subsequent development in cask and bottle, complementary to but not the same as aroma (q.v.). Embraces all the subtle and fragrant elements that combine and arise. The bouquet of a fine mature wine is one of the features most appreciated by the connoisseur. "Bouquet" can also be used loosely as a synonym for the nose or general smell of a wine.

Breed. An abstract qualitative term. A fine wine of good pedigree should display breed.

Burnt. Descriptive, analogous, like singed (q.v.). Red wines, dessert wines and hot-vintage wines can have a burnt character on the nose.

Capsule. "Cap" for short. Usually lead, sometimes a wax seal over the cork. *See also Goût de capsule.*

Caramel. Sweet, toffee-like smell. Sometimes indicates an acceptable degree of maderization as in old Sauternes.

Cedar. A cedarwood, cigar-box smell characteristic of many fine clarets.

Chaptalized. A French term for adding sugar to the grape must in years when the natural grape sugar is deficient. Without it these wines would be lacking in alcohol and unstable. Chaptalized wines tend not to keep well, though they can be attractive when young.

Characteristic. A characteristic wine possesses all the strengths or weaknesses normally expected of its grape type, district, style, vintage, age.

Cheesy. Or cheese rind: a descriptive term, not usually derogatory, applied to some clarets. Frankly, I do not know the cause; it might just be a stage of development. Sourness is not implied.

Chocolaty. Also descriptive, applying to the nose. I associate the term mainly with some of the sweeter, heavier, usually blended but not unattractive burgundies. Usually weighty and chunky on the palate.

Chunky. A term I often use to describe a hefty, somewhat coarse-textured red wine.

Clean. Nose particularly; but also taste. Fresh and free from faults.

Cracking-up. A disintegrating wine, usually over-mature and oxidized.

Crème-brûlée. The rich, burnt toffee and butter smell of very mature Sauternes.

Crisp. Firm, brisk, refreshing, zestful. Indicates good level of acidity, particularly in dry whites.

Depth. Depends on the context: a wine can have depth, i.e., richness of colour; depth of nose — the opposite to superficial, one has to sniff long and hard to detect its latent fruit and character; depth of flavour, richness, complexity.

Developed. Usually qualified. e.g. undeveloped, still immature but implying potential. *See also* Well developed.

Dry. In relation to wine always means not sweet (q.v.): sugar fully fermented out. *See also* Medium dry.

Dumb. Usually used in the context of an immature fine red wine with an undeveloped bouquet. Sometimes the dormant bouquet can be aroused by patiently warming the glass in cupped hands.

Earthy. Evocative and descriptive, nose or taste. Not derogatory in normal contexts. Red Graves can have an earthy taste, so, in a different way, can some Australian and California wines.

Esters. Smells are conveyed by volatile esters and aldehydes to the receptors in the nose, a chemical process. The nervous system then takes over.

Estery. Peardrops, a faulty, chemical smell.

Extract. To do with the body of a wine and frequently loosely used. Soluble solids, excluding sugar, which add to the richness and substance of wine, essentially from ripe grapes; a measure of quality.

Fading. Can apply to colour loss and general decline of bouquet and flavour; the result of age.

Fat. Usually referring to a combination of sweetness, alcohol, high extract, possibly glycerine, and implies a slight lack of counterbalancing acidity.

Finesse. An abstract qualitative term related to refinement, elegance.

Finish. The end taste. A good positive finish is essential in a fine well-balanced wine. A poor finish indicates lack of quality, follow-through and acidity.

Firm. Sound constitution, positive. A desirable quality on the palate.

Fixed acidity. Part of the essential make-up of any wine; its backbone or, perhaps a closer analogy, its nervous system. *See also* Volatile acidity.

Flabby. Soft, feeble, lacking acidity on the palate.

Flat. The next stage after flabby, well beyond bland (q.v.). Total lack of vigour on nose and on palate; lack of acidity; oxidation.

Flowery. Evocative. Can refer to nose: fragrant, fresh aroma; developed bouquet, or taste.

Fluffy. This is a term I sometimes use when I note a loose-knit, distinctly unfirm, "hollow" wine.

Fortified wine. A wine that has had brandy or neutral spirit added during fermentation, or after the wine has been made, or both. Port, sherry, madeira, marsala and the muscats of Australia are all fortified.

Forward. A word I frequently use to indicate a wine that is quickly developing, mature for its age.

Fragrant. Self-explanatory and highly attractive. Can be applied to aroma, bouquet, flavour or aftertaste.

Fresh. Displaying or retaining attractive youthful properties on nose and palate.

Fruity. Rarely grapy. More a positive, fleshy quality of nose and flavour derived from sound, ripe grapes.

Full. Must be qualified or used clearly in a particular context: e.g., full coloured (better to say deep coloured), full of flavour. Most often used in relation to weight. (q.v.).

Full bodied. A big wine, high alcoholic content and extract; a mouth-filling table wine or a robust young port.

Goût de capsule. A curious "lead-cap", slightly metallic smell associated with some claret.

Grapy. Self-descriptive. Aroma and taste usually associated with very ripe Rieslings and Muscatel-type grapes.

Green. Unripe, raw, youthful on nose or palate. Strictly speaking, resulting from unripe grapes, but also loosely used to describe an immature, acidic wine.

Green tinged. Self-descriptive colour.

Gristly. Gristle: tough textured.

Gritty. Coarse texture.

Hard. On the palate, severe, probably still tannic. Not a fault in a young wine.

Heavy. Overendowed with alcohol, more than full bodied; clumsy, lacking finesse.

High toned. This is a tricky one. It is an expression I frequently use for the nose of a particularly marked but light volatile character, often associated with considerable fragrance but can verge on, and is probably associated with, highish volatile acidity (q.v.).

Hollow. A wine that has a first taste, something of a finish but no middle palate.

Honeyed. Self-descriptive. Some young, natural dessert wines, if good, have a distinct smell of honey that deepens with age. Even dry wines, if of good vintages, can develop a mellow, honeyed bouquet as they mature.

Hot-vintage character. The smell or taste of grapes baked in a particularly hot summer sun or from an area with a normally hot climate. Tends to be associated with high alcoholic content; peppery (q.v.).

Iron. A character derived from the soil, noticeable more on palate than nose. Lahte often has it, so has Cheval Blanc. And in a swingeingly metallic, harsh tannic-acid way I have noted it in one or two young Australian and California wines.

Kernel. Or kernelly. Not nutty; for me an undesirable bitter-walnut smell and taste or, worse, bitter almonds (q.v.).

Lean. Self-descriptive. On the palate, sinewy, firm; often the sign of a "long-distance runner".

Legs. The viscous droplets that form and ease down the sides of the glass when the wine is swirled.

Light. Referring to body: low alcohol content. Also light colour (pale is a less ambiguous word), light nose (little bouquet).

Long. Refers to length of flavour. A sign of quality.

Macération carbonique. A modern method of vinification that at best produces appealingly fresh and fruity wines, at worst superficial, flimsy, tinny ones. What worries me is that more districts are abandoning traditional wine-making methods. *Macération carbonique* is an easy way out, but I now think of wines made in this way as "whole fruit drinks". The method seems to reduce wine to its lowest common denominator, blurring boundaries, reducing character.

Maderized. Heavy, flat, "brown" smell and taste of an overmature oxidized wine.

Malic acid. A mouthwatering, raw-cooking-apple smell and tartness on the palate due to unripe grapes.

Mawkish. Hard to define: more unpleasant than insipid. Stale character.

Meaty. Rich "chunky" nose, almost chewable flavour.

Medium. A term that ought always to be qualified. Medium colour, medium body, etc.

Medium dry. Half dry, some residual sugar, for example a *demi-sec*. Vouvray and very many German wines. Or a slightly sweetened fortified wine.

Medium sweet. Self-explanatory. Usually too sweet to accompany a main course. A light dessert wine.

Mercaptan. An unpleasant rubbery smell of old sulphur, mainly on very old white wines.

Milky. A milk-like smell. Lactic acid. Not a good sign but not necessarily bad or undrinkable.

Moreish. Rather a childish term for something temptingly tasty one wants more of.

Mousy. Refers to both a smell and taste. A sign of a bacteriological disease; also the curious "droppings" taste of wine made from hail-damaged grapes.

Murky. More than deep coloured: not bright, turbid. Mainly a red wine fault.

Must. Grape juice in the cask or vat before it is converted into wine.

Nose. The overall smell of wine. Also, to nose, nosing.

Nutty. The smell of cob nuts (tawny port), and a particular and pleasant quality I associate with oak and the *Chardonnay* grape and with some old amontillado sherries.

Oak. A smell deriving from maturation in small French oak casks. Adds a certain character and style but can be overdone.

Oily. Can apply to a particularly unctuous smell or a texture. A highly viscous white wine can also have an oily look.

Old. In a wine context an old nose or old taste implies signs of decay beyond normal maturity.

Open knit. Can apply to nose or taste/texture of a fairly fully developed wine. Forthcoming, loose-knit, loose textured.

Overblown. The somewhat unpleasant smell of an overmature or faulty wine.

Oxidized. "Brown," old straw smell; flat stale taste of a wine destroyed by the action of air in cask or in bottle through a faulty or shrunken cork.

Pasty. I use this in relation to a particular sort of smell and taste, so I suppose I should try to define it: raw, lactic, slightly rough texture.

Peach-like. Evokes the smell of the fruit, e.g., a ripe Ruwer wine (German).

Peacock's tail. The way the flavour of certain great burgundies can open up and fan out in the mouth.

Peardrops. An acetone, spirit-glue smell. A fault, usually in white wines.

Peppery. The effect of a high alcoholic content in a young wine, noticeably vintage port. Almost a physical, peppery assault on the nose, accompanied by a hot, peppery texture.

Piquant. A high-toned, overfragrant fruity nose verging on sharp, usually confirmed by an overacidic end taste. Can still be a refreshing, flavoury drink, but not one to keep.

Plummy. Can apply to both colour and taste. A thick red-purple appearance; fruit, some coarseness on palate, often indicating an in-between state of maturity, or a particular style.

Powerful. Really self-explanatory. Assertive, usually full bodied.

Pricked. Distinctly sharper than piquant. Acetic smell, tart. An irremediable fault.

Prickly. On nose and palate, sharp edged, raw, acidic.

Pungent. Powerful, assertive smell, linked to a high level of volatile acidity, e.g., certain old madeiras.

Ripe. Highly desirable in any context: ripe grapes (with full complement of natural sugar); ripe smell and taste, both exhibiting the softness and sweetness resulting from ripe grapes.

Robe. A rather elegant French term for the colour of wine. An expression I personally use only in relation to fine red burgundy.

Round. On the palate, a feature of a complete, well-balanced, mature wine. No hard edges.

Severe. Self-descriptive. Hard, unyielding wine.

Sharp. Acidity on the nose and palate somewhere between piquant and pricked (q.v.). Usually indicating a fault.

Silky. Refers only to texture, the feel of a ripe Pomerol, for example.

Sinewy. Lean, muscular on the palate. Usually a wine of some potential.

Singed. An analogous term that I use to describe the smell of some red wines of hot vintages.

Smoky. Both evocative and descriptive: the smell of burnt oak chips, of wood smoke. For me a pleasant type of smell that I associate with the bouquet of good burgundy and certain other wines.

Spanish root. A smell that reminds me of this root, a sort of liquorice. Certain ports have it.

Spicy. Self-descriptive, recognizable on nose and palate. A good Gewürztraminer is an example.

Spritzig. Or *spritz* for short. A German term. First detectable visually as tiny specks of air in the wine and then as a crisp prickle of youthful acidity and carbon dioxide in the mouth.

Stalky. Nose and taste. Not necessarily a fault, but undesirable; common, not an attribute of fine wines. Probably due to unripe grapes or prolonged contact with stalks during fermentation.

Stewed. An unimpressive, fudged-up, compounded sort of aroma lacking clear-cut fruit. Often from blended, sugared wines. Quality generally lacking.

Stringy. A texture: on the thin and scrawny side, lacking equability.

Sulphury. The prickle on the nose, rather like a whiff of a burnt match or coke oven, announcing the presence of sulphur dioxide, a common white wine preservative. Not a fault. Often wears off in the glass but should not be too intrusive.

Supple. Texture, balance: pleasant combination of vigour and harmony. Highly desirable in a properly developing red wine.

Sweet. A wine with a high sugar content, natural or added. A property of all dessert wines. Wine can smell sweet, but sweetness is primarily detected on the tongue. The sweetness of Sauternes and German *Beerenauslesen* is the result of fermenting overripe grapes containing a particularly high natural sugar content. Port is made by the addition of brandy, which stops the fermentation, leaving the desired degree of unconverted sugar; sweet sherry is made by adding sweetening wine.

Tang, tangy. Rich, high-toned, zestful bouquet and end taste, particularly in old madeira, tokay and some other old fortified wines.

Tannin. An essential preservative extracted from the skins of red grapes during fermentation. It dries the mouth.

Tart. Sharp, nose catching, tongue curling. Americans occasionally use this as a synonym for the natural acidity in wine, but in English wine circles it has an unattractive, even faulty connotation. A tart wine may be drinkable but is less than pleasing.

Tête de cuvée. No hard and fast definition, varies according to district, but definitely implies "the pick of the bunch", from the best cask or casks in a grower's cellar.

Thin. Deficient, watery, lacking body. Usually used in a derogatory sense. Not a synonym for light.

Tinny. Metallic, acidic at the back of the palate. A fault, but often tolerable.

Toffee-nosed. A literal description: sweet toffee, caramel-like smell. Possibly the first evidence of approaching maderization, but attractive. Nothing to do with being a wine snob.

Tuilé. A colour: tile red. To my eyes the colour of sun-weathered tiles in Provence, not newly made red tiles.

Unripe. A condition of wine arising from the use of unripe grapes containing malic acid, which gives the wine a smell of cooking apples and a raw, somewhat tart, end taste. A word sometimes loosely used as a synonym for immature.

Vanilla. A descriptive word for a smell generally associated with certain cask-aged wines.

Varietal. A distinctive aroma and taste deriving from a specific grape variety.

Velvety. A textural description: silky, smooth, a certain opulence on the palate.

Vin de garde. A wine that needs keeping, ageing.

Vinifying, vinification. The processes of wine making: preparing and fermenting grapes.

Vinosity. An abstract term indicating an intrinsic richness of quality stemming from fine ripe fruit, balanced, supple.

Vinous. Having a pleasant enough, positive winey smell and taste but lacking a recognizable varietal (q.v.) character.

Volatile acidity. A normal component of wine but undesirable in excess, the danger signs being a vinegary smell and bitter/acid end taste. Excess volatile acidity cannot be remedied.

Weight. A measure of the body, *see* Alcohol.

Well balanced. All the components of the wine — fruit, acid, tannin, alcohol, etc. — in equilibrium. A highly desirable state and certainly expected of fine vintage wine, particularly when mature.

Well developed. Component parts blended together, a desirable state of full maturity.

Wishy-washy. Feeble, weak, loose, unknit components. Lack of character and quality.

Woody. In relation to a wine nose or taste, a perjorative term, as opposed to oak (q.v.), which is desirable. The result of wine kept too long in cask, particularly old casks with rotten staves.

Yeasty. Undesirable smell, usually accompanied by an unclean, beery end taste.

Zest, zing. Terms used to describe a wine with an abundance of life and, metaphorically, sparkle, racy acidity. An attractive quality.

VARIATIONS in the COLOUR of WINE

In the natural order of things, the first sense brought into play by wine is the sense of sight. But there is much more to it than a beguiling or beautiful colour: the experienced eye can tell whether the wine is young or old, full bodied or light, immature, approaching its peak, going downhill or out of condition; the colour can give a clue to the style of wine, the sort of area – sometimes the district – in which it is grown, and even the grape.

The appearance of wine
Generally speaking dry wines look cool, fresh, mouthwatering, inviting; sweet white wines are golden hued, anticipating their honeyed richness of smell and taste. The colour of a rosé – and it can vary from the pale onion-skin of Provence, the orange pink of Anjou, to the pink red of Tavel – is its principal attraction. As for the reds, the variations are endless and often most meaningful: from the light, pink purple of a fresh young beaujolais, through claret red, garnet, to the rich *robe* of a great burgundy. All the natural colours of fine red table wines, and the vast range of dessert wines, are enhanced by a good table setting, brilliant crystal decanters, silver candelabra and thin-sided, elegantly shaped stemmed glasses.

But quite apart from aesthetic considerations, it is the relative depth of colour and the variations in hue which, in combination, yield so much advance information, to be supplemented by our sense of smell and confirmed and augmented on the palate.

The notes and illustrations
Under a heading indicating the type and age of the example illustrated, the salient features of its appearance are described. Beneath each drawing is the name of the wine portrayed, the colour within the lines of the tasting glass being an indication of its depth and hue. Each illustration is based on transparencies of the actual wine photographed in tasting glasses tilted at an angle over a matt white background to eliminate distracting shadows and highlights.

Selection of wines
The wines have been selected to illustrate a wide range of colour combinations rather than to represent every major wine district. Wine is notoriously difficult to reproduce in colour, and white wines, particularly the paler types, virtually impossible. The descriptions are based on the actual wine; the colours reproduced must be taken as an approximation to lead the eye into the text.

An immature 1-year-old red Bordeaux.
High quality and good vintage.
Considerable depth, virtually opaque at the centre of the bowl, shading through a deep mulberry colour to a still intense and youthful violet rim.
Vintages such as 1945, 1959 and 1961 would have been still deeper at this age, whereas middling-quality vintages such as 1969 and 1973 were originally less deep, and poor vintages such as 1956 and 1968 palish pink.

Semi-mature 10-year-old red Bordeaux.
Good quality, of a very good but slowly maturing vintage.
Originally deep purple, now a distinctly less deep but fine claret red, the colour leading in gradual steps to a less intense and maturing red-brown edge.
Quite typical of 1970 claret. The equivalent quality '71 slightly less deep and more mature-looking at this stage.

Ch. Palmer, vintage 1978.
Margaux, 3me cru classé (Médoc).
Cask sample drawn just over a year after the vintage.

Ch. Gruaud-Larose, vintage 1970.
St-Julien, 2me cru classé (Médoc).
Château bottled, cellared in London.

Perfectly mature 27-year-old red Bordeaux.
Good classed-growth quality, and of an outstanding
though not heavyweight vintage.
Medium-deep, warm garnet-claret red with a
beautifully even gradation from the bowl to a glowing,
mature, red-brown rim.

Overmature 56-year-old red Bordeaux.
Good classed-growth quality, good vintage, but in poor
condition. Although deep when young, the depth here is
partly due to oxidation resulting from poor cork and
slight ullage. Earthy at centre ranging through old
mahogany to overmature amber rim.
Haut-Brion of this age can be excellent; Lafite paler but
redder and healthier.

Ch. Grand-Puy-Lacoste, vintage 1953.
Pauillac, 5me cru classé (Médoc).
Château bottled.

Ch. Lagrange, vintage 1924.
St-Julien, 3me cru classé (Médoc).
Château bottled. From an ullaged half-bottle.

Mature 6-year-old dry white Bordeaux.
Good quality, fair-to-middling vintage. Unexceptional dry white wine colour: pale yellow tapering off to colourless rim. This class of wine will deepen in colour but will not improve further with age.

Maturing 9-year-old sweet white Bordeaux.
Good quality, good vintage but middleweight.
A deeper yellow at birth becoming a positive yellow gold as it approaches maturity. Colour at this age shades off to very pale rim. Suduiraut, particularly in a good vintage, tends to be a deep buttery yellow; Lafaurie-Peyraguey in recent vintages is pale, more green tinged.

Ch. Carbonnieux, vintage 1974.
Léognan, cru classé (Graves).
Château bottled. Berry Bros selection.

Ch. Suduiraut, vintage 1971.
Preignac, 1er cru classé (Sauternes).
Château bottled.

Mature 13-year-old sweet white Bordeaux.
From the greatest Sauternes vineyard, an outstanding, mature vintage.
Gold-tinged yellow at birth, now a pure amber gold with positive yellow-gold rim – a subtle range of warm golden colours much enhanced by cut glass and candle-light, which brings out the highlights.
Although perfect now this wine has 20 or more years of development. It will gradually deepen in colour, losing some sweetness but gaining other nuances of flavour.

Fully mature 52-year-old classic sweet white Bordeaux.
From the finest vineyard in the Barsac commune, great vintage, fully mature.
An amazingly bright and lively gold, with warm, slightly orange tinge shading off to an amber-gold rim. The whole effect would be much enlivened by candle-light, giving the wine interwoven shades of colour like shot taffeta.
The 1929 Climens is a deeper old-gold colour and also perfection.

Ch. d'Yquem, vintage 1967.
Sauternes, 1er grand cru classé.
Château bottled, half-bottle.

Ch. Climens, vintage 1928.
Barsac, 1er cru classé (Sauternes).
Château bottled. Alas, my last bottle!

Typical young 18-month-old beaujolais.
Nice quality, good vintage.
Light and fresh looking: medium-pale plummy purple
with faint but distinct pink-purple rim.
For drinking, lacking the body and balance to develop
further. With age the colour will change to a pale
burgundy red, and later will take on an onion-skin tinge.
Only outstanding beaujolais vintages such as 1976 are
worth keeping.

**A 4-year-old burgundy of good vintage, starting
to mature.**
A good-quality village wine from the middle of the Côte
de Nuits.
Medium depth, attractive pure burgundy red shading
off to a paler rim showing just a trace of red-brown
maturity.
Fairly typical. Other '76s can be slightly deeper or paler.
Will gradually lose colour and become more brown at
the rim.

Brouilly, vintage 1978.
Beaujolais Villages.
Bottled in France for Harveys of Bristol.

Morey St-Denis, vintage 1976.
Côte de Nuits.
French bottled. Harvey's selection.

Fully mature 31-year-old burgundy.
Originally a quite good-quality village wine, and of a great vintage.
Still wearing the colour of an outstanding vintage: quite intense, a deep burgundy red shading off to a very positive, mature mahogany-amber rim.

Fully mature 61-year-old burgundy.
Good quality, great classic vintage.
Beautiful colour still: medium garnet-red centre, tinged with orange, leading through a warm mahogany colour to a pure amber rim.
Although never recorked, and with slight ullage, the wine had benefited from undisturbed storage in a good cool French cellar.

Nuits St-Georges, vintage 1949.
Côte de Nuits.
French bottled. Alfred Giraud. Half-bottle.

Richebourg, vintage 1919.
Côte de Nuits, grand cru.
French bottled: Calvet.

Young recently bottled fino-style sherry.
Basically a fully fermented dry white wine with light
fortification. No sweetening or "color" wine added.
Fresh looking, very pale straw yellow with hint of green,
tailing away to a completely colourless edge. Will not
improve with bottle-age: the yellow will merely deepen
and eventually look rather drab, with taste to match.

Standard medium amontillado sherry.
A medium-dry proprietory brand of nice quality.
Bright amber colour due partly to cask age, shading off
to a colourless rim.
The finest and most expensive old amontillados, aged in
wood, will be a more positive, possibly deeper amber
colour with intensely yellow-amber rim.

Manzanilla.
Sanlucar de Barrameda.
Bottled in Bristol by Harvey's.

Club Amontillado.
Of the fino family, matured and blended in Jerez.
Bottled in Bristol by Harvey's.

An old-bottled oloroso sherry.
Basically a deeper, heavier and sweeter style than amontillado though it begins life pale and dry like all other sherries. With age in cask and bottle, now a warm, golden, amber brown with a marked amber-gold colour near the rim. Depth of colour can vary, and lesser commercial oloroso blends tend to be less incisive and tail off at the rim – and on the palate.

A high-quality dessert "brown" sherry from an old solera.
Appropriately deep and brown in colour with a warm, singed character; intense, and with a pronounced amber rim indicative of age and quality.

Oloroso, bottled in 1954.
Matured and blended in Jerez, Spain.
Bottled in Bristol by Harvey's.

Finest Old Brown sherry.
Aged and blended in the Jerez area.
Bottled by Berry Bros & Rudd, London.

25

Immature 2-year-old vintage port.
Classic British style and quality, good vintage.
Opaque – black as Egypt's night – in the centre, the
depth of colour continuing to an intense, immature-
purple rim.
Ready for bottling. A wine like this will need 12 years in
bottle before approaching its maturity, and will develop,
losing colour, softening, for a further 20 years, and
fading gradually, mellowing, for another 20.

A good example of a traditional style of wood port.
Distinctly ruby in colour: red with a hint of plummy
youthful purple, the concession to some maturity being
in the touch of red brown at rim.

Dow, vintage 1977.
The main brand of Silva and Cosens.
A cask sample from Vila Nova de Gaia, Portugal.

Cockburn's Special Reserve.
Cockburn, Smithes & Ca., Oporto.
Made and blended in Oporto, bottled in Bristol.

Mature 33-year-old vintage port.
One of the best-known British port shippers and a very good immediate postwar vintage, shipped in cask; matured in bottle for 31 years.
Totally different from a young vintage port: considerable colour loss, now medium, "warm" ruby with an orange-brown shade of maturity penetrating and becoming very apparent towards the rim, which finally becomes a palish red brown.

Fine-quality old tawny port.
Port loses its colour far quicker in wood, genuine old tawnies being surprisingly pale, with a glowing, sometimes slightly orange hue, gradating evenly to a very mature, gentle, pale straw rim.
These old wood ports are bottled at their peak of maturity and do not benefit from further bottle-age.

Cockburn, vintage 1947.
Shipped in wood and bottled in 1949.
Matured in bottle in an English cellar.

His Eminence's Choice.
Delaforce Sons & Ca.
Matured and bottled in Oporto.

A young fine-quality hock from the Palatinate.
Ready at 3 years of age, but will keep and improve.
Palish straw yellow, bright and appealing.
Frankly one can see why some of the tall German wine
glasses have a green stem: the reflection gives the wine a
little more zing and appeal.
The dessert wines, many described in the main text,
start life with more colour and become a buttery gold
with age.

A good-quality, mature, 27-year-old Rhine wine.
Fine-quality unsugared Rhine wines of good vintages
keep remarkably well – much depends on storage
conditions and the staying power of the rather short
corks. Originally pale, now a lovely golden buttery
yellow.

**Ruppertsberger Giesböhl Riesling Spätlese,
vintage 1976.**
Palatinate. Original bottling: Dr. Bürklin-Wolf.

Steinberger Naturrein, vintage 1953.
Rheingau, Staatsweingut.

An overmature, 35-year-old white burgundy.
Fairly high quality; a great and scarce postwar vintage.
A somewhat drab and off-putting old straw colour, not
very bright and with slight sediment. Despite
appearances, the wine was hanging on to life, and its
original quality pushed through, full of flavour and
character. Contrary to general belief, dry white wines,
if of high quality, not only keep well but develop extra
degrees of richness if stored in a cool dark cellar.

A classic Australian Muscat.
A rare, intensely sweet, fortified dessert wine from the
ubiquitous muscat grape, aged in wood (part of the
blend could well be 60-year-old wine).
Glowing rich colour, ruddier than Bual or Malmsey
madeira, shading off to a positive amber-gold rim – the
sure sign of high extract, high quality and age.

Montrachet, vintage 1945.
Côte de Beaune, grand cru.
French bottled: Grivelet Père et Fils.

Bundarra Special Muscat Liqueur.
Glenrowan, north-east Victoria.
Aged in wood and bottled by Bailey's.

One of the new classics from northern California.
An immature, 4-year-old, natural high-strength table wine from late-picked Zinfandel grapes with high sugar content producing 17.5 per cent alcohol.
The sheer power and concentration apparent from the opacity, and its youthful potential in the intense purple and bright violet rim.
Clearly half a century of life ahead.

Six-year-old California Cabernet-Sauvignon.
A high-quality Napa Valley red wine of an exceptionally good vintage.
Exhibiting the depth and richness of wine made from the classic Bordeaux grape variety in the warmer climate of northern California. Initially opaque, purple, now a deep ruby, intensely red at the rim.
A long future. Colour loss and change will be slow.

Mayacamas late-harvest Zinfandel, 1976.
Mayacamas Winery, in the hills east of Napa Valley.
Matured and bottled after two years.

Clos du Val, vintage 1974.
Napa Valley Cabernet-Sauvignon.
A magnum from the winery, London stored.

A semi-mature, 11-year-old Rhône red.
The real thing: a Châteauneuf-du-Pape made on a
great estate in a good vintage.
Depth of colour one associates with red wine made
from grapes in the hot Rhône valley: the "warm" red
of a 14° wine, purple when young, now a ruby-garnet
colour, red brown at the rim; showing maturity but
clearly another 10 or 20 year development potential.

A 5-year-old Australian "claret".
A wine of good quality made from Cabernet-
Sauvignon and Shiraz grapes in the broad Barossa
Valley.
Deep, intense ruby anticipating fairly high alcoholic
content and the strong purple rim indicating its
relative immaturity.
Like all good reds this will slowly lighten in colour, the
outer edge turning through red to a red mahogany then
to a warm amber and lastly to a pale brown.

Ch. de Rayas, vintage 1969.
Châteauneuf-du-Pape, southern Rhône, France.
Château bottled. Imported by Loeb & Co., London.

Yalumba Walter's Blend claret, vintage 1975.
Angaston, Barossa Valley, South Australia.
Produced and bottled at the Yalumba Winery.

Standard blend of (dry) Sercial madeira.
Rather deeper – and richer on the palate – than its
counterpart, a fino sherry.
A straw-amber gold with a faintly warm orange tinge
shading off through yellow to a pale watery rim.
Bottled for immediate drinking. Even good
commercial blends do not improve in bottle.

A rich – just over a century old – madeira.
A high-quality, straight-vintage wine from the Bual or
Boal grape, with at least 50 years in cask, then
probably stored in demijohns before bottling in the
1950s.
With the glowing vibrant colour of fine old madeira:
burnt umber with a hint of orange leading through
amber to a very intense buttercup yellow, sometimes
green-gold tinged. The highlights in old madeira are
fabulous, deserving an appreciative palate.

"Good Company" Sercial.
Cossart, Gordon & Cia., Funchal.
Bottled by Cossart, Gordon & Co., in England.

Boal, 1874.
Produced and matured in Madeira.
Blandy's, Funchal.

RED
BORDEAUX

If Bordeaux claims a large share of this book it is because of the dominating role it has played in my life as a wine merchant and auctioneer, and as an enthusiastic *amateur*, in the French sense. And in the world of the connoisseur, red Bordeaux is the wine that generally occupies most cellar space, graces more tables and is discussed most avidly.

The reasons are many. Putting first things first, claret — the term for red Bordeaux amongst the English-speaking peoples — is a first-rate beverage. It is light, it is dry, it cleans the palate and aids digestion. Frankly, if it were not a basically satisfactory drink it would have got no further. What gives claret endless appeal is its range and diversity and, in the higher realms, its complexity. As far as the English are concerned, there is also its historical background, and for the newer wine-producing countries, Australia and the United States in particular, the best claret acts as a touchstone, a standard against which their own Cabernet-Sauvignons can be compared.

I mentioned complexity. To give an idea of the permutations, "the bible of Bordeaux" by Cocks et Féret lists over 3,500 individual Bordeaux vineyards, most graced with the prefix "château". Now, not only does each château make a wine of a slightly different style and character, but no vintage is entirely like another. Permutations are further multiplied by the effect of age, which differs according to a château's potential and, widely, from one vintage to another. This in essence is what this book is all about.

A word about the selection of wines noted. On the face of things, it would appear that I am a fearful snob. First growths and great names abound. The reason for this is far more mundane. Only wines of good quality, made well and in good years, benefit from keeping; only wines of high quality, from the best vineyard sites and of the finest years, actually gain extra dimensions of bouquet and flavour through the ageing process; and, in private cellars, it tends to be the finest, most cherished and most prestigious wines that are kept longest, before finally coming to light as rarities. My experience at Christie's is that one member of a family is keen on wine and lays down good stocks; the next generation is less or not at all interested; the generation after that has either forgotten the wine or finds it too old. This was certainly the case with the Glamis Castle and the Gladstone cellars, Sir George Meyrick's and Sir John Thompson's, and several others referred to in the text.

Minor wines from small, less well-sited vineyards, or of poor years, do not develop beyond a certain point. Age confers a certain rarity value and stimulates a little curiosity, but no more. Like the proverbial man in the street, the *petit château* is at best decent and pleasant. It is the Churchills of this world who stand out, rise to the heights, inspire — and are most worthy of record.

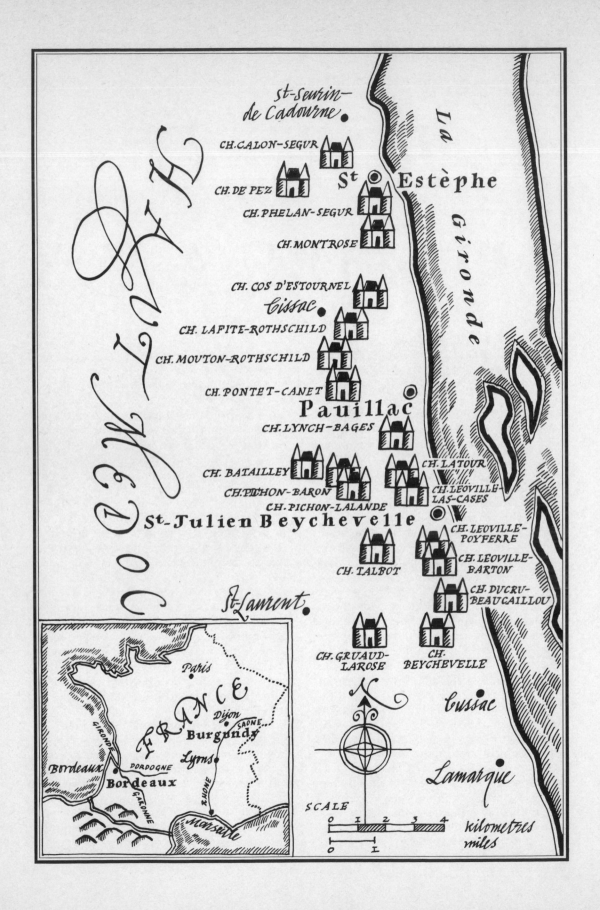

St-seurin-de Cadourne

CH. CALON-SEGUR

CH. DE PEZ

St Estèphe

CH. PHELAN-SEGUR

CH. MONTROSE

CH. COS D'ESTOURNEL

Cissac

CH. LAFITE-ROTHSCHILD

CH. MOUTON-ROTHSCHILD

CH. PONTET-CANET

Pauillac

CH. LYNCH-BAGES

CH. BATAILLEY

CH. LATOUR

CH. PICHON-BARON

CH. LEOVILLE-LAS-CASES

CH. PICHON-LALANDE

St-Julien Beychevelle

CH. LEOVILLE-POYFERRE

CH. LEOVILLE-BARTON

CH. TALBOT

CH. DUCRU-BEAUCAILLOU

St-Laurent

CH. GRUAUD-LAROSE

CH. BEYCHEVELLE

Cissac

Lamarque

La Gironde

MÉDOC HAUT

Paris

FRANCE

Dijon

Burgundy

Lyons

Bordeaux

Bordeaux

GIRONDE

DORDOGNE

GARONNE

SAÔNE

RHÔNE

Marseille

N

SCALE

0 1 2 3 4 kilometres

0 1 miles

1771

"Excellent fine flavoured Claret of the year 1771," the first Bordeaux vintage to appear in a Christie's catalogue, in March 1776.

1784

"It is one of the best vintages which has happened in nine years ... Château Margau [*sic*] bought by myself on the spot" — Thomas Jefferson, in a letter.

1785

In a catalogue of 1792 "One case containing 50 quart bottles of the growth of Latour of the Vintage 1785".

1788

The year in which Bordeaux châteaux were first mentioned by name in a Christie's catalogue: "Lafete" and "Ch. Margeau", in sale of French ambassador's stock.

1791

Six hogsheads of first-growth claret of 1791 "considered the best that France has produced for many years, and similar is difficult at this time to be obtained, and now in order for bottling" — from a Christie's wine sale catalogue of 23 May, 1797.

1795

A very good year.

1796–1797

Mediocre.

1798

A great year; a good crop of excellent, full-bodied, velvety wines. "1798, Ch. Margot's Celebrated Vintage, bottled in London 1802" sold for the high price of £9 2s. 6d. per dozen at Christie's in March 1811.

1799

Picking began on 5 October; an above-average crop.
Ch. Lafite. Despite the poor rating in Cocks et Féret a bottle produced from the private cellars at the château for the Overton tasting in Fort Worth was very much alive: fabulous colour, warm palish *tuilé* (the colour of a sun-faded old tile in Provence); a gently fragrant bouquet, with a touch of decay when first opened which cleared, held and even developed in the glass; light though still a meaty little wine, faded but fascinating, the finish a little dried up and tart. Bottle recorked in 1953.
Tasted May 1979 ★★★★★ (for survival).

1800–1801

1800, a bad vintage. 1801, passable.

1802

Very good, but not up to the 1798.

1803

Picking began 25 September. A good year.
Ch. Lafite. Medium light, warm amber with a touch of red, very appealing; bouquet low-keyed at first but sound as a bell, blossoming in the glass, amazingly clean and fragrant; dry, lightish, a bit lean and raw on the palate but some fruit left, very much alive with a firm backbone and acidity. Last recorked in the mid-1950s.
At the Overton tasting, May 1979 ★★★★★

1804–1813

1804, mediocre. 1805, abundant but no better. 1806, not highly regarded at the time though a bottle tasted by a client in New York in 1979 was faded but excellent. 1807, small crop, good wines. 1808, variable. 1809, worst vintage of the period. 1810, passable. 1811, the famous "Comet" year, notable throughout Europe for the remarkable quality of the wine. Picking began 14 September. A magnificent and abundant vintage. Lafite, drinking gracefully at the age of 115, considered the finest red Bordeaux ever made and the pioneer of great vintage clarets. 1812, ordinary. 1813, flat, mediocre.

1814

Picking began on 20 September. Smallish crop, quality moderate to very good.
Ch. Lafite. A light, faded orange amber, some warmth and life, but with a watery rim; very little nose, a bit thin and spirity but it appeared very healthy and held well in the glass, with glimmerings of gentle fruitiness; on the palate dry, light but firm, alcohol but no fruit, very clean and, surprisingly, tasted much better after a couple of hours. Last recorked at the château in the 1950s.
At the Overton tasting, May 1979 ★★

1815–1824

1815, the year of Waterloo. "A remarkable year in every respect. The wines agreeable and perfumed, having both body and richness." (H. Cocks, quoting Mr Franck, in *Bordeaux: its wines and the claret country*, 1846.) On a par with 1798 and 1811. 1816, very wet spring and summer; disastrous. 1817, almost as bad. 1818, small crop, hard wines, high prices. 1819, abundant, good. 1820, lacking colour, hard. 1821, bad vintage, abundant but poor. 1822, small crop of high-priced wines, which developed well, hard. 1823, rain during vintage, low priced but Médocs turned out well. 1824, bad; minimal yield, hard acid wines.

1825

Picking began on 11 September. A celebrated vintage. Slow developing. After preceding poor vintages, wines snapped up at excessive prices.
Ch. Lafite. Lovely orange-amber colour; a ravishingly delicate and fragrant bouquet, faint at first but developed richly — outstanding, with flavour to match, a touch of piquancy but altogether enchanting and the true Lafite style. Recorked, good level.
At the Overton tasting, May 1979 ★★★★★
Ch. Gruaud-Larose. Surprisingly deep plummy colour, not bright as it had no time to settle; very rich old *Cabernet* aroma, ripe mulberry, just a touch of decay; a ripeness on the palate, lovely rich flavour leading to a light dry finish. Recorked at the château.
Amazing condition considering that it was drunk at a great old-wine dinner given in my honour by Len Evans, attended by the prime minister and 12 of the best palates in Australia, the very evening I and the bottle arrived in Sydney in February 1977 ★★★★

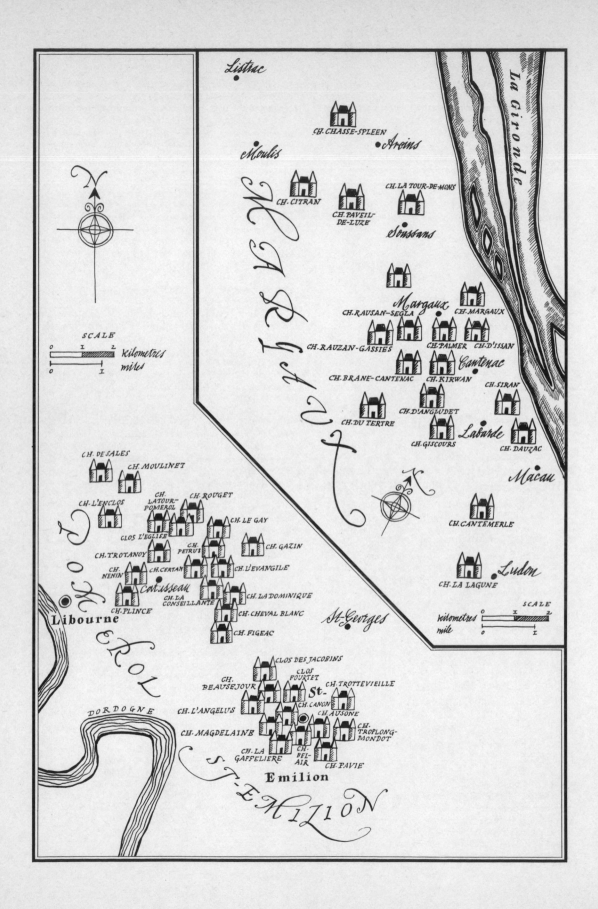

Listrac

La Gironde

CH. CHASSE-SPLEEN   • Arcins

Moulis

MARGAUX

CH. CITRAN

CH. LA TOUR-DE-MONS

CH. PAVEIL-
DE-LUZE

Soussans

Margaux   CH. MARGAUX

CH. RAUSAN-SEGLA

CH. RAUZAN-GASSIES   CH. PALMER   CH. D'ISSAN

Cantenac

CH. BRANE-CANTENAC   CH. KIRWAN

CH. SIRAN

CH. D'ANGLUDET

CH. DU TERTRE   Labarde

CH. GISCOURS   CH. DAUZAC

Macau

CH. CANTEMERLE

SCALE
0   1   2   kilometres
0   1   miles

CH. DE SALES

CH. MOULINET

CH. ROUGET

CH. L'ENCLOS   CH.
LATOUR-
POMEROL

CLOS L'EGLISE   CH. LE GAY

CH. TROTANOY   CH.
PETRUS   CH. GAZIN

CH.
NENIN   CH. CERTAN   CH. L'EVANGILE

CH. LA LAGUNE   • Ludon

Catusseau   CH. LA
CONSEILLANTE   CH. LA DOMINIQUE

SCALE
kilometres   0   1   2
mile   0   1

CH. PLINCE   CH. CHEVAL BLANC   St-Georges

Libourne   CH. FIGEAC

POMEROL

CLOS DES JACOBINS

CLOS
FOURTET

CH.
BEAUSEJOUR   CH. TROTTEVIEILLE

St-

CH. CANON

CH. L'ANGELUS   CH. AUSONE

DORDOGNE

CH. MAGDELAINE   CH.
TROPLONG-
MONDOT

CH. LA
GAFFELIERE   CH.
BEL-
AIR   CH. PAVIE

ST-EMILION

Emilion

36

1826–1840

1826, cool, rainy; reds weak. 1827, abundant, good colour and body. 1828, warm summer, rain during vintage; light but fine perfumed claret. 1829, latter part cold and wet; green (unripe grapes and meagre wine). 1830, severe winter affected growth; small vintage, minor wines. 1831, first rate, small crop, rich wines. 1832, very hot and dry, reds lacked softness and bouquet. 1833, abundant, hard wines. 1834, storm, hail; small crop but some very fine wines, celebrated and high priced. 1835, abundant; Médocs best, though light, fragrant. 1836, hard, acid wines. 1837, abundant; good quality. 1838, generally poor, low prices. 1839, frost reduced crop; ordinary. 1840, abundant; good colour and flavour but "its want of body unsuitable for the English Market"!

1841

Picking began 18 September. Excellent year: wines rich, highly coloured and firm, "much liked in England. . . . Prices moderate until the quality became known, and then very high." (From the summary record kept by successive *régisseurs* at Lafite.)
St-Emilion. From an old French cellar: good colour; bouquet old and sour but still vinous; dry, light, slightly tart, faded but interesting.
At the Heublein tasting, May 1976.

1842–1843

1842, average crop, moderate quality, lacking body. Prices low. 1843, small and bad.

1844

Picking began 7 October. A first-rate vintage, reckoned at the time to be the best since 1815. Below average crop. High prices.
Ch. Lafite. Fine deep colour considering its age, intense to rim; fine cedary nose, very sound; dry, medium body, gentle, complete though not long. Remarkable. Recorked at the château in 1953. Good level.
At the Heublein tasting in New Orleans, May 1976 ★★★★

1845–1847

1845, bad weather, deficient wines. 1846, hot; good big wines. 1847, an abundance of light flavoury wines not to the English taste of the time. Practically all shipped to Germany, Holland and the United States.

1848

Cold winter, moderate spring, very hot summer through to picking on 20 September. Abundant and good: full, deep coloured, yet soft and with remarkable finesse.
Ch. Lafite. Still incredibly deep, rich and intense in colour; very rich bouquet, trace of iron, very fragrant and spicy — a touch of eucalyptus and resin; rich on the palate, still fairly full bodied, enormously fruity — almost a citrus-like character, rich and still tannic. An astonishing wine. Recently recorked at the château.
At the Overton tasting, May 1979 ★★★★★

1849–1857

1849, picking began 22 September. Moderate ordinary vintage. 1850, hot, humid; abundant, light and ordinary wines. 1851, good spring, excessively hot summer; reduced quantity, good big wines. 1852, frost, hail, *coulure*, rain; average crop, light wines. 1853, exceptionally wet, tiny rotten crop, one of worst years of the mid-19th century. 1854, noted for the onset of oidium, a disease as serious as the pest, phylloxera. A minimal crop; taste of rot. 1855, oidium unchecked, tiny crop, passable high-priced wines. 1856 as 1855. 1857, oidium cured by sulphur but vines weakened; a better crop, better wines.

1858 ★★★★★

Favourable winter and spring, hot summer. A good crop; picking began on 20 September. Wines have deep colour, power, *sève*, fragrance and finesse. The first vintage of the two decades destined to be known as the golden age of Bordeaux.
Ch. Lafite. A fine healthy colour, similar to the 1864; a bouquet that made me think of mushrooms cooking in butter, aromatic, spicy; a very dry wine, lightish and faded, flavoury, piquant but positive, slightly faded and dried-out finish. Bouquet, flavour held well in glass.
Tasted on four occasions, first from a bottle from Lord Rosebery's cellars (sold at Christie's in May 1967), and the latest a recorked bottle from the private reserves at the château. At the Overton tasting, May 1979 ★★★★

1859–1862

1859, above average production; ordinary wine. 1860, cold and wet; abundant crop of thin, bad wine. 1861, terrible frost on 6 May decimated the crop, remaining vines produced very good, high-priced wine. 1862, above average crop, average quality.

1863

Picking began 23 September. A smallish crop of mediocre quality.
Ch. Latour. Very dark colour, virtually opaque, incredible depth and life for its age; bouquet gentle, nutty — a bit varnishy at first but it cleared, developed and held well; slightly sweet, full bodied but soft and harmonious, beautiful flavour and balance, wonderful finish. A very great wine and a perfect drink.
At dinner at the château, March 1970 ★★★★★
Laroze [*sic*]. Bottled by Claridge's, 24 dozen binned in 1865. Long unbranded corks, good level. Palish red; rich old nose; dry, light, slightly piquant but fruity.
From Sir George Meyrick's cellars in Anglesey, August 1970 ★

1864 ★★★★★

A truly *grande année*. Great heat prior to picking on 17 September. Wines of pronounced bouquet, sap, finesse, softness and elegance.
Ch. Lafite. A Cockburn & Campbell bottling, believed to be Lafite, was perfect tasted in November 1976, and the $18,000 jeroboam of Lafite I opened and decanted at "the Feast for St. Jude's" charity dinner in Memphis in October 1978 was also remarkable, its innate richness and fruit overcoming the trace of sourness generated by the considerable (low shoulder) ullage. More recently: fine colour, slightly lighter than the 1865; gentle, perfect bouquet — fragrant, slightly smoky (oak shavings) and fruit; touch of sweetness on entry, the hallmark of a perfectly mature wine made from perfectly ripe grapes, leading to a very dry finish. Moderately full bodied, firm, perfectly balanced. No decay, no oxidation, no overacidity or tiredness. Just perfection. Recorked.
At the Overton tasting, May 1979 ★★★★★

Ch. Mouton-Rothschild. Sourness and acid finish spoiling the fruit, but another from the same cellar, ullaged just below mid-shoulder, surprisingly sound, fruity, delightful. Original cork poor and greasy.
Both at Heublein tastings, May 1979.

Ch. Léoville. Medium light, fine mature colour; perfect bouquet and flavour; gentle, sweet, no signs of decay. Lovely drink. Bottled by Greenwell, Hutchinson. Long unbranded cork, 1½-inch ullage.
From the cellars of Fasque, the Scottish seat of Sir Thomas Gladstone, the brother of the great Liberal prime minister, and tasted just before the sale at Christie's in May 1972 ★★★★★

1865 ★★★★★

Another magnificent year, the second half of the first great pre-phylloxera twin vintages. Favourable conditions led to the early picking (6 September) of perfectly ripe grapes. Wines full of colour, body and all the characteristics of *une grande année*.

Ch. Lafite. Tasted on four occasions, all bottles from Sir George Meyrick's cellars (sold at Christie's in 1970) which, although never recorked, had been preserved for a century by the cold and very damp conditions at Bodorgan, in Anglesey. Most recently: a lovely and lively colour, still remarkably youthful; the last bottle tasted was ullaged to just above low shoulder — it must either have been one of the seconds or the cork had lost its grip during its nine years in American cellars — despite the ullage, the bouquet was rich and cheesy, with deep vinosity and fruit and held well, without strain, for well over two hours; still fairly full bodied it was amazingly good on the palate, rich, chewy, good tannin and acidity (which had preserved the wine all those years).
Provided by Lloyd Flatt for the Overton tasting, May 1979 ★★★★

Ch. Latour. Opaque, even younger looking than the 1920; very fragrant bouquet, rich, high toned, tough, too much volatile acidity; slightly sweet, fullish body, very silky, fabulous flavour, fractionally marred by a twist of end acidity.
Tasted in 1977 and at the château in April 1978 ★★★★

Ch. Kirwan. A wonderful deep colour; lovely nose, sweet, fragrant, no signs of age or "off" odours; slightly sweet, lovely flavour, perfect balance.
An unusual find in the Bodorgan cellars of Sir George Meyrick. I do not make a practice of opening old wines in clients' cellars, but these bottles were unlabelled and unidentifiable. Happily the corks were clearly branded Kirwan 1865 and levels good. Sir George and I finished off the bottle for lunch. Another opened at the pre-sale tasting in October 1970 was identical ★★★★

Ch. Gruaud-Larose. Pale autumnal colour but healthy; extremely rich and pungent bouquet — touch of sourness which might have worn off. A powerful wine which had lost some body and dried out somewhat. Good. Recorked at the château.
At the Cordier pre-sale tasting at Christie's in September 1976 ★★

1866–1867

1866, an extremely humid year resulting in unripe vines and feeble green wines. 1867, hail and *coulure* reduced yield; mediocre quality. Prices too high.

1868 ★★

Curious conditions: hot May to July, exceptionally wet in August, extremely hot before and during the early vintage, 7 September. Some good wines but prices, particularly for Lafite and Margaux, unbelievably high. Possibly a reflection of the enormous price paid for the Lafite estate by Baron James de Rothschild that year.

Ch. Lafitte [*sic*]. Bottled by Cruse. Pristine appearance save for the low level, below shoulder. Loose cork. Nevertheless a surprisingly good colour and bouquet for ullage and age; dry yet rich, with high extract.
From the cool, dry, Ten Broeck mansion in New Jersey, at the Heublein tasting, May 1978.

Ch. Pichon-Longueville. Manskopf & Sons. Ullaged. Brown and oxidized.
Tasted 1972.

1869 ★★★★

For some unknown reason, 1869 and 1870 have never been twinned like, for example, the 1874/75, 1899/1900, 1928/29. 1869 was one of those rare years that combined superabundance and high quality, following perfect weather for growing and vintaging (15 September).

Ch. Lafite. In magnum, with original short cork now black and greasy with age. Lovely garnet red colour, with touch of tawny; mushroomy and a trifle sour on the nose at first, but like an old man with stiff joints, after a little exercise — fresh air, and coaxing — it recovered, softened and cleared, the bouquet blossoming in the glass; on the palate very rich, soft, languorous and velvety, just a touch of decay at the edges but otherwise complete, with a mouth-drying finish.
At the Coq Hardy in Bougival, at an unforgettable lunch given by Peter Palumbo to mark the wine's centenary, in May 1969.

Ch. Montrose. Bottled by Geo. Claridge. Lovely colour, very healthy, quite deep; rich old leathery nose; dry — still tannic, fairly full bodied, good aftertaste. Others, ullaged, were similar but a bit on the tart side.
From Sir George Meyrick's cellar. Twenty-five dozen had been laid down at Hinton Admiral in Hampshire, in May 1888; 22 dozen remained in the bin. Tasted prior to sale, in April 1970.

1870 ★★★★★

Vying with the 1864 as the greatest pre-phylloxera vintage and, possibly, of all time. Frost reduced the crop, July heat baked the grapes, and the vintage started early, on 10 September, in excellent conditions. The wine was massive, *très corsé, très vineux*, but so hard and unyielding that (like the Latour 1928 in its turn) it took 50 years for it to become drinkable. Quite the most reliable of all the old vintages.

Ch. Lafite. I confess I have been privileged to taste the 1870 Lafite on some ten occasions, mainly from three great private cellars, Glamis Castle, Sir John Thompson's and the Ten Broeck mansion. Undoubtedly the finest, bottled by Coningham's, were from Glamis (an untouched bin of 40 magnums was sold at Christie's in 1971). Perfect wax seal, cork and level: amazingly deep colour, more like a 1945; perfect bouquet, not a whiff of decay, very rich, complete; slightly sweet, still fairly full bodied, a wonderfully rich mouthful, holding the tannin that had kept it all those years (and which, in excess, had made the wine unpleasantly undrinkable until the late 1920s).
A dinner at Christie's with Cyril Ray, Edmund Penning-Rowsell, Hugh Johnson, Harry Waugh and others, June 1971 ★★★★★

Ch. Latour. Also remarkably deep colour; deep and rich on nose and palate. Soft, rounded. Marvellous.
Tasted January 1969 ★★★★★

Ch. Montrose. Bottled by Cruse. Also deep and fine; rich, leathery; complex, holding well.
Tasted 1973 ★★★

Ch. Pichon. Very deep; fabulous *Cabernet* nose; crisp, flavoury but lacking the length of flavour of Latour.
Tasted 1967 ★★★

1871 ★★★

Picking began 18 September. Smallish crop following coldest winter since 1829/30 and uneven maturation of grapes. Red wines lacked colour and alcohol, but some turned out elegantly.

Ch. Lafite. With château capsule and branded cork, remarkable level (only ¼ inch between cork and wine). Fine deep colour; lovely bouquet which blossomed beautifully; a certain richness, medium light, lovely extended flavour. Perfect.
From the very cold cellars of Fasque, where it had been laid down by the second Gladstone baronet. Tasted May 1972 ★★★★★

Ch. Léoville-Las-Cases. Bottled by Bell, Rannie of Perth. Two-inch ullage. Not as deep as Lafite, a palish mature colour though still ruddy; touch of sourness on the nose but good fruit under; similar sweetness and weight as Lafite but shorter — class will out — nice flavour.
Also from Fasque. Tasted May 1972 ★★★

1872 ★

Picking began 20 September but, because of rain, could not be completed until 15 October. Regarded as an ordinary year.

Ch. Lafite. Fully mature mahogany red colour, pale but healthy; delicate, slightly smoky bouquet; dry, light, faded but pleasant.
Tasted on two occasions, from different cellars in Paris, both recorked by Lafite staff, 1976, May 1977 ★★

1873

Terrible frost on 28 April destroyed three-quarters of the crop. Picking began 20 September. Ordinary quality. Not tasted.

1874 ★★★★

Picking began 14 September. An enormous crop of high-quality wine.

Ch. Lafite. Tasted on ten occasions, different bottlings, different provenance. Of all old wines this seems to benefit most from long exposure to air, in decanter and glass. The best tasted recently came from Sir John Thompson's cellar, the following notes being an amalgam. All excellent level bottles. Medium depth, very pretty colour, a lively brick red; usually a touch of sourness on the nose when first opened (which is the reason for so many old wines being condemned — they are not given a chance to get over the shock of exposure after a century of being cooped up in a bottle) but rich and interesting — the last was at its fruity best after four hours; medium body, firm, gentle flavour, still with tannin and acidity preserving the wine and giving it a dry finish.
Tasted 1967 — May 1979 ★★★★

Ch. Latour. Beautiful colour, still quite deep; rich, fruity — fine bouquet and flavour, perfect balance. Holding marvellously well.
From Lord Rosebery's cellar, at Christie's pre-sale tasting, May 1967 ★★★★★

Ch. Mouton-Rothschild. Quite deep, excellent colour; fruity, rich bouquet with the overripe sweetness and age the French call *gibier* or *faisandé*, gamy; soft, velvety, nice acidity, exquisite long finish.
At Heublein's in the United States and at the Coq Hardy, Bougival, both a century after the vintage, in May 1974 ★★★★

1875 ★★★★★

An even greater crop than 1874, in fact the biggest production of wine in the Gironde from the start of records until the mid-1960s. This was due not just to favourable weather but to the greatly increased acreage under vines following nearly 20 years of prosperity — with higher and higher prices for magnificent wines. Boom time for Bordeaux, as the fanciful châteaux built during this time bear evidence. 1875 clarets made up in delicacy and finesse what they lacked in body. The English trade not only found them too light but some feared to buy them as they felt they were too delicate to survive. They were so lacking in tannin that most were drunk within ten years. A total contrast to 1870. The weather pattern of a year described at the time to be "prodigious in quantity and quality": good flowering (though some ominous complaints about phylloxera, foreshadowing the disaster to come); bad weather in June; July uncertain; early August sunshine, later great heat; September fine with showers; harvest began 24 September in good warm weather.

Ch. Lafite. Many of the few remaining bottles one comes across are from the formerly untouched bins (over 12 dozen bottles in perfect condition) at Bodorgan, the Meyrick family seat in North Wales, that were sold at Christie's in 1970. First tasted in my office with the late Jack Rutherford, the last *grand seigneur* of the English wine trade — the wine was perfection: palish, but a lovely garnet red, mellow and attractive; a faint old lady when first opened, but the bouquet developed delicate fruit, richness and the warm wholemeal-biscuit character which, for me, is the hallmark of the finest claret as it blossoms in the glass (oxidation is too clumsy a term for this magical transformation); on the palate slightly sweet — for a red wine — lightish, rich but soft and gentle, silky texture, delicate end acidity. The most lovely drink.
It is not often I finish off a bottle. I did on this occasion, in May 1970 ★★★★★

Mind you, some have not survived. An ullaged bottle had a drab, amber colour; maderized banana-skin nose; some fruit and richness, battling unsuccessfully with a stale, grubby finish.
At the Overton tasting, May 1979.

Ch. Mouton-Rothschild. Loose greasy cork, low shoulder. Pale colour; in spite of unavoidable decay there was a fragrance of bouquet; the flavour was also delicate and lovely although there was marked acidity. Perfect bottles must be delectable.
From the Ten Broeck mansion, Heublein pre-sale tasting, May 1979 ★★

Ch. Pichon-Lalande. Fine, fully branded cork, exceptionally good level, preserved at a damp 48°F in the Gladstone cellars at Fasque. Fine lively colour; perfect bouquet, gentle, rich, sweet, very fruity; firm flavour, just a touch of astringency on the finish.
Tasted May 1972 ★★★★

1876

Poor conditions, small crop. Picking began 26 September. Not very attractive, mediocre, uneven wines in the Médoc. Rarely seen; none tasted (phylloxera appeared that year in the vineyards of Lafite).

1877 ★★

Long wet winter and spring. Phylloxera "making rapid progress". Picking began 20 September. Above-average crop of light but charming wines.

Ch. Lafite. A magnum, from the château. Remarkably deep ruby colour; lovely bouquet which developed in glass; rich, silky, full flavoured, dry finish. Remarkable.
At André Simon's 90th birthday dinner at the Connaught Hotel, March 1967 ★★★★

Ch. Branaire-Duluc-Ducru. Sheer perfection. Original branded cork, very good level. Light in colour, pink and delicate; sweet, gentle, fragrant bouquet; distinctly sweet on the palate, soft, light, delicate, lovely flavour and finish. Lavender and old lace.
From the cellar in Bordeaux of Mme Teysonneau, J. Calvet label. At a Bordeaux Club dinner at Christie's, December 1979 ★★★★★

Ch. Haut-Bailly. Remarkably full coloured, deeper than Pétrus 1955, very ruby but mature rim; touch of death on the nose at first but it cleared and held well; slightly sweet, medium full bodied, very good rich flavour, dry finish.
From a magnum at André Simon's dinner, March 1967 ★★★★

Ch. Peyrabon (St-Sauveur). Fine deepish colour, mahogany rim; old nose but very rich and sound; dry and austere (but it was probably both when young), sound though slightly edgy.
From Glamis Castle, April 1971 ★

1878 ★★★★

Generally described as the last of the pre-phylloxera vintages. In fact phylloxera started in the Bordeaux vineyards in the mid-1870s and wines continued to be made from ungrafted vines until after the turn of the century. What is certain is that 1878 was the last of a string of quite exceptional vintages. A growing year of variable conditions but favourable from 1 September. Picking began 19 September. Big crop, very good wines.

Ch. Mouton-Rothschild. Several low-shoulder bottles tasted, all remarkably good considering the ullage, with delicate fragrant bouquet, firm and good acidity.
Stock of pristine appearance, never recorked, from the Ten Broeck mansion at Heublein's in May 1978, 1979 ★★★★★

Ch. Langoa. Deep and red for age; sound, rich nose; a big flavoury dry wine.
Tasted July 1967 ★★★

Ch. Rausan-Ségla. From the cellars of the once renowned Café Voisin, Paris. Probably recorked prewar. Ullaged mid-shoulder. Very fine colour; no decay, very rich, fragrant bouquet and flavour; exquisite aftertaste. Lovely wine.
Tasted June 1977 ★★★★

Ch. Mouton d'Armailhacq. Bottled by Harvey's. Good colour; old but complete, firm, fruity; developed and held well, touch of end acidity.
Tasted 1976 ★★★

Ch. Peyrabon (St-Sauveur). Good level, deepish, very good sound nose and flavour.
Tasted at Len Evans's dinner in Sydney, February 1977 ★★★★

1879

Poor spring; bad flowering; *coulure*; dismal summer; a small crop of ordinary wine, picked 9 October. Never tasted.

1880

Fairly similar though the late summer was hot. Picking began 21 September. Small crop. Some quite attractive classed growths made. Otherwise ordinary.

Ch. Mouton-Rothschild. Levels varying from mid- to low shoulder, soft crumbly corks. Faded colour though a glimmering glow of life; bouquet varied from bottle stink, old bananas and smoky bacon rind to curiously appealing waxy *Cabernet*; some sweetness, some fruit, almost all were better on the palate than nose.
From the Ten Broeck mansion, at the Heublein tastings, May 1978, 1979.

1881 ★

Difficult climatic conditions. Phylloxera spreading to the Médoc and Château Lafite affected. Picking began 12 September. Smallish crop of hard, charmless wines.

Ch. Latour. Sir George Meyrick at Hinton Admiral had 27 dozen in two bins left over from the 30 dozen laid down by his grandfather in May 1894, and one can see why: the wine must have been like red ink. The best bottle I tasted (1¼-inch ullage — very good for age) still had an impressively deep colour; nose old but fine; a very dry austere wine, full bodied and powerful, still loaded with the tannin and acidity of its raw youth. Severe but good.
Tasted October and December 1970 ★★

Ch. Gruaud-Larose. Paler, but a very healthy colour; old but rich; dry and sound but a bit astringent.
Tasted September 1976 ★★

1882–1883

1882, picking began 28 September. Crop depredated by phylloxera and tainted by mildew. Very light. 1883, picking began 27 September. Weather and quality uneven. Average crop, light wines.

1884 ★

More mildew but a good summer. Phylloxera "wearing itself out". Picking began 25 September. Two-thirds of the average crop. Variable quality, Margaux better than Pauillac.

Ch. Giscours. Bottled by Harvey's. Excellent level. Lovely colour; gentle attractive bouquet; attractive flavour, slightly sweet, light. Creaking a little but holding well for age and vintage.
Tasted July 1971 ★★

1885–1886

1885, picking began 29 September. Half crop due to mildew and the ravages of phylloxera. Ordinary wines.

1886, severe frost, mildew but good late-vintage weather. Picking began 25 September. Two-thirds of the normal crop. Ordinary quantity.

1887 ★★

The best vintage between 1878 and 1893. A warm summer and excellent harvesting conditions from 19 September (Lafite began picking on 28th). Still only half the average crop though mildew under control. Sound, healthy, full-bodied wines, now fading.

Ch. Lafite. Branded cork, very slight ullage. Light but pleasant colour, an autumnal tawny; very pleasant delicate bouquet, with the slightly singed character I associate with sun-baked grapes and the ivy-leaf smell from mildew; fragrant, nice aftertaste.
From a Rothschild cellar in Paris, May 1976 ★★

Ch. Margaux. Lightish, very mature looking but lovely colour; good, fragrant, mint-leaf bouquet; lovely flavour, firm, nice refreshing tang, despite ivy-leaf taste of mildew recognized by Bernard Ginestet.
Both bottles from the Glamis Castle cellars, one at the pre-sale tasting in May and the other at Berkmann's Margaux dinner in November 1971 ★★★

Graves de Cussac (Médoc). Light but still red and pretty; lovely soft charming nose; flavour affected by mildewed overtones and edgy finish.
From Glamis Castle, 1971 ★★

Ch. Gruaud-Larose. Fine colour; good nose with tinge of ivy leaf; very dry, lightish, excellent condition but slight astringency.
At the Cordier pre-sale tasting, September 1976 ★★

1888 ★★

Depressingly poor summer saved by brilliant September, the vintage starting on 28th (though later at Lafite: 2 October). A much bigger crop and more elegant wines than 1887. Good.

Ch. Lafite. Larose & Cie, Bordeaux. Branded cork. Very light colour; surprisingly charming and flavoury for an ullaged half-bottle.
From a Scottish cellar, November 1970 ★★

Ch. Margaux. Slightly deeper than the 1887; light, delicate, fragrant *Cabernet* bouquet and flavour. A lovely drink.
From Glamis Castle, May and November 1971 ★★★

Ch. Gruaud-Larose. Lightish, pretty colour; ivy-leaf bouquet (which I happen to find very attractive); a delicate and delicious wine. Recorked, good level.
Lunch at the château, March 1977 ★★★

Ch. Léoville. Lovely faded garnet red; little bouquet; dried out and faded though sound and complete.
Tasted 1970 ★★

1889 ★

Late flowering, as in 1888, led to a late vintage, 29 September (Lafite: 6 October), fortunately in good weather. More colour and body than the 1888. Elegant and good.

Ch. Lafite. Soft crumbly cork but good level. Light in colour but a healthy glow; enchanting bouquet, delicate fruit; flavour — like a pink-cheeked old lady — frail, still lovely, but a slightly bitter finish.
Tasted May 1975 ★★

Ch. Mouton-Rothschild. Very similar. Another frail,

faded but sparkling-eyed old lady. Fruity middle, slightly short.
At the Coq Hardy, Bougival, May 1974 ★★

1890 ★

Cold spring, another year of late flowering and retarded vintage. Picking began 29 September. Moderately warm summer and lovely September — which makes all the difference: colour and body at the expense of quantity, which was average.

Ch. Lafite. Very good level. Beautiful colour, bright, with excellent gradation from ruddy red to warm mahogany; an exquisite bouquet — sweet, ripe, delicate; some richness leading to a dry finish. Rich, attractive.
From a Rothschild cellar in Paris, May 1976 ★★★★

Ch. Margaux. Branded cork. Good level and colour; quite sound and good, but austere, tannic and more interesting than appealing.
Tasted April 1975 ★

Ch. Latour. Medium colour, very mature; sweet, gamy nose and flavour.
From the château, May 1977 ★★

1891

An uncanny resemblance to previous years: very late flowering, very late vintage 2 October, happily in good conditions, just saving complete unripeness. Yield severely reduced by the pestilential *cochylis* (who would be a vine grower?). Green, mediocre wines.

Ch. Lafite. Recorked at the château in 1957. Medium light, attractive colour; elegant bouquet — cedar and tea; dry, light, sound and very attractive.
From a Paris cellar, May 1976 ★★

Ch. Latour. Château capsule, unbranded cork, ullaged low shoulder. Deepish colour but sour, oxidized nose and flavour. Some fruit but poor condition.
Tasted 1974.

Ch. Léoville-Poyferré. Similar colour to Lafite; overripe, gamy, but fragrant; delicate and attractive in a perverse sort of way.
Tasted February 1978 ★★

1892 ★

Picking began 22 September. Half-sized crop following two severe frosts and a 110°F shrivelling sirocco mid-August. A hailstorm then ravaged Pauillac. Irregular quantity and quality, little colour but elegant.

Ch. Lafite. Recorked 1957. Lightish but pleasant colour; sound, delicate and attractive bouquet and flavour. Light, elegant, dry finish.
Tasted May 1976 ★★★

Ch. Canon (St-Emilion). Light, bright warm tawny; very perfumed and attractive old nose, high toned and forthcoming; touch of initial sweetness, light, an interesting, warm, singed, ivy-leaf taste, excellent acidity. A charming, delightful wine. Holding well.
At Mme Teysonneau's in Bordeaux, April 1979 ★★★

1893 ★★★★

A complete contrast to the previous 15 rather dismal years: no ravaging by frosts, diseases or pests. Warm spring, early flowering, a baking hot summer and the earliest start to the harvest on record, 15 August. Biggest crop since 1875, good quality. It was first thought outstanding, some later disappointments.

Ch. Lafite. Condition depends, as always, on cork and level. Tasted on five occasions, two bottles oxidized, three good. Deepish colour; a sweet, meaty, singed bouquet — in fact rather unusually raisiny; very rich on the palate, almost caramelly, still tannin and acidity.
Last tasted at the Overton tasting, May 1979 ★★★

Ch. Margaux. Tasted four times since 1971. Consistently impressive. Very fine deep colour; sweet, soft, most excellent bouquet — Margaux's greatest feature — crystallized violets, no decay; on the palate, sweet (for a red wine), soft, creamy, incredibly rich. A fabulously complete wine.
From Sir John Thompson's cellar, December 1976 ★★★★★

Ch. Mouton-Rothschild. Medium colour, good for age; wonderfully stylish, smoky (snuffed candle) bouquet; again the distinct sweetness of fully ripe grapes, an opulent complex flavour. Complete, good finish, remarkable condition.
Tasted 1971, March 1972 ★★★★★

Ch. Gruaud-Larose. Opaque, big vintage colour; old rich nose but dried out and austere on the palate.
At the château, April 1976 ★★

Ch. Pape-Clément. Shipped by Pfungst Lacy. Lovely mahogany colour; gentle cedary bouquet; soft, gentle and attractive flavour. Thinner than Margaux.
From Sir John Thompson's cellar, December 1976 ★★★

Ch. Léoville-Poyferré. Deepish; sound, fruity; a bit old and tired but good for an ullaged half-bottle.
Tasted 1977 ★

Ch. des Laurets (a minor St-Emilion). Old but rich, spoilt by end acidity, "must have been a 'big vintage' wine", I wrote at the time.
Tasted 1969 ★

1894

As a result of the extreme heat the previous year vines did not sprout as they should (a phenomenon that included trees and shrubs); *coulure*, rain, changeable weather. Picking began 5 October. Crop half that of 1893. Quality uneven, thin.

Ch. Ausone. The only 1894 I have tasted. Slightly ullaged, lightish, browning colour; bouquet old, delicate but holding on; old on the palate, too, reminding me of the earth floor of a *chai*. Unclean finish.
Tasted February 1977.

1895 ★(★★★)

Very uneven conditions. Wet until end July; good weather August and September — but devoid of any beneficial rain. Picking began 22 September in exceptional heat which made wine making difficult. Some grapes raisin-like. Those saved turned out remarkably.

Ch. Lafite. The manager saved his wine by asking a scientist for his advice, which was to draw off some of the overheated must (unfermented grape juice), cool it overnight and return it to the fermenting vats. Other châteaux learned too late, after the heat and microbes had spoilt the wine. Good level. Medium-deep colour, very mature; lovely old cedar-like bouquet, slightly peppery, developed well; soft, lovely old flavour. Better than Lafite 1893.
Tasted at Marquis de Vasselot's, April 1975 ★★★★

Ch. La Mission-Haut-Brion. Recorked 1950. Light-

ish, attractive, very mature looking; fragrant bouquet which made me think of vine roots; delicate, charming, delightful wine — on the edge, a touch of overacidity.
At the château, September 1978 ★★★

1896 ★★★★

Favourable weather, good flowering. August to start of vintage changeable, but cleared for the picking on 20 September. Abundant crop, good wines, fine, delicate, distinguished.

Ch. Lafite. Excellent level. Deepish attractive colour; distinctly sweet, ripe and appealing bouquet, developing richly; a dry wine, lightish body, good but not long flavour, touch of piquant acidity.
From a Rothschild family cellar in Paris, May 1976 ★★★

Ch. Latour. Light, delicate, but dried out for a Latour.
Tasted June 1971 ★

Ch. Montrose. Good level. Lightish, very mature but a good healthy glow; bouquet of old cedar with some *Cabernet* fruit; dry, lightish, gentle and no tannin left. Very good.
Tasted May 1976 ★★★★

1897 ★

Smallest crop between 1863 and 1910 due to unusual salt winds off the sea "scorching" young shoots, and *coulure*. Good weather before harvest (20 September) saved it from complete mediocrity.

Ch. Lafite. Recorked at château in 1957. Lightish, pretty colour; pleasant nose; dry end to end but elegant. (Ullaged bottles with original corks overripe and tart.)
From a private cellar in Paris, May 1976 ★★

1898 ★★

Picking began 23 September. Half average crop. Variable weather, variable quality. Some good, if somewhat hard, wines made. They took time to soften.

Ch. Lafite. Recorked. Light ruddy-tawny colour, similar to the 1887; curious light tarry smell and flavour. Developed well. Dry, lightish, firm, slightly short.
Tasted May 1976 ★★

Ch. Mouton-Rothschild. Medium deep, quite full for its age, healthy, brown rim; very rich old man, sweet and complex bouquet, flavour. Nice acidity. Holding well.
Tasted September 1975 ★★★

Ch. Villemaurine (St-Emilion). Pretty deep for age; the sweetness of overripeness and slight decay; delicate, flavoury, excellent aftertaste.
Tasted at Len Evans's old-wine dinner in Sydney, February 1977 ★★★★

1899 ★★★★

The first of the great *fin de siècle* twins. Abundant harvest, 24 September. *Très grande année*: outstanding.

Ch. Lafite. Tasted on five occasions, none better than the last. Good level. Very bright and appealing colour; delicate, slightly smoky, incredibly beautiful bouquet and flavour. Dryish, clean as a whistle, exquisite.
At the Overton tasting some thought it better than the 1900, others argued otherwise. For me it was excellent but different. May 1979 ★★★★★

Ch. Latour. Tasted four times. Medium deep; a bit musty at first, reminded me of plasticine, but cleared to reveal remarkable richness and fruit; dryish, full, soft, attractive. Lovely finish.

Tasted 1967, 1976 and at the château, June 1977 ★★★★

Ch. Margaux. Very pale, with faint ruddy glow; rich, very fragrant, scented bouquet; drying out, touch of decay. Two bottles fascinating but disappointing.

At the château, April 1972 ★★

Ch. Mouton-Rothschild. Two identical notes: dry, silky, faded, agreeable.

Tasted 1969, 1972 ★★★

Of the 16 other 1899s tasted the best were:

Ch. Beychevelle. Pale rosy-tinted mahogany; delicate; faded but complete flavour arching across the palate. Firm, silky.

Tasted 1970 ★★★★

Ch. Brane-Cantenac. Rich bouquet and flavour, refined.

Tasted 1971 ★★★★

Ch. Gruaud-Larose. Recorked, excellent level. Fine colour; rich old thoroughbred-stables nose and flavour. Highish acidity.

Tasted 1976 ★★

Ch. La Lagune. Soft, complete, rich, better than Mouton. Half-bottle.

Tasted 1969 ★★★★

Ch. Léoville-Barton. Good level. Similar to Gruaud, slightly redder colour; delicate *Cabernet* bouquet which developed richly; gentle and attractive. Good finish.

Tasted 1976 ★★★

Ch. Moulin-Riche. Soft and meaty.

From Glamis Castle, 1971 ★★★

1900 ★★★★★

This century opened with one of the most perfect vintages ever. A superabundant crop of very fine wines. Hotter than 1899. Excellent weather conditions through to harvest 24 September. Well-cellared wines with sound corks and good levels can still be excellent.

Ch. Lafite. Very good level. Medium-light colour, warm and attractive; very rich almost spicy bouquet which blossomed opulently; rich, full of flavour though not full bodied (Lafite at its best), still with tannin and acidity holding it firmly together. Magnificent.

At the Overton tasting, May 1979 ★★★★★

Ch. Latour. Deep coloured, magnificent; a tinge of old age on the nose but fine; ripe, not as full bodied as I expected but full of flavour, dry, somewhat austere finish.

At the château in 1970 and from a magnum, October 1978 ★★★

Ch. Margaux. Described by the recent owners as the greatest Margaux this century. Tasted and enjoyed by me on three occasions. Still remarkably deep coloured — a huge-looking wine; deep, rich, waxy bouquet, like a ripe burgundy at first but with Margaux delicacy and finesse; rich, fairly full bodied, silky, perfectly balanced — all the component parts in harmony. A perfect wine.

Tasted 1969, November 1971 ★★★★★

Ch. Margaux. *2me vin.* It is interesting to note that in this prolific vintage, and in others around this period, they kept the finest casks for their *1er vin*, the rest being designated *2me vin*. I came across a small stock in Bordeaux. The bottle tasted had quite a good level. Deep, mature, very rich colour; slightly singed, meaty bouquet — toasted, fern-like — anyway I liked it; rich,

ripe — almost overripe — on the palate. Moderately full bodied, warm and velvety. Very good finish and aftertaste.

At Mme Teysonneau's, April 1979 ★★★★

Ch. Mouton-Rothschild. One bottle deep brown and acetic. Another bottle with good healthy colour; rich, ripe, high-toned *Cabernet* bouquet; excellent flavour, balance and freshness of acidity.

Both tasted 1970. At best ★★★★

Ch. Léoville-Las-Cases. De Luze label. Excellent level. Fullish, lovely colour; the most beautiful, fragrant, cedar-like bouquet; soft, rich but delicate, excellent balance. A most fabulous, elegant wine.

From Glamis Castle (preceding the magnum of 1870 Lafite at dinner), June 1971 ★★★★★

Ch. Rausan-Ségla. Also perfection.

Tasted May 1976 ★★★★★

Ch. Pape-Clément. London bottled. Good level and colour; excellent long flavour.

Tasted 1973.

1901

Vegetation backward, a summer mixture of intense heat, rain and fog resulted in scorching and brown rot. Picking began 15 September, hampered by lack of labour. Big harvest, bad to just passable wines. Not tasted.

1902

Summer conditions not unlike 1901 but a better late vintage (27 September). Moderately large crop, light ordinary wines.

Ch. Lafite. Short cork. Level upper mid-shoulder. Lightish, fully mature colour; a surprisingly exquisite bouquet and flavour — rich, delicate, faded in the glass. Fleetingly appealing.

At the Overton tasting, May 1979 ★★

1903

Temperatures below freezing in April reduced crop. Poor sunless summer but better conditions in September through to picking on 28th. Poor wines.

Ch. Latour. Pale in colour; thin decaying bouquet; dry, delicate, slightly tart end. Interesting but the antithesis of Latour.

At the special preview tasting prior to the Latour sale, June 1977.

1904 ★★★

A return to good times, good conditions: summer with plenty of sun and enough rain to ripen and swell the grapes. An abundant crop gathered in excellent vintage conditions 19 September. Did not live up to expectations.

Ch. Lafite. Faded colour, very mature; sweet and fragrant on the nose; dry, light, faintly astringent. Interesting, but not as good as Haut-Brion.

Tasted October 1970 ★ *Two bottles with poor corks and low levels were oxidized and sour. Tasted 1976.*

Ch. Latour. Reputed to be good.

Ch. Haut-Brion. Lightish, pretty colour; rich, earthy Graves aroma; light, drying out but charming bouquet and flavour. A lovely drink.

Tasted October 1970 ★★★

Ch. Cheval-Blanc. Long cork, good level for age. Pale autumnal brown, with a glow of red; gentle, old, faintly decayed but appealing bouquet; slightly sweet, lovely

flavour — clean, attractive, slight twist of end acidity though gentle finish.
From the Kressmann family cellar, Bordeaux, December 1977 ★★★

Ch. Durfort. German bottled. Sound and flavoury.
Tasted 1977 ★★

Ch. Cantemerle. Kressmann bottling. Fragrant, delicate, attractive.
Tasted 1976 ★★★

1905 ★★★

Generally quite good weather conditions but rain throughout the two weeks of picking, which began 18 September, produced an abundant crop of light wines, with some elegance.

Ch. Lafite. Recorked. Medium, very attractive finely graduated colour; sweet, gentle, stem-ginger bouquet; dry, lightish and delicate. Pleasant dry finish.
From a Rothschild cellar in Paris, May 1976 ★★★

Ch. Margaux. Good healthy mature colour; bouquet rather resinous and varnishy at first but developed beautifully in the glass and lingered; pleasantly dry, light, soft, silky texture, nice acidity well in check. Short middle flavour and end but very enjoyable.
Decanted at 6.45 pm, poured at 8.45 pm, lingered fragrantly in the glass until around 10.30 pm. At Anthony Berry's, June 1969 ★★★★

Ch. Mouton-Rothschild. Plain unbranded cork, ullaged mid-shoulder. Lightish, fully mature amber; surprisingly sound and delicate on nose and palate. A little lacking but fine.
From a Paris cellar, July 1977 ★★★

Ch. Gruaud-Larose. Good colour; smoky bouquet; dry, a bit stringy and a touch of tartness.
Tasted May 1979.

1906 ★★★

Singularly favourable weather conditions but excessive heat and drought in August reduced yield. Good harvest 17 September. Robust wines of high quality.

Ch. Lafite. Tasted twice. First: faded in colour but rich on nose and palate, lovely flavour in 1973. The second: recorked, similar colour to the 1905 but livelier; a sweet rather medicinal nose; nice flavour, tangy and tannic.
From a Paris cellar, May 1976 ★★

Ch. Margaux. Tasted on four occasions. Beautiful faded autumnal colour; delicate and faded, but completely sound on nose and palate; soft yet a very unfeminine Margaux. A good if dry and austere finish.
Tasted 1970 — May 1975 ★★★

Ch. Haut-Brion. A somewhat sickly, decayed bottle in 1972, but later, from the Dillon cellar, a beauty despite greasy cork and very slight ullage. Mature, lively colour; lovely rich bouquet; slightly sweet, medium body, excellent rich fruit. Dry finish.
Last tasted November 1979 ★★★

Ch. Calon-Ségur. Recorked. Very mature, faded but sound and attractive.
Tasted 1972.

Ch. Léoville-Poyferré. Cruse. Healthy colour; gentle, medicinal *Cabernet* bouquet and flavour. Unexpectedly nice.
Tasted June 1976 ★★

1907 ★★

Picking began 25 September. Abundant year of useful, light and appealing wines not unlike the 1905s.

Ch. Margaux. Believed to have been bottled in Vienna. A gently attractive palish colour; lovely fragrant bouquet, smoky and flowery; dry, lightish, delicate yet a certain austerity. Fragrant aftertaste.
Tasted November 1975 ★★★

Ch. Pétrus. Medium colour; good rather bland bouquet which held well; dry, lightish, rich, elegant, fine. Past its best but holding firmly. Character reminds me of the 1929s. The oldest Pétrus I have tasted.
A half-bottle, July 1967 ★★★

Ch. Gruaud-Larose. Recorked. Medium colour; very sweet gentle bouquet; lightish, flavoury. Good.
Tasted twice, at the château and at the pre-sale tasting, September 1976 ★★★

1908 ★★

Picking began 21 September. Average conditions, average crop, middling quality — "a little hard, without charm", to quote a contemporary report.

Ch. Latour. Tasted twice, both excellent. Medium, very mature colour; sweet bouquet, completely sound, held well; a distinctly dry wine, lightish style for Latour but still tannic, lovely flavour and delicious dry finish.
From the de Beaumont family cellar in 1974 and one recorked 1966, at the Overton tasting, May 1976 ★★★★

Ch. Lafite. Recorked 1957. Lightish, pretty, very mature-looking; light, gentle, yet rich and stably; very sound, dry, good but short flavour, nice end tang.
From a Paris cellar, May 1976 ★★★

Ch. Haut-Brion. From an *impériale* (eight-bottle size), original cork poor and black. Wine opaque — a massive, completely mature brown; very old, very earthy smell, malty, volcanic, molasses; a huge earthy wine, rich silky texture, unusual style and character. Seemed to be in danger of collapsing when first opened at table, but improved. Impressive but curious.
Tasted December 1969 ★

1909 ★

Vines luxuriant until August storms and hail; indifferent September but hot sunny harvest around 26th. Average crop; light wines.

Ch. Lafite. Tasted four times. Depth varied from very pale to medium, but all were very brown; bouquet consistently better, some richness, spicy, *Cabernet*, curious but not unattractive; light and thin, little fruit. Not dead but faded.
Tasted 1955 — October 1969.

Ch. Latour. Fine long cork but ullaged mid-shoulder. Lightish, very mature; smoky, fruity, held well; dry, light for Latour, thinning but fruity and very pleasant.
From the de Beaumont cellar, June 1974 ★★

Ch. Léoville-Poyferré. Lightish, very mature colour but some life; sweet, gently decayed but holding; dry, fairly light, gentle, faded but sound.
From the cellars of the late Lionel Cruse, December 1975 ★★

Ch. Palmer. Palish; sweet, sound bouquet; a charming old lady. Better than the Lafite.
Tasted October 1969 ★★

1910

Bad vintage. Disheartening conditions, cold, rain, unsettled to end July; August better, but nights cold.

Weather improved at very end of September for a very late harvest, 10 October. Quarter of normal crop; insubstantial wines.

Ch. Haut-Brion. Reputed to be the best in an otherwise poor, mildewy year. Good cork, reasonable level. Medium, mature, quite brown; light yet forthcoming, an easy, high-toned *Cabernet* bouquet reminding me of Lafite 1912; dryish, light, gentle, faded but holding on. *Tasted April 1971* ★★

1911 ★★

Vines retarded, storms inducing mildew and pests, the latter being killed off by summer heat and drought. Good harvest of small ripe grapes on 20 September. Yield small, quality good.

Ch. Margaux. Of the ten châteaux of this vintage that I have tasted, this was the best. Good levels, plain corks — almost certainly recorked. Deeper and richer looking than Latour, very fine colour; bouquet rich, flavoury and fragrant; dryish, slightly austere but with attractive and positive flavour, complete and sound. *From a private cellar in Paris, 1976, November 1977* ★★★

Ch. Latour. Excellent level, recorked. Medium light, autumnal, tawny red; gentle, sweet, fragrant but showing age and a touch of peppermint; lightish, faded but pleasant, fragrant. One bottle a bit tart. *Tasted May, September 1976* ★★

Ch. Mouton-Rothschild. Medium, mature; light, gentle, faded but sound bouquet; slightly sweet, out of its own class and style, but a pleasant surprise. *At Joe Berkmann's Mouton tasting, March 1972* ★★

Ch. Cos d'Estournel. Recorked, excellent level. Palish but attractive colour; very pleasant bouquet, rich, delicate, vinous; attractive flavour, enough richness to cover piquant acidity, but with a slightly bitter finish. *From a Paris cellar, May 1976* ★★

Ch. Rausan-Ségla. Fragrant ivy-leaf nose and flavour. *Tasted November 1977* ★★

Ch. Cheval-Blanc. Original cork. Curious meaty nose, rich interesting texture and balance, bit short, dried out. *Tasted 1976, November 1977.*

1912 ★

May hot; unsettled at flowering; July satisfactory; August cold and wet; September fine and warm. Abundant harvest 26 September. Quality considered fairly satisfactory, though light.

Ch. Lafite. Tasted five times. All recorked at château. A palish, completely mature but attractive warm-amber colour; most appealing bouquet — fragrant, minty *Cabernet*, trace of eucalyptus/ginger; dry, light, faded but refreshing, cedary. *From a Rothschild family cellar and another in Paris, 1969, 1970, 1976, May 1979* ★★★

1913

Good opening to year upset by oppressive, sunless and pestilential July and August. Improvement before harvest on 25 September averted complete disaster. Abundant; mediocre, sick wines.

Ch. Latour. Lightish colour and body for Latour, mature; fragrant; dry, flavoury, some tannin and acid preserving the wine. *At the Latour pre-sale tasting, June 1977* ★

1914 ★★

Fine May, then extended and delayed flowering. Hot August. Harvest 20 September in good conditions. Average crop. First assessed very good; turned out disappointing though some excellent wines.

Ch. Lafite. Recorked. Lovely colour; light, delicate, fragrant cedar-like bouquet; dry, lightish, positive, a certain piquancy. Lacking length of a great vintage but attractive. *Tasted 1976, May 1977* ★★

Ch. Cos d'Estournel. Fine colour; old mushroomy nose but good fruit under; good flavour, long finish. *Tasted October 1969* ★

Ch. Moulin-Riche. *2me vin* of Léoville-Poyferré. Lightish but good colour; sweet, attractive nose; dry, flavoury, piquant. *Tasted 1976* ★

Ch. le Burck (Mérignac). Ullaged. Overripe, faded, edgy but still fruity and drinkable. Rare wine. *Tasted March 1979.*

1915

Crop reduced by half due to wet midsummer, mildew and pests. Wartime shortage of treatments and labour. Fine weather from August completely ripened remaining grapes by 22 September, but due to shortage of pickers many vineyards were abandoned. Quality at time reported to vary from satisfactory to bad. Never tasted.

1916 ★★

Wet spring; early June flowering, warm August and fine vintage, 26 September. Average crop of good if somewhat hard wines lacking charm.

Ch. Latour. Fairly deep, fine colour; hard, unyielding at first but as soft as it will ever get; flavoury, tannic. *Tasted 1974, at the château in 1976 and, recorked, May 1976* ★

Ch. La Mission-Haut-Brion. Recorked. Lovely appealing garnet red; very fragrant, earthy bouquet; dry, fullish, fairly powerful positive flavour. Firm, complete. *At the château, April 1978* ★★★

Ch. Capbern. Full, firm. *Tasted 1972, 1976* ★★

Ch. d'Issan. Deepish mahogany, rich tannic nose and flavour. Tough but with fruit. *Tasted 1973* ★

Ch. La Lagune. Bottled by Moll & Moll: good colour, austere but flavoury. *From the Castlemilk cellars. Tasted on six occasions, 1967 — 1969* ★★ Château bottled: old roasted nose and flavour, smoky, dried up but rich. *Tasted 1973* ★★

Ch. Léoville-Las-Cases. Rich colour, sound nose and flavour, tannic, leathery. *Tasted 1974* ★

Ch. Léoville-Poyferré. Autumnal, astringent but good. *Tasted 1970* ★★

Ch. Le Marque (possibly Lamarque). English bottled. Delightful delicacy of colour, bouquet and flavour: gentle *Cabernet* fruit, rosy blush in colour reflected in rather high end acidity — but delicious with pheasant. *Tasted December 1979* ★★

Ch. Montrose. Fullish, mahogany, leathery. *Tasted 1958* ★

1917 **

Complete contrast of style to 1916. Good, light, supple, fragrant wines. Warm May, good flowering; excessively hot June; July and August poor, changeable. Moderately early vintage, 19 September, in good conditions. Average crop partly due to labour shortage.

Ch. Lafite. Good, deepish colour; rich, attractive, slightly medicinal nose; ripe on palate, rich, dry finish. Attractive wine.
From a family cellar in Paris, June 1976 ***

Ch. Latour. Four notes on this. Colour varying from enormous, fresh and young-looking (at Berkmann's tasting of Latours in 1973) to medium, but rich and attractive; bouquet needs time to clear; but overall ripe, rich, flavoury wine with dry finish and good aftertaste.
Last tasted September 1976 ***

Ch. Gruaud-Larose. Tasted three times. Consistently fine, deep, rich tawny colour; sweet, gamy, overripe nose and flavour, but tailed off to dry astringent finish.
Tasted 1976 — June 1977 *

Ch. Léoville-Barton. Fine, rich, old *Cabernet* nose; rich, firm, silky wine with long flavour.
Tasted January 1969 ***

1918 ***

Fine spring, irregular flowering; warm summer, beneficial rain prior to harvest on 24 September. Crop slightly bigger than 1917. Good colour, sound, reasonable body. "Healthy but rough" (de Luze).

Ch. Lafite. Variable including two bad bottles. At best, medium light, very mature colour; rich, spicy old nose (needs time to clear); dried out a little, lightish but lovely flavour, variable end acidity.
Tasted 1969 — May 1977. Up to **

Ch. Latour. Also variable, from an oxidized magnum to a fine bottle: deep, fine, classic-year colour; very good bouquet, some age showing; medium dry, fairly full bodied, high quality, soft, perfect balance though not rounded like the 1920.
Last tasted at dinner at Mme Cordier's, July 1976 ***

Ch. Margaux. *2me vin.* Deeper than the 1919; old but fragrant bouquet; dry, lightish, crisp, nice flavour, holding well.
In Delor's tasting room (wine bought at Paris auction as 1er cru), April 1973 **

Ch. Léoville-Poyferré. Lovely old mahogany colour; some bottle-stink cleared to reveal rich, wholemeal bouquet; rich but lightish, elegant and silky. Lovely flavour. Perfect.
Tasted May 1970 ****

Ch. La Mission-Haut-Brion. Recorked. Medium colour; light, peppery, *gibier*; dry from start to finish. Thinning out.
Tasted at château, April 1978 *

Ch. Pavie. Poor cork, ullaged and sour in 1977. Belgian bottled: low shoulder. Old, rich; iron and ivy nose but excellent flavour and finish.
Tasted November 1977 **

Ch. Gruaud-Larose. Lovely colour, deepish, rich, *tuilé*; sweet, complex, cinnamon bouquet; ripe, rich and fruity very dry tannic finish, excellent condition.
Tasted at château in July and at Cordier pre-sale tasting, September 1976 ****

Ch. Haut-Bailly. Sound despite ullage.
Tasted 1976 *

Ch. Certan. Overripe, old, but rich and interesting.
Tasted 1975 *

1919 ***

Good spring and flowering; damp July with oidium, mildew, followed by hot summer, drought, scorched grapes. Harvest 24 September, some areas reduced, abundance at Lafite. Quality good, though light.

Ch. Lafite. Good colour, light flavoury wine.
Tasted June 1976 ***

Ch. Latour. Variable. Two bottles dusty and decomposed (1971 and 1973). Recorked bottle had attractive colour; well-knit, sound if gamy bouquet; sweet, soft, nice flavour but no great length.
Last tasted September 1976 **

Ch. Margaux. *2me vin.* Good appearance. Corks also branded "*Deuxième vin*". Deepish, browner rim than the 1918; more age on the nose, at first some decay which cleared; still a bit overacid.
In Delor's tasting room, April 1973 *

Ch. Gruaud-Larose. Magnum. Fairly deep, firm, mature colour; nose like old tobacco and damp leaves but cleared; slightly sweet, fullish, rich, still tannic, twist of acidity at end. Good aftertaste.
Tasted July 1976 **

Ch. La Mission-Haut-Brion. One bottle ullaged and oxidized in 1975. More recently: medium light, very mature; rich, ripe, appealing *gibier* nose; dry, soft, nice condition. Attractive if you like your pheasant high and your Brie runny.
Tasted December 1978 **

Ch. La Serre-Maquin (St-Emilion). Old but holding well.
Tasted 1975, 1977.

1920 ****

The first unqualified *grande année* after 1900, and if well kept, holding well. *Climate*: wet, mild winter; excellent spring, growth advanced, no frosts; flowering perfect, prospects good — then July and August exceptionally cold, with oidium and black rot which reduced an otherwise bountiful crop. September fine, with rain to swell grapes, but yield at harvest, 22 September, one-third of 1919. Quality good; healthy child turns into fine young man despite teenage problems.

Ch. Lafite. "Probably the most perfect claret now. Full, rich, with charm and softness." (Kathleen Bourke reporting in January 1967 on a dinner with Harry Waugh at Ronald Barton's.) I have tasted this wine only once. Very good level. Lovely warm colour; very attractive sweet ripe bouquet which developed and held well; some sweetness on the palate, the perfect Lafite weight, medium light, lovely gentle fragrant flavour. Clean. Lafite epitomizing red Bordeaux at its most refreshing and refined.
At the Overton tasting, May 1979 *****

Ch. Latour. "Best of all the first growths." (Edouard Cruse.) Tasted four times, and consistently good. Most recently, recorked bottle: very fine deep rich colour; excellent bouquet, mature but still peppery, rich and cedary; dry but rich, fairly full bodied, magnificent flavour, soft, velvety, well balanced.
Last noted at the Overton tasting, May 1976 ****

Ch. Margaux. Fullish colour; very rich bouquet, some decay but holding well; a huge, dry, rather austere wine, but good.
Tasted November 1971 ★★★

Ch. Mouton-Rothschild. Fullish, mature-looking; magnificent bouquet, very rich, spicy, mature; a dry, medium-bodied, lovely well-balanced wine.
Tasted September 1972 ★★★★

Ch. Cheval-Blanc. Badly ullaged. Old tawny, oxidized yet soft and drinkable.
Tasted 1978.

Ch. Brane-Cantenac. Recorked. Good colour; sound, delicate bouquet and flavour.
Tasted 1976 ★★

Ch. Durfort-Vivens. Quite good level. Sweet and ripe.
Tasted 1978 ★★

Ch. Gruaud-Larose. Very mature colour; rich, ripe; overmature but flavoury.
Tasted 1976 ★★

Ch. La Mission-Haut-Brion. Good, fully mature colour; lovely old roasted bouquet, honeyed, perfect; very rich with crumbly dry end.
At the pre-sale tasting, December 1978. Bouquet ★★★★ *Taste* ★★★

Ch. Palmer. Very fine deep colour and nose; full and fine. Holding well.
Tasted 1973 ★★★

Ch. Petit-Village. Ullaged mid-shoulder. Lovely colour, rich mahogany-amber rim; lovely rich smoky nose and flavour; dry, still slightly tannic. Very clean finish.
Tasted December 1979 ★★

Ch. Phélan-Ségur. At best: lovely colour, gentle, very flavoury.
Tasted 1976, 1977, 1978 ★ *to* ★★★

Half a dozen other wines tasted, good to overripe to oxidized, depending on state of cork and level.

1921 ★★★

A year, like 1895, noted for its exceptional heat and attendant problems of vinification. April frosts, hail, excellent flowering then exceptional and continuous heat. Picking commenced fairly early, 15 September. Moderate quantity. Good wine makers made magnificent wine. Cheval-Blanc made its reputation with this vintage (repeated in 1947). Baked grapes have thick skins and high sugar content, resulting in deep-coloured wines full of alcohol and tannin. (Lafite not tasted; Latour — one deep brown, oxidized bottle.)

Ch. Mouton-Rothschild. Good level. Very deep, fine colour; huge alcoholic nose, waxy, fruit, developed well; rich, full-bodied, strapping wine, touch of iron, loaded with tannin. Long dry finish. Impressive.
Tasted 1972, June 1975 ★★★★

Ch. Haut-Brion. An attractive bottle in 1972. Later, from the Dillon cellar (puffy cork, good level): colour not as deep as expected but lovely bright garnet; slightly sweet, delicate nose; sweet, medium light, some delicacy. Good texture, elegant and complete. Very good. Dry end.
Tasted October 1979 ★★★★

Ch. Léoville-Poyferré. Fine colour, not too deep, very mature; baked character on nose and palate. Earthy for a St-Julien, but stylish and sound.
Tasted 1972 ★★★

Ch. La Mission-Haut-Brion. Deep mature colour;

incredibly rich roasted-toasted bouquet; dry, full, rich cheesy flavour. Still lots of tannin and acidity. Excellent.
Tasted December 1978 ★★★★

Brief notes on some other wines:

Ch. Margaux. Lovely colour, rich but cracking up.
Tasted 1970.

Ch. Gruaud-Larose. Rich, singed nose and flavour.
Tasted 1976.

Ch. La Lagune. Lively, old but soft; fragrant, fruity; edgy acidity but attractive.
Tasted twice, in 1975.

Ch. Marquis-de-Terme. Deep, rich.
Tasted 1973.

Ch. Palmer. Rich, overripe but appealing.
Tasted 1973.

Ch. Pichon-Lalande. Flavoury, charming.
Tasted 1973.

Ch. Rauzan-Gassies. Lovely colour; singed fruit bouquet; good rich flavour, very dry finish. Holding well.
Tasted 1977.

Ch. Terrefort. Fine deep colour, austere yet silky.
Tasted twice, in 1967.

1922

High hopes in spring and early summer, with favourable flowering, dampened by cold wet September. Picking began early, on 19th, but those who waited benefited. Enormous crop of uneven quality.

Ch. Latour. Firm, lovely colour; old but good *Cabernet* nose; lightish, faded but surprisingly nice.
Tasted 1975, June 1977 ★★

Ch. Haut-Brion. Similar "weight" of colour as the 1953; gentle, fine old earthy Graves bouquet; dry wine, fairly light, soft, elegant, holding well.
Tasted 1971, November 1972 ★★★

Ch. Calon-Ségur. Ullaged. Old but interesting, one of the better '22s.
Tasted 1977, 1978 ★

Ch. L'Evangile. Slight ullage. Deep, fine colour; surprisingly full bodied; dry, leathery but good flavour.
Tasted March 1976 ★★

Ch. Martinens. Attractive, sound.
Tasted 1974, 1976 ★★

1923 ★★

Almost the opposite weather conditions: cold wet spring; warm summer, lacking rain; moderate, late vintage 1 October. Average quantity, quite good quality. Some charm, lacking colour.

Ch. Latour. Huge: almost as deep as the '26; curious old chocolaty bouquet; sweet, rich, slightly short and dry finish.
Tasted March 1973 ★★

Ch. Margaux. Fine deep colour; delicious, deep and aromatic bouquet, sound; rich, velvety but lightish in body and style, clean dry edge.
Tasted 1960, June 1970 ★★★

Ch. Haut-Brion. Tasted twice. First, a double magnum: old, almost deathly bouquet; an incredibly rich and impressive old flavour in 1969. More recently, a bottle with good level. Palish, very mature; sweet, sickly nose; soft, flavoury, touch of acidity.
Last tasted March 1976 ★

Ch. Calon-Ségur. Tasted twice. One bottle well past its best, but interesting, in 1967. Later, another bottle, fragrant, piquant.
Last tasted 1972. (Another 2nd growth St-Estèphe, Cos d'Estournel, is said to be one of the best.)
Ch. Montrose. Very dry, flavoury, a good drink.
Tasted 1958 ★★

1924 ★★★

Une bonne année and abundant despite severe winter, poor spring and wet summer — "worst August in living memory". Transformation due to three wonderful weeks in September (as in 1978), picking from 19th in variable conditions. Now overripe and drying out, but the best bottles full of flavour and charm.
Ch. Lafite. Medium pale, finely graduated rose-hued tawny colour; delicate arboreal, very fragrant bouquet, exquisite after some time in glass; on the palate distinctly sweet, delicately balanced, attractive.
Tasted 1971, 1977; showed well at the Overton tasting, May 1979, and, better still, from the Dillon cellar, October 1979 ★★★★ to ★★★★★
Ch. Latour. Very fine deep mahogany; rich old nose, developed well; full flavoured, tannic. Plenty of life.
Tasted 1976, May 1977 ★★★★
Ch. Margaux. Fine, bright, mature colour; ripe but drying out; faded elegance.
Tasted 1970, 1971 ★★★
Ch. Haut-Brion. Dubious in 1972. Later, two samples from the Dillon cellar excellent: rich colour, intense rim; sweet, rich, ripe gamy nose and flavour; dry, medium light, firm, positive, more acidity and less good finish than the excellent 1926.
Tasted November and December 1979 ★★★★
Of the 27 other '24s I have tasted the best were:
Ch. Beychevelle. Tasted ten times, all from half-bottles, varying levels. Some astringency but at best a deliciously rich, ripe fragrant wine, charming, delicate.
Tasted 1976 — December 1978 ★★ to ★★★
Ch. Capbern. Gentle, faded but nice and sound.
Tasted 1972 ★★
Ch. Chasse-Spleen. Dry, flavoury, piquant, charming.
Tasted 1975 ★★
Ch. Desmirail. Half-bottle: lovely, rich; delicate; delicious.
Tasted June 1976 ★★★
Ch. Ducru-Beaucaillou. Old looking; better flavour than nose.
Tasted 1967, 1969, 1976 ★
Ch. Giscours. Fine, rich but somewhat dry leathery flavour, yet some softness.
Tasted 1971, 1975 ★★
Ch. La Mission-Haut-Brion. Marvellous deep colour; fabulous bouquet; very rich, like singed earth; drying out but a lovely flavour, surprising delicacy.
At pre-sale tasting, December 1978 ★★★
Ch. Nenin. Fragrant, silky, light but firm in 1964. More recently, a low-shoulder bottle, oxidized, falling apart.
Last tasted 1975. Up to ★★
Ch. Palmer. Lively colour; exquisite bouquet; charming and elegant in 1975. Later, from an *impériale*: fine, deep colour; fragrant but overripe nose; dry, medium light, very rich but fading and with edgy end acidity, a *demi-mondaine* of advancing age but opulent charms.
Tasted at Kerry Payne's dinner at Brooks's club, June 1977 ★★★

Ch. Pichon-Lalande. Looked like a '52; overripe at first but developed warmly in glass; dry, lightish, refined, smooth and silky. Long dry finish. Perfect. A lingering thoroughbred.
Tasted December 1969 ★★★★
Ch. La Pointe. At best retaining fruit, lovely balance and that silky Pomerol texture. Ullaged bottles poor.
Tasted 1971, 1977. To ★★★
Ch. Rausan-Ségla. Decaying, overripe but very flavoury — like well-hung pheasant.
Tasted 1975 ★★

1925 ★

A somewhat unripe year due to lack of sun. June and the flowering were good; otherwise, cold, wet, dull. Late vintage, 3 October, to take advantage of improved conditions. Abundant. Because there were so many good vintages in the 1920s, very few '25s were shipped to England; the few examples I have tasted coming from overseas cellars. Cos d'Estournel was reputed to be one of the best. An overripe vintage which needs drinking up.
Ch. Lafite. One bottle colourless and acetic; another with 2-inch ullage, pale, but light, elegant and quite flavoury.
From a cellar in New York, tasted 1971 ★
Ch. Léoville-Las-Cases. Half-bottle. Palish but lovely colour; curious, thinning but holding on to life.
Tasted 1969.
Ch. Beychevelle. Good level, very mature, old and tailing off.
Tasted 1976.
Dom. de Chevalier. Richer and more interesting.
Tasted 1976 ★
Ch. Ferrière. A wine from Margaux rarely seen in any vintage. It had a good long branded cork and reasonable level, just below top of shoulder. Medium pale, rich and attractive, brown edge; touch of decay at first, but overall sweet bouquet; overripe sweetness on the palate too, but delicate and pleasant drink.
Tasted November 1979 ★

1926 ★★★★

Une très bonne année but small crop due to poor flowering after long winter, cold spring and drought during long, very hot dry summer (similar to 1865), which continued through to late harvest, 4 October. Very high prices due to small quantity and boom period.
Ch. Lafite. Came on the market at an exorbitant price. Once had all the trappings of a hot year: deep colour, rich and ripe. Now losing colour though still a rich ruddy hue; at best rich, fragrant, cedary bouquet and flavour but overripe with traces of acidity. Dangerous but rewarding.
Tasted 1975, 1977, May 1979 ★★ to ★★★
Ch. Latour. Consistently good, very deep still, like the 1955; bouquet absolute perfection — sweet, rich, deep *Cabernet* aroma; a fairly full, rich wine, powerful yet delicate flavour, crisp, excellent finish.
Tasted five times between 1966 and 1978, twice at the château. One of the best wines at the Latour tasting organized by Joseph Berkmann in 1973 and at Dr Overton's in 1976 ★★★★★
Ch. Margaux. Very deep colour; very fine, smoky bouquet; sweetish, rich, soft, ripe, long and dry finish.
Tasted November 1975 ★★★★

Ch. Haut-Brion. First tasted in 1971: deep, port-like though austere. Then from the Dillon stock at pre-sale tastings. Good levels and corks. Very deep, rich attractive colour; sweet, broad, harmonious nose, which opened up and developed to delicate perfection; lovely flavour and balance. Excellent, perfect dry finish. One bottle not quite as impressive, deep, burnt, prune-like nose, some acidity.
Last tasted October and twice in December 1979. At best ★★★★★

Ch. Cheval-Blanc. The decade of the 1920s was good at this château. The '26 memorable for me for when I first drank it, lunching at Berry Bros, in 1967, I could not believe it was from Bordeaux — more like the plumpest, ripest and most velvety burgundy (just as the '47 is almost port wine). Medium light yet rich mahogany colour; full but delicate bouquet, honeyed, harmonious; fairly sweet for claret, lovely rich flavour, perfect weight and balance. In fact a perfect wine. Decanted four hours prior, from bottles never moved from Berry's cellars.
Tasted on three occasions since, in 1970, 1974 ★★★★★

Other good '26s tasted:

Ch. Beychevelle. Opaque; solid rich bouquet and flavour.
Tasted 1973 ★★★★

Ch. Cos d'Estournel. Silky, fading but nice.
Tasted 1970 ★★★

Ch. Ducru-Beaucaillou. Very deep; fine cedar bouquet; drying out, austere.
Tasted June 1975 ★★

Ch. La Mission-Haut-Brion. Fabulous colour, very lively and as deep as the '28; soft, delicate, wonderful bouquet, still full of fruit; medium dry, silky, rich, elegant, dry finish.
Tasted 1973 and at the pre-sale tasting in December 1978 ★★★★

Ch. Mouton d'Armailhacq. Lightish; old cedar; flavoury.
Tasted 1974, 1976 ★★★

Ch. Pouget. Most excellent: delicate flavour and balance.
Tasted 1975 ★★★

Ch. Talbot. Mature; slightly sweet, some astringency but good.
Tasted 1970 ★★

1927

A poor vintage, certainly the worst of the 1920s. After good flowering and hot July the weather deteriorated: cold, wet, windy through to picking 27 September. Reports at the time expected normal yield and some quality. Ignored by the trade; an abundance of good vintages either side, so rarely seen.

Ch. Latour. Good colour, medium deep, very mature; delicate, peppery, *Cabernet-Sauvignon* bouquet; lightish, surprisingly nice, refreshing acidity, soft, slightly short.
From the cellars of the Comtesse de Beaumont, 1974, and a recorked bottle from the château on my 50th birthday, May 1977 ★★

Ch. Margaux. Good cork. Excellent appearance. Lightish mature red; sweet, *Cabernet* bouquet and flavour. Remarkably attractive for a year of ill-repute. Reminded me of Lafite 1912. Much better than the '27 Romanée-Conti tasted at same time.
Tasted April 1971 ★★

Ch. Loudenne. Deep colour, very brown; old, mushroomy but some fragrance; dry, lightish. Holding well.
At the château, April 1979 ★

1928 ★★★★★

A monumental year: flowering under good conditions; splendid summer, excessive August heat tempered by beneficial rain; harvest 25 September in promising conditions. Of all the vintages of this decade, the most massively constituted and holding best.

Ch. Latour. I am putting this first, because it is archetypal and probably the best '28 now. Like the 1870 Lafite, it was overloaded with tannin and took half a century to soften. I remember dining at the Sichel home in the mid-1950s when young Peter told me that his father was drinking the '28 Latour as his house wine and that it would never come round in his lifetime. Alas, he was right. It is still enormously deep in colour, a beautiful shade, rich; rich also on nose and palate, full bodied, still laden with tannin but softening with almost velvety dry finish.
Last tasted at a Bordeaux Club dinner at Caius College, Cambridge, February 1980 ★★★★

Ch. Lafite. Not remotely in the 1870 class, but with rich attractive colour; crumbling nose — some fragrance and spice; better on palate — dry, beefy, tannic, some astringency, dull. On the last two occasions with the original crumbly corks.
Last tasted May 1979 ★

Ch. Margaux. Reputed to be the best since 1900. Fine deep colour, strong mature rim; touch of old age on nose but deep and attractive; full, firm well-balanced wine. Iron fist in velvet glove.
Tasted 1971, August 1976 ★★★★

Ch. Mouton-Rothschild. Very deep, crisp red brown; a dangerously exciting nose and flavour — fruity, peppery, mature, attractive, plenty of substance to mask fairly high acidity.
Tasted 1967, 1972, September 1977 ★★

Ch. Haut-Brion. A most curious wine, as if made from singed raisins and prunes. Opaque; burnt nose, high acidity in 1970 and 1974. From the Dillon cellar, one corked bottle, another with opulent, overripe nose — living dangerously; slightly sweet, full, rich, exaggerated style, better balanced than the '29. Most extraordinary and perversely impressive wine.
Tasted October and December 1979 ★★★

Ch. Cheval-Blanc. Certainly unusual, soft, unlike any other '28, with little tannin left. As always, storage and state of cork is a critical factor.
Tasted three times, 1955 — 1978 ★

Other '28s showing well:

Ch. d'Angludet. Fabulous, very mature; showing a lot of age with slight sweetness of decay — overripe pheasant; good but not lengthy flavour, attractive, dry finish.
Tasted September 1978 ★★★

Ch. Beychevelle. Ripe, attractive.
Tasted 1970, 1978 ★★★

Ch. Bouscaut. Deep mahogany; wonderful, singed, earthy flavour, tough but serene, virile yet an old man.
Tasted 1969 ★★★

Ch. Brane-Cantenac. Perfectly lovely in early 1960s. Later, a bit severe.
Last tasted 1971 ★ to ★★★

Ch. Calon-Ségur. Almost opaque; a full, rich, leathery wine.
Consistent on seven occasions, 1954 — May 1976 ★★★
Ch. Capbern. Rich, lovely.
Tasted 1972, 1976 ★★★
Ch. Cos d'Estournel. Almost opaque; rich, full, very good flavour, silk and leather texture.
Tasted 1973, 1976 ★★★
Ch. L'Evangile. Opaque; sweaty old nose; soft, delightful flavour with the velvety texture of a fine Pomerol.
Tasted 1977, March 1978 ★★★
Ch. Figeac. Bouquet like mushroom soup. Rich, gentle. First rate in 1968. Later, still holding well.
Last tasted January 1977 ★★
Ch. Gazin. Variable, at best slightly sweet, soft, elegant and attractive.
Tasted 1966 — 1975 ★★
Ch. Gruaud-Larose. Fine, deep; sweet ripe bouquet; rich but dry.
Tasted 1956, 1974, September 1976 ★★★
Ch. Lagrange. Fruit and charm, flavoury, acidity showing through.
Tasted June 1977 ★
Ch. La Lagune. Very forthcoming, rich, lovely bouquet and flavour.
Tasted 1970, and 1975 when at its best ★★★
Ch. Latour-Pomerol. Fragrant, delicate, nice balance.
Tasted May 1977 ★★★★
Ch. Malescot-St-Exupéry. Marvellous depth; fine old *Cabernet* nose and flavour. Dry, rich, good finish.
Tasted 1976 ★★★
Ch. La Mission-Haut-Brion. Deep colour but, surprisingly, lighter than the '29; rich, fruity, rather overdeveloped, but flavoury with crispness and very dry end.
Tasted 1973, 1975 and twice recorked ex-château, April and December 1978 ★★★
Ch. Mouton-d'Armailhacq. Beautiful garnet red; ripe, fascinating, sweet, *gibier*; rich, tannic.
Tasted 1969, 1971 ★★★
Ch. Smith-Haut-Lafitte. Lightish colour for a '28; rich, interesting, high-toned bouquet, cinnamon; soft, pleasant. Holding well.
Tasted 1976 ★★
Ch. Talbot. Half-bottle: lovely colour, nose and flavour. Tannic but not heavy.
Tasted 1976 ★★★
Of the twenty other '28s tasted, some notes are rather old and possibly no longer applicable. For example:
Ch. Langoa-Barton. I noted: "magnificent, full of goodness and character" in 1955. But 25 years later it will surely be less so.

1929 ★★★★★

Considered the best vintage since 1900. A complete contrast in style to its twin, 1928. Soft, elegant wines of great finesse and delicacy. The early part of the year was generally favourable. Flowering started in good weather but became irregular due to rain. July, August and September were unusually hot and dry, though there was beneficial rain mid-September prior to picking on 26th. As in 1928, an average-size crop. The best (and best-kept) wines still retain the hallmark of finesse and suppleness, but, less sturdily constituted than '28s, they are fading and those left should be drunk.

Ch. Latour. Of the 55 different '29s I have tasted over the years, Latour is the most consistently beautiful. I prefer it to the renowned 1928; it is in the same league as the great pre-phylloxera vintages and the 1900 and 1920. Fine deep colour with rich mahogany edge; rich, gentle, ripe cedar and *Cabernet* bouquet; a rich opulent wine, soft, luscious, complete.
Tasted eight times, once in 1955, mainly in the 1970s, last in June 1977 ★★★★★
Ch. Mouton-Rothschild. For some years the idol of the salerooms, particularly in jeroboams. Like Mistinguett, Marlene Dietrich, Greta Garbo: ineffable, unattainable, full of mystique and star quality — even when past its prime. To me, in gastronomic terms, it is like a well-hung pheasant, gamy, expensive. I have wallowed in its *de luxe* corruption on several occasions, the last from a jeroboam: in fact I found the bouquet very fragrant, very exciting; opulent fruit, really a glorious flavour and excellent aftertaste but showing distinct signs of cracking up. Past its best, but what a best that must have been. The thrill was to catch the bird before extinction.
Six notes from 1968 to the Kerry Payne dinner at Brooks's, June 1977 ★★★★
Ch. Lafite. Lafite was not as successful in the 1920s as some of the other first growths. There are considerable arguments about the '29. I have tasted it on only four occasions, all in the United States and all from mid-shoulder-level bottles. One, in 1975, I thought old but exquisite; the others astringent, dried out. There must be better bottles but at best it will be showing its age.
Tasted 1972–1979.
Ch. Margaux. The '29 did not have the reputation of the '28. I have tasted it only twice, once at the château, and found it disappointing. Medium-light colour; lacking the bouquet that is Margaux's pride and joy; a bit mean and stingy on the palate. (Note to try again.)
Tasted 1971, 1975 ★
Ch. Haut-Brion. With its almost identical twin, the '28, one of the most idiosyncratic, assertive, strangely impressive of wines. Tasted five times. First in 1972 when I noted an incredible scent, very odd, more like a tokay essence. Always very deep, concentrated brown, amber rimmed, occasionally overacid. Nearly came to blows with the great Len Evans at his memorable dinner in Sydney — only the large-framed Mr Fraser, the prime minister, sitting between us, kept us apart. Len thought it magnificent; I thought it overblown. Most recently tasted from the Dillon cellar: original cork, long and greasy. Intense depth; rich, malt-extract nose; immensely rich, slightly sweet, full bodied, highest extract after the '28 I have ever known — more like port. Mountainous, perverse. A matter of taste. I now have a feeling that we were both right.
Last tasted October 1979 ★★★
Ch. Cheval-Blanc. One of the really great '29s. Now lightish, colour fading; beautiful, delicate, fragrant, minty *Cabernet* bouquet; distinctly sweet, ripe, delicious, charming ethereal flavour and exquisite finish. Like Marlene Dietrich, as I remember her in cabaret in the 1950s.
Tasted 1971, 1972, January 1978 ★★★★
Ch. Léoville-Poyferré. Also reputed to have been one of the most exquisite '29s. I have tasted it only once,

from a magnum: fine, deepish, very mature colour; very rich, positively sweet-ripe *Cabernet* bouquet — fabulous; distinctly sweet and ripe on the palate, fullish, rich, some tannin holding it together firmly, lovely finish. A remarkable wine altogether.
Tasted December 1960 ★★★★★

Ch. La Mission-Haut-Brion. Described by the Woltner family as "a no problem wine", it has an incredibly deep colour, virtually opaque; exceedingly rich nose, sweet, meaty, burnt cocoa, which developed and held well; ripe, full of body and flavour, very rich, *à point*.
Tasted 1973 and three times in 1978 ★★★★★

Tasted in the 1960s:

Ch. Beychevelle. Soft, feminine, lovely.
Tasted 1968 ★★★★

Dom. de Chevalier. Full coloured; honeyed bouquet; fine silky wine.
Tasted 1968 ★★★★

Ch. Lascombes. Quiet, firm, balanced — the perfect gentleman.
Tasted 1969 ★★★★

Ch. La Tour-Carnet. Full, silky but dry, more like a 1928.
Tasted twice in 1969 ★★★

Of the wines tasted, or last tasted, in the 1970s:

Ch. Batailley. Fragrant, delightful, *à point*.
Tasted 1972 ★★★★

Ch. Calon-Ségur. Outstandingly rich colour; rich yet refined; great vinosity, lovely finish.
Tasted 1967, 1971, 1972 ★★★★

Ch. Canon. One of my favourite St-Emilions. Deep garnet red, mahogany edge; rich, mature, perfect bouquet, flavour and balance. No signs of cracking up.
Tasted April 1978 ★★★★

Ch. Capbern. Attractive but short.
Tasted 1972, 1976 ★★

Ch. Ducru-Beaucaillou. Deep, showing considerable age in colour and on nose but wonderfully rich, beautifully balanced and no decay.
Tasted 1975 ★★★★

Ch. Duhart-Milon. Dry, austere but lovely drink.
Tasted 1961, 1970 ★★★

Ch. Laburthe-Brivazac. Like a reincarnation, tasting a wine from a château long since overrun by the Bordeaux suburban sprawl. A fine deep classic colour, more like a '28; touch of death on the nose, fungi and acidity; but dry, silky texture, rich yet austere. More graves than Graves, but fascinating.
Tasted 1971 ★★

Ch. La Lagune. Rich, elegant but touch of sourness.
Tasted 1975 ★★

Ch. Montrose. Half-bottle. Dry, elegant, touch of acidity but good aftertaste.
Tasted 1976 ★★★

Ch. Nenin. Calm, cedar bouquet; rich, good, sound.
Tasted 1974 ★★★★

Ch. Pavie. Very deep, rich, good but not great.
Tasted 1972 ★★★

Ch. Rausan-Ségla. Very fine deep colour; exceedingly rich, thoroughbred stables bouquet; positively sweet on palate, overripe, very flavoury.
Tasted six times, 1965–1975 ★★★★

Ch. Rouget. Deep, sweet, *gibier*.
Tasted 1973 ★★★

Ch. Talbot. Outstanding, almost exotically rich and characterful, though some Talbot leanness and masculinity.
Tasted 1968 and twice, from magnums, in 1978 ★★★★

Ch. Terrefort de Fortissan. Opaque; *gibier*.
Tasted 1974, 1975 ★

Ch. La Tour-Haut-Brion. Deep, ripe, good.
Tasted October 1978 ★★★

The following were on the slippery slope (on dates in brackets):

Ch. Desmirail (*twice in 1969*); **Ch. La Dominique** (*1970*); **Ch. Durfort-Vivens** (*1979*); **Ch. Figeac** (*1969, 1975*); **Ch. Gruaud-Larose** (*1969*); **Ch. Léoville-Barton** (*1972, 1974, 1978*); **Ch. Marquis-de-Terme** (*three times in 1976*).

I think in fact most of the great '29s were really at their peak in the 1950s for I have many notes throughout this decade: "lovely, perfection, crystallized violets, complete". These include:

Ch. Brane-Cantenac; Ch. Cantenac-Brown; Clos Fourtet; Ch. La Grave-Trigant; Ch. Lynch-Bages; Ch. Meyney; Ch. Pichon-Baron; Ch. La Pointe; Ch. Pontet-Canet.

1930

Heralded the entry of the three most dismal consecutive vintages of Bordeaux's most dreary decade. It seems that bad weather, bad wines and bad times go together. The weather had no redeeming features: continual rain in June and July, very little warmth when needed. A trade paper reported "this year's crop [picked 1 October] is a complete failure as regards quality and quantity". Not tasted.

1931

Nearly as bad. Rainy spring, fine June, then cold and wet. Beautiful autumn enabled an average crop of mediocre grapes to be picked 25 September

Ch. Latour. In poor condition. Ullaged. Old socks, a trifle sour but just drinkable.
At the Overton tasting, May 1976.

Ch. Haut-Brion. Two notes, first at the pre-sale tasting of Dillon stock in December 1979. Half-bottle, good level for age (upper shoulder). Very good colour for an "off" year; curious meaty/varnishy nose and flavour. And, more recently, at home (I bought some because it is the year of my wife's birth): similar, a sort of '29 concentrated must character. Extraordinary.
Last tasted February 1980 ★

1932

The latest harvest on record, starting 10–15 October under indifferent conditions and ending 1 December. Half crop, execrable quality.

Ch. Latour. The only '32 I have tasted. Latour has the reputation of being able to make decent wine even in bad years. A bottle from the château, presumably recorked: modest colour but not totally pale and lifeless; nose of rotten grapes and ginger biscuits (sugary old *Cabernet*); a bit pasty on the palate, but not bad.
Tasted June 1977.

1933 ★★

A generally overlooked and underrated vintage. Poor

weather impaired flowering; lack of rain in July and hot dry winds in August reduced crop. Moderately early harvest, 22 September, in fine weather. Light flavoury wines.

Ch. Lafite. Medium colour, fine, mature; completely ripe bouquet; dry, lightish, touch of acidity but nice. *Tasted only once, from Caves Maxim, at Heublein's, May 1978* ★★

Ch. Latour. A rich, complex, very ripe wine, still fairly deep, lovely colour; magnificent, fragrant, cedary bouquet; fruity, but not heavy. Elegant, flavoury, opulent yet lean.
Tasted five times since 1964. Considerable arguments at Dr Overton's tasting, half of the guests preferring the '34. Last tasted May 1976 ★★★

Ch. Margaux. I rated it near to perfection, with superfine bouquet and flavour. Dry, elegant, refined.
Tasted 1957, 1966 ★★★★

Ch. Cheval-Blanc. Tasted once, English bottled. Palish, very mature; extraordinary bouquet, very scented, butter-drops (an old English toffee); slightly sweet, very light in body, fading, ethereal but no decay. Fragile, charming, exquisite aftertaste.
Tasted 1975 ★★★

Ch. La Mission-Haut-Brion. Very mature brown colour; rich, ripe, open ivy-leaf tinged bouquet; flavoury but crumbling. Dry finish.
Twice, at pre-sale tastings, December 1978 ★★

Ch. Ducru-Beaucaillou. Lovely colour; rich, cheesy nose, which developed well in the glass; gentle, fruity, good balance.
Tasted 1970 ★★★

1934 ★★★

Undoubtedly the best vintage of the 1930s. Drought conditions in June and July were followed by sufficient rain to swell the grapes for a good, early (15 September) and abundant harvest: double that of 1933. Sound and deep wines, the best still excellent. But they are not improving and some distinctly cracking up.

Ch. Lafite. Despite the reports (in 1953) of it going downhill, it is clearly enjoying the ride. Notes at three tastings in recent years have been consistent: lightish colour, very mature-looking but lively and attractive; bouquet and flavour delicate but rich, complex, showing age but charming.
Tasted 1972, 1974 and at the Overton tasting May 1979 ★★★

Ch. Latour. Deep, soft and perfect in the 1950s, my later notes indicate browning; bouquet spicy but spiked (a sharpness on nose leading to tartness on palate). At the Overton tasting in May 1976 I felt it was overripe with flesh hanging loose. Others liked it. Most recently at the Coq Hardy, Bougival: old nose — celery and boiled fennel, trace of paint stripper (estery), very flavoury but drying out and acidic.
Last tasted February 1980 ★

Ch. Margaux. First tasted in 1954 (my note is a terse VG — very good). I next drank it with pheasant in chocolate sauce! Its delicacy did not stand a chance. More recent exposures have varied according to state of cork and levels. It is a surprisingly deep-coloured wine and at its best has that unequalled Margaux fragrance of bouquet, with flavour and elegance to match on the palate. Rich, ripe, old but saucy.
Last tasted July 1978 ★★★

Ch. Mouton-Rothschild. Ten tasting notes, from 1955, when it was very deep coloured and "just reaching its apogee" (to quote Harry Waugh, tasting it in 1953). Now less deep, but marvellously rich looking; rich, fragrant, flavoury but acidity beginning to show through.
Last tasted May 1977 ★★ *to* ★★★★

Ch. Haut-Brion. Deep rich colour; concentrated bouquet; rich earthy character: a good '34.
Tasted 1955, 1972 and from the Dillon cellar, October 1979 ★★★

Ch. Cheval-Blanc. Danish bottled. Good level, light but lovely colour; nose a bit varnishy at first but developed richness and delicacy; lovely finish. Exquisite.
Tasted June 1978 ★★★★

Ch. La Mission-Haut-Brion. Fabulous colour, deep, bright; fragrant, slightly scented nose; sweet rich wine.
At the pre-sale tasting, December 1978 ★★★★

Other interesting '34s tasted:

Ch. Canon-La Gaffelière. One, Belgian bottled, meaty, rich; another oxidized.
Tasted 1978 to ★★

Ch. Cos d'Estournel. Deep brown; dry, peppery, austere old man.
Tasted 1956, 1965, 1974, 1977.

Ch. Le Couvent (St-Emilion). Belgian bottled. Sound and attractive.
Tasted 1978 ★★

Ch. Langoa-Barton. Lovely colour; rich old stably nose; a big wine, somewhat astringent but characterful.
Tasted 1968, 1969 ★★

Ch. Léoville-Poyferré.
Tasted 1954, 1975, 1978.

Ch. Pichon-Baron. Delicious in 1955, attractive in 1967. Not tasted recently.

1935 ★

An overlooked vintage. Late flowering, hot dry summer but very wet September. Picking began late, 30 September, presumably in the hopes of last minute sun which did not arrive. Early pickers did best. Abundant (rain filled out grapes); quality irregular, green. Rarely seen.

Ch. Latour. Deepish; rich, peppery, *Cabernet* bouquet, held well; dry, fairly full bodied, touch of volatile acidity but quite a nice wine.
Tasted June 1974 ★★

Ch. La Mission-Haut-Brion. Deep, like the '34 but somewhat drab; curious nose — compost and sour cream; a dry, lightish austere wine, with flavour of boiled sweets.
At the pre-sale tasting, December 1978.

Ch. Lestage. Fine colour; nose and palate sound, dry, slightly short.
Tasted 1976 ★

Ch. Pontet-Canet. English bottled. Poor corks and ullaged, varnishy, oxidized.
Tasted November 1979.

1936 ★

An equally overlooked vintage. When bottled in 1938, the trade, just recovering from the slump, was probably working off its stock of '29s and looking forward to the much acclaimed '37s. Almost diametrically opposite weather conditions: wet summer, fine September, late picking 1–4 October. Rather tart wines, rarely seen, but I prefer them to the '35s.

Ch. Latour. Fullish, mature; rich old gamy bouquet — attractive in a perverse sort of way; charming and flavoury in 1976. Later, a trifle green and tart.
Last tasted 1978 ★★

Ch. La Mission-Haut-Brion. Deepish colour, very fine and bright; a singed, sugared-sweet nose but fragrant; flavoury and nice acidity.
Tasted 1978 ★★

Ch. Cheval-Blanc. Half-bottle. Maderized and flat.
Tasted 1976.

Ch. Mouton-d'Armailhacq. A pretty wine; piquant *Cabernet* bouquet and flavour.
Tasted 1976 ★

Ch. Cantenac-Prieuré (now **Prieuré-Lichine**). Similar.
Tasted 1976 ★

Ch. Lagrange. Somewhat tart but flavoury.
Tasted twice, in 1976.

Ch. Branaire-Duluc-Ducru. Full coloured, severe.
Tasted 1973.

Ch. Coufran (St-Estèphe). Good colour; attractive; sound and flavoury. A constant delight.
Tasted nine times, 1968 — 1970 ★★

1937 ★★

A curious year: drought without excessive heat from May to the second week of September, when there was welcome rain. Harvest 20 September, under ideal conditions. Quantity average, quality thought promising at the time but the wines, whilst often fragrant, are mostly dried up and astringent.

Ch. Lafite. Not easy to generalize. Several magnums, probably poorly kept, and some slightly ullaged, were astringent and oxidized at tastings in the United States in 1974 and 1975. A recent bottle surprised me with its very attractive warm colour; gentle fragrant cedar bouquet; very positive and appealing flavour, good acidity. Improved in glass.
At the Overton tasting, May 1979. To ★★★

Ch. Margaux. I have always considered this the best of the '37s. Fine, pretty colour; very rich, wholesome bouquet; dry, delicate, also a dry finish but not the usual '37 acidity. A middle-aged but charming lady.
Tasted 1970 — June 1978 ★★★

Ch. Latour. Not my favourite Latour. In 1955 I noted that it had lost all its tannin; in 1965, tired watery finish; in 1966, lovely flavour but astringent end. More recently, spicy medicinal nose but high acidity, even tart.
Tasted 1975, 1976, December 1978.

Ch. Mouton-Rothschild. A huge tough-looking wine; rich, opulently scented; quite nice flavour but some decay and swingeing acidity.
Tasted only once, in March 1972 ★

Ch. Haut-Brion. A fairly astringent specimen at a Heublein tasting in 1975, but two good bottles from the Dillon cellar, levels mid- and upper shoulder: fairly deep intense colour; very rich, concentrated though low-keyed bouquet, very sound; dry, lovely flavour and fruit but fairly obtrusive '37 tannic acid.
Tasted October and December 1979 ★★

Ch. La Mission-Haut-Brion. Deep; fruity but aged and a bit short — still one of the better '37s.
Tasted 1973 ★★

Ch. Ausone. Deep brown, oxidized in 1975. Later, not

bad: chocolaty — old straw nose, dry, austere, tailed off.
Last tasted 1976.

Ch. Cheval-Blanc. Mature, slight orange tinge; rich old nose; dry, leathery.
Tasted 1970, 1977 ★

Ch. Batailley. Attractive colour; old but fragrant.
Tasted May 1978 ★★

Ch. Beychevelle. Charming but a bit leathery.
Tasted 1971 ★★

Ch. Calon-Ségur. Deep, lemon-mahogany rim; unknit but intriguing and fragrant bouquet; flavoury. A bit edgy but not a bad '37.
Tasted 1954, 1961, May 1979 ★

Ch. Cos d'Estournel. Deep, rich; leathery; tannic.
Tasted 1970, 1974 ★

Ch. Giscours. Fine deep colour; old and rather full classic nose and flavour, but also austere, leathery.
Tasted 1971, 1975 ★★

Ch. Lascombes. Good mature colour; gentle, rich yet dry, tannin and acidity but a good '37.
Tasted May 1979 ★★

Ch. Gruaud-Larose. Old, like decaying leaves, astringent and unappealing.
Tasted twice, in 1976.

Ch. Marquis-de-Terme. Flavoury but spoiled by rasping acidity.
Tasted four times in 1976.

Ch. Palmer. Very deep; sweet nose; rich and flavoury.
Tasted twice, in 1976 ★★★

1937s were frequently seen in my early days in the trade, so I have quite a few old and now fairly irrelevant notes, for example: **Ch. Montrose.** Big and black in colour and far too hard and tannic, bouquet the best feature (in 1955). In the 1960s I quite liked **Ch. Capbern, Ch. Mouton d'Armailhacq** and one or two others. I did not care for the vintage then and care less for it now, 32 wines and over 60 tastes later.

1938 ★

Lack of sun delayed ripening. Late vintage, 28 September. Slightly below average in quantity and quality. Bottled in the early days of the war and now rarely seen. Light wines, mostly with acidity showing through now.

Ch. Latour. Tasted four times. Fullish, lovely colour; a good, rich, if somewhat unknit bouquet and flavour. Soft, ripe. Acidity a bit obtrusive.
Tasted 1966 — December 1978 ★★

Ch. Cheval-Blanc. Attractive *tuilé* colour; light, curious but nice bouquet and flavour. Slightly sweet, dry finish.
Tasted 1976 ★

Ch. La Mission-Haut-Brion. Same weight as the '36. Piquant.
Tasted December 1978 ★

Ch. Rausan-Ségla. Fine deep colour; good rich fragrant cedary nose; a lightish style, nice. Finished weakly.
Tasted 1975 ★

Ch. Coufran. Attractive but with a bitter finish.
Tasted 1968.

1939

Six weeks from end of June cold and stormy. Abundant but very late harvest, 2 October. Light, but fragrant.
Ch. Latour. Deep coloured, as ever, amber-brown rim;

rich old nose; dry, getting tired, yet elegant, interesting.
Tasted 1964, 1976, December 1978 ★★

Ch. Margaux. Smooth, velvety, distinctly flavoury and attractive.
But this was in 1954 ★★★

Ch. Mouton-Rothschild. Lightish in colour; sound and nice bouquet; with an acceptable twist of acidity.
At the Heublein tasting, May 1978 ★

1940 ★★

Picking began 26 September. Vines suffered from wartime neglect. Average crop of variable wines. No reports in trade press of the time. Can still be attractive.

Ch. Latour. Surprisingly deep even for Latour; sweet, almost overrich but fragrant *Cabernet* bouquet; not quite as attractive on the palate — chunky, dry finish. Best were recorked at the château. One in the United States was oxidized.
Tasted on seven occasions between 1967 and May 1979 ★★

Ch. Haut-Brion. Good level. Beautiful garnet red; rich, meaty/iron bouquet; medium dry, medium body, attractive, flavoury, holding well.
From the Dillon cellar, October 1979 ★★★

Ch. La Mission-Haut-Brion. Very fragrant bouquet, crystallized violets; dry, light, very flavoury, attractive.
At the pre-sale tasting, December 1978 ★★★

Ch. Cantemerle. Kressmann's bottles variable. Faded old fruit in 1974. Acetic in 1975. Later, flavoury but breaking up, slightly ullaged.
Last tasted 1976.

Ch. Palmer. Rich; smoky, intriguing; sound and flavoury, though short.
Tasted 1973 ★★

Ch. Calon-Ségur. Deep coloured; big and tannic.
Tasted 1957, 1960 ★★

1941 ★

Very cold winter, mediocre spring but good summer. Vines suffered from diseases, due to neglect. Small and late (3 October) vintage of mediocre wines.

Ch. Latour. Deep, rich and attractive looking; rich, quite good but unripe *Cabernet* bouquet; fullish, very dry and austere.
Tasted 1969, December 1978 ★

Ch. La Mission-Haut-Brion. Better colour than the '40; some richness but delicate; flavoury.
Tasted December 1978 ★★

1942

Another very long cold winter; dry and warm spring and summer; poor September. Picking commenced 19 September. Small crop of light, pleasant and useful wines.

Ch. Lafite. Fine, medium colour, rich and attractive looking; gentle old nose; stringy, showing age but nice.
Tasted 1974, 1975, December 1976 ★★

Ch. Latour. Opaque in 1964. More recently: still quite deep; hard, dusty bouquet, some fruit; very dry, tannic. Powerful but no follow through. One bottle oxidized.
Last tasted September 1976 ★

1943 ★★★

Cold winter, good flowering, hot and dry summer. The best of the wartime vintages. Average crop (picking began 19 September). Mainly good, some great. Out of

the 20 or so châteaux tasted, overall impression is of richness and fruit, nice quality but lacking persistence: blunt.

Ch. Latour. Deep, rich, in 1954. More recently: losing colour; rich peppery *Cabernet* nose; velvety yet tough.
Last tasted at Dr Overton's, May 1976 ★★

Ch. Margaux. Mature colour; delicate yet rich bouquet and flavour. Good condition, attractive but short.
Tasted at the château in 1975, and in the U.S.A., May 1978 ★★

Ch. Mouton-Rothschild. Rich, old cedar; not as good on the palate, some style no charm.
Tasted in Australia, 1975 ★

Ch. Haut-Brion. Good in 1959. Velvety and rich, twice in 1975. Recently: a touch of sourness, ripe but edgy.
The last three tastings in the U.S.A., 1978 ★

Ch. Gruaud-Larose. Fine colour; very ripe scented burgundy-like bouquet; dry and austere on the palate. Fine flavour, but lacking length, abrupt finish.
Tasted 1975. ★★

Ch. Cantemerle. Deep, ripe, complete good flavour. Elegant and not as blunt as most '43s.
Tasted 1973, 1977, January 1980 ★★★

Ch. Cheval Blanc. Faded but not unpleasing.
Tasted 1974 ★

Ch. Damluc (Camblanes, 1ère côtes). A château not seen before — I bought it, out of curiosity, at one of my own sales. Lightish mature colour; sound, sweet, pleasant stably nose; attractive flavour, slightly bitter edge.
Tasted 1971, January 1978 ★

Most of my notes are from the mid-1950s when the wine was just over ten years old and the St-Emilions and Pomerols seemed the most attractive. Amongst more recent disappointments have been both Pichons (in 1974 and 1975) and Ch. Léoville-Las-Cases, described as "useless" by Harry Waugh in 1953, and by me as "tired" and "so-so" in 1976.

1944 ★★

Cold dry winter; fairly good spring; hot thundery summer. Slightly bigger crop. Picking began 27 September. Quality irregular due to rain towards end of harvest. Lightish wines, short, flavoury but prone to acidity. Turned out better than expected.

Ch. Lafite. Lightish in colour and body but some charm in 1953. More recently: nose improved after a shaky start; silky soft middle marred by distinct acid edge.
Last tasted October 1968 ★★

Ch. Latour. Consistent notes on three occasions. Fairly deep colour; good *Cabernet-Sauvignon* aroma; very dry, flavoury, fruit, slightly unbalanced, noticeable acidity.
Tasted 1958, 1963, 1976 ★

Ch. Haut-Brion. Samples from the Dillon family cellar, New Jersey: lightish but healthy colour; light, delicate, fragrant (touch of decay on a mid-shoulder ullaged bottle); light, gentle but crisp, earthy, fragrant, attractive.
Tasted November and December 1979 ★★

Ch. La Mission-Haut-Brion. Fully mature; lacked nose; dry, smoky, interesting flavour but....
Tasted May 1977 ★

Ch. Pontet-Canet. Probably London bottled by Cruse's agents. Fairly deep, rich fine colour; very rich, gamy bouquet; slightly sweet, '47-like richness, excellent flavour, dry finish. Remarkable for a "light" year.
Tasted November 1979 ★★★

1945 ★★★★★

As a sort of recompense for the years of misery, war, deprivation, dreary vintages, 1945 heralded a string of vintages the quality of which matched and sometimes exceeded the wealth of the decade of the 1920s, even the pre-phylloxera years. 1945 itself was, and arguably still is, one of the greatest of all vintages, for me certainly one of the top three this century. Climate: the crop was severely reduced by heavy May frosts followed by hail, disease and exceptional drought during the summer and during the early harvest (13 September). Characteristics: reported at the time to have a very full colour and inclined to an excess of tannin — both facets that have been retained. By and large they are great wines: deep, concentrated, packed with flavour — as if the remaining grapes (half the crop of 1944) had striven to suck from the soil every available ounce of nourishment. Which indeed is what they did — the result of Mother Nature's severe pruning. Some, however, are now drying out.

Ch. Lafite
Pauillac

More restrained than the massive Latour and the spectacularly opulent Mouton, Lafite '45 needs all one's attention, but it is supremely rewarding. Tasted on eight occasions since 1967, it showed consistently and continued to improve. Fairly deep in colour for Lafite, it has the '45 hallmark of intense colour right to the rim; a concentrated spicy bouquet which needs time to blossom in the glass; rich, complex, almost chewy flavour, supported by tannin and acidity. A marvellous wine. Last tasted at Dr Overton's, May 1979 ★★★★ Drink now — 2010 or longer if kept well.

Ch. Latour
Pauillac

Tasted nine times. Deep, packed, vigorous and strapping in 1965. More recently, magnificently huge, opaque in appearance; a bouquet like gnarled old cedar; rich yet dry, massive, intense, loaded with tannin and acidity. Tasted October 1977 ★★★★(★) Drink now — 2020?

Ch. Margaux
Margaux

First tasted as late as 1971 and four times since. One of the most massive and masculine Margaux ever. Very deep coloured; intensely rich and fragrant bouquet, classic, cedar-pencil/cigar-box character, Cabernet *fruit more like mulberry than blackcurrant; but, though velvet textured and magnificent, a touch too powerful and austere.* Tasted January 1978 ★★★★(★) At its peak in 1985–2005.

Ch. Mouton-Rothschild
Pauillac

This is not claret, it is Mouton '45, surely one of the giants of all time — and one of the few wines I might lay claim to identify almost on sight, certainly on nose. A Churchill of a wine. First tasted in 1954 and noted, after just two years in the wine trade, that the nose was "amazing . . . quite unlike any other claret, reminiscent of mango chutney". Tasted on 14 occasions over the past quarter-century. It still has a magnificent, deep, almost opaque appearance, ruby with a pronounced mahogany rim; fabulous and, I like to think, totally unmistakable bouquet — highly concentrated, intense blackcurrant Cabernet-Sauvignon *aroma, touch of cinnamon — and flavour to match. Ripe, rich yet with the body and component parts to keep it in balance for years to come.* Last tasted November 1978 ★★★★★ Drink now — 2050.

Ch. Haut-Brion
Pessac, Graves

Absolute perfection. Indeed from this vintage on, I find, looking back, that I have had more unalloyed pleasure from Haut-Brion than almost any other claret: down to earth yet suave, somehow fewer mannerisms and criticizable facets than most other great châteaux. Described by Harry Waugh in 1953 as a "really good, heavenly wine". I first tasted it in July 1959: "full yet soft . . . really great wine of a great year" and have enjoyed it exactly a dozen times since. Still fairly deep, fine mature colour, shade of sun-baked red brick; fine, rich, fragrant and complex bouquet; slight sweetness of wine made from fully ripe grapes, magnificent, chewy, chunky yet smooth. Magnificent aftertaste. Last tasted May 1979 ***** Drink now — 2000.

Ch. Ausone St-Emilion	Only tasted twice. Big, black and nowhere near ready in 1955. More recently, a deep iron flavour, somewhat astringent. Last tasted 1974. I must reserve my judgement.
Ch. Cheval-Blanc St-Emilion	Deep, very fine colour; fragrant forthcoming nose; rich, fine consistency, long dry finish. Tasted only once, June 1977 *** Drink now — 1995.
Ch. Pétrus Pomerol	A wonderfully deep, velvety appearance, but the bottle that was to have been the highlight of a Bordeaux Club dinner, hosted by Harry Waugh, was corked: a stale, woody nose. It should have been great, and doubtless normally is. Tasted November 1974 (****) Drink now — 1990.

Other growths. Of the 56 non first-growth châteaux I have tasted, what strikes me is the opulence, quality and state of preservation of the Pomerols and St-Emilions. Amongst the outstanding:

Ch. Certan de May Pomerol	Sweet, almost port-like in its richness. Tasted 1974 **** Drink now — 1990.
Ch. La Croix de Gay Pomerol	Lovely red-brown colour; beautiful sweet, ripe, bouquet; fruity, leathery but rich. Tasted 1962 and, Harvey bottled, in 1965. Drink now — 1988.
Ch. La Dominique St-Emilion	Almost opaque; bouquet fruity and exciting, mellow but acid showing through; huge, dry, but soft furry edge masking remnants of tannin and highlighting acidity — flavour like sarsaparilla. Tasted 1954, 1961, 1962, March and December 1979 *** Drink now — 1985.
Ch. L'Enclos Pomerol	Rich, earthy bouquet which developed extraordinarily, drier at its peak. Shipped and bottled by Cruse's London agents. Tasted 1974 *** Drink now — 1985.
Ch. La Fleur Gazin Pomerol	Lovely, excellent condition. Tasted 1972 **** Drink now — 1990.
Ch. Gazin Pomerol	Tasted eight times, first in 1964: deep red, mahogany tinged. Perfection of balance in 1967. Rich, tangy yet soft in 1969 — probably the first occasion I used "iron fist in velvet glove" analogy. Various bottlings: at the château, Bordeaux bottled by Hanappier and, when last tasted, a Harvey bottling. Sometimes with tar-like overtones on the nose; high toned; magnificent. Last tasted March 1974 **** Drink now — 1985.
Ch. Magdelaine St-Emilion	Opaque; bouquet seemed deeper and sweeter even than Gazin; rich, full, soft yet tough, and holding well. Touch of iron on the finish. Tasted once, unforgettably, in 1969 **** Drink now — 1988.
Clos René Pomerol	Deep; slightly burnt cedary bouquet; rich, fabulous flavour and balance. Perfection. Tasted 1974 ***** Drink now — 1990.
Ch. Ripeau St-Emilion	Opaque; magnificent; very dry and tannic but sound, fine, slowly developing wine. Tasted 1972 *** Drink now — 1990.

Vieux Ch. Certan Pomerol	*Deep, magnificent, fantastically concentrated.* Tasted 1973 **** Drink now — 2000.

Other notable '45s:

Ch. Batailley Pauillac	*Deep; rich, fruity; drying out but firm and fine.* Tasted 1957, 1972 *** Drink now — 1990.
Ch. Bel-Orme St-Estèphe	*Deep; velvety; rich, lovely. Notable, for a bourgeois claret.* Tasted 1968 — 1969 *** Drink now — 1995.
Ch. Langoa-Barton St-Julien	*Sound, mature, attractive, firm, long finish.* Tasted 1974 *** Drink now — 1990.
Ch. Léoville-Barton St-Julien	*Raw and tannic in 1954. Still hard and unready in 1957. Berry Bros bottling: fine, elegant, classic in 1971. Château bottled: deep; rich; dry but concentrated and in perfect state. Magnificent.* Last tasted 1972 ***** Drink now — 1995.
Ch. La Mission-Haut-Brion Talence, Graves	*Fine, deep; earthy nose and flavour, twice in 1973. More recently: beautiful deep colour (though not as deep as the '47 or '49); tobacco-like bouquet; rich, powerful, dry finish.* Tasted twice, in 1978 **** Drink now — 1990.
Ch. Palmer Margaux	*Fine in 1971. Later, an interesting comparison of a rather stale, acidic London bottling against one château bottled showing magnificently.* Last tasted 1973 *** to **** Drink now — 1990.
Ch. Pichon-Baron Pauillac	*Deep, rich brown; old stably nose; showing age but rich and magnificent flavour.* Tasted 1972 *** Drink up.
Ch. Pontet-Canet Pauillac	*A nose like boiled beetroot and full but hard and raw in 1954. Still deep red brown; smoky, rich well-developed bouquet; hot-vintage character — powerful, chunky but lovely flavour and balance.* Last tasted at château, April 1978 **** Drink now — 1995.
Ch. Talbot St-Julien	*Deep; old, tough, cedar nose; rich but austere, touch of iron.* Tasted 1976 *** Drink now — 1990.
Ch. La Tour-Haut-Brion Graves	*Deeper than its "elder brother", La Mission; touch of acidity on the nose; some sweetness, fruity, acidity and gravelly iodine aftertaste. A very idiosyncratic red Graves.* Tasted 1978 ** Drink up.

Amongst the variable I put:

Ch. Beychevelle St-Julien	*Tasted nine times since 1957. All very deep in colour; at its best with a calm, beautiful classic bouquet and lovely flavour though with fairly severe tannic-acid finish. Château bottlings fairly consistent. A Christopher's bottling very attractive but short. Most recently, another London bottling, acetic.* Last tasted 1977. Up to **** Drink now — 1990.
Ch. Gruaud-Larose St-Julien	*Big and fruity in 1954. Fragrant and lovely but also a poor bottle, thin and green, in 1960. A certain greenness marring a lovely bouquet in 1961, 1967 and 1969. More recently: full marks for fine depth of colour; richness and complexity of bouquet — Cabernet blackcurrants and vanilla; long and rich on palate.* Last tasted 1973. Up to **** Drink now — 1988.

Amongst those that seem unbalanced, either drying out, overaustere or showing signs of age and acidity are:

Ch. Calon-Ségur St-Estèphe	*Tasted ten times. Rounded and pleasing in the mid-1950s. Packed with punch and impressive in 1970. Getting austere and leathery in the late 1970s; one specimen woody, oxidized.* Last tasted 1978. Variable. Drink up.
Ch. La Conseillante Pomerol	*Bright; sharp, concentrated, rapier-like flavour.* Tasted June 1977 ★★★ Drink up.
Ch. Cos d'Estournel St-Estèphe	*Soft yet big and unready in 1959. Fruity but raw in 1962. More recently: excellent deep old cedar bouquet; rich flavour, plenty of life but a hint of volatile acidity.* Last tasted November 1972. Drink up.
Ch. Croizet-Bages Pauillac	*Deep, raw in 1968. Very fine quality, classic in March 1969, but perhaps overloaded with tannin. Later I noted it had developed into a great minor wine.* Last tasted 1969 ★★★ Should be better developed now. Drink now — 1995.
Ch. Ducru-Beaucaillou St-Julien	*Rough and tannic in 1952. Hard and searingly dry from a double-magnum in 1973. More recently, complete but not too impressive.* Last tasted 1975. Up to ★★ Drink up.
Clos Fourtet St-Emilion	*Fine colour, nicely made but dry, austere, Médoc-like. Long finish.* Tasted 1971 and at Berry Bros in 1972 ★★★ Drink now — 1990.
Ch. Léoville-Las-Cases St-Julien	*Variable notes in 1954. Elegant nose and a fine, classic, well-balanced wine in 1971. Later: bland, dry and thinning out, probably a poor bottle.* Last tasted in the United States in 1972 ★★★? Drink now — 1988.
Ch. Léoville-Poyferré St-Julien	*Consistently beautiful bouquet but dry, raw and astringent.* Tasted in 1954, 1955, 1963, 1967, 1977. Hard to evaluate. Might soften a little.
Ch. Mouton d'Armailhacq Pauillac	*Another wine living dangerously. Fine colour; high-toned* Cabernet *bouquet — a sort of caricature of Mouton-Rothschild; very flavoury, some characteristic d'Armailhacq delicacy but marked end acidity.* Tasted four times from 1968 to May 1977 ★★ Drink up.
Ch. Rausan-Ségla Margaux	*Opaque; rich mulberry aroma; dry, full, deep, impressive but severe.* Tasted in 1965, twice in 1968, 1975, 1977 and, in magnum, in October 1979 ★★★ Drink now — 1992.
Ch. Rauzan-Gassies Margaux	*Flavoury but spoilt for me by a rather raw, loose acidity.* Tasted three times in 1950s and 1960 ★ Drink up.
Ch. Latour-Pomerol Pomerol	*Deep; high-toned, peppery/fruity bouquet; very rich and fruity, hard acidic finish.* Tasted 1972 ★★★ Drink up.

1946

More an "odd" vintage than an "off" vintage, including an unusual invasion of locusts. Climate: perverse weather, dry spring, rain almost daily from early May to mid-June delayed flowering. Fairly hot summer, but first half of September cold and wet — improvement in second half. Picking began on 30 September and continued in unusually hot October sunshine. Crop two-thirds average. Not surprisingly, quality variable. Not often seen.

Ch. Latour Pauillac	*Tasted four times. Opaque; remarkably good if "blackstrap" flavour in 1964. More recently, still fairly deep, fine colour; sweet plummy nose, rich, fruity; dry, very flavoury, a little raw and short.* Last tasted May 1976 ★★★ for flavour and novelty. Drink up.

Ch. Mouton-Rothschild *Pauillac*	*Very deep — could only be Latour or Mouton; a calm, deep, rich classic bouquet — no edginess of overmaturity or decay; dry, pronounced* Cabernet-Sauvignon *flavour. In 1971 I described it as thick and fruity, really more drinkable than the '45, but at Lenoir Josey's in Houston I found it rather more lean and with a touch of stalky greenness, still excellent for such a year.* Last tasted October 1978 ★★★ *Drink up.*
Ch. Mouton d'Armailhacq *Pauillac*	*Mean, astringent — rather tart.* Tasted 1969. Drink up.
Ch. La Gaffelière-Naudes *St-Emilion*	*Belgian bottled. Deep, curious nose, like a milking parlour; dry, nice flavour but unripe lactic acid.* Tasted 1977. Drink up, cautiously.
Ch. La Mission-Haut-Brion *Talence, Graves*	*Lovely colour; dry, flavoury, a trifle acidic.* At the pre-sale tasting, 1978 ★ *Drink up.*

1947 ★★★★

Another postwar milestone. Altogether different in style to the 1945: big, warm, fleshy, generous wines following an "Edwardian" summer. Climate: good late spring; fine June; successful flowering; fine July; August hot with some night rain; fine September, the picking beginning on 19th in almost tropical heat. The trade press reported that the sugar content had reached unprecedented heights. But, as in 1921, the heat was a mixed blessing — some wine makers had difficulty in controlling the fermentation, which is why some wines were "pricked" and many show signs of acidity taking over. But there are some rich, ripe, exciting wines.

Ch. Lafite *Pauillac*	*Tasted eight times. Very deep, lovely in 1958. Beautiful bouquet developing but acid edge noted in 1959, 1967, 1968, 1969 and 1975. Seemed to have regained balance in 1976: medium, mature colour; delicate, rich and attractive bouquet; soft, fruity, good balance. When last tasted: similar depth of colour to Lafite 1949 though richer and ruddier; singed, seaweed (iron) Lafite nose; rich, warm, very flavoury, dry but not overacid finish.* Last tasted at Overtons, May 1979 ★★★★ *Drink now.*
Ch. Latour *Pauillac*	*A massive wine in 1954. Unready in 1964, varying degrees of acidity showing. An acetically inclined bottle in 1966 and a poor bottle, old and sour, in 1976. Of the eight notes the best was in 1974: huge, opaque; bouquet dumb and peppery at first but developed rich cedar; full, rich, expansive wine with a dry finish. Choose well-stored bottles.* At its best ★★★★ *Drink up.*
Ch. Margaux *Margaux*	*A well-endowed dowager rather than a pretty debutante. Big yet soft and lovely in 1958. Velvety but lacking Margaux femininity and charm in 1966. Still magnificently deep, a big, ripe, hot-vintage colour; bouquet to match, very mature but no signs of decay; on the palate, velvety, towering yet delicate, rich yet dry. Tasted five times.* Last tasted at a Saintsbury Club dinner, October 1977 ★★★★ *Drink now — 1990.*
Ch. Mouton-Rothschild *Pauillac*	*An opulent wine: very deep brick-red colour; magnificent, gingery, Mouton-*Cabernet *nose; great rich flavour, perfect balance and condition, exquisite aftertaste. Consistent since early 1960s.* I felt it was at its peak of perfection when last tasted in September 1979 ★★★★★ *Drink now — 1990.*

Ch. Haut-Brion *Pessac, Graves*	*Tasted only twice. I felt it was magnificent but far too strong to drink with enjoyment in 1957. More recently: stylish, high toned, a bit steely and distinctly not opulent. Last tasted 1971. Must defer judgement.*
Ch. Ausone *St-Emilion*	*Harry Waugh reported this as pleasant but not great in 1955. I found the colour excellent; nose sound and attractive; a soft easy wine with lovely flavour and balance, holding well in magnum. Tasted only once, in May 1976 ★★★ Drink now — 1990.*
Ch. Cheval-Blanc *St-Emilion*	*For those who were unaware of its success in 1921 and 1929, 1947 was the first really eye-opening vintage of Cheval-Blanc. It did for this château what the '31 vintage did for Quinta Noval: set it on a pedestal. I have been privileged to taste Cheval-Blanc '47 on ten occasions from 1959, when it was impressive but seemed unready, through the 1960s, when it was consistently rich and lovely. Three bottled by Harvey's were excellent; two Belgian bottlings, rich but showing some end acidity in 1977. Last tasted from a château-bottled magnum: colour still very deep and fine; a complacent, abundantly confident bouquet, calm, rich, distinguished — but it did not open up and blossom in the glass like a great Médoc; slightly sweet, plump, almost fat, ripe, incredibly rich, high in alcohol. A magnificent wine, almost port-like. Last tasted at a Saintsbury Club dinner, April 1980 ★★★★★ Drink now — ad infinitum?*
Ch. Pétrus *Pomerol*	*1945, 1947 and 1949 were marvellous years for Pomerols and Pétrus '47 is probably the summit. Tasted only twice, the first château bottled: it was incredibly deep coloured, opaque, fully mature — brown tinged; heavy, hot vintage "burnt" bouquet, classic, showing considerable maturity; like Cheval-Blanc, slightly sweet, fairly full, rich, rounded, but more noticeable (and in this case more welcome) acidity. A fabulous wine. At a luncheon of the "jeunes négociants" (I sat between two septuagenarians!) in Bordeaux, August 1971. A Belgian bottling was also very good in May 1977 ★★★★★ Drink now — 1995?*

It is perhaps appropriate to mention here that when I entered the wine trade in 1952, at the not-so-tender age of 25, 1947s were part of the normal stock-in-trade. It is hardly surprising therefore that I have notes of nearly 70 châteaux, some tasted many times. It is probably best to split my notes on other growths into sections. Non first growths enjoyed recently:

Ch. Calon-Ségur *St-Estèphe*	*A lovely big wine in 1954. Rich but tannic in 1972. Three years later, very fine colour, deep for its age; a warm old nose; rich, ripe, complete and highly satisfactory. Tasted July 1975 ★★★★ Drink now — 1995.*
Ch. Cantemerle *Macau*	*Deep; very fragrant, rich, delightful; elegant, fruity, touch of '47 acidity. Tasted July 1978 ★★★★ Drink up.*
Ch. Ducru-Beaucaillou *St-Julien*	*Deepish red brown; very ripe, fruit; soft and lovely in 1962. Fine in May 1977 ★★★★★ Drink now — 1995?*
Clos L'Eglise *Pomerol*	*Very deep; rich, masculine; excellent. Tasted 1970, 1976 ★★★★★ Drink now — 1992.*
Ch. La Fleur *Pomerol*	*Blossoming bouquet; very rich, charming, lovely flavour, long finish. English bottled, tasted 1974 and Belgian bottled in 1977 ★★★★ Drink now — 1990.*
Ch. La Gaffelière-Naudes *St-Emilion*	*Very mature; excellent flavour, rich, plenty of grip still and fine aftertaste. Belgian bottled. Tasted May 1977 ★★★★ Drink now — 1988.*
Ch. La Garde *Graves*	*Fine mature colour; fragrant, silky, honeyed bouquet; a plump, soft, well-balanced wine. Tasted 1969, 1975 ★★★ Drink now — 1985.*

Ch. Gruaud-Larose St-Julien	*Fruity and advanced in 1954. More recently: sweet, rich, very ripe and lovely.* Tasted twice, in 1974 ★★★★ *Drink now — 1988.*
Ch. Léoville-Las-Cases St-Julien	*Loaded with tannin and "hard as hell" noted in 1954 and a rather contradictory note a year later. A flavoury but overacid bottle in 1965. Ten years later a lovely mature-looking wine; gentle cedary bouquet; lovely, soft, excellent flavour with good, dry, lightly tannic finish.* Tasted July 1975. At best ★★★★ *Drink now — 1995.*
Ch. Meyney St-Estèphe	*Deep; old rich cedar; good middle flavour but a bit edgy.* Tasted in magnum, 1977. *Drink up.*
Ch. La Mission-Haut-Brion Talence, Graves	*Brown, mature; rich, gnarled old bouquet; slightly sweet, excellent, tobacco-like, red Graves flavour.* Tasted 1973 and twice at, and from, the château in 1978 ★★★★ *Drink now — 1990.*
Ch. Moulinet Pomerol	*Magnificent colour, mature but vigorous; gentle, sound nose; slightly sweet, soft, velvety, rich. Lovely wine, drying out at finish. Bottled by Justerini & Brooks.* Tasted 1974 ★★★★ *Drink now — 1988.*
Ch. Pontet-Canet Pauillac	*Lovely Pauillac aroma but unready in 1956. Wonderfully preserved in jeroboam in 1973. More recently: a lovely deepish brick red; sweet, fragrant, overripe but sound bouquet; lovely flavour, elegant, still holding its tannin and acidity but elegant.* Tasted March 1978 ★★★★ *Drink now — 1992.*
Ch. Rausan-Ségla Margaux	*Fine, deep, very mature; fabulous if somewhat singed and overripe nose; elegant, very flavoury, dry finish.* Tasted 1977, February 1978 ★★★★ *Drink now — 1988.*
Ch. Talbot St-Julien	*Nose fragrant but creaking a bit; lovely flavour, soft, fruity.* Tasted 1968 and, à point, 1974 ★★★★ *Drink now — 1985.*

Notes on other wines last tasted from 1960 to mid-1970s:

Ch. Cos d'Estournel St-Estèphe	*Fullish, very good nose; soft, well balanced, lovely, rich but touch of St-Estèphe austerity.* Tasted 1961, 1969.
Ch. La Dominique St-Emilion	*Four slightly variable notes, overall very good.* Tasted 1955–1961.
Ch. Duhart-Milon Pauillac	*Considered by many shippers one of the very best '47s in the early 1950s. In its youth I was not unduly impressed, but later found it dryish, well-knit, mature and attractive.* Tasted 1963.
Ch. Grand-Puy-Lacoste Pauillac	*Fine depth and length.* Tasted 1965.
Ch. Lascombes Margaux	*Big, soft and velvety but I felt it would not improve further.* Tasted 1967.
Ch. Montrose St-Estèphe	*Attractive; fine rich wine — a half-bottle only.* Tasted 1969.

Less satisfactory bottles:

Ch. Beychevelle St-Julien	*Lacking usual charm.* Tasted 1961, 1973.
Ch. La Croix de Gay Pomerol	*Hard and green in 1955. More recently, sweet and cracking up.* Tasted 1971.

Ch. Gazin *Pomerol*	*Soft, light, not a patch on the 1945.* Tasted 1960.
Ch. Léoville-Poyferré *St-Julien*	*Charming blackcurrant cordial nose; good fruit but dry, acidic finish.* Tasted 1971.
Ch. Palmer *Margaux*	*Good in 1955. Harvey bottling: rich, ripe but with excess volatile acidity. (The château bottling might be better.)* Last tasted in 1966.
Ch. de Pez *St-Estèphe*	*Leathery in 1958. Later, old and austere.* Last tasted 1976.
Ch. Pichon-Baron *Pauillac*	*Tart in 1955. Astringent in 1971. Later, acidity and sharpness.* Tasted twice in 1976.
Ch. Pichon-Lalande *Pauillac*	*Good and big in 1954. Later, though attractive and flavoury some evidence of imbalance.* Tasted 1966 and twice in 1969.

1948 ★★★

What with its somewhat unabashed toughness and the fact that it was sandwiched between two infinitely more attractive vintages, '48 has always been neglected; a rough diamond, a character, but lacking polish and charm. Climate: weather conditions, the cause of character, were somewhat perverse — good spring, quite exceptional heat (110°F in the sun) in mid-May, followed by cold wet weather through June. Crop losses through *coulure*. July at first cold and dry, then warmer. Beneficial rain early August then too wet, cold, rot. The critical month of September fine, warm and dry right through picking from 27th. Crop three-quarters that of 1947. Quality was expected to be good. It was; but the trade and its customers preferred the '47s and '49s and were probably right.

Ch. Lafite *Pauillac*	*Harry Waugh, buying for Harvey's, noted in 1953 that it was good and quite reasonably priced. I first tasted it in 1954 and found it "lovely", an adjective which recurred in 1956, 1959 and 1960. Recently: fairly deep; rich, overripe but exciting bouquet; soft, full flavoured, stylish, characterful.* Last tasted August 1979 ★★★ Drink now — 1990.
Ch. Latour *Pauillac*	*Tasted five times. Big, black, huge, "green" and raw but very good in 1956. Still exceptionally deep coloured; very rich, peppery, alcoholic and still unknit bouquet; strong* Cabernet *flavour, very rich, attractive but somewhat aggressively tannic. A good mouthful now, will probably improve.* Last tasted October 1976 ★★★(★) Drink now — 1995.
Ch. Margaux *Margaux*	*Tasted twice: very deep, distinctly red tinged, heavy, full, rich "legs". In 1975 I thought it sweet, very rich but with high acidity. But, very recently, at the Coq Hardy, Bougival, it was exquisite: a very light, delicately fragrant nose, no old age or acidity; drying out, but very firm and harmonious. Still tannic but not a beefy '48.* Last tasted February 1980 ★★★★ Drink now — 1990.
Ch. Mouton-Rothschild *Pauillac*	*Deeper than the '47; fabulous, rich, forthcoming bouquet, reminiscent of the '45 with cinnamon-like overtones. A dry wine. Slightly bitter finish. Massive.* Tasted 1969, June 1975 ★★ Drink now — 1995.
Ch. Haut-Brion *Pessac, Graves*	*Tasted on only two occasions, and notes not too consistent or satisfactory. Fine quality but somewhat astringent.* Tasted in 1959 and two bottles in 1967, one with high acidity. Judgement deferred.

Ch. Cheval-Blanc St-Emilion	*Tasted five times. Big, fruity, severe, unready in 1961. Tasted alongside the '47: same depth of colour but holding more of its pristine purple; rather prickly, peppery, high-toned, fruity bouquet and flavour to match. Higher acidity and, not surprisingly, less well balanced than the '47. Edmund Penning-Rowsell preferred it. Certainly more challenging than the plump and complacent '47 Cheval-Blanc.* Last tasted in magnum, June 1978 ★★★ Drink now — 1985.

Some other growths:

Ch. Léoville-Barton St-Julien	*Reputed to be one of the most perfect '48s, a claim well substantiated on the one occasion I have drunk the wine: a really lovely garnet red; fabulous bouquet and flavour, rich, slightly sweet, and ripe, verging on overripe. Beautiful balance, Léoville-Barton — and claret — at its elegant best. Second bottle identical.* Host, Rob Kewley, M.W., September 1971 ★★★★★ Drink up.
Ch. Léoville-Las-Cases St-Julien	*Tasted five times, various bottlings. Tannin and acidity predominant in the 1960s.* Showing well when last tasted in July 1975 ★★★
Ch. Lynch-Bages Pauillac	*Marvellously rich blackcurrant aroma; full, flavoury, condensed, chunky, '48 dryness and grip.* Tasted 1958, 1960 and 1973 ★★★★ Drink now.
Ch. La Mission-Haut-Brion Talence, Graves	*Fabulous is the only word: for colour, bouquet and flavour. Fine, full, rich, earthy/smoky. Fragrant aftertaste.* 1962 and at the pre-sale tasting in December 1978 ★★★★★ Drink now — 1990.
Ch. Mouton d'Armailhacq Pauillac	*Severe but flavoury in 1969. Later, English bottlings coarse and unbalanced.* Tasted 1970, 1972.
Ch. de Pez St-Estèphe	*Extremely deep coloured still; deep, fruity, peppery nose; huge, soft, rich, perfectly balanced.* Tasted April 1979 ★★★ Drink now — 1990.

Older notes of some interesting wines:

Ch. Calon-Ségur St-Estèphe	*Still big, undrinkably full of tannin and acidity.* Tasted 1960.
Ch. Cantemerle Macau	*Unusually black; nose like fresh asparagus; big but not hard in 1956. Later lovely* Cabernet *nose and flavour.* Last tasted 1961.
Dom. de Chevalier Léognan, Graves	*Appearance described as "deep and crisp and even". Dry, big, fine balance.* I noted "twenty years of life left" in 1962.
Ch. La Dominique St-Emilion	*Full flavoured but green, in 1964. Later, a Harvey bottling was perfect.* Last tasted 1965.
Ch. Grand-Puy-Ducasse Pauillac	*Tough as old boots.* Tasted 1969.
Ch. Haut-Bailly Graves	*One of my favourite red Graves. Huge, very attractive but overladen with tannin and acidity.* Tasted 1971.
Ch. Léoville-Poyferré, the Pichons, Ch. Brane-Cantenac	*All fairly big, black, severe but impressive in the mid-1950s, the latter still severe and austere in 1967.*
Ch. Palmer Margaux	*Big and fruity in 1954. More recently: some colour lost, and browner, but still huge, fruity and tannic.* Last tasted 1970.
Ch. Pape-Clément Pessac, Graves	*Lovely, silky textured, green but coming round.* Tasted 1961.

1949 ★★★★★

A great vintage. Fine, supple, beautifully balanced wines. Extraordinary weather conditions. Climate: January and February the driest months on record; flowering in cold and rain caused most disastrous *coulure* ever remembered; second half of June fine and warm; July the hottest and driest ever, equalling 1893. Temperature of 145°F recorded in the Médoc on 11 July. August lacked rain, even dew. Grapes small. Storms early September; harvest began on 27th in fine hot weather tempered with a little benign rain. October driest on record. Quantity below average, quality *très bonne année*. Characteristics: resembling the '47s in many ways, perhaps with more finesse and elegance. They are holding fairly well: less dried out than the '45s, firmer than the '47s. Claret at its middleweight, fragrant, superfine best.

Ch. Lafite Pauillac	*The life cycle of this wine has been as curious and perverse as the weather that made it. Tasted on 13 occasions. I tasted it three times in 1955 and found it consistently disappointing: hard, lacking fruit. There was a gap of 15 years before I tasted it again and still, in the early 1970s, found it thin and not really good enough. Fragrant and flavoury in the mid-1970s, though an acid edge noted twice. Tasted four times in 1979: at a Saintsbury Club dinner, at the Heublein tasting, from an* impériale *(from the château via Christie's) at Dr Overton's, and at the great Lafite tasting the following evening. To sum up, it has a medium (not deep) but very rich mature colour; fragrant, slightly cheesy bouquet; medium dry, lightish in weight and style, flavoury but on the decline. It lacks the balance and majesty of Latour, the elegance of Margaux and the grace and delicacy of Mouton '49.* Last tasted May 1979 ★★★ Drink up.*
Ch. Latour Pauillac	*Tasted 14 times: dark, big and raw in 1954; maturing and blossoming in the late 1960s; magnificent throughout the 1970s. Still an impressive depth of colour; deep, sweet — almost honeyed, cedary bouquet; on the palate full and rich, soft yet firm and perfectly balanced. Great depth, length of flavour and marvellous aftertaste.* Last tasted June 1979 ★★★★ Drink now to beyond the year 2000.*
Ch. Margaux Margaux	*I must confess that I have been an almost secondhand admirer of Margaux '49; I had not realized, until looking up my notes for this paragraph, how few times I have had the wine. I certainly do recall, and of course noted, the first time I drank it — at a dinner party after a wedding reception at the Windermere Hydro. Despite my querying their mistake (I had ordered the generic Margaux '49, not being able to afford a first growth in a restaurant even in those inexpensive days), the management insisted that Château Margaux '49 was the same thing, so we enjoyed several bottles with our friends. Deep, fine; soft and rounded at 15s. (75p) per bottle. What is more we complained so bitterly about the food and the service that we paid only for the wine. This was in May 1956. Later, in the 1970s, I noted a twist of cracking-up acidity to mar the otherwise rich flavour. Should be good, but. . . .* Tasted 1970, 1971 (a London bottling) and 1974 ★★★★ Drink up.*
Ch. Mouton-Rothschild Pauillac	*A great wine. I confess I recall being surprised when Baron Philippe de Rothschild told me that it was the favourite of all his "children". I thought he would have put the '45 first. But I did not have my notes with me at the time, and Philippe's high opinion was confirmed a short time later at a Bordeaux Club dinner hosted*

by Harry Waugh who, incidentally, in 1955 described the '49 as "very deep in colour", with a "beautiful, fragrant" bouquet, and as "a lovely big wine packed with fruit and flavour. Surprisingly forward." A lot of these '47s and '49s were quite delicious even as early as the mid-1950s. I first tasted Mouton '49 in 1963 and on the six occasions since my notes have been rapturous: medium colour, fine, mature; fabulous flowery bouquet — a sort of quintessence of Cabernet-Sauvignon; *medium dry, medium body now, very flavoury, combining great delicacy with richness. A lovely wine, incredibly attractive and in perfect condition. Impossible to put its complexity and delight into words any more than one can describe the rarest orchid or a Mozart piano concerto.* Last tasted September 1976 ★★★★★ *Perfect now, will keep though gently fading.*

Ch. Haut-Brion Pessac, Graves	*Good. A style all of its own. Eight notes fairly well spaced from February 1956 when it had a good flavour but was unready. Soft in 1959; good but not great in 1967; elegant and rich in 1971. My best note on the wine was in May 1974: deeper than Latour; sweet, rich, velvety nose; very rich, complex, earthy wine, slight, astringent finish. A year later: holding its magnificent depth of colour; a lovely rich Graves-earthy (hot pebbles) bouquet; drying out a little. Sound, characterful.* Last tasted October 1975 ★★★★ *Drink now — 1990.*
Ch. Ausone St-Emilion	*Tasted three times. Full flavoured and good, twice in 1957. More recently: deep, browning; distinctly old on nose, but rich; very dry, austere, almost 1948 severity, burnt flavour, full of character but not very attractive.* Last tasted August 1972 ★★? *Drink up.*
Ch. Cheval-Blanc St-Emilion	*Tasted 16 times from August 1954, when I found it more advanced and rounded than the '50 and "very pricey" at 23s. (£1.15) on the Saccone & Speed list. (I worked in their "carriage trade" offices — they did not have a shop. My distinguished clients were surprisingly price conscious even in those days.) By November 1959 I thought it beautifully balanced, one of the best '49s. Soft, rich and elegant in the mid-1970s. The three most recent notes: magnificent colour; bouquet of mulberries and crushed fruit; magnificent flavour. Rich, at Dr King's in Atlanta, May 1958. Next, bottled by Justerini & Brooks: fabulous deep rich colour; very rich, ripe plummy mulberry bouquet, great scent; slightly sweet, soft, fruity, well composed, dry finish, in October 1978. Later, one bottled by Corney & Barrow very similar, very attractive — which just goes to show how well English wine merchants bottled in the late 1940s and 1950s.* Last tasted June 1979 ★★★★★ *Drink now — 1990.*
Ch. Pétrus Pomerol	*Not tasted. Tiny production, as always. Reputed to be excellent.*

Other growths: over 50 other châteaux of the 1949 vintage tasted; just over half noted in the 1950s and 1960s but not since. So I will concentrate on more recent notes, to give an idea of quality and development.

Ch. Beychevelle St-Julien	*Well developed in 1960. Lovely and soft in 1965. Later, somehow holding its fine vintage colour; bouquet high toned, fruity; dry, elegant, flavoury, touch of leathery tannin, intriguing.* Tasted 1974, June 1975 ★★★ *Drink now — 1985.*
Ch. Bouscaut Graves	*Deeper than the '53 or '55; a curious bouquet; attractive flavour, rich but piquant.* Tasted 1969, 1970 ★★ *Drink up.*

Ch. Branaire-Ducru St-Julien	*Very deep, plummy; complex old nose, fruit and bottle-age, opened up well; a huge dry wine, fruit, depth but slightly volatile-acid edge.* Tasted June 1970 ★ Drink up.
Ch. Calon-Ségur St-Estèphe	*Honeyed nose and delightful in 1954. Seven notes later: fine deep colour; rich magnificent bouquet (consistently a dominant feature); very rich, very fine, some of its original tannin holding well giving it a dry finish.* Last tasted September 1976 ★★★ Drink now — 1995.
Ch. Cantemerle Macau	*One of my favourite wines. Like Charles Keene, the artist's artist, Cantemerle is the claret man's claret. (Philippe de Rothschild likes Cantemerle best after his own.) Fabulous colour, lovely garnet red, autumnal at edge; exquisitely perfumed bouquet, high toned, delicate* Cabernet; *dry, fullish but not plump like a '49 Pomerol, elegant, refreshing — just lacking the length of a first growth.* Tasted 1966, April 1977 ★★★ Drink now — 1985.
Ch. Certan Pomerol	*Shipped by Cruse, bottled by their London agents and from the cellars of the late Jack Rutherford. Even lovelier than the Clos René. Less deep, more mature; bouquet more delicate, developed beautifully; soft, velvety Pomerol texture, wonderful flavour.* Tasted January 1974 ★★★★ Drink now — 1990.
Ch. La Dominique St-Emilion	*Berry Bros slip label, but Block, Grey & Block capsule, so assume bottled by the latter. Good long cork, high level. Fine mature colour; slightly dusty at first but developed and held well; marvellous fruit. Flavoury but thinning with dry, slightly acid-etched finish.* Tasted December 1979 ★★ Drink up.
Ch. Ducru-Beaucaillou St-Julien	*Tasted only once: fullish colour; calm, rich nose; slightly sweet, medium body, fully developed, attractive, light finish.* Tasted May 1974 ★★★ Drink now — 1985.
Ch. Gruaud-Larose St-Julien	*A lovely wine from the outset: soft, most pleasant in 1952. Hint of burgundy-like softness in 1953. Delicious in 1955. Very flavoury and attractive in 1974. Rich mulberry nose blossoming in 1978. More recently, soft, velvety, perfect balance.* Last tasted May 1979 ★★★★ Drink now — 1990.
Ch. Lynch-Bages Pauillac	*Very deep; magnificent* Cabernet *nose but unready in 1961. More recently: less deep but firm; exquisite, fruity, blackcurrant bouquet; dry, rapier-like* Cabernet *flavour, the poor man's Mouton. Very good, holding well.* Tasted 1974 and May 1975 ★★★★ Drink now — 1990.
Ch. La Mission-Haut-Brion Talence, Graves	*Tasted four times from 1971. Most recently: very deep, like the '48, with its brownness but perhaps lacking its brightness; rich bouquet, earthy-stably, fruit, perfect condition; rich, concentrated, yet soft and elegant. Beautifully shaped.* At the pre-sale tasting, December 1978 ★★★★ Drink now — 1995.
Ch. Pape-Clément Pessac, Graves	*Another of my favourite wines. When young, it was just pleasant but piquant, flavoury but with a hint of raw youthful acidity. Tasted twice in 1955. By 1970 the bouquet had developed and I found it almost Pauillac-like: a fine, deepish, mature but not over-brown colour; a most pronounced gingery-*Cabernet *aroma, almost too good to be true, like Mouton; very earthy but exceedingly fine crisp flavour. Most attractive.* Last tasted December 1972 ★★★★ Drink up.
Ch. Pontet-Canet Pauillac	*Deep, raw and ungracious in 1956. In full bloom by the mid-1970s. It retained great depth of colour, opaque really; excellent cedar-*

	like nose, rich, ripe; rich on entry but with a dry finish. Fullish body, positive flavour. Fine and impressive. Last tasted at the château, April 1979.★★★★ Drink now — 1995.
Clos René Pomerol	*Shipped by Cruse, bottled by their London agents and from the cellars of the late Jack Rutherford. One of the perfect Pomerols of this period: fine deep colour; very forthcoming, meaty, fine bouquet; lovely rich yet crisp flavour, fine dry finish. In perfect condition.* With Jack, at lunch at Christie's, January 1974 ★★★★ Drink now — 1995.
Ch. Rouget Pomerol	*Deep mahogany; beautiful nose; silky Pomerol texture but burnt-earth flavour of Graves. A character.* Tasted 1970, 1972 ★★
Ch. Talbot St-Julien	*Rich, high toned, fragrant, but with a touch of austerity.* Tasted 1962, 1975 and twice prior to the Cordier sale in September 1976 ★★★ Drink now — 1990?
Ch. Vrai-Canon-Boyer Fronsac	*Just to show how a well-kept, Belgian-bottled wine from the small Fronsac district can keep. Good lively colour; rich; flavoury, complete.* Tasted May 1977 ★★★ Drink now — 1990.

Some '49s not tasted recently but particularly good:

Ch. La Conseillante Pomerol	*A beautiful wine.* Tasted 1966.
Ch. Lagrange	*A lesser rated classed growth of St-Julien, lovely.* Tasted 1954, 1965.
Ch. La Tour-de-Mons	*A consistently well-made bourgeois wine from Soussans.* Tasted 1961.

1950 ★★

After the encouragement provided by the great postwar vintages, nature tactfully added to this bounty an abundant one, albeit of uneven quality, to fill the war-depleted cellars of the trade. Climate: a good flowering, hot summer (heavy, thundery August) and damp September. A large crop, nearly double that of 1949, harvested in changeable weather, 23 September. Characteristics: middleweight, flavoury, lacking the charm and balance of 1949 but can be surprisingly nice. Not often seen.

Ch. Lafite Pauillac	*Tasted five times. More colour than expected; lovely bouquet, attractive and supple in 1959. More recently, very flavoury.* Last tasted January 1975 ★★★ Drink up.
Ch. Latour Pauillac	*Tasted on eight occasions since 1960 when it was full yet reasonably soft and nice to drink. Consistently satisfying since and when last tasted: a deep mature colour; lovely, rich but delicate, gentle nose; rich, fruity, elegant, dry tannic finish.* Tasted June 1979 ★★★ Drink now — 1990.
Ch. Margaux Margaux	*Reputed to be one of the best '50s. Harry Waugh, tasting it as it was being bottled in April 1953, thought it charming and elegant and "liked immensely. Should be ready early." I have tasted it on ten occasions since 1956, most memorably in 1968 at the second annual dinner of the Masters of Wine, perfect in magnums. Later at the château in 1972: very mature, lovely colour; excellent ripe bouquet which opened up and blossomed in the glass; slightly sweet, medium body, soft, delicate, well balanced. At its peak in 1973. Most recently: although rich, showing a bit of age.* Last tasted at lunch at the château, September 1975 ★★★★ Drink now.

Ch. Mouton-Rothschild Pauillac	*Lightish in style, soft and nice in 1956. Variable in 1970 and 1972. More recently: deep coloured; lovely bouquet; flavoury and quite a lot of grip.* Last tasted June 1975 ★★★ Drink now — 1985.
Ch. Haut-Brion Pessac, Graves	*Not much liked in 1955. Better in 1970. Later: fine red-brown colour; rich, fully ripe, biscuity nose and flavour.* Last tasted June 1975 ★★★ Drink now — 1985.
Ch. Ausone St-Emilion	*Seemed prematurely mature.* Tasted only once in 1957 ★★? Drink up?
Ch. Cheval-Blanc St-Emilion	*For some reason I have been exposed to Cheval-Blanc more than any other '50 claret. I found it disappointing after the Médocs in 1954. Then, pleasing through the late 1950s and 1960s. Out of 14 notes the best was in America in 1975, when I found it attractive, soft and rich, still with tannin and acidity. Most recently: a poor Bordeaux-bottled specimen.* Last tasted 1976. Variable. At best ★★★ Drink up.
Ch. Pétrus Pomerol	*Not tasted, but I recall Harry Waugh's note in 1953: "excellent. Asked for quote". Those were the days. Now one is lucky to be allocated any, and only at a price.*
Carruades de Ch. Lafite Pauillac	*Lovely, ripe, flavoury.* Tasted 1954, 1959, 1970 ★★★
Ch. La Gaffelière-Naudes St-Emilion	*Lovely wine, full of fruit and flavour and "best '50 yet" in 1956. More recently: extraordinarily rich and attractive.* Last tasted September 1976 ★★★★ Drink now — 1985.
Ch. Grand-Puy-Ducasse Pauillac	*Surprisingly full and fine; soft, rich, flavoury.* Tasted 1972 ★★★
Ch. La Mission-Haut-Brion Talence, Graves	*Consistently rich, ripe and exciting on eight occasions since 1960. Perhaps at its peak, fully developed, silky, in 1972. More recently: fairly deep, very fine colour; old, earthy, cedary nose and flavour. Dry.* Last tasted April 1977 ★★★ Drink now — 1985.
Ch. Rausan-Ségla Margaux	*Waxy, elegant, very sound in 1977. Later: fragrant, dry, thinning a little but attractive and flavoury.* Tasted twice in 1978 ★★ Drink now — 1985.
Ch. Troplong-Mondot St-Emilion	*A consistently reliable St-Emilion. Soft, ripe, most attractive.* Tasted three times in 1976 ★★★ Drink now — 1985.
Tasted recently, now variable:	*Ch. La Bégorce-Zédé; Ch. Cantemerle; Ch. Haut-Bailly; Ch. Montrose; Ch. de Pez; Ch. Pichon-Baron.*
Outstanding when tasted prior to the mid-1960s:	*Ch. Beychevelle; Ch. Brane-Cantenac; Ch. La Conseillante; Ch. Croque-Michotte; Ch. Figeac; Ch. La Lagune; Ch. Léoville-Barton; Ch. Lynch-Bages; Ch. Malescot-St-Exupéry; Ch. de Sales; Ch. Smith-Haut-Lafitte; Vieux Ch. Certan.*

1951

A strong contender for the worst vintage in Bordeaux since the early 1930s. Indeed one of the poorest ever. Climate: miserably wet and cold April/May; June foul; July hot but thundery; August incredibly cold; a few hot days and cold nights in September. Grapes ripened slowly, unevenly, some not in time for the very late vintage, 9 October. Nature's overcompensation: average crop of thin and acid wines. Assessment: virtually untouchable. Thin, acid, decaying.

Ch. Latour *Pauillac*	*They say that good wines can be made at Latour even in a bad year; 1951 is the exception that proves the rule. Raw in 1956. Oxidized and woody in 1969. Not very attractive though not undrinkable in 1975. Later: surprisingly deep for an "off" vintage; hard, dull nose, with what is known as* goût de capsule; *dry, austere, no fruit.* Last tasted May 1976.
Ch. Mouton-Rothschild *Pauillac*	*Green, stalky, raw, just drinkable.* Tasted 1963.
Ch. Cheval-Blanc *St-Emilion*	*One of the few pleasant, light, drinkable '51s when young. A faint semblance of bouquet; overmature but flavoury, a touch too much acidity.* Last tasted 1971.
Ch. La Gaffelière-Naudes *St-Emilion*	*Described by Harry Waugh, tasting in 1953, as easily the most successful of its year. Perhaps its own microclimate, tucked down the valley, was more favourable. I found it fresh and beaujolais-like on the nose, a trifle negative but quite a pleasant flavour.* Tasted November 1955. Doubtless merely a blithe spirit by now.

1952 ★★★ to ★★★★

A good vintage, rather stern and unyielding in the Médoc, better in the Graves and excellent in Pomerol and St-Emilion. Climate: warm spring; hot June — flowering under exceptionally good conditions; July and August hot (with some rain); September cold and picking on 17th in unfavourable conditions. Quantity below average. Assessment: considered a *bonne année* at the time, but many wines lack vinosity and charm. The most superb were in Pomerol and St-Emilion. The Médocs were, and still are, hard though good, firm, long lasting but lacking plump flesh.

Ch. Lafite *Pauillac*	*Not my favourite vintage of Lafite. Back in 1953, Harry Waugh (long before he became a director of Château Latour) observed that Lafite was behind all the first growths in this vintage, though Allan Sichel liked it. I have tasted it nine times: first in 1963, and again in 1965, when I thought it had nice quality, fruit and balance. I found the bouquet fragrant and forthcoming in the late 1960s, best in October 1970 and less good in the mid- to late 1970s. At the Overton tasting, it was more mature looking, less attractive and weaker in colour than the '53; a bit ungenerous and faded on the nose (also noted in 1975 and 1977); some delicacy on the palate but with a hard, dry finish.* Last tasted May 1979 ★★? Hopefully it might enjoy an Indian summer.
Ch. Latour *Pauillac*	*One would have thought that the combination of Latour weight and the tough '52 vintage would result in an undrinkable giant. Not so. Ranked "top of the tree with Mouton" in 1953, and the following year "better than the '53". I quote Harry Waugh's notes, brief but to the point. I first tasted the '52 Latour when it was ten years old, and have had it 11 times since. At the Overton Latour tasting it was the deepest of the group of surrounding vintages; rather peppery and alcoholic on the nose, but developed well; a big dry wine, full of fruit, the tannin finish beginning to dominate.* Last tasted February 1980 ★★★ Will last for decades but likely to dry out.
Ch. Margaux *Margaux*	*Fragrant (the bouquet of Margaux is its hallmark) but severe and unforthcoming in 1968. It has remained mean, moody but*

magnificent: very deep colour, though browning; really a fairly massive wine, velvety with, seemingly, a whole cask of bouquet and flavour waiting to burst out. But when? Tasted five times, last in February 1977 **(**) Optimistically 1985–1995.

Ch. Mouton-Rothschild Pauillac	*Three notes, in 1967, 1972 and, the most recent: deep, fine, flavoury with silky/leathery texture.* Last tasted June 1975 *** Drink now — 1995.
Ch. Haut-Brion Pessac, Graves	*Preferred it in the mid-1960s. It had a sweet, honeyed nose and soft, lovely, pronounced Graves earthiness. Later the tannic finish became more noticeable. But I like it; it has character.* Last tasted May 1974 *** Probably holding well.
Ch. Ausone St-Emilion	*For years Ausone has gone its own sweet way — "the only one in step". Around this time the practice was to keep the grapes on the vine until the last possible moment and to comb the vineyard, as at Yquem. The '52 was unusually pale in colour, almost brown at the outset: "a pretty, light wine" (Waugh in 1953); "should develop early and well" (Calvet, also in 1953). I first tasted it in 1960 and noted its "most odd colour, like a '29", but a sweet, honeyed yet leathery nose — most curious, as was the flavour. Exceedingly dry but not tannic. Like a soft red Graves. Despite the brown, teak-edged colour, it has survived very well. Good in 1961 and two excellent Belgian bottlings, with bouquet more root-like than fruit-like and firm, positive flavour. Eccentric perhaps, but sane and healthy.* Very sound when last tasted in 1977 ** Drink now — ?
Ch. Cheval-Blanc St-Emilion	*No nose, raw and rather dull when first tasted in 1954. It has developed consistently well over the years. Gloag's bottling lovely in 1960. Harvey bottlings fine in the mid-1960s. Two château bottlings tasted in 1969 and three years later: deep lovely colour; very fragrant, gentle, touch of iron from the soil; medium body, soft, silky — lovely texture in the mouth, gentle but firm dry finish.* Last tasted November 1972 **** Drink now — 1990.
Ch. Pétrus Pomerol	*Lovely full rich wine when young. Still deepish; a bit unforthcoming on the nose; soft, fine textured and unobtrusively powerful.* At three Heublein pre-sale tastings in May 1973, 1974 and 1976 ****(*) Drink now — 1995?

Of the 90-odd other '52 châteaux of which I have notes, many were tasted mainly in the late 1950s and 1960s. Of those '52s tasted recently and showing outstandingly well are:

Ch. Branaire-Ducru St-Julien	*Four good notes, promising in mid-1950s, maturing nicely in 1963 but still not fully developed in 1970. Most recent note: deep, fine, healthy colour; warm, deep, gentle bouquet; dry, velvety yet firm, quite tannic. Really a very attractive '52 Médoc beginning to show softness behind its severe face. Should develop further.* Last tasted June 1974 ***(*)? Drink now — 1992.
Ch. Calon-Ségur St-Estèphe	*Nearly a dozen notes from 1954. Not a very appealing wine. The owner, M. Gasqueton, preferred his '53. A fairly deep-coloured wine; a rather old-fashioned classic. Good but tough and tannic in early 1970s. Later, a Justerini & Brooks bottling with rather high acidity.* Last tasted March 1975 ** Might soften. Drink now? — 1985.
Ch. Cantemerle Macau	*For once, not its usual charming self: deep, almost blackstrap — a hot, burnt, brown-rimmed colour; an old man, stern, weather-beaten; dry, fairly full bodied, tough and lacking suppleness. Could either soften a little or dry up.* Tasted April 1971 **(*)?

Carruades de Ch. Lafite Pauillac	*Three notes. First bottled (well) by Harvey's: full, dry but some charm in 1961. Showing a bit of strain in 1966. Eleven years later: less colour, more mature; nose a bit woody but with fruit and held well; dry, lightish, fully mature, soft but a bit flat.* Last tasted May 1977★★ Drink up.
Ch. La Dominique St-Emilion	*Deep, rôtie nose when young, still fairly deep and very good, fine flavoured, iron, tangy, even in half-bottles.* Tasted 1974, 1976 ★★★
Ch. Ducru-Beaucaillou St-Julien	*Tasted four times — about my least favourite Ducru vintage. I found it dull and lacking in January 1956; developing a little by 1962; stodgy and unremarkable in 1965. Most recently, Dutch bottled: fine deep mature colour; heavy burnt character, sound but severe nose; dry, fairly full bodied, stern, masculine, tannic.* Last tasted November 1978 ★ I can only see it drying out.
Ch. La Gaffelière St-Emilion	*Seemed to be a high-water period for this château. Harry Waugh ruted it the best of the St-Emilions after Cheval-Blanc in 1953. The two English bottlings I tasted in 1958 and 1961 were somewhat unremarkable however. Later, a château-bottled half-bottle was sound but a little lacking.* Last tasted 1976 ★★ to ★★★ Drink up.
Ch. Le Gay Pomerol	*Dutch bottled: fairly deep fine colour; lovely rich nose, with well-developed bottle-age; ripe, silky, medium weight, firm texture, nice balance.* Tasted July 1972 ★★★
Ch. Gruaud-Larose St-Julien	*One of the most attractive '52 Médocs, which had finesse even when young, and was better than the '45 in 1961. Lovely, soft and agreeable in 1966. Fruity, "10 years more life" in 1972. Later: fine mature colour; rich, forthcoming, open, easy bouquet and flavour; sweet, fruity, rich middle palate and somewhat abrupt tannic dry finish. Good though.* Last tasted 1975 ★★★ Drink now — 1985.
Ch. Haut-Bages-Libéral Pauillac	*One of the least seen classed-growths: medium colour, mature looking. Two lovely bottles in 1969, both shipped by Calvet and bottled in London by G. Barnes. More recently, a château-bottled half with a nose like old cedar stumps; a bit gnarled on the palate but rich.* Last tasted October 1973 ★★ Drink up.
Ch. Léoville-Las-Cases St-Julien	*Reported as being much too light in cask. My notes start in 1958, since when I have tasted it half a dozen times including three English bottlings. It seemed at its best in the mid-1960s. Later, an Avery bottling: astringent and rather unattractive.* Last tasted October 1973. Drink up.
Ch. Léoville-Poyferré St-Julien	*Quite nice. I have seven notes, including another Avery bottling in 1973, slightly better than the Las-Cases and four château bottlings since. Seemed at its best in 1974. Most recently: deep, mature looking; old nose but interesting; quite well balanced but tired and dry.* Last tasted June 1979 ★ Drink up.
Ch. Lynch-Bages Pauillac	*Not tasted recently but a dozen enthusiastic notes from the cask to the autumn of 1968. It was a stunning wine, full (13° alcohol) and fruity. Probably still is.* Last tasted September 1968 ★★★? Drink up.
Ch. Magdelaine St-Emilion	*Not dissimilar in looks to the '61, perhaps deeper and certainly browner; complex fragrant bouquet, crisp, touch of hardness; medium dryness and body, some softness, holding well, firm, slightly tough dry finish. Characterful.* Tasted December 1978 ★★★ Drink now — 1990.

Ch. Montrose St-Estèphe	*Not surprisingly, being Montrose and a '52, tough and hard in cask. By early 1970s it had developed remarkably and was elegant and stylish. Most recently, a château-bottled half: still deep in colour but not brown, a lively brick red; very fresh for its age, sweetish bouquet; ripe on the palate, fairly full bodied, excellent flavour and condition — soft, harmonious, most agreeable.* Last tasted January 1975 ★★★★ Drink now — 1990.
Ch. Moulinet Pomerol	*Five notes, all in mid-1970s. Fairly deep colour; rich iron and cedar nose, slow to develop; dry, silky, Pomerol texture, nice consistency and balance. One deep brown and oxidized bottle.* Tasted 1974–September 1976. At best ★★★★ Drink now — 1986.
Ch. Pape-Clément Pessac, Graves	*Beautiful colour — lovely garnet red; good, high-toned, hot, vintage bouquet; ripe, medium light yet with a big hard vintage flavour and very pronounced Graves earthiness, fairly high fixed acidity. Tough but fine.* Tasted December 1971 ★★★(★) Drink now — 1990.
Ch. Pichon-Lalande Pauillac	*A couple of good London bottlings in 1969 and 1971. Most recently, from a* Marie-Jeanne*: very deep, almost opaque and still youthful looking; fragrant cedar/cigar-box bouquet, slightly peppery; dry and still tannic but rich and impressive. Broad shouldered but well tailored.* Last tasted December 1978 ★★★(★) Drink 1982–1995.
Ch. Plince Pomerol	*Medium pale, lovely colour; bouquet rather shy at first but developed well; ripe, soft, lightish, pleasant. An easy wine, no great character but nice.* Tasted January 1975 ★★ Drink up.
Ch. Taillefer Pomerol	*Bottled by Avery's: medium, mature; very good nose; absolutely delightful flavour, balance, condition. Pomerol charm and weight.* Tasted September 1978 ★★★★ Perfect now. Drink up.
Vieux Ch. Certan Pomerol	*Reported to be good but all sold by early 1953. I have eight notes from 1965. I liked it best when it was just about 15 years old, firm but velvety. Disappointing, unyielding in early 1970s. A fairly good recent note: deep fine colour; lovely, soft, harmonious bouquet and flavour though dry overall.* Last tasted May 1978 ★★★ Drink now — 1985.

1953 ★★★★★

Perhaps the most attractive of all the postwar vintages and, for me, a personification of claret at its most charming and elegant best. Climate: early spring, dry with frost every night for two months; flowering started well but cold and rain caused some *coulure*; end of June hot and thundery; one of the finest Augusts in memory — *août fait le moût* — good weather until mid-September, then excessive rain delayed the harvest. Picking started 2 October in perfect weather. Average, ample yield. Assessment: as it happens, this is the first vintage I was able to taste in the cask, on my first visit to Bordeaux — a busman's holiday (one of very many as my wife will testify) in August 1955. It was appealing even in cask and, a rare thing for a vintage, the wines never to my knowledge went through a hard period: the 1953 vintage was a beautiful baby, a delightful child, uneventful puberty, no spots and no adolescent traumas, married and lived happily ever after. The best are still perfectly lovely but, to mix my metaphors, many are now enjoying the serenity of an early autumn, intensely beautiful but browning at the edges.

Ch. Lafite Pauillac	*The epitome of elegance, yet quite a big production (202 tonneaux compared with 90 in 1945 and just over 100 in 1947 and 1949), which was — I was told — bottled over an extended (nine months) period. I was new in the trade and not privileged to taste it in cask,*

though *Harry Waugh did and in 1954 noted the nose "lovely" and the palate "rather light and delicious but well made". I myself have tasted it on 20 occasions since 1960. It started being a really lovely drink in the mid-1960s, and was at its peak — fully developed but still firm — when 20 years old. Last noted at the Overton tasting: beautiful colour, not deep, a wonderfully developed garnet red, shading off to a rich, glowing mahogany rim; an open, relaxed, fully developed bouquet, sweet cedar, fragrant; lightish and dry — as a good claret should be — delicate yet generous, lovely flavour, finish and aftertaste.* Last tasted May 1979 ★★★★★ Drink now until an ethereal old age in the 1990s.

Ch. Latour Pauillac	*For some reason or other, not tops. Perhaps the style of Latour and the nature of the vintage were incompatible. When new in cask* Harry Waugh *noted "very deep [colour], fine full bouquet, plenty of body but not as hard as usual". Big crop. Not as good a wine as '52 or '55. Curiously, my most admiring notes on this wine were between 1968 and 1973. It seems to be going through a less than charming, introspective period — still deep coloured and fairly massive. It could open out again. Tasted on 17 occasions.* Last tasted May 1978 ★★★ Drink 1983–1995?
Ch. Margaux Margaux	*Margaux at its best. First tasted in March 1961 — quite unready then and later that year. Developing nicely mid-1960s and, judging from my notes the wine seemed to have reached the peak of perfection in 1971: medium full, lovely garnet hue, rich almost viscous rim; magnificent bouquet; rich, waxy, elegant, soft and silky, excellent balance. Most recently I noted particularly its long fragrant aftertaste.* Last tasted May 1975 ★★★★★ Drink now — 1993?
Ch. Mouton-Rothschild Pauillac	*Another luscious beauty, deeper than Latour, browner than Lafite; glorious Mouton aroma of celestial blackcurrants, cinnamon and stem ginger; very rich, very fine, very flavoury. Seven notes from 1963.* Last tasted March 1978 ★★★★★ Drink now — 2000.
Ch. Haut-Brion Pessac, Graves	*Its qualities fully developed by the mid-1960s, seemingly at its peak in 1972/73, holding well. Tasted ten times since 1966. Most recently: fine deep earthy-brown colour; lovely rich Graves — earthy aroma and flavour; great depth, richness, vinosity.* Last tasted May 1979 ★★★★★ Drink now — 1990s.
Ch. Ausone St-Emilion	*Soft and gentle when young. Curiously attractive bouquet, deep, meaty, rather Graves-like.* But tasted only four times between 1956 and 1973 ★★★? Doubtless fully mature.
Ch. Cheval-Blanc St-Emilion	*Magnificent colour, deep though mature; fine bouquet with shades of iron/earth/warm tea leaves — sounds a bit odd, but most attractive; very rich, lovely, distinctive flavour, velvety, firm finish. A dozen notes since 1956.* Last tasted January 1978 ★★★★★ Drink now — 1990.
Ch. Pétrus Pomerol	Harry Waugh, *tasting from the cask in 1954: "Deep . . . fine in every way, subtle with much breed. A beauty." I cannot improve on his notes. First tasted by me in 1956, next in 1959. It seemed fully developed by 1960, a firm, most attractive wine. Tasted five times since: lovely colour, deep but lighter and prettier than the '52; fabulously fragrant bouquet; unbelievably rich and soft with a trace of iron and earth, beautiful acidity, dry finish.* Last tasted May 1976 ★★★★★ Drink now — 1990s.

Of the 117 other '53 châteaux of which I have notes, many were tasted mainly in the late 1950s and 1960s. Of those '53s tasted recently and showing outstandingly well are:

Ch. Beychevelle
St-Julien

Elegant and pleasing from cask onwards. Tasted on 12 occasions, various bottlings. The most recent was château-bottled: mature looking, rich, lovely, soft, velvety and at its peak. Last tasted 1972 ★★★★ Drink now — 1985.

Ch. Cantemerle
Macau

Deliciously drinkable. Consistently attractive from first tasting in 1959 to nearly 20 notes later. One of my most favourite clarets: elegant, soft and ripe, sheer perfection. At its peak in 1973. Still lovely when last tasted in September 1976 ★★★★ Drink now — end 1980s.

Ch. Cos d'Estournel
St-Estèphe

Five notes from 1960. Still fairly deep; bouquet well developed; dry, firm, fruity, good balance. Last tasted April 1977 ★★★★ Drink now — 1990.

Ch. Ducru-Beaucaillou
St-Julien

Deep; cedar-box bouquet; fine, gentle, elegant, holding well. Tasted 1967, April 1977 ★★★★ Drink now — late 1980s.

Ch. La Gaffelière-Naudes
St-Emilion

Medium light, mature; slightly sweet, gentle, rich, lovely flavour. Tasted 1970, 1971 ★★★★

Ch. Giscours
Margaux

Lovely ripe colour; cedary, well-developed bouquet; lovely flavour. Perfect weight, condition and finish. Tasted October 1975 ★★★★ Drink up.

Ch. Grand-Puy-Lacoste
Pauillac

First tasted, and was immensely impressed by it, in 1973. A fine, deep, rich colour, mature; lovely fragrant unobtrusively Cabernet nose; lovely flavour, vinosity, balance. For me, claret at its best. Last tasted October 1979 ★★★★ Drink now — 1987.

Ch. Gruaud-Larose
St-Julien

Lovely, rich, spicy. Tasted 1958, 1961, September 1976 ★★★★ Drink now — 1990s.

Ch. de Heby
Castelnau

First time I had come across, indeed heard of, this small property. Tempted by price and an Avery bottling. Lovely weathered brick red; gentle, ripe; some '53 vinosity and charm. At Thornbury Castle, July 1979 ★★★ Drink up.

Ch. Lagrange
St-Julien

A somewhat under-regarded château. The '53 is good. Lovely bouquet in 1964. Good note in 1971 and, a year later: gentle, soft, excellent, silky and well balanced — a very good mouthful. Last tasted 1972 ★★★★ Drink now — 1980s.

Ch. Léoville-Barton
St-Julien

A lovely wine. Good Harvey bottlings tasted in 1950s. Some good château bottlings in 1960s. On last five occasions all bottled by Berry Bros: elegant, cedary. Last tasted 1975 ★★★★ Drink now — 1988.

Ch. Lynch-Bages
Pauillac

One of the peak vintages made by the present owner's father, "the wizard of Pauillac". Harry Waugh, tasting in cask, noted in 1954: "Delicious. Beautifully full flavour. A wine to gamble on. Would like at least 40 hogsheads at £30"! Note the price: £30, not for a bottle, not for a dozen, but for a cask of roughly 25 dozen — for shipment to Harvey's for bottling in Bristol. In retrospect, it does not seem much of a gamble. I noted it was magnificent, one of the best '53s in 1956. More recently, rich but completely mature. Last tasted May 1972 ★★★★ Drink up.

Ch. Magdelaine
St-Emilion

Rich, soft, mature. Tasted 1956, 1960, 1964, December 1978 ★★★★ Drink now.

Ch. La Mission-Haut-Brion
Talence, Graves

Consistently lovely wine though considered too expensive at the time. Tasted ten times from 1955. Now fullish, lovely autumnal *colour; fragrant, excellent bouquet; rich, ripe, great vinosity. Marvellously symmetrical.* Last tasted December 1978 ***** Drink now — 1990s.

Ch. Montrose St-Estèphe	*Probably the best vintage of Montrose ever tasted. Very deep and full bodied when young. First tasted in 1956 and on ten occasions since then, improving all the time. Most recently: very beautiful colour; perfect classic bouquet — fruity, rich, honeyed; still full bodied and with tannin and acidity, but excellent.* Last tasted May 1978 ***** Drink now — late 1990s.
Ch. Palmer Margaux	*A curious wine and, for me, untypical of '53. The most unusual (raspberry flavoured) wine at a Sichel tasting in 1955. Uneven notes in 1960s. More recently: fine, very mature colour; curious hard nose, which did not develop; very rich and flavoury.* Last tasted May 1975 ** to *** Drink now — late 1980s?
Ch. Pichon-Lalande Pauillac	*Tasted only twice. Surprisingly deep coloured still; lovely classic bouquet, gentle, vinous; dry yet soft, elegant, stylish, wonderful texture.* Tasted 1972, and from a Marie-Jeanne at the '45 Club dinner, December 1978 **** Drink now — 1990s.
Ch. Pontac-Monplaisir Graves	*Fine brick red; fresh, slightly austere but attractive.* Tasted March 1975 ** Drink up.
Ch. Pontet-Canet Pauillac	*Generally harmonious. Several bottlings, English and Bordeaux. Deep, fine colour; very rich, cedary, mature bouquet; silky and elegant, at the château in 1975. Later: almost opaque; rich but age showing on nose and drying out on palate. English bottled.* Last tasted October 1977 ** to **** Drink now — late 1980s.
Ch. Rausan-Ségla Margaux	*Originally very promising. Variable notes. David Sandeman bottling rich in 1968. Most recent note: strong, firm wine, still hard and unready for age and vintage.* Tasted March 1975 ** to *** Hard to advise.
Ch. Talbot St-Julien	*Slow developing, perhaps lacking a little charm but surprisingly deep coloured, like a '59 or '61; magnificent nose and taste. Six notes from 1956.* Last tasted March 1978 *** Drink now — late 1990s.
Ch. La Tour-de-Mons Soussans	*A perfect example of how good a well-made bourgeois claret can be. Excellent from the outset. Eight notes later: a very pleasant easy wine, soft, agreeably fair finish. At peak.* Last tasted February 1975 *** Drink up.

Good wines not tasted since 1970. Probably all fully mature and need drinking:

Ch. Batailley Pauillac	*Fullish, mature; deep rich Cabernet nose; full of fruit, soft yet dry finish. Five notes from 1960.* Last tasted 1965 ***
Ch. La Conseillante Pomerol	*Lovely wine, perfect balance, beautiful aftertaste.* Tasted May 1969 ***
Ch. Croizet-Bages Pauillac	*Not one of my favourite châteaux but excellent in '53. Rich, chunky, silky texture.* Tasted 1963, 1968, 1971 ***
Ch. Gloria St-Julien	*The first vintage I ever tasted of this brilliantly managed bourgeois château. Soft, fruity and flavoury in 1958. Later, remarkably attractive, with great character and style, perfectly balanced.* Last tasted August 1968 ***
Ch. Lafon-Rochet St-Estèphe	*Very deep, big and firm St-Estèphe character.* Tasted 1969 ***

Ch. Léoville-Las-Cases St-Julien	A good '53, multi-starred when first tasted in cask, in February 1955. Twelve years later, a lovely mature wine, from British Transport Hotels bottling. Last tasted 1967 ★★★★
Ch. Nenin Pomerol	Initially a fine full-bodied wine. Later, softened and excellent. Last tasted early 1960s. Probably holding well.
Outstanding when tasted prior to 1960:	Probably still good: Ch. Beauséjour; Ch. Belgrave; Ch. Calon-Ségur; Ch. Certan de May; Ch. Cissac; Ch. L'Eglise-Clinet; Ch. Figeac; Ch. Gazin; Ch. Grand-Corbin; Ch. Grand-Puy-Ducasse; Ch. Lagrange (Pomerol); Ch. Lanessan; Ch. Langoa-Barton; Ch. Mouton d'Armailhacq; Ch. Pavie; Ch. de Pez; Clos. René; Ch. Pierre Sevaistre.

1954 ★

Not very good but not wholly bad. Climate: what a year. Late hard winter as in 1945; fine spring; first half of July coldest since 1880; August probably coldest on record followed by continuous rain; early September hot, then worst weather in living memory. Late harvest, 11 October, in best weather of the year which saved the crop. Chaptalization authorized. Reduced crop. Assessment: despite this climatic track record some quite nice wine made. Not often seen now but worth a gamble.

Ch. Lafite Pauillac	Fair quality: forward and flavoury in the mid-1960s. A very attractive drink. Last tasted March 1969 ★★ Drink up.
Ch. Latour Pauillac	A good example of how they can make a most attractive wine at Latour in a moderate vintage. Good colour; pronounced Cabernet aroma, deep, rich, cedary; essentially dry, chunky, surprisingly good mouthful. Seven consistent notes from 1964. Last tasted June 1975 ★★★ Drink now — 1989.
Ch. Margaux Margaux	Dry, lightish, mature. Nothing special. Tasted 1971, April 1976. Drink up.
Ch. Mouton-Rothschild Pauillac	Thin in cask. No recent notes.
Ch. Haut-Brion Pessac, Graves	Unimpressive in cask. Austere and fair acidity. Last tasted 1963. Drink up.
Ch. Cheval-Blanc St-Emilion	Ripe, soft, cheesy. Quite attractive. Tasted 1973, September 1976 ★ Drink up.

1955 ★★★

A good but under-appreciated vintage. Climate: the weather pattern alternating early in year — January very wet; late February spring-like; March cold, frosty; April warm, May cold, both dry; flowering in fine weather then rain, hot days in June; July perfect; August hot and dry; welcome rain in September, fine conditions for harvest on 22nd. Reports at the time said: "wines cannot fail to be good". Yet they were not as attractive as the heavily bought '53s. Assessment: they have quietly blossomed in recent years.

Ch. Lafite Pauillac	When first tasted, in 1961 (it was on Harvey's retail list "for laying down" at 36s. or £1.80 a bottle) I rated it highly but noted

that it was showing signs of early maturity. In 1971 there was little change but the last five years have seen a rich development: holding its colour; very rich, complex Lafite/iron bouquet; charming, elegant, excellent flavour and aftertaste. Tasted a dozen times. Last tasted April 1979 ★★★ *Drink now — 1990.*

Ch. Latour Pauillac	*Distinctly finer than the 1953. Deep purple-black in 1961, packed and concentrated. A dozen tastings later: still deep, rich in colour; the nose opening up — tea and ginger; fullish, fine powerful wine. Classic.* Last tasted May 1976 ★★★(★) *Drink now — 2000.*
Ch. Margaux Margaux	*A lightish style of Margaux, soft, charming, a little insubstantial. Tasted five times from 1961.* Last tasted May 1979 ★★★ *Drink now — 1985.*
Ch. Mouton-Rothschild Pauillac	*Very deep yet looked a quick developer when young. Tasted 17 times since 1961, consistently attractive. Now medium-full colour; high-toned* Cabernet *aroma settled down to a beautiful, calm, dignified Pauillac bouquet; delicate, flavoury, nice balance, very attractive.* Last tasted December 1976 ★★★★ *Drink now — 1990.*
Ch. Haut-Brion Pessac, Graves	*A good '55. Fine colour, mature; soft gentle bouquet; Graves earthy, slightly charred flavour with typical Haut-Brion elegance. An easy attractive wine. Ten tastings from 1961.* Last tasted October 1979 ★★★★ *Drink now — 1990.*
Ch. Ausone St-Emilion	*A gap. Never tasted.*
Ch. Cheval-Blanc St-Emilion	*Frankly variable. I have tasted it 15 times since 1962, various bottlings: Berry Bros, Calvet shipped and English bottled, Tyler's and château bottled. Some distinctly volatile and overripe. The best was from a double magnum: deep brick red; rich, pronounced bouquet (iron from soil); rich and soft on the palate. Lovely.* Tasted May 1978 ★ to ★★★ *Drink up.*
Ch. Pétrus Pomerol	*Still fairly deep coloured; delicate bouquet, slow to develop, unusual style, complex, mint leaf; dry, velvety yet austere. Needs time in decanter, really unready. Tasted ten times from 1967.* Last tasted October 1976 ★★(★★?) *Drink now — 1990.*

Other châteaux: '55s featured heavily on the wine lists of my mid-trade career. I have tasted (and drunk) over 150 non first-growth châteaux, most in the late 1950s to mid-1960s. The following châteaux tasted more recently, and relevantly:

Ch. Bel-Air-Marquis-d'Aligre Soussans	*There are lots of Bel-Airs in Bordeaux but none so distinguished sounding as this wine, not often seen in England. Attractive brick red; good nose; stylish, elegant, perfect luncheon claret.* Tasted 1967 and twice in September 1979 ★★★ *Drink now — 1985.*
Ch. Calon-Ségur St-Estèphe	*Fine deep colour; lovely, gentle, cedar bouquet; slightly sweet, rich, soft yet piquant flavour.* Tasted 1959, 1965, 1969, May 1978 ★★★ *Drink now — 1988.*
Ch. Ducru-Beaucaillou St-Julien	*Lovely in cask in 1956. Tasted ten times since, English, Dutch and château bottled. Consistent development. Dry, good flavour, texture and balance.* Last tasted November 1978 ★★★ *Drink now — 1985.*
Ch. Duhart-Milon Pauillac	*Opaque (from high proportion of old vines); very fine rich* Cabernet *nose; ripe and rich on the palate, full bodied yet soft. Excellent. Seems one of the best '55s.* Tasted only once in April 1978 ★★★★ *Drink now — 1990.*

Ch. Grand-Puy-Lacoste Pauillac	*Very full flavoured in cask, and consistently flavoury in 1973 and 1977. More recently: fruity, elegant, but a touch of acidity beginning to show.* Last tasted September 1979 ★★★ *Drink up.*
Ch. Léoville-Las-Cases St-Julien	*Lovely colour, tuilé; fine, rich, cedary bouquet; excellent flavour, mature but holding well. What good claret is all about.* Tasted 1964, 1967, 1969, July 1977 ★★★★ *Drink now — 1990.*
Ch. Lynch-Bages Pauillac	*First tasted in the chai in 1958 and half a dozen times since, the last two English bottled. A fairly deep, flavoury, plausible wine, but not great.* Last tasted January 1977 ★★★ *Drink up.*
Ch. Malartic-Lagravière Graves	*Deep plummy burgundy-red; open-knit, slightly stewed fruit nose; nice balance, attractive flavour and texture. Long, slightly raw finish.* Tasted July 1979 ★★ *Drink now — 1985.*
Ch. La Mission-Haut-Brion Talence, Graves	*A powerful wine when young, still showing a youthful bitterness in mid-1960s. Subsequent tastings in 1973 and 1975 showed development to perfection: fine colour, curiously not as deep as '52 or '53; gentle, delicate, fragrant, perfectly formed bouquet; rich, lovely flavour, balance.* Tasted September and December 1978 ★★★★★ *Drink now — 1995.*
Ch. Pontet-Canet Pauillac	*Very good, well balanced in cask. Two bottlings with tinny acidity (one a Harvey bottling) in 1969 and 1971. More recently, at the château: fairly deep; calm almost creamy bouquet; soft, rich, good balance. Excellent.* Last tasted March 1979 ★★★★ *Drink now — 1990.*
Ch. Siran Labarde, Margaux	*Brick-red rim; sound and attractive bouquet and flavour. Dry, elegant.* Tasted July 1976 ★★★ *Drink now — 1988.*
Ch. Talbot St-Julien	*Tasted eight times, both château and English bottled, since 1959. At its most perfect in 1975, bottled by Harvey's: medium, lovely brick red; wonderful bouquet, gentle, ripe, cedary; medium dry, medium light, perfect flavour and balance. Château bottled also lovely in 1976. Most recently: Harvey bottling, less harmonious on nose, but perfect Sunday lunch claret.* Last tasted December 1978 ★★★ *Drink now — 1985.*
Ch. Trotanoy Pomerol	*Some signs of cork failure. Good colour; a bit aged and edgy on nose at first, but calmed; fruit and elegance, but drying out.* Tasted April 1979 ★★ *Drink up.*

1955s showing particularly well between mid-1960s and mid-1970s but not tasted recently:

Ch. Cantemerle Macau	*Surely one of the very best '55s. Wonderful vinosity and balance in 1967 and 1969. Seemed at its peak in 1970. Later: lovely but tannic finish.* Last tasted 1972.
Ch. Cos d'Estournel St-Estèphe	*Lovely bouquet, very attractive.* Tasted only once, in 1972.
Ch. La Dominique St-Emilion	*One of my favourite '55s. Deep, soft, earthy.* Tasted eight times between 1969 and 1975.
Ch. Gaffelière-Naudes St-Emilion	*Very good indeed.* Tasted 1965, 1969, 1970.
Ch. Gloria St-Julien	*Gloria began its upward climb in the mid-1950s. The '55 vintage tasted eight times, mainly Harvey bottlings, from 1959. An attractive, positive wine.* Last tasted 1966. Probably fully mature now.

Ch. La Grave-Trigant-de-Boisset Pomerol	*Sweet, earthy, wonderful claret. Tasted a dozen times from 1956 in cask and various bottlings. Last tasted 1974.*
Ch. Gruaud-Larose St-Julien	*Consistently attractive. Various bottlings tasted between 1961 and 1973.*
Ch. Langoa-Barton St-Julien	*A bit piquant and green from 1961 to 1965. Later: attained a lovely refined flavour. Last tasted 1966.*
Ch. Lascombes Margaux	*Consistently attractive in 1958, 1966 and 1969. Fully mature when tasted in 1973.*
Ch. Montrose St-Estèphe	*Magnificent, one of the best '55s and, for me, one of the loveliest vintages of this excellent but austere wine. Tasted 1968, 1970.*
Ch. Moulinet Pomerol	*Various bottlings, consistently fragrant and silky. Last tasted 1969.*
Ch. Pape-Clément Pessac, Graves	*Tasted over a dozen times. At its best in early to mid-1960s. Last tasted 1974.*
Ch. Phélan-Ségur St-Estèphe	*Not my most favourite wine in recent vintages but the '55 good in cask and perfect more recently. Last tasted 1971.*
Ch. de Sales Pomerol	*Harvey bottling: silky, soft and subtle. Tasted 1956, 1961.*
Ch. La Tour-de-Mons Soussans, Margaux	*Lovely flavour and balance. Tasted 1973, 1976.*
Some disappointing '55s, variable or fading:	*Ch. Batailley; Ch. La Fleur-Pétrus; Ch. Nenin; Ch. Pichon-Lalande.*
Ch. Léoville-Barton St-Julien	*Acidic and charmless in 1967. Thin, quite good flavour in 1969. More recently: spoiled by bitter finish. Last tasted 1976.*
Ch. Léoville-Poyferré St-Julien	*Variable bottlings, one good, two acid, one corked. Tasted 1969–1975.*
Ch. Palmer Margaux	*Yes, Palmer — quite luscious when tasted in 1961 but three times since, once in magnum, showing too much acidity, little middle flavour and rather dull. Last tasted November 1975.*
Ch. Petit-Village Pomerol	*One of the few disappointing Pomerols, flavoury but high acidity. Tasted five times, in 1968 and 1969.*

1956

One of the most dismal postwar vintages. Climate: appalling, reported to be the most severe winter since 1709; three inches of snow late February; unprecedented bad March; vines damaged, some killed, late development; cold August; excessive rain in September; weather picked up briefly 10 October, picking began 14 October. Small crop, roughly a quarter of average. The vintage was not touched by the trade which by then had a surfeit of '52s, '53s and '55s. The wines were far from execrable, but must be thin and *passé* by now.

Ch. Latour Pauillac	*Surprisingly deep coloured for an "off" year. Full, flavoury but short in 1970. A bit tart but flavoury in 1975. More recently: little nose but Cabernet flavour, again short. Last tasted May 1979. Drink up.*

Ch. Margaux Margaux	*Only sampled once, in cask. Though light in colour and body it was flavoury, attractive but acidic.* Tasted September 1958. Of little interest now.
Ch. Mouton-Rothschild Pauillac	*Again, like Latour, deep for an "off" year; medicated Cabernet aroma; very flavoury, piquant.* Tasted December 1973.
Ch. Ausone St-Emilion	*Surprisingly deep; sound cheesy nose; dry, austere but sound.* Tasted September 1976.

I have not tasted Lafite or any other first growths except those noted above, and of the other half-dozen classed-growths five are listed below:

Ch. Gruaud-Larose St-Julien	*Light, astringent, bitty and bitter, but curiously attractive.* Tasted in cask, 1958.
Ch. Montrose St-Estèphe	*Easily the best; fruity, nice, drinkable, well balanced.* Tasted 1967, 1968.
Ch. Mouton-Baron Philippe Pauillac	*Light, agreeable in 1963. Later: sugared fruity nose, lightweight, thin and peeky.* Last tasted 1969.
Ch. Palmer Margaux	*Maturing quickly, piquant acidity but a flavoury drink.* Tasted 1962.
Ch. Rauzan-Gassies Margaux	*Light but pleasant in colour, on nose and on palate. Not bad at all.* Tasted 1968.

1957 *

Not my favourite vintage: uneven, aggressive. It reminds me constantly of 1937 though, as with the latter, there are some attractive surprises. Climate: a most perverse year; one of the mildest Februarys on record; March incredibly hot; early April frost and heavy frost in May; cold delayed flowering, which occurred in June under the worst possible conditions — cold, rain, then hot and thundery; July cold and wet; August coldest on record. Small crop. Picking began on 1 October in record heat. Eighty-eight châteaux tasted. By and large my recommendation is: drink up.

Ch. Lafite Pauillac	*Surprisingly (for the year) attractive in cask. Soft, cassis flavour but acidity showing in 1973 and 1974. Later: pleasant bouquet, very flavoury but a trifle dry, short and raw.* Last tasted 1975 * Drink up.
Ch. Latour Pauillac	*Big and black in cask, "green" but flavoury. Still purple and restrained, loaded with tannin and acidity but flavoury in early to late 1960s. Found it hard, austere and unattractive in 1974. Later: raw acidity.* Last tasted 1976. Hard to know what to advise. If you have a small amount, keep it another ten years; if a large stock, hedge your bets and thin out.
Ch. Margaux Margaux	*Dry, flavoury — touch of bitterness in cask. Later: good soft ripe bouquet, chunky but unrelaxed ("screwed up" in my notes).* Last tasted 1974. Judgement reserved.
Ch. Mouton-Rothschild Pauillac	*Lively deep red colour; appealing, somewhat piquant Cabernet-Sauvignon aroma; very flavoury, richness masking '57 acidity.* Tasted 1961, 1970, 1974. Probably nice now and will keep.
Ch. Haut-Brion Pessac, Graves	*Tasted six times since 1958. Deep rich flavour in mid-1960s. By mid-1970s less attractive: loose-knit, leathery.* Last tasted May 1975.

Ch. Ausone St-Emilion	*Rich, most attractive; almost burgundy-like nose; soft, curious chocolaty flavour in cask. Always looked mature but though flavoury had a raw acid edge. Tasted six times. Last tasted 1971. Do not keep.*
Ch. Cheval-Blanc St-Emilion	*Green in cask and in early 1960s. Most recently, a British Transport Hotels bottling: firm, rich, mature colour; light stylish nose and flavour. Fruity. Refreshing acidity. Last tasted October 1971 ⋆ Probably needs drinking.*
Ch. Pétrus Pomerol	*Not tasted.*

Some other growths tasted in the 1970s:

Ch. Cantemerle Macau	*Soft, pleasant, happily without excessive acidity. A good flavoury '57. Tasted 1971.*
Ch. Cos d'Estournel St-Estèphe	*Lovely flavour spoiled by excess acidity. Tasted 1963, 1968, 1970, 1971. Drink up.*
Ch. Ducru-Beaucaillou St-Julien	*Nice in cask, showing well in 1960s. Recently, a Saccone & Speed bottling: oxidized. Tasted eight times from 1958. Last tasted 1972.*
Ch. Giscours Margaux	*I did not like this in cask but two English bottlings impressed me: fragrant, lovely refined Cabernet flavour, good texture and dry finish. Tasted 1967, 1971.*
Ch. Grand-Puy-Ducasse Pauillac	*A surprisingly attractive '57. Tasted four times in 1969, and in 1974.*
Ch. d'Issan Margaux	*Charming in cask. Flavoury, good texture, tannin and acidity in 1961. More recently, good Army & Navy Stores bottling. Last tasted November 1971*
Ch. La Lagune Ludon	*Fairly deep coloured, fruity, a bit raw but not overacid. Tasted 1969, 1970.*
Ch. Lascombes Margaux	*Touch of pleasing softness, flavoury, leading to stalky end acidity. Tasted 1971, 1973.*
Ch. Léoville-Las-Cases St-Julien	*Tasted in cask, and ten times since. Attractive when young but towards late 1960s showed overmaturity and bitter/acid finish. Later: quite nice and flavoury. Last tasted 1973. Drink up.*
Ch. Léoville-Poyferré St-Julien	*Lightish, not bad, various bottlings. Tasted 1967, 1972, 1974.*
Ch. Lynch-Bages Pauillac	*In cask, blackcurrant aroma and dry. It still has typical, almost exaggerated, Cabernet nose; very flavoury. Tasted ten times. Last tasted November 1978 ⋆⋆⋆*
Ch. Malescot-St-Exupéry Margaux	*Flavoury in cask. Fine deep colour; rich peppery Cabernet aroma; dry, good fruit, very agreeable "bite". A good '57. Tasted March 1974. Drink now.*
Ch. La Mission-Haut-Brion Talence, Graves	*Amazingly deep, almost opaque; attractive, characterful peppery/iodine nose and flavour. Rich but dry and not overacid finish. Tasted several times. Last tasted December 1978 ⋆⋆⋆*
Ch. Montrose St-Estèphe	*A big, impressive wine in cask, though green. Overimbued with tannin/acidity in the mid-1960s. Two Justerini & Brooks*

	bottlings overacid in 1971 and 1977. But a good château bottling, best of a group of '57s in 1970. So hard to recommend.
Ch. Pape-Clément Pessac, Graves	*Deepish, mature brown colour; rich but earthy brown flavour. Austere. Tasted 1976 ★*
Ch. Rausan-Ségla Margaux	*Extravagantly cassis in cask, though green. Tasted five times since. Consistent, flavoury but very high '57 acidity. Last tasted November 1970. Drink up.*
Ch. Rauzan-Gassies Margaux	*Dry, unappealing. Tasted five times, 1963–1970.*
Ch. Talbot St-Julien	*Rather raw in 1967. More recently: quite good flavour with short tannin/acid finish. Last tasted September 1976 ★*

Some '57s tasted prior to 1970:

Ch. Batailley Pauillac	*Flavoury but crumbling. Tasted 1958, 1965, 1967, 1968.*
Ch. Brane-Cantenac Margaux	*Sweet, attractive bouquet, light and delicious for a '57, no over-acidity. Tasted 1967, 1968.*
Ch. Canon St-Emilion	*Variable bottlings, one attractive but all overacid. Tasted 1968, 1969.*
Ch. Croizet-Bages Pauillac	*Austere, acidic, refreshing perhaps but not very attractive. Tasted 1967, 1968.*
Ch. La Dominique St-Emilion	*Nice nose, a bit lean and severe but attractive. Tasted four times in 1967 and 1968.*
Clos Fourtet St-Emilion	*Intriguing flavour but no middle. Acidity. Tasted 1958, 1961.*
Ch. Grand-Puy-Lacoste Pauillac	*Well made as usual. Attractive, flavoury Pauillac/Cabernet style. Tasted 1967.*
Ch. Léoville-Barton St-Julien	*Good, deep, rich bouquet, flavoury but marked acidity. Tasted 1967, 1968.*
Ch. Mouton-Baron Philippe Pauillac	*Fragrant, piquant. Tasted 1967, 1969.*
Ch. Nexon-Lemoyne Ludon	*Rarely seen château: nice flavoury wine. Tasted 1967, 1968.*
Ch. Les Ormes-de-Pez St-Estèphe	*Remarkable blackcurrant aroma and flavour. Tasted 1958, 1963, 1969.*
Ch. Petit-Faurie-de-Soutard St-Emilion	*Most attractive little wine. Tasted 1961, 1964.*
Ch. de Pez St-Estèphe	*Very flavoury, plenty of tannin and acidity. Tasted 1958, 1961.*
Ch. Pichon-Baron Pauillac	*Flavoury, austere, '57 acidity. Tasted 1958, 1969.*
Ch. Pichon-Lalande	*Dry, astringent. Tasted 1961, 1965.*

Ch. Pontet-Canet Pauillac	*Fairly big wine in cask. Seven variable notes in 1960s. Cruse bottling better than a tart English one.* Tasted 1961–1968. Drink up.
Clos René Pomerol	*Sweet, silky and attractive.* Tasted 1969.

1958 ★★

A curiously attractive but frequently maligned vintage, bypassed by the English trade who had bought '57s and then invested heavily in the '59s. Climate: mild February; March cold with snow and hail; April abnormally cold; early May exceptionally fine, but then cold and rainy; good flowering in June; warm and dry end July/early August. Late harvest, 10 October, in good conditions. Summary: soft, very flavoury wines still under-appreciated and under-priced, but many need drinking up. Forty-one châteaux tasted.

Ch. Lafite Pauillac	*Medium colour, mature; attractive, classic bouquet; ripe, gentle, feminine, flavoury. Touch of bitterness at end, but also a touch of class.* Tasted June 1975 ★★ Drink up.
Ch. Latour Pauillac	*Tasted seven times, slightly variable notes, the worst being dull and stodgy. Very deep coloured in early 1960s, seemed at best in 1970: singularly attractive, excellent mouthful. A bit short.* Last tasted May 1976 ★ Drink now — 1985.
Ch. Margaux Margaux	*Unimpressed. Light, high toned, short piquant flavour in 1963. But more recently a half-bottle pleased.* Last tasted 1971. Drink up.
Ch. Mouton-Rothschild Pauillac	*Deep coloured; very attractive, chunky, rich Cabernet nose; exciting flavour.* Tasted only once, in June 1978 ★★ Drink now — 1985.
Ch. Haut-Brion Pessac, Graves	*Tasted nine times. Poorish notes in late 1960s but seems to have got its second breath in the 1970s. Fairly deep, rich, mature colour; singed, earthy/fruity bouquet which developed well; medium dryness and body, flavoury, in good order, dry finish.* Last tasted March 1979 ★★ Drink up.
Ch. Cheval-Blanc St-Emilion	*Sweetish, soft, agreeable.* Tasted 1969, 1970, 1972, 1973. Drink up.
Ch. Ausone St-Emilion	*Fully mature in late 1960s. More recently: loose-knit, ripe, some richness.* Last tasted September 1976 ★★ Drink up.
Ch. Pétrus Pomerol	*Fairly deep velvety appearance; unforthcoming nose, developed slightly; medium dry, medium body, rich, soft, fluffy sort of wine. Balanced but appeared stunned.* Tasted only once, in May 1973.

Other growths tasted during the past ten years:

Ch. Beychevelle St-Julien	*Very mature colour; very ripe bouquet; attractive in a bitty, superficial way.* Tasted four times 1967–May 1976 ★ Drink up.
Ch. Calon-Ségur St-Estèphe	*Brown in 1968. Later: quite appealing though orange-tinged maturity; rich, stewed old nose; soft, slightly medicinal (iron) flavour. Not bad.* Last tasted 1976. Drink up.
Ch. Cantemerle Margaux	*Good bouquet, charming.* Tasted 1962, 1971, 1973.

Carruades de Ch. Lafite Pauillac	*Light, very mature looking; a charmer — rich, biscuity, well-developed bouquet; dry, firm but fading.* Tasted 1964, November 1978 ⋆ *Drink up.*
Ch. Chasse-Spleen Moulis	*Fine deepish colour; attractive nose and finish. Nice wine.* Tasted 1972.
Ch. Cos d'Estournel St-Estèphe	*Nice wine. Soft, flavoury, some richness.* Tasted twice in 1973.
Ch. La Dominique St-Emilion	*Slightly lactic nose, but cedary; flavoury, attractive though a little edgy.* Tasted 1976, May and December 1977 ⋆ Drink up.
Ch. Figeac St-Emilion	*Curious* Cabernet *nose; soft, earthy, mild, yet twist of acidity. So-so.* Tasted 1973.
Ch. Gazin Pomerol	*Lovely colour; rich, open bouquet; fruit and charm, dry finish.* Tasted 1967, 1968, 1969, 1973.
Ch. Gruaud-Larose St-Julien	*Fine colour; rich cedary nose and flavour. Slightly short but pleasant and ready.* Tasted 1969, 1974, September 1976 ⋆⋆.
Ch. Léoville-Poyferré St-Julien	*Lightish, very mature; bland nose; quite nice flavour and style, but edgy acidity.* Tasted 1972. Drink up.
Ch. La Mission-Haut-Brion Talence, Graves	*Very deep, rich colour; fabulous bouquet; a huge, dry, earthy wine; soft, remarkably good.* Tasted 1975, 1976, December 1978 ⋆⋆⋆ Drink now — 1985.
Ch. Pape-Clément Pessac, Graves	*Lightish, fully mature; overripe nose; dry, quite nice. A bit lean and stringy.* Tasted 1974.
Ch. Talbot St-Julien	*Soft, fruity but dry, short, unknit acid finish.* Tasted twice, in 1976. Drink up.

1959 ⋆⋆⋆⋆⋆

"The vintage of the century"; and perhaps because of the early adulation of the Press (egged on by the Bordelaise) it has its detractors — "too little acidity", "cracking up", etc. Widely bought by the English trade and certainly one of the most massively constituted wines of the postwar era. Climate: one of the finest Februarys in living memory — frost at night, early morning mist and hot sun; March equally good; April hot, cold, rain and storms; May improved later; June good; July almost too hot; August fine and warm; September hot, a lot of rain from 13th but good weather for picking which started on 23rd. Average quantity; rated *très grands vins*. Summary: a challenging year, my notes full of contradictions of style and a plethora of variable English bottlings. At best (as Mouton) masculine and magnificent; others living dangerously.

Ch. Lafite Pauillac	*I had to wait until 1975 to taste this, then three times in three months. Most recently: deep, magnificently rich colour; dumb at first but developed fragrance in glass; the antithesis of the delicate '53, a massive wine, fat, loaded with tannin and acidity, yet elegant. Lots of life.* At the Overton tasting, May 1979 ⋆⋆⋆⋆(⋆) Drink 1985–2000.
Ch. Latour Pauillac	*If Lafite was huge in this vintage, the weight of Latour can be imagined. Tasted 17 times since 1963. Black/purple when young, still opaque but beginning to show maturity; nose dumb and peppery; packed with component parts. An enormous wine, dry, full of alcohol, fruit, extract. Quite unready.* Last tasted March 1978 ⋆⋆⋆(⋆⋆) Drink 1990–2050.

Ch. Margaux Margaux	*A dozen notes since 1964. Still fairly deep coloured but maturing; rich, cedary scented bouquet — needs time to develop; fairly full bodied, rich, velvety, certainly no lack of acidity. One dull, slightly oxidized bottle.* Last tasted 1977 ★★★(★) Drink 1990–2010.
Ch. Mouton-Rothschild Pauillac	*Sixteen consistently ecstatic notes since 1963. Still enormously deep in colour; wonderfully concentrated* Cabernet-Sauvignon *aroma, cedar and blackcurrants; fairly dry, full bodied, massive yet soft, velvety, packed with flavour.* Last tasted December 1976 ★★★★(★) Drink now — 2030.
Ch. Haut-Brion Pessac, Graves	*Twenty notes from 1963. Very deep rich colour, browner than any of the first-growth Médocs; deep, magnificent tobacco-like bouquet; an excellent earthy heavyweight with dry tannic finish.* Last tasted September 1978 ★★★(★★) Drink 1985–2010.
Ch. Ausone St-Emilion	*Deep, fine mature colour; dumb but rich/singed bouquet; slightly sweet yet austere, fairly full bodied, idiosyncratic as ever.* Tasted only twice in March and July 1971 ★★★ Drink now — 1990?
Ch. Cheval-Blanc St-Emilion	*Deep, hot-vintage colour but showing distinct maturity in appearance; sweet and fruity bouquet; ripe, full, rich, soft. Dry finish. Fully developed. Tasted six times in 1970s.* Last tasted January 1979 ★★★★ Drink now — 1990.
Ch. Pétrus Pomerol	*Fairly deep, mature looking; an incredible bouquet, rich, fishy (in the Chambertin sense); full, deep, velvety, rich, rich, rich. Dry finish.* Tasted only once, in May 1972 ★★★★(★) Drink now — 2000.

Of the 134 other châteaux of this vintage tasted, the following are the most significant noted over the past ten years:

Ch. Batailley Pauillac	*Nine notes from 1961. Consistent. Chunky, plummy, attractive, fruity but a touch of coarseness.* Last tasted 1973 ★★★ Drink now.
Ch. Belair St-Emilion	*Fine, simple, flavoury wine. Nice.* Tasted 1971 ★★★ Drink now.
Ch. Bel-Air Marquis d'Aligre Soussans	*Despite its grand title, just a* grand cru exceptionnel — bourgeois supérieur. *Unready in 1968. More recently: delicious — garnet/mahogany colour; gently mature bouquet; lovely mellow-brick flavour.* Last tasted October 1977 ★★★ Drink now — 1985.
Ch. Beychevelle St-Julien	*Not its usual delicate self, more robust — Batailley-like. First tasted in 1964. Perfect Lyons bottling in 1967 and by British Transport Hotels in 1968. Château bottled: high toned, fruity nose; attractive, charming in 1972. Later: a rich but otherwise disappointing Army & Navy Stores bottling.* Last tasted 1973 ★★
Ch. Brane-Cantenac Margaux	*Deepish, mature; meaty, medicinal bouquet; rich, fair finish — various bottlings.* Tasted 1972 — May 1978 ★★ to ★★★
Ch. Cantemerle Macau	*First tasted in 1965. Claret at its very best in 1967. Most recently: deep, fine, classic colour; gentle harmonious bouquet; soft and flavoury but with sustaining tannin/acidity.* Last tasted May 1977 ★★★★ Drink now — 1990.
Ch. Cantenac-Brown Margaux	*Two English bottlings and one château bottled, consistent, showing marked end acidity. One overripe, one (the château bottling) woody.* Tasted 1968, 1969, 1972.

Carruades de Ch. Lafite Pauillac	*Very attractive, medium deep, warm garnet red; gentle, fragrant, ripe, cedary bouquet and flavour. Consistently attractive on six occasions from 1969.* Last tasted May 1979 **** Drink now.
Dom. de Chevalier Graves	*Rich, attractive fruity bouquet; excellent flavour and balance. Not an earthy Graves.* Tasted 1971 **** Drink now.
Ch. Cos d'Estournel St-Estèphe	*Beautifully made, well balanced. A full, firm, beefy wine. First tasted 1965.* Last tasted 1971 **(**) Should be good now — 1995.
Ch. Coufran St-Estèphe	*Consistently reliable bourgeois growth. Excellent flavour, balance and finish in its class.* Tasted 1969, June 1978 ***
Ch. La Dominique St-Emilion	*Dry, rich, long.* Tasted 1976 **** Drink now — 1990.
Ch. Ducru-Beaucaillou St-Julien	*Tasted five times from 1968, Berry Bros and château bottlings. Consistent notes: deep, fine big wine, well balanced, understated.* Last tasted May 1975 ***(*) Drink now — 1990.
Ch. Dutruch-Grand-Poujeaux Moulis	*Several bottlings, consistently good. Rich, chunky, forward.* Tasted 1968, 1969, 1978, March 1979 *** Drink now — 1990.
Ch. Fieuzal Graves	*Forthcoming, nice flavour and balance.* Tasted 1975 *** Drink now.
Ch. Giscours Margaux	*Attractive, well bred, fairly marked tannin and acidity.* Tasted 1968, 1970. Probably softened now.
Ch. Gloria St-Julien	*Bottled by The Wine Society. Deep; developed well in glass; good but noticeable acidity.* Tasted 1977 ** Drink up.
Ch. Grand-Puy-Lacoste Pauillac	*Fruity, crisp, somewhat astringent cedar-wood flavour.* Tasted 1968, 1974. Drink up.
Ch. Gruaud-Larose St-Julien	*Fifteen notes starting in 1967, all reasonably consistent. Various bottlings. Most recently, a château-bottled half: fine, deep, mature colour, heavy bead (legs); rich, meaty, showing a bit of age and touch of overacidity. Very flavoury.* Last tasted July 1976 ** Drink up.
Ch. Langoa-Barton St-Julien	*Full, sweet. Excellent mouthful.* Tasted 1970. Then ** Drink up.
Ch. Lascombes Margaux	*Maturing; sweet bouquet; good balance, holding well.* Tasted 1967 — May 1979 *** Drink now — 1990.
Ch. Léoville-Barton St-Julien	*Well made. Lovely and almost ready to drink in 1963; a bad Victoria Wine/Tyler's bottling in 1972. Most recently: a deepish brick-red colour (the wine and my host, Mr Ray); very attractive well-developed nose and flavour; gentle, mellow-brick/cedar.* At lunch with Cyril Ray in Albany, July 1979 **** Drink now — 1985.
Ch. Léoville-Las-Cases St-Julien	*Eight notes from 1962. Seemed to gain in colour, certainly at its deepest and best in 1973 and 1975. More recently: rich fruit, heavyweight but velvety, still fairly massive.* At the Heublein tasting, May 1979 **** Drink now — 1990.
Ch. Léoville-Poyferré St-Julien	*A noticeable end acidity in most bottlings (Harvey's, British Transport Hotels, Blayney's, château) tasted since 1967. Seems to be gaining in depth of colour, with enough plumpness and extract to counter-balance the acidity.* Last tasted March 1977 ** Drink up.

Ch. Lynch-Bages Pauillac	*A château always popular in England. I found the '59 a bit raw and coarse from 1965 to 1968, lovely in 1969 but, summing up, untypical. Berry Bros bottling had fine deep colour; rich but muted nose (Lynch-Bages normally has marked* Cabernet *aroma); soft, flavoury, nice balance.* Last tasted February 1972 ** Drink now — 1985?
Ch. Lynch-Moussas Pauillac	*Ten notes (various bottlings) from 1961, mostly qualified: green, not well-knit, sweet and sour. Most recently, a château bottling: a bit odd, slightly sour.* Last tasted 1970.
Ch. Malescot-St-Exupéry Margaux	*Big-vintage colour; characteristic scented* Cabernet *plus elderberry aroma; deep, chunky, fruity wine.* Tasted 1970 **
Ch. La Mission-Haut-Brion Talence, Graves	*Chunky, deep plummy colour; fragrant; heavily laden, with dry tannic finish. Impressive. Tasted four times from 1973.* Last tasted December 1978 **** Drink 1985–2010.
Ch. Montrose St-Estèphe	*Tasted 11 times, six different bottlings, but consistently impressive, austere and tannic in mid-1960s. More recently: deep, mature, rich rimmed; extremely good classic bouquet; rich, full bodied, massive yet soft (iron fist in velvet glove), very dry finish. A broad-shouldered wine.* Last tasted June 1979 **** Drink now — 2000.
Ch. Nenin Pomerol	*Disappointing, hard and charmless.* Tasted 1970.
Ch. Palmer Margaux	*Rich-vintage colour, 1929 style but still youthful; high toned, almost burgundy-like in its vegetable richness; slightly sweet, impressive, very fragrant. Some English bottlings showing acidity.* Best out of château-bottled magnums, in 1979 and January 1980 **** Drink now — 1990.
Ch. Pape-Clément Pessac, Graves	*British Transport Hotels bottlings, elegant and refined in 1968 and 1969. Later, château bottled: fragrant and charming.* Last tasted 1972 ** Probably at peak now.
Ch. Phélan-Ségur St-Estèphe	*English bottlings: light and watery in 1965; astringent in 1967. More recently: austere with twist of acidity.* Last tasted 1973.
Ch. Pichon-Baron Pauillac	*Fairly deep, firm, positive colour; magnificent classic* Cabernet *bouquet and flavour. Touch of piquancy. Interesting to see its development.* Tasted 1971, 1972, March 1977 *** Drink now — 1990.
Ch. Pichon-Lalande Pauillac	*A well-balanced, slowly maturing wine. First tasted 1966. Three bad, pricked, Kinloch bottlings in 1969. Dolamore's: flavoury but showing acidity in 1976. The same year a château-bottled magnum was nubile but virginal: soft, rounded but unyielding.* Last tasted August 1976 ***(*) Drink 1983–1995.
Ch. Plince Pomerol	*Two perfect London bottlings in 1971: fat, flavoury, well balanced. Later, a vinegary one bottled by Saccone & Speed.* Last tasted 1972.
Ch. Pontet-Canet Pauillac	*An unwitting demonstration of bottling variations. Bordeaux bottled by Cruse: chunky, not very exciting in 1967, 1969 and 1970. Army & Navy Stores bottling: woody nosed, positive flavour and acidity in 1971. Berry Bros bottling: sweet, soft and nice in 1972. London bottled by Rutherford's (the Cruse agents) noted as mature looking, sweet on nose but dry on palate in 1976. And, most recently, at the château: rather deep and immature; fragrant, fruity nose; rich and firm.* Last tasted April 1979. So take your pick. At best *** Drink now — 1990.

Ch. Rausan-Ségla *Margaux*	*Deep coloured; positive, stylish and attractive wine.* Tasted 1967– 1971 ✱✱✱ *Probably holding well.*
Ch. Rauzan-Gassies *Margaux*	*Seven notes, only two of which are good. Seemed not too well balanced in 1963; green, with a touch of volatile acidity twice in 1967. More recently: mature, creaking a bit with age, velvety but acidic.* Last tasted 1973.
Clos René *Pomerol*	*Soft, rounded, a nice drink but curious burnt tang and touch of acidity.* Tasted 1969, 1976 ✱
Ch. St-Pierre-Sevaistre *St-Julien*	*Two English bottlings, both delicious.* Tasted 1969, 1971 ✱✱✱
Ch. Talbot *St-Julien*	*Four different English bottlings and two château bottlings, all consistent. Not as dry and masculine as usual. Mature, soft and flavoury. No great length but good.* Tasted 1967–September 1976 ✱✱✱ *Drink now — 1988.*
Ch. La Tour-Haut-Brion *Graves*	*The number two red of La Mission: opaque; bouquet closed up, needing time; rich, with body and bite.* Tasted 1978 ✱✱✱✱ *Drink 1985–2000.*
Ch. La Tour-de-Mons *Soussans*	*Normally reliable, but three poor English bottlings, including Justerini & Brooks, in 1967, 1968 and 1969. Later, sound and flavoury.* Last tasted 1972. At best ✱✱
Ch. Troplong-Mondot *St-Emilion*	*Forward and mature in colour, nose and taste. Soft. Little to it.* Tasted 1971 ✱
Vieux Ch. Certan *Pomerol*	*Charming, tough, unready in 1967. At its silky/leathery textured, rounded best in early 1970s. More recently, showing signs of cracking up, though still attractive.* Last tasted October 1975.

1960 ✱

A curious, somewhat overlooked year as was 1958, but more deservedly. Treated, probably rightly, with a certain amount of disdain by the trade, which was full to the bung with '59s anyway. Not a *vin de garde* but some flavoury wines made. Climate: despite a cold January and frosts in April and May, perfect flowering weather around 25 May. Warm and dry June augured well but July/August rainy and below average temperatures. Rain and sun alternated in September, the harvest being stretched between 12 and 15 October.

Ch. Lafite *Pauillac*	*Seven notes from 1967. Not very good, little to it, probably at best mid-1970s. Now lightish, mature; getting gamy and overripe on the nose; light, flavoury but short with twist of end acidity.* Last tasted November 1978 ✱ *Drink up.*
Ch. Latour *Pauillac*	*Reputed to be one of the best 1960s. First tasted in 1968. Six evenly spread notes since. Most recently: strong Cabernet character but short, still surprisingly deep coloured; peppery nose, class showing, also acidity which is reiterated at the finish. A big dry wine.* Last tasted May 1976 ✱✱ *With care 1985–1990.*
Ch. Margaux *Margaux*	*Tasted only twice: obscure nose; lightweight and astringent in 1964. More recently: dry, somewhat severe.* Last tasted 1971.
Ch. Mouton-Rothschild *Pauillac*	*Tasted only four times but prefer it to Lafite and Latour. A rather dishy mouthful in 1971, very pronounced cedar and blackcurrant*

Mouton aroma; very flavoury, exciting but short. Last tasted June 1976 ⋆⋆ Drink now — 1985.

Ch. Haut-Brion Pessac, Graves	Compared to other vintages, relatively light, soft, forward when tasted in 1964. Well made in difficult circumstances but touch of end acidity, showing overmaturity. Last tasted 1971 ⋆ Drink up.
Ch. Ausone St-Emilion	Tasted only once: lightish mature colour; broad, mature, chaptalized bouquet; slightly sweet, soft, quite nice condition. Bland and ready. Tasted 1971 ⋆ Drink up.
Ch. Cheval-Blanc St-Emilion	Not too good. Gave me that old uncertain feeling in the mouth in 1968. Raw in 1969. More recently: an aged taste — could have been a poor bottle. Last tasted September 1976. Be circumspect.
Ch. Pétrus Pomerol	Not tasted.

Of the 62 other châteaux noted, the two which enjoyed the best reputation certainly warranted it. I put them first:

Ch. Palmer Margaux	Remarkably mature and drinkable in 1965, has continued (apart from a somewhat tart Berry Bros bottling in 1967) consistently soft and agreeable since. Still attractive in May 1977 ⋆⋆ But drink up.
Ch. Léoville-Las-Cases St-Julien	Tasted 15 times, various bottlings: English, Scottish, Dutch and even Austrian. Delightful in the mid-1960s. Though cedary and flavoury, showing signs of cracking up. Last tasted July 1978 ⋆ Drink up.

Others tasted recently:

Ch. Calon-Ségur St-Estèphe	Nine notes: fruity, soft but raw in mid-1960s. A bit uneven, stewed fruit. Last tasted December 1976. Drink up.
Ch. Figeac St-Emilion	Attractive strawberry fruitiness and flavoury in 1965. More recently: a very aged bottle. Last tasted 1976. Drink up.
Ch. Lafon-Rochet St-Estèphe	Lightish colour, nose and body, but some fruit, developed well. Delightful little wine. Tasted March 1978 ⋆⋆ Drink now — 1985.
Ch. La Mission-Haut-Brion Talence, Graves	One of the deepest looking '60s; good bouquet — reminded me of mince pies; soft, flavoury, at best in the late 1960s to early 1970s. Later: blunt, short and touch of acidity. Last tasted December 1978 ⋆ Drink up.
Ch. Montrose St-Estèphe	One can rely on Mr Charmoluë, the owner, to do his best. Soft, fruity, well made and showing consistently well four times in 1968. Later: maturing but still tannic. Last tasted 1972 ⋆⋆ Drink now — 1985?
Ch. Pontet-Canet Pauillac	Seven rather variable notes from 1967, but a Cruse half-bottle proved a surprise: unexpectedly deep in colour; gentle, good, sound bouquet which held well; slightly sweet, soft, open, fully developed, the brownness of colour being endorsed by an edge of acidity. Attractive though short — which about sums up the best 1960s. At a Decanter Magazine tasting, August 1979 ⋆⋆ Drink up.
Ch. Soutard St-Emilion	Frequently delighted with this infrequently seen château. Chaptalized, fully mature but a pleasant little wine in 1973, 1975. Last tasted September 1976 ⋆⋆ Drink up.
Ch. Talbot St-Julien	Tasted only twice, but impressed: good rich nose; dry, nicely put together. Both in 1976 ⋆⋆ Drink now — 1985.

1960s showing well prior to the early 1970s. Most should have been drunk by now:	*Ch. Beauregard; Ch. Cantemerle; Carruades de Ch. Lafite; Ch. Chasse-Spleen; Ch. Ducru-Beaucaillou; Ch. Dutruch-Grand-Poujeaux; Ch. L'Eglise-Clinet; Ch. Giscours; Ch. Gloria; Ch. Grand-Barrail; Ch. Grand-Puy-Lacoste; Ch. Gruaud-Larose; Ch. Lagrange; Ch. La Lagune; Ch. Lascombes; Ch. Léoville-Poyferré; Ch. Malescot-St-Exupéry; Ch. Meyney; Ch. Nenin; Ch. Pichon-Baron; Ch. Pichon-Lalande; Ch. Prieuré-Lichine; Ch. Rausan-Ségla; Ch. Siran; Ch. de Terrefort.*
Not showing well in the 1960s:	*Ch. Beychevelle; Ch. Haut-Batailley; Ch. Léoville-Barton; Ch. Rauzan-Gassies; Ch. de Sales.*

1961 ★★★★★

Undoubtedly the greatest postwar vintage and one of the four best of the century. Deep, rich, concentrated, long lasting. As with 1945, more by luck than good management (see climate conditions which follow). Unlike 1945, more flesh and fat and likely not to dry out as severely as some of even the most renowned of that vintage. But only time will tell. Climate: despite frost at the end of March, vegetation was advanced. Cold during flowering with rain which washed away the pollen. This had the immediate result of reducing the potential crop. Rain at end of July, persistent drought in August followed by a very sunny September. In fact, nature effected a severe pruning; the remaining grapes, small and concentrated due to drought, benefited from the abundance of nutrients (drawn from the soil), which would otherwise have been distributed amongst a normal-sized crop. The preharvest sun brought those remaining small grapes to full maturity, thickening the skins to provide depth of colour. Vintage began 27 September, very small harvest, highest quality. Market: tiny crop plus high quality equals high asking price. There was some trade resistance (would the consumer pay the price?) particularly from those who had big stocks of '59s. Offered at retail prices ranging from the equivalent of £1.35 per bottle for a good second growth to £3.50 for the leading first growths, their value has since increased consistently and considerably, fetching at auction in 1979 an average of £16 and £60 per bottle respectively. As stocks dwindle, so prices will increase. 1961s are the gold dust of the wine world. Summary: the hallmarks of the '61 *grands vins* are intense depth of colour, concentrated bouquet and flavour; the sweetness of fully ripe grapes, high extract, flesh, tannin and acid for long keeping, length and aftertaste. And if ever there was a case made for mandatory bottling at the château, this vintage provides much evidence.

Ch. Lafite Pauillac	*Although I have been selling this wine since it first came on the market I did not taste it until 1975, since when I have had it half a dozen times. At the great Overton tasting of Lafite it was the deepest of the first group of vintages; subdued, restrained but rich and elegant nose; a very dry, even austere wine, full bodied, concentrated, quite unready. Needs much longer in bottle, and like the 1870 may take ages to come round. Unfortunately there were two dud, prematurely old, woody bottles at the tasting of 20 leading châteaux of the 1961 vintage given by Dr John Taams in Holland in May 1978.* Last tasted May 1979 ★★(★★★) Drink 1990–2030?
Ch. Latour Pauillac	*As can be imagined, an enormous wine. Tasted nine times since 1968, consistently impressive: intense colour, the least mature, most purple of all the '61s at the Taams tasting in 1978; deep, alcoholic, port-like nose, still peppery; medium dry, very full bodied, packed, beefy but beautiful balance.* Last tasted May 1978 ★★(★★★) Drink 1990–2030. It will be interesting for posterity to see how Lafite and Latour develop.
Ch. Margaux Margaux	*If the hallmark of Lafite is refinement, of Latour masculinity, of Mouton concentrated fruit, then the outstanding characteristic of*

Margaux is intense fragrance. The '61 has it but needs nursing out of the decanter and glass. Tasted eight times since 1964: deep colour, showing some maturity; the bouquet is extraordinary — rich, singed creosote, cedary, intense, lovely; rich, silky, elegant, long flavour, very dry finish. *Last tasted September 1978* ***(**) *Drink 1985–2010.*

Ch. Mouton-Rothschild
Pauillac

First tasted in 1963. A stunning wine: still very deep but beginning to show a little maturity; amazing richness and ripeness of grape, concentrated Cabernet-Sauvignon bouquet, flavour; magnificent, balanced, unready. *Last tasted May 1978* ***(**) *Drink 1985–2020.*

Ch. Haut-Brion
Pessac, Graves

First tasted in 1963. Surprisingly soft and lovely on the palate even in the mid-1960s but the nose curiously waxy and dumb, developing its characteristic hot, earthy/pebbly bouquet only latterly. Ripe, soft, lovely texture, but not as demonstrably or obtrusively a '61 as the other first growths. Fine, gentlemanly, understated. *Last tasted November 1979* ***(**) *Drink 1985–2010.*

Ch. Ausone
St-Emilion

Tasted once. Well-defined colour, stylish, lighter and elegant version of Ausone 1959. Not great but good. *March 1971* *** *Drink now — 1990?*

Ch. Cheval-Blanc
St-Emilion

Rich and velvety when first tasted in 1967. A bit adolescent in 1972. Showing well at the Taams tasting: marvellous colour, deep but mature; mulberry aroma, rich, port-like (reminiscent of the '47); distinct sweetness of fully ripe grapes, soft, open, a little loose-knit after the Médocs, gentle but firm finish. *Last tasted May 1978* ***(*) *Drink now — 2000.*

Ch. Pétrus
Pomerol

Tasted only twice. Extremely deep coloured; magnificent bouquet, amazing fruit; a lovely, rich, velvety wine. Scarce and very high priced. *Last tasted April 1968* ***(**) *Drink 1985–2010.*

Of the 152 other châteaux tasted many are, not surprisingly, magnificent. The '61s have an added dimension: intense richness. But one wine is absolutely outstanding and another supreme. Indeed, it could be argued that both the following wines might be placed in the second rank of first growths, above the line, as it were, with Ausone, Cheval-Blanc and Pétrus.

Ch. Palmer
Margaux

First tasted — a Berry Bros bottling — in 1972 and just three times since, all château bottled. At Dr Taams's remarkable tasting of '61s in Holland all 20 participants, professionals and gifted amateurs, rated it top (only Pétrus, of the great growths, was not in the tasting). Exceptionally deep, strongly coloured right to the edge of the meniscus, showing maturity; amazingly concentrated fruit with that mulberry character I associate with fully ripe grapes, a touch of iron, complex, fragrant; enormously rich on the palate, fruit, softness yet with firm underlying tannin and acidity. As great as its reputation. *Last tasted May 1978* ****(*) *Drink now — 2000.*

Ch. La Mission-Haut-Brion
Talence, Graves

First tasted in 1973, deep, rich and velvety. Four times in 1978: enormous depth of colour, virtually opaque but maturing; rich, ripe, port-reminiscent nose; magnificent wine, sweetness of ripe grapes, vast but fleshy — not severe. *Last noted at the pre-sale tasting, December 1978* ****(*) *Drink now — 1995.*

Other '61s tasted recently:

Ch. Beychevelle
St-Julien

Tasted nine times since 1963. Showed extremely well at the Taams tasting: deep; very rich, spicy bouquet; a marvellous scent which developed its complexity in the glass; a rich, soft, ripe wine packed with flavour. *Last tasted May 1978* ****(*) *Drink now — 1995.*

Ch. Branaire-Ducru *St-Julien*	*Three English bottlings, one overacid. Last tasted, château bottled: very deep colour; very fine, rich but delicate bouquet; dry, full, velvety but tannic, good but unready.* Last tasted with Sam and Michael Aaron in New York, October 1979 ★★(★★) Drink 1985–2000.
Ch. Brane-Cantenac *Margaux*	*Mature looking; sweet, attractive, cedar-Cabernet nose and flavour. Overall dry, tannic. Tasted only three times.* Last tasted June 1977 ★★★(★)? Drink now — 1990.
Ch. Calon-Ségur *St-Estèphe*	*Tasted a dozen times since 1967, mostly château bottled. Colour not as deep as expected and showing some maturity belied by a markedly dry tannic finish; bouquet undeveloped and unknit as yet. Good quality but not great.* Tasted May 1978 ★(★★)? Drink 1990–2000.
Ch. Cos d'Estournel *St-Estèphe*	*Magnificent depth of colour, bouquet and flavour. Very tannic.* Tasted May 1978 ★★(★★) Drink 1985–2010.
Ch. Ducru-Beaucaillou *St-Julien*	*Tasted many times since 1967 with the most consistently enthusiastic notes. Deep, rich mahogany colour; concentrated cedar and fruit; complex, fairly tough still, but beautifully balanced.* Last tasted August 1979 ★★★★(★) Drink 1983–2000.
Ch. L'Enclos *Pomerol*	*Rich, magnificent. Tasted only once, bottled by the Swedish State Monopoly.* In Malmö, June 1978 ★★★★ Drink now — 1990.
Ch. de Ferrière *Margaux*	*One hardly ever sees Ferrière — this was only the third tasted of any vintage. London bottled by Morgan Furze: deep and lively colour; a very fragrant bouquet; very flavoury, nice weight, not heavy, refreshing acidity.* Tasted February 1980 ★★★ Drink now — 1990.
Ch. La Gaffelière *St-Emilion*	*A touch too much redness, like a 1962; attractive, fully developed, high-toned bouquet; rich, very flavoury, with a twist of acidity.* Tasted July 1979 ★★★ Drink now — 1985.
Ch. Gazin *Pomerol*	*Various bottlings, tasted eight times since 1969. Basically a nice wine, easy, well-knit but not in the same class as second-growth Médocs.* Last tasted May 1976 ★★★ Drink now — 1985.
Ch. Giscours *Margaux*	*Deepened in colour between 1969 and 1975. Virtually opaque, but maturing rim; slightly scented, almost burgundian bouquet; a good foursquare but stylish wine.* Tasted March 1975 ★★★ Drink now — 1990.
Ch. Gloria *St-Julien*	*Four good notes, the last an outstanding Berry Bros bottling: fabulous colour; ripe, mulberry bouquet; ripe, most attractive.* Last tasted October 1978 ★★★★ Drink now — 1990.
Ch. Grand-Puy-Lacoste *Pauillac*	*Elegant, fruity, soft yet with a touch of austerity.* Tasted August 1979 ★★★(★) Drink 1985–1995.
Ch. Gruaud-Larose *St-Julien*	*Seven consistently impressive notes from 1969. Deep, mature edge; a broad, open, sweet and fragrant bouquet, touch of fern and cedar; medium dry on entry, with dry tannic finish. In between, full, rich yet elegant, complex, with good texture. A very fine wine.* Last tasted May 1978 ★★★★(★) Drink now — 1995.
Ch. Lafon-Rochet *St-Estèphe*	*First tasted (a good Christopher's bottling) in 1971, a rich, complete wine with sweet nose, great depth, dry overall, good length and lovely end taste.* Last tasted August 1979 ★★★(★) Drink 1985–2000.
Ch. Lagrange *St-Julien*	*Tasted a dozen times since 1968, including four good Christopher's bottlings. A dry, fragrant wine, full flavoured yet some delicacy.* Last tasted June 1977 ★★★★ Drink now — 1990?

Ch. Lascombes Margaux	*Tasted seven times since 1970, one with rave notices in January 1978, two showing a bit of raw acidity, in particular at the Taams tasting in May 1978. Most recently: fine, deep, great-vintage colour though clearly mature mahogany edge; peppery high-alcohol nose, fruity, developed well in glass; slightly sweet on entry, rich, ripe chunky wine with lovely consistency and long dry finish.* Last tasted at a picnic lunch in Hugh Johnson's garden, July 1979 ***(*) Drink now — 1995.
Ch. Léoville-Barton St-Julien	*Beautiful colour; soft, sweet — cold tea and wet cedar-box — bouquet; an elegant, dry wine, with touch of iron and lovely leathery texture. Distinctive, characterful.* Tasted 1976, 1978, March 1979 ****(*) Drink 1985–1995?
Ch. Léoville-Las-Cases St-Julien	*A sequence of admiring notes punctuated by two dull London bottlings ("Chaville" on the label) in 1976, and two poor château bottlings at the Taams tasting: one woody, one dried up, but saved by a third bottle which was sweet on the nose and very good.* Last tasted May 1978. At best **** Drink now — 1990.
Ch. Léoville-Poyferré St-Julien	*Various bottlings tasted on seven occasions from 1967, all consistently good. Rich colour but not as deep as some '61s; rich, open, developed bouquet; soft, delicate, refined, shapely, elegant, delicious.* Last tasted October 1979 ***(*) Drink now — 1990.
Ch. Lestage Listrac	*A relatively minor wine, to demonstrate that not all '61s are great: deep coloured; slightly volatile, kernel-like nose; fruity, overacid* Tasted November 1978. Drink up.
Ch. Lynch-Bages Pauillac	*Tasted 18 times, various bottlings since 1967. Lupton's bottling (shipped by Cruse) was good. Saccone & Speed's (shipped by Schröder & Schÿler) was not a patch on the château bottling tasted at the same time in 1970. The château bottling showed well enough at the Taams tasting: medium deep, not displaying much maturity yet; marked cinnamon-Cabernet nose, the hallmark of Lynch-Bages; rich, fine, very flavoury, tannic finish.* Last tasted, a good Dutch bottling, November 1978. At best ****(*) Drink 1985–1995.
Ch. Magdelaine St-Emilion	*Three top notes in 1970, 1972 and 1978. Magnificently rich, plummy robe; nose- and palate-filling. Slightly sweet at first, dry iron finish. Almost port-like. Great character.* December 1978 ****(*) Drink now — 1990.
Ch. Malescot-St-Exupéry Margaux	*Deep; characteristic Malescot raw blackcurrants nose; a strapping dry wine, flavoury, concentrated.* Tasted 1967, October 1977 ***(**) Drink 1985–1995.
Ch. Montrose St-Estèphe	*A dozen consistently good notes from 1967 including one shipped by Lebègue and bottled by Collie's of Aberdeen. Very deep colour; fine but peppery, dumb nose; a massive wine, tannic, unready but lovely. Worth the wait.* Last tasted November 1978 **(***) Drink 1985–2020.
Ch. Mouton-Baron Philippe Pauillac	*Deep, still purple in 1975, consistently good, excellent drink. Interesting to see what nature's pruning and a hot summer can do with a customarily light, easy style of wine.* Last tasted October 1976 **** Drink now — 1990.
Ch. Nenin Pomerol	*A flavoury but slightly suspect (overacid) Hedges & Butler bottling tasted in 1969. A good Justerini & Brooks bottling with lovely texture in 1975. Later: a fine, soft, château-bottled example.* Last tasted March 1976. At best **** Drink now — 1990.

Ch. Les Ormes-de-Pez St-Estèphe	*Fairly deep, rich, fruity. Approaching classed-growth standard.* Tasted 1967 — May 1975 **** Drink now — 1990.
Ch. Pape-Clément Pessac, Graves	*Not as deep coloured as most good '61s; fragrant, damp fern/tobacco leaf Graves aroma; calm, fruity, rich, ripe. Excellent.* At the Taams tasting, May 1978 ***** Drink now — 1990.
Ch. Pavie St-Emilion	*Noticed a bitter edge in 1963 recurring with two English bottlings in 1971 and 1972. Last tasted, château bottled: '61 depth of colour; cinnamon/spicy bouquet; dry, firm, nice balance but unspectacular.* Last tasted February 1978. At best *** Drink now — 1985.
Ch. de Pez St-Estèphe	*Excellent, full, dry, tannic and unready.* Tasted December 1968 *(***) Drink 1985–1995.
Ch. Pichon-Baron Pauillac	*Tasted only three times and all good English bottlings: Justerini & Brooks, Bouchard Ainé, and by the anonymous* par l'importateur *who made such a mess of the Rauzan-Gassies.* Last tasted in May 1976 ***
Ch. Pichon-Lalande Pauillac	*Deep, lively, rich mulberry-like nose; lovely flavour, fat yet tannic, fragrant aftertaste.* Last tasted out of a jeroboam and a double magnum in November 1978 ***(**) Drink 1983–2000.
Ch. Pontet-Canet Pauillac	*A magnificent wine, but you would not think so from some of the bottlings: Liggins', hard and acidic in 1967; Lyons', stalky in 1968; Stowell's, too much volatile acidity in 1972; Ellis Son & Vidler, a spongy, worm-eaten cork (possibly not their fault) in 1974. And some good bottlings by Joule's of Stone, Avery's of Bristol, Christopher's and the Army & Navy Stores, tasted between 1969 and 1975. Most recently, one bottled in Bordeaux by Cruse, the then proprietors of the château: impressive '61 depth of colour; incredibly rich nose, ripe and mulberry-like (a sort of Californian warmth and opulence); positively sweet, full of body, flavour, extract. Almost up to Palmer standard. Excellent.* Last tasted at a Studley Priory wine weekend, November 1979 ****(*) Drink now — 1985.
Ch. Rauzan-Gassies Margaux	*Tasted only twice: rich, leathery, good in 1968 and, later, an English bottling speciously labelled* mise en bouteilles par l'importateur, *with a stewed, cardboardy nose; dry and short on the palate.* Last tasted May 1976. Judgement reserved.
Ch. Respide Graves	*Orange tinged; curiously attractive medicinal bouquet; soft, pleasant, earthy. Lovibond bottling.* Tasted March 1978 ** Drink up.
Ch. Smith-Haut-Lafitte Graves	*Tasted 11 times. Slightly variable notes, including a couple of poor, acid-edged Bordeaux bottlings in 1976 and 1977. Sweet, ripe and flavoury, rich but slightly worrying high-toned, volatile, peppery nose and end taste.* Last tasted October 1978 * To be on the safe side, drink up.
Ch. Talbot St-Julien	*Best note was on a magnum in 1978: pleasant cedary bouquet; positively sweet, chewy, lovely. A half-bottle at the same time showing more age, and most recently a rather chocolaty Dutch bottling.* Last tasted November 1978. At best **** Drink now — 1990?
Ch. Tertre-Daugay St-Emilion	*A bland Dutch bottling in 1972. Later, two caramelly nosed, skinny and undistinguished château bottlings.* At the Heublein tasting, May 1978 * Drink up.
Ch. Trotanoy Pomerol	*A beautiful wine, tasted in 1973, 1977. Impressive but unready at Taams tasting in 1978, and showing great breeding at the Gault-*

Millau tasting in Paris: very deep, very richly coloured, mature; the bouquet developed to perfection in the glass; wonderful finesse, great length. Last tasted June 1979 ★★★★ *Drink now — 1990.*

1961s impressive but not tasted recently:	*Ch. Batailley; Ch. Bellegrave; Ch. Bourdieu-la-Valade; Ch. Cissac; Ch. Citran; Ch. La Conseillante; Ch. Figeac; Ch. Fonbadet; Ch. Fourcas-Hosten; Clos Fourtet; Ch. La Garde; Ch. Grand-Puy-Ducasse; Ch. Haut-Marbuzet; Ch. d'Issan; Clos des Jacobins; Ch. La Lagune; Ch. Laroze; Ch. de Lisse; Ch. Moulinet; Ch. Paveil-de-Luze; Ch. Pédesclaux; Ch. Plince; Ch. Prieuré-Lichine; Ch. Rausan-Ségla; Ch. St-Georges; Clos St-Martin; Ch. de Sales; Ch. Simard; Ch. Siran; Ch. La Tour-de-Mons; Ch. Villegeorge.*
Not showing well, tasted prior to 1970 (very minor wines omitted):	*Ch. Cap de Mourlin; Ch. Le Gay; Ch. Grand-Corbin; Ch. Gros-Caillou; Ch. Lagüe; Ch. Meyney; Ch. Patâche d'Aux; Ch. Pomys; Ch. Ripeau; Ch. La Tour-de-By.*
Other variable bottlings:	*Ch. Beauregard; Ch. Bel-Orme; Ch. Chasse-Spleen; Ch. Croizet-Bages; Ch. du Glana; Ch. Haut-Batailley; Ch. Liversan.*

1962 ★★★

A good vintage overshadowed, not surprisingly, by the incomparable 1961. Climate: cold and rainy conditions to the end of May. Flowering mid-June in good weather, very hot summer with some rain, September hot and sunny, tempered by welcome showers to swell the berries. Late harvest under good conditions, 9 October. Abundant crop, *une très bonne année.* Market: a commercial vintage, reasonably priced. Assessment: a firm, well-coloured vintage, with some of the leanness of the '66, thrown into the shade not only by the '61s, but to some extent by the '64s. Never fully appreciated, indeed did not really blossom until the mid- to late 1970s, though some were most attractive and flavoursome when young. Positive, fruity but many showing some overacidity. With certain exceptions, drink up.

Ch. Lafite Pauillac	*Not tasted until 1971 when I thought it surprisingly full and unready, nice in five to ten years. Good note in 1972 but still green in 1975. My best notes, rating 20/20, in February and September 1977 — refined and elegant. Last noted at the Overton tasting, when I observed the pronounced sharp redness of colour which I associate with '62s; a curious varnishy nose, but nice and fragrant, if not completely harmonious; dry, very flavoury, still elegant but with a touch of rawness and '62 piquancy.* Tasted twice in May 1979 ★★★ *On the decline but will probably last a surprising length of time. Drink now — 1990.*
Ch. Latour Pauillac	*Ten consistent notes since 1965 when it was purple, packed, raw and tannic. Still deep, though beginning to show maturity; a rich, soft, cedary, classic* Cabernet *nose; fullish, excellent flavour and balance, hard, dry, tannic finish. A fine classic wine.* Unready when last tasted in August 1976 ★★(★★) *Drink 1985–2010.*
Ch. Margaux Margaux	*Tasted in cask, then a year after bottling and in 1967 — a lightish somewhat delicate wine. Developed well. A pleasant mature colour; fragrant, smoky, very fine bouquet and flavour. Richness and delicacy. A good '62.* Last tasted November 1975 ★★★(★) *Drink now — 1990.*
Ch. Mouton-Rothschild Pauillac	*First tasted in 1965: at that time, and for the next ten years, a bit green, skinny, austere and peppery nosed. When last tasted seemed to have gained and developed in every way: very deep*

coloured; outstanding blackcurrant/mulberry bouquet; dry but very flavoury. Good texture. *September 1977 ***(*) Drink now — 1990.*

Ch. Haut-Brion Pessac, Graves	Tasted only five times but showing an interesting development, from 1964 in cask, through its blossoming in 1971 and 1972, to the mid-1970s. Latterly, deep and still youthful in appearance; curious almost La Tâche-like nose; fairly full bodied, rich, velvety, with fine, long flavour and lots of life. *Last tasted September 1975 ***(*) Drink now — 1995.*
Ch. Ausone St-Emilion	Lightish, fully mature; sweet, nicely developed nose; pleasant wine, somewhat lightweight and indeterminate. *Tasted 1971, September 1976 ** Drink now — 1985.*
Ch. Cheval-Blanc St-Emilion	Tasted a dozen times since 1965. Reasonably consistent notes. Seemed at its peak in 1976. Latterly, more mature and less aggressively red than '62 Médocs; mild, rich but gentle cedary bouquet; lightish in weight and style, soft, elegant, nice balance. Good but not overimpressive. *Last tasted July 1978 *** Drink now — 1990.*
Ch. Pétrus Pomerol	Tasted once in 1967, twice in 1971: fine deep colour; deep, subtle, rich but not fully developed bouquet; sweet, rich, velvety, good balance. A sleeping beauty. *Last tasted March 1971 **(**) Drink 1983–1995.*

Of the 165 other châteaux tasted, the following are more recent notes:

Ch. Beychevelle St-Julien	Fairly light and forward in 1964. An excellent Harvey bottling in 1966. More recently seemed to have a rather tinny, acidic finish, though with positive fruity flavour. *Last tasted March 1978 ** Drink up.*
Ch. Calon-Ségur St-Estèphe	Distinctly raw and green in the mid-1960s. Lovely brick-red colour; rich well-developed nose; very flavoury but twist of acidity in mid-1970s. Various bottlings, preferred château bottled. *Last tasted 1974 ** Drink up.*
Ch. Cantemerle Macau	Tasted only once. Lovely colour; beautiful, fragrant bouquet; usual Cantemerle elegance. Very attractive wine. *May 1976 **** Drink now — 1985.*
Ch. Cantenac-Brown Margaux	A typical indeterminate '62. Colour deep and immature; bouquet and flavour partly developed, partly still unripe, with touch of acidity. But attractive, soft and refreshing in 1969 and 1973. *Last tasted March 1976 ** Best to drink up.*
Carruades de Ch. Lafite Pauillac	A charmer, scented, pretty. At its best in the early 1970s. Cedary, attractive but losing its bloom. *Last tasted January 1978 *** Drink up.*
Ch. Cos d'Estournel St-Estèphe	Tasted only twice. Classic but unready in 1969. Later, a somewhat unstable nose and a bit short. *Last tasted September 1977. Must retaste.*
Ch. Croizet-Bages Pauillac	A most attractive little wine. Four tasting notes from 1968, the last two being Justerini & Brooks bottlings: rich, fruity, flavoury, dry finish. *Last tasted July 1977 *** Drink now — 1985.*
Ch. La Dominique St-Emilion	One of my favourite châteaux. A soft, fruity, mature wine. Developed quickly and very good when last tasted. *September 1976 **** Drink now — 1985.*
Ch. Ducru-Beaucaillou St-Julien	Attractive when young. Consistent. Various bottlings including a notable Berry Bros in 1970. Deepish, with '62 redness; touch of sweetness on nose and palate, flavoury, good finish and aftertaste. *Last tasted June 1979 **** Drink now — 1988.*

Ch. Duhart-Milon Pauillac	*Tasted twice, both high toned, piquant. So-so, in 1968.* Last tasted September 1977 ∗ Drink up.
Ch. Figeac St-Emilion	*Good wine. Garnet red; sweet, gentle bouquet; characteristic iron sub-flavour. Distinctive.* Tasted 1966 — May 1978 ∗∗∗∗ Drink now — 1985.
Ch. Fourcas-Hosten Listrac	*A flavoury Bordeaux bottling (Schröder & Schÿler) spoilt by bitter finish. Château bottled: firm, deep, crisp Cabernet nose; firm positive flavour. A minor wine.* Tasted December 1975 ∗∗ Drink up.
Ch. Gazin Pomerol	*Eight variable notes, various bottlings, from 1966. Recently, a rich, chunky, piquant half-bottle.* Last tasted May 1978 ∗∗ Drink up.
Ch. Giscours Margaux	*Lovely in mid-1960s. Seems to have gained depth of colour with age; a dry wine, very flavoury but with peppery, high-toned bouquet and acid edge.* Last tasted March 1979 ∗∗ Do not keep.
Ch. Grand-Puy-Lacoste Pauillac	*Better and fuller than Ducasse when tasted in 1967. A poor English bottling (Hibbert-Solent), a good Justerini & Brooks and an anonymous woody bottle in 1977. Most recent, château bottled: deep red; bouquet and flavour very good indeed, crisp Pauillac fruit.* Last tasted November 1978 ∗∗ to ∗∗∗∗ Drink now — 1990.
Ch. Gruaud-Larose St-Julien	*Eleven fairly consistent notes. A good, chunky, flavoury wine, attractive when young. Has maintained considerable depth of colour; lovely sweet nose which develops well; fullish, rich, complete, dry finish with slight twist of acidity.* Last tasted July 1977 ∗∗∗ Drink now — 1985.
Ch. Haut-Bailly Graves	*Deepish; rich, pebbly Graves nose; maturing nicely but with a touch of acidity.* Tasted October 1978 ∗∗ Drink up.
Ch. Lagrange St-Julien	*Peppery, fruity, high toned, acidic, somewhat charmless — but flavoury.* Tasted 1972, 1976 ∗ Drink up.
Ch. Léoville-Barton St-Julien	*Touch of austerity, but a stylish wine. Berry Bros bottling: fine colour; very good, fresh fruity bouquet and flavour. Never a heavyweight, a trim welterweight.* Tasted three times, in June 1975 ∗∗∗ Drink now — 1985.
Ch. Léoville-Las-Cases St-Julien	*Eight notes: a thoroughly nice wine from the first tasting in 1965. An understated classic Berry Bros bottling in 1968. On the plateau of perfection in 1973 and still there: almost opaque colour; fine, iron-tinged, sweet bouquet and flavour. Most attractive.* Last tasted November 1976 ∗∗∗∗ Drink now — 1990.
Ch. Lynch-Bages Pauillac	*As obvious in style as Malescot, but more crisp and less coarse. Nine notes: interesting and attractive bottlings (Seager's, Paten's, The Wine Society, Berry Bros and château): pronounced redness; spicy, cinnamon/blackcurrants bouquet; chunky, flavoury, the château-bottled being gentler, sweeter and perhaps more refined than the Berry Bros, which seemed alongside, more peppery and piquant.* Both last tasted in October 1978 ∗∗∗ Drink now — 1988.
Ch. Magdelaine St-Emilion	*Only slightly less deep than the 1961, but redder; rich, iron-earthy nose, with good fruit which developed richly; slightly sweet, rich, chunky yet soft delicious flavour, lovely aftertaste. Fine wine.* Tasted 1976, December 1978 ∗∗∗∗ Drink now — 1988.
Ch. Malescot-St-Exupéry Margaux	*Copybook Malescot: loads of flavour, sound, chunky Cabernet-Sauvignon aroma, though a trifle coarse and obvious. Appealing*

mouthful though, in 1968, twice in 1969. Last tasted April 1976 ★★★ Drink now — 1990.

Ch. Meyney St-Estèphe	*Pretty reliable yeoman-farmer type of wine: deep, good rich nose and very flavoury. Slightly tinny edge. Tasted four times. Last tasted November 1978 ★★★ Drink up.*
Ch. La Mission-Haut-Brion Talence, Graves	*Deep, slow maturing; pronounced earthy/iron Graves nose and flavour; rich, tannic in 1973 and 1976. The last bottle was woody. December 1978 ★★(★★) Drink 1983–1993.*
Ch. Montrose St-Estèphe	*One cannot help but admire the steady, sturdy reliability of style and structure of Montrose. Like Ducru, consistently well made by a family who "live above the shop". But the wine is such a slow developer. Impressive but dumb in late 1960s. Two excellent Justerini & Brooks bottlings in 1972. Fine, positive brick-red colour; full cedary, fruity nose; fine, firm, soft, agreeable middle flavour, yet still tannic on finish. A man's wine. Last tasted January 1975 ★★★(★) Drink now — 1995.*
Ch. Palmer Margaux	*Consistently attractive. A good Harvey bottling noted in 1965, possibly at peak in early 1970s. Latterly, a deep, crisp colour; cedary, vinous bouquet; slight sweetness leading to dry tannic end. Rich, flavoury. Last tasted December 1976 ★★★★ Drink now — 1988.*
Ch. Pape-Clément Pessac, Graves	*Over a dozen notes. Certainly one of the best '62s, crisp and lovely when young. Steady consistent development. Still fairly deep though maturing; deep, crisp, scented earth/cedar Graves bouquet and flavour. Distinct firm Cabernet flavour. Complete. Last tasted September 1977 ★★★★ Drink now — 1990.*
Ch. de Pez St-Estèphe	*Seven notes, six bottlings: a somewhat rough, tough little wine. Last tasted April 1976 ★ Not worth keeping.*
Ch. Pichon-Baron Pauillac	*Variable notes. On balance seems quite nice, though dry and lacking charm. Tasted 1969 — October 1975 ★★? Drink up.*
Ch. Pontet-Canet Pauillac	*Fifteen notes, various bottlings: William Standring's good. Lyons' late-bottled and peeky. Paten's overacid. Even Cruse's own bottling a bit sharp. Yet consistently flavoury, dry, firm and challenging. Last tasted March 1979. At best ★★ Drink up.*
Ch. Rausan-Ségla Margaux	*Tasted eight times since 1964. Fairly consistently lean, green, refreshing, but a little unknit and lacking charm. Masculine, uncompromising. Age may soften. Last tasted September 1975 ★(★) Drink 1982–1990.*
Ch. Talbot St-Julien	*Eleven notes dating from April 1966. Various bottlings: Harvey's and Paten's good, Saccone's overacid twice in 1976. The most recent, château bottled: fairly deep colour, heavy sediment; complex cedary nose and flavour, with body and an appealing, refreshing piquancy. Last tasted December 1977 ★★ Drink now — 1985.*
Ch. La Tour-Haut-Brion Graves	*Very deep and immature looking; curious, sweet, high-toned, raspberry-like nose; rich, flavoury, dry finish. Tasted September 1978 ★★(★) Drink 1982–1990.*
Ch. Troplong-Mondot St-Emilion	*A really impressive, almost 1961-quality wine when tasted in 1968. Eight years later, notes marred by a distinctly vinegary Justerini & Brooks bottling. Last tasted 1976. At best ★★★ Drink now — 1985.*

Ch. Trotanoy Pomerol	*Tasted only once: fine pronounced colour; positive ivy-leaf bouquet; interesting flavour and texture. Overall rich and ripe but with '62 acid finish.* November 1977 ★★★ Drink up.
Ch. Villegeorge Avensan	*Fruity but green.* Tasted November 1977 ★ Drink up.
Some other wines showing well in late 1960s to mid-1970s:	*Ch. L'Angélus; Ch. d'Angludet; Ch. Branaire-Ducru; Ch. Citran; Ch. Corbin; Ch. Durfort-Vivens; Ch. Ferrière; Ch. La Fleur-Pétrus; Ch. Fonroque; Ch. Gaffelière-Naudes; Ch. Gloria; Ch. Grand-Pontet; Ch. Gressier-Grand-Poujeaux; Ch. Haut-Batailley; Ch. d'Issan; Clos des Jacobins; Ch. Lafon-Rochet; Ch. Lagüe; Ch. La Lagune; Ch. Langoa-Barton; Ch. Lascombes; Ch. Moulinet; Ch. Mouton-Baron Philippe; Ch. Nenin; Ch. Pédesclaux; Ch. Pichon-Lalande; Ch. La Pointe; Ch. Rauzan-Gassies; Clos René; Ch. de Sales; Ch. Smith Haut-Lafitte; Ch. Tronquoy-Lalande.*
Wines tasted late 1960s to mid-1970s and not showing too well:	*Ch. Batailley; Ch. Belgrave; Ch. Brane-Cantenac; Ch. Chasse-Spleen; Ch. Cos-Labory; Ch. Fombrauge; Ch. La Garde; Ch. Grand-Puy-Ducasse; Ch. Kirwan; Ch. Laujac; Ch. Léoville-Poyferré; Ch. Pavie; Ch. Petit-Village; Ch. Pontet-Clauzure; Ch. de Terrefort; Ch. Tertre-Daugay; Ch. Trottevieille.*

1963

A poor vintage though stopping short of being execrable. Climate: a hard winter but no spring frost damage. Flowering in unfavourable conditions. June to September unusually cold and wet, causing rot, frustrating growth and ripening, though there was continuous good weather and sunshine during the harvest, which began late, on 10 October. Below-average crop of light insubstantial wines. Market: the trade did not need this vintage, and the advent of the '64s endorsed their disinterest. Assessment: never a *vin de garde*, those that are not already consumed should be, and rapidly.

Ch. Lafite Pauillac	*Tasted only once. Light, dry, thin, somewhat acidic. Not Lafite, but not unpleasant.* November 1967.
Ch. Latour Pauillac	*Half a dozen notes: a relatively sound wine due to the high percentage of* Cabernet-Sauvignon *and old vines. Light, stalky and quite nice if somewhat "cooked" in 1968. Seemed to gain colour and peppery richness though lacking length. Not bad but not Latour.* Tasted November 1977 ★
Ch. Margaux Margaux	*Light and unripe in cask. Developed a little, though no depth; sugared nose; sweet, flavoury, quite nice, but not first-growth quality.* Tasted September 1976 ★
Ch. Mouton-Rothschild Pauillac	*Tasted only twice. One quite attractive, in cask, the other alongside Lafite: sweet, clean bouquet; broader flavour, better balanced and less skinny.* Tasted November 1967 ★★
Ch. Haut-Brion Pessac, Graves	*Green, appley nose, curious and raw in cask. Later: dull colour; medicinal, chaptalized; plausible flavour.* Last tasted December 1973.

Of the 18 other '63s I have tasted the best were:

Ch. Beychevelle St-Julien	*Although unknit and plausible, an attractive light drinkable wine as in 1968. Tasted seven times.* Last tasted September 1976 ★★

Ch. Cantemerle Macau	*Mature, gentle, pleasantly sweet nose, light in body and style, piquant but nice drink.* Tasted November 1971 **
Ch. Cos d'Estournel St-Estèphe	*Probably the deepest coloured of the '63s; some fruit, better than Margaux in 1969; piquant, flavoury.* Seven consistent notes 1967–1971 *
Ch. Léoville-Las-Cases St-Julien	*Charming, fragrant, attractive, not a bad finish.* Tasted 1969 *
Ch. Pontet-Canet Pauillac	*Pretty colour; odd, piquant, flavoury and not unappealing.* Tasted 1971 *

Marginal '63s:

Ch. Ducru-Beaucaillou St-Julien	*Attractive mature colour; not bad nose and flavour.* Tasted May 1973.
Ch. La Mission-Haut-Brion Talence, Graves	*Good colour for '63; stewed-fruit nose; slightly sweet, a bit wishy-washy.* Tasted twice, in 1978.
Others quite attractive in the mid- to late 1960s:	*Ch. Croizet-Bages; Ch. Haut-Batailley; Ch. d'Issan; Ch. Poujeaux; Ch. Rauzan-Gassies.*

Non-starters in the '63 handicap:

Ch. Branaire-Ducru St-Julien	*Chocolaty in 1967. Poor nose, little flavour, high acidity a year later.* Last tasted 1968.
Ch. Calon-Ségur St-Estèphe	*Like an Anjou rosé in cask. Developed slightly in 1968 and 1969. Later, prematurely aged in colour and on nose.* Last tasted 1972.
Ch. Giscours Margaux	*Like sugared Dettol. Dry, ropy half-bottle in 1973. Three years later, life hanging by a thread but drinkable.* Last tasted 1976.
Ch. Montrose St-Estèphe	*A brief rake's progress: light but charming in 1967. Muffled nose and marked acidity in 1968. Later sour.* Last tasted September 1976.
Ch. Tronquoy-Lalande St-Estèphe	*Raw, slightly bitter, brown tinged.* Tasted 1969, 1970.

1964 ** to ***

On the whole a very good vintage. Far too much has been made of the "picking after the rain" problems for the wines have given, and still give, a lot of pleasure. Climate: mild wet winter; rather warm spring; very good flowering conditions; summer hot and dry; by mid-September a sound, healthy, ripe crop. Conditions at the start of the harvest were good but the second half was seriously affected by two weeks of continual rain, which was particularly bad in parts of the Médoc. It is well known that Latour picked early and Lafite late (28 September). An abundant crop, one of the biggest since the war. Market: by and large the trade found this vintage appealing and, because of the quantity, prices were moderate. Present condition: after the 1970 vintage, I suppose I have tasted more '64s than the wines of any other year. The unevenness of English bottlings is more apparent than ever, possibly because of some inherent instability, a pricked, overacid condition being the main fault. At their best they are agreeable, chunky, fruity and flavoury wines. Nice now, particularly St-Emilions and Pomerols. A lot of minor wines are thin and acid.

Ch. Lafite Pauillac	*It was said that the start of picking was delayed until an important (foreign) member of the family was due to stay the weekend at the château; anyway, whatever the reason, the picking was delayed*

and, as luck would have it, they were caught by the rain. No amount of protestations can deny the fact that the wine has the thinness and piquancy of a much poorer vintage. I did not taste the wine until 1973, when I found it flavoury, superficially attractive but not great; plausible but not unpleasing in 1974. The following year I was able to see it in its true perspective at a tasting of first-growth '64s at Edmund Penning-Rowsell's. It had a surprisingly good colour, better than expected; a high-toned, cedary bouquet, but showing excess volatile acidity and a trace of the smell I associate with a wine which is cracking up — banana skins; on the palate dry, lightish, rather thin and short, with a piquant twist of acidity on the finish. It did not develop in the glass and will not, in my opinion, develop further in bottle. Last tasted March 1975 ★ Drink up.

Ch. Latour
Pauillac

The management had better luck and, as is common knowledge, picked early and made a magnificently beefy wine. A sample from the cask in 1965 was impressively sweet and fruity. At the comparative tasting referred to above, in 1975, it showed a fine, deep colour; a deep, even, rather restrained Cabernet nose; distinctly dry and austere, full of alcohol, fruit and extract, clearly unready. It ranked top with Pétrus. I have since tasted the wine on five occasions. Most recently: still deep; a good but dumb, peppery nose; chunky, packed with flavour and component parts but a little blunt. Might possibly develop like the '43s. Last tasted March 1978 ★★(★★) Drink 1990–2030?

Ch. Margaux
Margaux

Tasted only half a dozen times, beginning with a fine cask sample in the spring of 1965. It was lovely as early as March 1971, and somewhat bland, feminine, in December of that year. A bit odd in 1974. Most recently, at the Penning-Rowsell tasting: fine deep colour; bouquet rather like a clenched fist, unforthcoming at first but developed a sugary fragrance like Mouton; slightly sweet, pleasant, even toned, reasonable length, dry, slightly acidic finish. Last tasted March 1975 ★★ Drink now — 1995?

Ch. Mouton-Rothschild
Pauillac

Another late-picked wine. The cask sample in May 1965 lacked colour and the characteristic Mouton concentrated Cabernet-Sauvignon aroma. Thin, stalky and tart in 1973. Nondescript in 1974. At the Penning-Rowsell tasting of first growths in March 1975, it was unimpressive: paler than Lafite; lacking fruit on the nose; rather skinny, short and tailed off. Tasted three times since, last in 1976. However much I admire Baron Philippe, not even his genius could turn this vintage into a fine wine. Drink up.

Ch. Haut-Brion
Pessac, Graves

Although I understand this was also picked late, it was soft and agreeable, if light, in March 1965 and has since gradually, somehow, gathered strength. It showed very well (the ladies gave it and Cheval-Blanc high marks) at the Penning-Rowsell tasting: fairly deep colour; bouquet developed slowly but well; dry, fruity, some Graves earthiness, fairly high end acidity. A year later I found it attractively opened up, the bouquet better developed than the 1966. Latterly, a fine mature colour, brown rimmed; deep, rich, round, flavour, smooth, fruity. Probably at peak in March 1977 ★★★★ Drink now — 1990.

Ch. Ausone
St-Emilion

Tasted only three times. Good in cask. A touch austere in 1976. More recently: deep coloured but very mature looking; an impressive, powerful, but somewhat unyielding tobacco-like bouquet; medium body, firm, good middle flavour, still a long way to go. Last tasted January 1978 ★★(★★)? Drink 1985–1995.

Ch. Cheval-Blanc St-Emilion	*St-Emilion and Pomerol did not suffer from the same torrential rain as in the Médoc, and I have 14 consistently good notes of the Cheval-Blanc since first tasting it in cask, which demonstrates the quality admirably. Seemed to promise fast maturity in 1969 but has developed steadily. At the Penning-Rowsell tasting in 1975 it showed a fairly deep colour; its bouquet blossomed pleasantly in the glass; a rich, medium-full, flavoury and most agreeable wine. Good but by no means great. More recently: mature, soft and completely ready.* Last tasted November 1978 **** Drink now — 1990.
Ch. Pétrus Pomerol	*Arguably the finest '64. Tasted six times since 1976. Head and shoulders above the rest. The most impressive of the first growths at the Penning-Rowsell tasting in 1975: incredibly deep and immature looking; liquorice and blackberry aroma, developed great richness; dry, severe, extremely full bodied — probably maximum natural level of alcohol (familiar to devotees of California and Australian giant reds). Tasted twice since then: still opaque in the middle; magnificent ripe, slowly awakening bouquet; full, rich, velvety, port-like.* Last tasted January 1978 ***(**) Drink 1985–2015.

Of the 230-odd châteaux of this vintage tasted, the following are the best of those most recently noted:

Ch. Beychevelle St-Julien	*One of the best '64s. A dozen consistently good notes. From a cask sample in 1965, and from five English bottlings, notably Army & Navy Stores, and on the last occasion Berry Bros: a deep, rich, chunky, well-balanced wine.* Last tasted September 1978 **** Drink now — 1988.
Ch. Boyd-Cantenac Margaux	*Three good English bottlings in early 1970s: Paten's (twice) and Berry Bros. Most recently, château bottled: fairly full rich colour; sweet, complex, attractive nose; on the sweet side, fullish, rich, rather chocolaty but very appealing.* Last tasted November 1976 ***
Ch. Brane-Cantenac Margaux	*Seven notes. Soft, sugared.* Tasted 1967 — 1974. Drink up.
Ch. Carbonnieux Graves	*Raspberry-tinged and rasping in 1968. A more settled earthy Graves character in 1973. Latterly, deep, calm, well-knit, dry finish.* Last tasted July 1975 ** Drink now — 1985.
Dom. de Chevalier Graves	*Fine deep red colour, shading off to considerable maturity; good-class bouquet, difficult to define, which developed well; ripe, excellent Graves flavour — earthy/iron undertones, rather dry tannic finish.* Tasted July 1979 *** Drink now — 1990.
Ch. Citran Avensan	*Six notes. Now mature looking; interesting, spicy, citrus-like bouquet; chunky, good balance, attractive.* Last tasted July 1978 *** Drink now — 1988.
Ch. Cos d'Estournel St-Estèphe	*Ten rather variable notes dating from cask samples in 1965 and including three very uneven château bottlings tried with the proprietor at lunch at the Savoy: the first was woody and raw; the second slightly acidic, less full but better knit; the third better in colour, nose and flavour. The château owner was somewhat embarrassed. I preferred Berry Bros bottling, also two excellent Army & Navy Stores bottlings: deep, rich, chunky in 1971.* Good in December 1976. At best *** Drink now — 1990.
Ch. Coufran St-Estèphe	*A thoroughly satisfactory, well-made bourgeois claret. Seven good notes from 1968. Autumnal colour; rich cold-tea smell and taste, attractive, short, dry finish.* Last tasted July 1978 *** Drink now — 1985.

Ch. Ducru-Beaucaillou St-Julien	*A dozen notes. Not very inspiring when young, and not blemish-free in early 1970s. At the* Decanter Magazine *tasting it showed quite well: overall dry, chunky, somewhat stodgy. Most recently: deepish, good, chunky. Pleasant drink. No finesse.* Last tasted October 1979 ★★ Drink now — 1985.
Ch. Figeac St-Emilion	*First tasted in cask in 1965. Inconsistent notes included "bland", "insubstantial" as well as "soft" and "agreeable" up to 1973. The wine seemed to have opened up in 1976, though holding well. Still quite deep coloured; good bouquet; rich, firm finish.* Last tasted April 1979 ★★(★)? Drink now — 1990.
Ch. La Fleur-Pétrus Pomerol	*Fine deepish colour; attractive bouquet; rich, balanced, excellent condition.* Tasted June 1977 ★★★ Drink now — 1990.
Clos Fourtet St-Emilion	*So often disappointing, this potentially good growth was nice, firm and fruity in this vintage. First tasted 1973. Good Justerini & Brooks and château bottlings.* Both tasted September 1975 ★★★ Drink now — 1988.
Ch. Gazin Pomerol	*Consistently good on five occasions since 1967. The last, an Army & Navy Stores bottling: excellent deep colour; rich fine bouquet and flavour, lovely texture and balance.* Last tasted December 1976 ★★★★ Drink now — 1990.
Ch. Gombaude-Guillot Pomerol	*Rich, excellent flavour, dry finish.* Tasted April 1976 ★★★ Drink now — 1985.
Ch. Gruaud-Larose St-Julien	*Twelve notes, variable bottlings. Paten's and Army & Navy Stores good. Robert Jackson's and Cockburn's of Leith (twice) raw and acidic. Enjoyable fruity mouthful in 1968. More recently: a rich, chunky wine.* Last tasted September 1976. At best ★★★ Drink now — 1985.
Ch. Haut-Batailley Pauillac	*Medium, mature, firm, elegant, holding well.* Tasted 1967, March 1977 ★★★ Drink now — 1984.
Ch. Lafon-Rochet St-Estèphe	*Fruity, agreeable, well-knit, unready in 1968. Immature, tannin and acidity noticeable in 1973. More recently: well developed, good colour; open cedary nose; broad full flavour.* Last tasted August 1979 ★★★ Drink now — 1985.
Ch. Lagrange St-Julien	*Fruity, flavoury but raw and overacid judging by one passable Bauly's London bottling in 1971 and two less passable by Justerini & Brooks in 1977 and 1978.* Last tasted July 1978. Drink up.
Ch. La Lagune Ludon	*Soft and forward in 1967. A bit betwixt-and-between in 1972 and 1973. Later: deep coloured; rich mustard-and-cress nose; rich, curiously individual on the palate, short dry finish.* Last tasted April 1975 ★★ Drink now — 1985?
Ch. Léoville-Barton St-Julien	*Unimpressive in 1965 and 1969. Later, a fine deep-coloured, surprisingly (after earlier notes) Cabernet nose and flavour.* Last tasted 1972. Probably needs drinking up now.
Ch. Léoville-Las-Cases St-Julien	*A good '64 which now seems to be showing signs of cracking up. A nice copybook claret in 1967. Cedary, nice texture, unassuming, balanced and at best in 1971 to 1973. Acid edge appearing in 1975 and more noticeably acid, though very flavoury, a year later.* Last tasted March 1976 ★★ Drink up.
Ch. Léoville-Poyferré St-Julien	*Twelve variable notes from 1967, including two good (Bauly's and Paten's) and three bad — tinny, cloudy, overacid (two Hibbert-*

*Solent and an unknown English bottling, the latter most recently).
A good château bottling: deep, still youthful looking; sweet
chunky/fruity nose and flavour, lively, developed well.* Last tasted
February 1978 ★★ *Select with care, drink now — 1985.*

Ch. Magdelaine St-Emilion	*Deep, loose-knit, full, attractive in 1976.* Last tasted June 1977 ★★★ *Drink now — 1985.*
Ch. Malescot-St-Exupéry Margaux	*A zestful '64. Six consistent notes from 1969, at best in 1971: "the poor man's Mouton", bottled by Army & Navy Stores. Later, the same bottling losing a bit of that zest.* Last tasted December 1976 ★★ *Drink up.*
Ch. Meyney St-Estèphe	*A noticeably dry tannic wine, raw in 1973. Developed nicely though still tannic in 1977.* Last tasted November 1978 ★(★)? *Drink now — 1988.*
Ch. La Mission-Haut-Brion Talence, Graves	*Seems to have gained colour and beefiness since 1970. A deep-coloured wine; huge, peppery, high-toned; fine, rich, chunky flavour, tannin and acidity.* Last tasted December 1978 ★★(★★) *Drink 1982–1990.*
Ch. Montrose St-Estèphe	*A fine strapping wine, almost '59-like. Fifteen fairly consistent notes from 1965.* Still tannic in March 1977 ★★★(★) *Drink 1985–1995.*
Ch. Nenin Pomerol	*Both château bottled and Army & Navy Stores bottling tasted within two months of each other: very deep, less mature looking than Gazin; soft, gentle, richly vinous bouquet; dry on the palate, an interesting flavour, less rounded than Gazin, more tannic.* Last tasted December 1976 ★★★ *Drink 1983–1993.*
Ch. Palmer Margaux	*Not one of the better '64s, indeed a notable pause in a range of successful Palmer vintages. About a dozen variable notes from 1965. Army & Navy Stores and château bottling best. Three Sichel (London) bottlings: one just good enough, one dull, one oxidized.* The last two, and a pleasantly fruity château bottling, tasted March 1978 ★ to ★★ *Drink up.*
Ch. Pape-Clément Pessac, Graves	*Soft, earthy, pleasant though unready in 1973. Three years later, a poor grubby British Transport Hotels bottling.* Last tasted October 1976. *Probably ★★★ at best. Drink now — 1985?*
Ch. Petit-Faurie-de-Soutard St-Emilion	*Deep coloured; sweet, rich, fragrant and rounded.* Tasted September 1975 ★★★ *Drink now — 1990.*
Ch. Petit-Village Pomerol	*An agreeable wine, fragrant in 1973. Fruity in 1976. More recently: deep attractive colour; fruity nose; soft, meaty, ripe flavour.* Last tasted August 1978 ★★★ *Drink now — 1985.*
Ch. de Pez St-Estèphe	*Good but raw in 1968. More recently: soft, pleasantly open-knit and ready.* Last tasted March 1976 ★★ *Drink now — 1985.*
Ch. Pichon-Lalande Pauillac	*Five notes since 1967, the last from an* impériale: *crisp, fruity wine, slight touch of aniseed, dry finish.* Last tasted November 1978 ★★★ *Drink now — 1990.*
Ch. Pontet-Canet Pauillac	*It was quite nice in cask but suffered the handicap of some pretty dull, occasionally raw English bottlings. Later, bottled by Cruse in Bordeaux: medium deep, mature looking; bouquet well developed, fruity, scented; an attractive, rich fruity wine, ready for drinking.* Last tasted December 1976. *At best ★★★ Drink now — 1988.*
Ch. Pontet-Clauzure St-Emilion	*Deepish; disappointing nose, a bit stewed; drying out, austere, quite nice middle flavour, slightly bitter finish.* Tasted April 1976.

Clos René Pomerol	*Harvey bottled: quaffable in 1968. Softened by 1971. More recently: delicious.* Last tasted January 1979 ★★★ Drink up.
Ch. Rouget Pomerol	*Deep coloured; good nose; fairly tough and leathery but rich and attractive in 1975.* Last tasted August 1976 ★★★ Drink now — 1988.
Ch. de Sales Pomerol	*Château bottled, woody in 1965. Recently, a good Harvey bottling.* Last tasted 1979. At best ★★★ Drink up.
Ch. Talbot St-Julien	*Not as good as its big sister, Gruaud-Larose. Fruity but raw in 1968, 1972 and 1973. A good but immature Army & Navy Stores bottling in 1971. Château bottled loose-knit in 1976 and plum coloured, fruity nose and taste two years later.* Last tasted November 1978 ★★ Drink now — 1985.
Ch. La Tour-du-Pin-Figeac St-Emilion	*Lovely wine, château bottled in 1971. Later, a Dutch bottling: mature, pleasant but tailing off.* Last tasted November 1977 ★★ Drink up.
Ch. La Tour-Haut-Brion Graves	*Deep youthful colour; good fruit, slightly peppery on nose; fruity, flavoury, attractively piquant.* Tasted September 1978 ★★★ Drink now — 1988.
Ch. Troplong-Mondot St-Emilion	*A good Christopher's bottling in 1968. Four excellent château bottlings from 1969 to 1970. Showing well as an André Simon selection in 1971. One rich but overacidic Justerini & Brooks bottling in 1973. Most recently: a rich, attractive, nicely textured wine bottled by City Cellars.* Last tasted February 1975 ★★★ Drink now — 1985.
Ch. Trotanoy Pomerol	*Interesting wine: rich colour; curious charred-heather, deep, low-keyed bouquet; medium-full body, foursquare, rich, flavoury with quite a punch at the end.* Tasted 1972, November 1977 ★★★ Drink now — 1985.
Ch. Trottevieille St-Emilion	*Rich, delicious, balanced, mature.* Tasted 1976, November 1978 ★★★ Drink now — 1988.
Vieux Ch. Certan Pomerol	*Gentle, soft, fruity, stylish wine. Dry finish.* Tasted 1972, 1973, October 1975 ★★★ Drink now — 1988.
Pleasant '64s	*Ch. Bourgneuf; Ch. Bouscaut; Ch. Clerc-Milon-Mondot; Ch. La Conseillante; Ch. Croix de Gay; Ch. Croizet-Bages; Ch. Curé Bon La Madeleine; Ch. La Dauphine; Ch. Fonbadet; Ch. Grand-Pontet; Ch. Laroze; Ch. Larrivet-Haut-Brion; Ch. Moulinet; Ch. Pédesclaux; Ch. Respide.*
Not showing well	*Recently tasted '64s: Ch. Belgrave; Ch. Chasse-Spleen; Ch. Crabitey; Clos L'Eglise; Ch. Le Gay; Ch. Maucaillou; Ch. Soutard; Ch. Villegeorge.*
Showing well	*1964s tasted mid-1960s to mid-1970s: Ch. d'Angludet; Ch. Cantemerle; Ch. Cantenac-Brown; Ch. La Dominique; Ch. Fourcas-Hosten; Ch. Giscours; Ch. Grand-Puy-Lacoste; Ch. d'Issan; Ch. Lanessan; Ch. Loudenne; Ch. Malartic-Lagravière; Ch. Moulin-Pey-Labrie; Ch. Paveil-de-Luze; Ch. Pavie; Ch. St-Pierre-Sevaistre; Ch. La Tour-Martillac; Ch. Tronquoy-Lalande.*
Tasted in mid-1960s to mid-1970s, not showing well:	*Ch. Belair; Ch. Branaire-Ducru; Ch. Calon-Ségur; Carruades de Ch. Lafite; Ch. Cissac; Ch. Duhart-Milon; Ch. La Gaffelière; Ch. Junayme; Ch. Langoa-Barton; Ch. Lynch-Bages; Ch. Phélan-Ségur; Ch. Pichon-Baron; Ch. Puy-Blanquet; Ch. Rauzan-Gassies; Ch. St-Georges; Ch. Tertre-Daugay.*

1965

One of the four worst postwar vintages. Wines ranging from insignificant to execrable. Whose fault? The weather's. Climate: uneven and protracted flowering after a long winter; heavy rains throughout the summer; September wet and humid, causing rot. The remaining grapes ripened late and irregularly. Weather improved for a late harvest, 15 October. Smallish crop of very light and thin wines. Recommendation: drink up.

Ch. Lafite Pauillac	*Pale; stalky* Cabernet *nose; dry, light, passable luncheon wine. I really do feel that it harms the reputation of Lafite to sell a wine of this negligible stature under the château label, shaking the credibility of the first growths as a whole.* Tasted February 1974. Drink up.
Ch. Latour Pauillac	*As usual, Latour manages to make the best of a bad job. Jean-Paul Gardère remarked in 1967 that "it will make a charming bottle. Light, with some elegance." Certainly better than Lafite in February 1974: deeper; the same raw* Cabernet *nose, but more fruit on the palate. Tasted twice since: pale and light for Latour, an easy, sugared, quite flavoury, indeed pleasant, wine.* Last tasted June 1976 ⋆ Drink up.
Ch. Mouton-Rothschild Pauillac	*Tasted twice. Lost what little colour it had, very brown; none of the usual fruity intensity of aroma; a dry, thin shadow of Mouton, but flavoury and drinkable.* Last tasted March 1976. Drink up.
Ch. Haut-Brion Pessac, Graves	*Tasted twice: not a bad colour; "mealy", seawater smell; better flavour and finish than Mouton.* Tasted 1973, March 1976.

No other first growths tasted. Of the 17 other '65s, the best were:

Ch. Beychevelle St-Julien	*Charming. Lacking substance but surely one of the best '65s.* Tasted 1967, 1976, March 1978 ⋆
Ch. Montrose St-Estèphe	*Some fruit but raw and short. Better than the '63.* Tasted September 1976.

Some just passable '65s:

Ch. Brane-Cantenac Margaux	*Wishy-washy but not unsound.* Tasted 1967, 1973, September 1976.
Ch. Cantenac-Brown Margaux	*Quite nice.* Tasted 1971.
Ch. Ducru-Beaucaillou St-Julien	*Positive flavour, acid finish.* Tasted September 1976.
Ch. Giscours Margaux	*Better colour than most. Not bad.* Tasted 1967, 1973, September 1976.
Ch. Gruaud-Larose St-Julien	*Better than the '68. Some richness and tolerable end acidity.* Tasted twice in 1976 ⋆
Ch. Léoville-Poyferré St-Julien	*Superficially attractive, but short acid end.* Tasted 1970.
Ch. La Mission-Haut-Brion Talence, Graves	*Tart and unattractive in 1971. More recently a better impression, albeit with an iodine character.* Tasted December 1978.

Ch. Prieuré-Lichine *Margaux*	*Bland, hollow.* Tasted 1967.
Ch. du Tertre *Margaux*	*Stalky, raw but passable.* Tasted 1971.
Ch. Tronquoy-Lalande *St-Estèphe*	*Curiously attractive, piquant.* Tasted 1969, 1970.
Not particularly pleasant:	*Ch. Lanessan; Ch. Lascombes; Ch. Pichon-Baron.*

1966 ★★★★

An excellent vintage. Stylish, elegant, well balanced. Lean rather than plump, though with good firm flesh. A long-distance runner. Climate: after a mild winter and early spring the flowering was completed in fine weather. The summer was cool and drier than average although July was rainy. The lack of sunshine in August was made up for by a very hot, sunny September. Although the weather became unsettled before the vintage, there was no rot and grapes were harvested on 6 October under perfect conditions. Assessment: though immediately appealing when young, many '66s, particularly the Médocs, have been going through a long, rather hard and closed-up period. But there is real quality and style; Bordeaux at its most elegant. Should blossom into lissom flavoury wines; could develop into the five-star class.

Ch. Lafite *Pauillac*	*Tasted only half a dozen times. Complete, showing length in 1969. Firm, showing fine potential in 1975. Fragrant cedar bouquet, some complexity in 1978. A musty bottle immediately replaced by an excellent back-up bottle at the Overton tasting: fine* tuilé *red; richness on nose and palate; dry, stylish, mouth-filling flavour, length and lovely aftertaste.* Last tasted May 1979 ★★★★(★) Drink 1982–1996.
Ch. Latour *Pauillac*	*Only three notes, all ten years after the vintage. Magnificent colour; bouquet and flavour packed and closed in, but an enormous rich wine. Dry, yet velvet-lined. Should develop stunningly.* Last tasted October 1976 ★★★(★★) Drink 1986–2010 plus.
Ch. Margaux *Margaux*	*Lovely Cabernet aroma and flavour a year after the vintage. Developing well through the mid-1970s. Later, rich, fruity, elegant bouquet and flavour, some plumpness but slim, elegant yet with fine structure. An archetypal '66.* Last tasted September 1978 ★★★★(★) Drink now — 2010.
Ch. Mouton-Rothschild *Pauillac*	*Tasted only three times. A bit austere, green but flavoury in 1975. A year later: plummy colour; magnificently pointed Cabernet-Sauvignon aroma; dry, stylish but unready.* Last tasted October 1976 ★★★(★★) It should be excellent. Time will tell. Drink 1986–2000 plus.
Ch. Haut-Brion *Pessac, Graves*	*Half a dozen notes. Rich in cask, consistent development through mid-1970s. Deep coloured; magnificent bouquet — warm, earthy, fruity; noticeable ripe sweetness; fine, big velvety wine.* Tasted May 1978 ★★★★★ Drink now — 2000.
Ch. Ausone *St-Emilion*	*Most attractive. Stylish, elegant; well developed in 1971. Later, lovely rich flavour and balance in 1976.* Last tasted October 1976 ★★★★ Drink now — 1995.
Ch. Cheval-Blanc, **Ch. Pétrus**	*I see I have tasted neither of these since they were in cask. Both promised well. Both should be top class.*

On analysis I probably have a higher percentage of good notes for this vintage than for any other. Of the 204 other châteaux tasted, few have fallen below a remarkably high standard; indeed the notes are so consistent that they would be boringly repetitive if I detailed them all, château by château. What I propose, therefore, is to list the better wines, limiting some comments just to the star rating (bearing in mind the class of wine) and a few salient features. Maturity and drinkability: generally speaking Graves and St-Emilion are perfect now. Minor châteaux of all districts might as well be drunk now though they are sound and will keep. The better Médocs and Pomerols are a bit backward and should be at peak between 1983 and 1995.

Ch. L'Angélus St-Emilion	*Soft, easy wine.* Tasted 1969–1974 ★★★
Ch. d'Angludet Margaux	*Deep coloured and fruity.* Not tasted since 1969 and 1971 ★★★ Probably now — 1990.
Ch. Anseillan Pauillac	*Deep, delicious, disarmingly charming. A bit too soft?* Tasted 1976 ★★★ Drink now — 1986.
Ch. Batailley Pauillac	*One acidic bottling, otherwise fruity, chunky, but a bit coarse for its class.* Tasted 1969–1978 ★★★ Drink now — 1990.
Ch. Beychevelle St-Julien	*Firm, elegant style. Delicious.* Tasted many times. 1967–1979 ★★★(★) Drink now — 1996.
Ch. Branaire-Ducru St-Julien	*Elegant, rich, dry, good aftertaste.* Tasted September 1978 ★★★ Drink now — 1992.
Ch. Brane-Cantenac Margaux	*Rich, ripe, cedary, broader style of wine. Complete. Much better than some more recent vintages.* Tasted 1974, 1976, 1978, January 1980 ★★★★ Drink now — 1996.
Ch. Calon-Ségur St-Estèphe	*Raw and tannic in 1969. Seven notes and seven years later a classic cedary nose; deep, dry, firm, classy.* Tasted 1976 ★★(★★) Drink 1982–1996.
Ch. Canon St-Emilion	*A highly regarded château in Bordeaux, not well enough known elsewhere. An excellent example.* Tasted 1975 ★★★★ Drink now — 1988.
Ch. Canon la Gaffelière St-Emilion	*Quick maturing easy wine.* Tasted 1970 ★★★ Drink up.
Ch. Cantemerle Macau	*Stylish as ever but slow to attain harmony in this vintage.* Tasted 1975–1978 ★★(★★)? Drink 1983–1993.
Ch. Cantenac-Brown Margaux	*Attractive, fruity, dry, elegant.* Tasted 1971–1976 ★★★★ Drink now — 1990.
Ch. Cardinal-Villemaurine St-Emilion	*Blancmange nose; soft, nice.* Tasted 1974 ★★ Drink now — 1986.
Carruades de Ch. Lafite Pauillac	*Gentle, rounded, subdued cedary nose; dry, nice weight and balance, some charm and delicacy.* Tasted March 1978 ★★★ Drink now — 1990.
Dom. de Chevalier Graves	*Fine quality, texture, balance.* Tasted 1975, 1978 ★★★★ Drink now — 1990.
Ch. Cissac Cissac	*As so often, a good, reliable, refreshing claret.* Tasted 1975 ★★(★) Drink now — 1990.
Ch. Citran Avensan	*Lovely in cask; rich citrus-like fragrance.* Seven notes from 1967–1977 ★★★ Drink now — 1992.

Ch. du Colombier-Monpelou Pauillac	*Very pleasant little wine.* Tasted 1976 ★★★ *Drink now — 1990.*
Ch. La Conseillante Pomerol	*Beautiful wine: fine colour; well developed, fragrant; perfect Pomerol texture.* Tasted 1976 — November 1978 ★★★★ *Drink now — 1996.*
Ch. Cormey-Figeac St-Emilion	*Soft, delicious.* Tasted twice in 1975 ★★★ *Drink now — 1986.*
Ch. Cos d'Estournel St-Estèphe	*Deep, tannic.* Tasted 1967–1978 ★★(★★) *Drink 1984–2000.*
Ch. Coufran St-Estèphe	*Spicy, chunky, agreeable — a consistently well-made bourgeois wine.* Tasted 1969–1978 ★★★ *Drink now — 1992.*
Ch. Croizet-Bages Pauillac	*Five consistent notes from 1969. Delicious Cabernet nose and flavour.* Last tasted March 1979 ★★★ *Drink now — 1992.*
Ch. La Dauphine Fronsac	*Attractive fruity bouquet; Pomerol-like style and texture. Very well constituted.* Tasted 1970 ★★★ *Drink now — 1990.*
Ch. Dauzac Margaux	*Fruity, stylish, attractive.* Tasted 1970, 1973, 1975 ★★★
Ch. La Dominique St-Emilion	*Attractive, balanced, needs time.* Tasted 1976 ★★★(★) *Drink now — 1990.*
Ch. Ducru-Beaucaillou St-Julien	*Very fine wine. Classic, gentlemanly, unassertive. Rich garnet red; rich minty/cedar bouquet; dry, lovely flavour, excellent texture. Needs more time.* Many notes from 1970–1979 ★★★(★) *Drink 1982–1996.*
Ch. Duhart-Milon Pauillac	*Very rich colour; extraordinarily pronounced raw blackcurrant aroma due to high proportion of young vines. Very flavoury but raw.* Tasted May 1979 ★★(★) *Drink 1982–1990.*
Ch. Durfort-Vivens Margaux	*Fruit and flavour.* Tasted 1972 ★★(★) *Drink now — 1986.*
Clos L'Eglise Pomerol	*Opaque, enormous wine, very fine, unready.* Tasted 1973 ★★(★★) *Drink 1982–2010.*
Dom. de L'Eglise Pomerol	*Deepish; attractive stylish wine, lovely flavour, texture and balance.* Tasted 1970–1977 ★★★★ *Drink now — 1990.*
Ch. L'Enclos Pomerol	Tasted 1970 ★★★
Ch. L'Evangile Pomerol	*Deep '66 Pomerol; gentle, well-knit bouquet; full and fruity.* Tasted 1975 ★★★(★)
Ch. Figeac St-Emilion	*Lovely garnet colour; broad, expansive, good quality and character in 1975. Later, fragrant, rich, attractive.* Last tasted 1978 ★★★★ *Drink now — 1990.*
Ch. Fombrauge St-Emilion	*Sweet, chunky.* Tasted 1973 ★★★ *Drink now — 1990.*
Ch. Fonbadet Pauillac	*Plummy; good fruit; medium weight, firm, nice balance.* Tasted 1972, 1976 ★★★ *Drink now — 1992.*
Les Forts de Latour Pauillac	*The first vintage this wine was marketed. Made from the younger vines at Latour, it is like an uncertain son following in the footsteps*

of a distinguished father. A chip off the old block but, in this vintage, no more. Tasted 1972–1975 ★★(★) Drink now — 1990.

Clos Fourtet
St-Emilion

Deep coloured; rich but tough. Tasted 1977 ★★(★) Drink now — 1990.

Fronsac wines

Tasted a fascinating cross-section with Harry Waugh in Fronsac and in London prior to a special sale. Twenty-five châteaux of decent, stocky, yeoman-farmer quality, varying in fruit and charm. Outstanding was La Dauphine. From ★★ to ★★★

Ch. Gazin
Pomerol

Tasted first in 1967. Still unready. Last tasted 1976 ★★(★) Drink now — 2000.

Ch. Giscours
Margaux

Firm. Tasted 1971, 1976 ★★(★) Drink now — 1996.

Ch. Gloria
St-Julien

Deepish; attractive bouquet and flavour. Refreshing. Five notes all in 1972 and 1973 ★★★ Drink now — 1990.

Ch. Gombaude-Guillot
Pomerol

A wine little seen in England: fine colour; cheesy nose; dry but plump and attractive. Dinner with Yves Pardes of Delor in Bordeaux, September 1976 ★★★ Drink now — 1990.

Ch. Grand-Puy-Lacoste
Pauillac

Good colour; crisp, intense Cabernet *aroma; wonderful fruit, but lean and attractive, perhaps lacking finish?* Tasted 1971, August 1979 ★★★(★) Drink 1983–1996.

Ch. Gruaud-Larose
St-Julien

Exceptionally good, full fruity wine which needs quite a bit of coaxing. Unready. Eleven consistent notes from 1974 to July 1979 ★★★(★) Drink 1983–2000.

Ch. Haut-Bages-Monpelou
Pauillac

Delicious Cabernet *flavour.* Tasted 1969, 1972 ★★★ Drink now — 1990.

Ch. Haut-Bailly
Graves

Wonderfully earthy Graves with style and quality. Tasted 1973 — November 1978 ★★★★ Drink now — 1996.

Ch. Haut-Batailley
Pauillac

Fairly deep; peppery, fruity nose and taste, some elegance. Tasted 1974–1977 ★★★(★) Drink now — 1992.

Ch. Haut-Marbuzet
St-Estèphe

Firm, with fruit. Tasted 1973 ★★(★) Drink now — 1992.

Ch. Kirwan
Margaux

Attractive but not enough to it. A third growth that frequently fails to impress. Tasted 1973, 1975 ★★ Drink now — 1986.

Ch. Lafon-Rochet
St-Estèphe

Three notes from 1967: deep colour; rich, elegant vinous nose; lean firm, crisp and flavoury. Last tasted August 1979 ★★(★) Drink 1983–1993.

Ch. Lagrange
St-Julien

Another faltering third growth. Pleasant but lacking style and finish. Tasted 1974 ★★ Drink now — 1986.

Ch. La Lagune
Ludon

A bit chocolaty. Four notes, including one Dutch and two English bottlings. Judgement reserved. Tasted 1970–1977 ★(★★)? Drink up.

Ch. Lanessan
Cussac

Ten notes. Deep coloured; clean, attractive, nice weight but still a bit lean and raw. Tasted 1973 — October 1978 ★★(★) Drink now — 1990.

Ch. Langoa-Barton
St-Julien

Delicious fruit, elegant, refreshing. Tasted 1975, 1977 ★★★ Drink now — 1990.

Ch. Lascombes Margaux	*Only tasted once, but lovely.* Tasted 1971 ***(*) Drink now — 1990.
Ch. Léoville-Barton St-Julien	*A good Léoville and a fine middle-Médoc. Good colour, not too deep, maturing; extremely good classic Cabernet nose which, like all wine of real quality, developed in the glass; a ripeness to soften its firm dry style. Excellent.* Tasted 1971, 1972, 1973, January 1980 ***(*) Drink now — 1996.
Ch. Léoville-Las-Cases St-Julien	*Copybook claret. Lovely weight and balance. Dry.* Tasted 1967–1978 ***(*) Drink now — 1996.
Ch. Léoville-Poyferré St-Julien	*Elegant, complete.* Tasted 1969–1977 ***(*) Drink 1982–1996.
Ch. Liversan St-Sauveur	*Quality of vintage adds style and complexity to this decent bourgeois claret.* Tasted 1975 *** Drink now — 1990.
Ch. La Louvière Graves	*An excellently run property whose wine is rarely seen in England. Full of bounce.* Tasted 1975 **(*) Drink now — 1986.
Ch. Lynch-Bages Pauillac	*Five different bottlings showing slight variations. Flavoury but not as stylish as it should be.* Tasted 1970–1978 **(*)? Drink now — 1992.
Ch. Magdelaine St-Emilion	*Deep, complex, rich.* Tasted 1974 — December 1978 ***(*) Drink 1982–1996.
Ch. Malartic-Lagravière Graves	*Better than usual: deep colour; good Cabernet nose; soft, fruity.* Tasted 1977 *** Drink now — 1986.
Ch. Marquis-de-Terme Margaux	*Attractive, piquant-fruit style of wine.* Tasted 1974 ** Drink now — 1985.
Ch. Meyney St-Estèphe	*Straightforward, good fruit, firm backbone, some style.* Tasted 1970, 1974 **(*) Drink 1982–1992.
Ch. La Mission-Haut-Brion Talence, Graves	*A no-problem vintage with record production at the Domaines Woltner. Considered perfection. Certainly a fine wine with rich, hot-pebbles, Graves bouquet and flavour, plump, rich, well-knit, great length. A vintage which definitely puts La Mission in the second rank of the first growths.* Tasted 1973 — December 1978 ****(*) Drink 1982–2010.
Ch. Montrose St-Estèphe	*Dry, tannic but classic. For long keeping.* Tasted 1967–1978 **(**) Drink 1986–2010.
Ch. Mouton-Baron Philippe Pauillac	*The baron himself prefers this to his first growth. One can see why: it is not as heavy as Mouton-Rothschild yet attractive and stylish. The '66 particularly flavoury and pleasant.* Tasted 1974, 1975 **** Drink now — 1992.
Ch. Nenin Pomerol	*Elegant.* Tasted 1973 *** Drink now — 1990.
Ch. Palmer Margaux	*A fine deep wine; a ripe mulberry bouquet and rich mouthful. Seven consistent notes including Berry Bros, Army & Navy Stores, and Quellyn Roberts bottlings.* Tasted 1971 — May 1978 **** Drink now — 1996.
Ch. Pape-Clément Pessac, Graves	*Lovely wine of almost Médoc style: cedary, firm. Eight notes, including several good Berry Bros and Army & Navy Stores bottlings.* Tasted 1972 — July 1979 **** Drink now — 1996.

Ch. Paveil-de-Luze Soussans	*Full, earthy. A wine that is best drunk young though this will develop further.* Tasted 1972–1975 ★★(★) Drink now — 1986.
Ch. Pavie St-Emilion	*Mature; soft and plausible.* Tasted 1972, 1974 ★★ Drink up.
Ch. de Pez St-Estèphe	*Well made, sturdy. One bad (Dubos Frères) bottling.* Tasted 1970–1976 ★(★) Drink 1983–1993.
Ch. Pichon-Baron Pauillac	*Concentrated, close-knit.* Tasted 1974 — October 1979 ★★(★) Drink 1984–1996.
Ch. Pichon-Lalande Pauillac	*Deep, cedary, developing.* Tasted 1974 — November 1979 ★★(★★) Drink 1982–2000.
Ch. Plince Pomerol	*Maturing; harmonious bouquet; smooth, silky.* Tasted only once, in 1972 ★★★ Drink up.
Ch. La Pointe Pomerol	*Stylish, attractive.* Tasted 1969–1976 ★★(★) Drink now — 1992.
Ch. Pontet-Canet Pauillac	*Ripe, stylish.* Tasted 1972 — November 1979 ★★★(★) Drink 1982–1996.
Ch. Rausan-Ségla Margaux	*Deepish, maturing; good, classic claret smell, dumb at first but developed in glass; dry, firm, well balanced.* Tasted 1967–1975 ★★(★) Drink 1982–1996.
Clos René Pomerol	*Mature; charming in a sugary way.* Tasted 1971 ★★★ Drink now — 1986.
Ch. St-Pierre St-Julien	*One so rarely sees this Dutch-owned classed growth. Flavoury.* Tasted once, in 1969 ★★★ Drink now — 1996.
Ch. Siran Margaux	*Garnet red; good nose, clean, spicy. Elegant little wine.* Tasted 1970–1977 ★★★ Drink now — 1990.
Ch. Soutard St-Emilion	*Lovely, sweet little wine.* Tasted 1975 ★★★ Drink now — 1986.
Ch. Talbot St-Julien	*A bit lean and austere.* Tasted 1970–1977 ★★(★) Drink 1983–1996.
Ch. La Tour-Haut-Brion Graves	*The number two wine at La Mission. A sweet, ripe, spicy Graves.* Tasted September 1978 ★★★ Drink now — 1990.
Ch. La Tour-Martillac Graves	*Dry, earthy/iron Graves style.* Tasted 1973 ★★ Drink now — 1986.
Ch. La Tour-de-Mons Soussans	*Really lovely tile-red colour; cedary; dry, lovely texture and balance. In its class, excellent.* Tasted 1973, 1976 ★★★★ Drink now — 1990.
Ch. Tronquoy-Lalande St-Estèphe	*Sound. A bit green.* Tasted 1969–1970 ★★(★)? Drink now — 1986.
Ch. Troplong-Mondot St-Emilion	*Firm, fruity, nice balance.* Tasted 1975 ★★★ Drink now — 1988.
Ch. Trotanoy Pomerol	*Most distinctive and stylish: rich colour; curious charred-heather bouquet; dry, firm, elegant and beautiful but unready.* Tasted November 1977 ★★★(★) Drink 1982–2000.
Ch. Villegeorge Avensan	*Dry, flavoury.* Tasted 1977, June 1979 ★★★ Drink now — 1986.

Some of the borderline, or just dull châteaux tasted in the 1970s:	Ch. de Barbe; Ch. Chasse-Spleen; Ch. Fonréaud; Ch. Haut-Sarpe; Ch. Larrivet-Haut-Brion; Ch. Lestage; Ch. Lynch-Moussas; Ch. Pontet-Clauzure; Ch. La Rivière; Ch. La Tour-St-Pierre.
Least impressive of good bourgeois and classed-growth level tasted recently:	Ch. Fourcas-Hosten; Ch. Gaffelière-Naudes; Ch. Malescot; Ch. Phélan-Ségur; Ch. Rauzan-Gassies.
Minor châteaux and minor districts not showing well at recent tastings:	Ch. Bernard-Raymond; Clos Cheval-Blanc; Ch. Cros-Figeac; Ch. Grand-Barrail-Lamarzelle-Figeac; Ch. Lolan; Clos des Menuts; Ch. St-Ignan; Ch. Pierre-Bibian; Dom. de Segonzac; Ch. Sémeillan; Ch. La Serre; Ch. La Vieille-France; Ch. Vigneau.

1967 **

Quite attractive when young and one of the last really good-value vintages of claret for the trade, following as it did the much-bought '64s and '66s. Climate: mild winter; flowering a bit late; July/August hot and dry; the first three weeks of September cold and wet; the last week hot. First week of October cool and damp (picking at Lafite started on 3rd) and some ensuing good weather interrupted by heavy rain. Uneven results and general chaptalization. The climate from July to early October virtually the reverse of 1966. The addition of sugar enabled agreeable wines to be made. Assessment: they now resemble a girl well past her bloom of youth, whose heavy make-up is wearing thin, revealing a distinctly washed-out and blemished complexion underneath. In short, most '67s are losing whatever charm and lustre they had and need drinking up.

Ch. Lafite Pauillac	Definitely a powdered lady. Raw and purple in cask; nose and flavour developed by the mid-1970s. Now losing colour, weak rimmed; a superficially attractive fragrance and delicacy, but no follow through. Not without appeal. Last tasted March 1978 ** Drink up.
Ch. Latour Pauillac	Certainly one of the best '67s. Deep coloured; huge, peppery nose; slightly sweet at first, fairly massive, unrefined, with dry finish. Eight notes. Tasted from 1969 — June 1979 **(*) Drink now — 1990.
Ch. Margaux Margaux	Three good notes: soft, pleasant, in the mid-1970s. At the comparative tasting of first-growth '67s at Edmund Penning-Rowsell's, it was fairly deep in colour; nose healthy and fragrant though a touch hard; agreeably made, pleasant, tailed off to a mildly dry, hard end. Last tasted March 1978 ** Drink now — 1986.
Ch. Mouton-Rothschild Pauillac	Best in the mid-1970s, its sweet chaptalized nose at its most developed. With a fluffy, high-toned Cabernet-Sauvignon bouquet and flavour. Fruity, but what finish there is, is faintly tart and bitter. Eight notes. Last tasted March 1978 ** Drink up.
Ch. Haut-Brion Pessac, Graves	A nice wine. Consistent notes: surprisingly deep colour; nose a bit peppery and undeveloped; some richness, distinctly earthy Graves flavour. Nice condition. Tasted 1974 — January 1979 *** Drink now — 1985.
Ch. Ausone St-Emilion	Palish colour; bland, slightly sweet nose and taste; fully developed and pleasant. Tasted only once in March 1971 ** Drink up.
Ch. Cheval-Blanc St-Emilion	Most drinkable, even attractive, but not well constituted. Although deeper than expected, somewhat insubstantial; a bland creamy/lactic, molasses nose which faded; dry, flavoury, but with

citrus-fruit background and coarse blanket of acidity. No future. Eight notes. Tasted 1974 — March 1978 ** Drink up.

Ch. Pétrus *Pomerol*	*Tasted only once, at the Penning-Rowsell tasting where we all put it top (at least the men did — the wives preferred Haut-Brion and Cheval-Blanc). A rich zestful colour; bouquet deep and fruity but as yet undeveloped; a full, rich, well-knit, velvety wine, yet seeming to lack the shape of a truly* grand vin. Tasted March 1978 ***(*)? Drink 1983–1993?

I have divided the 159 other châteaux tasted and noted into three categories: the best made and showing well, the moderately good to passable, and the unbalanced and least satisfactory. First, the better '67s tasted in the 1970s:

Ch. Bel-Air-Marquis d'Aligre *Soussans*	*Soft, easy, well developed.* Tasted 1976 ** Drink now — 1985.
Ch. Canon *St-Emilion*	*Reliable pedigree and good wine making is responsible for a very attractive wine.* Tasted December 1974 *** Drink now — 1985.
Ch. Cantemerle *Macau*	*Nicely made, but a bit raw edged.* Tasted 1973 — November 1979 **(*)? Drink now — 1987.
Ch. Cantenac-Brown *Margaux*	*Pleasant, well contrived, easy. A good '67.* Tasted 1976, 1977 *** Drink now — 1986.
Dom. de Chevalier *Graves*	*Lovely colour and nose, at best in early 1970s, developing a slightly bitter finish.* Tasted 1973 — November 1975 ** Drink up.
Ch. Crabitey *Graves*	*Good colour; fruity aroma and flavour. Attractive minor wine.* Tasted 1972, November 1978 *** For its class. Drink up.
Ch. Croizet-Bages *Pauillac*	*Palish; quite nice nose and flavour; lightish, maturing quickly.* Tasted twice in 1973 ** Drink up.
Ch. Dauzac *Margaux*	*Pleasant, mature.* Tasted 1973, 1974 ** Drink up.
Ch. Ducru-Beaucaillou *St-Julien*	*A good '67 but, as with others, better in the 1970 to 1976 period. Plum coloured; quite good fruit. Not for long keeping.* Last tasted August 1979 *** Drink up.
Ch. Duhart-Milon-Rothschild *Pauillac*	*This was the first year that the owners suffixed the Rothschild name to their property. It was a pleasant enough luncheon wine when they conceded this endorsement but the '67 has never risen above that level.* Tasted 1971 — January 1975 ** Drink up.
Ch. L'Evangile *Pomerol*	*Typical of the lighter sugary style of Pomerol: attractive bouquet; bland, silky delicacy slightly marred by raw finish.* Nice though in 1974, 1975 *** Drink up.
Ch. La Fleur *Pomerol*	*Deep, fullish, firm.* Tasted 1975, 1976 ***
Les Forts de Latour *Pauillac*	*The prodigal son. I expected it to be lighter than the '66 when first tasted in 1972, but at that and subsequent tastings it has greatly impressed: it has a deep, velvety colour with flavour to match; a good* Cabernet-Sauvignon *nose. Like a robust schoolboy, lacking a little charm. But a good '67.* Tasted July 1978 **(*) Drink 1982–1992.

Ch. Giscours
Margaux

Best in the early to mid-1970s. Pleasant, agreeable, a bit gutless.
Tasted 1969 — March 1977 ★★ Drink up.

Ch. Grand-Puy-Lacoste
Pauillac

Positive, deepish colour; peppery; steely fruit but showing quality and style in 1974, 1975. Recently a pricked (tart) bottle. Last tasted September 1978. At best ★★★ Drink now — 1986.

Ch. Gruaud-Larose
St-Julien

Eight slightly variable notes. Clearly chaptalized, with a gentle cinnamon overtone; a bit stalky but not (yet) baring its '67 acidity. Tasted 1970 — January 1979 ★★ Drink now — 1986.

Ch. Haut-Bages-Monpelou
Pauillac

Both Berry Bros and château bottling attractive. Tasted 1974 ★★★ Drink up.

Ch. Haut-Bailly
Graves

A lovely, gentle, soft, earthy wine in the mid-1970s but showing a little strain and edginess in 1978. Later, a soft, ripe bottle. Last tasted July 1979 ★★★ Drink up.

Ch. d'Issan
Margaux

Surprisingly nice in 1971. Pleasant, acidity noticeable but refreshing in 1973. Last tasted January 1976 ★★ Drink up.

Ch. Lafon-Rochet
St-Estèphe

Fairly deep though mature rim; curious high-toned, fruity/medicinal nose; dry, lacking some substance but rich and raw. In short, lacking balance but a flavoury mouthful. Tasted 1971–1978 ★★ Drink now — 1986.

Ch. Lague
Fronsac

Easy, attractive. Tasted 1973, 1975 ★ Drink up.

Ch. La Lagune
Ludon

A very attractive '67. Good colour and bouquet, medium dry, fair body, a chunky fruity character not unlike a '64. Notes from 1970 — February 1979 ★★★ Drink now — 1990.

Ch. Langoa-Barton
St-Julien

Tasted twice, in 1976 ★★ Drink now — 1986.

Ch. Léoville-Barton
St-Julien

Elegant, refined, altogether delightful in mid-1970s. Latterly, fully developed and a bit of raw acidity showing. Tasted May and November 1979 ★★★ Drink up.

Ch. Léoville-Las-Cases
St-Julien

Consistent notes showing an agreeable, fragrant, forward wine in the early 1970s, but acidity beginning to show from 1976. Seven notes. Tasted from 1969 — October 1978 ★★ Drink up.

Ch. Léoville-Poyferré
St-Julien

One of the nicest '67s that I tasted in cask. Consistently agreeable notes. Last tasted November 1976 ★★★ Drink now — 1986.

Ch. La Louvière
Graves

Well-run property, well-made wine. Fine, deep, attractive colour; rich, peppery, iron/earth Graves aroma; medium dryness and body, soft, fruity. A good '67. Tasted 1975 ★★★ Drink now — 1985.

Ch. Lynch-Bages
Pauillac

Only tasted twice. Light, fruity and very flavoury. Tasted 1969, October 1976 ★★ Drink now — 1986.

Ch. Magdelaine
St-Emilion

Characterful, idiosyncratic, a slightly overdone bouquet, fragrant but unsettled; soft, nice texture, quality, dry finish. Six notes. Tasted 1975 — December 1978 ★★★

Ch. La Mission-Haut-Brion
Talence, Graves

A deep and impressive '67. Rich and velvety in mid-1970s. Still fairly deep and immature; getting a bit lean and austere. Characterful. Tasted 1974 — March 1979 ★★★ Drink now — 1990.

Ch. Montrose St-Estèphe	*Consistent notes: plum coloured; bouquet pleasant but shy; nice vinosity, chunky, a bit severe — as Montrose usually is — until fully mature.* Tasted 1970 — March 1976 **(*) Drink 1982–1992.
Ch. Mouton-Baron Philippe Pauillac	*Mature, fragrant, attractive but insubstantial. Probably on decline.* Tasted 1974, 1975 ** Drink up.
Ch. Nenin Pomerol	*Deep, good, immature.* Tasted 1975 ** Drink now — 1987.
Ch. Palmer Margaux	*Four agreeable bottles in 1975 and 1976, but three disastrous English bottlings, Berry Bros and Corney & Barrow's both "jam tarts" (jammy with high volatile acidity) and a completely oxidized bottle in January 1979.* Last tasted 1979 ** (but beware). Drink up.
Ch. Pape-Clément Pessac, Graves	*Most attractive from 1967 to 1976. Showing full maturity of colour; lovely claret nose, but with prickle of raw acidity showing through.* Last tasted June 1978 *** to ** Drink up.
Ch. Paveil-de-Luze Soussans	*Nice flavour and balance.* Tasted 1973 ** Drink up.
Ch. Pichon-Baron Pauillac	*Some depth of colour; round, well-knit bouquet; ripe and fleshy for a '67. Good structure, mouth-filling, good aftertaste.* Tasted March 1978 *** Drink now — 1988.
Ch. La Pointe Pomerol	*Attractive flavour, texture.* Tasted 1973, October 1976 ** Drink now — 1985.
Ch. Rausan-Ségla Margaux	*Easy, piquant, flavoury.* Tasted 1974, 1975, November 1979 ** Drink up.
Ch. Rauzan-Gassies Margaux	*Lovely flavour.* Tasted 1969, 1970, May 1979 *** Drink now — 1987.
Ch. de Sales Pomerol	*Medium, mature; rich cheesy nose; good flavour and texture.* Tasted 1970, September 1976 *** Drink now — 1986.
Ch. Simard St-Emilion	*Palish; nice but insubstantial.* Tasted 1973 ** Drink up.
Ch. Talbot St-Julien	*Pretty colour, good fruit. Shorter than Gruaud-Larose. A good '67.* Tasted 1974 — September 1976 *** Drink now — 1987.
Ch. Trotanoy Pomerol	*One of the best '67s. Fairly deep; appealing Merlot-plus-iron aroma; medium dry, remarkable, rich, gentle finish. Very attractive.* Tasted 1977, August 1978 *** Drink now — 1990.
The moderately good to passable. Drink up:	*Ch. d'Angludet; Ch. Cissac; Ch. Citran; Ch. Le Crock; Ch. Fourcas-Hosten; Ch. Les Grandes-Murailles; Ch. Larrivet-Haut-Brion; Ch. Moulinet; Ch. de Pez; Ch. La Tour-Carnet; Ch. La Tour-Haut-Brion; Ch. Villegeorge.*
From the less satisfactory for their class, to the positively poor:	*Ch. L'Angélus; Ch. Beychevelle; Ch. Branaire-Ducru; Ch. Brane-Cantenac; Ch. Calon-Ségur; Ch. Canon La-Gaffelière; Ch. Capet-Guillet; Ch. Carbonnieux; Ch. Cos d'Estournel; Ch. Curé Bon La Madeleine; Ch. Figeac; Ch. Lascombes; Ch. Malescot-St-Exupéry; Ch. Marquis-de-Terme; Ch. Meyney; Ch. Phélan-Ségur; Ch. Pichon-Lalande; Ch. Pontet-Canet; Ch. Pontet-Clauzure; Ch. Robert; Ch. St-Pierre; Ch. La Tour-de-Mons; Vieux Ch. Certan.*

1968

A poor vintage, arguably the worst since 1951. Climate: cold spring, flowering in less than perfect conditions, sunless summer, though July was fine, August being the coldest and wettest for 20 years (similar to 1951). A little sunshine in September. An abundant crop of immature grapes picked in fine weather starting 4 October. Assessment: this sort of vintage exposes as sheer nonsense the glib saying that some good wines are made even in a poor vintage. Light and drinkable perhaps, but not good. Few remain, which is perhaps as well.

Ch. Lafite Pauillac	*It is of course arguable (and none of our business) whether a* premier grand cru *does its reputation — or that of Bordeaux — any good by selling a wine under its own name in a vintage like this. But in the 1971 to 1973 wine boom period, when this and other '68s were put on the market, the ignorant and the gullible would buy anything. What did they get? A very pale-coloured wine, pink rosé in the early 1970s; a wine becoming distinctly brown at the edges by 1976 though with a quite attractive, delicately piquant,* Cabernet *aroma, and a tiny flavour, pleasant enough, but little to it.* Notes in 1974, and twice in March 1976. Drink up.
Ch. Latour Pauillac	*As so often in a poor year, Latour did better than most. Much deeper in colour than Lafite and Mouton; a pleasant, open-knit* Cabernet *aroma; distinctly dry, thin and short.* Tasted in cask, and twice in 1976 ⋆ Not for keeping.
Ch. Mouton-Rothschild Pauillac	*What a vintage to live down. What a poor advertisement for Mouton: light and very brown coloured; sugared nose; dry, thin, flavoury but tart.* Tasted 1975, 1976.
Ch. Haut-Brion Pessac, Graves	*Probably the best of the 1968 first growths.* Quite nice in 1974 ⋆
Ch. Pétrus Pomerol	*Medium colour, mature; stewed nose; slightly sweet, chunky wine; raw finish.* Tasted November 1979 ⋆

Of the 13 other '68s noted the most outstanding were:

Ch. Beychevelle, **Ch. Ducru-Beaucaillou,** **Ch. Gruaud-Larose** St-Julien	*"Were" is the operative word. The first two were nice in 1972 but a bit skinny and raspingly tart in 1976. The Gruaud-Larose was still good to drink in 1976.*

Other quite nice wines noted:

Les Forts de Latour Pauillac	*Positive and peppery.* Tasted 1976.
Ch. Giscours Margaux	*Very agreeable.* Tasted 1971.
Ch. La Lagune Ludon	*Thin but flavoury.* Tasted 1973, 1975.

Amongst the remaining "also rans":

Ch. Chasse-Spleen Moulis	*Pale, acid.* Tasted 1974.
Ch. Marquis-de-Terme Margaux	*Stewed, short and hard.* Tasted 1975.

Ch. Talbot St-Julien	*Stalky.* Tasted 1974, 1976.
Ch. La Tour-Carnet St-Laurent	*Piquant, fruit and acidity.* Tasted 1975.

1969 *

After a moderately promising start this has turned out to be one of the most unsatisfactory vintages of the period. A flash in the pan: flavoury but overrapid development. Some attractive wines, but. . . . Climate: vines flowered in bad weather, which immediately reduced the potential crop; a cold June followed by favourable weather in July and August. The first two weeks of September rainy, followed by fine and sunny weather through to the vintage, which started 6 October. The smallest crop for 20 years. Market: due to the smallness of the crop, the disastrous previous year's vintage and the active market, the wines were snapped up. But in any case, the price was still relatively reasonable. Assessment: judging by the number of notes, a wide range of '69s have been circulating in England. At best lunchtime refreshers — fairly pale, insubstantial, piquant — some distinctly overacid. Not for keeping. Buy carefully, and drink up.

Ch. Lafite Pauillac	*Tasted only three times. Fragrant and flavoury in 1974 and 1976, but noted most critically at Edmund Penning-Rowsell's tasting of '69 first growths: fairly deep colour; a low-keyed albeit classic nose, fragrant, some complexity but somewhat medicinal; lightish, flavoury, piquant, intriguing but a bit thin. Very fragrant aftertaste.* Last tasted March 1979 ** Drink now — 1985.
Ch. Latour Pauillac	*Deep, concentrated and raw in 1970. Three subsequently qualified notes, but at the Penning-Rowsell tasting: the deepest of the first growths, crisp looking; fairly impressive nose, clear-cut but mouth-watering acidity; a dry, medium-bodied (for Latour), straightforward mouthful. A bit dull.* Last tasted March 1979 ** Probably worth keeping a while to soften.
Ch. Margaux Margaux	*Elegant, leathery velvety feel, though astringent in 1970. Three moderate notes in 1974 and 1975. At the Penning-Rowsell tasting: medium colour; light, delicate bouquet which developed a little; a dry, skinny wine, quite flavoury but short.* Last tasted March 1979 * Not worth keeping.
Ch. Mouton-Rothschild Pauillac	*Really quite forward and pleasing in 1970. Qualified notes in 1974, 1976 and 1977. Deeper than Lafite; curious, milky, un-Mouton-like nose, though it developed quite well; distinctly dry and green. Long, peppery, acidic finish but pleasant aftertaste.* Last tasted March 1979 * Not much future.
Ch. Haut-Brion Pessac, Graves	*Although I found this a bit raw but quite nice in 1970, 1974 and 1976, in comparison with Lafite and Mouton at the Penning-Rowsell tasting it was positively plump, with a fine, deep colour; a rather static earthy/iron Graves nose; medium dry, some softness yet firm, a little earthy, austere.* Last tasted March 1979 ** Drink now — 1985.
Ch. Ausone St-Emilion	*Tasted only twice. Mature looking; pleasant bouquet; flavoury, piquant.* Tasted 1974, 1976 **? Drink up.
Ch. Cheval-Blanc St-Emilion	*Although I had previously noted this (on five occasions) as lightish and fully mature, in comparison with the other first growths, it was deep; a sweet, high-toned, stewed — almost varnishy — nose, and*

volatile acidity; some body, chunky, with characteristic touch of iron from the soil, but loose-knit edge and twist of end acidity. The worst of the group. Last tasted March 1979. Drink up.

Ch. Pétrus Pomerol	*Quite the best: very deep, still purple; deep, undeveloped bouquet, yet fat and fragrant, liquorice-root and alcohol; on the palate, full bodied with some ripeness, relatively fat and complete. The most rounded of the first growths.* Tasted 1975, 1977, 1979 ★★★ Drink 1983–1989.

Of the 139 other '69s tasted I have listed the best, the average and the worst, omitting completely minor wines or wines tasted only once and perhaps unfair to grade. Bear in mind that lightness of colour, thinness and acidity are the prevailing features. The following are the best '69s. All are two stars with the exception of Ch. Gruaud-Larose, which is three stars.

Some of the better '69s:	*Ch. Batailley; Ch. Beychevelle; Ch. Canon; Ch. La Croix de Gay; Ch. Croizet-Bages; Ch. Ducru-Beaucaillou; Ch. L'Evangile; Ch. Fonroque; Ch. Giscours; Ch. Gloria; Ch. Gruaud-Larose; Ch. Haut-Bailly; Ch. Latour-Pomerol; Ch. Laujac; Ch. Lynch-Bages; Ch. Magdelaine; Ch. La Mission-Haut-Brion; Ch. Montrose; Ch. Mouton-Baron Philippe; Ch. Pontet-Canet; Ch. Talbot.*
Average, passable '69s all with one star:	*Ch. L'Angélus; Ch. Branaire-Ducru; Ch. Calon-Ségur; Ch. Canon-La Gaffelière; Ch. Citran; Ch. Cos-Labory; Ch. Dauzac; Ch. Fieuzal; Ch. Gaffelière-Naudes; Ch. Grand-Corbin Despagne; Ch. Grand Puy-Ducasse; Ch. Grand Puy-Lacoste; Ch. Grandes-Murailles; Ch. Haut-Batailley; Ch. Liversan; Ch. Malartic-Lagravière; Ch. Malescot-St-Exupéry; Ch. Marquis d'Alesme; Ch. Marquis-de-Terme; Ch. Moulinet; Ch. Pavie; Ch. Pichon-Lalande; Ch. La Pointe; Ch. Prieuré-Lichine; Ch. Rausan-Ségla; Ch. Rauzan-Gassies; Ch. de Sales; Ch. La Tour-Figeac.*
Less attractive to downright unattractive '69s, most tasted several times:	*Ch. Léoville Las-Cases eight times, from 1970 to 1979. No stars: Ch. Bel-Air; Ch. Bernard-Raymond; Ch. Cantemerle; Ch. Cantenac-Brown; Ch. Cos d'Estournel; Dom. de Chevalier; Ch. Lafon-Rochet; Ch. La Lagune; Ch. Lynch-Moussas; Ch. Palmer; Ch. Pape-Clément; Ch. Petit-Village; Ch. de Pez; Ch. Pichon-Baron; Ch. La Tour-du-Pin-Figeac.*

1970 ★★★★

An outstanding vintage with that rare combination of bumper crop and high quality; moreover, it was avidly welcomed by an appreciative international market. Climate: spring late, but blossoming took place in good weather; great heat and drought in July; August rainy and cooler, with hot intervals; beginning of September cold and stormy but thereafter a long run of hot sunshine through the vintage, 4 October to November. *Très abondante, très bonne année.* Another relatively unusual feature was that all the main grape varieties, *Cabernet-Sauvignon, Cabernet-Franc, Merlot* and even the *Petit Verdot* ripened fully and around the same time. Characteristics: depth of colour, body, alcoholic content due to the heat and a roundness and softness from the fully ripe grapes; full of fruit and vigour. Long lasting. Assessment: many wines are nicely developed but the minor wines — of which hundreds crept out of the backwoods at the time — might as well be drunk. The top wines should be kept.

Ch. Lafite Pauillac	*A fine, monumental wine. First tasted in cask (the* maître de chai *was most reluctant to waste it on me) in August 1971: a fine, deep*

elegant wine. Consistently good notes. The word elegant being repeated in 1974, 1975 and 1977. The last considered assessment was at the great Overton tasting in Texas: medium full, rich, attractive but still undeveloped; intense bouquet, Cabernet-Sauvignon *and iron, which developed a rich, biscuity quality in the glass; ripe (slightly sweet, soft), fairly full bodied — almost beefy for Lafite — round, excellent flavour and incredible aftertaste.* Last tasted May 1979 ★★★(★) Drink 1985–2020.

Ch. Latour Pauillac	*Tasted in cask in January 1971 and March 1972: opaque and purple; full of fruit, alcohol, tannin and acidity, but all in balance. Consistently impressive. Most recently, fabulous colour; rich* Cabernet-Sauvignon *aroma; packed with fruit, flavour, alcohol, tannin, acidity — all the component parts, still austere.* Last tasted October 1977 ★★★(★★) Drink 1990–2020.
Ch. Margaux Margaux	*Deep coloured, fine; its best feature a fabulous bouquet, complex, fruity; medium dry, rich, chunky, perhaps lacking the follow-through of the other first growths but a good future.* Tasted 1974 — September 1978 ★★★(★) Drink 1985–2000.
Ch. Mouton-Rothschild Pauillac	*Fairly deep, still youthful looking; fine but undeveloped nose, still peppery, characteristic* Cabernet-Sauvignon *aroma tucked under; a fairly powerful dry wine, more lean and austere than its fellow peers.* Tasted 1974 — September 1977 ★★★(★)? Drink 1988–2010.
Ch. Haut-Brion Pessac, Graves	*Deep, fine colour, maturing; bouquet reined in, but rich and complex; fairly full bodied, rich, firm, powerful. Long dry finish.* Tasted 1973 — October 1976 ★★★(★) Drink 1985–2000.
Ch. Ausone St-Emilion	*Tasted only twice, in the same year. I found it attractive and fine: plummy, quick-maturing colour; broad, earthy, rich bouquet, good fruit; medium dry, soft, lovely biscuity flavour. Good finish. Not in front rank of first growths but very good.* Last tasted October 1976 ★★★ Drink now — 1990.
Ch. Cheval-Blanc St-Emilion	*First tasted in cask in the spring of 1972 and noted its surprising lack of purple, its spiciness and length. A good note in 1974. More recently: maturing well; very firm bouquet; an overall elegant wine though still a little severe and perhaps not at the very top of the tree.* Last tasted October 1976 ★★★(★) Drink now — 1995.
Ch. Pétrus Pomerol	*Tasted in cask the same day as the Cheval-Blanc. Hugely impressive, spicy, silky. Tasted only once since: fairly deep, fine mature colour; bouquet high toned but closed up though it developed in the glass; a fine, intensely rich wine, soft, wonderful flavour, perfect tannin and acid balance. A great future.* Last tasted October 1976 ★★★(★★) Drink 1985–2010.

I suppose I have tasted more '70s than any other vintage, nearly 300 different châteaux, many of them several times, from cask until recently. Without delving into statistics, the overall impression is of a thoroughly satisfactory vintage though not as uniformly excellent (this is just my impression) as 1966. With a vintage that is under ten years old at the time of writing, with so many slight variations of condition and states of development, it would be both foolish and misleading to try to rate the wines too precisely, so I propose to divide the wines into groups, using my broad star classification for intrinsic quality, indicating lastly the period of optimum development. The following are totally satisfactory '70s with further potential:

Ch. Batailley Pauillac	*Typical plummy, chunky specimen.* Tasted 1975, 1976 ★★★ Drink now — 1990.

Ch. Beychevelle St-Julien	*Lovely fruit, weight and balance. A charmer.* Tasted 1971 — March 1978 ***(*) Drink now — 1995.
Ch. Branaire-Ducru St-Julien	*Plummy, soft and chocolaty in cask. Not tasted since. Probably fully mature.* Tasted April 1972 ***?
Ch. Brane-Cantenac Margaux	*Spread of five notes, from cask in 1972. Not as deep coloured as some, and more fully developed on nose and palate. Sweet, easy, lovely, and lively enough.* Last tasted July 1978 *** Drink now — 1988.
Ch. Calon-Ségur St-Estèphe	*Attractive in cask. Still fairly purple, with an elegant vinous bouquet and attractive flavour, but a bit too easy and plausible for a great '70.* Last tasted January 1978 *** Drink now — 1990.
Ch. Canon St-Emilion	*Fine colour; lovely, sweet, fragrant nose; very attractive.* Four notes, 1974 — November 1975 ***
Ch. Cantenac-Brown Margaux	*Opaque, massive, almost baked, most impressive for years.* Tasted 1971 — March 1979 **(**)? Drink 1983–1998.
Ch. Carbonnieux Graves	*Fairly deep; peppery nose; fullish, chunky, stocky earthy/iron flavour. Austere.* Tasted 1973, April 1976 **(*) Drink 1983–1995.
Ch. Chasse-Spleen Moulis	*Deep coloured; fairly tough but nicely made.* Tasted 1974 — October 1977 **(*) in its class. Drink now — 1990.
Dom. de Chevalier Graves	*Deeper colour than Pape-Clément, but maturing; good, earthy Graves nose; slightly sweet on the palate, soft, fruity, fragrant aftertaste.* Tasted 1977 — September 1978 **** Drink now — 1990.
Ch. Citran Avensan	*Fairly deep; sweet, fragrant bouquet; "deep and crisp and even". Excellent, bourgeois.* Tasted 1976, 1977, 1978, January 1979 *** Drink now — 1990.
Ch. Clerc-Milon Pauillac	*Deep, slow developer; fragrant, fruity.* Tasted 1975, 1976, May 1978 **(*) Drink 1982–1995.
Ch. La Conseillante Pomerol	*Magnificent in cask. Star rating based on this and its reputation.* Tasted May 1971 ***(*) Drink now — 1990.
Ch. Cos d'Estournel St-Estèphe	*Fairly deep coloured; curious, sweet chocolaty nose; ripe and rich, interesting shape and texture, dry finish. Not as impressively classic as Montrose.* Tasted 1975 — September 1977 **(*) Drink 1982–1992.
Ch. Coufran St-Estèphe	*Maturing; fruity, firm, most attractive. Relatively minor wine consistently well made.* Tasted 1977, July 1978 **(*) Drink now — 1992.
Ch. Ducru-Beaucaillou St-Julien	*Concentrated in cask. Still deep and immature looking; classic but undeveloped bouquet; dry, stern and unyielding, but great potential.* Last tasted August 1979 **(**) Drink 1985–2010.
Ch. Duhart-Milon-Rothschild Pauillac	*Positive colour; farmyard-rich Cabernet aroma; full of fruit, a bit brash.* Tasted 1975 — September 1977 **(*) Drink 1982–1992.
Ch. Figeac St-Emilion	*Deep but maturing; big, soft, velvety, excellent wine.* Tasted 1975 — March 1979 **** Drink now — 1990.
Ch. La Fleur Pomerol	*Deep; quite a bite, good potential.* Tasted May 1977 **(*) Drink now — 1990.
Les Forts de Latour Pauillac	*Purple and excessively raw in cask. Softening a little but core of iron.* Last tasted March 1975 *(**)? Drink 1985–1995?

Clos Fourtet St-Emilion	*Still immature and closed up, though good firm flavour and balance.* Last tasted March 1980 ★★(★) Drink 1981–1990.
Ch. La Gaffelière St-Emilion	*Quick maturing, very attractive garnet red; sweet on nose; a sweet, rich, warm, open-knit flavour and texture.* Six consistent notes, March 1975 — October 1977 ★★★
Ch. Gazin Pomerol	*Rich, maturing.* Tasted twice, in 1976 ★★★ Drink now — 1992.
Ch. Giscours Margaux	*Deep, well constituted, tannic.* Tasted 1971–1976 ★★(★) Drink 1982–1997.
Ch. Gloria St-Julien	*Thoroughly attractive, fragrant.* Six notes, 1975 — April 1979 ★★★ Drink now — 1990.
Ch. Grand-Puy-Lacoste Pauillac	*Opaque and mouth-filling in cask. Still a very deep, rich colour; crisp, fruity upper-register bouquet; a dry wine, firm, more lean and sinewy than most '70s.* Tasted four times in 1979 ★★★(★) Drink 1983–1995.
Ch. Gruaud-Larose St-Julien	*Beginning to lose its plummy purple colour; well-knit fruity wine, rich, flavoury, well balanced. Still a bit hard.* Six notes, 1976 — March 1980 ★★★(★) Drink 1983–2000.
Ch. Haut-Bages-Monpelou Pauillac	*Army & Navy Stores bottling: fruity, chunky.* Tasted December 1976 ★★
Ch. Haut-Bailly Graves	*Stood out amongst other '70s at a comparative tasting of cask samples at Château Loudenne in April 1972. Since then it has developed well: fairly deep but maturing; ripe, blossoming earthy fruity aroma; a touch of ripe sweetness, soft yet firm. Excellent balance.* Last tasted January 1978 ★★★★ Drink now — 1990.
Ch. Haut-Batailley Pauillac	*Deep and still immature in appearance; undeveloped, slightly medicinal, crisp Pauillac nose; dry, firm, lean. Good finish.* Tasted July 1978 ★★(★) Drink 1983–1995.
Ch. Lafon-Rochet St-Estèphe	*Deep, still plummy purple; rich, fruity aroma; dry, powerful, good aftertaste.* Tasted 1975 — September 1979 ★★(★) Drink 1983–1998.
Ch. Lagrange St-Julien	*Deep; fruity; substantial. One of the best Lagranges of recent years.* Five notes, 1974 — October 1979 ★★★ Drink 1982–1995.
Ch. La Lagune Ludon	*Richly purple in cask. Still immature looking in mid-1970s. Always (from the early 1960s) a decidedly different style of claret, more plummy, rich and open-knit, sometimes rather burgundy-like. But invariably seems to hold well.* Last tasted December 1976 ★★(★)? Drink now — 1990.
Ch. Lascombes Margaux	*Good colour, nose and balance. Attractive wine.* Tasted June 1977★★★ Drink now — 1990.
Ch. Laujac Bégadan	*Good rich Cruse bottling in 1974. Later, a fragrant, dry, Army & Navy Stores bottling.* Last tasted December 1976 ★★★
Ch. Léoville-Barton St-Julien	*Plummy, still immature looking; rich, sweet, attractive nose; dry and somewhat austere on the palate. Good future.* Tasted March 1979 ★★(★★) Drink 1983–1996.
Ch. Léoville-Las-Cases St-Julien	*Good in cask in 1972. Fairly deep, fine, youthful colour; lovely, rich, stylish nose; a dry wine, fullish, fine, elegant.* Last tasted June 1976 ★★★(★) Drink now — 1995.

Ch. Lynch-Bages Pauillac	*Opaque in cask. Tight-knit through the mid-1970s. Still dark; deep cedar/Cabernet aroma; ripe fruitiness, cinnamon overtones, loads of tannin and acidity. Long life ahead.* Last tasted February 1978 ★★★(★) Drink 1984–2000.
Ch. Magdelaine St-Emilion	*Deep coloured; gentle, sweet nose; rich, soft, mouth-filling, good tannin and acidity. Fine.* Tasted December 1978 ★★★(★) Drink 1981–1995.
Ch. Marquis-d'Alesme-Becker Margaux	*Two good, deep-coloured Dutch bottlings in 1977. Château bottled: firm, well constituted.* Last tasted February 1978 ★★(★) Drink 1982–1992.
Ch. La Mission-Haut-Brion Talence, Graves	*Opaque and highly concentrated in cask. Seven notes since: still deep and relatively immature looking; tremendous earthiness, rich and alcoholic on the nose; a monumental wine, still tannic.* Last tasted December 1978 ★★★(★★) Drink 1985–2020.
Ch. Montrose St-Estèphe	*Opaque, huge and tannic when first tasted in February 1975. One bad (British Transport Hotels) bottling in 1976. A year later: still deep; developing a rich classic nose; dry, full of fruit and extract.* Last tasted January 1977 ★★★(★) Drink 1985–2000.
Ch. Mouton-Baron Philippe Pauillac	*Fairly quick developer, very flavoury.* Tasted 1975, twice in 1977, and July 1978 ★★★ Drink now — 1990.
Ch. Palmer Margaux	*Strange that I have only tasted this once, and quite recently. Fairly deep, firmly coloured to the rim — always a good sign; unforthcoming aroma as yet; concentrated, gripping. Great potential.* Tasted May 1979 ★★★(★★)? Drink 1985–2010.
Ch. Pape-Clément Pessac, Graves	*I always expect a lot from this stylish red Graves. It has a sweet almost caramelly nose; dryish, quite nicely constituted but uneven development.* Five notes, 1973 — October 1977 ★★★(★)? Drink 1983–1995.
Ch. Patâche d'Aux Bégadan	*Deep and fruity but minor. Unready.* Tasted 1976 ★(★) Drink now — 1986.
Ch. de Pez St-Estèphe	*Because all the cépages had developed so fully and evenly, Martin Bamford (in charge of IDV/Gilbeys operations in France) persuaded the owner to make a cask of each grape variety separately. I was fortunate enough to taste each in cask in March 1972 and in bottle in March 1976. Here are my notes on the wine made from the individual grape varieties, then the final blend:* *Cabernet-Sauvignon: deep purple; deep fruity/peppery (alcoholic) nose with the wholemeal biscuit quality developing — I associate this with fine claret; on the palate, dry, concentrated, loads of tannin and acidity.* *Cabernet-Franc: the deepest and most purple in cask and bottle; nose hard and green, reminding me of the smell of the chai in which the casks are housed; less dry, not as full bodied, flavoury long finish. More velvety in bottle.* *Merlot: fine deep purple; gentle, shy, the least pronounced in cask and bottle, raspberry tinge; broader on the palate, soft, gentle, dry finish. Velvety but very firm in bottle. Very good.* *Petit Verdot: habitually the slowest grape to mature. Fine deep colour; different sort of aroma, waxy, sappy and green; dry, rather raw in cask, stylish, shorter flavour and astringent end. Dry, fruity but austere in bottle.* *The blend (as marketed): 70 per cent Cabernet-Sauvignon, 15 per cent Cabernet-Franc, 10 per cent Merlot, 5 per cent Petit*

Verdot. *In cask: fairly deep; fruity, stalky aroma; round, firm, opened up in the mouth. In bottle: rich, though (in 1974) still unknit, but very good, with long flavour and finish. Tasted twice since: deep, plum coloured; fabulous nose developing; on the palate dry, full, beefy. What is more, it demonstrated how the overall blend was better than each individual part.* Last tasted September 1977 ★★★(★) in its class. Drink 1985–2000.

Ch. Pichon-Lalande Pauillac	*Good* Cabernet *character in cask. Most recently: deep; very pleasant, sweet, peppery* Cabernet-Sauvignon *nose and flavour. Dry, unready.* Last tasted November 1975 ★★★(★) Drink 1983–1995.
Clos René Pomerol	*Rather disappointing de Luze bottling in 1976 made up for by château bottling: deep, mature; easy, elegant Pomerol style; deep, long, lovely flavour.* Last tasted July 1978 ★★★ Drink now — 1990.
La Rose-Pauillac Pauillac	*Not a château but the name of the wine made and marketed by the Pauillac co-operative. Quite impressive, powerful with a long flavour, tannin and acidity.* Tasted September 1977 ★★(★) Drink now — 1990.
Ch. St-Pierre-Sevaistre St-Julien	*Deep and immature; fragrant* Cabernet *aroma; rich, flavoury.* Three notes, 1975, October 1976 ★★(★) Drink 1982–1994.
Ch. Talbot St-Julien	*Medium dry, lean, masculine.* Tasted 1974–1976 ★★(★) Drink 1983–1995.
Ch. du Tertre Margaux	*Just beginning to mature; good fruit and flavour, tannin and acidity.* Tasted twice, in November and December 1976 ★★(★) Drink now — 1990.
Ch. La Tour-de-By Bégadan	*Minor.* Tasted 1975, 1976 ★ Drink now — 1985.
Ch. La Tour-Haut-Brion Graves	*Massive in cask. Like its big brother, La Mission, an intensely deep, strong wine, but more coarse and raw.* Last tasted 1978 ★★(★) Drink 1985–2000.
Ch. Trotanoy Pomerol	*Deep, fine colour, maturing rim; rich, meaty, high toned; mouth-filling, long dry finish.* Tasted November 1977 ★★(★★) Drink 1983–1995.
Vieux Ch. Certan Pomerol	*Rich, soft, flavoury, well balanced.* Tasted 1976, November 1978 ★★★

Tasted once or twice and quite nice:

Ch. L'Angélus St-Emilion	*Pink, gentle, feminine.* Tasted 1975 ★★ Drink now — 1985.
Ch. d'Angludet Margaux	*Very flavoury.* Tasted twice, in 1976 ★★ Drink now — 1990.
Ch. Bel-Orme-Tronquoy- de-Lalande St-Estèphe	*Fine colour; hard, alcoholic, immature on nose and palate. Stern and tannic. Slow to develop but really worth waiting for.* Tasted October 1979 ★(★★)? Drink 1984–1990.
Ch. Le Bourdieu Vertheuil	*Fruity.* Tasted 1975 ★★ Drink up.
Ch. Bourgneuf Pomerol	*A modestly reliable wine. Little bouquet but nice flavour. Army & Navy Stores bottling.* Tasted 1976 ★★ Drink up.
Ch. Cissac Cissac	*Sweet nose; dry, a bit skinny.* Tasted 1977 ★(★) Drink now — 1985.

Ch. Croizet-Bages Pauillac	*Fruity.* Tasted 1974 **(*) Drink 1982–1992.
Ch. La Dauphine Fronsac	*A consistently good wine from this honest-to-goodness, second-rank district. Fine, deep colour; lovely nose; depth but no great length.* Tasted 1974 **(*) Drink now — 1990.
Ch. L'Evangile Pomerol	*Minty, tangy, curious, interesting.* Tasted 1976 **(*) Must retaste.
Ch. La Fontaine Fronsac	*Fruity, easy.* Tasted 1975 * Drink soon.
Ch. Fourcas-Dupré Listrac	*Good Army & Navy Stores bottling. Full flavour, good finish.* Tasted 1976 * Drink up.
Ch. Le Gay Pomerol	*Not so much attractive as impressive: very deep, tough.* Tasted 1974 ***? Has probably developed well.
Ch. Haut-Coutelin St-Estèphe	*Intensely coloured; well filled.* Tasted 1976 ** Drink now — 1986.
Ch. Haut-Fonrazade St-Emilion	*Plummy colour; sweet attractive nose; dry, flavoury.* Tasted 1976 ** Drink now — 1984.
Ch. Haut St-Lambert Pauillac	*Fruity, short.* Tasted 1975 * Drink up.
Ch. Jauma St-Emilion	*Minor, nice wine.* Tasted 1974 ** Drink now.
Ch. de Lamarque Médoc	*Firm.* Tasted 1976 ** Drink now — 1985.
Ch. Lamouroux Margaux	*Minor, pleasant.* Tasted 1975 ** Drink now — 1984.
Ch. Lanessan Cussac	*Deep; low-keyed bouquet; tannic, unready.* Tasted October 1979 **(*) Drink 1983–1995.
Ch. Langoa-Barton St-Julien	*Deep, dry but rich.* Tasted 1976 **(*) Drink 1982–1992.
Ch. Lestage Parsac, St-Emilion	*Pleasant luncheon wine. Light.* Tasted 1974 ** Drink up.
Ch. Lolan Médoc	*Ordinary but nice.* Tasted 1975 * Drink up.
Ch. Maucaillou Moulis	*Deep, fruity, tannic.* Tasted 1975 ** Drink now — 1986.
Ch. Meyney St-Estèphe	*Developing nicely; bouquet, as so often, is least interesting feature. Stolidly reliable.* Tasted October 1979 ** Drink now — 1988.
Ch. Montlabert St-Emilion	*Classified — on the label — somewhat ingenuously "2me 1er cru, Graves de St. Emilion". In fact, modest but ripe and agreeable.* Tasted December 1979 ** Drink now.
Ch. Moulin-Pey-Labrie Fronsac	*Good example of a reliable Fronsac château: deep coloured; positive and attractive nose, fullish, soft — for Fronsac; good flavour and balance.* Tasted 1976 *** Drink now — 1990.

Clos de l'Oratoire St-Emilion	*Weak colour; light; sugared.* Tasted 1976 ⋆ Drink up.
Ch. Padarnac Pauillac	*Full, coarse.* Tasted 1977 ⋆ Drink now — 1985.
Ch. Pontoise-Cabarrus St-Seurin	*Deep, still immature in colour, nose and palate. But good cedary aroma. Nicely made.* Tasted June 1978 ⋆(⋆) Drink now — 1986.
Ch. Rausan-Ségla Margaux	Tasted 1975 ⋆⋆(⋆)? Must retaste.
Ch. Roquetaillade-La-Grange Graves	*Plummy; earthy nose and flavour; austere.* Tasted 1976 ⋆⋆ Will keep.
Ch. Rozier St-Emilion	*Soft, chunky.* Tasted 1976 ⋆
Ch. St-Pierre Pomerol	*Not to be confused with the classed growth St-Julien. Not tasted before, but most impressive. Bottled by the Swedish State Monopoly: a beautiful, mouth-filling wine, flavoury, soft, round.* Tasted in Sweden, June 1978 ⋆⋆⋆ Drink now — 1984.
Ch. Simard St-Emilion	*One corky bottle, the other delicious, with dry iron-tinged flavour.* Tasted April 1978 ⋆⋆
Ch. Siran Labarde	*Firm and upright.* Tasted 1975 ⋆⋆(⋆) Drink 1982–1990.
Ch. Soutard St-Emilion	*Deep youthful colour; dry, medium body, pleasant, rounded though still with some bite.* Tasted 1975 ⋆⋆ Drink now — 1985.
Ch. Tessendey Fronsac	*One of a myriad wine farms in Fronsac, one of the most consistently reliable secondary districts of Bordeaux. Fullish, maturing nicely; good nose and flavour, straightforward.* Tasted 1975 ⋆ Drink now — 1985.
Ch. La Tour-Figeac St-Emilion	*Tuilé colour; nice cheesy bouquet; chunky, straightforward.* Tasted October 1978 ⋆⋆ Drink now — 1985.
Ch. Les Trois-Croix Fronsac	*Deep; decent, straightforward.* Tasted twice, in 1976 ⋆⋆ Drink now — 1988.
1970s particularly attractive when young:	*Ch. Canon la Gaffelière; Ch. Cantemerle; Ch. Les Carmes-Haut-Brion; Ch. La Croix St-Georges; Ch. Fieuzal; Ch. Lagüe; Ch. Lalène; Ch. Tour-du-Roc-Milon; Ch. Troplong-Mondot; Ch. Vernon.*
Pleasant enough '70s reaching their peak:	*Ch. Beauséjour; Ch. Calon-St-Georges; Ch. Cap de Mourlin; Ch. Cos Labory; Ch. Dauzac; Ch. Fombrauge; Ch. Gombaude-Guillot; Ch. Grand-Corbin-Despagne; Ch. Les Grandes-Murailles; Ch. Kirwan; Ch. Le Pape; Ch. Pavie; Ch. Petit-Faurie-de-Soutard; Ch. Pontet-Clazure; Ch. de Sales; Ch. La Tonnelle; Ch. La Tour-du-Pin-Figeac; Ch. La Tour-du-Roc; Ch. la Vieille-Tour-La-Rose.*
1970s I have found somewhat uninteresting:	*Ch. Beau-Rivage; Ch. Beau-Site; Ch. Belgrave; Ch. Bezineau; Ch. Bouscaut; Ch. du Bousquet; Ch. Boyd-Cantenac; Ch. Cheret-Pitres; Ch. La Croix de Gay; Ch. Curé Bon la Madeleine; Ch. Ferrande; Ch. Fonbadet; Ch. Fontrose; Ch. d'Issan; Ch. Liversan; Ch. Lynch-Moussas; Ch. Monlot-Capet; Ch. Phélan-Ségur; Ch. Pipeau; Ch. La Pointe; Ch. Pontet-Canet;*

	Ch. Respide; Ch. Rocher-Bellevue-Figeac; Ch. St-Georges; Ch. Smith-Haut-Lafitte; Ch. La Tour-Carnet; Ch. La Tour-Martillac; Ch. La Tour-de-Mons; Ch. La Tour-St-Bonnet.
Some unattractive '70s tasted in mid-1970s:	*Ch. Andron-Blanquet; Ch. Beaumont-de-Bolivar; Ch. Chapelle d'Espagnet; Cru Coutelin-Merville; Ch. Croque-Michotte; Ch. Grâce-Dieu; Ch. Grand-Pontet; Ch. Greysac; Ch. Junayme; Ch. Livran; Ch. Macquin-St-Georges; Ch. Maderot; Ch. de Marbuzet; Ch. Petit-Village.*
1970s unpleasant when young:	*Ch. La Barde; Dom. Barreau-Taillefer; Ch. Bellegarde; Ch. Bellevue-Gazin; Ch. Haut-Liscoud; Ch. Haut-Montignac; Ch. Haut-Sociondo; Ch. Laussac; Ch. des Maines; Ch. Malartic-Lagravière; Ch. La Pey de Bie; Ch. de Portets; Ch. La Tour-Tabenot; Ch. Tourteran.*

1971 ★★★

A good vintage with some stylish elegant wines. Uneven — but what vintage is not? — the Pomerol district outstanding and some excellent Médocs. Climate: cold wet spring; May and June cold and rainy; summer warm and sunny with some light rain — an ideal combination; fine weather in October with picking starting on 4th. Production and quality: a word about crop size or yield. In 1971 it was described as *faible* and, certainly, in comparison with the previous vintage, it was half-size. But, to put things into perspective, the production in 1971 was as high as any in the first half of this century. To what extent the higher figures from 1950 have been due to the planting of more vines and to what extent to a greater yield per acre is a matter for the statistician and agrarian economist. Undoubtedly increased world demand and high prices encouraged extra planting of vines. Equally, the greater use of fertilizers, more efficient control of pests and diseases — and less severe pruning — have all combined to increase plant yield. But only in exceptional years do quantity and quality go hand in hand. And we have already seen — in 1945 and 1961 — how nature's severe "pruning" concentrates and enhances the quality of grapes and wine. Market: due to the pressure of world demand, probably at its most overheated about the time the '71s came on the market, and because of the small crop in relation to the 1970 vintage, prices asked and obtained by the growers were high. 1971 was notable also for the "discovery" and marketing of a large number of really rather uninteresting *petits châteaux* — each like "a poor player that struts and frets his hour upon the stage, And then is heard no more". Assessment: the selection noted — and please remember that there has been no consciously arranged comparative tasting, they are noted as they crop up in the tasting room before a sale or out at dinner — provides a pretty fair cross-section summary. Most of the minor wines should be drunk, not kept, and many '71s of quality are delicious now. Most of the better growths will keep but might not improve all that much except for the greats like Pétrus.

Ch. Lafite Pauillac	*First tasted in November 1974: not very impressive colour but a good nose. Tasted four times since, most recently at the Overton tasting, where it looked extraordinarily light in colour and fast-maturing; some elegance and cedar on the nose which opened a little then faded; a dry wine, lightish, easy, lissom, flavoury but not a long-lasting classic.* Last tasted May 1979. Rated ★★★ as a very pleasant drink, but perhaps only ★★ for Lafite. Drink now — 1985.
Ch. Latour Pauillac	*Six notes. Raw in cask in April 1972. Peppery in mid-1970s. Not as deep, indeed a totally different style and weight to the 1970 Latour, more charm, more elegance, but still dry and raw.* Last tasted September 1978 ★★(★★) Drink 1983–2000 plus.
Ch. Margaux Margaux	*Tasted only once: youthful but not very deep coloured; undeveloped bouquet; flavoury, nice aftertaste.* Tasted December 1974. Probably developing well but I am not in a position to give a useful first-hand opinion.

Ch. Mouton-Rothschild *Pauillac*	*Four notes from 1974. Similar depth to Latour; more forward than the Mouton '70, with a sweet fruit-bush/Cabernet-Sauvignon aroma; a dry, well-constituted, fruity and attractive wine. Might conceivably attain some of the delicacy and elegance of the wonderful '49.* Last tasted September 1978 ★★(★) Drink 1982–2010.
Ch. Haut-Brion *Pessac, Graves*	*Tasted only once. Slightly deeper and less developed than the '70; dry, firm, earthy.* Tasted March 1976 ★★★(★) Drink 1982–2000.
Ch. Ausone *St-Emilion*	*Tasted in cask, April 1972: fascinating, spicy, clove-like flavour. Only once since: deeper than the '70; well-knit nose; soft yet firm.* Last tasted March 1976 ★★★ Drink now — 1990?
Ch. Cheval-Blanc *St-Emilion*	*Tasted twice, on the same dates as Ausone. Fragrant in cask. Later: fairly deep but maturing; very good nose and flavour, with characteristic earthy/iron overtone, lovely finish.* Last tasted March 1976 ★★★(★) Drink now — 1995.
Ch. Pétrus *Pomerol*	*13.5° alcohol. Rich and "loaded" in cask. More recently: rich, deep colour; fabulous bouquet reminiscent of ripe mulberries and boiled sweets; a fat, hefty, velvety wine, enormous fruit and character. Surely one of the best '71s, if not the best.* Last tasted September 1978 ★★★★(★) Drink 1985–2010.

Of the 160-odd other châteaux tasted, quite a few were the newly "discovered" *petits châteaux*, sought after by merchants to replace the overpriced classed growths. What follows then are two sections: classed growths or near equivalents, then the lesser bourgeois and *petits châteaux*. First the classed growths (or equivalent quality):

Ch. d'Angludet *Margaux*	*Very attractive maturing colour; calm, gentle, creamy bouquet — all very misleading, as the wine was somewhat raw and austere on the palate.* Tasted November 1979 ★★(★)? Will be interesting to see how it develops.
Ch. Batailley *Pauillac*	*Noticed curious touch of marzipan on nose and palate in 1974. Dry, lightish but firm in 1976. Most recently: deep, plummy; rather neutral nose; positive flavour.* Last tasted March 1980 ★★ Drink now — 1986.
Ch. Beychevelle *St-Julien*	*Fine colour, more developed than the '70; gentle, elegant Cabernet bouquet; medium body, some richness, very attractive. Stylish.* Tasted 1976, 1977, March 1978 ★★★★ Drink now — 1990.
Ch. Branaire-Ducru *St-Julien*	*Quick-developing colour, nose and palate. Sweet, fragrant, but no depth.* Tasted twice, in 1976 ★★ Probably best to drink up.
Ch. Brane-Cantenac *Margaux*	*Although this château has a good reputation I have been in two minds about it in some recent vintages. Occasionally rather strange, particularly in this vintage, which I have tasted seven times. The '71 was attractive in 1974. Rich, chocolaty, medicinal nose and loose-knit in 1975 and 1976. Developing richness and texture in 1977, though still a bit peppery and raw. Most recently: some richness and flesh.* Last tasted March 1979 ★★(★)? Drink now — 1988.
Ch. Calon-Ségur *St-Estèphe*	*Once the beefy, characterful stand-by of all good English merchants, Calon-Ségur seems to have lost out a little. I have tasted the '71 only once: quick-maturing in appearance and on the palate; nice though undeveloped on the nose; dry, firm, lightish style. Nice enough but. . . .* Tasted March 1976 ★★ Drink now — 1986?
Ch. Canon-La Gaffelière *St-Emilion*	*Medium pale, showing maturity; rich little wine.* Tasted 1976 ★★

Ch. Cantemerle Macau	*In cask: firm, elegant, impressive. Should be good.* Tasted only once, in September 1973.
Ch. Cantenac-Brown Margaux	*Skinny in cask; unimpressive.* Last tasted May 1978 *(*)
Ch. Carbonnieux Graves	*Good colour; elegant bouquet and flavour, fairly rich, attractive.* Tasted 1976 *** Drink now.
Ch. Clerc-Milon Pauillac	*Fine colour; light, gentle, fruit; dry, very flavoury, neat texture. Refreshing acidity.* Tasted May 1978 **(*) Drink now — 1986.
Ch. La Conseillante Pomerol	*An easy style of Pomerol: lightish, mature, not much middle flavour but agreeable.* Tasted 1974, 1975, and twice in 1976 *** Drink up.
Ch. Cos d'Estournel St-Estèphe	*Not very deep; a plausible, attractive, easy wine — perhaps not what one expects from a second-growth St-Estèphe. Thinner than the '70 but nice.* Tasted 1974, 1975 *** Drink now — 1986.
Ch. Cos-Labory St-Estèphe	*Six consistently less-than-satisfactory notes from 1975, including a very tart Sichel selection, English bottled. But even château bottlings light and insipid.* Last tasted February 1978.
Ch. La Croix de Gay Pomerol	*Disappointing: good colour but curious woody nose.* Tasted September 1976. Retaste. Should be better.
Ch. Croizet-Bages Pauillac	*Firm, positive colour and flavour, crisp and dry.* Tasted 1976 **(*) Drink now — 1988.
Ch. Croque-Michotte St-Emilion	*Lightish, mature, very fragrant, attractive.* Tasted 1976, 1977. Drink up.
Ch. Dauzac Labarde	*Forward; pretty little wine.* Tasted 1973, 1974, 1975, 1976 **
Ch. Ducru-Beaucaillou St-Julien	*Four notes from 1974. Now maturing nicely; sweet, cedary nose; soft, easy, very attractive. Not in the front rank of Ducrus but a good drink.* Last tasted August 1979 *** Drink now — 1988.
Ch. Durfort-Vivens Margaux	*Deep coloured; calm, chocolaty nose; nice texture, tannin and acidity. Capable of development.* Tasted June 1978 **(*) Drink 1982–1990?
Ch. Figeac St-Emilion	*Fine mature colour; sweet, soft, flowery, almost spicy bouquet; slightly sweet at first sip but light, dry end. Almost too easy and charming.* Four notes, 1976 — March 1979 *** At peak, drink up.
Ch. La Fleur-Pétrus Pomerol	*Fairly deep; pleasant though unexceptional nose; soft, fruity, pleasing flavour. Dry finish.* Tasted September 1978 *** Drink now — 1986.
Ch. Fombrauge St-Emilion	*Very attractive. Four consistent notes.* Tasted 1975, 1977 *** Drink up.
Les Forts de Latour Pauillac	*Very attractive; rich, good nose, flavour and balance. For those who cannot afford to keep the company of its first-growth father, a worthy son.* Tasted March 1979 *** Drink now — 1990.
Ch. Fourcas-Hosten Listrac	*Medium, mature; sweet, attractive nose and flavour.* Tasted 1975 ** Drink now.
Ch. La Gaffelière St-Emilion	*Medium light, mature looking; sweet and salty nose; very pleasant but tailed off a bit.* Tasted 1976, October 1977 ** Drink up.

Ch. Gazin Pomerol	*Medium colour; rich, somewhat medicinal, bouquet; nice flavour, some richness and elegance but not as impressive as it should be.* Tasted twice, in 1976. Prefer to retaste before giving it a rating.
Ch. Giscours Margaux	*Impressively deep, indeed opaque and immature; rather dry and hard, but firm fruit.* Tasted only once, in June 1976 ★★(★)? Drink 1982–1995.
Ch. Gloria St-Julien	Gloria in excelsis: *a splendid '71. Deep colour; nice, gentle, cedary bouquet; ripe, lovely flavour and fruit. Soft, touch of iron from the soil.* Supplied by Harvey's for the Decanter Magazine dinner at the World Wine Fair, Bristol, July 1979 ★★★★ Drink now — 1990.
Ch. Grand-Puy-Lacoste Pauillac	*A good, flavoury, stylish '71.* Four notes, 1976 — October 1979 ★★★(★) Drink 1983–1993.
Ch. Gruaud-Larose St-Julien	Seven consistent notes from 1974. *A very satisfactory '71, fairly plummy and deep as Gruaud often is; a comparatively low-keyed nose with fruit and mint; some ripeness on palate, chunky, flavoury but lacking finesse.* Last tasted October 1979 ★★(★) Drink 1982–1992.
Ch. Haut-Batailley Pauillac	*Plum coloured; sweet nose; very flavoury, competently made. Not for long keeping.* Three notes, 1976, 1977 ★★★ Drink now — 1985?
Ch. Kirwan Margaux	*Unimpressive colour; ordinary nose; quite nice flavour.* Tasted 1976 ★★ Drink up.
Ch. Lagrange St-Julien	*A fruity little wine.* Tasted only once, in 1975 ★★ Drink now.
Ch. La Lagune Ludon	*A youthful looking, rather jammy wine. Idiosyncratic as ever, but always flavoury.* Tasted 1974, twice in 1976 ★★ to ★★★(★) according to one's personal taste. Drink now — 1990.
Ch. Larrivet-Haut-Brion Graves	*Deep; sweet nose; good* Cabernet *flavour.* Tasted November 1975 ★★★ Drink now — 1986.
Ch. Léoville-Barton St-Julien	*Quick maturing; pleasant, broad, sugary nose; fragrant easy wine. Good style, but a bit lacking.* Tasted in June 1977 ★★ Drink now — 1985.
Ch. Léoville-Las-Cases St-Julien	*The owner of this big estate quietly gets on with making excellent wine. Like Ducru, can be relied upon to make the best of the material available. Relatively deep coloured; a dry wine, somewhat severe but underlying richness. Classic form.* Tasted 1974, 1976, March 1979 ★★★(★) Drink 1982–1990.
Ch. Léoville-Poyferré St-Julien	*Medium weight, rich and flavoury.* Tasted only once, in 1976 ★★★
Ch. Lynch-Bages Pauillac	*Gingery and plausible in 1974. Later, noted richness of colour, nose and palate.* Last tasted September 1976 ★★★ Drink now — 1988.
Ch. Magdelaine St-Emilion	*Mature looking; sweet, soft, easy, elegant — like a lighter style Pomerol.* Tasted December 1978 ★★★ Drink now — 1988.
Ch. La Mission-Haut-Brion Talence, Graves	*Excellent in cask. Three notes since. Still deep coloured and youthful but more advanced than the '70; good* Cabernet *nose; some richness and sweetness, elegant, very flavoury. A top '71.* Last tasted December 1978 ★★★(★) Drink now — 1995.
Ch. Montrose St-Estèphe	*A notably good '71. Lovely fragrant bouquet developing, with flavour to match. Dry but rich.* Tasted only twice, in 1974, 1976 ★★★(★)? Drink 1982–1995.

Ch. Mouton-Baron Philippe Pauillac	*Bright attractive colour; pleasant* Cabernet *aroma; dry, fruity, lightish style.* Tasted November 1977 ★★★ Drink now — 1988.
Ch. Nenin Pomerol	*A good rich wine.* Tasted 1976 ★★★ Drink now — 1988.
Ch. Palmer Margaux	*Frankly I often find Palmer difficult to recognize, describe and assess — save in exceptional vintages such as the '61. Four notes from 1974, when I found it fragrant and flavoury. Most recently: fine deep colour; indefinable nose — sweet, plummy, even-tempered, a bit cardboardy — which failed to develop in the glass; fairly dry, fullish, quite a strong backbone but not yet well-knit.* Last tasted November 1978 ★★(★)? Drink 1982 – 1992?
Ch. Pape-Clément Pessac, Graves	*Lightish, forward, a bit stalky in 1976. Later: palish, plummy; plausibly attractive nose; some richness, elegant and nicely textured.* Last tasted June 1978 ★★★ Drink now — 1990.
Ch. de Pez St-Estèphe	*Consistently well-made bourgeois growth. Good fruit.* Tasted 1972, 1974, 1976 ★★(★)
Ch. Phélan-Ségur St-Estèphe	*Five consistent notes, all reasonably good for this somewhat inconsistent château. Pretty colour; cedary, sugared nose; a dry wine of a light, easy style.* Tasted 1976 — February 1980 ★★ Drink now — 1985.
Ch. Pichon-Baron Pauillac	*Tasted only once but unimpressed. Boiled-sweets nose; dry, astringent finish.* Tasted 1976 ★ Probably fairest to retaste.
Ch. La Pointe Pomerol	*Borderline: a bit too pale, forward and easy. Feeble really.* Tasted 1975 – 1976.
Ch. Pontet-Canet Pauillac	*A Bordeaux bottling by Cruse: lacking fruit; easy, chaptalized, rather dull.* Tasted July 1978. Borderline ★ Drink now — 1985.
Ch. Prieuré-Lichine Margaux	*Unfair to classify as tasted only once when fairly young: rather hard and green. Should be a pleasant, flavoury wine.* Tasted 1975.
Ch. Rauzan-Gassies Margaux	*Good colour; a bit stalky and piquant; quite attractive flavour but dry, bitter finish.* Tasted 1976 — September 1978 ★(★) Might soften a little.
Clos René Pomerol	*Good colour; attractive nose; good flavour, nice weight and balance. A good '71.* Tasted June 1979 ★★★ Drink now — 1990.
Ch. St-Pierre-Sevaistre St-Julien	*Flavoury château bottlings in 1975 and 1976, but a year later a couple of unsatisfactory English bottlings.* Last tasted 1977. At best ★★★ Drink now — 1990.
Ch. de Sales Pomerol	*Never a cheap wine, usually a well-made one, and a good '71: mature; sweet, almost strawberry-like, ripe* Merlot *aroma; sweet, soft, very attractive.* Tasted 1976, twice in 1978 ★★★★ Drink now — 1986.
Ch. Soutard St-Emilion	*Stewed, sugary, uninspiring. Should have been better.* Tasted 1974.
Ch. Talbot St-Julien	*More lean than Gruaud-Larose but developing nicely: style, fruit, firm flesh. A very good '71.* Tasted 1974 — July 1978 ★★★★ Drink now — 1992.
Ch. du Tertre Margaux	*A minor classed growth: fruity, sugared, light tinny finish.* Tasted 1976 ★
Ch. La Tour-Carnet St-Laurent	*So many bourgeois wines are better than this classed growth. Lightish and pink; stalky scented* Cabernet *aroma.* Unimpressive in 1975. Hard to foresee much development.

Ch. La Tour-Haut-Brion *Talence, Graves*	*Raw and short compared with its elder brother La Mission, but perhaps an overreaction to the latter.* Tasted 1972, September 1978 ★★(★) Drink 1982–1995.
Ch. Troplong-Mondot *St-Emilion*	*Good colour; lovely fruit.* Tasted 1974 — March 1980 ★★★ Drink now — 1984.
Ch. Trotanoy *Pomerol*	*One of the most stylish and elegant '71s. Four consistently excellent notes. Maturing; lovely fruit and vinosity; svelte, nice silky texture, good aftertaste.* Last tasted November 1977 ★★★★ Drink now — 1990.
Vieux Ch. Certan *Pomerol*	*Very attractive colour, maturing, good "legs"; a soft, fruity, supple wine on nose and palate; expands nicely, charming, slightly lacking finish. Not only good legs but a nubile, willowy body. But I did taste it first in the spring when the sap was rising (in 1978). Later, also showing well, elegant.* Last tasted June 1979 ★★★ Drink now — 1986.

Some lesser '71 bourgeois and *"petits châteaux"*:

Ch. de l' Abbaye-Skinner *Vertheuil*	*Dusty, peppery, Cabernet nose; lightish, high toned, flavoury, very dry end. Any resemblance between this and the good doctor of that name — a leading American connoisseur — entirely coincidental.* Tasted October 1977 ★
Ch. d'Arcins *Arcins*	*Positive, flavoury.* Tasted June 1979 ★★ Drink now — 1985.
Ch. Beauséjour *St-Emilion*	*There are not as many Beauséjours as Bel-Airs but watch out. As it happens this one was a pretty, Pomerol-style wine.* Tasted 1975 ★★
Ch. Bel-Air *Puisseguin, St-Emilion*	*There are about 30 châteaux in Bordeaux entitled, or prefixed, Bel-Air. So beware. This was stewed and raw in 1974 and a bit woody four years later.* Last tasted December 1978.
Ch. de Breuil *Cissac*	*Chaptalized and short.* Tasted twice, in 1976.
Ch. Cantegrive *Montbazon*	*Light, sugared.* Tasted 1975.
Ch. Cantelaudette *Bordeaux Supérieur*	*Typical of the myriad minor wines which made a market début in this vintage. Presumably previously destined for domestic (French) consumption or sold to a shipper for his blends. High toned, flavoury but not well balanced.* Tasted 1973, 1974. Probably — hopefully — dead and buried by now.
Ch. Canteloup *St-Estèphe*	*Cardboardy and raw.* Tasted July 1977.
Ch. Caruel *Bourg*	*Borderline: fruity and nice when young in 1974 and early 1977. Later, like old socks.* Last tasted December 1977.
Ch. Cazeau *Blayais*	*Sweet and easy.* Tasted 1975 ★
Ch. Certan-Giraud *Pomerol*	*Dry, nice wine.* Tasted 1975, 1976 ★★
Ch. Chasse-Spleen *Moulis*	*Deep colour and nice in 1974 and 1975. Two years later, marked acidity. Normally fairly reliable.* Last tasted May 1977. Judgement reserved.
Dom. de Cheval-Blanc *St-André de Cubzac*	*Not Ch. Cheval-Blanc but like Ch. Gazin, Côtes de Bourg, an ingenuously good-for-trade name. As it happens, it was a rather*

fragrant little wine, and inexpensive. Pity about the name though, more than a trifle misleading. Tasted 1975, 1976 ★★

Ch. Cissac Cissac	*Disappointing: palish, mature; superficially attractive nose and flavour but a trifle flat with touch of bitterness.* Tasted March 1979.
Ch. Citran Avensan	*Although I do not normally regard Citran as a minor wine, it is not up to its usual high standard in this vintage: hard, woody nose; dry, lean and higher acidity than usual.* Tasted 1977, July 1978.
Ch. Coufran St-Estèphe	*Not as good as usual. Nose developed, but dry and a trifle green on the palate.* Tasted July 1978 ★ Drink up.
Ch. Croix-de-Bertinat St-Emilion	*Fruity.* Tasted 1975 ★ Drink up.
Ch. La Croix-Millorit Bourg	*Fruity.* Tasted 1975 ★
Ch. L'Elysée du Pape Puisseguin, St-Emilion	*A pompously named château from the nether regions of St-Emilion. Indecisive colour; common, stalky nose and taste. Very dull.* Tasted 1976.
Ch. L'Enclos Haut-Mazeyres Pomerol	*A sugary little wine, stringy. Acid edge.* Tasted 1976.
Ch. Ferrande Graves	*Plummy and pleasant.* Tasted 1975 ★★
Ch. Fonbadet Pauillac	*Quick maturing; plausibly attractive.* Tasted 1975, 1976. Drink up.
Ch. Fontrose Médoc	*Curious nose; dry, light, a bit more life than the '70.* Tasted 1975 ★
Ch. La Garde Graves	*Attractive bouquet and flavour but a bit thin.* Tasted 1976 ★★
Ch. Garraud Lalande-de-Pomerol	*Borderline: plummy, cloudy; sharply etched fruitiness; flavoury but not harmonious.* Tasted March 1979 ★
Ch. Gobinaud Listrac	*Borderline: curious but not unattractive. A bit common.* Tasted October 1976.
Ch. des Graves Graves	*Brick red, stalky, severe.* Tasted 1975.
Ch. Haut Bel-Air Bourg	*Pink, raw and twisted.* Tasted 1976.
Ch. Haut-Brignon 1ères Côtes	*What this was like when young I do not know but it did not survive the ravages of time. Minor. Tinny in 1975. Most recently: vinegary.* Last tasted March 1979.
Ch. Haut-Mazeyres Fronsac	*Deep, nicely graded colour; good nose; soft, fruit, very nice wine.* Tasted March 1979 ★★★
Ch. Hosten-Marbuzet St-Estèphe	*Palish, browning; tinny, dusty, high-toned nose; not bad but tailed off.* Tasted January 1978 ★
Ch. Jubile	*Totally unknown. Had it appeared in the Cocks et Féret index it*

would have been sandwiched between Dom. de Joyeaux and Ch. du Juge. However, it is neither happy nor wise; and more bronze than silver jubilé. *Dry, just drinkable.* Tasted July 1977.

Ch. Lassegne St-Emilion	*Borderline: lightish, forward; sweet nose; soft. Pleasant enough.* Tasted October 1978 ★
Ch. Livran Médoc	*Stewed, unimpressive.* Tasted 1976.
Ch. Loudenne St-Yzans-de-Médoc	*Fragrant in cask. An appealing light and ripe luncheon wine.* Tasted March 1978 ★★
Ch. Maderot Graves	*Minor, pleasant enough, but a bit raw.* Tasted 1976.
Ch. Melin Sables-St-Emilion	*Soft and light. Minor wine.* Tasted 1976. Drink up.
Ch. Mont-Celestin Verdelais, Premières Côtes	*Scented, more like a young Beaujolais; flavour of boiled sweets. Presumably* macération carbonique. *Quite unsuitable or at least uncharacteristic for any Bordeaux with a château name.* Tasted twice, in 1977 ★
Ch. Les Ormes-de-Pez St-Estèphe	*Fairly full, dry and unready.* Tasted May 1978 ★★(★) Drink 1983–1993.
Ch. Pomys St-Estèphe	*Palish; stalky; not bad, little to it.* Tasted October 1976 ★
Ch. Pontet-Clauzure St-Emilion	*One of the best of a string of indifferent vintages. Mature; touch of aniseed on the nose; dry, reasonably good finish.* Tasted 1976 ★★
Ch. Potensac Médoc	*Zippy little wine.* Tasted November 1977 ★★
Ch. Puy-Blanquet St-Emilion	*Borderline: a bit stewed and jammy on the nose. Minor wine.* Tasted 1977, January 1979 ★
Ch. La Rivère Fronsac	*Borderline: typical deep Fronsac colour; nice nose; dry, quite nice but a bit raw. The trouble is that Fronsac wines, decent, honest and straightforward as they are, do not soften or develop much.* Tasted January 1978 ★(★)
La Rose-Pauillac Pauillac	*The co-operative wine, this one bottled in Holland. Delicious.* Tasted November 1978 ★★
Ch. Ségur Médoc	*Not to be confused with Calon-Ségur. Light, chaptalized, flavoury but nothing to it.* Tasted twice, in 1976. Drink up.
Ch. La Tour-de-Mons Soussans	*Not up to usual standard.* Tasted twice, in 1975.
Ch. La Tour-St-Bonnet St-Christoly	*A Médoc backwoodsman, stalky and stringy.* Tasted 1974, 1975. Probably withered by now.
Ch. Villemaurine St-Emilion	*Lightish, soft, pleasant.* Tasted 1975 ★
Ch. Yon-Figeac St-Emilion	*Agreeable.* Tasted 1976 ★★ Drink up.

1972 *

A mean, uneven vintage remembered more for its overpricing, which triggered the collapse of the Bordeaux market. Climate: cold spring, late flowering. Miserable summer though July very warm. Cold snap in August with heavy rain. September and October fine and dry. Grapes healthy but, with 1932 and 1956, one of the latest vintages since records began. Reasonably big crop, immature grapes. Market: as mentioned above, it was the price asked for the wines of this vintage that finally brought the house down. The market was severely overheated with excessive demand from merchants, in England and the United States particularly, who were either buying feverishly for customers — private individuals, financial groups, institutions, all jumping on the commodity investment bandwagon — or buying heavily to anticipate further steep price rises and further fuelling inflation.

Some of the very experienced *négociants* in Bordeaux, and some of the more level-headed merchants in the United Kingdom, began cautiously to act solely as brokers, not buying for stock. The poor quality of the '72 vintage was known from the start, and the price demanded in Bordeaux added insult to injury. The market stalled. Speculators, seeing no further price rises ahead, started pulling out. In these circumstances prices do not ease back, they plummet. To make matters worse, by the autumn of 1974, the entire property and commodity market slumped and the West's banking system nearly collapsed. Loans were called in and several wine firms failed. Others, even important brewery-backed wine groups, unloaded huge stocks. With cut-price wine flooding the western European and American wine markets, trade in Bordeaux came to a halt. Many châteaux had no income, no cash flow, in the 1975/76 period. The rival Rothschild owners of Châteaux Lafite and Mouton got together to offer a substantial quantity of wine at Christie's in the summer of 1976, and happily the boldness of the move not only replenished the coffers at those estates, but gave the market the reassurance it badly needed. But 1972 taught a severe lesson. Assessment: uneven and generally uninteresting. Those wines tasted in the mid-1970s are now either crumbling or undergoing a temporary revival or second wind. If bought cheaply they are fair enough. I would rather have a modest '72 than a totally indifferent branded *vin de table*.

Ch. Lafite Pauillac	*Tasted only once, when three years old: medium colour, beginning to mature; a light, pleasant nose; medium dry, medium light, surprisingly nice fragrant flavour. Certainly for me, the best of 43 leading growths noted at a comparative tasting of '72s organized by the Institute of Masters of Wine.* November 1975 *** as a wine ** for Lafite. Interesting to see how this develops.*
Ch. Latour Pauillac	*Tasted twice: deepish, plummy colour, similar to the '69, and weak at the rim; stalky unattractive nose in 1975, some fruit, sugared; distinctly dry, rather raw and hard. Weak finish. Not a good Latour.* Last tasted May 1976 * Might soften and open up a little . . . ?
Ch. Margaux Margaux	*Tasted three times: two bottles, one magnum. Fruity but short in 1974 and rated by me equal second in the big M.W. tasting of '72s. Certainly one of the deepest; the bouquet trying very hard to keep up the Margaux standards of fragrance; fruity and attractive on the palate but with a slightly hard, short, bitter finish.* Tasted November 1975 **(*) The bitterness might wear off, but it cannot increase in length or finesse.*
Ch. Mouton-Rothschild Pauillac	*Tasted twice, once in cask, a year old. Plummy, indecisive colour; not the usual Mouton intensity of aroma; dry, lacking body, with raw dry end.* Not very attractive at the tasting in November 1975 but doubtless flavoury enough with a meal now *?
Ch. Haut-Brion and **Ch. Ausone**	*Not tasted.*

Ch. Cheval-Blanc St-Emilion	*Palish, pretty colour; light but nice nose and flavour. Neither raw nor dry, and with a reasonably good finish.* One of the most attractive wines at the tasting in November 1975 **? Drink now — 1985. Interesting to see how it develops.
Ch. Pétrus Pomerol	*Some richness but a shadow of its normal self.* Tasted November 1975 **? Drink now — 1988.

Of the 21 other châteaux of this vintage I have tasted the best are:

Ch. L'Abbé-Gorsse-de-Gorsse Margaux	*Fairly deep and relatively immature looking; piquant* Cabernet *aroma and taste. Some richness but no softness. Not too well balanced.* Tasted July 1978 ** Drink now — 1984.
Ch. Batailley Pauillac	*A noticeably consistent château: ploughs a steady if slightly uninspired furrow. A pleasant enough wine, in the usual plummy style.* Tasted November 1975 ** Drink now — 1985.
Ch. Branaire-Ducru St-Julien	*Palish purple, weak rim; unusual scented nose; quite good firm flavour, but short.* Tasted November 1975 ** Drink now — 1985.
Ch. Canon St-Emilion	*Pleasant but short.* Tasted November 1975 ** Drink up.
Ch. Cantemerle Macau	*Surprisingly deep, fragrant and fruity in cask. But started to shed colour early, now medium and very pretty; light, feathery; some charm but a loose-knit dry finish.* Tasted November 1975 ** Drink now — 1985.
Ch. Citran Avensan	*Very appealing when tasted in 1977. Later, nose developed a little, some fruit but stalky. Slight, thin, short and austere.* Last tasted July 1978 * Drink up.
Ch. Clerc-Milon Pauillac	*Lightweight. Very pronounced* Cabernet-Sauvignon *aroma and flavour, but skinny and raw.* Tasted May 1978 * Drink up.
Ch. Ducru-Beaucaillou St-Julien	*Some cedary fragrance but a little disappointing at the tasting of '72s in November 1975. More recently: pretty colour, mature; pleasant nose, rather jammy fruitiness; lightish, flavoury, dry finish.* Last tasted October 1979 ** Drink now — 1986.
Ch. Grand-Puy-Lacoste Pauillac	*Maturing; sweet, curious but pleasant nose; dry, relatively well balanced.* Tasted November 1975 ** Drink now — 1986.
Ch. Gruaud-Larose St-Julien	*Pleasant colour; good fruit but short.* Tasted November 1975 ** Drink now — 1986.
Ch. Haut-Batailley Pauillac	*Unimpressive colour; nice, open, pretty bouquet; quite delicious.* Tasted October 1979 ** Drink now — 1984.
Ch. Hosten-Marbuzet St-Estèphe	*Surprise, surprise — some depth of colour, plummy; interesting bouquet — tea, mint and cheese rind (in fact quite attractive); medium dry, easy, soft (for a '72 and for a St-Estèphe).* Tasted January and October 1979 ** Drink now — 1983.
Ch. La Lagune Ludon	*Clever wine making resulting in a hint of the La Lagune richness, and one of the few '72s with a real aftertaste.* Tasted November 1975 ** Drink now — 1986.
Ch. Langoa-Barton St-Julien	*Pleasant brick red; sweet, chunky nose and flavour. Nice enough but not firmly constituted.* Tasted November 1975 ** Drink now — 1983.
Ch. Lascombes Margaux	*Sweet, attractive nose; fruity and some richness but pasty dry end.* Tasted November 1975 ** Drink now — 1984.

Ch. Léoville-Barton St-Julien	*Not much colour; charming, fruity but loose-knit. Not much basis for development, probably hanging on a thread.* Tasted November 1975 ✶✶ Drink up.
Ch. Léoville-Las-Cases St-Julien	*Fairly good, rich, plummy colour; pleasant nose; agreeable flavour, trying hard in November 1975. Rather loose-knit Cabernet aroma; dry, with yeasty finish four years later. Either poor bottle or cracking up.* Last tasted November 1979. Retaste.
Ch. Marquis-d'Alesme-Becker Margaux	*Marginal: pretty, maturing; tight, peppery nose; attractive and flavoury but weak finish.* Tasted November 1975 ✶✶ Drink up.
Ch. La Mission-Haut-Brion Talence, Graves	*A good '72 but a raw, stalky La Mission.* Three notes, 1975 — December 1978 ✶✶ Drink 1982–1986.
Ch. Montrose St-Estèphe	*Pretty colour; curious waxy/cheesy nose; nice flavour, short dry end.* Tasted November 1975 ✶✶ Drink now — 1988.
Ch. Pontet-Canet Pauillac	*Three notes: stewed fruit nose in 1978. Most recent: paler than the '73 and much browner; chocolaty bouquet which held well; not very clear-cut but pronounced Cabernet fruitiness, unbalanced, flavoury, green.* Tasted November 1979 ✶ Drink now — 1983.
Ch. Prieuré-Lichine Margaux	*Sugar covering a multitude of sins. Light, piquant/fruity.* Tasted November 1975 ✶ Drink up.
Ch. Rausan-Ségla Margaux	*Three consistent notes: fruity but unknit, crumbling finish. A quite nice '72 but no future.* Tasted 1975, November 1976 ✶✶ Drink up.
Ch. La Rose Trindaudon St-Laurent	*Sold in André Simon wine shops anonymously and honourably as Haut-Médoc, and for this reason both good value and interesting: palish; bouquet slightly sweet, speciously attractive fruitiness; flavoury but insubstantial.* Tasted August 1976 ✶✶ Drink up.
Ch. St-Pierre-Sevaistre St-Julien	*Tasted twice: one of the deepest '72s in the M.W. tasting; an appealing piquant Cabernet aroma and flavour. Dry, light, short.* Tasted October and November 1975 ✶✶ Drink now — 1986.
Ch. La Tour-de-Grenet Lussac-St-Emilion	*Has Lussac its own microclimate? Surprisingly fruity and attractive.* Tasted October 1975 ✶✶ Drink now.
Ch. Trotanoy Pomerol	*Marginal: pronounced colour; nose not too clean cut, or indeed clean; quite nice flavour and balance, but green, unripe end.* Tasted November 1977 ✶ Drink now — 1983.
Ch. Verdignan St-Estèphe	*Light but distinctly appealing. An inexpensive, easy wine, some charm but slightly bitter end.* Four notes, 1977 — July 1978 ✶ Drink up.
Vieux Ch. Certan Pomerol	*Pleasant nose and flavour; some sweetness, but short.* Tasted November 1975 ✶✶ Drink now — 1985.

1972s that are dull, or lacking, or earnest and trying:

Ch. d'Angludet Margaux	*Cinnamon nose; a bit thin and dull.* Tasted November and December 1975 ✶ Drink up.
Ch. Camensac St-Laurent	*Trying hard. Pleasant colour; some fruit, but stalky; light tannic end.* Tasted November 1975 ✶ Drink now — 1984.
Ch. Cissac Cissac	*Palish, immature; quite a jolly, piquant, Cabernet aroma, but light and little to it. Bitter finish.* Tasted April 1976. Drink up.

Ch. Cos d'Estournel St-Estèphe	*Lacking colour for a second growth St-Estèphe; curious, common nose; bitty, not very appealing.* Tasted November 1975. Drink up.
Ch. Cos Labory St-Estèphe	*Weak, unimpressive.* Tasted November 1975.
Ch. Coufran St-Estèphe	*Mature; chunky but short.* Tasted July 1977 ★★ Drink now — 1985.
Ch. Fieuzal Graves	*Caramelly, quite nice.* Tasted May 1977 ★ Drink up.
Ch. Giscours Margaux	*Quite a good colour; unknit, cheesy nose; moderately pleasant, but tails off.* Tasted November 1975 ★ Drink now — 1984.
Ch. Haut-Bailly Graves	*Pale; little of anything.* Tasted November 1975. Drink up.
Ch. Haut-Cluzeau	*Surely a Martin Bamford joke name for a minor wine from the Loudenne vats? Nose has a dash of vanilla, a soupçon of jam, stewed, scented — drinkable.* Tasted June 1979 ★ Drink up.
Ch. d'Issan Margaux	*Rather common nose; some fruit, weak finish.* Tasted November 1975. Drink up.
Clos des Jacobins St-Emilion	*Pink and weak looking; dry, chunky, stewed fruit on nose and palate.* Tasted March and October 1977 ★ Drink now — 1983.
Ch. Léoville-Poyferré St-Julien	*In the better rank when tasted in 1975. Piquant and flavoury though green in 1977. Most recently: raw, medicinal with unripe, stalky nose and flavour.* Last tasted June 1978. No future.
Ch. Loudenne St-Yzans-de-Médoc	*Pleasant little wine.* Tasted November 1975 ★ Drink up.
Ch. Magdelaine St-Emilion	*Pretty; light and insignificant bouquet; short dry finish.* Tasted November 1975 ★ Drink up.
Ch. Malescot-St-Exupéry Margaux	*Colour developing quickly; peppery, loose-knit, some fruit.* Tasted 1975, October 1977 ★ Drink now — 1984.
Ch. Les Ormes-de-Pez St-Estèphe	*Dry, raw. Some fruit.* Tasted 1977 ★ Drink now — 1985.
Ch. Palmer Margaux	*Maturing quickly; sweet, unknit nose; some fruit but light and short.* Tasted November and December 1975 ★ Drink now — 1984.
Ch. de Pez St-Estèphe	*Someone I was tasting with, who knows the château well, rated this quite highly. I gave it almost my lowest marks: pale, pink tinged; a high-toned nose; pasty, severe end. Not even on a dark night with sausages. But, in all fairness, I must try it again.* Tasted November 1975.
Ch. Phélan-Ségur St-Estèphe	*Mature looking; dull, not clear cut; raw but not bad.* Tasted October 1979 ★ Drink now — 1984.
Ch. Pichon-Baron Pauillac	*Insubstantial colour, nose and flavour but quite pleasant.* Tasted November 1975 ★ Drink up.
Ch. Pichon-Lalande Pauillac	*Borderline: distinctly better colour than the Pichon-Baron; undeveloped nose; pleasant flavour but no middle.* Tasted November 1975 ★★ Drink now — 1984.

Ch. Pontet-Clauzure St-Emilion	*Pink tinged; piquant; quite attractive. Squeeze-of-lemon acidity.* Tasted May 1976 ★ Drink up.
Ch. Smith-Haut-Lafitte Graves	*Smells like a poor Côtes du Rhône; very ordinary. One of the worst '72s at the M.W. tasting, November 1975. The sporting would give it another chance. I might.*
Ch. Soutard St-Emilion	*Unknit; plausible; short, poor finish.* Tasted November 1975. Drink up.
Dom. des Taste et Tuilleries Bourg	*Not just a pretty name: not a bad colour, nose or flavour. Dry.* Tasted 1974 ★★ Drink up.
Minor '72s:	*A string of minor wines imported, presumably in sheer desperation, and tasted without relish in 1974 and 1975, including: Ch. d'Ardennes; Ch. Bernard-Raymond; Ch. Le Bourdieu; Ch. Canuet; Ch. La Croix-Millorit; Ch. Guionne; Dom. de la Jarry; Ch. Mont-Célestin; Ch. Moulin-Bellegrave; Ch. Moulin-Pey-Labrie; Ch. Pierredon; Ch. La Tour-Bicheau.*

1973 ★★★

A fairly light, abundant vintage. Climate: initial growth affected by early dry conditions; April/May fine, with good conditions for flowering; July very wet, with little sunshine; August exceptionally hot and sunny; the first half of September fine, thereafter variable with hard and frequent rain. Vintage started 1 October under satisfactory conditions. Some rain — swelling grapes — followed by sunshine. A huge crop. The late pickers made the best wine. Market: this would have been welcomed as a useful commercial vintage had it not come on to the market in the middle of a severe wine recession. But it was too late to retrieve the situation then. They are proving useful now. Assessment: most '73s need drinking fairly quickly. Some, as can be seen, are better than others, but the majority lack colour and have at most a specious charm. A raw, ungracious vintage for red Graves, and insufficient fruit and body to mask the underlying coarseness of secondary districts, minor wines. But many flavoury and attractive wines.

Many of the notes that follow are based on two or three unusually interesting tastings, the most comprehensive being in Paris, organized by Gault-Millau — I was on the '73 Bordeaux panel. One of the German participants considered the arbitrary mixing of different districts and classes unfair and, the following year, invited an international panel to Bremen to taste three vintages from Pauillac including twenty '73s. It was a salutory experience. The first growths did not stand out immediately but blossomed and improved in the glass, gradually revealing great complexity; the other classed growths were up to standard but did not open up as fully; and the minor wines just ranged from dull and short to quite nice, and did not develop at all. A range of '73 St-Juliens were tasted blind, with proprietors, at Langoa-Barton in 1975. The rest of the notes are gleaned from pre-sale tastings and a variety of other occasions.

Ch. Lafite Pauillac	*Showed its paces well at the remarkable tasting of Pauillacs in Bremen. Medium-deep colour; nose evasive at first but developed beautifully in the glass over the course of an hour; a charming, dry wine, still a little hard but with blossoming flavour.* Tasted September 1977 ★★★(★) Drink 1983–1993.
Ch. Latour Pauillac	*Fairly deep, purple becoming plummy; gentle and charming — rather more feminine than usual; dry, medium body (for Latour).* Tasted 1977, September 1979 ★★★(★) Drink 1983–1996 or longer.
Ch. Margaux Margaux	*Lighter coloured, maturing more quickly than other first growths; charming, fragrant, somewhat sugary bouquet and flavour. Overall a lightweight wine.* Tasted September 1978 ★★★ Drink now — 1993.

Ch. Mouton-Rothschild Pauillac	*Tasted only once, at the Pauillac tasting in Bremen: fairly deep, still youthful looking; undeveloped bouquet, hard but refined; good long flavour, tannin and acidity. Stood out, with Lafite, above all the other '73s.* Tasted September 1977 ★★'(★★)? Drink 1985–1998.
Ch. Haut-Brion and Ch. Cheval-Blanc	*Not tasted.*
Ch. Pétrus Pomerol	*Tasted only once. A cask sample: deep, purple; huge, rich, peppery nose; slightly sweet at first sip, fairly full bodied but loose-knit, very dry tannic finish.* Tasted July 1974 ★★(★★) Drink 1985–2000.

To date I have tasted 110 other châteaux of this vintage, well under half as many as some of the older vintages. This is indicative of the nature of my business, which tends to specialize in mature wines. So what I have done is to list the better-known growths with comments and rating (tentative if only noted once, or not tasted since 1974 or 1975) and then list the lesser growths, similarly. I hope this will give the reader a bird's-eye summary of salient features and the variations.

Ch. L'Angélus St-Emilion	*A good '73. Fragrant, reasonably well balanced.* Tasted October 1976 ★★★ Drink now — 1985.
Ch. Bel-Air-Marquis- d'Aligre Soussans	*Good colour; dumb and dusty on the nose but some fruit; nice texture, pleasant flavour, dry, raw finish.* Tasted October 1976 ★★ Drink now — 1985.
Ch. Beychevelle St-Julien	*Good colour; straightforward nose and flavour, dry yet soft, nice balance.* Tasted 1974, 1975, March 1980 ★★(★) Drink now — 1990.
Ch. Boyd-Cantenac Margaux	*Lightish, dry, pleasant.* Tasted March 1979 ★★ Drink now — 1985.
Ch. Brane-Cantenac Margaux	*First noted at the Gault-Millau Bordeaux tasting in October 1976. It came in third but I did not rank it highly: fairly deep, maturing; a prematurely aged nose which I did not like, though it had a rich, complex character; some richness, tannic, short. I found it old and oily again in 1978 (a distinguished Bordeaux shipper and château proprietor thought it might be due to concentration of must). Latterly: brick red; oily, unpleasant mercaptan nose — I got no further.* Last noted October 1979.
Ch. Calon-Ségur St-Estèphe	*A charmer: fully mature; broad, pleasant, well-chaptalized nose; slightly sweet and easy. No length, no future, but nice.* Three notes, 1976 — September 1978 ★★★ Drink up.
Ch. Canon St-Emilion	*Very pretty colour; bouquet of cinnamon and iron; agreeable, light style, refreshing end acidity.* Tasted October 1976 ★★ Drink up.
Ch. Cantenac-Brown Margaux	*Very pale, pink tinged; chocolaty nose; fruity, piquant and insubstantial.* Tasted 1974 ★★ Drink up.
Ch. Chasse-Spleen Moulis	*Fairly deep and purple; peppery and immature nose but fragrant and concentrated, touch of cinnamon; dry, fairly full bodied, excellent flavour, tannin/acidity and good finish. In its class an impressive '73.* Tasted October 1976 ★★★ Drink now — 1986.
Ch. Clerc-Milon Pauillac	*Deep, purple; agreeable, better on palate than on nose. Positive flavour, nice balance, texture.* Tasted 1977, May 1978 ★★ Drink now — 1986.
Ch. Cos d'Estournel St-Estèphe	*Plummy pink; dry, hard, unyielding. Might soften and open up a little, but not for long keeping.* Three notes, twice in 1977 and September 1978 ★(★)? Drink now — 1984.

Ch. Ducru-Beaucaillou St-Julien	*Impressive colour, fruit and bite in 1975. Maturing; bouquet opening up but slightly short and bitter edged in 1978. A year later distinctly disappointing.* Last tasted October 1979 ★★ Could be going through a bad period but . . . ?
Ch. Duhart-Milon-Rothschild Pauillac	*Fairly deep plummy colour; fruity/stalky fragrance; hard. Of moderate quality.* Tasted 1976, September 1977 ★(★)? Drink now — 1985.
Ch. Durfort-Vivens Margaux	*Marginal: dumb, dull, hard and tannic.* Tasted October 1976 ★ Might have softened a little by now.
Ch. Fourcas-Hosten Listrac	*Good colour; fragrant but unmellow; positive and flavoury, fairly high but refreshing acidity.* Tasted 1976, October 1977 ★★ Drink now — 1984.
Ch. La Gaffelière St-Emilion	*Somewhat unyielding nose and flavour but nice quality.* Tasted October 1976 ★★ Drink now — 1985.
Ch. Gloria St-Julien	*Lightish pink-and-healthy colour; insubstantial but pleasant cedary bouquet; medium dry, modest weight, nice easy flavour but dry, slightly raw end.* Tasted 1975, 1976, February 1978 ★★ Drink now — 1985.
Ch. Grand-Barrail-Lamarzelle-Figeac St-Emilion	*Good colour, attractive but lacking development capability.* Tasted twice, in October 1976 ★★ Drink now — 1984.
Ch. Grand-Puy-Lacoste Pauillac	*Five consistent notes from 1976. Never very deep, now pink and pretty; fruity, fragrant bouquet, almost citrus-like in its refreshing piquancy. With charm and style, but not for long keeping.* Last tasted January 1979 ★★★ Drink before 1983.
Ch. Gruaud-Larose St-Julien	*Seven notes. Severe with a lot of tannin and acidity in 1975 and 1976; green, mouth-watering acidity in 1978, but developing into a nice fruity wine. A year later, pleasant, very flavoury. A bit short.* Last tasted October 1979 ★★★ Drink now — 1988.
Ch. Haut-Bailly Graves	*Hard, raw, fruity aroma; medium dry, some body, firm. One of the best '73 Graves.* Tasted 1976, February 1978 ★★ Drink now — 1985.
Ch. Haut-Batailley Pauillac	*Fragrant, well made, nice balance.* Tasted October 1976 ★★★ Drink now — 1986.
Ch. d'Issan Margaux	*Some colour; rather unyielding bouquet; but some fruit, straightforward.* Tasted 1974, September 1978 ★(★) Drink now — 1988.
Clos des Jacobins St-Emilion	*Rich appearance; fragrant, sugared nose; surprisingly pronounced flavour. A very attractive, easy drink, nice quality and good aftertaste.* Tasted October 1976 ★★★ Drink now — 1986.
Ch. Lafon-Rochet St-Estèphe	*Pale, very mature looking; strange leathery/medicinal nose and flavour — yet some fragrance and an open, easy, not unattractive wine.* Tasted 1977, August 1979 ★★ Drink up.
Ch. Lagrange St-Julien	*Pale, pink, chaptalized. Little to it.* Tasted 1976, May 1979 ★ Drink up.
Ch. La Lagune Ludon	*Three notes. Good colour, now mature; a sweet, soft, fruity wine, very agreeable.* Tasted 1974 — October 1979 ★★★ Drink now — 1988.
Ch. Lanessan Cussac	*Often a dull wine, but the '73 very pleasant colour, bouquet and flavour. Fruity, positive, nice, dry, refreshing finish.* Tasted 1976, September 1978 ★★★ Drink now — 1986.

Ch. Langoa-Barton St-Julien	*Rather feeble plummy colour; curious spicy aroma; piquant, positive, a bit scraggy.* Tasted October 1975 ** Drink now — 1985.
Ch. Lascombes Margaux	*Deep, rich and impressive at the Gault-Millau tasting in October 1976, but now seems to be falling apart: although surprisingly deep it is very brown; some fruit on the nose but unknit and slightly oxidized; a clumsy wine, no charm, uneven, no future judging by various bottles from different sources.* Last tasted January and February 1979. Must retaste.
Ch. Laujac Bégadan	*Pale, pink tinged; little nose; pleasant enough.* Tasted 1974, 1976 * Drink up.
Ch. Léoville-Barton St-Julien	*Slightly deeper than Poyferré; straightforward; dry, lightish, touch of stalkiness and vanilla. Should develop reasonably well.* Tasted at the château when young, in October 1975 **(*)? Drink now — 1988.
Ch. Léoville-Poyferré St-Julien	*Not much colour, a bit insubstantial in 1975. More recently: a touch of sweetness and fruit but not impressive.* Last tasted July 1978 ** Drink now — 1988.
Ch. Lynch-Bages Pauillac	*Fine deep colour; nose dumb and unyielding; very dry, a rather dull classic.* Tasted October 1976 **(*) Might develop.
Ch. Marquis-de-Terme Margaux	*Low-keyed but flowery Margaux style of bouquet; delightful touch of sweetness, some charm, maturing nicely. One of the few '73s without a raw, dry finish.* Tasted January 1978 *** Drink now — 1985.
Ch. La Mission-Haut-Brion Talence, Graves	*Came out badly in the Gault-Millau tasting in October 1976 mainly, I think, because its idiosyncratic Graves style appeared strange in the middle of all the Médocs and St-Emilions. Showed better at the Domaine Woltner pre-sale tastings at Christie's: quick maturing; burnt, gravelly nose; sweet, easy, flavoury.* Last tasted December 1978 *** Drink now — 1985.
Ch. Moulinet Pomerol	*Very pleasant light wine; fruity little bouquet; dry.* Tasted October 1979 ** Drink now — 1984.
Ch. Mouton-Baron Philippe Pauillac	*Four consistent notes, ranging from the Gault-Millau tasting in 1976 to a recent lunch at the Connaught Hotel. Pretty, pink tinged; undistinguished in every way though a pleasant enough luncheon wine.* Last tasted November 1979 * Drink up.
Ch. Nenin Pomerol	*Fragrant but a bit cardboardy on the nose; quite pleasant flavour but tails off.* Tasted October 1976 * Drink up.
Ch. Les Ormes-de-Pez St-Estèphe	*Good colour; quite nice though undeveloped bouquet; chunky, positive, fruity. Pleasant enough but no follow-through.* Tasted 1976, July 1978 ** Drink now — 1984.
Ch. Palmer Margaux	*Very fragrant but rather superficial smell and taste. Attractive but not up to the high Palmer standards.* Tasted 1978, May 1979 ** Drink now — 1985.
Ch. Phélan-Ségur St-Estèphe	*Not at all impressive at Gault-Millau tasting in 1976: poor nose; tailed off. More recently, a reasonably agreeable half-bottle.* Last tasted March 1979 * Drink up.
Ch. La Pointe Pomerol	*Fine deep colour for a '73; rich, attractive, concentrated fruity nose; good flavour and quality, though a little austere.* Tasted October 1976 **(*) Drink now — 1986?

Ch. Pontet-Canet Pauillac	*Six consistent notes. Quite attractive lightish garnet red; light, fragrant, easy bouquet and flavour. Some charm and elegance. Nice aftertaste. Perfect luncheon claret.* Tasted 1974 — November 1979 ★★★ Drink now — 1986.
Ch. Rausan-Ségla Margaux	*Fragrant, nicely made.* Tasted in cask, and in September 1978 ★★ Drink now — 1988.
Ch. St-Pierre-Sevaistre St-Julien	*Deep and lovely — high marks at the St-Julien tasting at Langoa-Barton in 1975 but all the signs of an early developer; light cedar, a touch of* Cabernet *on the nose; pleasant, easy, not much tannin but nice balance and "feel".* Last tasted July 1976 ★★★ Drink now — 1986.
Ch. de Sales Pomerol	*Fairly nondescript at Gault-Millau tasting in 1976. Recently, I found it quite richly developed, soft and fragrant.* Last tasted March 1979 ★★★ Drink now — 1986.
Ch. Smith-Haut-Lafitte Graves	*Palish; high toned, fragrant; some style and fruit but raw. Might soften a little.* Tasted October 1976 ★ Drink now — 1984.
Ch. Talbot St-Julien	*Deep, peppery, stalky and moderate marks at the tasting of '73 St-Juliens in 1975. Losing colour quite rapidly but developing into a pretty, fairly lightweight but attractive wine.* Tasted 1975 — September 1978 ★★★ Drink now — 1988.
Ch. Trotanoy Pomerol	*Light, pretty, pleasant, short.* Tasted November 1977 ★★ Drink now — 1984.

Lesser growths, both good and poor, virtually all to be drunk now and not kept:

Ch. Balestard La Tonnelle St-Emilion	*One of the many* 1er cru *St-Emilion châteaux, not often seen in export markets. Palish; not too clean; a bit coarse but some richness.* Tasted October 1976 ★
Ch. Beau-Site St-Estèphe	*Quite attractive, chaptalized, lightweight. Minor wine.* Tasted March 1977 ★★
Ch. Bel-Air La Clotte Bordeaux Supérieur	*Emphasis on the last word. Pale orange rose.* Tasted 1976.
Ch. Bel-Orme-Tronquoy-de-Lalande St-Estèphe	*One is tempted to suggest that the quality of a château might be in inverse proportion to the number of syllables in its name. A poor wine, prematurely pale and mature; curious tinny nose; light, thin, acidic.* Tasted October 1976.
Ch. Bonnet Entre-Deux-Mers	*A minor wine but pink, fresh and charming.* Tasted 1975 ★★
Ch. Bouscaut Graves	*Despite the care and attention lavished on it by its American owners, it is not possible to change the subsoil and influence the weather. Light wine; rather singed, medicinal nose; dry, quite good but slightly bitter finish — which might wear off.* Tasted October 1976 ★
Ch. Cantemerle Blaye	*Beware, an ambiguously named château. Not the Médoc classed growth. Plummy and ordinary.* Tasted 1974.
Clos Cantenac Lansac	*Nor is this, as one might assume, a Margaux, but amongst the table of* crus bourgeois et premiers artisans *in a minor commune across the river from the Médoc. It should have stayed there. A curious, powerful, coarse wine.* Tasted October 1976.
Ch. Caronne-St-Gemme St-Laurent	*Good red hue; some fruit on nose which faded and then seemed to revive; dry, light, flavoury.* Tasted January 1980 ★★

Ch. Chanteclerc Pauillac	*Rich plummy colour; hard, stalky nose and taste. Minor wine. Very dry.* Tasted September 1977 ⋆
Ch. Chicane Graves	*New to me. Minor wine, but fragrant, pleasing.* Tasted August 1979 ⋆⋆
Ch. Citran Avensan	*Surprisingly deep and youthful; fruity but green; dry, a bit austere, pleasant aftertaste.* Tasted 1978, January 1979 ⋆(⋆)
Ch. Cos Labory St-Estèphe	*Inconsistent notes. Hard, curious in 1977. A year later: nice fruit and positive flavour.* Last tasted February 1978 ⋆?
Ch. Coufran St-Estèphe	*Charming, fruity, dry.* Tasted July 1978 ⋆⋆
Ch. Dassault St-Emilion	*Peppery, fruity, quite good.* Tasted October 1976 ⋆⋆
Ch. de Ferrand St-Emilion	*A light, pretty, fragrant, agreeably sugared wine.* Tasted October 1976 ⋆⋆
Ch. La Fleur-Milon Pauillac	*Plummy; curious, cold, hard. Not thrilling.* Tasted September 1977 ⋆
Ch. Gazin Côtes de Bourg	*Another teaser shown by the shipper of the Cantemerle from Blaye. Light and fluffy (the wine, not the shipper — an old friend who surprised me by producing these ambiguously named châteaux).* Tasted 1974.
Ch. Grâce-Dieu St-Emilion	*Like de Ferrand, a pretty little wine.* Tasted October 1976 ⋆⋆
Ch. Grand-Corbin-Despagne St-Emilion	*Beautiful colour; spicy, rich iron/earthy aroma and taste. Nice quality.* Tasted September 1976 ⋆⋆⋆
Ch. Haut-Bages-Monpelou Pauillac	*Pleasant enough, light, refreshing.* Tasted 1976 ⋆⋆
Ch. Haut-Brignon 1ères Côtes	*Fragrant, light, minor.* Tasted 1975 ⋆
Ch. Haut-Milon Pauillac	*Unimpressive colour; some fragrance; rather strong and coarse.* Tasted September 1977 ⋆
Ch. Haut-Pauillac Pauillac	*One of the surprises of the Bremen Pauillac tasting. A lovely, fragrant, stylish wine with nice texture.* Tasted September 1977 ⋆⋆⋆
Ch. Lafitte-Gaujac Caudrot	*At least it is spelt with two t's. Despite the unappetizing name of the district (which is in the Entre-Deux-Mers), a surprisingly nice little wine.* Tasted 1974 ⋆⋆
Ch. Larcis-Ducasse St-Emilion	*Good colour; fragrant; flavoury, some potential.* Tasted twice, in October 1976 ⋆⋆(⋆)
Ch. Larguet St-Emilion	*Almond kernels and iron; sweet, jammy, alcoholic wine bottled by the Swedish State Monopoly. Probably keeps the cold out.* Tasted June 1978.
Ch. Larrivet-Haut-Brion Graves	*Deepish; hard, ungracious.* Tasted October 1976 ⋆
Ch. Lescours St-Emilion	*Palish but plummy; thin high-toned aroma with associated piquant flavour, but elegant. Nice aftertaste.* Tasted October 1976 ⋆⋆

Ch. La Louvière
Graves

Fine colour; rich, scented, burnt Graves aroma; fine flavour and quality. *Tasted September 1976* ***

Ch. Lynch-Moussas
Pauillac

Pale, pink and peppery in 1974. Later: light; piquant, some fruit; but raw and overacid. *Last tasted July 1978.*

Ch. Malartic-Lagravière
Graves

Never my favourite wine. Palish and purple; fairly fragrant, oak on nose; dry, light, flavoury, but tails off — absolutely no finish. *Tasted October 1976.*

Ch. Maucaillou
Moulis

Deeper than expected; gentle, sweet complete nose; pleasant, flavoury wine with dry finish. *Tasted May 1978* ***

Ch. Monbousquet
St-Emilion

Reasonably good colour; pronounced dusty Cabernet-Sauvignon aroma and flavour. Rich yet austere. *Tasted September 1976* **

Ch. Montgrand-Milon
Pauillac

Fragrant, agreeable little wine. *Tasted September 1977* **

Ch. Padarnac
Pauillac

Peppery, powerful, Cabernet aroma and flavour. *Tasted September 1977* **

Ch. Patâche d'Aux
Bégadan

A nonentity — mentioned because it is a petit château much shipped to England in the wake of the overpriced classed growths. *Tasted February 1978.*

Ch. Peymartin
St-Julien

Light; pleasant enough, a bit stalky. *Tasted October 1975* *

Ch. de Pez
St-Estèphe

Light, soft for de Pez, slightly stalky on nose and palate. *Tasted 1976* *

Ch. Poujet-Theil
Moulis

A rarely seen wine, showing quite well at the Gault-Millau tasting: good colour; nice classic quality though undeveloped and a little short. *Tasted October 1976* **

Clos René
Pomerol

Not exactly a minor wine. Quite attractive, but harsh. *Tasted October 1976* * *Might soften a little?*

La Rose-Pauillac

From the Pauillac co-operative. Dull, hard, unforthcoming. *Tasted September 1977.*

Ch. Rouet
Fronsac

Pink, light and pleasant. *Tasted twice, in November 1978* *

Ch. Ségur
Parempuyre

A nonentity. *Tasted October 1978.*

Ch. Soutard
St-Emilion

Palish, immature; scented nose; dry, short but agreeable. A pretty little wine. *Tasted October 1976* **

Ch. du Taillan
Médoc

Light, pleasant enough. *Tasted 1974, 1976* *

Ch. La Tour-de-By
Bégadan

Deep for a '73; rich Merlot nose but, paradoxically, coarse and green on palate. *Tasted September 1976.*

Ch. La Tour-du-Roc-Milon
Pauillac

Good colour; positive and immediate Cabernet aroma; nice, easy little wine. *Tasted September 1977* **

Ch. La Tour-St-Bonnet
St-Christoly

Insipid; minty nose. *Tasted 1976.*

Ch. Verdignan
St-Estèphe

Pink, but deeper than the '72; a dry, light, easy charmer. Four notes. *Last tasted July 1978* **

1974 ★

A superabundant vintage of moderate, uneven quality. Climate: good flowering weather; fine hot, dry summer; variable and more than average rainfall in September. Grapes swelled in thick skins. Rain at the beginning of the harvest on 3 October, continuing cold and wet. Production about the second highest on record. Market: the picking was completed at about the most miserably foreboding moment — the collapse of the financial system was imminent. The wine was bottled at the depth of the wine slump, châteaux cellars were bulging, and it seemed as though the glut could never be absorbed by the Bordeaux market. Following the revival of trade the "wine lake" was speedily drained — but '74 has never been found an attractive or popular commercial vintage. Assessment: raw, aggressive, ungracious vintage and one of my least favourite. It is just possible that, like a nasty, pimply schoolboy, with a spell of further education (in bottle — too late for the *éleveur*) and a decent job (resting in our cellars) it might settle down and behave respectably. But what do they say about making a silk purse out of a sow's ear? Worth buying cheaply and keeping a little on the off chance. Tasting notes: most have been culled from miscellaneous pre-sale and shippers' tastings for the London trade, notably de Luze and Nathaniel Johnston, and I presided recently over an interesting comparative tasting of '74 red Bordeaux against American Cabernet-Sauvignon in Holland.

Ch. Latour Pauillac	*Tasted only twice: deep, plummy purple; not very interesting nose; fullish and short in September 1976. A purple, stewed, unattractive bottle from the château (Jean-Paul Gardère, the manager, thought it might be corked) a year later.* Last tasted June 1977. Need to retaste.
Ch. Mouton-Rothschild Pauillac	*Tasted twice. In 1978, medium colour; surprisingly forward, attractive iron/Cabernet aroma. More recently: somewhat indecisive colour; fruity nose which opened up nicely; dry, medium body, straightforward, a bit short and raw.* Last tasted October 1979 ★★(★)? Interesting to see how it develops.
Ch. Haut-Brion Pessac, Graves	*Medium, quick maturing; undeveloped nose; lightish style, though with a chunky/fruity flavour. Short.* Tasted only once, in September 1979 ★★(★) Drink 1982–1990.
Ch. Ausone St-Emilion	*Medium, maturing; some fruit on nose; slightly sweet, rich, interesting aftertaste. Quite an attractive '74.* Tasted February 1978 ★★★ Drink 1982–1990.

No other first growths tasted to date. Of the three dozen or so other châteaux tasted, I put at the head the one really exceptional wine, La Mission, followed by a range of notes in alphabetical order.

Ch. La Mission-Haut-Brion Talence, Graves	*Immensely impressive colour, deep and purple; powerful aroma, peppery, whole fruit plus skins; fairly full bodied, rich, tangy — earthy/iron/pebbles/seaweed — raw dry finish.* Three notes, April 1978 — October 1979 ★★(★) Drink 1982–1992.
Ch. L'Angélus St-Emilion	*Rather feeble colour and nose; slightly sweet, easy but flat on the finish.* Tasted September 1976 ★ Drink up.
Ch. Branaire-Ducru St-Julien	*Very attractive colour, maturing nicely; aroma of fruit, raspberries, but unharmonious; a bit hollow and feeble, but not unattractive.* Tasted June 1979 ★ Drink soon.
Ch. Brane-Cantenac Margaux	*Found it very odd at the Nathaniel Johnston tasting in 1976: smelly, curious scent and taste. At the Elsevier-Bouquet tasting of*

'74s, it had a similar colour to Mouton; touch of aniseed on the nose; little character, dull, neutral but reasonable balance. Last tasted October 1979 ★ Drink now — 1986.

Ch. Camensac St-Laurent	One of the least often seen classed growths of the Médoc. Medium weight, pleasant, bright colour; curious overblown, rather smelly nose; dry, raw, cheesy, short raw end. At the Elsevier-Bouquet tasting of '74s, the Napa Valley Cabernet-Sauvignons made this wine creep back into the woodwork. Tasted October 1979. Not worth keeping.
Ch. Chasse-Spleen Moulis	Pale with an unhealthy orange tinge; cheesy nose; dry and raw. Tasted June 1979.
Ch. Clerc-Milon Pauillac	Plausible, positive, quite nice, maturing but still slightly bitter on the finish. Tasted May 1978 ★ Drink 1981?–1984.
Ch. Cos d'Estournel St-Estèphe	Plummy, immature looking; good fruit; a bit raw and short. Should round off a little. Tasted November 1977 ★(★) Drink 1982–1990.
Ch. Cos-Labory St-Estèphe	Lightish colour; pleasant nose; forward, little to it. Tasted February 1978 ★ Drink up.
Ch. Coufran St-Estèphe	Immature looking; quite nice chunky/fruity aroma; somewhat raw and ungracious but, as usual, decently made and should soften a little. Tasted January 1979 ★ Drink 1982–1986.
Ch. Ducru-Beaucaillou St-Julien	Quite good colour, still purple/red; sweet, fruity nose; not the usual finesse but a pleasant chunky wine. At shippers' tastings 1976, October 1979 ★★(★) Drink now — 1988.
Ch. Figeac St-Emilion	Jammy fruitiness with the characteristic iron overtone. Soft, pleasant, lacking real harmony and balance, but an agreeable '74. Tasted April 1979 ★★(★) Drink 1981–1986.
Clos Fourtet St-Emilion	Quick developer? Fruity and agreeable. Tasted in cask, September 1975 ★★(★) Drink soon.
Ch. Gazin Pomerol	Lightish and developing very quickly; light minty aroma; showing nothing like its true class. Short, tails off. Tasted September 1976. Drink up.
Ch. Giscours Margaux	Nothing impressive except its very deep colour; cheese rind nose, some fruit; dry, raw, tannic, short. The antithesis of Margaux elegance and charm. But might soften and find its second wind. Tasted April 1979. Drink 1982?–1986.
Ch. Grand-Puy-Lacoste Pauillac	Youthful; crisp, fruit-bush Pauillac Cabernet aroma; dry, a bit raw, but could develop into an agreeable flavoury wine. Tasted October 1979 ★(★) Drink 1982–1988.
Ch. Gruaud-Larose St-Julien	Fruity, firm, fair potential. Tasted in cask, April 1976 ★★(★)? Drink 1984–1994.
Ch. Haut-Batailley Pauillac	Light, forward; very attractive bouquet and flavour. An agreeable '74. Tasted 1976, October 1979 ★★★ Drink now — 1986.
Ch. Lafon-Rochet St-Estèphe	Plummy, looser-knit than Pontet-Canet; crushed fruit nose, quite nice; chunky, some richness but a bit raw. Time should soften it a little. At the Decanter Magazine tasting, August 1979 ★(★) Drink 1982–1988.
Ch. Lamouroux Margaux	Thin, watery edged; chaptalized; insubstantial — but a nice little drink. Tasted June 1978 ★ Drink up.

Ch. Lascombes Margaux	*High toned, flavoury, a little medicinal.* Tasted November 1977 *(*) Drink now — 1984.
Ch. Léoville-Las-Cases St-Julien	*Medium colour, youthful; sweet pasty nose; dry, loose-knit and raw. With this pedigree and capability the wine should round off a little.* Tasted June 1978 *(*) Drink 1982-1986?
Ch. Lynch-Bages Pauillac	*Very mature; interesting medicinal/iron Pauillac aroma and flavour, with a certain silkiness of texture. One of the least aggressive '74s.* Tasted June 1978 ** Drink now — 1984.
Ch. de Marbuzet St-Estèphe	*Deep, immature, raw. Probably all right with Lancashire hotpot and pickles.* Tasted May 1978 * Drink 1982-1986.
Ch. du Paradis St-Emilion, Vignonet	*Light structured, low keyed, modest. Will not last the course.* Tasted November 1978.
Ch. Patâche d'Aux Bégadan	*An early developer; sweet nose, some fruit, but raw and short.* Tasted February 1978, June 1979 * Drink now — 1984.
Ch. Pontet-Canet Pauillac	*A pleasant '74: reasonable colour, maturing, not a very firm rim but attractive; fruity Pauillac nose; agreeable and easy in cask in September 1975. More recently: dry, flavoury, citrus character.* Last tasted August 1979 ** Probably best drunk soon.
Ch. Rausan-Ségla Margaux	*Fairly deep, very purple; fruity, flavoury, fair tannin and acidity.* Cask sample September 1975 **(*) Reasonable potential. Drink 1984-1990.
Dom. du Sablot Lalande-de-Pomerol	*Minor wine, Bordeaux bottled. Deep coloured; youthful yet soft and nice.* Tasted June 1976 * Drink up.
Ch. Siran Labarde	*Light and lean.* Tasted February 1978 *(*) Drink 1982-1988.
Ch. Talbot St-Julien	*Deeper coloured yet softer in cask than Gruaud. Very attractive aroma; tannic finish. Some potential.* Tasted April 1979 **(*) Drink 1984-1994.
Ch. La Tour-Carnet St-Laurent	*Lovely colour, wonderful bright garnet hue; nose dumb but sound, cheesy, developed a little fragrance; dry and lean, hard but some elegance.* At the Elsevier-Bouquet tasting of '74s, October 1979 **(*) Drink 1982-1988.
Ch. La Tour-Haut-Brion Graves	*Deep; good raw fruity nose and flavour. Masculine, aggressive but a jolly good mouthful.* Tasted December 1979 *(*) Drink 1982-1990.
Ch. Trotanoy Pomerol	*Fairly deep, purple; sweet yet immature nose; dry, fullish, firm, raw and powerful. A good '74 but lacking Trotanoy flesh and finesse. Should improve and soften up a little.* Tasted November 1977 **(*)? Drink 1982-1988.
Ch. Verdignan St-Estèphe	*Plummy; not bad, a chunky little wine. Touch of end bitterness which should wear off.* Tasted April 1978 * Drink now — 1984.

1975 ★★★★

A timely vintage of undoubtedly high quality. Whether it will turn out to be a great vintage only time will tell; but at least, unlike the three preceding vintages, it is a *vin de garde* year, with impressively deep-coloured wines worth — indeed needing — cellaring. Climate: mild winter with quite heavy rainfall; warm start to spring, with cold spells and some frost; flowering under favourable conditions; summer very hot and dry; gentle, welcome, rain before the harvest, which began on 26 September. A few hailstorms, one very severe, otherwise dry and sunny throughout vintage. Small crop due to hot, dry summer conditions. The sun-baked skins contained deep pigment, resulting in dark-coloured wine; high sugar content assured a satisfactory level of alcohol. Market conditions: although vintaged in the depth of the wine depression, the wine was bottled at a more opportune period: trade had recovered, the previous vintage surpluses were mopped up; its reputation was high and the quantity available relatively modest. In fact the '75s, particularly the top growths, were keenly sought even at high prices. Assessment: certainly impressive. Some fine deep wines. It does seem to me that, as so often, the really well-run properties made outstanding wine; some were more lax. A perfect Pomerol vintage, but some Médocs lacked "puppy fat" and flesh. The best should develop well.

Ch. Lafite Pauillac	*Although no two vintages are alike, it is quite interesting to note that the production of Lafite (158 tonneaux: the equivalent of roughly 190,000 bottles) and the date of picking were similar to 1959. I have just four notes: as usual, not a big black wine but fine looking, with reasonable depth. Lovely and spicy in cask. Full marks at the M.W. tasting of '75s in March 1979. Outstanding in its complexity at a comparative, blind tasting of '75s at the Vintners' Club in San Francisco, and impressive, if hastily tasted, at the opening of the great Overton showing of Lafite in Texas later the same month. Summing up: medium deep, excellent colour; lovely fruity bouquet, peppery and closed up at first but swelling fragrantly in the glass; slight touch of sweet ripeness on entering the mouth, good body — neither light nor massive — lovely middle flavour, elegant, lean but shapely, firm tannic finish. Good aftertaste.* Last tasted May 1979 ★★★★(★)? Drink 1985–2010?
Ch. Latour Pauillac	*Five notes. Opaque, classic, rich in cask, September 1976. Slightly less massive than expected at the M.W. tasting of '75s, and at the Vintners' Club: deepish, attractive colour, beginning to mature; dumb and slow to develop in the glass — peppery, toasted, with innate fragrance; a big dry wine, packed with flavour, rich, hard, tannic. Quite unready.* Last tasted May 1979 ★★★(★★)? Drink 1985–2020?
Ch. Margaux Margaux	*Not tasted, but I was there as the grapes were being brought in. The juice was magnificently deep and the cellar-master said the must weight was as high as he had ever measured. 1975 turned out better for the wine than for the owners.*
Ch. Mouton-Rothschild Pauillac	*Tasted only twice. Fine and fruity at the M.W. tasting in March 1979. At the Vintners' Club, San Francisco: hard and unyielding nose at first, fragrant but alcoholic, yet developed magnificently in the glass; on the palate, a dry, very hard, concentrated, fruity wine of unmistakably first-growth quality. Plenty of tannin and acidity. A long laster.* Last tasted May 1979 ★★★(★★) Drink 1985–2020.
Ch. Haut-Brion Pessac, Graves	*Five notes, from "in cask", September 1976. Showed particularly well at the M.W. tasting of '75s and, in its characteristic Graves way, at the Vintners' Club. Summing up: fairly deep, good colour, velvety, starting to mature; totally different from the first-growth Médocs — bouquet more open-knit, sweet, elegant, touch of vanilla, a little jammy, opening up, warm and biscuity, in the glass; ripe, fruity, with Graves iron/earthy flavour, smoky, firm tannin structure, good aftertaste.* Last tasted May 1979 ★★★★(★) Drink 1982–2010.
Ch. Ausone St-Emilion	*Fairly deep colour; sweet, almost chocolaty, fragrant nose; good, firm.* Tasted March 1979 ★★(★) Drink 1982–1992.

Ch. Cheval-Blanc St-Emilion	Three notes. Complex in 1978. Then 17/20 at the M.W. tasting, March 1979. At the Vintners' Club: deepish plummy colour; fragrant, rich, easy bouquet that developed well; fairly full bodied, chunky flavour, leathery/tannic finish, and good after-taste. *Last tasted May 1979 ⋆⋆⋆(⋆) Drink 1984–2000.*
Ch. Pétrus Pomerol	Tasted twice. Full marks at the M.W. tasting of leading '75s, though I liked it least of the first growths tasted blind at the Vintners' Club. Trying to summarize: an undoubtedly deep, velvety appearance; sweet bouquet, full of fruit, with characteristic mulberry richness, but it did not blossom and open up — perhaps it needs far more time in bottle; slightly sweet on the palate, full bodied, fruity, rich and open-knit, but still a bit hard and stalky. Long tannic finish. *Last tasted May 1979 ⋆⋆⋆(⋆⋆)? Drink 1985–2000?*

A representative selection of notes on other châteaux follows:

Ch. Batailley Pauillac	Usual chunky wine but lacking flesh and fat. Severe. Bottle-age should help. *Tasted November 1978 ⋆(⋆⋆) Drink 1985–1995?*
Ch. Beychevelle St-Julien	Very attractive colour, nose and flavour. Dry, supple, elegant. *Tasted October 1979 ⋆⋆⋆(⋆) Drink 1982–1995.*
Ch. du Bousquet Bourg	Palish pink purple; pleasant enough minor wine. *Tasted June and October 1979 ⋆ For quaffing.*
Ch. Boyd-Cantenac Margaux	Deep, rich, crisp, purple; hard unyielding nose; dry, firm, nicely made. *Tasted October 1979 ⋆⋆(⋆) Drink 1982–1992.*
Ch. Brane-Cantenac Margaux	Tasted twice. As with an earlier vintage, I found the nose objectionable — old sulphur, manure — at the Nathaniel Johnston tasting in September 1976. Perhaps just a poor cask sample. More recently: medium deep, maturing; pleasant, sweet; an easy, flavoury wine, attractive but not for long keeping. Frankly not as impressive as it should be. *Last tasted November 1978 ⋆⋆ Drink now — 1986?*
Ch. Cambes Bourg	Medium colour with light purple — immature — rim; youthful, clean cut, rich, even nose; warm and appealing. Alcoholic but happily without the usual Côtes de Bourg coarseness. *Tasted August 1979. Although immature there is a tendency for wines of this class, even in good years, to develop only up to a certain point. So ⋆⋆(⋆) Drink 1982–1988.*
Ch. Cantemerle Macau	Clear-cut purple; crisp, high-toned aroma and flavour. Attractive. A bit lean? Good finish. *Tasted November 1978 ⋆⋆⋆(⋆) Drink 1985–1995?*
Ch. Cantenac-Brown Margaux	Open-knit, scented, unready. *Tasted January 1978 ⋆(⋆⋆) Drink 1983–1995.*
Dom. de Chevalier Graves	Fairly deep, immature; light, fruity nose and flavour. A bit green still. *Tasted at La Mission, September 1978 ⋆(⋆⋆)*
Ch. Clerc-Milon-Rothschild Pauillac	Three notes. Most recently: plummy colour; hard nose with piquant fruitiness; very positive, stylish, some ripeness but overall lean and dry. *Last tasted March 1979 ⋆⋆(⋆)*
Ch. Cos d'Estournel St-Estèphe	In cask: a deep, classic, pleasant but tannic, long-lasting wine. *Tasted only once, in April 1977 ⋆⋆(⋆⋆) Drink 1985–2000.*
Ch. Cos Labory St-Estèphe	Frankly, a too frequently unappealing château. This vintage tasted twice. Some fruit but hard edged and not much of a finish. *Last tasted March 1979 ⋆*

Ch. Ducru-Beaucaillou St-Julien	*Seven notes dating from a good cask sample in 1976. Showed well at two major comparative tastings, but appears to be going through a rather hard, ungraceful period. Most recently: deep coloured; gentle, understated, cinnamon/cedar bouquet; full bodied, hard. Not as long or distinguished as expected, and unless it develops belatedly, not a great '75.* Last tasted October 1979 ★★(★★)? Drink 1985–?
Ch. L'Evangile Pomerol	*Not very deep; light, pleasant, liquorice-like aroma leading to a dry, firm, rather tough, lean mouthful. Nice potential though.* Tasted November 1978 ★★(★) Drink 1982–1995.
Ch. Figeac St-Emilion	*Top class: lovely hot-vintage colour but starting to mature; lovely, fragrant, harmonious and forthcoming bouquet which held well in the glass; slightly sweet, reasonably full bodied, soft, heavenly, flavoury, good balance.* Tasted March and June 1979 ★★★★ Drink now — 1992.
Ch. Fourcas-Dupré Listrac	*Rich, but maturing quickly; intensely sweet* Cabernet *aroma; a ripe little wine with dry finish.* Tasted May 1979 ★★★ Drink now — 1990
Ch. Fourcas-Hosten Listrac	*Closed up in 1977. More recently: a fine deep colour; curiously scented, unknit and alcoholic; a hot, hard wine. This is the sort of '75 which might not be worth waiting for.* Last tasted June 1979 ★(★)?
Clos Fourtet St-Emilion	*Medium deep; good nose; dry medium body, very flavoury.* Tasted June 1979 ★★★ Drink 1983–1995.
Ch. Giscours Margaux	*Deep attractive colour and bouquet — reminded me of a Cox's Orange Pippin. Overall dry, flavoury, just enough flesh over the bones.* Tasted March 1979 ★★(★) Drink 1984–1994.
Ch. du Glana St-Julien	*Deepish, plum coloured, ripe, harmonious mulberry nose; dry, pleasing weight and flavour.* Tasted June 1978 ★★★ Drink now — 1990.
Ch. Gloria St-Julien	*Two notes, the most recent: fairly deep; immature citrus-fruit aroma; light style, a bit lacking in flesh and length. Flavoury.* Last tasted March 1979 ★(★★)? Drink 1985–1993.
Ch. Grand-Puy-Lacoste Pauillac	*Three notes. Most recently: good colour; lovely aroma of blackberries and mulberries, still tight-knit; most attractive, lots of fruit.* Last tasted October 1979 ★★★(★) Drink 1983–1995.
Ch. Gruaud-Larose St-Julien	*Opaque and concentrated in cask. Hard but rich in 1978. More recently: deep coloured; peppery, hard, and a little stalky; dry, rich but severe. More like Talbot in style, masculine, austere. Impressive, unready.* Last tasted March 1979 ★★(★★)? Drink 1985–2000?
Ch. Haut-Bailly Graves	*The least deep coloured of a group of '75 Graves tasted at La Mission: broader, open style; a bit skinny and lacking body.* Tasted September 1978 ★(★★) Drink 1983–1990.
Ch. Haut-Batailley Pauillac	*Fruity, dry and stolid in cask in 1977. A bit peppery and severe in 1978. Latterly: deep colour; a rather high-toned bouquet; dry and unforthcoming. Lacking usual style and charm. But a sleeper?* Tasted October 1979 ★(★★)? Drink 1985–?
Ch. Huissant St-Estèphe	*A lightish, quickly maturing, flavoury little wine.* Tasted October 1978 ★★ Drink now — 1985.
Ch. Kirwan Margaux	*Medium deep; nose both spirity and sweet; crisp, fruity, lacking length?* Tasted March 1979 ★(★) Drink 1983–1990.

Ch. Lafon-Rochet St-Estèphe	*Plummy, pink rimmed, less firm than Pontet-Canet; immature, fruit, pleasant enough; flavoury medium body but raw edged. Charmless. Needs time.* Tasted November 1979 **(*) Drink 1985–1995.
Ch. La Lagune Ludon	*A lovely full, fruity wine. So often La Lagune seems, when young, too sweet and fruity to last. But the wine making is cunning and its future is usually assured.* Tasted only once, in September 1976 ***(*) Drink now — 1995?
Ch. Langoa-Barton St-Julien	*Deep, hard, crisp, fruity, with notably dry end acidity. Needs ameliorating bottle-age.* Tasted October 1978 *(**)? Drink 1983–1993.
Ch. Lascombes Margaux	*Two poor bottles at the M.W. tasting: unimpressive colour; curious nose, showing distinctly high volatile acidity; stalky taste leading to tinny end acidity. Not exactly promising.* Tasted March 1979. Must retaste.
Ch. Léoville-Barton St-Julien	*Deeper and more purple than Langoa; dumb but fine, gentle fruit waiting in the wings; some ripeness, nice weight, soft, rich, very pleasant.* Tasted October 1978 **(**) Drink 1983–1995.
Ch. Léoville-Las-Cases St-Julien	*Two notes. A most attractive wine: extremely fine, deep; ripe, fruity; concentrated and long. Great future.* Last tasted March 1979 ***(*) Drink 1983–2000.
Ch. Léoville-Poyferré St-Julien	*From a cask sample in London: deep, rich but rather curious nose and flavour.* Tasted only once, in September 1976. Must retaste.
Ch. La Libarde Bourg	*Admittedly a minor wine. A pretty pink, and pretty feeble (for a '75) colour; sweet, even sugared on nose and palate. Soft entry but stalky bitter finish. Which just shows how variable wines can be, even in a good vintage.* Tasted October 1979 ** No future.
Ch. Lynch-Bages Pauillac	*Four notes: frankly disappointing. Trace of oxidation in 1978. Unknit, rather common, stalky, unripe aroma at the M.W. tasting. One of the least interesting '75s at the Vintners' Club tasting. Most recently: good enough colour but neither deep nor too impressive; rather common, stalky nose; flavoury. Consistently better on palate than on nose. Perhaps I was expecting too much of a usually attractive wine.* Last tasted October 1979 **(*)? Drink 1985–1995?
Ch. Magdelaine St-Emilion	*Fruity, alcoholic; earthy, characterful.* Tasted December 1978 **(**) Drink 1982–1995.
Ch. Malescot-St-Exupéry Margaux	*Not very deep; aroma of fruit, cinnamon; overall dry, with fruit but lacking flesh.* At a tasting in Denmark, March 1979 **(*) Drink now — 1988.
Ch. Marquis-d'Alesme-Becker Margaux	*Pretty colour; sweet, rich, well-developed bouquet; fruit, stylish, firm. Attractive, no great length.* Tasted March 1979 *** Drink now — 1988.
Ch. Meyney St-Estèphe	*Deeper even than Montrose; prickly, fruit-bush aroma; dry, mouth-filling, quite unready.* At a tasting tutorial in Odense, Denmark, June 1978 *(**) Drink 1985–1995.
Ch. La Mission-Haut-Brion Talence, Graves	*Five notes. Most recently: deepest of the group of '75 Graves tasted at La Mission; most characterful, cedary/spiciness, great depth, developed well; a tough, concentrated wine, full of all the right component parts but severe.* Last tasted May 1979 **(***) Drink 1985–2010.
Ch. Montrose St-Estèphe	*Five notes dating from 1976. Fine wine, slow developer. Deep purple colour; classic nose with depth of fruit, but still dumb and*

peppery; dry, with ripeness and good flesh but severe tannin and acidity. For those who like a massive, chewy, gutsy wine — or wait 20 years. Last tasted March 1979 ★★(★★) Drink 1986–2010.

Ch. Mouton-Baron Philippe
Pauillac

Medium colour; sweet, intriguing, persistent aroma; elegant, easy, fruity wine of considerable charm and nice weight. Tasted March 1979 ★★★ Drink now — 1990.

Ch. Nenin
Pomerol

Plum coloured; light, fragrant, biscuity and emerged intriguingly from the glass; dry, but easy style of wine. Quite a lot to it. One of the best Nenins in years. In fact, using the misleading method of averaging scores, this came out top at the Vintners' Club tasting. Tasted May 1979 ★★★(★)? Drink now — 1992.

Ch. Palmer
Margaux

Showing well at the M.W. tasting of '75s: deep, rich colour; ripe fruit aroma — mulberries and cinnamon; rich, concentrated, firm. Recent tasting showed a touch of sharpness on the nose but possibly five stars. Last tasted October 1979 ★★★(★) Drink 1985–1995.

Ch. Pape-Clément
Pessac, Graves

Similar colour to Haut-Brion; curious nose, some depth; well made, dry, firm, considerable depth. The most Médoc-like in style. Tasted at La Mission, September 1978 ★★(★★) Drink 1985–1995.

Ch. Patâche d'Aux
Bégadan

Lightish, but purple; nice nose; dry, raw, minor. Tasted June 1979 ★(★) Drink 1982–1987.

Ch. Pavie
St-Emilion

After years of rather second-rate wines, Pavie in 1975 suddenly shows a touch of class: "deep and crisp and even" (from a cask sample), almost as deep as Montrose in 1978, but less impressive looking at the M.W. tasting. It has, however, a pleasant, sweet, fruity bouquet and flavour, supported by a good hard core. Tasted March 1979 ★★★ Drink now — 1990.

Ch. Pichon-Lalande
Pauillac

Deep, complete purple; broad, fruity classic nose; good fruit, flavour and balance. Very satisfactory. Tasted November 1978 ★★★(★) Drink 1983–1995.

Ch. Pontet-Canet
Pauillac

Ruby coloured; undeveloped nose but good depth of fruit under; a stern, solid, immature wine, immensely tannic. Slow starter, interesting future. At a Decanter Magazine tasting in August and at Studley Priory wine weekend tasting in November 1979 ★★(★★)? Drink 1985–2000.

Ch. Pontet-Latour

A branded wine as calculated as its name: very pale, hardly a '75 colour; thin nose, boiled sweets; light, easy. Tasted 1978 ★ Drink up.

Ch. Ramage-La Batisse
St-Sauveur

One of the many pretty, inveigling, minor château names: like a fly catcher. Attractive colour; iodine/medicinal nose and flavour. But hard, raw and not very pleasant. Might soften a little. Perfectly suitable with goulash. Tasted October 1979 ★(★)

Ch. Rausan-Ségla
Margaux

Lightish, attractive, forward; rich bouquet; fruity, attractive, nice consistency and aftertaste. Tasted March 1979 ★★★ Drink now — 1990.

Ch. St-Pierre-Sevaistre
St-Julien

Deep purple; sweet jammy nose; good fruit, nice balance. Tasted March 1979 ★★★(★) Drink 1983–1995.

Ch. de Sales
Pomerol

Deep warm colour; good Pomerol style, soft and agreeable. Tasted October 1979 ★★★★ Drink now — 1990.

Ch. Siran
Labarde

Deep; steely but supple. Tasted February 1978 ★★(★)? Drink 1983–1995.

Ch. Talbot St-Julien	*Three notes. Deep in cask; immature but excellent fruit at the M.W. tasting of '75s in March 1979. Impressive at the Vintners' Club: rich colour, one of the deepest '75s; ripe, sweet aroma, crisp fruit, fragrant, developed well in glass; touch of sweetness leading to a very dry finish, good fruit and more elegant and feminine than usual.* Last tasted May 1979 ***(*) Drink 1983–2000.
Ch. La Tour-Haut-Brion Graves	*Deep plummy purple; fragrant but immature; fruity, peppery and dry. Good mouthful but a trace of coarseness.* Tasted September 1978 *(**) Drink 1985–1995.
Ch. La Tour-St-Vincent St-Christoly	*Just to demonstrate that minor wines do not automatically rise to the occasion, even if the weather is right: immature; insubstantial; macération carbonique sort of nose — plausible, tinny fruit; not without appeal, but bitter/acid finish.* Tasted January 1979.
Ch. Trotanoy Pomerol	*At the tasting of '75s at the Vintners' Club: attractive looking, medium deep, mature (all the '75s in San Francisco looked more advanced than in London or Bordeaux); pleasant Pomerol nose — sweet, touch of vanilla and slightly medicinal, nice vinosity, developed fragrance in the glass; slight sweetness on the palate, ripe, soft, leading to firm, dry, tannic finish. A thoroughly attractive, well-made — one is tempted to say plausible — and stylish wine.* Last tasted May 1979 ***(*) Drink 1982–1995.
Ch. Verdignan St-Estèphe	*Three notes. Most recently: youthful; crisp, fruity aroma, nice vinosity, honeycomb smell; dry, fruity.* Last tasted January 1979 **
Vieux Ch. Certan Pomerol	*Fairly deep but looked a quick-maturing wine; nose undeveloped; dry and still hard.* Tasted June 1979 *(**) Drink 1983–1995?

1976 ★★★

A good vintage, not outstanding, but some immediately satisfactory wines which should stand us in good stead. It is tempting to think of the many twin vintages — 1899 and 1900, '28 and '29, '33 and '34, '52 and '53 — not exactly as twins, any of them, but as pairs. 1976 is to '75 what '62 was to '61, but less so; more likely an amalgam of what '71 was to '70 and '67 to '66. But this is a game. The 1976 has its own character and the wines will develop in their own different ways, as usual. Climate: a hot, dry, wonderful summer — remember? The year of the rather alarming heat and drought in northern Europe. The weather broke in September, ruining the grape harvest in England and interrupting the picking in Bordeaux which began on 15 September. Market: following the high-priced '75s, some resistance was building up so there was no repeat of the 1970/71 situation. 1976 prices remained reasonable — albeit at a level that made the decade of the 1960s look ridiculously cheap, and the 1950s another world. Assessment: useful wines. At best, claret at its most pleasantly refreshing, but quite a few wines, from high to low class, lack flesh; more lean and hungry than elegantly svelte and supple. As can be seen from the profusion of tiny "towers" (La Tour-de-this and La Tour-de-that), it is hard work to find nice claret at an acceptable price for members of West End clubs. Such a pity because claret is the perfect beverage, stylish, light, refreshing. Helps down those endless lamb chops. A vintage worth buying carefully and keeping a while.

Ch. Lafite Pauillac	*In November 1978: deep, purple; good fruit but of course undeveloped; a dry, very flavoury wine. Most recently: maturing; intense flavour, length and aftertaste. Elegant and fine.* Last tasted March 1980 **(**) Drink 1983–1995.

Ch. Latour Pauillac	*Three notes: the usual tremendous depth of colour; rich, complex aroma, good fruit; some richness and ripeness, which balanced.* Last tasted March 1980 *(***) Drink 1988–2000.
Ch. Margaux Margaux	*Not tasted.*
Ch. Mouton-Rothschild Pauillac	*A poor, woody sample in November 1978. Almost a year later, at the Elsevier-Bouquet tasting of the '76 Bordeaux versus Napa Valley Cabernet-Sauvignon, it showed pretty well: deep coloured, just starting to mature; sweet, high-toned bouquet, touch of vanilla (oak); good fruit under. An overall dry wine with medium body, good Mouton flavour and well balanced.* Last noted at the M.W. tasting, March 1980 **(**) Drink 1986–2000.
Ch. Haut-Brion Pessac, Graves	*Three notes. A good cask sample in May 1977: deepish, maturing quite quickly; broad, sweet nose, rich vinosity (totally different from the crisper more restrained Médocs); a broad earthy flavour leading to a dry tannic finish. Attractive, well-made, stylish wine.* Last tasted March 1980 **(**) Drink 1982–2000.
Ch. Ausone St-Emilion	*One rather severe, austere cask sample. Seemed to tail off.* Tasted April 1978. Assessment reserved.
Ch. Cheval-Blanc St-Emilion	*Deep; distinct earthy/iron hallmark; very dry. Seemed well-enough constituted, good aftertaste* Tasted in cask and at the M.W. tasting, March 1980 *(**) Drink 1984–1994.
Ch. Pétrus Pomerol	*Fairly intense colour; deep mulberry-like* Merlot *aroma; dry but rich, broad style, peppery still.* At the M.W. tasting, March 1980 **(**) Drink 1985–2000.

Of the 70 or so other châteaux tasted — not many so far, because dealing in young wines is not my business — I have noted here only those tasted more than once, or, if only once, at a comparative tasting where a reasonably fair assessment, in a controlled context could be made. For example, the blind tastings at Boodle's in November 1978, and of the wine committee at Brooks's in December 1979 and January 1980.

Ch. de Barbe Bourg	*Lightish; high toned, fruity, not too clean on the nose; a too easy, sugared, early developer.* Tasted December 1979 *
Ch. Beychevelle St-Julien	*Fine deep colour; elegant, fruity; well made, good texture.* Tasted March 1980 ***(*) Drink 1984–1996.
Ch. Branaire-Ducru St-Julien	*Three notes. A sweet and chunky cask sample in May 1977. Developing well; curious open-knit earthy but attractive bouquet and taste. Very flavoury.* Last tasted March 1980 **(*) Drink 1981–1988.
Ch. Brane-Cantenac Margaux	*Very attractive colour, maturing quickly; open, fruity style; excellent classic shape, stylish, appeared forward but still hard.* At the Elsevier-Bouquet tasting of '76s, October 1979, March 1980 *(***)? Drink 1984–1994.
Ch. Camensac St-Laurent	*Seven notes. At the Elsevier-Bouquet '76 tasting: deepish; raw nose with noticeably high volatile acidity; iron flavour, firm, quite impressive but raw edge. Most recent: plummy; peppery high-toned aroma; straightforward but green and raw. Not good enough for a 5me cru classé.* At Brooks's, January 1980.
Ch. Cantemerle Macau	*A good '76: pretty colour; delicate fruit; slightly sweet, well-knit, with charm and good aftertaste.* Tasted March 1980 ***(*) Drink 1984–1994.

Ch. Les Carmes-Haut-Brion Graves	*Palish; quite nice, innocuous nose. An easy minor wine.* Tasted *January 1980* ** *Drink 1981–1985.*
Ch. Cissac Cissac	*Deep; fruity; a trifle overacid.* Tasted *January 1980* * *Drink 1983–1988.*
Clos de Clocher Pomerol	*Very appealing; sweet, harmonious; dry and tannic but good quality.* The dark horse at the Brooks's wine committee tasting, *January 1980* **(*) *Drink 1982–1988.*
Ch. Cos d'Estournel St-Estèphe	*Tasted in cask in April 1977: fruity, some elegance, notable acidity, clearly a quicker developer than the '75 tasted alongside Deepish colour; broad open bouquet which did not develop; dry overall, piquant, flavoury.* At Boodle's tasting, November 1978 **(*)? *Drink 1982–1990?*
Ch. Coufran St-Estèphe	*Deepish; fruity, high toned; a bit raw still.* Tasted December 1979 *(*) *Drink 1984–1992.*
Ch. La Courolle Montagne, St-Emilion	*A minor wine from the backwoods. Odd, not very reassuring nose though quite flavoury.* Tasted November 1978. *Drink 1982–1986.*
Ch. Ducru-Beaucaillou St-Julien	*Five notes. Impressive in cask in April 1977 and seemed to me more attractive and successful than the '75. Most recently showed distinct development: now a pretty plummy colour; nose elusive at first but distinct style and charm, opened up and sweetened a little in the glass, but firm foundation; a soft, fruity, charming wine. Should make a first-class bottle for mid-term drinking.* At the Decanter Magazine tasting, August 1979 ***(*) *Drink 1981–1988.*
Ch. Duhart-Milon-Rothschild Pauillac	*Stalky aroma but good flavour, nice finish.* Tasted November 1978 **(*) *Drink 1983–1988.*
Ch. Figeac St-Emilion	*Deep; good fruit; still hard, a bit short.* Tasted 1978, March 1980 *(**) *Drink 1983–1989.*
Ch. Fombrauge St-Emilion	*Medium, maturing; pleasant, bland, plausible nose; nicely put together, soft, loose limbed. Easy, short term.* Tasted January 1980 ** *Drink now — 1985.*
Ch. Gazin Pomerol	*Medium colour; forward: hard unyielding nose and flavour in 1978. Most recently: developing well, fragrant, forthcoming; good finish.* Last tasted March 1980 ***(*) *Drink 1982–1990.*
Ch. Giscours Margaux	*Deepest of the group; nose uptight, a bitter fragrance; some ripeness, firm, classic, leathery texture, very dry tannic finish.* Tasted October 1979 and at the M.W. tasting, March 1980 *(***) *Drink 1985–1995.*
Ch. Gloria St-Julien	*Two notes: rich, meaty nose but rather hard wooden flavour in November 1978. More recently, showed better, developing quite well.* Last tasted January 1980 **(*)? *Drink 1982–1987.*
Ch. Grand-Puy-Lacoste Pauillac	*Stalky, hard, immature but good. Should develop stylishly.* Tasted November 1978 **(*) *Drink 1983–1988.*
Ch. Les Grandes-Murailles St-Emilion	*Too pale, quick maturing, and rather feeble looking; easy chaptalized nose and flavour. Pleasant enough but little to it.* Tasted November 1978 * *Drink now — 1985.*
Ch. Gruaud-Larose St-Julien	*Deepish but developing; nose a bit stalky; very dry, fruity, flavoury but lacking fat and flesh. Should soften a little and make a flavoury drink.* Tasted November 1978, March 1980 **(*) *Drink 1983–1988.*

Ch. Haut-Batailley Pauillac	*Most attractive in cask in April 1977: fine colour; crisp* Cabernet *aroma; elegant, good fruit. Tannin noticeably as high as the '75. Recently: very deep, youthful colour; good, young fruit, still hard; distinctly dry and still severe but good balance and finish. Should turn into a well-formed, elegant wine.* Last tasted March 1980 ★★(★) Drink 1982–1990.
Dom. de L'Ile Margaux	*Rarely seen minor wine. Quite nice, light and fruity.* Tasted November 1978 ★★ For quick drinking.
Ch. Lafon-Rochet St-Estèphe	*A poor stalky bottle prior to a* Decanter Magazine *tasting. At a later comparative tasting, less deep in colour and more forward than Pontet-Canet, broader style, more open character.* Last tasted March 1980 ★★(★) Drink 1983–1989.
Ch. La Lagune Ludon	*Two notes: plum coloured; the usual plausible fruitiness — the wine maker must like Wagner and Tchaikovsky — undoubtedly attractive, but not for dedicated, hypercritical, fault-finding claret fanciers.* Last tasted November 1978 ★★★ Drink now — 1990.
Ch. Léoville-Barton St-Julien	*Fairly deep; some richness, delicacy and charm.* Tasted March 1980 ★★(★) Drink 1982–1988.
Ch. Léoville-Las-Cases St-Julien	*Four notes: more and more impressed with this château as the years go by. It should be good and it is quietly and consistently so. Elegant, showing real quality in cask, May 1977. Full flavoured and rich, at Boodle's, November 1978. Medium colour, rich, attractive; lovely fruit and character; touch of ripeness and sweetness on the palate, nice weight and balance. Not great but well made for mid-term drinking.* Last tasted March 1980 ★★★(★) Drink 1981–1988.
Ch. Lynch-Bages Pauillac	*Three notes. Cask sample May 1977: immature but with the pronounced blackcurrant* Cabernet-Sauvignon *aroma associated with this château. Next: peppery, attractive nose, but lacking a little fruit; chunky flavour and body at Boodle's, November 1978. More recently: losing colour (naturally, but quicker than in a big vintage), slightly plummy; rather bland, sweet, chaptalized nose; agreeable, reasonable fruit, tannic finish. Not a stayer but attractive before the bloom of youth (and sugar) wears off.* Last tasted March 1980 ★★ Drink 1981–1986.
Ch. Lynch-Moussas Pauillac	*Not much colour, weak rimmed; some fragrance but a lean and skinny wine.* Tasted January 1980 ★(★) Drink 1982–1987.
Ch. La Mission-Haut-Brion Talence, Graves	*Marvellous depth of fruit; positively sweet, rich, almost chewable. Fine finish.* Tasted March 1980 ★★★(★) Drink 1982–1992.
Ch. Montrose St-Estèphe	*Attractive cask sample in May 1977. Eighteen months later: fairly deep; fragrant, fruity aroma; fairly full bodied, soft, long flavour and good finish. Overall immature but an agreeable wine.* Last tasted March 1980 ★★(★★)? Drink 1985–1996.
Ch. Moulin des Carraudes	*An interesting development from the Domaine Société Civile de Lafite-Rothschild. Medium light in colour; nose a bit cold and undeveloped but stylish; nice body, some softness, very good flavour and finish. Stylish, at just over the price of a good bourgeois Médoc.* Tasted January 1980 ★★(★) Drink 1981–1987.
Ch. Moulinet Pomerol	*Medium light, youthful appearance, bright and attractive; light Pomerol style of nose, fruity, immature; dry, good body, firm, flavoury, very stylish.* Tasted January 1980 ★★(★) Drink 1982–1988.

Ch. Palmer Margaux	*Outstanding: most original and intriguing bouquet; crisp, fruity, spicy, excellent aftertaste.* Tasted March 1980 ★★★(★) Drink 1984–1998.
Ch. Pavie St-Emilion	*Medium, maturing; rather hard and ordinary nose; dry, short. Not a patch on the '75.* Tasted November 1978 ★(★) Drink 1981–1986.
Ch. de Pez St-Estèphe	*The deepest of the '76s at the Boodle's tasting. Good flavour but dumb and unyielding.* Tasted November 1978 ★(★)? Drink 1984 1990.
Ch. Phélan-Ségur St-Estèphe	*Palish; quite nice nose and flavour, some richness and fruit.* Tasted January 1980 ★★ Drink 1981–1985.
Ch. Pichon-Lalande Pauillac	*Three notes. May 1977 in cask: nice sweet nose but seemed a bit short. Next: maturing; fairly deep, rich bouquet; dry, a bit austere but good flavour. Richness, concentration, lovely aftertaste.* Last tasted March 1980 ★★(★★) Drink 1983–1993.
Ch. Pontet-Canet Pauillac	*Three notes: tasted in cask shortly after it had received a fining in April 1978. Alfred Tesseron, who is responsible for the wine making following the purchase of the property from the Cruse family in the early 1970s, told me that because of the very hot summer of 1976 there was a very small crop of Cabernet-Sauvignon. Tasted for a* Decanter Magazine *article with Harry Waugh and Edmund Penning-Rowsell in August 1979 and again at the Studley Priory wine weekend: deeper than expected, good colour, still immature; good, sweet fruit-bush aroma; dry, medium body, firm, crisp Pauillac style. Very dry finish. Good aftertaste.* Last tasted March 1980 ★★(★★) Drink 1982–1990.
Ch. Rausan-Ségla Margaux	*Palish and maturing fast; plausible, attractive nose; delicious.* Tasted March 1980 ★★★ Drink now — 1986.
Ch. Talbot St-Julien	*Deeper than Gruaud; piquant, spicy nose; very flavoury; dry finish.* Tasted March 1980 ★★(★) Drink 1984–1996.
Ch. La Tour-de-By Bégadan	*Deepish; uneven, woody nose and taste.* Tasted December 1979.
Ch. La Tour-Carnet St-Laurent	*Light style, pink tinged; little bouquet; touch of overacidity, but elegant, lively flavour with good aftertaste. But so it should have: it is, as one so often needs reminding, a 4me cru classé.* At the Elsevier-Bouquet tasting, October 1979 ★★(★)
Ch. La Tour-Haut-Caussen Blaignon, St-Estèphe	*Hard, stalky, not bad but minor and uninteresting.* Tasted December 1979 ★
Ch. La Tour-Haut-Moulin Cissac	*Deepish; dumb; nice texture, tannic, good enough.* Tasted December 1979 ★(★) Drink 1983–1988.
Ch. La Tour-du-Mirail Cissac	*Deep; some richness, agreeable, but not too good a finish.* Tasted December 1979 ★
Ch. La Tour-St-Bonnet St-Christoly	*Eliminated: high volatile acidity (vinegary — nothing to be done with it, except for salad dressing).* Tasted December 1979.
Ch. Tronquoy-Lalande St-Estèphe	*Deepish purple; dumb, peppery, good fruit under; touch of sweetness and richness, good fruit and alcohol. Nice wine after all the oh-so-boring "La Tours".* Tasted January 1980 ★★(★) Drink 1981–1987.
Ch. Verdignan St-Estèphe	*Three notes. Extremely attractive in cask, also in January 1979. And showing well at Brooks's tasting: shedding depth of colour but still youthful; pretty bouquet, nice fruit; dry, lightish, good texture and finish. Consistently good inexpensive claret.* Last tasted December 1970 ★★(★) in its class. Drink 1981–1985.

Vieux Ch. Certan Pomerol	*Tasted in cask in April 1978. Agreeable, for bottling early. Then at a pre-sale tasting in Amsterdam: lightish but lovely colour; a bit dry and lean.* Last tasted June 1979 *(**) Drink 1983–1993.

1977 *

One of the least inspiring vintages of the decade. Too early to tell exactly how it will develop but likely to be thin and short lived. Climate: almost the entire reverse of 1976. Some disastrous frosts in the spring; late flowering; June cold and wet; unusually high rainfall in July; first half of August hot and dry, the remainder cool and damp. Then, as in 1976, a complete change round, this time for the better: the driest September since 1851 with sunshine through to a short, latish harvest starting on 4 October, under almost ideal weather conditions. (In St-Emilion the start was later — 10 October.) In short, one of the most dismal summers in memory was just saved by a glorious prolonged autumn. The crop varied in the different districts but was moderate-sized, overall, the late summer sunshine producing beautiful well-coloured grapes, almost a deep blue, but not very sweet and a little acidic. Market: as ever, complicated. Despite a serious attempt by the authorities, leading shippers and growers to regulate the market, the plain fact is that the traditional *négociants*, who used to carry big buffer stocks, have never really recovered from the 1974/75 collapse. In any case those who did survive have the hurdle of high interest rates to cope with. Consequently, stocks congregated either at the château or, in an unregulated way, elsewhere in third-party hands. Because of the demand for '75s and '76s, and because the '77 vintage was relatively small, the price, just after that vintage, was something like 70 per cent higher than that prevailing in November 1976. The quality did not warrant it. Assessment: this is not considered an exciting vintage, either from the point of view of the drinker or commercially — except that some wines could turn out to be reasonably interesting and good value. Tasting notes: at the time of writing, few '77s are in bottle, and I have neither made a systematic tasting of the wines in cask nor been exposed to many at trade tastings of samples in London. In regard to my not infrequent visits to Bordeaux, I should point out that I spend most of my time underground assessing old wines rather than dipping my nose into casks of young vintages in *chais* — this is the job of the broker and merchant. I have tasted none of the first growths; and of the few dozen other growths, I noticed most were deep coloured and very purple. From two shippers' selections shown in London, by de Luze and Kressmann, I particularly noted the following:

Ch. Léoville-Las-Cases St-Julien	*At the de Luze tasting in May 1978 this was impressive and flavoury. And at the Kressmann presentation at the Café Royal in June 1979 it was head and shoulders above the other '77s: a surprisingly good colour, with a ripeness and amount of fruit noticeably lacking in most of the others on show.* Last tasted June 1979 **(*) Good short- to mid-term potential, say 1984–1989.
Ch. Ducru-Beaucaillou St-Julien	*First tasted in cask at the château in April 1978. Jean-Eugène Borie, one of the most highly respected proprietors in Bordeaux, told me his total production in 1977 was 75 per cent of his average, and, after grading every cask, he set aside only 50 per cent to sell under the Ducru label. M. Borie reckoned that this selected wine was better than his '73 and '74. At the de Luze tasting a month later I thought it was a pleasant, lightish in style (though deep coloured) fruity wine, chunky, with some richness and a dry finish.* Last tasted May 1978 **(*)? Drink 1984–1989.

Also showing well at the de Luze tasting:

Ch. Cantenac-Brown Margaux	*Deep purple; rich nose; a chunky, flavoury wine as usual, with tannin and acidity.* Tasted May 1978 (***)

Ch. Gazin Pomerol	*Deepish; a bit low keyed, but it often is when young.* Tasted May 1978 *(*)
Ch. La Lagune Ludon	*Much the least satisfactory of recent vintages tasted: skinny, stalky, lacking its usual fruit, fat and fun.* Tasted June 1979.
Ch. Lynch-Bages Pauillac	*Deep purple; fruity, immature; dry, piquant, flavoury, a bit raw.* Tasted May 1978.
Ch. Malescot-St-Exupéry Margaux	*Palish; unknit stalky nose; dry, skinny.* Tasted June 1979.
Ch. La Mission-Haut-Brion Talence, Graves	*Fairly deep purple; vinous but stalky; fruit and flavour.* Tasted in cask, September 1978.
Ch. Paveil-de-Luze Soussans	*Attractive* Cabernet *aroma; easy fruity flavour. A wine with immediate appeal for fairly quick drinking.* Tasted May 1978 *(*)
Ch. Pichon-Lalande Pauillac	*Good fruit, agreeably balanced, quick maturing.* Tasted May 1978 Possibly *(**)
Ch. La Tour-Haut-Brion Graves	*Assertive as ever, but raw.* Cask sample, May 1978.
Ch. La Tour-Léognan Graves	*Medium deep, youthful purple; an unusual aroma, fruit; soft, vinous, with pleasant character.* Tasted May 1978 *(*)

Postscript to 1977. These are early days. Let the *négociants* make their selections and the merchants choose the best and, hopefully, after all this sifting, the public will be left with *la crème de la crème*, or at least the best of the skimmed milk.

1978 ★★★(★)

A good vintage, but it only just made it. What Harry Waugh describes as "the year of the miracle", with wines intriguing enough to satisfy the most critical claret lovers. Climate: late spring; lengthy uneven flowering; dismal summer. Up until mid-August almost everything that could go wrong did go wrong. But as in 1977, a sudden burst of sun and heat which, miraculously, kept up right through to a late vintage — heat permanent but not excessive, tempered by Atlantic breezes and summer-rain-moistened soil. The vines were surprisingly healthy and the vintage, around 9 October, went without a hitch. The quantity was variable from district to district. Médoc average, Pomerol small. Market: in the spring of 1979 a report in *Wine & Spirit*, England's leading wine trade monthly, suggested that the '78 vintage was "a good one with the attractive qualities and [I would have written "but"] none of the irksome characteristics of a long-lasting year". In other words all the pundits and classicists love a *grande année*, but few these days can afford to tie up their capital, with interest rates as high as they currently are, for the length of time needed to nurse the wines through to maturity. 1978 seems to be the instant classic. An appealing sort of wine, buyable and sellable. Assessment: it is too early to tell, though it does seem that we have here an attractive vintage, one to have in the cellar for characterful mid-term drinking. Tasting notes: I was, in fact, staying at Château La Mission-Haut-Brion as the guest of Francis and Françoise Dewavrin-Woltner (Françoise is the daughter of the late Fernand Woltner, the genius behind the remarkable postwar development of La Mission) just before picking began. The vines looked magnificently healthy and I just felt in my bones that a good vintage would emerge. I tasted a few of the '78s in cask during a brief visit to Bordeaux in April 1979 — I was there mainly to pack up Mme Teysonneau's outstanding cellar of old wines (sold at Christie's the following September). Also a small range was noted at the Kressmann tasting in London in June, but the most interesting tasting took place in January 1980. It was a selection of thirty '78s offered by Harvey's *en primeur*, ranging from minor Côtes de Blaye to first-growths. I have since tasted two further ranges, from minor to classed-growth quality, but they were austere and not showing well. Time will tell.

Ch. Latour Pauillac	*At the Harvey* en primeur *tasting, very much what one would expect from a youthful Latour of this class of vintage: opaque; dumb, that is to say closed up, with some pretty concentrated* Cabernet *underneath, peppery — a combination of high alcoholic content and immature component parts like vital tannin and acidity (all this on the nose); medium dry, a touch of sweetness on entry, intense, concentrated, with dry tannic finish. Quite unready as a drink but all the signals set for a good future mouthful.* Tasted January 1980 (★★★★) Drink 1987–2000 plus.
Ch. Margaux Margaux	*A* Merlot *ensemble tasted in cask in March 1979: deep; soft, supple; good length. Promising. At the Harvey tasting: intense purple colour; good nose; a sweet ripe feel in the mouth, fragrant, peppery finish, good aftertaste. Should be a charmer.* Last tasted January 1980 (★★★★) Drink 1986–2000.
Ch. Haut-Brion Pessac, Graves	*Deep but far less intense than Margaux, noticeably rich, judging by the "legs"; much more forthcoming on the nose, which was pleasant, relaxed, slightly vanilla (or oak as our American friends would say); slightly sweet, immediately agreeable, gentle, elegant. Totally different in style from the firm, comparatively steely Médocs. But do not be misled: these fine Graves, often precociously attractive in their youth, retain their good looks long after some of the hard-faced Médocs have developed wrinkles.* At the Harvey tasting, January 1980 (★★★★) Drink 1984–2000.

No other first growths tasted yet, neither Lafite nor Mouton being available for the Harvey *en primeur* tasting. The following list is necessarily sparse and incomplete, but I feel I should list those wines which appeared noticeably good at the Kressmann tasting of cask samples in 1979, at the Harvey tasting and at Brooks's:

Ch. Canon St-Emilion	*Glad to see this at the Harvey tasting. Surely one of the best and most reliable St-Emilions, too little known outside France. An impressive colour; fragrant, and what Harry Waugh would, I think, describe as cheesy; a lovely wine, firm, well constituted. Dry finish.* Tasted January 1980 (★★★★) Drink 1983–1995.
Ch. Chasse-Spleen Moulis	*With La Tour-de-Mons, this has been one of the most consistent top bourgeois clarets. Seems exceptionally so, almost classed-growth standard, in '78: intense colour, purple to the edge of the meniscus; very impressive nose; excellent on the palate, concentrated, tough and dry. Likely to be a slow developer, but do not keep it too long as this class of wine rarely, if ever, develops the nuances and complexity that age confers on the great growths.* Tasted January 1980 (★★★) Drink 1985–1995.
Ch. Cos d'Estournel St-Estèphe	*A winner: intense purple rim; crisp fruit-bush aroma, reminded me of ripe raspberries; very attractive flavour, an innate softness, fleshy, good length and aftertaste. One of the best Cos's for years.* Tasted January 1980 (★★★★) Drink 1988–2000.
Ch. Ducru-Beaucaillou St-Julien	*Very deep and showing wonderful richness and class in June 1979. Still deep; a sweet, rich, gentle, nicely developing nose; flavour to match. A very straightforward wine, with toughness to ensure a good future. Though a great admirer of Ducru, I think that the Las-Cases had the edge.* Tasted January 1980 (★★★★) Drink 1986–2000.
Ch. Haut-Batailley Pauillac	*A pleasant young wine at the Kressmann tasting; fruit but a bit stalky on the nose; a sweet and easy wine but lacking length? Nice though.* Last tasted January 1980 (★★★)? Drink 1984–1994.

Ch. La Lagune Ludon	*Back to form in 1978, showing its customary deep, rich, sweet, chunky, open-knit, fruity style at the Kressmann tasting.* June 1979 (★★★) *Drink 1984–1995.*
Ch. Léoville-Las-Cases St-Julien	*Very impressive at the Kressmann tasting, June 1979, even more so with the benefit of further ageing at Harvey's in January 1980: fine, deep purple; most pronounced aroma, a real bouquet in the bunch of flowers sense, but still peppery; flavour to match. More intense than Ducru. Excellent aftertaste. Consistently and deservedly amongst the top second growths — and under half the price of the firsts. Most recently: as above but tough and with a good long finish.* Last tasted at Brooks's, January 1980 (★★★★) *Drink 1986–2000.*
Ch. Montrose St-Estèphe	*Cos and Montrose seem to have reversed their roles, their style and weight in 1978 — judging by their appearance alongside each other at the Harvey tasting. Not as deep as expected but a very pleasant colour; surprisingly open nose, soft and sweet, some oak — usually Montrose is noticeably closed up when young; very flavoury but not yet all of a piece, hot, dry end tannin and acidity. Unless I have misread the signals, should develop far quicker than the customary tough, long-distance classic.* Tasted January 1980 (★★★) ? *Drink 1985–2000.*
Ch. Nenin Pomerol	*A very relaxed and fairly reliable sort of wine. I had a greater regard for it, and Pavie, in the early 1950s. Showed nicely at the Harvey tasting: medium colour, pleasantly shaded; an open, fragrant nose; nice sweetness and agreeable balance. Good, never great.* Tasted January 1980 (★★★) *Drink 1982–1990.*
Ch. Palmer Margaux	*Attractively deep coloured but not crisply opaque, somehow broad, rich and plummy; the nose undeveloped but with an innate opulence, expansive, mulberry rich; on the palate beautifully rounded, well assembled, good grip. Seems to have an uncanny desire to be a '61 without the latter's intensity and concentration.* Tasted January 1980 (★★★★) *Drink 1984–2000.*
Other pleasant '78s:	*Ch. d'Angludet; Ch. Batailley; Ch. Brane-Cantenac; Ch. Fombrauge; Ch. Moulinet; Ch. Patâche d'Aux.*

1979

Better than expected but too early to rate. An enormous crop, the biggest in Bordeaux since 1934. Climate: a prolonged and extremely wet winter merged into a very damp and dismal spring. Good conditions in June for a highly satisfactory flowering. July dry but not hot, August dry but unusually cold, September little better. The result: a huge crop of small, healthy, but not fully swelled and ripened grapes. Because the ratio of skin to grape flesh is high, the colour of the wine is very deep. Tasting notes: a range of nearly thirty '79s tasted with Harry Waugh at the French Wine Farmers' offices in London in April 1980 revealed a consistently impressive depth of colour and a fair amount of fruit. Clearly a useful, prolific and, hopefully, reasonably priced vintage. Of the bourgeois Médocs I liked Cissac, Maucaillou and Les Ormes-de-Pez; of the classed growths I gave high marks to Châteaux Beychevelle, Ducru-Beaucaillou, Grand-Puy-Lacoste, Pichon-Lalande, Léoville-Las-Cases and, across the river, Châteaux L'Angélus and Trotanoy. A vintage to watch.

WHITE
BORDEAUX

White Bordeaux is not just Sauternes. Strictly speaking it embraces every dry, medium or sweet white wine made in the Gironde department and entitled to the appropriate appellation. For the purposes of this book, however, which is concerned with the good, the classic and the *crème de la crème*, the title embraces mainly the two districts of Graves and Sauternes.

Stretching from the suburbs of Bordeaux, the Graves district produces both red and white wine. Historically it is really the cradle of fine claret, for the Médoc was hardly planted in the days when Pepys's "O-Bryan" (Haut-Brion) was the most highly regarded *premier cru* in London. White Graves vary from almost bone dry to medium dry. The best keep well; the very best need bottle-age — the longer the better. The style depends on the balance of *Semillon* and *Sauvignon-Blanc*. The former, more yellow, soft and buttery (always reminds me of lanolin) on the nose and broader on the palate, gives it its main Graves character; the *Sauvignon-Blanc*, a crisper, fruitier, more acidic grape, gives it its refreshing quality. I probably stand alone in deploring the overuse of this grape and the smart modern wine making which is turning so many Bordeaux whites into pale imitations of Sancerre, but perhaps they *are* an improvement on the carelessly made, flabby and over-sulphured Graves and near-Graves of the past.

Sauternes usually begins life with a deeper yellow colour than any other white wine except for the great dessert wines of Germany. This is probably due to a combination of high sugar content and general richness, but the main tincture must stem from the colouring matter extracted from the sun-tanned skins.

Sauternes is distinctly sweet and rich on the nose and, in a good year, the honey tones indicative of a high sugar content and the overripeness due to *pourriture* are immediately apparent. This gets deeper, richer and more harmonious with age, developing what I always recognize as a crème-brûlée character.

On the palate, Sauternes is always sweet, from the medium sweet of a Barsac of a lighter year, to the intense sweetness of Yquem of a great vintage. Cassagnac suggested there was sweetness in the soil, "for all its produce is impregnated with it; peas, asparagus and even lentils: fruits too; greengages, peaches and strawberries have a matchless sweetness". Sauternes is also rich, developing a soft lusciousness with age, but with counterbalancing acidity to prevent it from cloying.

The lesser quality Sauternes have a lighter colour, often almost green tinged when young, and are rather grass-like on the nose, refreshing, perhaps, but not rich — no signs of honeyed noble rot. They are medium sweet, lightish in style and lack finish.

The finest quality Sauternes, particularly when mature, develop a depth and beauty of colour, bright amber shot with gold, and have

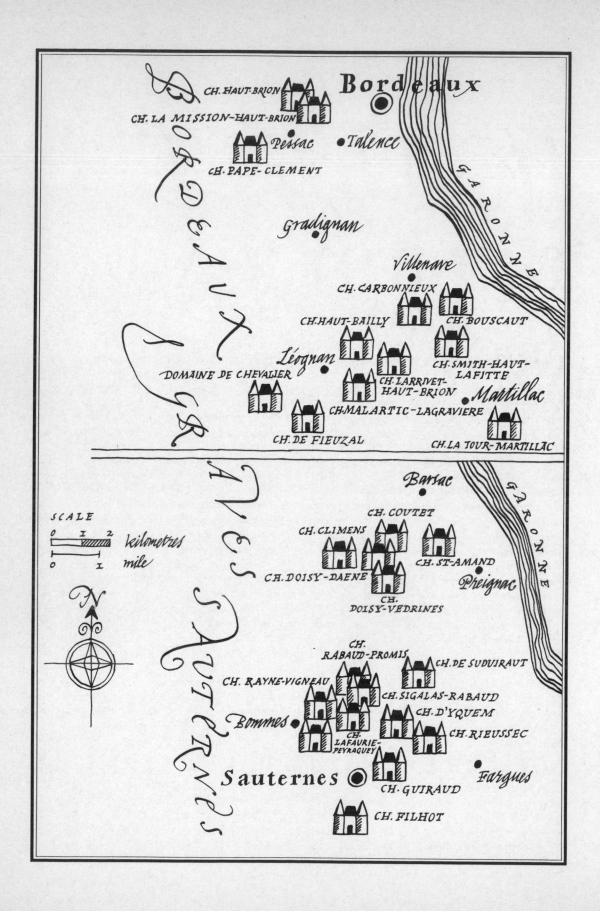

CH. HAUT-BRION
CH. LA MISSION-HAUT-BRION
Bordeaux
Pessac • Talence
CH. PAPE-CLEMENT

BORDEAUX

Gradignan

GARONNE

Villenave
CH. CARBONNIEUX
CH. HAUT-BAILLY
CH. BOUSCAUT
Léognan
DOMAINE DE CHEVALIER
CH. SMITH-HAUT-LAFITTE
CH. LARRIVET-HAUT-BRION
Martillac
CH. MALARTIC-LAGRAVIERE
CH. DE FIEUZAL
CH. LA TOUR-MARTILLAC

GRAVES

Barsac
GARONNE
CH. COUTET
CH. CLIMENS
CH. ST-AMAND
CH. DOISY-DAENE
Preignac
CH. DOISY-VEDRINES

SCALE
0   1   2 kilometres
0   1 mile

N

SAUTERNES

CH. RABAUD-PROMIS
CH. DE SUDUIRAUT
CH. RAYNE-VIGNEAU
CH. SIGALAS-RABAUD
CH. D'YQUEM
Bommes •
CH. RIEUSSEC
CH. LAFAURIE-PEYRAGUEY
Sauternes ◉
Fargues
CH. GUIRAUD
CH. FILHOT

a radiant intensity of bouquet, complex but complete, rich and honeyed, with flavour to match. With age, the sweetness fades — sometimes drying out almost completely — leaving a gentle richness and long, lingering flavour which can be delightful unless the acidity has taken over.

Of the non-fortified wines, Sauternes is one of the longest keeping. Traditionally the best châteaux have always used long corks and these seem to survive longer than other old wine corks. I can only assume that the natural "fat" of Sauternes keeps the cork moist and oiled. Rarely have I found old Sauternes recorked; rarely have they needed recorking. The best will outlive us all.

The notes have been culled from my white Bordeaux index, which contains tasting notes on some 87 châteaux and 78 different vintages over a period of 26 years. The extracts are therefore highly selective and I have aimed at the best and more recent examples. If Yquem appears rather repetitively as the sole example of older vintages, this is simply because, like Lafite, it is the wine that has the greatest staying power and happens to be most frequently found in the residue of great private cellars.

1777

The first appearance of *Vin de Graves* in a Christie's catalogue. Barsac made its saleroom début in 1787, Prignac [*sic*] in 1788 but *Vin de Sauterne* [*sic*] not until 1808.

1784

Thomas Jefferson wrote in 1787 to M. Diquem [*sic*], "I know that yours is of the best crus of Sauterne. . . . Permit me then Sir, to ask if you have some of the first quality of the year 1784." He received a positive response from the Comte de Lur-Saluces, M. d'Yquem's son-in-law and "the owner of all his assets". Jefferson, then American ambassador to France, reported that the wine "turns out very fine".

1811 ★★★★★

"Very Fine Sauterne" of this, the "Comet" vintage, sold at Christie's in June 1837.

1819 ★★★

Barton & Guestier's "*vin de Sauterne*, red seal" of this vintage sold in 1827.

1822 ★★

First *vintage* of Barsac to appear at Christie's (in 1829).

1825 ★★★★

A good Sauternes vintage, sold at Christie's in March 1840.

1847 ★★★★★

A vintage that heralded the début of a great era of Sauternes. The Russian Tsar paid a phenomenal sum to Lur-Saluces for his 1847 Yquem. "Ch. Yquem" sold for 120s. (£6) a dozen at Christie's in May 1867, and in several subsequent sales.

1848 ★★★★

1851 ★★★

Ch. Yquem of this vintage first appeared in the saleroom in May 1867.

1858 ★★★★

The start of the two "golden" pre-phylloxera decades. "Ch. Guiraud bottled in France" fetched 80s. (£4) per dozen, the highest price in a 1,306 lot sale of fine wines at Christie's in March 1870. "Ch. Yquem, *Vin de Goute*, Vintage 1858" sold March 1886.

1864 ★★★★

1865 ★★★★

1867 ★★

A moderately good pre-phylloxera vintage, better for white than red.
Ch. d'Yquem. Bottles with levels varying from mid-shoulder to three-quarters full. Very deep old amber (the three-quarters-full bottle was a worryingly brown amber), clearly maderized but alive; amazingly rich bouquet — deep, caramelly but clean; still retaining some sweetness, with rich, meaty flavour, lovely acidity, firm and surprisingly sound.
From the cellars of Elmore Court, Gloucestershire. Tasted four times, 1970 — June 1972 ★★

1868 ★

Not a particularly notable vintage in Bordeaux. Again probably better for white.
Ch. d'Yquem. No ullage. Orange-amber colour, not too deep, remarkable for its age; gentle, rich, classic old Sauternes bouquet, good rich bottle-age; dried out, hardly any sweetness remaining, nice flavour, but spoilt by slight bitterness and tingling end acidity.
Tasted June 1971 ★
Ch. Coutet. Imported by Pfungst & Co., and cellared in Oxfordshire from around mid-1870s. Good levels. Excellent, medium, warm amber colour; very fragrant, crème-brûlée bouquet — perfection, held well; still surprisingly sweet, excellent full flavour, touch of end acidity, but marvellous flavour and condition.
From the cellars of Sir John Thomson. Tasted twice, 1977 ★★★★

1869 ★★★

A very good vintage.
Ch. d'Yquem. Very full, pure deep amber colour, like an oloroso, with lemon rim, very bright; pure, clean, full crème-brûlée bouquet, very sound; medium dry, fairly

full and very rich. Perfect condition and balance, lovely acidity, clean, dry finish.
At the Coq Hardy, Bougival, a century after the wine was made. November 1969 ★★★★★

1874 ★★★★

A great pre-phylloxera vintage.
Ch. d'Yquem. Colour ranging from warm old gold to brown amber depending on ullage and oxidation; bouquet also varied from rich, lovely, honeyed bottle-age to distinct mushrooms and caramel; all medium sweet, fairly full bodied and better flavour than nose. The best had a lovely old flavour and dry meaty end.
Tasted 1972 — September 1975 ★ *to* ★★★

1875 ★★★★

Noted for delicacy and elegance.
Ch. d'Yquem. Bottled by Brandenburg Frères, Bordeaux. Loose cork, level low shoulder. Very deep brown like California syrup of figs; bouquet surprisingly good, crème brûlée (accent on brûlée), but rich and deep; still sweet, thick, rich, concentrated, good acidity.
At the Heublein tasting, May 1978 ★★

1878 ★★★★

The last of the relatively phylloxera-free vintages.
Ch. Filhot. Not too deep but very brown and unhealthy; old and oxidized nose; dried out, faded and thin, with acid end taste. Disappointing bottle.
Tasted May 1971.

1884 ★

The best vintage of a dismal period (1879–1886).
Ch. de Rayne-Vigneau. Château bottled. Lovely bright deep amber; very sound, gentle bouquet; medium sweet, lovely flavour but slightly short.
From an old Paris cellar, May 1976 ★★

1887 ★★

1888 ★★

Light wines produced, as in 1887, in continuing difficulties, both climatical and commercial.
Ch. d'Yquem. Medium-deep amber, very old maderized appearance; a bouquet of old *Semillon*, golden botrytis and bottle-age; drying out, medium light, high acidity — rather harsh and austere.
Tasted February 1977.

1890 ★★

A moderate vintage.
Ch. d'Yquem. Medium-deep yellow gold, pale for age; soft, rich lanolin, very fine and sound bouquet; medium sweet, soft, lovely wine, good aftertaste. Holding well.
Tasted 1971, April and June 1975 ★★★★

1892 ★★

Not a particularly notable vintage.
Ch. d'Yquem. Very bright, deepish yellow; bouquet rich, but slightly rubbery; medium, drying out though flavoury and tangy. Dry finish. Not as good a bouquet as 1890 and a little thin on flavour.
From the cellars of Château de la Fot, April and June 1975 ★

1893 ★★

A bakingly hot summer.

1894 and 1895

Undistinguished.

1896 ★

Ch. Filhot. Bright yellow-amber gold; rich, deep but some decay and old sulphur; drying out, some richness, fading but interesting.
Tasted April and June 1975 ★
Ch. Sigalas-Rabaud. Good level. Fine amber-gold; very rich honeyed-lanolin bouquet; medium sweet, medium body, rich, tangy wine, dry finish.
Both from Château de la Fot in the Creuse, April 1975 ★★★

1897 and 1898

Undistinguished.

1899 ★★★

One of the most famous twin vintages of Bordeaux.
Ch. d'Yquem. Deep coloured; old but sound nose; drying out. Touch of overmaderization, tired, lacking acidity. Old but interesting.
Tasted April 1973 ★

1900 ★★★★★

The best and sturdiest of the twins. A great classic.
Ch. d'Yquem. Fine, bright, warm amber colour; very good sound bouquet; still sweet, soft, attractive and in lovely condition.
Tasted November 1972 (two ullaged bottles tasted since have been deeper, duller and not in the same class, though interesting and drinkable). At best ★★★★

1901–1903

Not very good and rarely seen.

1904 ★★★★

A great vintage.
Ch. Coutet. I bought this at the Restaurant Darroze cellar sale. Despite a crumbly cork the level was good and the colour a marvellously warm, bright old gold (I had decanted it); perfect bouquet, fragrant, intense; drying out a little but rich, lovely flavour, perfect condition, excellent finish.
At a Bordeaux Club dinner at Christie's, December 1979 ★★★★★
Ch. de Rayne-Vigneau. Lovely old gold with amber-green rim; beautiful old crème-brûlée bouquet; medium sweet, very rich burnt toffee flavour, high acidity masked by richness.
Tasted May 1976 ★★★★

1905

Not very good and rarely seen.

1906 ★★★

Ch. Lafaurie-Peyraguey. This was the oldest of a remarkable range from the château: deep, very fine colour; very rich, fabulous bouquet; medium sweet, with powerful flavour and lovely finish.
At the pre-sale tasting, September 1976 ★★★★
Ch. Pontac. Originally imported by Morton & Co., a New York wine merchant and supplied, prior to World War I, to a San Francisco gentleman. A half-bottle:

despite very slight ullage, a very good amber colour; gently maderized but good; medium sweet, lightish, butterscotch flavour, nice acidity.
After lunch at Joe Heitz's in the Napa Valley, May 1979 ★★

1909 ★★

Ch. Lafaurie-Peyraguey. Medium-deep old gold with green rim; deep, very rich bouquet; medium sweet, rich, lovely acidity. Beautiful wine.
At the pre-sale tasting at Christie's, September 1976 ★★★★

1913 ★★

Ch. Lafaurie-Peyraguey. Medium amber gold, green rim; very, very rich, lovely bouquet; medium sweet, lovely flavour, lighter and more zest than 1914.
At the pre-sale tasting at Christie's, September 1976 ★★★

1914 ★★★

Some authorities give this vintage only 4/10 but I believe this is not borne out by results. Picking began early, for Sauternes, on 20 September. Now, of course, rare.
Ch. d'Yquem. Fine gold colour; excellent bouquet, rich honeyed bottle-age; drying out a little but very fine rich flavour and finish.
Tasted 1969, June and July 1973 ★★★★
Ch. de Rayne-Vigneau. Fine, bright; rich, sound; medium sweet, fine condition.
Tasted May 1975 ★★★
Ch. Lafaurie-Peyraguey. Fabulous topaz colour; beautiful nose; medium sweet — sugar still retained. Medium-light body, excellent flavour.
At the pre-sale tasting, September 1976 ★★★★

1915 ★★

Quite good but rarely seen. Drying out now.
Ch. Lafaurie-Peyraguey. Unbranded corks, probably Bordeaux bottled. Yellow gold; variable; drying out, one nice, the other austere and dull. Half-bottles.
Tasted May and June 1976 ★

1916 ★★★

A good, rather tough vintage. Rarely seen.

1917 ★★★

Softer and riper from the outset. Not a long laster.
Ch. Lafaurie-Peyraguey. A fairly deep old amber — not too lively or healthy; smell of old leaves; drying out, dusty, slight bitterness. Short.
At the pre-sale tasting, September 1976.

1918 ★★

Moderately good. Firmer than the 1917.
Ch. d'Arche. Bordeaux bottled. Fine lemon gold, pale for age; bouquet variable — sometimes old and smoky, at best like old Graves; medium sweet, better flavour than nose. At best pleasant and holding well.
Six notes, January — March 1974 ★★

1919 ★

Not very successful. Picking began 20 September (Y 15.9°) †*See footnote.*
Cru Haut-Peyraguey. Colour deepish; nose caramelized but sound; palate drying out, old, a bit severe and

charmless but clean and interesting.
Tasted June 1973.

1920 ★★★

A good vintage. Picking began 15 September.
Ch. d'Yquem (16°). Fine bright colour; feeling of quality but going downhill rapidly.
Tasted August 1955 ★
Ch. Coutet. Deepish old amber; excellent though slightly maderized and drying out a little.
Tasted October 1974 ★★★
Ch. Lafaurie-Peyraguey. Deepish amber gold; very sweet, honeyed bouquet; still very sweet, fat and magnificent though easing off towards finish.
At the château with pâté de foie gras in April and at the pre-sale tasting, September 1976 ★★★★
Ch. Palmer Margaux. Blanc. Château bottled. Very rare. Very slight ullage. Old-gold colour, good for age; slightly maderized but richness underneath; dry, rather dull and a little tart but one for the collection. (I can see why they now only make red.)
Tasted April 1976 ★

1921 ★★★★★

An exceptionally hot summer. Picking began 14 September in great heat. Great for white wines everywhere.
Ch. d'Yquem (19.9°). In my experience, Sauternes with high sugar and extract (exceptional richness) have a depth of colour that to the half-knowledgeable would indicate "finished, maderized". Yquem '21 is a case in point. I have drunk this wine on seven occasions since 1967, in London, Paris, New York and Sydney. It is undoubtedly a great, highly concentrated wine. Very deep amber gold, with slight variations — if too brown or too orange tinted, not likely to be at best; intense, fragrant, honeyed crème brûlée — in concentration the nearest bouquet to tokay essence; sweet, full bodied, exceptionally rich and concentrated, powerful yet soft and ripe, excellent acidity, long lingering finish. Surely the greatest?
Last tasted October 1978 ★★★★★ *Drink now — 2000.*
Ch. Coutet. Deep amber gold, green-amber rim; very rich, excellent bouquet; only medium sweet now but rich, lovely flavour and length.
Tasted March 1973 ★★★★★ *Drink now — 1990.*
Ch. Lafaurie-Peyraguey. Medium-deep amber green; drying out on bouquet and palate, yet lovely old flavour, somehow beyond ripeness, excellent end acidity.
At the pre-sale tasting, November 1968 ★★★★ *Drink now.*
Ch. Guiraud. Old gold and lemon; unexciting, soft madeira-like nose; better on palate. Nice flavour. Holding well.
Tasted June 1969 ★★ *Drink now — 1985.*
Ch. de Rayne-Vigneau. Very fine colour; slow to unfold but developed gentle, rich, honeyed bouquet; drying out a little but powerful, rich yet austere. One with soft cork, deeper colour and yeasty aftertaste.
Tasted November 1976. At best ★★★★
Ch. Suduiraut. Fine old gold; excellent, rich bouquet; medium sweet, very rich, fine flavour, dry finish.
Tasted May 1975 ★★★★ *Drink now — 1990.*
Ch. Climens. Good but somehow lacking '21 richness and follow through.
Tasted September 1977 ★★★

---

† *From records at Yquem: alcoholic degree plus sugar content. These figures give some indication of the relative quality and richness of each vintage. The figure follows Yquem in the text or, if no note on Yquem, in brackets in the introductory paragraph.*

Ch. Blanchon. A minor wine that I had never come across before. It was delightful: lemon gold, pale for its age; lovely almost pungently fragrant bouquet; still sweet, soft, delicate, with a lively finish.
From Maxim's, Paris, at a Heublein tasting, May 1978 ★★★

1922 ★

An abundant vintage but considered light, flat and lacking quality. Picking began 12 September.
Ch. d'Yquem (16.8°). Looking and smelling a bit tired. Not quite right. Drying out, lightish but holding quite well. Interesting but not a great wine.
Tasted February 1971 ★
Ch. de Rayne-Vigneau. Pale for age; good sound nose and flavour, gentle, balanced.
Tasted November 1971 ★★
Ch. Lafaurie-Peyraguey. Amber; low-keyed but sound bouquet; medium sweet, light, nice but short.
Tasted September 1976 ★★

1923 ★★

Quite good. Picking began 27 September. Holding reasonably well.
Ch. d'Yquem (16.5°). Deepish amber; good broad lanolin bouquet; drying out though nice firm flavour and crisp end acidity.
Tasted November 1977 ★★★
Ch. Coutet. Old gold; gentle — rather like an old Vouvray — developed richly in glass; drying out but rich and fine. Nice acidity. Holding well.
Tasted August 1971 ★★★

1924 ★★★

A ripe attractive vintage. Picking began 16 September.
Ch. d'Yquem (17°). Old gold, orange tinge; fragrant, fruity, crème brûlée; medium sweet, verging on over-ripe. Lush.
Tasted June 1977 ★★★ Drink up.
Ch. St-Amand. A curiosity from the Preignac district which flowed through the saleroom in the early 1970s. Extremely nice when first tasted in May 1974, in fact lovely colour, pale for age; deep, sound, mellow bouquet; still sweet and firm. But a batch (with worn labels and incorrectly thought to be 1926) bought for a wine weekend turned out to be variable: levels, brightness and sweetness. Bouquet best; flavour good but short.
At Studley Priory, November 1979. At best ★★ Drink up.
Ch. Lafaurie-Peyraguey. Cork soft and crumbly. Full golden colour; terrible bottle stink lasted two hours; fat, succulent, magnificent flavour, spoilt by cork.
Tasted February 1955 ★★★★
Ch. La Tour-Blanche. Nutty, drying out. Interesting.
Tasted October 1970 ★
Ch. Guiraud. Variable in colour. One woody, oily and slightly tart. Another sweet, maderized but attractive.
Tasted from half-bottles, June 1976. At best ★★
Ch. Climens. Loose cork but lovely colour and bouquet; quite sweet though marked end acidity.
Tasted April 1977 ★
Ch. Filhot. Good level. Medium amber gold; rich, sound, crème brûlée bouquet; medium sweet — drying out, medium body, very rich flavour, excellent condition and dry finish.
Dinner at Thornbury Castle, July 1979 ★★★

1925 ★★

Quite good. Picking began 27 September. Variable now.
Ch. d'Yquem (15.8°). Deep amber; old nose; dried out but powerful. Long finish. Turned bitter in glass.
Tasted February 1968.
Ch. Lafaurie-Peyraguey. 1925 happens to be the château owner's year of birth. Deepish old gold; excellent, fully developed old Sauternes nose, very sound; still sweet, fairly full, fat and rich. Extremely good.
At lunch with Jean Cordier, April 1976 ★★★★

1926 ★★★★

A very good vintage. Picking began 22 September.
Ch. d'Yquem (17.4°). Fine deep amber gold; wonderfully rich bouquet; rich, sweet and holding very well.
Tasted March 1975 ★★★★
Ch. Climens. It was this wine, first tasted in 1955, which revealed to me the beguiling beauty of old Sauternes: pure gold in colour; deep old honeyed nectar; rich and luscious though drying out. Fading gracefully.
Tasted for the eighth time, July 1960 ★★★
Ch. de Rayne-Vigneau. Fabulous bouquet. Liquid gold.
Tasted April 1969 ★★★★
Ch. Filhot. Half-bottle: chlorine smell; dry, horrid.
Tasted April 1976.
Ch. Rabaud-Promis. Half-bottle a little dull, disappointing. A slightly ullaged full-size bottle had somewhat sickly resinous nose but lovely flavour.
Tasted May 1977 ★
Ch. Carbonnieux. Ullaged mid-shoulder. Very bright yellow; old, quite good *Semillon* aroma; dry, firm, twist of lemon peel, most interesting.
Tasted January 1977 ★

1927 ★★

Reputation tainted by disastrous reds, some of the worst ever. But the late autumn weather improved, with some surprising results. Picking in Sauternes began 20 September (Y 15.5°).
Ch. Climens. Interesting colour, fairly deep, warm orange amber shot with gold; consistently good nose — honeyed, rich old lanolin; medium sweet, remarkably rich and powerful for an unregarded vintage. Slightly harsh end acidity.
Tasted three times, last on my fiftieth birthday, May 1977 ★★★
Ch. La Tour-Blanche. Similar colour; almost as good as the Climens — just a bit short.
Tasted five times. Last tasted September 1977 ★★
Ch. Lafaurie-Peyraguey. Again, surprisingly good, deep and rich but with marked end acidity.
At the pre-sale tasting, September 1976 ★★

1928 ★★★★

Picking began 18 September. With '29 one of the great twin vintages. Firm, distinguished wines. The best are holding well.
Ch. d'Yquem (18.2°). Generally pale for its age, a fabulous lemon gold; rich yet delicate, full of fruit, honeyed; seems to vary from drying out to very sweet and concentrated. Beautiful balance and long life ahead. The deeper, amber-coloured '28s are more tangy and caramelly. Seven notes from 1971. Magnificent.
Last at the Heublein pre-sale tasting, May 1980 ★★★★★
Ch. Lafaurie-Peyraguey. Bright but brown; sweet

nose and flavour but slightly bitter and disappointing.
Tasted only once, December 1966.

Ch. Filhot. Medium pale, pronounced lemon rim; faded bouquet; drying out, lightish but firm, lovely flavour, crisp. One slightly ullaged bottle was dried out and somewhat maderized.
Tasted February 1976. At best ★★★

Ch. Climens. Old gold, with slight sediment; honey and lanolin (ripe *Semillon*), rich; drying out but wonderful flavour and long finish.
Tasted on four occasions, the last March 1980 ★★★★ Drink now.

Ch. Fayot; Ch. Boisson; Ch. Myrat and Ch. Bastor-Lamontagne. All good.
Tasted 1967–1973.

1929 ★★★★★

Probably the best Sauternes vintage after 1921 and decidedly the most lusciously "copybook". Picking began 23 September. The best are still beautiful.

Ch. d'Yquem (21.2°). Deeper coloured than the '28, almost as deep as the '21, rich, with green rim; big, classic bouquet, very rich, complex, mature; medium sweet, concentrated, fabulous, lingering.
Last tasted June 1972 ★★★★★

Ch. Climens. Tasted twice in 1965: pure amber gold; highly developed, deep old bottle-age; medium sweet, extremely rich, unctuous, fat, completely ripe and long firm finish. Also at recent Heublein tastings: absolute perfection; soft creamy bouquet; still quite sweet, smooth, silky, at its zenith but no signs of tiredness. Surely one of the best ever Climens?
Last tasted May 1980 ★★★★★

Ch. Filhot. Warm old amber; gentle creamy bouquet, developed in glass; medium sweet, medium body, soft, rich, excellent old flavour. Holding well.
Tasted July 1972 ★★★★

Ch. Rieussec. Deep but very fine colour; honey, caramel and cream; still sweet and very rich. An exceptionally fine wine.
Tasted May 1977 ★★★★★

Ch. La Tour-Martillac. Rare to find Graves of this age. Bright yellow; interesting bouquet — some honeyed bottle-age, pronounced old *Semillon* aroma; fairly dry, medium body, a bit austere and abrupt but very sound and most interesting.
At office luncheons in 1974, 1975 and September 1976 ★★

Ch. Laville (Preignac). High toned, a little volatile.
Tasted 1978 ★

Ch. Bastor-Lamontagne. Extremely good.
Tasted 1973 ★★★

1930

A non-starter. Yquem not made.

1931 ★

No reputation and presumably no market — depression. But not bad. Picking began 21 September.

Ch. d'Yquem (16.6°). Very fine healthy golden colour; rather heavy nose, bottle-age; medium sweet, good sound flavour, with curious piquancy.
Tasted March 1968 ★★

1932

Disastrous. No alcohol, no sweetness (Y 5.0°).

1933 ★

Not a noted Sauternes vintage. Picking began 20 September (Y 16.3°).

Ch. Filhot. Loose cork, ullaged; dried out, sharp.
Tasted October 1978.

Ch. Lafaurie-Peyraguey. Lovely colour, with sediment; one slightly oily on the nose, another fine; some richness and fine flavour.
Tasted September 1976. At best ★★★

Ch. La Tour-Martillac. Pale, bright; gentle, sound vanilla nose; dryish, soft, very pleasant.
Tasted May 1976 ★★★

1934 ★★★★

Next to 1937 the best of the 1930s. Picking began 17 September (Y 18.0°).

Ch. Lafaurie-Peyraguey. From half-bottles: marvellous old amber gold; creamy, honeyed; medium sweet, fullish, rich, positive flavour and excellent finish.
Tasted 1977, May 1978 ★★★★

Ch. Lafite. Blanc. Labelled *"Vin de Château Lafite 1934"* with Carruades corks. Wine made for family use only. This was one of a small consignment given by Baron Elie de Rothschild to John Grimston (later the sixth Earl of Verulam). Excellent cork and level. Fine light gold, very attractive; lovely bouquet, sweet, honeyed bottle-age; dry, medium body, good flavour and excellent acidity. In remarkable condition and very pleasant to drink but a straight statement, short and no subtleties. Which is why they stick to red!
Tasted at Gorhambury, March 1978 ★★★

Ch. de Tastes (Ste-Croix-du-Mont). Château bottled. From a rarely seen but good property across the river from Sauternes: deep amber; rich, honeyed, slightly resinous nose; medium dry, lovely, rich flavoured.
Tasted April 1979 ★★★

1935 ★★

Quite good. Picking began 25 September. Bottled just before the war and rarely seen since.

Ch. d'Yquem (15.9°). When first tasted, in 1970, quite pale; good gentle but pasty nose; holding quite well but with acidity roughening its edges. Later, mid-shoulder ullaged bottle: deeper; rich but hard and a trifle tart.
Last tasted April 1976.

1936 ★★

Mediocre year. Picking began 2 October (Y 17.7°).

Ch. Lafaurie-Peyraguey. Good colour but not very bright; a bit hard; drying out but good flavour, firm.
At the pre-sale tasting, September 1976 ★★

Ch. Filhot. Light, unbalanced, drying effect, no finish.
Tasted October 1976.

1937 ★★★★★

A great classic year for Sauternes. Picking began 20 September. The high acidity that spoiled the '37 reds serves to crisp up and preserve the whites. The best will keep for another 20 years.

Ch. d'Yquem (19.1°). Very fine, deep amber gold; very rich, very fine bouquet; still quite sweet, its lusciousness perfectly balanced by lovely firm acidity.
Tasted April and May 1973 ★★★★★

Ch. Climens. Deep amber, with a shade of onion-skin; rich, golden bouquet, with the calm gentle *Semillon*

influence; medium sweet — drying out but very rich and powerful, firm and excellent acidity.
Tasted five times, 1966 — April 1976 *****

Ch. Lafaurie-Peyraguey. Old gold; excellent honeyed bouquet; excellent rich old Sauternes flavour but drying out. Crisp.
Tasted November 1972 ****

Ch. Coutet. Very deep old gold; fabulous bouquet; very, very rich, fat, but losing sweetness. Lovely finish.
Tasted March 1977 ***** *Drink now — 1990.*

Ch. de Ricaud. A *têté de cuvée* from Loupiac, between Barsac and Graves. This small district produces attractive bourgeois wines but one rarely comes across old vintages. This batch came from a particularly good cellar near Versailles and demonstrated how beautiful the best wine of even a minor district can be if it is of a great year and well stored. Fabulous colour, very bright topaz; lovely, rich, honeyed *Semillon* bouquet; sweet, rich, Barsac-like flavour, weight and balance, plump but nice acidity and fresh as a daisy (perhaps "buttercup" would be more appropriate). It is sensible to decant old white wines: they often have a slight sediment. In any case the golden colour looks even more spectacular in a fine cut-glass decanter.
Last tasted at a boardroom lunch, November 1979 ****

Two Graves of the 1937 vintage:
Ch. Pontac. Rather Loupiac-like in style, medium sweet, very pleasant.
Tasted 1976 **

Ch. La Tour-Martillac. Medium dry, rather four-square and unexciting but good in its way.
Tasted 1973, 1977 **

1938 **

Moderate only. Suffered from wartime preoccupation, and occupation. Picking began 26 September (Y 17.6°).
Ch. Lafaurie-Peyraguey. Powerful yellow colour; light lemony nose; dryish, light, short but quite nice.
Tasted September 1976 **

Ch. de Rayne-Vigneau. Very bright green gold; rich old nose; sweet, lovely, nice acidity.
Tasted October 1971 ***

Ch. Laville Haut-Brion (Talence). The oldest vintage I have tasted of this distinguished Graves. Old gold; unusual old *Semillon* nose, honeyed bottle-age under peppermint; dry, medium body, very drying end acidity.
At the château, September 1978.

1939 ***

Quite good. Picking began 20 September.
Ch. d'Yquem (17.8°). Palish lively amber gold; good; medium sweet, fine flavour, not full but rapier-like, with excellent long finish.
Tasted June 1972 ***

Ch. Climens. Bright; unusual, grapefruit-peel aroma; drying out, showing age, fairly marked acidity.
Tasted April 1966. Probably finished now.

Ch. Rabaud-Promis. Bright old gold; sweet, gentle, good bouquet and flavour but high acidity.
Tasted April 1976 **

Ch. La Tour Blanche. Bright yellow gold; sweet, vanilla aroma; sweet, medium light, dry finish.
Tasted April 1976 **

1940 *

Pretty poor wartime vintage. Rarely seen. Picking began 25 September (Y 17.1°).
Ch. Climens. Fine gold colour with fine hazy sediment; wax, fudge and old apples; drying out and not attractive.
Tasted May 1976.

1941

Poor vintage. Picking began 30 September (Y 17.6°). Meagre dry wines. None tasted.

1942 ****

Picking began 30 September. Very rich wines with finesse and bouquet.
Ch. d'Yquem (20.7°). A great surprise: fairly deep, warm and bright orange amber; perfect bouquet, rich honeyed crème brûlée; medium sweet, excellent body, balance, acidity. Excellent.
In the great French tradition, with pâté de foie gras at the Coq Hardy, Bougival, February 1980 ****

Ch. Climens. Yellow gold; good lanolin bouquet — *Semillon*, not much *pourriture noble*; medium sweet, some fruit, pleasant tingling acidity.
Tasted April 1976 ***

Ch. Coutet. Very pronounced old gold colour; light, good lanolin nose again; still quite sweet, medium light, very pleasant flavour and balance.
Tasted January 1977 ***

1943 ****

Very rich, vigorous, with breeding. Picking began 15 September.
Ch. d'Yquem (21.8°). Medium gold; honeyed bouquet, pretty good; lost a lot of the initial sugar, good but not outstanding. Worth looking out for.
Only tasted once, September 1972 ***

Ch. Caillou. Relatively minor wine showing very well indeed. Still sweet and rich.
Tasted November 1977 ***

Ch. Climens. Deepish, pleasant old gold colour; strong, honeyed bouquet; still quite sweet, perfect balance — soft yet firm and crisp. Lovely wine.
Tasted July 1970 ****

Ch. Coutet. Fullish colour; fine botrytis/bottle-age bouquet; losing sugar but rich and fine.
Tasted October 1958 ****

Ch. de Rayne-Vigneau. Fine gold; rich, tangy, good bouquet and taste, but showing age.
Tasted May 1975 ***

Ch. Rieussec. Distinctly orange tinged; fine, rich classic old Sauternes bouquet and flavour; losing sugar but still fat. Very mature.
Tasted December 1971 **

1944 **

Picking began 24 September. Despite high reading at Yquem (20.7°), a light and variable vintage.
Ch. Lafaurie-Peyraguey. Medium-deep amber gold; rich, good bouquet; rich, medium sweetness and body, tangy acidity.
Tasted September 1976 **

Ch. La Tour-Blanche. Pronounced old green-gold rim; light, slightly mint-leaf aroma; medium sweet, slightly pasty acidity but not bad.
Tasted April 1976 *

1945 *****

An excellent classic vintage. Concentrated, firm, refined. Early harvest, 10 September. Small production due to frost.

Ch. d'Yquem	*(22.7°). Lovely old gold; sweet, rich, lovely but a little subdued; sweet, full — even heavy, powerful and concentrated. Fabulous quality and condition.* Last tasted February 1971 ***** Drink now — 2000.
Ch. Lafaurie-Peyraguey	*Fabulous colour and bouquet; not heavy but refined.* At the pre-sale tasting, September 1976 ****
Ch. Laville Haut-Brion	*Yellow gold; good* Semillon *aroma; dry, crisp, clean finish.* Tasted at the château, September 1978 **
Ch. Laville Haut-Brion Crème de tête	*Slightly deeper — perfect; good, gentle, rich, honeyed bouquet; magnificent flavour and balance. One of the greatest dry white wines, certainly from the Graves.* At the château, September 1978 *****
Ch. Suduiraut	*Fine, deepish; very attractive, honeyed; rich, fruity, excellent acidity holding the balance.* Tasted April 1973 **** Drink now — 1995.
Ch. La Tour-Blanche	*Rich amber-gold colour with pronounced sap-green edge; exquisite bouquet — subtle, ripe, honeyed; sweet, rich, concentrated, excellent acidity.* Last tasted May 1978 *****

1946 *

Not an effective Sauternes vintage and totally overshadowed by the '45, '47 and '49. Climate: rot in September, picking started on 30th and saved by incredibly hot weather in October. (Y 18.2°). See footnote on page 167.

Ch. Coutet	*Bright yellow; stuffy but sound; lightish, nice, some acidity.* Tasted April 1976 *
Ch. Lafaurie-Peyraguey	*Yellow amber; bland; dryish, not bad but short.* At the pre-sale tasting, September 1976 **
Ch. Laville Haut-Brion	*Deep orange gold; sound bouquet, some honey but hard; dry, austere, short.* Tasted September 1978 *

1947 *****

A great ripe classic Sauternes vintage. One of the best ever. Picking began 15 September. Wine made in conditions of great heat. 1945 will certainly outlive it.

Ch. d'Yquem	*(22.5°). Overpowering and incomparable when first tasted in 1954. More recently, on the ninth occasion: deep, rich, amber-gold colour; very rich, burnt hot-vintage character, high toned; still sweet, fairly full bodied, rich, velvety yet powerful with marked end acidity.* Last tasted November 1975 ***** Drink before acidity gets the better of it.

Ch. Climens	*Perfect in 1965. A Harvey bottling in 1976 had a fabulous nose that somehow reminded me of almonds in old-fashioned apricot jam. Most recently: perfect, beautiful golden colour; lovely rich honeyed bouquet; still sweet, rich, excellent flavour and balance.* Last tasted at Christopher Tatham's, January 1980 *****
Ch. Coutet	*Fine gold, not too deep; perfect bouquet, honeyed, most attractive; drying a fraction but fine flavour and balance. Lovely acidity.* Four notes. Last tasted (in magnum) March 1973 ****
Ch. Doisy-Védrines	*Orange gold; orange-sorbet scent; lovely but hint of volatile acidity.* Tasted May 1973 *** Drink up.
Graves Supérieur Susbielle	*Supplied in burgundy bottles due to postwar shortages and stored in the perfect cellars at the Villa d'Olivette near Menton. Remarkably attractive yellow gold; excellent lime-honey Semillon bouquet and flavour. Sound as a bell.* At the villa, December 1979 ***
Ch. Lafaurie-Peyraguey	*Deepish; very rich bouquet and flavour. Powerful, lovely finish.* At the pre-sale tasting, September 1976 ****
Ch. Laville Haut-Brion	*Buttery yellow, pale for age; bland, soft Semillon nose and flavour. Dry.* Tasted November 1978 ***
Ch. Rieussec	*First tasted in 1952: rich and strong. Eight notes later: rich yellow gold — one bottle had loose flaky sediment; deep, rich, Barsac-like bouquet; medium sweet, rich, fine flavour and condition.* Last tasted November 1969 ****
Ch. Suduiraut	*Remarkably orange tinged and deep for its age; exceedingly rich; excellent flavour, condition. Lively end acidity.* Tasted May 1970 *****

1948 ***

A good vintage but lacking opulent appeal and not often seen now. Picking began 22 September.

Ch. d'Yquem	*(19.9°). First tasted in 1954. The wine seemed best in 1961/62. More recently: amber gold; medium sweet; attractive but a bit short on flavour.* Last tasted June 1972 **
Ch. Coutet	*Full, rich. Delightful.* But not tasted since 1953 ***
Ch. Doisy-Védrines	*Palish gold; drying out but agreeable.* Tasted December 1977 **
Ch. Haut-Brion Blanc	*Powerful flavour, almost an acquired taste.* Tasted 1959 **

1949 *****

A great vintage with breeding and finesse, less opulent than '47 and less concentrated than 1945, but classically composed and holding well. Picking began 27 September and continued into the driest October on record.

Ch. d'Yquem	*(20.8°). Perfection in 1962. On the eighth occasion: fine amber-gold colour, not too deep; perfect condition, lovely honeyed crème*

	brûlée — both bottle-age and botrytis; fairly sweet still, medium full, very rich but not fat, lovely flavour, balance and acidity. Tasted March 1979 ***** Drink now — 1990.
Ch. Climens	*Six consistently good notes. Pure amber, pale for age; rich, very attractive bouquet; again, holding its sugar well, good lively flavour and finish.* Last tasted March 1977 ****
Ch. Coutet	*Very fine in 1956. Later a deepish old gold; excellent botrytis nose; fairly sweet, fine rich ripe flavour.* Last tasted December 1966 ****
Ch. Doisy-Daëne	*Fresh, light style, attractive.* Tasted 1975 ***
Ch. Guiraud	*Deep old gold. Three London-bottled examples spoilt by peardrops and bitter almonds. Château bottled also deep and with poor nose but with quite crisp flavour and balance.* Tasted 1970 — 1972.
Ch. Laville Haut-Brion	*Yellow gold; buttery, honeyed; firmly but not assertively dry, soft, attractive, slightly abrupt finish.* Tasted 1971, April 1978 and (two out of eight bottles corked) November 1979 ** to ***
Ch. Le Pape	*Lovely refreshing nose; dry, agreeable, well constituted, holding well.* Tasted March 1979 ***

1950 ****

Far more successful for Sauternes than for claret. Climate: picking began 17 September in damp weather but ended in a hot, ripening Indian summer. Assessment: sweet, generally holding well.

Ch. d'Yquem	*(24.4°). Incredibly high must readings. Consistently, on the seven occasions tasted since 1961, I have found a pronounced peach-kernel aroma that I personally do not like; otherwise the wine has been consistently rich and luscious. So, a matter of taste.* Last tasted May 1975 *** Drink now — 1990.
Ch. Climens	*Sweet, ripe yet refreshing.* Tasted only once, in May 1965 ****
Ch. Coutet	*16° G.L. and 6° Baumé at its birth. Magnificently well balanced when I first tasted it in 1954. Six notes later: good colour, pale for age; fragrant, lovely bottle-age; still quite sweet, fine, rich, firm. Lovely finish.* Last tasted June 1975 ****
Ch. Lafaurie-Peyraguey	*Medium yellow amber; lovely, sweet scented; medium sweet, lovely flavour, similar kernelly taste to Yquem.* Tasted March, September 1976 ***
Ch. Rieussec	*Deepish colour; good; big fine wine, showing well.* Tasted 1966 ***
Ch. de Tastes Ste-Croix-du-Mont	*Fine colour; lovely botrytis and honey bouquet; medium sweet, very pleasant, light Loupiac style.* Tasted March 1977 ***

1951

Picking began late, 4 October. An unsatisfactory vintage. Yquem not made. No '51s tasted.

1952 ★★★

Good, rich, crisp wines. Yquem crop devastated by hail and no wine made. Picking elsewhere began 17 September. Particularly good in Barsac and Graves.

Ch. Carbonnieux	*Dry. Beautifully balanced.* Tasted February 1978 ★★★
Ch. Climens	*From an indifferent shipper's sample in 1954 and the first tasting from the cask in 1955 (when I preferred the neighbouring Coutet) the wine has developed in colour from a lightish gold to deeper bright gold; always ripe and honeyed on the nose, now developing crème brûlée; losing its intense sweetness, but on the eleventh and most recent occasion, perfect richness, weight and balance.* Last tasted May 1976 ★★★
Ch. Coutet	*Fresh and delicious in the cask, and fuller than the '53. Most recently, a fine specimen bottled by Justerini & Brooks: deep old gold, greenish tinged; sweet, rich, slightly vanilla nose; drying out but crisp, honeyed, very attractive.* Tasted July 1972 ★★★ Drink now — 1990.
Ch. Doisy-Védrines	*Deep; excellent nose; medium sweet, fine, rich, dry finish.* Tasted at Prunier's in London, 1971 ★★★★
Ch. Haut-Brion Blanc	*Two perfect bottles when five years old: pale; incredible aroma, a cross between* Traminer *and the finest* Chardonnay; *dry, powerful but restrained.* Tasted August and September 1957. Probably still good ★★★★

1953 ★★★★

Lovely rich, ripe, soft wines of classic proportions. Climate: finest August in living memory; excessive rain in September, but late harvest from 28th in perfect weather.

Ch. d'Yquem	*(23°). Extremely rich and full in cask in 1955; fine medium pale gold; rich but piquant and minty, preferred the '55 Yquem. More recently: still fairly sweet, fine flavour, delicate, lovely aftertaste.* Last tasted November 1972 ★★★★
Ch. Carbonnieux	*Palish yellow gold; scented vanilla-noisette nose; good flavour, acidity and aftertaste.* Tasted April 1977 ★★★
Dom. de Chevalier	*A bone-dry wine, consistently good. First a pale, grapy flavoured Harvey bottling in 1956, then five château bottlings, deepening to a yellow gold in the 1960s. Still fresh, with sound honeyed bouquet, complete on the palate but austere.* Last tasted February 1970 ★★★
Ch. Coutet	*Good, but preferred the '52.* Tasted in cask, July 1955. Now ★★★
Ch. Climens	*Lovely in cask. Developed deepish yellow; good, high-toned Barsac nose; sweet, slightly nutty flavour.* Last tasted 1971 ★★★★
Ch. Filhot	*Nice but not outstanding.* Tasted 1970 ★★
Graves "Royale" de Luze	*Just to demonstrate again, as with the '47 Graves Supérieur, how good the plain old-fashioned Graves could be and how well they have lasted. This came from a country house cellar near Versailles.*

	I bought a dozen or so for office lunches in 1976 and it was consistently good: an appealing bright yellow; pleasant honeyed Semillon nose; medium in dryness and body, soft, not long but healthy and most attractive. Last tasted October 1979 ★★★
Ch. Guiraud	*Bottled by Harvey's: light, disappointing wine.* Tasted 1958.
Ch. Haut-Brion Blanc	*First tasted in 1957: richly coloured; vanilla (oak) nose; dry, like a fine white burgundy but strong. Twenty years later: buttercup yellow; rich, honeyed, oaky/smoky Semillon bouquet; medium dry, rich, ripe, flavoury.* Last tasted November 1977 ★★★★
Ch. Rieussec	*Sweet but a bit thin with a touch of bitterness in 1957. A good rich Harvey bottling in 1960, deepening in 1968. Most recently: bright deep gold; lovely bouquet and flavour, still sweet, perfect balance and condition.* Tasted March 1968 ★★★★
Ch. Roumieu	*A little-seen Barsac, perfect capsule, label, branded cork and level: lovely colour, very bright, positive gold with hint of lemon; rich but delicate bouquet, honeyed Semillon, slight twist of lemon-peel acidity on nose and end taste; fairly sweet still, medium light, soft and very flavoury, some fat but refreshing. Dry finish. Just caught before its decline.* Tasted October 1979 ★★★ Drink up.

1954

Poor vintage in general, a washout in Sauternes. Characteristics: weak, watery, ill-knit wines. Climate: about the coldest, wettest summer on record — the worst in living memory; very late start to vintage in October sun but damage already done. Bad frosts finished it off.

Ch. d'Yquem	*Deep gold but watery rim; thick, clumsy, pasty nose; unknit, rich, yet very high acidity.* Tasted October 1971. Drink up.
Ch. Laville Haut-Brion	*Clearly better for the earlier picked Graves: lovely bright gold; clean, fresh, honeyed; very dry, medium full bodied, lovely flavour and fine dry finish. No signs of fatigue.* Tasted August 1970 ★★★

1955 ★★★★★

A great vintage for white Bordeaux: well-constituted wines, fatter and more stylish than the reds. Climate: weather perfect in July; hot and dry in August; welcome rain in September, picking started around 21st. October fine and dry — classic combination of influences. Abundant crop. Assessment: frankly one of my favourite postwar Sauternes vintages. Perfect now.

Ch. d'Yquem	*(20.5°). Palish; restrained but syrupy nose; fat yet clean and strong in cask in October 1958. Perfection in early 1970s. More recently: a lovely medium-pale gold; lovely, rich, golden botrytis bouquet; still sweet, though starting to lose sugar, medium full, soft, lovely flavour, excellent acidity and beautiful aftertaste.* Last tasted March 1980 ★★★★
Ch. Coutet	*Feeble in 1959, dull, lacking fruit in 1960. Later, a sweet, soft Harvey bottling, not too clean a nose.* Last tasted January 1967.

Ch. Doisy-Védrines	*Ten consistently excellent notes from 1963. Most recently: fine golden colour; very good, rich, honeyed bouquet; now medium sweet, good body, perfect balance.* Last tasted July 1972 ****
Ch. Filhot	*Sweet, nice weight in 1964. Fully ripe in 1968. Beginning to dry out but fresh, fine, lovely.* Last tasted March 1971 ****
Ch. Guiraud	*Once again disappointing, with slightly bitter/acid finish.* Tasted January 1971.
Ch. Haut-Brion Blanc	*Clearly a great year for white Graves too. Haut-Brion, as always, excellent but almost too powerful and pungent when young: pale; vanilla; raspingly dry, strong flavoured, unready in 1958. Mature by mid-1960s. Ten years later: fine, bright, deepish yellow gold; rich complex old-stables-and-honey bouquet; medium body, rich tangy flavour, overall dry.* Last tasted May 1975 ****
Ch. Lafaurie-Peyraguey	*Medium-pale gold; lovely, rich lanolin bouquet; sweet, fabulously rich, flavoury, tingling acidity.* Tasted September 1976 ****
Ch. Laville Haut-Brion	*Five consistent notes from 1977: medium-pale attractive yellow; lovely waxy Semillon with honeyed bottle-age and twist of Sauvignon; dry, firm, excellent, flavoury, good balance, nice acidity. Perfect.* Last tasted at a Bordeaux Club dinner, December 1979 ****
Ch. Liot	*A minor but attractive Barsac. Four good notes, syrupy rich.* Tasted 1958, 1959 ***
Ch. de Rayne-Vigneau	*Three good notes in mid-1960s. Recently: lovely old gold; crème-brûlée bouquet; sweet, rich lanolin flavour but dry, slightly bitter, finish.* Last tasted July 1978 **
Ch. Rieussec	*Fairly sweet, though lighter Barsac-like style, refreshing finish.* Last tasted 1962 ***
Ch. Sigalas-Rabaud	*Scottish bottled, labelled Rabaud-Sigalas: deep, rich but drying a little in 1969. Most recently, château bottled: pronounced yellow colour; magnificent bouquet; sweet, very rich, concentrated.* Last tasted May 1977 ****
Ch. Suduiraut	*Six excellent notes in 1970 and 1971. Deep, fine, lively colour; full fruity bouquet and flavour, a sweet, lovely mouthful.* Last tasted December 1972 ****

1956 *

Pretty disastrous. Characteristics: constituents lacking and ill balanced. Unripe. High acidity. Climate: the opposite to 1955. All the worst conditions at the most critical times. Coldest vine-crippling winter; cold August; excessively wet September and early October. Ruin for reds but short improvement for picking from 10 October.

Ch. d'Yquem	*(19.5°). By picking late, managed to achieve 14.5° G.L. (degree of alcohol by weight) and 4.5° of sugar. Tasted in cask: pale; fruity nose and flavour. Acidity high in 1960. More recently: yellow gold; pleasant, some richness but restrained; fairly sweet, light for Yquem, crisp, attractive, like a Barsac of a lesser vintage.* Last tasted January 1961 * Probably faded now.

1957 ★★★

A good vintage, not a heavyweight. Characteristics: clean-cut, refreshing acidity; lean, lacking flesh. Climate: winter and spring, reverse of 1956. Mild February; hot March; May frosts; summer coldest on record; late harvest from 3 October, the hottest on record.

Ch. d'Yquem	*(19°). First tasted in 1964: sharp nose but quite nice on palate. Later: palish gold; raw bouquet, Yquem but not at its best; sweet, refreshing acidity, perfect with foie gras.* Last tasted at the Bass Charrington vintage dinner, October 1969 ★★
Ch. Coutet	*A dozen notes. First tasted in cask in 1958: pale; young, fresh nose; crisp, nice balance. Developed consistently, gaining colour, medium sweet, refreshing.* Last tasted 1967 ★★★★
Ch. Doisy-Daëne	*A nice minor Barsac bottled by Harvey's: fragrant, crisp.* Three good notes 1959–1967 ★★★
Ch. Lafaurie-Peyraguey	*Pale; sulphury nose; medium sweet, a bit lean and unexciting.* Tasted October 1970 ★
Ch. Rabaud-Sigalas	*Three notes, a little variable, from 1959. Surprisingly fat and rich, almost cloying in 1961. Later, fine and fruity.* Last tasted 1967 ★★★★
Ch. Rieussec	*Five good notes from 1958 when it seemed surprisingly rich and fat. Has gained colour, bright yellow; rich and refreshing on nose and palate. A good '57.* Last tasted December 1971 ★★★★
Ch. Suduiraut	*Deepish, as Suduiraut customarily has been in postwar vintages; deep, fruity, excellent bouquet; fairly sweet, medium body, excellent flavour and balance.* Tasted December 1970 ★★★★

1958 ★★

Rich and elegant but a Cinderella vintage, never accepted by the trade or the customer and certainly overshadowed by the vintages of the mid-1950s, the classic '55, the monumental '59. Climate: good summer and late harvest from 7 October in good conditions. Assessment: as with the reds, ripe, plump, surprisingly agreeable. Exciting, flavoury but not for long keeping.

Ch. d'Yquem	*(19.7°). Sweet, rich and ripe in 1964. Later: old gold, more like a '47 in appearance; good, rich, ripe bouquet and flavour, surprising quality for a sublimated vintage. Sweet.* At peak, last tasted in August 1969 ★★★ Drink now.
Ch. Climens	*Pale gold; fresh, clean, medium sweet; quite good but not great.* Tasted only once, May 1965 ★★
Ch. Coutet	*Four good notes from 1967. Recently: medium-pale gold, bitty sediment; sweet, pasty/vanilla, honeyed bottle-age — very rich and attractive; medium sweet, rich and quite classic.* Last tasted June 1978 ★★★ Drink now — 1990.
Ch. Doisy-Védrines	*Old gold; touch of almond kernels; sweet, rich, nice balance.* Tasted May 1970 ★★
Ch. Rieussec	*Palish; quite nice meaty/malty nose and flavour.* Tasted July 1969 ★★

Ch. Suduiraut	*Four notes from 1967. Fat but with lovely firm backbone. Recently: medium amber gold; soft, honeyed, very ripe; sweet, rich, excellent flavour, nice acidity.* Last tasted November 1968 **** Drink now — 1990.

1959 *****

A great year: probably the last of the heavyweight classics. Climate: long hot summer — June to mid-September — then rain, but fine for harvest 21 September. High sugar content. Assessment: rich, powerful, massively constituted.

Ch. d'Yquem	*(21°). First tasted in 1964: sweet, soft, ripe, luscious. Now a lovely amber gold, the last bottle having a hint of orange in the colour which accompanied highish acidity; deep, rich, magnificent bouquet, honeyed and fragrant; still very sweet, full-bodied, fat, concentrated wine.* Last tasted March 1979 ***** At peak?
Ch. Climens	*Rather a heavyweight Barsac: lovely bright gold; excellent bouquet, ripe grapes and honey; sweet, fat, fullish and fine.* Tasted July 1972 *****
Ch. Coutet	*Four notes from 1966. Now a deepish colour; excellent fully ripe bouquet, honeyed bottle-age and botrytis; consistently sweet yet with tingling acidity, beautiful wine.* Last tasted May 1972 *****
Ch. Guiraud	*Have tasted this on nine occasions, English and château bottled, since 1967. Variable comments: it does seem that postwar Guiraud has not hit the heights. Most recently: medium pale, light gold — unimpressive for a big vintage with bottle-age; quite nice bouquet, vanilla, honeyed; fairly sweet, less fat than it should be and a bit abrupt.* Last tasted May 1975 **
Ch. Lafaurie-Peyraguey	*Consistently good since 1965. Most recently: medium full amber gold; fabulous ripe, Beerenauslese-like aroma; sweet, fullish, very rich but with a refreshing tang. Marvellous fruit and acidity.* Tasted September 1976 ****
Ch. Rieussec	*Consistently not quite right, a little insubstantial and acidity noticeable.* Tasted 1964–1966.
Ch. Suduiraut	*Very yellow; gentle, fragrant; sweet, fullish, lovely rich classic style, nice acidity.* Tasted November 1978 ****

Some interesting dry white '59s:

Ch. Baret	*Crisp and refreshing in 1964. By the mid-1950s intense yellow; rich, honeyed — bottle-age gives even a dry Semillon a Sauternes-like bouquet; dry, rich, still firm and fresh.* Last tasted May 1975 ***
Ch. Haut-Brion Blanc	*One of the two best growths. Tasted six times since 1973. Most recently: buttercup yellow; fine bouquet — gentle rich Semillon nose with twist of lemon peel; a distinctly dry wine, fullish with firm, lovely flavour and excellent acidity. This sort of white wine needs bottle-age.* Last tasted January 1977 **** Drink now — 1985.
Ch. Lafite Blanc	*The last vintage in which white wine was made at Lafite (as a house wine and not for sale): pale, dry, sound, Graves-like. A singularly appropriate opener to the great Overton Lafite tasting in Texas, May 1979* **

Ch. Laville Haut-Brion	*Made from old vines roughly fifty-fifty* Semillon *and* Sauvignon. *First tasted in 1966. Now a similar colour to Haut-Brion; with a calm, waxy, honeyed nose; lovely flavour, a very complete wine but lacking a little finesse.* Last tasted March 1978 ★★★
Ch. Olivier	*Rather a freak bottle consumed recently in Oporto: pale for its age and appealingly bright. Although I did not like the nose — no fruit, all almond kernels — it was not at all bad on the palate, very dry, quite good flavour and length. Firm and holding well.* At David Delaforce's, November 1979 ★★
Ygrec	*Straw yellow; rich, honeyed and fruity but sulphur noticeable — presumably to keep some residual sugar in check; medium dryness and body, not quite a Graves in flavour, clean dry finish and aftertaste.* Tasted December 1961 ★★

1960 ★

Not a notable Sauternes vintage. Climate: good spring; early summer; July and August cold and wet; September variable. Early and prolonged harvest, from 9 September. Assessment: lightish, thin and green, acidity. The Graves quite good.

Ch. d'Yquem	*Tasted in cask as late as October 1964. Eight years later: yellow gold, with watery rim; quite attractive aroma, but green (unripe); medium sweet, fuller bodied than expected, good flavour, slightly hard bitter finish.* Last tasted June 1972 ★★
Ch. Guiraud	*Pale lemon gold; quite nice bouquet and flavour. Lightish.* Tasted July 1973 ★★
Ch. Laville Haut-Brion	*Pale, very bright; unknit but not unattractive* Sauvignon-Blanc *piquancy; dry, lightish, apricot kernels and a twist of lemon. Appealing in its way.* Tasted March 1978 ★
Ygrec	*Presumably, with the unlikelihood of making a* 1cr *grand cru Sauternes, the owners of Ch. d'Yquem decided again to turn some of their crop into a dry white. I have tasted Ygrec '60 on four occasions. A curious wine. Most recently: a pretty lemon-yellow colour; honeyed* Semillon, *Graves-like, with slightly stewed undertone; bone dry, some body, flavoury, with pasty end acidity. Intriguing.* Last tasted January 1979 ★

1961 ★★★

A moderately good vintage but nothing like as great as the '61 reds. Climate: poor flowering conditions severely reduced potential crop; drought in August; sunny September, picking began on 19th. Small crop. Characteristics: stylish wines, with shape and flavour but lacking lusciousness of the greatest vintages.

Ch. d'Yquem	*(17.6°). Fine, pronounced yellow gold; fabulous crème brûlée; sweet, rich, full, concentrated (though in 1972 and 1975 I noted a slightly bitter finish).* Last tasted May 1978 ★★★(★)
Ch. Climens	*Several notes. Sweet, lovely.* Last tasted April 1980 ★★★★
Ch. Coutet	*Attractive, not a heavyweight.* Tasted 1964–1975 ★★★

Ch. Doisy-Védrines	*Attractive but lacked depth.* Tasted 1964, 1975 **
Ch. Guiraud	*Consistently good notes from 1967. Most recently: old gold; soft, pourriture noble and honey; sweet, good flavour and balance.* Last tasted September 1976 ***
Ch. Lafaurie-Peyraguey	*Medium colour; good nose; fairly sweet, nice flavour.* At the pre-sale tasting, December 1976 ***
Ch. Rieussec	*Relatively lightweight.* Tasted 1965–1970 **

Of the white Graves:

Ch. Haut-Brion Blanc	*Somewhat raw and austere.* Tasted 1973, 1974 **
Ch. Larrivet Haut-Brion	*Good quality, copybook Graves.* Tasted 1967 ***
Ch. Laville Haut-Brion	*In 1965 I regarded this as the finest Graves ever tasted. The aroma a cross between Corton-Charlemagne and Sancerre. More recently: bright straw colour; high-quality bouquet, slow to develop, deep fruit; medium dry, fairly full, fat, rich, with complex Sauvignon-Blanc flintiness. Overall impression dry. Could have a firmer finish.* Last tasted September 1978 ****

1962 ★★★★

Successful in Sauternes: a fine classic vintage. Climate: hot summer, some rain; no disasters. Picking began 1 October. Abundant. Assessment: well balanced, elegant, long lasting.

Ch. d'Yquem	*(18.5°). Seven notes. Crisp and fruity in cask, developing well. Most recently: medium-pale gold; very good nose, fresh, light, honeyed; sweet, fairly full fine flavour and balance. Classic style. Elegant.* Last tasted March 1974 *** Drink now — 1990.
Ch. Climens	*First tasted in 1964. A very rich, beautifully balanced wine.* Last tasted May 1971 **** Drink now — 1995.
Ch. Coutet	*Consistently good notes. Most recently: light gold; very good positive bouquet and flavour, firm dry finish. Long lasting.* Last tasted July 1976 **** Drink now — 1990.
Ch. Doisy-Daëne	*Firm deep yellow gold; lovely honeyed bottle-age and* pourriture; *medium sweet, fine flavour, typical Barsac touch of lightness and delicacy.* Tasted February 1978 ***
Ch. Guiraud	*Disappointing.* Tasted only once, in 1973.
Ch. Laville Haut-Brion	*Five notes from 1967 when it was dry, soft and delicate. More recently: good bright colour; slightly overblown* Semillon *aroma, but honeyed; medium dry, soft, easy wine with mild dry finish.* Last tasted September 1978 **
Ch. de Malle	*One rarely sees the wine from this, the most beautiful château in Sauternes. Very attractive: medium sweet, crisp and flavoury.* Tasted only once, in 1967 ***
Ch. de Rayne-Vigneau	*Three notes. Sweet, fat, well-knit, twice in 1968. Most recently: paler than most '62s, lemon gold; shedding some of its puppy fat and now more of an elegant, high-toned Barsac style and weight. Good aftertaste.* Last tasted March 1973 ****

Ch. Rieussec	*A Barsac-like Sauternes: lovely, very distinctive bouquet, sweet, middleweight.* Tasted 1967, February 1973 ****
Ch. Roumieu-Lacoste	*A lesser known Barsac tasted three times. The first a soft, attractive Harvey bottling. Two château bottled: honeyed, nice acidity, lacking the length and finish of the greater growths.* Tasted January, February and March 1972 ***
Ch. Suduiraut	*Four excellent notes from 1967. Typical Suduiraut old-fashioned depth of colour; really lovely bouquet; sweet, rich, very attractive traditional Sauternes.* Last tasted July 1974 **** Drink now — 1995.

1963

A disastrous year. Little made, few seen. Climate: hard winter; poor flowering conditions; dreary summer but picked up in time for a late harvest from 3 October.

Ch. d'Yquem	*It would seem an unfortunate error of judgement, presumably on the part of the late Marquis de Lur-Saluces, to market this wine under the Yquem label. It was bought by the trade, and later rejected, quantities changing hands at low prices in the salerooms. Unmistakable colour — very deep amber brown with orange tinge; rich but curious tinny cheese-rind smell; fairly sweet, old, slightly singed flavour, flat yet acidic, short.* Last tasted September 1975.
Ch. Laville Haut-Brion	*Pale lemon colour; unclean, sulphury nose; dry, light, dull.* Tasted April 1968.

1964 *

A washout, literally. Climate: after a satisfactory spring and a hot, dry summer with sound ripe grapes, the heavens opened. The reds were caught mid-harvest. Sauternes washed out before they had begun. Remaining grapes picked from 21 September. Yquem not made. Characteristics: variable. Some châteaux managed to make passable wines, but they are not balanced, not for long keeping. The dry whites are better.

Ch. Climens	*Quite nice in 1968. By the mid-1970s: medium-pale yellow gold; quite nicely developed nose (one woody bottle in 1973); medium sweet, some richness but acidity noticeable.* Last tasted November 1975 *
Ch. Guiraud	*Indifferent nose but surprisingly sweet and crisp.* Tasted 1970 **
Ch. Lafaurie-Peyraguey	*Very yellow; waxy Semillon nose, with almond-kernel overtones; fairly sweet, some richness but a curious flat-ended acidity.* Last tasted January 1978 *
Ch. de Malle	*Medium sweet, passable.* Tasted once, in 1970 *
Ch. Pajot	*Described as "Enclave Yquem", but a poor neighbour; deep, dull gold though not all bad.* Tasted 1970.
Ch. de Rayne-Vigneau	*Pleasant when young.* Tasted once, in 1968 *
Ch. Rieussec	*Deepish colour; almond-kernel nose; sweet but not well-knit.* Tasted in 1969, 1973.

Ch. La Tour-Blanche	*Dull heavy Graves-like nose; quite rich, but marked end acidity.* Tasted 1968, 1970.

Of the dry whites:

Ch. Haut-Brion	*Good colour for age; touch of lemon, reminded me of a Hermitage Blanc, developed nicely; dry, fresh for its age, long flavour, very nice finish.* Tasted September 1976 ★★★
Ch. Laville Haut-Brion	*Normal* cuvée*: very buttery yellow; old kerosine-tinged nose; dry, rich but metallic acid end.* Four notes 1968–1978.
Ch. Laville Haut-Brion Crème de tête	*Brighter colour; much better bouquet; attractive flavour but un-assertive and a little unyielding.* Tasted April and September 1978 ★★

1965

A poor year, worse even than 1963. By now, all the vineyard proprietors must have lost heart and a great deal of money. Climate: this is what the farmers had to contend with — a long winter; flowering uneven and protracted; heavy rains throughout the summer; September wet and humid, a few rotten grapes picked early October.

Ch. d'Yquem	*(17.7°). The nose was all right and the wine was sweet, with some body. Not bad.* Tasted only once, from a trade cask sample, 1967 ★
Ch. Doisy-Daëne, Sec	*An example of a second-growth Barsac reduced to making a little dry white wine. Palish; rather Graves-like nose; dry, quite nice and crisp — better than most standard Graves.* Tasted 1969, 1970 ★★
Ch. Laville Haut-Brion	*Pale; sulphury nose; dry, raw.* Tasted December 1978.
Ch. Suduiraut	*Medium yellow amber, touch of gold; semi-rich, incomplete bouquet; surprisingly sweet and rich for an "off" year, with good character. Presumably saved by eliminating the rotten grapes and by some old-fashioned wine making.* Tasted March 1978 ★★

1966 ★★★

A charming but uneven year. Climate: overall satisfactory. Picking began 26 September. Characteristics: some of the elegance and firmness of the '66 red Bordeaux, but a lean, sinewy vintage, lacking the flesh of the great classic Sauternes. Highish acidity.

Ch. d'Yquem	*(19.3°). Gold; fruity, acidity on nose; fairly sweet, excellent flavour but lacking that extra richness and depth, some acidity.* Last tasted March 1976 ★★
Ch. Climens	*In 1970 I thought it was a bit thin and weedy for Climens, but subsequently found the wine attractive: firm, rich, well balanced.* Last tasted November 1975 ★★★
Ch. Lafaurie-Peyraguey	*Five notes from 1969. Most recently: pronounced yellow, greenish tinge; light, rather undistinguished, grass-like aroma, touch of honeyed bottle-age; medium sweet, pleasant, thin though fairly assertive flavour.* Last tasted September 1976 ★★ Drink up.
Ch. de Malle	*Piquant with a soft barley-sugar flavour when young.* Tasted 1967.

Ch. Roumieu	*Palish gold; pleasant bouquet; sweetish, lightish, attractive but not great.* Tasted July 1976 ★★
Ch. Sigalas-Rabaud	*Acidic, tailing off to a bitter finish in 1975. Later, fairly rich with highish acidity.* Last tasted 1976.
Ch. Suduiraut	*Fine colour; fruity but a bit unforthcoming and slightly oily; flavoury, a little piquant.* Tasted November 1978

Some dry whites:

Ch. Carbonnieux	*Earthy, surprisingly* spritzig. Tasted 1968, 1971 ★
Ch. Haut-Brion Blanc	*Straw gold; mild, well mannered but slightly short.* Tasted 1971 ★★
Ch. Laville Haut-Brion	*First tasted and impressed by it in 1971: a bright yellow colour which it retains; rather low-keyed bouquet but soft, beautiful, gentlemanly wine. Beautifully balanced.* Last tasted September 1978 ★★★
Ch. Loudenne Blanc	*One of the few white Médocs. This was one of the first wines made after replanting and, with new methods of vinification, resembled a very dry, light, refreshing Loire wine.* Tasted at the château in October 1968 ★★ For quick drinking.
Ch. La Louvière	*Fairly yellow; rich little bouquet; dryish, good balance, nice acidity.* Tasted September 1975 ★

1967 ★★★★

The opposite to 1966: far better for the white than for the red, and an outstanding year for Sauternes, the best since 1959. Climate: flowering late; hot dry summer; September rains weakened the reds but late September sun helped the Sauternes and picking began 27 September. Characteristics: the wines have breeding; good bones, well constituted, well proportioned, and with that quality of flesh that gives the wine its richness and shape. Add to this a healthy glowing complexion. Fine Sauternes.

Ch. d'Yquem	*(20°). Considered by the Comte Alexandre de Lur-Saluces to be one of the best Yquems of this century, which is high praise indeed. Noted on 19 occasions since first tasted at the château in 1973, I find consistent quality showing through. The original pale gold has deepened to pure amber gold; the aroma has opened up from mint leaf and muscatel to a fine, rich, classic bouquet — honeyed, overripe, botrytis grape smell; holding its sugar, fairly full-bodied, rich pronounced flavour, finish still a little hard and, if one is overcritical, lacking a little finesse. But will gain, in my opinion, with further age.* Last tasted November 1969 ★★★★(★) Drink 1985–2025.
Ch. Climens	*Variable. Bottles tasted in 1973: rich, good, plenty of life. But a recent half-bottle disappointing: palish; high-toned, slightly amylacetate nose; rich but raw, edgy, bitter finish.* Last tasted February 1978. At best ★★★ Drink up.
Ch. Coutet	*Tasted on ten occasions since 1974, six times in half-bottles, all château bottled and consistently disappointing: not bad but unimpressive; feeble nose — vanilla, caramel, lanolin; nice enough flavour but short.* Last tasted September 1978 ★ Drink up.
Ch. de Fargues	*A ruined castle in the village of that name, owned by the Lur-Saluces. The only vintage I have ever tasted of this wine but on*

	several occasions between 1974 and 1976 it gave the utmost pleasure. Fine gold; ripe, most attractive honeyed bouquet; sweet, lovely rich flavour and balance. *Last tasted June 1976* ★★★★ *Drink now — 1995.*
Ch. Guiraud	Two good fat bottles in 1974. Yellow gold; pourriture richness and cress; fairly sweet, rich, good flavour and finish. Better than earlier postwar vintages. *Last tasted December 1976* ★★★★ *Drink now — 1995.*
Ch. Lafaurie-Peyraguey	Attractive colour, medium, not very deep; very good rich ripe honeyed bouquet; sweet, fullish, very rich and meaty. Alongside Yquem, in 1976: just lacked that extra richness, complexity and length. Excellent though. *Last tasted May 1979* ★★★★ *Drink now — 2000.*
Ch. Liot	Palish for a Barsac, more like a Graves; pleasant youthful aroma; medium sweet, lightish and not altogether inappropriately served as an aperitif by my French hosts. *Tasted February 1971* ★★ *Drink now — 1988.*
Ch. Pajot	A great improvement on the '64: medium gold, very bright; rich, a touch of almonds; sweet, classic Sauternes style and weight. *Tasted January 1971* ★★★ *Drink now — 1988.*
Ch. Rieussec	Rich but, as usual, not heavy. *Tasted 1971* ★★★ *Drink now — 1990.*
Ch. Sigalas-Rabaud	Medium-pale yellow gold; very fragrant, slightly mint leaf; fairly sweet, luscious but not cloying, elegant. *Tasted 1974, 1975, 1976* ★★★★
Ch. Suduiraut	Eight consistently good notes since 1974. Most recently: curiously paler than '66, more lemon gold; very sweet, soft, rich bouquet; a sweet wine altogether, fairly full bodied, fat, rich but well balanced. My sort of wine. *Last tasted October 1979* ★★★★ *Drink now — 2000 plus.*

Amongst the dry whites:

Ch. Bouscaut	Quite nice, dry, uninspired. *Tasted 1973, 1974* ★ *Drink up.*
Dom. de Chevalier	Palish still; light waxy bouquet; medium dryness and weight, very harmonious oaky/vanilla. *Tasted September 1975* ★★★ *Drink now — 1985.*
Ch. Couhins	Unusual for a Graves: 100 per cent Sauvignon-Blanc, almond flavoured, light and short. *Tasted 1975.*
Ch. Haut-Brion Blanc	Pale colour; delicate, gentle, understated, fine Graves nose; dry, delicate, stylish, good acidity. *Tasted 1971, 1972* ★★★ *Drink now — 1986.*
Ch. Laville Haut-Brion	Variable notes since 1972. Recently: very bright straw yellow; curious — a calm, even, Semillon/lanolin aroma but with Sauvignon-Blanc piquancy on the palate. *Last tasted September 1978* ★★ *Drink up.*

1968

A disastrous and wholly declassified Sauternes vintage. Climate: cold spring; poor flowering conditions; sunless summer; August coldest and wettest for 20 years. Unripe grapes.

Ch. d'Yquem	Not marketed, but I was shown the wine, with some reluctance, when still in cask as I was curious to taste an Yquem "off" vintage. It had a fairly deep amber colour with a weak, watery rim; unforthcoming bouquet; quite sweet and some richness but with high acidity and touch of bitterness. *Tasted April 1973.*
Ch. Laville Haut-Brion	Bright yellow; good honeyed nose; very dry, kernelly flavour. *Tasted December 1978* ★

1969 ★★

Initially quite a good rating but, as with red Bordeaux, variable and meagre. Climate: the damage was done around flowering time and just after; early September wet, but there followed fine sunny weather through October which at least gave Sauternes a chance. Picking began 1 October. Characteristics: somewhat skinny and with high fixed acidity. Not unlike the '57s but lacking the latter's fruit. I doubt its stamina.

Ch. d' Yquem	*First tasted in cask in April 1973: the correct* pourriture *on the nose but crisp on the palate with fairly marked acidity. Noted that it was quite nice and might well turn into a light 1957-type wine. More recently: it has gained colour; nose and palate quite rich and sweet. Some end acidity.* Last tasted March 1976 ★(★)? Hard to assess future.
Ch. Climens	*I found this attractive in 1973, with good acidity. Later, un-impressive: pale, lemon tinged; grass-like nose and flavour, slightly hot kernelly acid end. Feeble.* Last tasted November 1976. Drink up.
Ch. Coutet	*Palish yellow; quite pleasant nose; medium sweet lacking fat, lightish but firm end flavour.* Tasted November 1975 ★★ Drink now — 1985.
Ch. Doisy-Védrines	*Château bottled: good with some colour, sweetness and fat in 1972. Two London bottled both paler; odd about the nose, oily and un-Barsac-like; less sweet, thin and disappointing.* Last tasted 1973. Château bottled probably ★★ Needs drinking.
Ch. Lafaurie-Peyraguey	*Quite nice but not very well-knit. Palish yellow gold; bouquet a little peppery and called to mind ivy leaves; touch of acidity.* Tasted twice, in September 1976 ★ Drink up.
Ch. Rieussec	*I always think of Rieussec as being light and Barsac-like and Climens fatter and Sauternes-like, but in 1969 the roles were reversed: the colour was more yellow, the nose and taste richer.* Tasted twice, in 1976 ★★★ Drink now — 1986.
Ch. Sigalas-Rabaud	*Very un-Sauternes looking — rather pale, with a greenish tinge; medium sweet, quite nice.* Tasted March 1976 ★ Drink up.
Ch. Suduiraut	*Yellow amber gold; attractive, peach-like; sweet, quite good flavour and a fair finish. One of best '69s.* Tasted April 1978 ★★ Drink now — 1988.

Of the dry whites:

Ch. Carbonnieux	*Palish, flat yellow colour; bland lanolin aroma; dryish, a smooth, broad flavour with nice finish.* Tasted 1974 ★★ Drink up.
Ch. Doisy-Daëne, Sec	*Pale; stewed and unappealing nose; dry, dull.* Tasted 1974.
Ch. Haut-Brion Blanc	*Intriguing, classic, very dry, high fixed acidity.* Tasted 1973, 1974.
Ch. Laville Haut-Brion	*Very dry, fresh, fairly high acidity.* Tasted April 1978 ★ Drink up.

1970 ★★★

Good reputation, but is it fully justified? Climate: the main significance for Sauternes was the long hot autumn, early September to November, which fully ripened the grapes but inhibited *pourriture noble*. Characteristics: a consistent lack of colour, richness and (for great Sauternes) fat and flesh, though the alcoholic content and extract can be high. Graves are good.

Ch. d'Yquem	*Lemon tinged in cask in 1973. Five notes and four years later : still too pale for a classic year; lovely pineapple bouquet; sweet, crisp, attractive flavour.* Last tasted April 1980 ***(*) Drink now — 1995.
Ch. Climens	*Pale, not much gold; honey, some botrytis; very pleasant flavou, some richness, nice balance. Good but not great.* Tasted February 1977 *** Drink now — 1992.
Ch. Coutet	*Five notes from 1974. Most recently: yellow but a bit pale for good Sauternes vintage; pleasant, cress-like undeveloped nose; medium sweet, pleasant but lightweight like the '67.* Tasted May 1978 **
Ch. Doisy-Védrines	*Yellow; honeyed, attractive nose and flavour. Lightish.* Tasted March 1978 ** Drink now — 1990.
Ch. Filhot	*When young: palish, lemon tinge; lovely fragrant aroma, a bit "green"; sweet, nice body, pleasant.* Tasted only once, in April 1974 ** Drink now — 1988.
Ch. Guiraud	*Preferred it when younger, in 1975/76. Now buttery yellow, too pale for a good vintage with bottle-age; waxy, light, undeveloped nose; medium sweet, earlier bottles rich, but recently I felt it disappointingly light in style.* Last tasted January 1979 ** Drink now — 1988.
Ch. Lafaurie-Peyraguey	*Six notes from 1975. Most recently: bright yellow; lightly honeyed* Semillon, *little or no honeyed botrytis on the nose; not very sweet, lacking fat, firm, attractive but not impressive.* Tasted December 1977 **
Ch. Rieussec	*Yellow, with the faintest gold tinge; nice, gently sweet, lightly honeyed nose; fairly sweet and full, some richness and good finish. One of the best Rieussecs for some time. Probably deeper now, developing well.* Tasted October 1975 ***(*) Drink now — 1992.
Ch. Suduiraut	*First tasted in 1975: sweet but not as plump as usual. In April 1978: palish lemon gold; honey and ripe peaches; very sweet, medium full bodied, lovely flavour and balance, though a more recent sample surprisingly pale with almond kernels and sulphur dioxide on the nose.* Last tasted November 1978 **(*) Drink now — 1988?
Ch. La Tour-Blanche	*Attractive light yellow gold; pleasant overripe* Semillon *character; medium sweet, but not weighty enough though attractive.* Tasted April 1977 **(*) Drink now — 1992.

Of the dry whites:

Ch. Baret	*Only mentioned because there are so many more interesting and exciting wines in the world than this sort of dull Graves: pale, colour; sulphury nose; dryish, lightish, quite nice but. . . .* Tasted 1975.
Ch. Carbonnieux	*Fruity, positive, ripe, one of best.* Last tasted February 1978 *** Drink now — 1985.
Dom. de Chevalier	*Very dry, firm, flavoury.* Tasted 1973–1975 *** Drink now — 1985.
Ch. Haut-Brion Blanc	*Powerful, rich and steely, almost raspingly immature.* Tasted 1973. *A wine that needs time* *** Drink now — 1995.
Ch. Laville Haut-Brion	*An extraordinary wine: lovely colour, pronounced yellow; rich, nutty, complex but slightly unknit; medium dry, full bodied (13° G.L., which is unusually high for a dry white wine), powerful, nutty, flavoury.* Tasted September 1978 **(**)? Drink now — 1995.

1971 ★★★

A good vintage. Climate: a slow (cool and damp) start with a better end. Picking started 1 October in good autumn weather. Assessment: although not overly impressive at first, they have the core and suppleness of a long-distance runner. Yquem not tasted.

Ch. d'Arche	Good yellow colour; a touch too hard; medium sweet, rich, alcoholic, some flesh. *Tasted September 1979 ★★(★) Drink 1982–1995.*
Ch. Climens	A most attractive wine: good nose and flavour, sweet enough, flesh but not fat, excellent balance. *At the Mérite dinner at Brooks's, June 1980 ★★★(★)*
Ch. Coutet	Lovely yellow, gold tinged; lovely, even, ripe, honeyed bouquet; sweet, perfect flavour and balance, good end acidity. Far better than Coutet '67 and '70 and should improve. *Tasted February 1979 ★★★(★) Drink now — 1990.*
Ch. Doisy-Daëne	Too pale; a bit grass-like, no richness but pleasant enough; medium sweet, some fat, soft but nothing great. *Tasted June 1979 ★★ Drink up.*
Ch. Lafaurie-Peyraguey	Palish, lemon tinged; lightly honeyed, grass-like; medium sweet, lightish — a new-style light Sauternes, attractive but not impressive. *Tasted October 1978 ★★ Drink now — 1986.*
Ch. Sigalas-Rabaud	Good bright yellow, fresh, mint leaf and honey, medium sweet, medium soft, fleshy, nice acidity. *Tasted July 1979 ★★★ Drink now — 1990.*
Ch. Suduiraut	Medium pale; attractive, fruity, high toned; medium sweet, light shortish end. Not at all the old Suduiraut style. *Tasted November 1978 ★★ Drink now — 1984.*

And one amazing 1971 Graves:

Ch. Laville Haut-Brion	Incredible colour, very bright; gentle, very rich, Barsac-like; dry but unusually full bodied (13.5° G.L.), very intense, firm, marked acidity — made from exceptionally ripe grapes deliberately left on the vines as long as possible. *Tasted September 1978 ★★★★*

1972

A poor vintage for Sauternes, many declassified; uneven for Graves. Not enough tasted to express a general opinion.

Ch. Broustet	Very pale; ordinary, sulphury nose; flavour of boiled sweets. *Tasted 1975.*
Ch. La Chartreuse	Admittedly a minor and inexpensive wine: very pale; stewed aroma; very sweet, bitty and short. *Tasted 1975.*
Ch. Nairac	Palish; pleasant nose; attractive flavour, refreshing acidity. Trying hard. *Tasted 1976 ★*
Ch. Suduiraut	Palish lemon; light, high toned; medium sweet, lightish, no length, twist of acidity. *Tasted April 1978. Drink up, do not keep.*

1973 ★★

Moderate, lightweight. Few tasted.

Ch. Carbonnieux	*Consistently reliable dry Graves: good colour; nice nose; fresh clean flavour, good balance.* Tasted April 1977 ★★ *Drink up.*
Ch. Climens	*Palish; pasty, vanilla aroma; medium sweet, light but firm. Quite nice.* Tasted June 1977 ★★ *Drink now — 1988.*
Ch. Lafaurie-Peyraguey	*Rather weak colour; vanilla aroma; fairly sweet and some richness.* Tasted September 1978 ★ *Drink now — 1986.*
Ch. Nairac	*Palish but pronounced yellow; light quite pleasant grass-like aroma; medium sweet, lightish. Liot-type wine.* Tasted August 1979 ★★ *Drink now — 1986.*

1974

The worst Sauternes vintage of what is clearly a dismal period. Cold rainy weather during the vintage. Graves also indifferent.

1975 ★★★

Moderately good, though better for red than for white Bordeaux. Picking started 29 September. A very wide range tasted recently which, frankly, I found generally disappointing. Time will sort out the men from the boys.

Ch. Coutet	*Medium pale; heavy, rich, herbal aroma; sweet, medium full body, rich, tangy, good aftertaste.* Tasted November 1978 ★★(★★) *Drink 1982–2000.*
Ch. Doisy-Védrines	*Palish yellow; gentle botrytis nose, touch of almond kernels — fining; sweet, lightish, very flavoury, nice acidity and aftertaste.* Tasted October 1978 ★★(★) *Drink 1982–1992.*
Ch. Filhot	*Palish, slightly green tinge; low-keyed, ripe but not overripe* Semillon *aroma; medium sweet, not a great deal of fruit.* Tasted November 1978 ★(★) *Drink 1982–1990.*
Ch. Guiraud	*Medium colour; curiously rich nose; medium sweetness and body, slightly piquant flavour.* Tasted November 1978 ★(★) *Drink 1982–1992.*
Ch. Lafaurie-Peyraguey	*Hardly recognizable as a Sauternes in cask in April 1976: pale, still not fallen bright; youthful fruit, light* Semillon, *touch of piquant* Sauvignon-Blanc *but no botrytis; medium sweet, fruity, youthful acidity. More recently: still fairly pale, faint green tinge; light herbaceous grass-like aroma; straightforward, no great depth.* Last tasted November 1978 ★(★) *Drink 1983–1993.*
Ch. de Rayne-Vigneau	*Palish; uninspiring nose, touch of oak/vanilla; sweet, medium full body, nicely made but rather untamed end acidity. Should develop a little.* Tasted November 1978 ★★(★) *Drink 1982–1995.*

Ch. Rieussec	*Good colour; quite rich waxy* Semillon *nose; fairly sweet, hot dry finish, raisiny aftertaste.* Tasted November 1978 *(**) Drink 1983–1995.
Ch. Sigalas-Rabaud	*Palish; crisp blackcurrant-like* Sauvignon-Blanc *predominant; medium sweetness and body, a bit short.* Tasted November 1978 *(*) Drink 1982–1990.
Ch. Suduiraut	*Still in cask: good colour; honeyed (botrytis) nose; sweet, fullish, good flavour and acidity, slightly bitter finish which should wear off in time.* Tasted April 1978 **(*) Drink 1984–2000.
Ch. La Tour-Blanche	*Sweet, clean, attractive in cask in September 1976. Later: palish; curious unknit nose — slightly sharp, high toned, resiny; medium sweetness and body, a piquant barley-sugar taste. Needs time to harmonize.* Last tasted November 1978 *(*) Drink 1984–1995.
Minor wines	*Showing well in 1978: Ch. St-Amand; Ch. Roumieu.*
Minor and unimpressive	*Tasted in 1978: Ch. d'Arche; Ch. Broustet; Ch. Chantegril; Ch. Doisy-Daëne; Ch. Haut-Bergeran; Ch. Liot; Ch. Raymond-Lafon.*

1976 ★★★★★

Potentially great, particularly for those made in the classic tradition. Picking started 21 September. Well worth selecting and keeping. Few tasted yet.

Ch. Filhot	*Yellow, with green tinge, attractive; appealing aroma — pineapple and honey; fairly sweet, attractive, flavoury, probably early developer. One of the best Filhots for years.* Tasted May 1977 ***
Clos du Pavillon Ste-Croix-du-Mont	*Just shows how attractive (and what good value) some of the sweet wines from across the Garonne can be: very bright; sweet, soft vanilla nose; sweet, fleshy, nice acidity. A modest charmer.* Tasted at Robin Don's, August 1979 **
Ch. Suduiraut	*The first reassuringly classic-style Sauternes of the 1970s. From the cask: very deep, magnificent colour; equally rich and magnificent aroma and flavour. Very sweet, positively fat, not a trace of youthful bitterness.* Tasted April 1978 ***(*)
Amongst the dry Graves:	
Ch. Bouscaut Blanc	*Palish yellow; ordinary, rather heavy but immature nose; dry, blunt, youthful acidity. Not very exciting.* Tasted September 1978 *
Ch. Carbonnieux	*Very pale, greenish, bright; fragrant nose, mixture of tilleul and kernels; dryish, flowery flavour but tailed off.* Tasted September 1978 ** Drink soon.
Ch. Haut-Brion Blanc	*Roughly 50 per cent* Semillon, *50 per cent* Sauvignon-Blanc. *Very pronounced yellow; honeyed* Semillon *uppermost, beautifully complex bouquet; dry, good body and flavour, assertive, backbone of firm acidity.* At a tasting with Alexis Bespaloff at the Windows of the World restaurant, New York, October 1979 **(**) Drink 1982–1995.
Ch. Laville Haut-Brion	*Pale yellow, very bright; outstanding bouquet — rich, generous, honeyed and well-knit; medium dry, lovely ripe flavour but lightish in style though firm, long.* Tasted September and December 1978 **(**) Drink 1982–2000.

Ch. La Louvière	*Made entirely from* Sauvignon-Blanc *grapes: palish; rather raw, mouthwatering, fruitbush aroma; bone dry, lightish — reminiscent of, but more solid than, Sancerre. Interesting. Refreshing.* Tasted *January 1978* ⁎⁎ *For quick drinking.*

1977

Poor vintage, late picking from 20 October, small crop.

Ch. Filhot	*The only '77 Sauternes tasted: very pale; rather light, high-toned, boiled-sweets nose; sweet enough, lightish and undistinguished.* Bottled at the château for a trade tasting in London, May 1978 ⁎

1978 ★★★

Good but not great. Climate: an appallingly dismal summer saved by a protracted Indian summer, which ripened the grapes but was not suitable for the formation of botrytis. As in 1970 it will have alcohol and extract due to the hot sun, rather than the lusciousness and sweetness resulting from overripe, botrytis-affected grapes.

1979 (★★★)?

Showing promise. Another late harvest, but this time with botrytis. Prediction: too early — at the time of writing — to taste, but 1979 might well be to 1978 what 1971 was to 1970.

RED
BURGUNDY

Burgundy is not Bordeaux. The climate is different: a continental climate as opposed to a maritime climate. The terrain is totally different: the main quality area, the *Côte d'Or*, is a long straight slope of vineyards looking south-east across a broad fertile valley towards the Jura and Switzerland beyond. The Médoc by contrast is flat and pebbly, between river and sea. Above all, the grape variety is different: *Pinot*, which gives the wine its special character.

At best, burgundy is rich and velvety to look at, but not necessarily deep coloured. I do not usually use the French expression *robe*, but it does seem to fit what one seeks in the appearance of a good red burgundy.

The *Pinot* aroma and flavour is hard to describe. Mint has a mint-like smell, garlic is garlic, *Pinot* is *Pinot* — more root-like in character as opposed to the fruit-bush crispness of *Cabernet-Sauvignon*. A lecturer once likened the *Pinot* aroma to boiled beetroot, and I know what he meant. The wines are softer — fine, mature burgundy is velvety, usually quite alcoholic, often heady. And even young, immature burgundy does not have the swingeingly tannic dryness, the astringency, of red Bordeaux.

Quality and longevity
It is commonly said, outside Burgundy, that the reds are no longer of the quality they used to be, they are too light and will not keep. I believe that even if partially true it is unfair and misleading. Take paleness of colour and lightness of style and body. Some growers, most noticeably in the 1960s, began to introduce speeded up wine-making methods. Shorten the fermentation and less colour is extracted. The wines are lighter, quicker maturing, easy to sell and can be drunk quickly. Good for business. But just because some wines are not deep coloured this does not mean to say that they are poor or will not keep. Only in certain years are the red wines naturally deep. My point really is that the English, and American, merchant and his customer have been brought up on burgundy coloured and strengthened by blending in wines from the south.

Well-constituted burgundy will last as long as a good Bordeaux. Lightness of colour and style can be misleading: the key is the intrinsic quality and balance of the component parts. I am sure that many '71s and the better constituted '76s will last well; so might many other lighter looking wines.

Red burgundy pre-1945
There can be no systematic tastings of old wines; one either has an opportunity — and finds it of interest — or one hasn't. What follows, therefore, is a record of some of those snatched opportunities. There is no point in including estimated life spans; all should have been drunk ages ago. To add perspective I have started with brief historical references to old vintages.

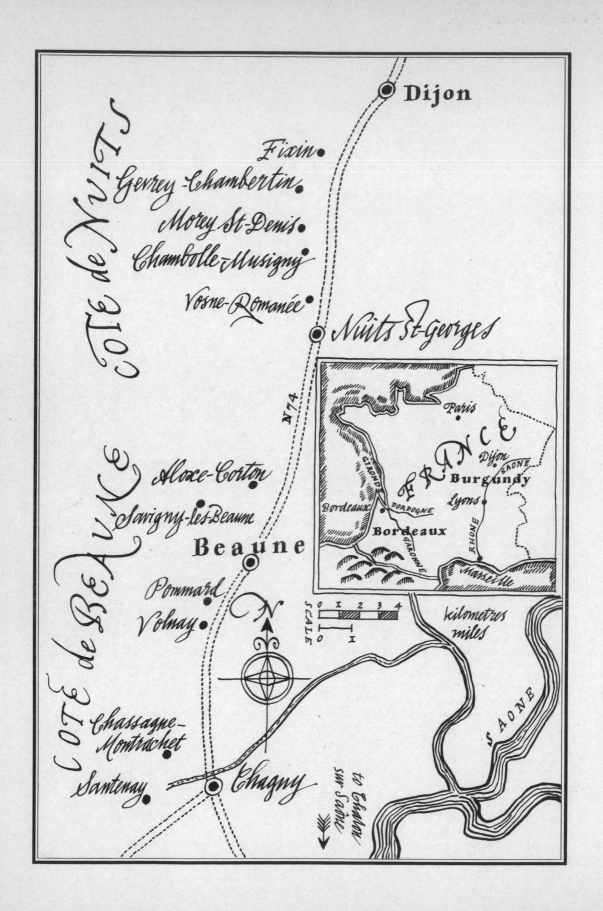

1753, 1755, 1757 and 1766 ★★★

All good vintages.

1768

On 24 January, the first appearance of burgundy in a Christie's sale.

1771, 1772 and 1774 ★★★

1778

The year in which Burgundy vineyards appear by name in a Christie's catalogue: Chambertin, Pommard, Nuits, Chassagnes from the cellar of the Marquis de Noailles.

1784 ★★★, 1788 and 1791 ★★★★

1795, 1798 ★★★

1801 ★★★, 1802 ★★★★, 1803 ★★★

1806 ★★★★, 1807 ★★★

1811 ★★★★★

The "Comet" vintage.

1815 ★★★★, 1818 ★★★

1819, 1822 and 1825 ★★★★, 1827 ★★★

1832

Chassagne-Rouge. The oldest burgundy that I have tasted; from a house near Lyons. The first bottle ullaged halfway down the deep sloping shoulder: very pale in colour, hardly any redness left, with a light, watery rim; tired, strained old bouquet, but still a touch of sweetness and richness; a positive flavour, slightly too acidic and astringent but drinkable — quite remarkable for a table wine nearly one and a half centuries old. Second bottle similar, slightly sweeter on the palate.
At a Heublein tasting in New Orleans, May 1977.

1834 ★★★★, 1840 ★★★, 1846 ★★★★★

1848 ★★★★, 1849 ★★★

1858 ★★★

Corton, Clos du Roi (Labaume Aîné). The oldest of a vast array of burgundies sold for the widow of the previous owner of Labaume. Good unbranded cork. Pale but lively; rich, meaty, fruity bouquet; faded, light but sound, clean and attractive. Very good for its age.
Tasted August 1967 ★★★

1859 ★★★★

1864 ★★★★

As in Bordeaux, the 20 years before the phylloxera finally took hold produced wines of remarkable quality, a fact supported by much circumstantial evidence: contemporary reports, connoisseurs like George Saintsbury writing at the time the wines were at their peak, and André Simon's notes between the wars. More directly, there is the extraordinary quality of some of the wines of this period still occasionally emerging from cellars. 1864 was one of those great pre-phylloxera vintages.
Beaune, Clos de la Mousse, Tête de Cuvée (Bouchard Père). From the cellar crypt of the Domaine du Château de Beaune. In a contemporary bottle but regularly recorked. Very attractive colour, fading, of course, and autumnal, but with a healthy blush of red; gentle old *Pinot* bouquet; soft, delicate, no decay, slightly roasted end taste. Very fine.
Tasted May 1974 ★★★★

1865 ★★★★★

One of the greatest mid-19th century vintages.
Corton (Loffet). My first experience of a pre-phylloxera burgundy. At the tasting before the sale of "Finest and Rarest Wines" that really put Christie's on the international fine-wine map. Originally purchased by the first Earl of Rosebery from the merchants, Loffet, and binned in 1894. Sold May 1967. Original cork, good level. A lovely medium-light, orange-red colour; fabulous old *Pinot* bouquet and flavour; medium dry, still a fair amount of body, rich, lovely warm finish. A revelation.
Tasted April 1967 ★★★★★
Beaune, Première Cuvée, Grizot (Bouchard Père). Grizot was a *vigneron à moitié*. He farmed and tended the vines and received in return half the production. Over the past few years the Bouchard family have produced from the cellars of the Domaine du Château de Beaune several bottles of this and the following wine for the annual Heublein auctions. All had been periodically recorked and when necessary topped up. Another bottle has had to be sacrificed for this. Beautiful healthy colour for its age; very pronounced and lovely, smoky, old *Pinot* bouquet; slightly sweet, rich but fading a little, really lovely flavour and fragrant aftertaste.
Tasted May 1977, 1978 ★★★★★
Volnay, Santenots. Also Bouchard Père. Equally good, but difficult to detect district differences at this age.
Tasted May 1978 ★★★★★
Clos Vougeot, Tête de Cuvée (Bouchard Père). Made before the break up of the *clos* into many small parcels in 1889. Last recorked in the middle 1960s, perfect fill. Fine deep colour, quite remarkable for its age; perfect bouquet — rich, slightly singed *Pinot*; almost sweet, the result of a rich, ripe vintage. Lovely flavour, deep but languorous, beautiful balance and condition.
At a Heublein pre-sale tasting, May 1978 ★★★★★

1868 ★★, 1869 ★★★★

1870 ★★★★

Fine rich wines made in this year.

1875 ★★★★★

A great vintage. Quality and abundant quantity. Stylish wines that kept well.
Chambertin, Tête de Cuvée (Charles Bernard). A sort of reincarnation: from a previously unopened wooden case from the Ten Broeck mansion, New Jersey. Case fully branded, including the rarely seen information "bottled 1878". Original straw sleeves, tissue wrappings, capsules and labels — all in mint condition.

Two bottles opened, both with very good levels: a lovely old tawny colour with a warm ruddy glow; distinctly old on the nose, cracking up, acidity uppermost; slightly sweet on the palate. One bottle had a soft, rich, long flavour, the other was faded and oxidized, overacid. *At Heublein pre-sale tastings, May 1977. At best* ★★★

Beaune (Geisweiler). Also from the Ten Broeck cellars, pristine, except for the level, five inches below cork — clearly the original cork had been losing its grip gradually for at least 50 years. Result: pale tawny colour; old overripe nose; light, tired and tart. *Tasted May 1977.*

1877 ★★★

"Vinous, soft and flavoury, with high character." (Bouchard Père in May 1979.) Little seen.

1878 ★★★★

Refined, well-constituted wines. *Climate:* very satisfactory budding and flowering, no frosts. Alarmingly wet August but magnificent vintage weather. An abundant crop of high-priced wines.

Unknown burgundy (Geo. Claridge). The only burgundy in Sir George Meyrick's magnificent cellars sold at Christie's in 1970. The bin label read "Claridge Burgandy [*sic*]/1878/No 330/10 dozen @ 42s./Packed [binned] Jan. 1888". Excellent but unbranded original cork, good level. Pale tawny red, very mature looking; lovely old *Pinot* bouquet and flavour; not a trace of decay but drying out and thinning. A fine quality wine.

Tasted August 1970 ★★★★★ *The reason why these corks — and the wine — had survived (and the Ten Broeck bottles were less good) was undoubtedly due to cellar conditions, for both had remained undisturbed for about a century. The Bodorgan cellar was consistently cold and extremely damp; Ten Broeck's were cool and clearly dust dry, possibly with seasonal temperature variations.*

1885 ★★★

A fairly good though not great year following a string of dismal vintages. *Climate:* slow start but backward vines blossomed in fine warm weather and continued favourably. Quality good. Quantity above average.

Chambertin, Tête de Cuvée (Bouchard Père). Pale, very faded colour but holding on to life; old but sound; light, faded but still a pleasant little flavour. *At a Heublein tasting, May 1973* ★★

1886 ★★★

A very good vintage, "delightful" according to George Saintsbury, but rarely seen now.

1887 ★★★★

An extremely good year. Favourable climatic conditions.

Clos Vougeot (Bouchard Père). A delightful wine, amazingly well preserved despite the size of bottle. Fairly pale and veering towards amber; light, delicate, almost syrupy sweet bouquet; faded though lovely flavour and good vinosity. Dry, firm edge and finish. *English stock, in half-bottles. Tasted first with Leslie Haworth, a Cheshire connoisseur, in 1958 and later with the (then) young and precocious Melvyn Master in December 1966* ★★★

1889 ★

Generally regarded the last "phylloxera-free" vintage.

1893 ★★★

Quality variable, some extremely good wines made in conditions of great heat. *Climate:* exceptionally hot, dry summer; unusually early harvest at end of August.

Savigny. Lightish but good colour; very attractive smell and taste, in good condition and with long finish. Remarkable for a minor district wine of this age. *From Glamis Castle, tasted prior to sale, June 1971* ★★★

Clos Vougeot. Slight ullage. Muddy, murky appearance; maderized nose; lifeless but not undrinkable. For vinous necrophiliacs. *From the Garvan cellars, New York. Tasted November 1971.*

1894 ★★★, 1898 ★★★

1900 ★★

Moderately good, variable. Not as uniformly fine as in Bordeaux. *Climate:* New Year mild and wet; cold March; good flowering; warm weather until end of August; storms and heavy rain in September prejudiced quality, but abundant yield.

Chambertin, Tête de Cuvée (F. Chauvenet). Good colour for age; amazingly rich, powerful bouquet; a bit overblown but exercising a dangerous fascination. A fabulous aftertaste. *From a New England cellar. Tasted May 1977* ★★★

Nuits (Calvet). This was believed to be 1900. It could just have been 1915. Good: rich old nose; distinctly sweet, soft, hot peppery finish. *From a good private cellar in Bordeaux. Tasted 1978, 1979* ★★

1904 ★★★★

Very good year, stylish and soft. *Climate:* weather pattern ideal, summer dryness compensated by rain at end of August. Harvest 17 September to end of month under optimistic conditions.

Clos Vougeot. Two-inch ullage (a good level for this age of burgundy). Very pale in colour; surprisingly sweet, scented vanilla nose and taste; very pleasant, remarkably rich and good. *From a New York cellar. Tasted November 1971* ★★★

Vosne, Première Cuvée. Good colour; excellent rich, perfumed old wine. *From Glamis Castle. Tasted June 1971* ★★★

Musigny (Bruninghaus). Magnificent and nowhere near the end of its life. Burnt amber colour; full flowery bouquet; fruit and still a little hard. *Tasted January 1955* ★★★

1906 ★★★★★

Excellent vintage, even better than 1904. Full, supple, fragrant wines, considered perfect. *Climate:* ideal for quality — no spring frosts, satisfactory flowering; hot summer reduced yield but concentrated quality. Harvest completed by end of September.

Clos de Corton, Tête de Cuvée (grower unknown). Rather low in the neck and with soft cork. Light colour but a good healthy glow; very fragrant bouquet, piquant, enticing, truffles and cats; firm, rapier-like on the palate. Curiously appealing. *Tasted May 1975* ★★★

1907 ★★★

Good but light wines, rarely seen.

1908

Poorish: light and "green" wines following capricious weather conditions.

Mercurey (v. Kapff). German bottled. Extremely good for a southern Burgundy wine of such age and reported only for this reason.

From a private cellar in Bremen. Tasted May 1977 ★★

1911 ★★★★★

A magnificent classic burgundy vintage. Below average yield. Excellent quality. *Climate:* cold winter; moderate spring; ideal flowering; July and August fine and hot for early ripening. Harvest in before end of September.

Chambertin (Lupé-Cholet). 1½-inch ullage, hard crumbly cork. Mahogany colour; gentle, pure old *Pinot* aroma, holding well; dry, refreshing, slightly overacid finish. Nice though.

From the Garvan cellar, New York. Tasted February 1971 ★★

Chassagne-Montrachet (Labaume Ainé). Lightish but fine colour; rich and complex nose; fine, rich and silky on the palate. Good acidity, excellent finish.

Tasted August 1967 ★★★

Musigny (Lupé-Cholet). Fairly good level. Fine, fullish colour for age; slightly sickly nose; sweet, rich, very flavoury, with peppery end acidity.

Also from the Garvan cellar. Tasted November 1971 ★

Santenay (Dr Barolet). Light colour, no red left; old, rich but a trifle sour on the nose and palate. Second bottle identical. Disappointing but successes followed.

At original tasting at Barolet house in Beaune, October 1969.

La Tâche-Romanée (Jules Regnier). Ullaged low shoulder but holding well despite this level and age: fairly deep, rich colour, mature brown but touch of red; rich, stably nose and flavour.

From a private cellar in Paris. Tasted May 1976 ★★

Clos Vougeot (Faiveley). Fullish, good colour; flowery bouquet; good flavour balance and condition.

From a West Country cellar. Tasted June 1971 ★★★

1915 ★★★★★

A great vintage; full, fruity wines with good colour. Considered perfect. *Climate:* favourable weather conditions through to early (mid-September) harvest. Grapes in superb condition. Above average yield.

Bonnes-Mares. Beautiful; rich, old *Pinot* bouquet and flavour; powerful yet silky. Extremely attractive.

At lunch with Sichel & Co, May 1967 ★★★★

Chambertin, Vieux Cépages (Labaume Ainé). From old vines: a lovely, old, refined bouquet and flavour, overripe *Pinot* on the nose; rich and honeyed on palate. Fading but delicious.

Tasted 1967, May 1968 ★★★

Musigny, Tête de Cuvée (Bouchard Père). Very pale indeed; old, refined, very mature but sound.

From the Bouchard cellars in Beaune. Tasted May 1973 ★★

Musigny (Labaume Ainé). Long, thin, wizened, fully branded cork, but good level. Pale colour, fully mature with slight orange tinge but lively and pretty; lovely refined *Pinot* bouquet, deliciously opulent overripe overtones; dry, light, flavour to match. Beautiful acidity. It was this wine that made me think of an overripe

burgundy being like well-hung game: exotic, flavoury but with a touch of rot and not to everyone's taste.

At pre-sale tasting, December 1970 ★★★★

Nuits, Cailles (Morin). Absolutely delicious, no signs of decay, firm, good body and exquisite flavour.

Tasted June 1972 ★★★★

1916 ★★

Not great, but considered "decent — light and stylish" at the time. *Climate:* almost identical to Bordeaux. Average yield, quality good. Firm wines.

Aloxe-Corton (Labaume Ainé). Very old looking; surprisingly rich, fine, extended bouquet; rich on palate, too, but unbalanced.

Tasted August 1967 ★★

1917 ★

Moderate quality; quantity disappointing. *Climate:* weather conditions similar to Bordeaux.

Beaune, Clos des Avaux (Labaume Ainé). Lovely colour but palish and very mature looking; earthy, slightly burnt, brackish nose; better on palate — attractive, piquant and refreshing.

Tasted May 1968 ★★

1918 ★★

Quality considered higher than 1917. Above average quantity. *Climate:* similar to Bordeaux: overhot summer with welcome rain in September. Fine harvest.

Chambolle-Musigny, Charmes (Labaume Ainé). Lightish but good colour; delicate, excellent bouquet; remarkable richness, elegance, fine balance.

Tasted August 1967 ★★★

1919 ★★★★★

Outstanding vintage. Quantity below average. Fruity and stylish. *Climate:* favourable for vines throughout the season but rather too hot and dry in August. Yield below average. I have notes of nearly 20 wines of this vintage so have selected a short illustrative range.

Beaune, Bressandes (Labaume Ainé). Pale but lovely colour; delicate bouquet and flavour.

Tasted August and October 1967 ★★★

Chambertin. No shipper's name on label, unbranded corks. Deepish, mature colour; very rich old bouquet, smoky and spicy; holding well (two bottles oxidized).

From a good private cellar in Belgium. Tasted February 1974 ★★

Chambolle-Musigny (Dr Barolet). Remarkably deep for its age, full of colour and life; unassertive at first, a delicate, rich, ripe old grouse, opening up in the glass — a nutty, wholemeal biscuity bouquet; distinctly sweet — the sweetness of a thoroughly ripe wine made from thoroughly ripe grapes — fine, firm, complete flavour, magnificently preserved. In Harry Waugh's opinion, the greatest wine of the entire Barolet collection.

Tasted twice. Last, dining with Harry Waugh in April 1970 ★★★★★

Corton, Tête de Cuvée. Originally from the Hotel St-Petersbourg, Paris. Fine colour; meaty, mature Corton nose; full, fine flavour, excellent acidity. No decay.

Tasted at Christie's, April and May 1978 ★★★

Grands-Echézeaux (shipper unknown). Palish but lovely colour; beautiful mature *Pinot* nose; rich, fine texture and condition.

Tasted October 1970 ★★★

'Hospices de Beaune' (Calvet). Precise vineyard/*cuvée* not stated on label. Excellent cork, long and firm. The deepest and finest of the Teysonneau burgundies from the "young wine" (1915–1929) cellar. Lovely colour, very bright, most appealing; rich, smoky, fragrant, sustained bouquet; sweet, medium body, soft, gentle, firm. Nice acidity. Still some tannin left. Perfect.
One of a fairly big stock of burgundies from Mme Teysonneau's mansion in Bordeaux. Her uncle was a Calvet. Tasted August 1979 ★★★★★

Richebourg. Fine colour; old, sound but curious bouquet — cold tea and cheese; lovely old flavour and finish. Holding well.
From the Restaurant Drouant-Est, Paris. Tasted April 1969 ★★★

Romanée-Conti, Tête de Cuvée (de Vilaine). Two-inch ullage — good. Surprisingly pale (old tawny) but a glimmer of red; charming, fragrant; delicate and faded.
From a fine private cellar in Paris. Tasted May 1976 ★★★

1920 ★★★

Good vintage, softer than 1919 and with less body. Small production. *Climate:* similar to Bordeaux but cryptogamic vine diseases damaged the crop and too little sun in July and August slowed ripening. Harvest late September under excellent conditions.

Aloxe-Corton (Calvet). Palish but warm ruddy colour, very mature; light, rather straw-like, stalky nose; sweet, the lightest of the group, complete but short.
Tasted August 1979 ★★★ *for age and class.*

Chambertin (Calvet). Good long cork, good level. Beautiful tile-red colour; rich bouquet which held well; distinctly sweet, fullish, fairly alcoholic, sustained flavour. Perfect condition and finish.
From the Teysonneau cellar, August 1979 ★★★★

Chambolle-Musigny (Calvet). Fairly loose, soft, crumbly cork. Orange-mahogany colour, very bright; soft, very rich, but low-keyed bouquet, fragrant; sweet, soft, rich, lovely. A very complete wine. Dry finish.
From the Teysonneau cellar, August 1979 ★★★★

Corton, Dumay (Dr Barolet). One of the few Hospices de Beaune wines in the enormous, two-tier, Barolet cellars. Medium colour, rich; marvellously rich old stably bouquet and flavour. Slightly astringent remains of tannin and acidity. Good for a half-bottle.
At a pre-sale tasting, December 1979 ★★★

Vosne-Romanée (Noirot-Carrière). Pleasant, medium, mature red; old waxy but interesting bouquet; dry, medium light in body. Quite good.
Tasted November 1971 ★★

1921 ★★★

A much better vintage for red wine in Burgundy than in Bordeaux, though variable. *Climate:* abnormally long hot summer. Harvest in perfect weather.

Beaune "Cardinal" (R. B. Smith, Perth). Pale but very pretty; a lovely soft, rich and earthy nose; slightly sweet, fading but charming. Held well by a residue of tannin and acidity.
Half-bottles of a locally bottled "ordinaire". From the cellars of Glamis Castle. Tasted April 1971 ★★

Chambolle-Musigny, Les Grandes Charmes (Belgian bottled). The owner's father, a noted connoisseur, had imported and bottled the wine locally. Lovely colour; beautiful, ripe *Pinot* nose which held well in the glass; still some sweetness, excellent flavour, sound, good acidity but getting just a little stringy.
At lunch in Charleroi, January 1977 ★★★★

Charmes-Chambertin (Dr Barolet). A magnificent colour, very rich; bouquet developed beautifully in the glass; a full, rich, harmonious wine — with the angel of death hovering overhead.
Tasted only once, at first tasting in Beaune, October 1969 ★★★★

Fleurie (Mari Père et Fils). Included as it is the oldest beaujolais I have ever tasted. Pale; light, fruity and sound. Touch of end acidity.
At a pre-sale tasting in Geneva, April 1971 ★

Nuits (Calvet). Loose cork which fell in. Not a bad colour, orange mahogany; rich, meaty, singed, hot-vintage bouquet; slightly sweet, soft, lovely rich flavour, excellent acidity. Obviously the old cork, despite giving up the ghost, had protected the wine until the last.
From Mme Teysonneau's cellar. Tasted August 1979 ★★★

Clos de la Roche (Dr Barolet). I have tasted this ubiquitous Barolet wine several times and there is still quite a lot of stock around. (Bottles are now dispersed all round Europe, the United States and Australia.) The full scale of the "Barolet collection" — an expression I coined prior to the Christie sale that brought the cellar on to the market — has never been appreciated. The two-level cellar housed thousands of dozens in old stone bins. There were three bins of Clos de La Roche '21 alone, containing hundreds of dozens. And not surprisingly they varied in condition. At its best it is still full coloured; rich on nose and flavour but a little short. Just to show that it (and I) can travel well, the best bottle of this wine I ever drank was at Len Evans's famous dinner in Sydney, in February 1977. The nose seemed to be more intense, a true fishy *Pinot*, aromatic; soft, lovely flavour and interesting acidity. At its worst, very brown; corky/woody nose; dried out and austere.
Tasted 1969–1978. At its best ★★★

1922 ★

An abundance of reasonably sound wines. *Climate:* weather ideal until middle of August, then cold delayed maturity. Harvest last week of September. *Market:* as will be seen with later vintages, even in the 1950s and 1960s, a year like this, surrounded by much better vintages, tends to be left out in the cold. Few shipped. None tasted by me.

1923 ★★★★

A very good vintage in Burgundy (far better than Bordeaux). Considered beautiful wines, nearly as good as 1915. *Climate:* not easy for the vines, March too wet, April and May cold and wet; June and July too dry. August excessively hot and dry, but some rain in September. Small production.

Beaune (Dr Barolet). Not too good. We did not select this for the Barolet auction in 1969, but some was shipped later. It let the Barolet name down.
Tasted June 1971.

Chambertin (Charleux & Co.). I had never come across this (Beaune) merchant's name before, but a half-bottle was delightful: fine colour; slightly sour at first but the nose cleared and there was a scented ripeness underneath; fading, but rich and attractive.
Tasted July 1972 ★★★

Côte de Nuits Villages (Dr Barolet). When tasting this in the cellars in October 1969 I was in some doubts whether to enter any for the sale; but it was curious and interesting. Appearance rather old and bitty; raspberry-like bouquet which I suspected would be short-lived. Not a bad flavour but a bit blunt — not surprisingly, as it was not a *grand cru* and was never meant to be kept.
Last tasted December 1969 ★

Grands-Echézeaux (Cuvée Engel). Fullish, good colour; old mushrooms but fruit under; sweetish, fairly full bodied, good flavour but marked acidity.
From the Drouant-Est, Paris. Tasted April 1969 ★

Nuits (P. Ponnelle). I picked up a small parcel of this wine for office luncheons and it has almost never failed to delight. Beautiful colour, what the French call *tuilé*; bouquet sometimes a little stuffy on opening but usually cleared well; fairly dry, good firm backbone, quite a bit of body, misleadingly alcoholic in fact, rich, spicy, smoky *Pinot* flavour. Well-nigh perfect. The levels were all good except for one bottle ullaged low shoulder, which was pricked and off.
Tasted 1975 — April 1979 ★★★★

Savigny, Fouquerand (Dr Barolet). An Hospices de Beaune wine bought and bottled by the late Dr Barolet's father (as were all the wines of this period). Medium deep, mature, lovely; light but distinguished bouquet; lightish, refined flavour and texture. Refreshing finish.
At the pre-sale tasting, December 1969 ★★★

1924 ★★★

Pleasant wines that developed well. *Climate:* little summer sunshine and bad weather during the vintage.
Beaune. Another purchase for office entertaining as no one else seemed to be interested in an anonymous old Beaune. In spite of worried anticipation each bottle gave us much pleasure. Fully mature looking; a rich, smoky old bouquet; always soft, fragrant and flavoury. A beguiling mouthful.
From the Drouant-Est. Tasted 1973–1978 ★★ *to* ★★★

Mercurey. From an obscure cellar near Burgundy. A curious orange-pekoe-tea shade; curious malty/ivy-leaf nose; dried out and acidity taking over.
Tasted March 1978.

Volnay, Santenots (Labaume Aîné). Fine old mahogany; remarkably sweet, honeyed, rich, forthcoming; soft, most agreeable, fully mature, excellent condition.
Tasted 1967, 1968 ★★★★

1925

Considered a poor vintage: light, dry, hard and astringent. Half the normal harvest due to the prevalence of a vineyard pest, *cochylis*.
Fleurie (Jaboulet-Verchère). The first really old beaujolais I ever drank. Lovely old bouquet, immediately attractive, which seemed to gulp in the air, on the verge of breakdown, but then held well; slightly sweet, light and charming flavour.
At a Berry Bros luncheon, September 1970 ★★

Santenay (Dr Barolet). Surprisingly good: fresh colour; nice nose; slightly sweet and most attractive.
At one of the pre-sale tastings, December 1969 ★★★

1926 ★★★★

Excellent but now variable. *Climate:* poor spring; cold weather during flowering reduced quantity to about one-third of normal; long summer drought.

Beaune, Hospices, Brunet (Labaume Aîné). Dusty, unattractive nose but nice flavour; good balance if light.
Tasted May 1968 ★

Beaune Grèves de l'Enfant Jésus (Bouchard Père). Fabulous rich velvety colour; extremely rich bouquet and flavour, a big wine but not heavy. Burgundy at its ripest and sweetest.
Tasted December 1966 ★★★★

Charmes-Chambertin (Bouchard Père). Light coloured; old but spicy and attractive; slightly spoiled by gnarled, dry, twisted end acidity. A half-bottle.
Tasted at Lloyd Flatt's in New Orleans, May 1977 ★

Latricières-Chambertin, Cuvée Camas Good corks, rather light coloured, very mature looking with heavy sediment; old, musky, some decay but still fruity; light but rich flavour. Better taste than smell.
Three half-bottles from the cellars of the Restaurant Drouant-Est, Paris, April 1969 ★★

Volnay. Grower unknown, bottled by the Restaurant Drouant-Est. Good colour; firm crisp, smoky *Pinot* bouquet and flavour. Nice acidity. The bottles varied.
Tasted at office luncheons, 1973–1977. At best ★★★

1927

A mouldy vintage in every respect. *Climate:* inclement. Harvest 12–19 September in poor conditions following a cold wet summer.

Romanée-Conti. As this was the only '27 burgundy to come up for sale in recent years, a bottle was opened to taste. It looked fairly pale and very mature but the bouquet was better than expected: light but slightly sweet old *Pinot*; dry, light, sound, though pretty feeble for the greatest name in Burgundy. Acidity very pronounced. As it was the year of my birth I bought a bottle, which I tasted alongside Château Margaux of the same vintage. The Margaux beat the Romanée-Conti hands down, possibly because of its better condition. The cork of the burgundy was wizened and there was a three-inch ullage. Hardly any red left; mushroomy, deathly nose; better on the palate. Though light and thin, it was still soft and drinkable.
Last tasted April 1971.

1928 ★★★★

Very good year. Fine firm wines. *Climate:* full of hazards — spring frosts; rain and hail in June; good summer but great heat and drought towards the end of August followed by beneficial showers. Hail then reduced the crop previously nipped in the bud. But the remaining grapes had quality.
Beaune, Les Avaux (Bouchard Père). Fine '28 depth of colour; very good, rich nose; dry, still tannic.
At a Heublein tasting, May 1977 ★★★

Beaune, Hospices, Brunet (Dr Barolet). Not as deep coloured as expected, but firm; very rich, verging on overripe bouquet and flavour. Attractive, gamy. Delicious but on the downward path.
At the main Barolet pre-sale tasting, December 1969 ★★★

Corton, Bressandes (Labaume Aîné). A meaty, strapping wine, on the wane. A bit too much acidity.
Tasted August 1967 ★

Fleurie Bottled by Gloag's of Perth. Sound, well

preserved. After all, only a beaujolais not Chambertin, so excellent for its age.
From Glamis Castle, tasted June 1971 ★★

Grands-Echézeaux (Dr Barolet). Lovely colour; excellent nose, deep; fabulous depth, dry finish.
Tasted February 1971 ★★★★

Nuits St-Georges. The oldest wine at the Leroy "50 years of Nuits St-Georges" tasting and from Mme Bize-Leroy's personal cellar. A deep, rich-looking wine; extremely good bouquet; very sweet, fairly full bodied, extremely rich but a fine masculine wine.
At the Domaine d'Auvernay, September 1979 ★★★★

Pommard, Epenots (Dr Barolet). One of the best Barolet wines. First tasted with Harry Waugh in the Barolet cellars, then at the pre-sale tasting in Paris (December 1969) and on three occasions since. I first noted its curiously attractive bouquet, which reminded me of *fraises des bois*, and its original flavour; then its Corton-like character, presumably due to that baking hot August. One bottle tasted later was cracking up: I put this down to subsequent rebottling and recorking. On the last occasion it was showing well: very rich, fragrant bouquet and flavour, a fine wine, well preserved.
At a Whitwham tasting in Altrincham, November 1975 ★★★★

Pommard, Rugiens (Dr Barolet). Also first tasted from the bin: fruity, rich, refreshing. And at Christie's pre-sale tasting in Geneva it stood out as a magnificent, nutty, sturdy wine with excellent finish (1969). Some were shipped under the Etienne Vergy label for the Heublein auction in 1970.
Last tasted 1970 ★★ *to* ★★★★ *depending on bottling.*

1929 ★★★★★

Abundant and high quality. Refined, ripe and elegant. *Characteristics:* as in Bordeaux, wines of immediate appeal. Softer, less firm, less tough than the '28s but supple and lasted well. *Climate:* excellent weather conditions. Hot end of summer compensated for by end-of-September rain. Big yield harvested under good conditions from 29 September. *Assessment:* if cellared well and corks are sound, the best can be silky perfection.

Beaune, Clos des Vignes Franches. Good rich nose; slightly sweet, very flavoury.
From the cellars Labaume Ainé et Fils, August 1967 ★★★★

Chambertin (T. Bassot). A *tête de cuvée* wine from an American cellar. Old fruity nose. Quite nice.
At a Heublein tasting, May 1977 ★★

Chambertin (Legrand Frères). Very attractive colour; lovely burnt old *Pinot* nose; sweet, warm, good finish.
From a Swiss cellar. Tasted April 1976 ★★★

Corton, Clos du Roy [*sic*] (Labaume). Lovely colour; excellent, honeyed, old *Pinot* nose and flavour.
Tasted May 1968 ★★★★

Clos des Lambrays (H. de Bahèzre). Another *tête de cuvée*: a bit low in the neck, poor corks. Good colour; both bottles flavoury and characterful but one a bit tart.
At Heublein tastings, May 1977 ★ *to* ★★★

Musigny (de Vogüé). Let down by the cork, a great disappointment. Too brown; a meaty/malty, somewhat oxidized nose and taste.
Tasted May 1977.

Nuits St-Georges (Dr Barolet). Lightish, very mature but lovely colour; old, slightly mushroomy nose; rich,

silky, almost oily textured, but with astringent edge.
Tasted December 1969 ★

Nuits St-Georges (Belgian bottled). Probably recorked. Good though fading colour; delicate, smoky *Pinot* bouquet; drying out but elegant and very sound.
At lunch in Charleroi, January 1977 ★★★

Nuits St-Georges, Les St-Georges (Leroy). In my opinion, the finest of the 38 wines at the Leroy tasting. A good-looking wine, not too deep, not too pale, with fine gradation of colour; sweet, rich, smoky *Pinot* bouquet, intensely fragrant. A thoroughly sweet, ripe wine, extremely elegant, sheer perfection.
Tasted at Ch. d'Auvernay, September 1979 ★★★★★

Pommard (Liger-Belair). Good branded cork. Slightly orange tinged; deep, rich old *Pinot* bouquet; fullish, fine deep flavour.
Tasted December 1970 ★★★

Pommard, Epenots (Labaume). Nice, light, elegant.
Tasted August 1967 ★★★

Romanée-Conti (de Villaine et J. Chambon). *The* Romanée-Conti. An old bottle with slender neck and very tight cork. Beautiful colour, lovely shade; really fine old *Pinot* nose, still fruity and holding well; very soft, very rich, fading a little — obviously thinner and less substantial than in its youth, but preserved by good tannin and acidity. Exquisite and extended flavour.
From Sir Gerald Kelly's cellar. Tasted November 1968 ★★★★★

Vosne-Romanée, Beaumonts (Dr Barolet). First tasted in Geneva before the original Barolet sale in December 1969: a fine-looking wine, still healthily red; well-developed bouquet, rich and sound; slightly sweet, medium body but rich, powerful flavour, rounded and velvety. Showed as well at the Paris tasting. Next, at a Heublein pre-sale tasting in May 1970, recorked and under the Etienne Vergy label: overblown and slightly oxidized. Later, a much better bottle: a touch of sourness on nose compensated for by its style and elegance.
Last tasted May 1972 ★★ *to* ★★★★

1930

An execrable vintage. Pale, thin, unbalanced wines. *Climate:* poor spring conditions, Easter frosts and summer rains adversely affected quality. Harvest 5 October. Yield lower than average.

Beaune, Clos des Mouches (Dr Barolet). When I made my first visit to the Barolet cellars in Beaune, the first thing I did, with Harry Waugh, was to look at some of the "off" vintages. Even the wizardry of the old doctor himself could not turn this into a fine wine, but it was surprisingly attractive: pale, very mature; soft, gentle nose and flavour. No firmness, no depth, but sound.
Tasted October 1969 ★

Morey St-Denis (Dr Barolet). A lightish and very lovely colour; old, slightly mushroomy nose; rich and silky, but also oily and astringent.
At the pre-sale tasting, December 1969.

1931

Another poor year. Light, thin, astringent. *Climate:* far too wet — cold and rain without interruption from July to mid-September. Weather good from 15 September and the vintage, starting 2 October, finished under sunny conditions. Quantity and quality low.

Chambolle-Musigny, Charmes (Dr Barolet). Again, Barolet has provided me with the only example of this old, "off" vintage. At the first cellar tasting: some depth of colour but too brown; the noticeably volatile and vinegary nose and taste spoiling a fleeting richness. There was a better sample prior to the sale: dry, slightly astringent but not at all bad.
Last tasted December 1969.

1932

The third disastrous vintage in a row. *Climate:* spring alternately cold and warm, thundery; normal flowering 25 June; July stormy; warm and dry through August to last week of September, when there were violent storms and much rain. Extremely late harvest 17 October. Average production. Not tasted.

1933 ★★★★

A very stylish vintage. Particularly welcome after the three preceding disasters but a good vintage in its own right. Nevertheless it tended to be overshadowed by the '34, which was more heavily bought and appreciated by English wine merchants and their customers. *Climate:* early hazards — frost damage in April, and hail and rain in June when vines were in bloom. Very warm and dry in July and August. Welcome rain at end of September, Vintage 2 October. Production small, half that of 1932. *Assessment:* the few '33s remaining, if from a good cellar, can still be delightful: sweet, fleshy and elegant.
Beaune, Vignes-Franches (L. Latour). Lovely limpid colour; distinctly sweet, very attractive.
Tasted February 1967 ★★★★
Beaune du Château (Bouchard Père). At best: fine, deep, mature colour; somewhat hard and unforthcoming nose; silky and fine in 1968.
At two Heublein tastings, last in May 1971 ★★★
Bonnes-Mares (Dr Barolet). First tasted in the courtyard above the doctor's cellars: a nice wine, charming and elegant. Next: showing its age, fading gently but sound (August and December 1969). And lastly: lovely colour but watery rim; rich, refined, stylish.
Last tasted December 1971 ★★★
Chambertin. Bottled by Skinner & Rook, a Nottingham firm still family owned. Not very deep; an old nose but sweet, pleasant; rich and attractive, with light end acidity. Ronald Avery thought it "quite nice but of Charmes or Latricières quality".
Tasted November 1972 ★★
Chambertin, Clos de Bèze (Damoy). A really beautiful colour; gentle, sweet nose; smooth, warm and silky on the palate. Not my first good '33, but the first that made me really notice its quality and style.
Tasted in the Damoy cellars, September 1958 ★★★★
Charmes-Chambertin (Dr Barolet). Not the deceased doctor's fault but there were also worms in the cork. Acetic.
Tasted December 1969.
Corton, Clos du Roi (Dr Barolet). Good, rich, meaty Corton style, but with '33 elegance.
At the original Barolet pre-sale tasting, December 1969 ★★★★
Romanée St-Vivant (P. Ponnelle). Bottled by Ellis, Wilson & Bacon Ltd in Brighton. Fabulous colour, fairly deep but mature; overwhelmingly fragrant bouquet, slightly burnt character, held well; fairly full bodied, a lovely rich, fruity wine, perfect balance/acidity, lovely aftertaste. A high tribute to the intrinsic quality of the wine, the reputation of the shipper and the ability and integrity of the English bottlers.
At an office lunch, January 1977 ★★★★★
Volnay. Another English-bottled wine, by W. Coates. Fine colour; good, slightly singed bouquet; very rich. Nice acidity.
Tasted May 1976 ★★★★
Volnay (Labaume). Lovely old wine, dry but velvety.
Tasted October 1967 ★★★

1934 ★★★★

The biggest and best vintage of the decade. Ripe, well-constituted wines. *Climate:* favourable throughout. If anything, too favourable, for the fine weather and warmth caused too-rapid growth in those vines that had not been short pruned: result, an overabundance of bunches on long canes. Fairly early vintage, 19 September. Unusually hot weather during the fermentation created some wine-making difficulties. *Assessment:* for those who like living dangerously or wooing a wanton. Rich, overripe wines reflecting the heat of the summer and some with acidity resulting from the overhot fermentation. Drink up.
Barolet burgundies: of the eight '34s tasted before the great Barolet sale in December 1969, outstanding were the two Pommards, Epenots and Ruglens, also the Chambolle-Musigny. Grands-Echézeaux was not grand enough, the Volnay rich, quite nice, and the Clos des Chênes fragrant but astringent.
Beaune, Vignes-Franches (L. Latour). Fairly deep; overripe but with richness masking overacidity.
Tasted October 1978 ★★
Chambertin (Gaston Roupel). First tasted in 1977. Showing a bit of old age but rich, ripe, good dry finish.
From a Belgian cellar. Last tasted June 1978 ★★★
Chambertin (Héritiers Latour). Fairly deep; distinctly old, rich, ripe and gamy on nose and palate. Like a perfectly hung pheasant.
At Louis Latour's dinner at Boodle's, October 1977 ★★★★
Chambertin (Heymann Bros). Probably French bottled. Astonishingly deep in colour, too brown; waxy nose; rich and soft but slightly acidic. Rather bloated.
Lunching with Edna (Tiny) Roberts, July 1979 ★★
Chambolle, Amoureuses (Dr Barolet). Rich colour; rich, ripe, gamy bouquet and flavour. Lovely.
Last tasted at dinner with Harry Waugh, April 1970 ★★★★
Chambolle-Musigny (Dr Barolet). Palish, very mature colour and bouquet; lovely *Pinot* nose and flavour, rich yet delicate. At the original pre-sale tasting in 1969; similar in 1971. But another bottle, three years later, almost the opposite: deep coloured; shy bouquet developed slowly; stylish but decaying a little.
Last tasted August 1974 ★ to ★★★
Charmes-Chambertin (P. A. André). Fairly deep; curious old cold-coffee nose and taste. A bit dried out.
Tasted November 1977 ★
Corton, Chaumes (L. Latour). Excellent colour; dry, nutty, some age, sound; silky, gentle, really quite sweet.
At lunch with Louis Latour, September 1975 ★★★

Echézeaux (Dr Barolet). Sweet, fading but attractive.
Tasted February 1971 ★★

Gevrey-Chambertin (Dr Barolet). I do not think this wine was in the original Barolet sale. I first noted it at the new London agents' tasting in 1971. It was lovely. Later the same year (original cork): dry, elegant, refined. Stylish and silky in 1972 and, most recently, still fairly deep; rich, well-developed nose, good but showing a bit of age.
Last tasted March 1979 ★★★ *but drink up.*

Latricières-Chambertin. My first ever '34. A nice wine, expensive — then — at 23s. (£1.15) retail.
Tasted 1954.

Meursault (Legrand). Unusually, a red Meursault and, surprisingly, a deep chocolaty colour; with a gentle fruity nose; sweet, attractive though a little short.
Tasted April 1976 ★★

Musigny (P. Ponnelle). Very deep coloured; a big, deep, rich wine. Dry finish. Not exactly my idea of an elegant feminine Musigny.
Tasted May 1976 ★★★

Nuits St-Georges, Clos des Porets (H. Gouges). Very good cork. Pale, almost rosé, but healthy; fabulously fragrant, Gouges-style smoky *Pinot*; gentle, rich, lovely swelling flavour leading to dry finish. Such a contrast to the clumsy, souped-up burgundies the English were brought up to admire.
Tasted May 1975 ★★★★

Nuits St-Georges, Vaucrains (H. Gouges). Tasted first in November 1977, from a good Belgian cellar. Medium-pale mature colour; beautiful sweet, typical Gouges smoky *Pinot* nose; rich, lovely smoky flavour, dry finish, good aftertaste. Majestic.
Last tasted June 1978 ★★★★

Richebourg (Quancard collection). A really lovely colour; gentle, delicate, rather fruity, berry-like bouquet; delicate, harmonious, beautiful.
One of Russell Hone's discoveries, tasted March 1978 ★★★★

Clos Vougeot (Legrand Frères). Curiously light and lovely, but old burnt-fruit smell and taste. Dried out.
Tasted April 1976 ★

1935 ★★★ to ★★★★

A pleasing but, in England, totally underrated vintage. *Climate:* hot dry summer; grapes set back by cold rainy September; quality regarded at the time of picking, 5 October, to be clean and sound "but probably lower than 1933/34". *Market:* an abundant crop, only slightly smaller than 1934. But the English trade had stocked up with '34s. *Assessment:* rarely seen but worth looking out for. With the two notable exceptions below, they tend to be faded, with acidity getting the upper hand, but flavoury and delicate.

Richebourg (Dom. de la Romanée-Conti). The first '35 I tasted and sold at Christie's. Medium colour, very mature; some signs of age on the nose but good fruit under; a good domaine flavour, rather lightweight in style for Richebourg. Interesting.
Tasted April 1969 ★★★

Savigny, Hospices, Cuvée Fouquerand (Dr Barolet). There was some confusion over the name (with Cyrot, the grower, appearing in the records) but none over the quality: very deep, a hot-vintage colour and nose; dry, fairly full bodied, rich, deep, sunburnt flavour, dry finish. Quite remarkable. Harry Waugh considered this

one of the two best Barolet wines.
At the pre-sale tasting, December 1969 ★★★★★

Vosne-Romanée, Malconsorts. Far too pale, too old and deathly on the nose but a remarkably rich flavour, with depth and aftertaste. Astonishing in 1969. Probably caught it ascending on the third day, for it was well and truly dead, recorked by de Villamont, in 1971.
Of the seven other '35s in the Barolet sale, all tasted autumn 1969:

Bonnes-Mares. Refined but a bit dried out.

Grands-Echézeaux. Lovely but too pale and faded.

Morey St-Denis. One of the very best: good colour, plenty of life; good nose; excellent flavour and balance. Not a hint of impending decay.

Pommard. Lightish; soft, fruity, nice acidity.

Clos Vougeot. Overmature, flavoury but acidic.

1936 ★

Variable, mainly below average. *Climate:* dismal damp and cool summer. Morning frosts during harvest (from 2 October). Half the crop of 1934 and 1935; quality not bad in better vineyards. There seemed to be a total lack of interest in this vintage, which cannot be put down to the intrusion of war as, subsequently, the '37 vintage was much traded-in. Probably a combination of a genuinely uninteresting vintage and good stocks of '34s remaining in post-depression conditions. Not tasted.

1937 ★★★★

A highly regarded vintage, firm, rich, stylish wines, certainly better balanced than in Bordeaux. *Climate:* warm weather from May throughout the summer. Regular ripening, and a welcome rainy spell in September. Harvest began 27 September in excellent conditions. Quantity smallish, about the same as 1936, due to lack of rain at judicious intervals to swell grapes. The trade press at the time reported quality to be "probably the best since 1929". *Assessment:* it was not until I assembled these notes that I realized what a lovely vintage this was, and still can be. For I have found many of the wines very rich and characterful.

Beaune du Château (Bouchard Père). Beautiful colour; nice flavour "but usual '37 acidity". I must have had the acidity of '37 Bordeaux in mind.
At a Heublein tasting, May 1968 ★★★

Chambolle-Musigny (Dr Barolet). Palish and unexciting. Acidity noticeable. A second-generation Barolet wine, certainly not amongst the 1969 discoveries.
Tasted June 1971.

Chambolle-Musigny, Vignes du Château (Grivelet). Deep; delicate scented bouquet; surprisingly sweet, and the acidity refreshing. No signs of overmaturity.
Tasted February 1970 ★★★

Chassagne. Bottled by Gloag's of Perth. Soft, delicate, quite delicious.
At a small restaurant in Cheshire, January 1960 ★★★★

Le Corton. A remarkable wine though I did not detect any *Pinot* character in the nose of the Corton — I thought it was a high-quality red Graves of a hot vintage. I did not note the shipper or domaine. Anyway, the wine was perfection: very rich, very fine, scented with an earthy, warm flavour.
At lunch with Jack Masters, November 1967 ★★★★★

Corton (Lebègue). A pronounced meaty/fishy *Pinot* aroma, mature; a big hot-vintage flavour and character, still full of tannin and acidity. At least I correctly placed this wine. (A decade ago I was much better at blind tasting than I am now. Sir Guy Fison, an old boss and mentor from Saccone & Speed days, was and still is, consistently the best taster in the Club, indeed, he has one of the very best palates in the country.)
At a III Form Club tasting, October 1968 ★★★★

Corton-Bressandes (Jaboulet-Vercherre). A *tête de cuvée* from Maxim's. Basically a fine rich wine but marred by a touch of sourness.
At a Heublein pre-sale tasting, May 1978 ★

Corton, Hospices, Dr Peste. Fine mahogany colour; ageing but rich and powerful.
Tasted April 1969 ★★★★

Gevrey-Chambertin (Dr Barolet). Original cork. Rich and excellent.
Tasted December 1971 ★★★★

Grands-Echézeaux (Remoissenet). Deep coloured, mature; an old burgundy nose; slightly sweet, incredibly soft and velvety.
Dining at John Avery's, July 1979 ★★★★

Morey St-Denis (Dr Barolet). Recorked by de Villamont. Lovely fragrant nose and flavour.
Tasted December 1971 ★★★

Prémeaux, Corvées Paget (C. Viénot). Rarely seen wine: very firm colour; a warm, curiously attractive, high-toned bouquet; slightly sweet, fullish flavour, long follow through and splendid finish.
Tasted November 1960 ★★★★

Romanée-Conti. A magnificent wine. First noted at a remarkable tasting of wines from the domaine at Christie's in 1972. More recently, a bottle from the late Clarence Dillon's cellars in New Jersey: marvellous colour, still fairly deep, rich burgundy red shading off to a ripe, mahogany rim; distinctly overripe and gamy on the nose, but opulently rich and attractive; slightly sweet, pleasant weight, lovely ripe flavour that seemed to extend and get richer in the glass.
At an office luncheon, October 1979 ★★★★★

La Tâche. Deep; beautiful; immense extract, intensity and palate-coating richness, length and aftertaste.
Tasted at the Coq Hardy, Bougival, February 1980 ★★★★★

Volnay, Champans (Sichel). The first '37 burgundy in my notebooks: deepish; nose like a '28 claret; flavoury, satisfying bite to it. Liked it the more I tasted it.
Tasted October 1957 ★★★

1938 ★★

A once quite good but rarely seen vintage. *Climate:* variable weather — frosty spring; heavy hailstorms in spring and summer. Vines slow maturing but free from disease. Vintage started 6 October but those who picked late, taking advantage of autumn sun, did best. Quantity about the same as 1937. Quality good. *Market:* hardly any remain, mainly drunk locally, or by the Germans. There was a shortage of bottles and some remained in cask until after the war. *Assessment:* really an "off" vintage and certainly long on the downhill slope.

Chambolle-Musigny (Labaume Aîné). Pale, not much deeper than the 1858 Corton from the same cellar; stuffy nosed; light, a bit of acidity, but not bad.
Tasted August 1967 ★

Corton (Dr Barolet). In the courtyard above the cellars, the wine nearly matched the autumn sunlight and golden leaves. A fine rich colour; a firm rich nose and taste.
Tasted with Harry Waugh in Beaune, October 1969 ★★★

Corton, Hospices, Charlotte Dumay. Bottled by Lovibonds. An unforgettable experience: my first really "corked" (for want of a better word) bottle. Nose not too bad when first opened: started to crack up after ten minutes, and after one hour in our decanter smelt like bad cabbages, quite overpowering the Limburger cheese at a tasting. Really foul.
At a young wine merchants' tasting, June 1955.

Grands-Echézeaux (Reine Pédauque). Tasted twice: sweet, delicate, old, sound but short, with a touch of acidity. Three months later I tried another bottle and suspected that it had been "refreshed". No character. Perfectly ordinary drink.
Last tasted April 1971 ★

Nuits St-Georges, La Richemone. The only representative of the decade of the 1930s at the Leroy tasting of Nuits St-Georges and unworthy of that honour: surprisingly deep but ominously brown — reminded me of the smell of an institutional kitchen (unclean); a twisted wine with a poor finish.
Tasted September 1979.

Romanée-Conti. Made from ungrafted vines. First noted at the Romanée-Conti tasting at Christie's in September 1972. Similar colour to the '56, though rather better; cold-tea nose; decaying on the palate, burst of acidity at end — in short, I was unimpressed. Totally different at an office lunch: fine but autumnal colour; very ripe, fine smoky *Pinot* nose; lovely flavour, balance and finish. So? . . .
Last tasted November 1973. At best ★★★★

1939 ★★

Moderately good. *Climate:* some frost, nipping the buds; flowering variable; disappointing summer, July cold and wet, mid-August to mid-September fine. Delayed harvest, 15 October, in unsettled conditions. Quantity average, quality deemed good, but needed careful selection. The war, in any case, kept it off the overseas markets. *Assessment:* frankly, I have not enough first-hand evidence on which to base an assessment. But as few '39s remain, I doubt if it matters.

Morey St-Denis (Dr Barolet). The one and only '39 to come my way. At a later Barolet pre-sale tasting, recorked by de Villamont: good colour; light, quite nice nose and flavour. A bit short but pleasant enough.
Tasted December 1971 ★★

1940 ★★

Moderate only. *Climate:* hard winter, very beautiful spring but, thanks to wartime difficulties, untreated mildew almost decimated the crop. *Assessment:* rarely seen, can be good.

Chambertin, Tête de Cuvée (T. Bassot). Mature; mushroomy nose. The *tête* was mushroom shaped.
From Maxim's cellars, at a Heublein tasting, April 1978.

Richebourg (Dom. de la Romanée-Conti). Fine mature colour with a warm orange hue; delicate high-toned bouquet; gentle, fading a little but with charm and elegance.
Tasted at the Coq Hardy, Bougival, February 1980 ★★★

Romanée-Conti. Deeper than the Richebourg and La Tâche; magnificently opulent bouquet reminiscent of coffee and crème brûlée; rich on the palate, lovely finish. *At the Coq Hardy tasting and lunch, February 1980.*

La Tâche. Very ripe "toasted" bouquet; rich and appealing, refreshing acidity. Needs drinking. *At the Coq Hardy, February 1980* ★★★

1941 ★

An uninspiring wartime vintage. Poor unripe wines. *Climate:* vines reasonably healthy, just a little mildew on the leaves; autumn mediocre, humidity and cold prevented ripening. Picking began on 10 October in difficult conditions. *Assessment:* hard to judge on the basis of just two examples of the late Dr Barolet's wizardry. Few '41s remain.

Corton (Dr Barolet). Despite a slightly wormy cork it showed well at the original pre-sale tasting in 1969: a lightish, mature, lovely colour; not very exciting cold-tea nose; rich, piquant flavour. Even better at a later pre-sale tasting: good bouquet, smoky, mature; soft, nice finish. Holding well. *Last tasted November 1971* ★★★

1942 ★★★

A good wartime vintage. *Climate:* spring and summer fine enough and dry enough. Hail ravaged vineyard areas in the Côte de Beaune on 13 September; picking started the day after — one of the earliest vintages for decades — and continued, with stops and starts, for four weeks. Thanks to short vinification (three to four days), wines that exceeded 12° avoided being tainted with the taste of hail. *Assessment:* judging by the small but varied selection tasted, a stylish vintage. Well-stored wines of quality worth looking out for — that is if you have a mind for this sort of exploration. One consolation: little-known vintages like this are usually inexpensive.

Beaune, Grèves (Bouchard Père). Medium pale, but fine mature colour; very good nose; rather light and rarified in style and weight, zestful but short. Nice. *From a magnum at a Heublein pre-sale tasting, May 1971* ★★★

Beaune, Theurons (Bouchard Père). Beautiful rich tile red; fabulous bouquet; slightly sweet, an elegant, scented, feminine wine though lacking length. *Tasted at Lloyd Flatt's in New Orleans, May 1977* ★★★

Richebourg (Dom. de la Romanée-Conti). Distinctly paler than the '43, more orange, very attractive; light, open, delicate bouquet, which developed beautifully in the glass; soft, gentle, good finish. *At the Coq Hardy tasting, February 1980.*

Ruchottes-Chambertin (T. Bassot). A considerable amount of colour lost, but quite good, old, smoky *Pinot* nose and flavour. Dry. Nice wine. *From Maxim's, Paris, at a Heublein tasting in Atlanta, May 1978* ★★

La Tâche The first '42 tasted in June 1967: a lovely deep colour; fine, sweet, ripe, slightly exotic bouquet; some richness, soft, ripe, nicely balanced. It was followed by Margaux '53, which was rather an odd order of service. Recently: richness and intensity; good texture and finish, refreshing acidity. *Last tasted at the Coq Hardy, February 1980* ★★★

1943 ★★★★

The best wartime vintage. Flavoury, well-constituted, excellent ripe wines. *Climate:* beautiful spring, summer and autumn, but the size of the crop reduced by frosts in May and hail on 21 July. Grapes ripened fully. No chaptalization needed. *Market:* perhaps as well that the grapes were full of natural sugar as there was a shortage of cane-sugar, also of bottles, corks and labour. Because of this, many wines had to be kept too long in cask, which made them dry out and decline. *Assessment:* good, and the best still worth looking out for.

Beaune, Clos de la Mousse (Bouchard Père). Lighter than the Grèves but rich and equally good. *From the Bouchard cellars, at a Heublein tasting, May 1971* ★★★

Beaune, Grèves (Bouchard Père). Tasted twice: good colour; fragrant; good silky flavour. *Also from Bouchard at Heublein's in 1971 and May 1972* ★★★

Pommard. From the so-called Quancard collection. A bit woody and dry but not bad (a note written long before I received a report from Louis Latour about the bottling problems quoted above). *Tasted June 1978* ★

Clos St-Denis (T. Bassot). Probably recorked. Rich *Pinot* nose; very flavoury. *From Maxim's, Paris, at a Heublein tasting, April 1978* ★★★

Richebourg (Dom. de la Romanée-Conti). Medium colour but rich, mature; lovely copybook "beetroot", ripe *Pinot* nose, rich and in excellent condition; the driest of the group of wartime Domaine wines tasted, crisp, wonderful uplifting and expanding second phase of flavour, excellent aftertaste. *At the Coq Hardy tasting, February 1980* ★★★★★

La Tâche Carried by my host, Berek Segan, in his car and consumed in a Chinese restaurant in Melbourne. It survived the shaking and the "sweet and sour": fine colour; ripe *Pinot* nose; dry, lightish and a bit fluffy and overblown, like an overripe Clos de Tart. But a provocatively flavoury wine. *Tasted March 1977* ★★★

Vosne-Romanée (Lejay-Lagoute). Medium colour; good deep nose; sweet, delicious flavour, plenty of life. *Tasted May 1967* ★★★★

1944 ★ to ★★★

Light wines, little colour yet fragrant, soft and some quite fine. *Climate:* fine weather until the beginning of September, the vines magnificent, healthy, sound, abundant and forward. Then on 8 September, the day Beaune was liberated, the rains came down and it poured continuously, delaying the picking, which started on 6 October and continued in detestable weather until the 28th. *Assessment:* judging by a solitary example from Burgundy's most prestigious vineyard and a good private cellar, a light, charming vintage, but probably passé now with the possible exception of a beefy Corton or a meaty Chambertin.

Romanée-Conti. Distinctly overmature looking, brownish, walnut tinged, watery rim; a top quality wine clearly, but with smelly overtones — perhaps decanted too long (three hours, I was told); light in style, piquant fruit, slightly too short and watery finish. Fascinating, very flavoury. *At a dinner given by Dr Brian Elliott, a keen young collector in my Harvey days in Manchester, in February 1959* ★★

1945 ★★★★★

A great vintage, substantial, well-constituted, mainly dry and firm wines. Climate: frosts in March and April inflicted the most damage on the lower-lying vineyards and reduced potential crop — nature's pruning; otherwise a beautiful spring with flowering beginning May (the earliest start between 1940 and 1977) and completing rapidly. At 5 pm on 21 June there was a sudden and severe cyclone, which ravaged ten of the principal villages of the Côte de Beaune from Puligny to Corton and which further reduced the crop there to one-sixteenth of that previously anticipated. What with the spring frost, low rainfall and the cyclone, it was inevitable that the total crop in 1945 would be small, but the grapes, as so often in such cases, was very concentrated and of high quality. Assessment: I have just over 30 notes on '45 burgundies, compared with 189 on claret of the same great vintage, which is less an indication of interest than evidence of greater exposure to, and availability of, Bordeaux, particularly on the English market. Having said that, the quality of this vintage was immensely impressive and, by and large, the wines have lasted well. Also notable was the amount of quality wine shipped in cask and the high standard of bottling in the immediate postwar period, when the wine trade was still old-family dominated, and traditional methods resumed despite the five-year interruption.

Beaune, Grèves Bouchard Père	*Smoky/oaky fragrant bouquet; very rich, long, dry, attenuated finish.* The best at Lloyd Flatt's Bouchard tasting in New Orleans, May 1977 ★★★★
Beaune, Grèves, **Vigne de l'Enfant Jésus**	*Shipped from the Bouchard cellars for a Heublein auction. Very mature looking; lovely mustard-and-cress nose.* Tasted May 1973 ★★★
Beaune, Hospices, **Nicholas Rolin**	*A broad, generous and attractive wine, but with a touch of decay appearing on the nose.* Tasted at the Peppercorn's, December 1967 ★★★
Bonnes-Mares de Vogüé	*Rather curiously the cork was branded Musigny, due either to a postwar shortage of corks or to careless labelling in the cellar of the domaine. No matter: a soft, velvety, most refined wine (probably Musigny), overall dryish, with long flavour and finish. Lovely, but at the time nowhere near its peak.* Tasted November 1960 ★★★(★)
Chambertin T. Bassot	*Still fine and deep coloured; beautiful, elegant, complex bouquet and flavour.* At a pre-sale tasting, November 1972 ★★★★
Chambertin Saccone & Speed de Monthélie Harvey's	*One of a whole range of excellent burgundies of the 1945, 1947 and 1949 vintages bottled by Saccone & Speed and tasted over a three-day period in the firm's tasting room in August 1954, demonstrating not only the massiveness of the '45 burgundies but the quality of London bottling during that postwar period. The Chambertin was magnificent, but still hard. The retail price, 15s. (75p) per bottle! The next, bottled in Burgundy by de Monthélie, was a fine, dry, velvety wine, still green and unready.* Tasted July 1960 ★★(★★) *Another bottled by Harvey's: deep and at 20 years of age still youthful and peppery; dry, well balanced.* Tasted October 1965 ★★★★
Chambertin, **Clos de Bèze** Bichot	*Keep on friendly terms with your shipping agents and you might be offered wine like this: massively deep-coloured; a full-bodied, powerful wine.* At lunch at Porter & Laker's in London, March 1976 ★★★★
Charmes-Chambertin Bouchard Père	*Also good. Gentle yet prolonged flavour.* Tasted May 1977 ★★★★
Corton Doudet-Naudin, Lejay-Lagoute	*The first time I had come across the iniquitous practice of the wine being decanted and rebottled just before shipment. The colour of the*

Doudet-Naudin was good; the nose less so; nevertheless a full, soft, burnt-Corton flavour. Tasted February 1967 ** *From the Dijon firm of Lejay-Lagoute: a thoroughly rich and pleasant mouthful.* Tasted May 1967 ***

Corton, Hospices, Charlotte Dumay

One of the best wines in the Quancard collection: good colour, not at all deep but very rich; deep, burnt, magnificently ripe Pinot *nose; good body, rich flavour leading to a dry finish. On the verge of decay and needed drinking.* Tasted March 1978 ****

Echézeaux
Doudet-Naudin

Brown tinged; chocolaty on the nose — not my idea of an old ripe Pinot. *Probably another decanted-before-shipment burgundy. Dry, but a soft classic Doudet-Naudin wine.* Tasted January 1971 **

Mazis-Chambertin and others
Saccone & Speed bottlings

The most unusual and least ready of the Saccone & Speed range, which also included a pleasant but pricey Gevrey-Chambertin (it was £1. 2s. 6d. [£1.12] more expensive than the Chambertin), an unready Corton, a rather sharp, green Chambolle-Musigny, and a smooth Volnay priced at 8s. (40p) a bottle. All tasted August 1954.

Musigny, Vieilles Vignes
de Vogüé

First tasted from a magnum on a Harvey grand tour in September 1958: very deep coloured; a wine of great depth and power, really rather outsize and unready. Later: still fullish, with a beautiful, silky, exquisite flavour, ready but firm and with time in hand. Tasted April 1961 *****

Nuits St-Georges, 1er cru

Representing the vintage at the big Leroy tasting of Nuits. Fine, evenly graded colour; rich cheese-rind nose, showing some age; a dry, lean, flavoury wine. Good finish. Tasted September 1979 ***

Nuits St-Georges
Hasenklever

Beginning to lose colour, and show fine maturity on the nose; lovely, silky wine. Tasted October 1968 ***

Richebourg

An indulgent magnum for the Harvey acolytes on the grand tour. Probably not from the Domaine de la Romanée-Conti. Certainly still very strong and hard. At Les Trois Faisans, Dijon, September 1958 ***

Clos de la Roche

From the cellars of Claridge's in Paris, via Burgundy and The Wine Society cellars. Original cork, rather small (corks were a problem in the immediate postwar period) but firm, good level. Lovely colour; attractive, ripe Pinot *nose, a bit stewed (perhaps a bit of old sulphur?); dry, firm, seemed in excellent condition.* At a pre-sale tasting, February 1978 ***

La Tâche
Dom. de la Romanée-Conti

Where I got this from I do not know but I see that I served it at a dinner party for Alain de Vogüé (of Veuve Clicquot) and my then chairman and his wife, in Bristol: very deep coloured; in fact depth — underlying the bouquet and flavour — was its hallmark. Big, rich, but at the time seemed just on the verge of budding. Tasted May 1961 ***(**) Should be at its peak now.

Clos Vougeot
Piat and another

I just mention this as it was the first '45 burgundy I ever tasted, noting that it was luscious, full, smooth and "perhaps the sweetest red yet drunk" — in September 1953, just a week before I sailed, with a cargo of empty pipes, from London to Oporto in the good ship Seamew. *Next tasted, shipper unknown: a lovely, rich, meaty wine, still very lively.* At a Saintsbury Club dinner — I was not a member then — the month my new department at Christie's resumed wine auctions, October 1966 ****

1946 ★

An unimportant vintage but by no means wholly bad. Climate: a good start, with plenty of sun and an abundant crop until hail damage on 10 August followed by a cold, rainy spell. Last ten days warm before harvest, 30 September to early October. Assessment: despite — perhaps because of — only three notes, I have the impression that, like the same vintage in Bordeaux, this was a minor charmer, unjustly but understandably ignored.

Beaune, Hospices, Deslandes Dr Barolet	*Surprisingly deep for an "off" vintage, but perhaps less surprisingly for a Barolet wine; light, curious, old chemical laboratory smell; the palate more in keeping with the colour, rich, a good flavour, with marked but tolerable acidity.* At the first Barolet tasting, in Paris, December 1969.
Chambertin Shipper unknown	*A medium, very mature colour; lovely ripe Pinot nose; dry, light, delicate, yet with quite a positive, rich flavour. Delightful.* One of the minor delights at a Heublein pre-sale tasting in San Francisco, April 1978 ★★★
Morey St-Denis Saccone & Speed	*The first '46 tasted: a "lovely little dinner wine" I noted, bottled by Saccone & Speed (for whom I worked at that time) and retailing at 13s. (65p). Full, yet well developed.* Tasted April 1954 ★★

1947 ★★★★

A first-rate vintage, rich, ripe, classic wines. Climate: in September the trade press reported that "since the beginning of the year there has been marvellous weather for the vines" and in November that the wines "should be remarkable". They were right. As a result of the good ripening summer, picking commenced early, on 16 September, but as so often in hot conditions there were wine-making difficulties. Those who coped well made great wines. Market: eagerly mopped up by the trade anxious to replenish their war-depleted cellars. Perfect, ripe, immediately attractive wines, and prices that were acceptable even in austerity-bound Britain. Assessment: not as reliable as the '45s, mainly because of the difficulty of vinifying a hot-vintage wine. They tend to crack up. But the best, well kept, still make a luscious mouthful.

Beaujolais **Moulin à Vent** **Fleurie** **Mercurey**	*I include these just to show how well the better old-style village wines can last in a good vintage like '47. My first '47 with bottle-age was a half of Moulin à Vent bottled by Justerini & Brooks (bought in a mixed parcel that included Cheval-Blanc): good colour; rich bouquet; nice flavour holding well — but not developed sufficiently to warrant keeping that long. Another Moulin à Vent, in a magnum this time, consumed at George Rainbird's for lunch: marvellous old Gamay nose that had begun to resemble a firm ripe Pinot; soft, excellent quality and condition. Next a quite good Fleurie (Quancard collection) in January 1978. By far the most outstanding was a Tête de Cuvée Mercurey of Bouchard Père, admittedly not a beaujolais, but a south Burgundy wine. It had a delightfully rich mulberry nose and flavour.* At a Heublein tasting in May 1977 ★★★
Beaune L. Latour Bouchard Père	*A memorably elegant Vignes-Franches of Louis Latour in 1958 and, in contrast to the faded Richebourg, two Bouchard wines showing very well earlier the same year: Clos de la Mousse, rich and still tannic though showing a touch of old age on the nose.*

| | *Beaune, Grèves, Vigne de l'Enfant Jésus: a fine, rich, burnt/ hot-vintage bouquet and flavour.* Tasted March and May 1969 ★★★ |

Chambertin
Dr Barolet

First tasted pre-sale in 1969: good, but not obviously outstanding on the nose; powerful and lively. I next drank it at my first dinner as a new member of the Bordeaux Club which, strangely enough, was devoted to burgundy, and which included four Barolet wines of which this was the youngest. A bit smelly and overripe on the nose at first, but it cleared and held well; a soft, completely ripe wine, really excellent. Last tasted August 1974 ★★★★

**Chambertin,
Tastevinage**
J. Drouhin

Equally perversely, and even more delightful, a great burgundy served by Comte Alexandre de Lur-Saluces at his home in Bordeaux: colour still fullish and fine; a perfect classic — inimitable and impossible to describe — Chambertin Pinot aroma; slightly sweet, rich but not at all heavy, elegant and very flavoury. Perfect condition. Tasted April 1978 ★★★★★

Chambertin
Harvey's
J. van der Meulen
Maxim's

A good, mature, flavoury Harvey bottling. Tasted August 1965. *An equally convincing Belgian bottling by J. van der Meulen.* Tasted May 1977. *A year later, an excellent Maxim's (Paris) bottling.* Tasted May 1978. All about ★★★★

**Chambertin,
Clos de Bèze**

First tasted bottled by Saccone's — a bigger wine than the '49, and 19s. (95p) per bottle in 1954. Next an unknown domaine bottling, drinking well. At lunch in the Council House, Bristol, 1961 ★★★

Charmes-Chambertin
Dr Barolet

Standing in the courtyard at the first tasting in October 1969 I thought this was a fine, rich and lovely wine. But it was less impressive at the pre-sale tasting, seeming to lack colour, with too much age on the nose. Nice only. Last tasted December 1969 ★★ to ★★★

Corton
English bottlings

Although originally excellent and doubtless still good, I see that I have tasted very few Cortons or indeed any other '47s since 1954. Of the earlier notes there were several excellent Saccone bottlings, of which Corton-Chaumes was outstanding, also the Bressandes, then rather hard. An Aloxe-Corton of Sichel's was a bit thick and chocolaty on the nose but quite good for its class and holding well. Tasted 1971.

Musigny
de Vogüé

Returned by a dissatisfied client in Los Angeles. Despite plain capsule, short unbranded cork and slight ullage, this much-travelled wine displayed a lovely colour and gentle, fragrant, old Pinot aroma. But it was a bit faded and, in truth, had a touch too much acidity. A distinctly unfathomable mystery from which a lesson or two might be learned but few firm conclusions reached. Tasted January 1975 ★

Nuits St-Georges
Lupé-Cholet
Justerini & Brooks
Chalié-Richards

At the beginning of my career in the wine trade, from the firm Lupé-Cholet (I was to meet the two indomitable Lupé sisters for the first time only in 1979), London bottled by their agents Cock Russell: rich and full, almost too sweet and velvety, firm fruity bouquet. Trade price 152s. (£7.60) per dozen. Tasted September 1952. *Next an odd half-bottle of Justerini & Brooks: a good, rich, ripe, hot-vintage wine.* Tasted 1968. *Later, a very mature, less good, Chalié-Richard bottling.* Tasted 1972.

Richebourg
Dom. de la Romanée-Conti

Frankly, this was a disappointment, from a good Paris cellar. Long, branded cork in excellent condition. Really rather light coloured and very mature looking; old, ripe Pinot *nose which held for an hour and faded after two; surprisingly little to it, classic but faded.* Tasted November 1969 ★★ *Must be a will-o'-the-wisp by now.*

Richebourg Saccone & Speed Grivelet	*The first '47 Richebourg I ever had was a beautiful wine bottled by Saccone & Speed described as "softer and rounder than most '47s".* Tasted 1954. *Next came a rather curious outsize wine from, and drunk at, the Domaine Grivelet: deep but browning; rich, languorous wine, not fruity or vinous; very strong — 15° — impressive but not to my taste.* Tasted 1958.
Romanée St-Vivant Lebègue-Bichot	*Lovely colour; rich, meaty bouquet which held well; still ripe sweetness, medium body, very good rich flavour, perfectly balanced, excellent dry finish.* At an office lunch, October 1979 ★★★★
Volnay Various bottlings	*Not much success here: only a rather dull Harvey bottling way back in 1955. More recently, a disappointingly sour Clos des Ducs, of d'Angerville's.* Last tasted May 1973.
Vosne-Romanée Dr Barolet	*Not in the original Barolet sale, and not a patch on the '49. Re-corked, no character, dull.* Tasted November 1971 ★
Vosne-Romanée Saccone & Speed Jules Laine Lejay-Lagoute Harvey's	*My first '47: a sweet-smelling but tannic Saccone & Speed bottling.* Tasted 1954. *A heavyweight, characterful, mature* Pinot *from Jules Laine of Nuits St-Georges.* Tasted 1971. *A rather stewed and somewhat stale Lejay-Lagoute specimen.* Tasted March 1973. *Most recently, an excellent Harvey bottling at a burgundy lunch at David Somerset's: very lively, rich-vintage colour, fully mature; unexciting bouquet; marvellous taste, sweet, incredibly rich, but not remotely heavy and with a good dry finish.* Tasted March 1975 ★★★
Clos Vougeot Saccone & Speed Justerini & Brooks	*A straightforward, unexciting — but fair enough for under 17s. (85p) a bottle — Saccone bottling.* Tasted 1954. *A rather nice Justerini & Brooks bottling: lots of good red colour; a gentle, unassuming, ripe* Pinot *nose and good firm flavour.* Tasted June 1968 ★★★

1948 ★

A good but bypassed vintage. Fairly beefily constituted, full and fruity wine. Climate: weather successively cold, rainy and fine. July and half August wet, some disease, but good weather from 15 August. Vintage 4 October. Reports at the time said, not too encouragingly, that the wines were "superior to 1946". Market: singular lack of interest, possibly due to lukewarm reports, or to the parallel unexcitement over the '48 Bordeaux, but mainly, I think, because of heavy buying of the '47s and the likelihood of a good commercial '49. Assessment: relatively few tasted and the notes, even though not very recent, speak for themselves. The best, well kept, should still be more than just interesting.

Richebourg Dom. de la Romanée-Conti	*My first '48, and from a magnum, at Bichot's in Beaune. Then just ten years old: a big and black wine; incredibly rich, high-toned nose; full, rich, most impressively fine.* Tasted September 1958 ★★★★ *If there is any left it will still be magnificent.*
La Tâche Dom. de la Romanée-Conti	*First tasted at a dinner party in October 1958. A marvellous wine: deep, lovely colour; attractive, indescribable La Tâche-style of bouquet; full bodied, packed with flavour but still green and immature. Perfect seven years later: deep; really ripe, rich bouquet and flavour; slightly sweet, soft. Still perfection.* Last tasted May 1980 ★★★★

Vosne-Romanée Pasquier-Desvignes	*I bought some in 1976 and served it at several dinner parties. It had a fine colour with a pleasantly singed* Pinot *bouquet and flavour, but I noticed that it oxidized if decanted early, and I had one acetic bottle. Generally flavoury and characterful.* Last tasted May 1977 **
Clos Vougeot F. Mugnier L. Gro	*Both palish, very mature, the Gros with a slight coppery tinge; the Mugnier nose with singed '48 character, Gros fine ripe; Mugnier tangy, Gros sweeter, refreshing.* From Maxim's, Paris, at a Heublein tasting in San Francisco, May 1980, both ****

1949 *****

An outstanding vintage. Well formed, full of grace. Burgundy at its most deeply refined and elegant. Climate: a worrying start: flowering in unsettled conditions with rain every day. Thereafter a very dry year with judicious rain to fill the berries before the vintage on 27 September. Market: bought by all the traditional buyers, and at prices that did not begin to reflect any of the pressures of demand from newly awakening markets. Doubtless the British trade at the time did not appreciate this, battling as it was with rationing and austerity. Assessment: still outstanding and keeping better than the '47s, being closer knit and, I think, trimmer and better balanced. Elegant burgundy at its best. Some good English bottlings crop up. Worth seeking out before they go the way of all flesh. Tasting notes: I have extracted from a substantial number of notes (though, as with 1945, a fraction of those of the same vintage of claret) those that seem to me to reflect the style, development and condition of the '49 vintage as a whole. First, notable '49s tasted since 1970:

Beaune, Hospices, **Rousseau-Deslandes**	*Tasted twice, both bottled by Barton & Guestier. An attractively autumnal colour; sweet, harmonious, ripe* Pinot *nose; soft, sweet, but with dry finish. Excellent condition. Very good but not great.* Tasted April 1972, March 1973 ****
Le Chambertin David Sandeman	*Bottled by David Sandeman, wine merchants, not to be confused with Geo. Sandeman, the port and sherry shippers. A most beautiful, mature ruddy colour but with a curious cheesy nose and flavour and wishy-washy end. Nice but disappointing.* Tasted April 1972 **
Chambolle-Musigny Justerini & Brooks	*A delightful wine, beautifully bottled by Justerini & Brooks, which boldly and successfully followed Lafite and Margaux '53 at a lunch party given for my colleague, Alan Taylor-Restell, and me by a client, a well-known actor. The wine had a really lovely colour, medium light, very mature; a rich, ripe, mature, true* Pinot *bouquet and flavour; soft, well preserved.* At John Barron's, June 1974 ***
Corton Doudet-Naudin	*Fairly deep coloured; lovely, rich, slightly medicinal flavour. I find the style of the Doudet-Naudin wines somewhat lacking in zest and stylishness, but they are at least consistent and keep very well.* Tasted November 1974 **
Corton, Clos du Roy de Villamont	*Burgundy spellings do vary. This is the old-fashioned "Roy". Palish, fully mature; fine scented bouquet; lovely flavour, stylish but lacking length and depth.* Tasted April 1974 **
Musigny de Vogüé	*For me, this wine embodies all the style and quality of vineyard and vintage. Medium deep, lovely colour (this was in a line-up of bottles at a pre-sale tasting; it looked like the crown jewels in a Georgian decanter); a glorious ripe, mature,* Pinot *scent — rare for Bordeaux to match this sort of harmony and opulence; slightly*

sweet, rich yet firm, not heavy or fat. Beautiful flavour sustaining acidity, prolonged finish. Tasted April 1972 ****(*) *Drink now — 1995.*

Nuits St-Georges Alfred Guiraud	*A variable batch of half-bottles, mature and attractive looking but some acetic. The best sweet and ripe, but lacking style and real quality.* Tasted February 1979. At best **
Nuits St-Georges, Argillières Leroy	*The second finest wine, after the '29 noted in the first section, at the remarkable "half-century" tasting of Nuits St-Georges at the home of Mme Bize-Leroy: medium deep, a lively colour, rich to the very rim; intensely fragrant, fully developed bouquet; a rich, majestic wine, beautifully balanced, and still kept on the firm path of development by its everpresent but undemonstrative tannin and acidity. Perfect.* Tasted September 1979 **** *Drink now — 1995.*
Pernand-Vergelesses Bichot	*An unusually attractive wine tasted on a seemingly unrepeatable occasion: a pre-sale tasting in the* Caves Municipal, *Vosne-Romanée. We had been invited to dispose of the cellar of the Restaurant Belin at Montbard, but the authorities frowned on this Christie incursion, though notable local growers like Clair-Daü and Drouhin-Laroze were courteous, attentive and helpful. This particular wine had a lovely old nose, fine flavour, excellent balance and was, I believe, bought by the grower.* Tasted December 1972 ***
Richebourg Harvey's	*Bottled by Harvey's: medium light, very mature colour; good mature* Pinot *nose; now dry, fading, a shade of the Richebourg meatiness, but very flavoury and complete.* Tasted November 1978 ***
Richebourg Lebègue	*The oldest wine in a mammoth tasting of burgundies presented by Roger Aldridge. Unhappily this was sadly out of condition: cloudy; almond-kernels nose; tired and pricked.* Tasted January 1971.
Romanée St-Vivant	*As the domaine or shipper of burgundies is never revealed at Saintsbury Club dinners, I can only assume this was Marey-Monge: fine, deep; fabulous, almost exotic bouquet; powerful burnt-*Pinot *flavour. Burgundy approaching its very best.* Tasted April 1974 ****
Vosne-Romanée Dr Barolet and Etienne-Vergy	*One of the two most outstanding postwar Barolet wines at the original pre-sale tasting in December 1969: delicate bouquet; fine backbone, well clothed, elegantly dry. Later, using a sous-nom of de Villamont under which some Barolet wines were shipped to the United States, two samples at Heublein pre-sale tastings. One had been recorked before shipment. The bottle with the original cork was distinctly better (the other was showing signs of age and strain) and was lovely, rich and characterful.* Tasted May 1970. At best ****

Some outstanding '49s tasted in the late 1960s:

Beaune du Château Bouchard Père	*Excellent. Rich, lovely wine, fine, open and frank.* Tasted May 1969 ****
Beaune, Grèves, Vigne de l'Enfant Jésus Bouchard Père	*First tasted in 1956: not very deep in colour; good nose; I found the style strange, somehow felt it ought to be a white wine. Anyway, it survived those early (and inexperienced) doubts, for it was perfect, shipped from the Bouchard cellars for the Heublein sale in Chicago: it had held its colour well; light, delicate bouquet; lightish body, lovely flavour, perfect.* Last tasted May 1969 ****
Bonnes-Mares Saccone & Speed Bichot	*Somehow, as with Musigny, this great vineyard seemed perfectly wedded to the vintage. First tasted, bottled by Saccone & Speed, in August 1954: a very full red colour; good aroma, slightly peaty*

overtone; delicious, fruity, stylish — and under £1 a bottle retail. Those were the days when no one thought twice of shipping in cask wines of this quality for bottling in London. It also showed extremely well at a burgundy evening at Dick Bridgman's (a founder member of a tasting club I had started for young "sprigs" in the trade) in 1955. It had "more guts and finesse" than a range of frankly taste-alike commercial samples from the shippers, Cock Russell. Later, when nearly 20 years old, a beautiful bottling by Bichot: lovely, ripe, deep, fruity bouquet and flavour with a twist of happily refreshing acidity at its finish, giving it a young-for-its-age feel. *Last tasted in Beaune, August 1968.*

Romanée St-Vivant *Marey-Monge*	*Shipped by Drouhin. Well-nigh perfect. Marvellous shape, style and richness. Tasted April 1969 ★★★★*

Notes on some other '49s:

Chambertin, Clos de Bèze	*Bottled by Mackay's in Guernsey. Real Chambertin opulence of aroma. At peak in 1965 ★★★★*
Corton, Bressandes	*Bottled by the Victoria Wine Company and making a good mouthful in 1959, around the time that a jingle appeared in advertisements in London underground trains: "Pamela's party was better than mine, the minx got her drinks from Victoria Wine" — and how well she was served in those days by that most extensive, but not expensive, chain of wine shops.*
Grands-Echézeaux	*Fabulous, unbelievably good. An Avery bottling — no wonder they have such a special reputation for burgundy. Tasted 1955 ★★★★*
Clos des Lambrays	*Rarely shipped to England, this one was bottled by Avery's. My notes read: "A thumping good wine with plenty of life." Tasted 1962 ★★★★*
Clos de Tart *Mommessin*	*On the pale side of medium; an overripe but attractive nose and flavour; rather sweet, peppery, in 1966, though I had thought it on the verge of death in 1960. A curiously overblown wine. Last tasted September 1966. At best ★★★*
Volnay, Santenots *Dom. Jaques Prieur*	*A Tastevinage wine: honeyed, silky, in 1959. A year later perfection. Last tasted 1960 ★★★★*
Vosne-Romanée *Lejay-Lagoute*	*One of three '49s from this Dijon firm, all with a similar colour. Good bouquet; nice flavour, soft but refreshing. Their Nuits St-Georges as good but the Beaune running to a touch of acidity. All tasted May 1967. At best ★★★*

1950 ★

Fairly light wines of moderate quality. Not as good as Bordeaux. Climate: dreaded hailstorms in July, August and September, the latter two months wet. Fairly early picking, 18 September. Abundant. Assessment: although only seven notes — which demonstrates how little they featured in English merchants' lists — they show a certain consistency: a lack of colour, quick maturing, a tendency to acidity, though they could be nice and flavoury. Only the better quality wines, perfectly stored, will be more than a curiosity now.

Nuits St-Georges *J. Regnier*	*The first two are mentioned because they made an interesting comparison in the Harvey's tasting room in June 1955. Regnier's*

H. Sichel Dr Barolet	*was youthful looking; quite nice nose; young, crisp, pleasant. Sichel's looked much more mature; much better flavour than nose, but dry, acid finish. The Barolet wine (the only '50 in the original Barolet sale) was very pleasant too: palish, but lovely mature colour; surprisingly chunky/chocolaty rich* Pinot *nose and flavour. Very nice wine.* Tasted December 1969 ***
Pommard Faiveley	*Belgian bottled. First tasted in a private cellar near Ostend. Although it had rather a spongy cork I thought it quite nice, with a reasonably good* Pinot *nose, but the acidity was a bit too high. A few months later, in Amsterdam, I noted it as very pale, with a curious open, mustard-and-cress nose; dry, flavoury — to which I added, somewhat ambiguously "a little tart". Another pre-sale sample was distinctly off.* Last tasted May 1977.
Clos de la Roche Chanson	*I have a feeling that Christopher Fielden gave me this at an extempore dinner at his house when he was sales director of Chanson in Beaune (an extraordinary position for a young Englishman to hold). Very mature, palish; old but sound, meaty/earthy, very attractive — reminded me of some of the wines made in the 1920s; medium dry leading to a dry finish, very pleasant flavour, noticeable but perfectly tolerable acidity.* Tasted September 1975 **
La Tâche Dom. de la Romanée-Conti	*Distinctly brown in colour; ripe, earthy, very mature bouquet; slightly sweet, soft, medium body, old ripe flavour. Absolutely mature.* At lunch with Pierre Ponnelle in Beaune, September 1963 **
Volnay, Hospices	*A rather skimpily labelled but interesting bottle from the Quancard collection, a rather anonymous cellar unearthed in the Burgundy area: good level, fairly pale, very mature, with a rather unconvincing light rim; a light, scented bouquet, showing some age yet with sweetness and elegance; medium dry, lightish. A delicate, flavoury little wine with a twist of end acidity.* At the pre-sale tasting, March 1978 **

1951

A dismal vintage. Vying with 1956 for the worst of the decade. Climate: dismal summer. Even delaying the vintage until 15 October did not help. Assessment: virtually untouched by the trade, not surprisingly, judging from the Chambertin noted below, that was shown to the inquisitive Harvey party. Barolet was such an unorthodox loner that I mention his '51 only because it is likely to be the only one an English or American collector will come across.

Chambertin, Clos de Bèze Damoy	*Pale and browning: a smelly wine which reminded me of the bad cabbage '38 Hospices wine previously noted, though it was not as pronounced. Full flavoured but a light bitter end.* One of a range of vintages tasted at the grower's house, September 1958.
Chambolle-Musigny Dr Barolet	*Trust the doctor to turn his ministrations to a sick vintage. As I particularly wanted to see if his "off" vintages were any good, this was one of the first that Harry Waugh and I tasted in the cellars in October 1969; and again, before a later sale. The notes were consistent: not a bad colour but with a watery rim; even more surprisingly, a sound and attractive flavour — some ripeness, lightish. Slightly peppery on nose and palate.* Last tasted June 1970 *

1952 ★★★

A satisfactory, well-constituted vintage. More stolid than the '53; more consistent, better balanced and more forthcoming than the '52 red Bordeaux. Climate: drought in June; hot in July/August but some welcome rain. Would have been a really great year but warmth lacking in September. Vintage 7 October. Quantity reduced but quality regarded excellent. Assessment: this has always been one of my favourite burgundy vintages. Soundly based, a little foursquare but with innate richness. Still made in the good old-fashioned way. The best are still excellent. Tasting notes: 91 notes largely concentrated in the period from 1954 to 1960 when, working in the old, traditional wine-merchant division of Saccone & Speed and, later, at Harvey's, I had to know our stock-in-trade, at a time when the 1952, 1953, 1955 and 1957 vintages dominated their lists. Relatively few '52 burgundies crop up in Christie's wine sales, and those that do tend to be in small quantities scarcely warranting extracting a sample. First the notable wines tasted in the 1970s.

Beaune Audiffred	*Palish, very mature; some '52 richness pervading, but cork tainted.* Tasted January 1971.
Beaune, Grèves Piat	*Endorsing my feelings for the '52s, this wine was first noted, very favourably, at a pre-sale tasting in Texas in November 1975. The dynamic Robert Sakowitz must have bought some for his own cellar for he produced it at a dinner party three years later: medium — holding its colour well; bouquet sheer perfection, soft, harmonious, with a slight touch of vanilla, slightly singed (hot vintage, burnt skins) smoky Pinot; slightly sweet, medium body, lovely flavour, perfect balance.* Last tasted in Houston, October 1978 ★★★★
Beaune, Perrières Auguste Moreau	*Mature; fabulous, fragrant; dry but rich oaky character.* At a Heublein tasting, May 1975 ★★★★
Le Corton Bouchard Père	*First tasted in 1959: a lovely, distinctive wine, with a very meaty, slightly burnt flavour; good wine for the price (£1 per bottle retail). Considered fully ripe in 1971. Caught out by a poor, woody, Bouchard Père magnum in 1972. Later, good colour; fairly deep and rich, reliable but uninspiring.* Last tasted May 1973 ★★★
Corton, Clos du Roi Chanson	*Medium, very mature colour; very good nose but age showing; fullish, rich, fine flavour, silky and perfect balance. The host: that epitome of English country wine merchants, Tom Abell.* At lunch at Edward Sheldon's, Shipston-on-Stour, March 1976 ★★★★
Gevrey-Chambertin Avery's	*Either different shipments, or very curious changes in bottle, or thoroughly unreliable note taking: lightish, very crisp and flavoury — very similar to the Harvey bottling — in 1963. More recently, distinctly chunky and chocolaty.* Last tasted in 1971. At best ★★★
Grands-Echézeaux J. Drouhin	*A magnificent wine: fullish, fine firm colour, mature rim; almost voluptuously ripe and fine; touch of sweetness, fair body, soft, rich easy, velvety.* At a Drouhin and Hugel lunch at Claridge's, September 1973 ★★★★★
Morey St-Denis Bouchard Père	*Fairly deep, very good, excellent bottle-age.* Tasted May 1971 ★★★
Musigny P. Ponnelle	*Very attractive, stylish wine.* Tasted April 1970 ★★★
Nuits St-Georges, Vaucrains	*At the Leroy tasting. A deeper colour than even the 1959 Nuits; showing some age on the nose but rich; drying out a bit and frankly*

	lacking charm, though it has good flesh and flavour. A touch of acidity, cracking up. Tasted September 1979 ★★
Richebourg *Dom. de la Romanée-Conti*	*First drunk at Gaddesby in March 1967: it was austerely rich and in perfect state. More recently, at a dinner hosted by the co-owners of the domaine: still very deep coloured; well-developed nose, impressive if not ravishing like the '53 Grands-Echézeaux; slightly sweet, fairly full bodied, a deep velvety wine, now soft, rounded flesh over firm bones.* At the Ritz Casino, London, March 1979 ★★★★
Romanée-Conti *Dom. de la Romanée-Conti*	*First tasted in September 1968: a magnificent* robe; *high-quality nose; great depth of flavour, burnt-earth character, still tough. Five years later: still deep and firm coloured; very rich, complex, excellent* Pinot *bouquet; rich, fine flavour and balance. Real Romanée-Conti quality. Holding well.* Last tasted August 1973 ★★★★★
Savigny, Guettes *Doudet-Naudin*	*Light, dry Savigny-les-Beaune style, with an iron tang. Holding well.* Tasted November 1974 ★★
Vosne-Romanée *Dr Barolet*	*Showed well at the original pre-sale tastings in Geneva and London, even though one had a wormy cork: good colour; lovely, firm, elegant Vosne style; silky, crisp in December 1969. Next, less good, recorked I suspect, dull, but sound.* Last tasted April 1974 ★ to ★★★
Vosne-Romanée, Suchots *H. Sichel*	*French bottled: a gentle mature nose; soft, rich, dry-burnt '52 character, nice balance, good acidity.* Tasted August 1970 ★★★
Clos Vougeot *Dufouleur*	*Quite nice ripe old* Pinot *nose; soft, attractive, but fading a little.* Tasted October, November and December 1971 ★★★
Clos Vougeot *Hatch, Mansfield*	*A first-rate London-bottled wine: deep coloured but showing complete maturity; lovely old* Pinot *nose and flavour; broad, meaty Vougeot style, firm, excellent condition.* Tasted May 1975 ★★★★
Clos Vougeot *D. Sandeman*	*Middle of the road, nothing like the distinction of Hatch Mansfield's bottling.* Tasted April and July 1972 ★★

Some of the more significant and, for me, interesting '52s tasted prior to 1970, beginning with four more Barolet wines all at pre-sale tastings in December 1969:

Aloxe-Corton	*Minor, attractive, short* ★★
Beaune	*Pretty, scented* ★★
Chambolle-Musigny	*The best of the group: a rich and lovely wine* ★★★★
Morey St-Denis	*Quite nice* ★★★
Pommard, Grands Epenots, Clos des Citeaux	*Bottled by Avery's: a very good wine with remarkable grip and time in hand.* Tasted June 1968 ★★★(★)
Romanée St-Vivant, Les Quatre Journaux *L. Latour*	*Deep old* Pinot *nose; sweet, rich, fine but still holding back, youthful, even peppery.* Tasted October 1968 ★★★(★)
La Tâche *Dom. de la Romanée-Conti*	*First tasted in 1961: although some depth it always seemed fully mature, with no red left; highly fragrant; soft, silky, beautiful but completely ready. Seven years later: fabulously rich, full-blossomed bouquet yet curiously light for a '52. Extraordinary wine; great finesse. Completely ripe.* Tasted September 1968 ★★★★

Clos de Tart Mommessin	*An attractive ripe wine.* Tasted February 1967 ★★★
Volnay, Caillerets Bouchard Père	*Rich and magnificent.* Tasted May 1969.
Amongst the Harvey bottlings:	*Beaune, Grèves, good in 1961 but became tart later. Beaune, Malconsorts, more like a Corton — lovely. Beaune, Theurons, overripe. Chambertin, completely mature. Chambolle-Musigny, full, dry and meaty in 1959. Corton, so-so, agreeable enough, needed drinking in 1965. Gevrey-Chambertin, good fruit, similar to Avery's in 1963. Grands-Echézeaux, touch of the real thing. Volnay Clos des Chênes, a rather uncharacteristic Volnay, big and meaty. But a good drink in 1959.*

Postscript: Having praised some English bottlings I must express certain misgivings about what I can only describe, in retrospect, as the bland, ingenuous relationships between wine merchants, their London shippers and agents and their principals in Burgundy, exemplified by a typical (blind) tasting of shippers' samples of '52 Nuits St-Georges in the summer of 1955. There were two pure *Gamay*-type wines, two toffee nosed, some casky, some with guts and some too soft — and prices ranged from 116s. to 132s. (£5.80–£6.60) per dozen duty paid and delivered. My point really is that there appeared at the time to be a blithe disregard of true style and quality — the right name, an approximation of type and price being the main considerations.

1953 ★★★★

An excellent vintage. Elegant, ripe, supple wines of distinction. Climate: long, wet winter; a promising mild April followed by bad weather. June and July cold and rainy but the vital ripening months of August and September warm and sunny. Harvest, 29 September, brought in under excellent conditions. Market: a delightful blossoming wine, easy and agreeable when young and appearing on an equally blossoming market, before the real pressures had begun to build up. Assessment: like the '53 clarets, delicious at the earliest age, they developed effortlessly and well, some peaking in the early to mid-1960s, though the best-balanced, well-kept, high-quality wines are still ravishing if ethereal: burgundy at its most fully developed and appealing. What strikes me is the way rather delicate but nicely constituted wines will retain their vigour and charm for long after they first reveal their full development. Tasting notes: I was fortunate to observe the birth and development of this attractive vintage and tasted a wide range at its peak. I have once again divided the notes into a summary of '53s tasted over the past ten years and a section on the most interesting and/or significant wines tasted prior to this period and not tasted since. Notes on '53s tasted since autumn 1969:

Beaune, Clos du Roi Doudet-Naudin	*Mature; quite a rich tangy wine with noticeable acidity.* Tasted in Geneva, November 1974 ★★
Bonnes-Mares Paul Bouchard	*The least seen (in England) of the three Bouchards. Sweet bouquet, almost too good to be true; flavoury and elegant, attractive but plausible, with a slightly tinny finish.* Tasted February 1971 ★★
Chambertin, Clos de Bèze Thorin	*Berry Bros selection. A curious wine noted in somewhat underlit and difficult circumstances: at the dinner following the opening of a new wine bar. Very odd nose: spicy herb garden; dry, chunky flavour, rich, attractive, but with neither strong* Pinot *character nor '53 sweetness and charm.* Tasted December 1972 ★★
Chambertin, Clos de Bèze Shipper unknown	*Deep "hot-vintage" colour; fine ripening nose of high quality; fullish, rich, classic Nuits, firm and stylish.* Tasted November 1969 ★★★★

Corton Doudet-Naudin	*Fairly deep, mature colour; rather dry singed nose; good meaty flavour.* At Marcel Doudin's, September 1975 ★★★
Corton, Clos du Roi	*London bottled by David Sandeman. Fine, rich colour; slightly scented nose; quite a nice meaty wine but not a patch on the same merchant's bottling of '49 Chambertin.* Tasted April 1972 ★★
Côte de Nuits Villages Dr Barolet	*First noted without enthusiasm at the original pre-sale tasting in 1969: no nose but quite nice. Later: deep, plummy, still immature; indifferent nose; rich but raw and peppery on the palate. Interesting but odd.* Last tasted August 1970 ★
Echézeaux Bouchard Père	Tête de cuvée: *palish; very ripe fine* Pinot *bouquet; dry but firm and flavoury.* At a Heublein tasting May 1970 ★★
Gevrey-Chambertin Dutch bottled	*Bottled by W. Kuijt in the curious dumpy shaped bottles sometimes encountered in Holland and Belgium. Very mature looking, almost like orange-pekoe tea; a lovely, true, rich, smoky* Pinot *nose and flavour.* At a pre-sale tasting, May 1977 ★★★
Grands-Echézeaux Bouchard Père	*A Hertford Wine Company bottling, rich but showing its acidity in 1967. Bettered by Bouchard's own bottling: palish, very mature looking; old, very ripe* Pinot *bouquet and flavour; again slightly tart.* Consistent notes 1969, March 1970 ★
Grands-Echézeaux Dom. de la Romanée-Conti	*Violet, fragrant bouquet; silky, lovely, full flavoured, several notes in 1963. Displaying the highest quality, fully developed in 1965. Yet, most recently, still surprisingly deep; incredibly rich bouquet — scented beetroot — radiantly forthcoming; slightly sweet, rich yet delicate, with fabulous aftertaste. The '53 vintage and "the domaine" at its ravishing best.* Last tasted with the domaine owners at the Ritz, March 1979 ★★★★★
Nuits St-Georges, Clos St-Marc C. Viénot	*Bottled in Geneva. Palish; little nose; dry, quite good quality but no vigour left.* At a pre-sale tasting in Düsseldorf, June 1973 ★
Richebourg Avery's	*Fragrant; very sweet, elegant but rather light — more like a Volnay in character.* Tasted August 1973 ★★
Richebourg Grivelet Père	*Very mature, flavoury but a bit strained and acidity gaining the upper hand, in July 1966. Later that autumn, it was sound but needed drinking. And recently: fullish; plausible, ripe* Pinot *nose and flavour—a sort of poor man's Romanée-Conti. Very drinkable.* Last tasted November 1969 ★★
Romanée-Conti Dom. de la Romanée-Conti	*Absolutely magnificent. Losing colour but lovely; an overpowering bouquet: fruity, smoky* Pinot; *slightly sweet at first sip, leading through a rich, warm, smoky/oaky flavour to a long lingering dry finish. Richness and elegance masking fairly high alcoholic content.* A present from Harry Yoxall and drunk, after a suitable rest period, at home with him as a guest. June 1975 ★★★★★
Clos Vougeot Bouchard Père	*Curious that the Heublein pre-sale tastings, all burgundies are labelled* tête de cuvée. *Anyway, this had a nice colour, very mature; rather old but nice rich nose; slightly sweet, lovely flavour but touch of piquancy.* Tasted 1970, May 1971 ★★
Clos Vougeot L. Latour	*Nearly spoiled through slipshod decanting. Still, a lovely ripe* Pinot *bouquet; slightly sweet, medium body. Lovely wine.* At the Capital Hotel, November 1978.

Clos Vougeot, **Le Prieuré** P. Ponnelle	*Soft and velvety in 1967. Later, surprisingly deep; slightly med-* *icinal nose which held well; soft, warm, pleasant. Good not great.* Last tasted December 1975 **
Romanée St-Vivant Bouchard Ainé	*Odd half-bottles and lukewarm notes: slightly unclean though* *some nice fruit and not unattractive in July 1969. Three months* *later, overmature and sharp.* Last tasted October 1969.
Romanée St-Vivant Bouchard Père	*Mature; ripe old* Pinot *bouquet and flavour. Good wine but* *slightly bitter finish.* Tasted October 1969 *
Romanée St-Vivant Marey-Monge	*A Grivelet bottling in 1966 was ripe and exciting but spoiled by a* *gritty acidity. A crisp Harvey bottling still green and unripe in* *1959. Recently at John Avery's, a fine colour; rather oversweet on* *the palate, rich open-knit very positive, delicious and opulently* *overripe.* Last tasted July 1979 ***
Ch. de Vosne-Romanée Dom. du Château	*Fine deep, classic vintage colour; very good mature* Pinot *nose,* *stylish, with a touch of burnt/volcanic character that made me* *think of Corton; slightly sweet, fairly full but elegant, rich and well* *balanced. Easy to drink and at its peak.* At Harvey's, January 1971 ***
Vosne-Romanée Dr Barolet	*Signs of cork weevil. Good colour; bouquet with slightly sickly* *overtones; not bad flavour, I wrote "retaste" — and never did.* At pre-sale tasting, Geneva. December 1969 *

Notable '53s tasted prior to autumn 1969, and not since:

Beaune, Hospices, **Guigone de Salins**	*A lovely wine shipped and probably bottled by Lebègue: ripe and* *mature.* Tasted in February 1967 ***
Chambolle-Musigny P. Ponnelle	*Sweet and lively, an excellent drink.* Tasted 1960 *
Chassagne-Montrachet, **Clos St-Jean** de Monthélie	*A soft, attractive, somewhat overripe wine beginning to fall apart,* *with a light, slightly acid finish.* Tasted October 1966 **
Corton P. Ponnelle	*A good ripe wine.* Tasted November 1966 ***
Gevrey-Chambertin Colcombet	*Ripe, waxy nose; nice flavour.* Tasted May 1969 **
Musigny Vieilles Vignes de Vogüé	*A perfect wine: deep, attractive, beautifully balanced, firm and* *elegant. Nice but not then fully developed.* Tasted May 1961 ****
Clos de la Roche A. Rousseau	*A most beautiful wine: soft, very flavoury and marvellously bal-* *anced. Quite lovely.* Tasted August 1960 ****
La Tâche Dom. de la Romanée-Conti	*Palish and very mature; a marvellously developed high-flying* *fragrance; seemed rather dry but had a lovely, long, delicate* *flavour and crisp finish.* At peak in April 1966 ****
Volnay, Clos des Chênes	*Light in colour even in 1960, soft, light style. Some charm and* *elegance.* Tasted May 1960.
Vosne-Romanée, Suchots Dom. Blée	*A Grivelet wine that appeared brown and overripe.* Even in January 1960.
Clos Vougeot Lebègue	*Well bottled by British Transport Hotels. Pale but attractive;* *thoroughly mature but alive and kicking.* Tasted May 1968 **

1954 ★★★

A variable, abundant and totally bypassed vintage. Climate: dry spring, fine blossoming; but a rainy summer put paid to early hopes though there was a late autumn reprieve. Picking began 7 October. Market: coming as it did after the much-bought '52s and '53s, the vintage was given a miss which, judging by the few I have tasted, is a pity. The same applied to the '54 vintage port and, to a lesser extent, claret. Assessment: all I can say is that if any '54s of good provenance come my way I will not hesitate to acquire a bottle or two.

Bonnes-Mares Grivelet	*Starting on rather a low note: my first '54 was rather off putting: hard, unbalanced and ungrateful.* Tasted September 1958.
Chambolle-Musigny Dr Barolet	*One of several eye-openers during my first visit, with Harry Waugh, to the two-tier cellars below the Barolet mansion in Beaune. This wine was still in cask in October 1969. It had lost a bit of colour in the wood but was fine looking; the nose was rich and sweet, rather strawberry-like; on the palate — soft, flavoury and completely sound. It was one of the most immediately attractive wines at the pre-sale tasting that we held in Geneva in December 1969: fabulously rich, mature* Pinot *nose and flavour. Latterly, still lovely.* Last tasted April 1974 ★★★★
Corton Mommessin	*Palish, mature; low-keyed nose and flavour; ripe, nice — good value at 135s. (£6.75) per dozen.* Tasted July 1968 ★★★
Côte de Nuits Villages Dr Barolet	*This was incredibly good, rich and fine — after ten years in cask!* Tasted October 1969 ★★★
Hospices de Nuits, Les St-Georges	*A rare and more than interesting '54: a fine-looking wine, fairly deep coloured; extraordinary fruit on the nose, rich, high-toned, honeyed bottle-age; a very intense and powerful wine. I rated it almost as high as the '49.* At the remarkable Leroy tasting, September 1979 ★★★★
Musigny de Vogüé	*Fairly deep, plummy, rather youthful looking; a good, slightly sugary nose with excellent* Pinot *character; a fine, feminine wine. Lovely.* At a pre-sale tasting in Geneva, April 1969 ★★★★
Romanée St-Vivant Bouchard Ainé	*Deep coloured but mature; sweet, ripe, a big hot flavour. Really quite nice.* Tasted February 1969 ★★★
Vosne-Romanée, Grande Rue H. Lamarche	*Grande Rue and '54: a double rarity. Curiously sweet, almost smelly on the nose; soft yet slightly leathery texture. But a good drink.* Tasted October 1958 ★★

1955 ★★★

Generally good, with finesse. Middleweight, lacking the depth and manliness of '52s and the grace, flesh and elegance of '53s. Climate: wet spring; cold June and a late flowering. By August the vines in fine condition. Harvested from 5 October in the best conditions for 20 years. Quantity down on 1954. Market: fairly popular and heavily bought vintage though it shared, with '55 Bordeaux, a rather low-keyed, sound but unexciting reputation. It was the Indian summer of English bottling. Most wine merchants were still shipping a large proportion of their wines, even fine wines, in cask and the standard of bottling was still high. Assessment: almost as instantly appealing as the '53s, the wines developed quickly. Although the Côte de Nuits had depth and style they always lacked length and finish and the alluring flesh and charm of the '53s; the Côte de Beaune were light and probably at their best in the mid- to late 1960s.

Tasting notes: I have nearly 200 notes, but over three-quarters were tasted prior to 1970, when most of the wines were being sold and drunk, and over half were tasted prior to 1964, when I was still wine-merchanting. Once again I have listed first those wines tasted over the past ten years that will give the reader an idea of the style, quality and condition of the '55s. The next section is a briefer summary, with highlights.

Aloxe-Corton L. Latour	*Palish, very mature colour, nose and palate. Rather stewed, warm flavour. Quite nice.* Tasted July 1971 **
Aloxe-Corton, Fournières H. Thévenot	*This was the oldest of a most attractive range of wines bottled at the Domaine H. Thévenot in Aloxe-Corton. The domaine was acquired by a M. Fournier, who maintained quality production. Upon his death in the early 1960s, his widow sold the domaine but retained a stock of some 25,000 bottles. The remainder was acquired by Jean-Pierre Bloud and a substantial portion offered for sale at Christie's. This particular wine was fairly pale in colour and completely mature; a sound, ripe nose; dry, lightish but with fine, rich flavour—much livelier and better balanced than the colour indicated.* At the pre-sale tasting, April 1972 ***
Chambertin Avery's	*Quite deep, lovely; marvellous, ripe* Pinot *bouquet and flavour; medium body. Elegant.* Tasted November 1970 ****
Chambertin Héritiers Latour	*A half-bottle, remarkably full and rich for a '55. Its sweet, opulent, smoky* Pinot *flavour opened up but then seemed to cut off abruptly, lacking the long, lingering farewell that a great wine would have in a great vintage.* Tasted December 1975 ****
Chambertin L. Jadot	*Fairly deep, mature; quite nice nose, expected more; a rich, smooth, rounded wine, with nice balance and warmth, but not great.* At the Masters of Wine jubilee dinner, March 1980 ***
Charmes-Chambertin H. Sichel	*At an end-of-seminar dinner in Houston: medium colour, very mature looking; rich, smoky, good mature nose and flavour. Dry, perfectly developed. Good acidity. At peak.* Tasted November 1974 ****
Corton H. Sichel	*Deep, richly coloured; fabulous, fully ripe flavour, fullish, meaty, very good but short.* Tasted October 1975 ***
Corton, Maréchaudes Doudet-Naudin	*Bouquet not very marked but a soft, nice wine. Tasted blind; I thought it was a '64.* Tasted October 1971 **
Gevrey-Chambertin Doudet-Naudin	*Decent colour; slightly sweet, a "good commercial", agreeably rich wine.* Tasted May 1971 **
Nuits St-Georges, 1er cru Leroy	*Fullish colour; curious overripe nose, fragrant but with a whiff of decay; drying out and getting thin. Too old, lacking flesh and charm.* At the Leroy tasting, September 1979 *
Pommard, Rugiens C. Breton	*Medium colour; good deep bouquet; rich, elegant, good backbone and finish.* Tasted January 1971 ***
Richebourg Bouchard Aîné	*Plum coloured; stewed prunes on the nose. I did not note its taste. Doubtless good for the bowels.* Tasted October 1972 *
Romanée St-Vivant Marey-Monge	*A lovely ripe wine, sweet, soft, perfectly balanced and at its peak.* At the Bass Charrington Vintage Dinner at Claridge's, October 1968 *****
Romanée St-Vivant Bouchard Aîné	*Bottled by British Transport Hotels. Variable: one bottle oxidized, the best overripe and not completely sound.* Tasted February 1971.

Romanée St-Vivant Marchand Bolnot	*Bottled in Geneva. Getting old. Dry, light, flavoury.* Tasted June 1973 **
Dom. St-Clément Hellmers	*Where my old friend Mr Scott found this I do not know, but it was a winner, a marvellously flavoury and mature* Pinot, *and excellent value at £13. 10s. (£13.50) per dozen to the trade.* Tasted July 1972 **
Savigny-Lavières Bouchard Père	*Pale, very mature looking; altogether old for its age and light in body and style, though a nice drink.* Tasted May 1971 **
Volnay Calvet	*Palish, very mature; very rich, highly mature, rather* faisandé *(gamy) nose; fabulously sweet, rich flavour to match, yet overall light and gentle.* Tasted January 1971 ***
Vosne-Romanée Patriarche	*Fairly deep, lively, mahogany-tinged colour; sweet, subtle and silky bouquet; rich, burnt, chunky flavour with nice tannin and acidity.* Tasted January 1971 ***
Vosne-Romanée, Beaumonts	*A superb Avery bottling: delicious, sweet, fragrant bouquet; lovely, delicate flavour. Perfect in its class.* Tasted February 1966 *****
Clos de Tart Belgian bottled	*Bottled by J. van der Meulen. A real jam tart: jammy flavour, tannic and tart. Nose curious but developed well.* Tasted May 1977.
Clos Vougeot Grivelet	*Grivelet at his opulent best. Rich, ripe, rounded.* Tasted April 1978 ***
Clos Vougeot London bottled	*A good Justerini & Brooks bottling: medium, mature; fine elegant nose; meaty. Absolutely right.* Tasted October 1972 ***
Harvey bottlings:	*I have notes of a whole string of generally very appealing Harvey bottlings, the best of those, not already mentioned, being: Bonnes Mares; Chambolle-Musigny, Charmes; Charmes-Chambertin; Grands-Echézeaux; Vosne-Romanée, Malconsorts; Vosne-Romanée, Tête de Cuvée.*
Santenay, le vrai	*This was one of the most salutary lessons of my wine-trade career, an eye-opener. Harry Waugh had taken three Harvey bottlings of Santenay to taste blind with Javillier the broker, in a grower's cellar. The first sample was of the wine that we thought our customers would consider an acceptable Santenay. It had a good colour, a clean nose, not unlike the next sample but a bit better. This wine, purchased from a Burgundian negociant via a London shipper was, the local growers and brokers pronounced, bonne cuisine — blended, but blended well. The second sample was fullish in colour, had a rather innocuous nose, was fairly full flavoured but had no particular character. Supplied by a well-known London shipper it was thought to be an Algerian blend plus alcohol. Goût américain was the verdict of the local experts! The third was so pale it was almost rosé, with a sweet, curious nose, a rather piquant flavour and slightly acid finish. I and the Harvey team found this strange and of unaccustomed style, but we were told that it was le vrai Santenay and needed a couple of years to shake off the acidity. In fact, all the '55 Côte de Beaune wines we tasted in growers' cellars were fairly pale in colour — a far cry from the souped-up wines the English merchants and their customers were accustomed to. The moral: all that glisters is not gold!*

1956

The worst vintage of the decade. Thin, deficient wines. Climate: intense cold and severe frosts in February, mainly affecting the lower slopes; a poor spring with vegetation a month behind, but by the end of June vines appeared healthy; cold and incessant rain throughout July and August, with vine diseases and pests gaining a hold; days of hot sunshine in September but too late to ripen the grapes for even a late harvest, which started 5 October, except in the Côte d'Or, where it was around 15th to 20th. Only about one-third to half the normal crop. Assessment: not generally shipped and rarely if ever seen under the vintage label. I do not hold with the "vintage chart" adage that good wines can be made in a bad vintage. But quite often the best is made of a bad job, as below:

Romanée-Conti *Dom. de la Romanée-Conti*	*This was craftily slipped into the domaine's tasting at Christie's and really was quite a surprise. Though palish and very mature looking, as one might expect, it had a lovely, ripe, old Pinot nose, far better than anticipated. A dry, sinewy — or rather thin and gristly — wine, but not bad.* Tasted September 1972 *

1957 ★★★

Flavoury wines, much better balanced and constituted than the '57 red Bordeaux, the high acidity adding to the flavour and zest. Climate: mild wet winter; fairly good early summer with extreme heat at end of June; July unsettled, first very hot, then cool and rainy, the grey days being attributed, by some locals, to atomic experiments. Vintage 7 October. Assessment: attractive firm wines, the tendency to overacidity being ameliorated by the heavier burgundy style. One must remember that Burgundy has a continental climate, more sheltered and balmy than the maritime climate of Bordeaux, which probably accounts for the softer, less abrasively acidic tendencies in this sort of vintage. The best '57s are still highly flavoured and still make an attractive drink. Tasting notes: I have a large number of notes, the vast proportion being made earlier than 1970, indeed well over half are prior to 1965, so I have concentrated on those wines which will, I hope, illuminate the nature, quality and condition of the vintage. Some '57s tasted within the past ten years:

Aloxe-Corton *Doudet-Naudin*	*Pure chocolate on the nose yet dry and austere on the palate.* Tasted October 1978 ★★
Beaune, Clos de Fèves *Chanson*	*Lovely garnet red; some age on the nose and signs of cracking up; dry, nice flavour, good acidity.* Tasted March 1976 * Needs drinking up.
Bonnes-Mares *Misserey*	*Maybe the context had something to do with it. Shortly after our safe arrival in Chicago in an American Airlines DC10 (just four days before the fatal accident that occurred the day we took off for Dallas), an old friend, Bill Contos, picked up my wife and me in his new Rolls and whisked us off to a delightful surprise dinner at his restaurant, Chez Paul. He has a marvellous wine list and I chose this '57 to see how it had developed. It was a most attractive wine: medium colour, mature; lovely, ripe Pinot nose, lightish, fading but attractive; a delicate, smoky flavour and good acidity. Delightful.* Tasted May 1979 ★★★ Drink up.
Chambertin, Clos de Bèze *Paul Bouchard*	*Deepish, pleasant enough; dry, quite nice, some acidity.* Tasted February 1971 *

Corton, Clos du Roi Paul Bouchard	*Meaty flavour, tinny finish.* Tasted February 1971 ⋆
Gevrey-Chambertin Jaffelin	*Palish, very mature looking; old but sound nose; slightly sweet, lightish, fully mature.* Tasted July 1972 ⋆⋆
Gevrey-Chambertin A. Rousseau	*Demonstrates what a good grower can make of a village wine in a moderate vintage: fairly deep; a very good, even, ripe Pinot nose; firm, flavoury and attractive.* Tasted February 1973 ⋆⋆⋆
Monthélie Ropiteau	*Palish; quite a nice, dry, flavoury little wine. Piquant.* Tasted July 1972 ⋆⋆
Nuits St-Georges, Porets Leroy	*Deep rich colour; showing a touch of age on the nose, but rich; excellent singed flavour and good acidity. A fine wine.* At the big Leroy tasting, September 1979 ⋆⋆⋆⋆
Richebourg Dom. de la Romanée-Conti	*Deepish, good colour; very fragrant, ripe, forthcoming and refreshing nose; getting lighter though not softer with age, but attractive, flavoury and refreshing. A piquant touch. Probably at best.* Tasted February 1971 ⋆⋆⋆⋆
Volnay, Santenots	*Probably a Mommessin wine, as I was dining with their London agent. An odd style, not very harmonious, chunky and bitty, with raw acidity — but, having said that, flavoury and a nice enough drink.* Tasted October 1973 ⋆
Clos Vougeot C. Brétin	*Fine, rich, mature burgundy red; sweet — oversweet really — with curious overtone like burnt-out fireworks; also slightly sweet on the palate, medium body, positive, but just misses.* Tasted January 1971 ⋆

Some attractive English-bottled '57s:

Bonnes-Mares	*Berry Bros: fading but fine.* Tasted April 1972 ⋆⋆
Romanée St-Vivant	*Tyler's: age showing but rich, refreshing '57 acidity.* Tasted March 1975 ⋆⋆
Clos Vougeot	*Marcilly. Bottled by British Transport Hotels. Scented, light, charming.* Tasted October 1971 ⋆⋆

Amongst the better '57s tasted prior to 1970:

Beaune, Hospices, Clos des Avaux Bottler unknown	*A very fine-looking wine; refined, most beautiful, very well-balanced bouquet; a dry wine, lovely, silky and firm. Excellent quality, most attractive.* Tasted December 1967 ⋆⋆⋆⋆
La Tâche Dom. de la Romanée-Conti	*Showing very well in its youth: light in style; very, very ripe, very fragrant, recognizable La Tâche nose; sweet, most attractive and immediately drinkable.* Tasted September 1960 ⋆⋆⋆⋆
Clos de Tart Mommessin	*Very attractive when first tasted in 1962: fabulous acidity and rarest violet flavour on palate and aftertaste. Lovely wine but I noted that it might need watching. Later, offered simply as a Côte de Nuits, unlabelled but with branded cork, it was very light and very mature looking; completely overripe nose; the acidity had caught up with it.* Last tasted October 1968.

1958 ★★

A moderate-quality vintage from all accounts and one entirely bypassed by the English trade. Climate: February mild but cold at the end of the month; the end of April and the whole of May were without frosts but there were some local storms; variable in June with warm and cold days; good flowering period; after a warm July the prospects for the vintage were good; heavy rain then affected the vines, but September was mainly fine with some rain at the end of the month. The harvest took place during a fine, sunny October, starting on 1st. Very large crop. Market: after substantial buying of '52s, '53s, '55s and '57s, and with the 1959 "vintage of the century" in the offing, it was no wonder that 1958 was given a miss. Tasting notes: to my surprise I see that I have not a single note of any 1958 burgundy, which would seem to endorse the unpopularity of this vintage with English wine merchants. What happened to the enormous production I do not know. Doubtless some slept for a year.

1959 ★★★★★

A great vintage and, in my opinion, one of the last classic heavyweights made in Burgundy. Climate: blossoming took place under the best conditions in June; dry weather followed in July and August and there was some rain to swell the grapes in September; early harvest, 14 September, in warm weather. A record crop of high-quality wine. Assessment: from the very outset these were big and attractive wines and, by and large, have kept well. They tend to be beautifully constituted with a good colour, good extract, lots of tannin and acidity and a great deal of flavour. Tasting notes: I have more notes on the '59s than on any burgundy vintage except 1964, two-thirds of which were tasted during the 1960s. As 20 years is quite a long span in the life of a normal, commercial red burgundy I shall deal with a cross-section of tasting notes made in the 1970s first and then summarize the pre-1970s notes.

Aloxe-Corton H. Thévenot	*Surprisingly youthful looking; scented, rather pasty nose; nice flavour, tannin and acidity.* At the Jean-Pierre Bloud tasting, April 1972 ★★★
Aloxe-Corton Tollot-Beaut	*A ripe Grivelet-type nose and taste. Not a beefy '59, nor of top quality, but very flavoury.* Tasted in magnum, December 1979 ★★ Drink up.
Aloxe-Corton, Fournières	*Another Thévenot wine, again deepish and still somewhat immature looking; a pretty good rich nose; sweeter and richer than the above wine.* Tasted in the cellars, April 1972 ★★★
Beaune, Bressandes Chauvenet	*Palish, very mature; rather overblown* Pinot *nose; light, delicate fruit with nice aftertaste.* Tasted May 1978 ★★ Drink up.
Beaune, Clos du Roi Doudet-Naudin	*Showing a bit of old age in 1971. Later: nice colour; a straightforward wine, though a touch of finings (like almond kernels) on the nose.* Last tasted October 1973 ★
Beaune, Hospices, Clos des Avaux	*A good Lebègue bottling: peppery but lovely in 1964. Later: deepish; excellent ripe nose; full bodied, fine flavour and finish.* Last tasted May 1972 ★★★★
Beaune, Vignes-Franches L. Latour	*Paler than some of the good Côte de Nuits and maturing in colour; very light on the nose; slightly sweet. A curious, full-flavoured but piquant wine. Stylish.* Tasted October 1971 ★★★
Bonnes-Mares Bouchard Père	*Bottled by the Army & Navy Stores. Fairly deep coloured; good nose; fine wine, rather hefty for lunch on a hot summer's day.* Tasted with Raymond Harcourt, the retired head of the A. & N. wine department, in August 1975 ★★★

Bonnes-Mares C. Viénot	*Bottled in Geneva. Medium colour; slight but sweet meaty nose; soft, good flavour, middleweight.* At a pre-sale tasting, June 1973 ★★
Chambertin, Clos de Bèze Lebègue	*One of the inevitable* tête de cuvée *burgundies at a Heublein tasting of wines from the "cellars" of the good ship* Queen Elizabeth. *One of the half-bottles that bobbed ashore: palish and completely mature.* Tasted May 1973 ★★
Chambolle-Musigny Hasenklever	*A rather indifferent nose but pleasant enough taste.* Tasted February 1971 ★
Chambolle-Musigny L. Latour	*Medium, plum coloured; moderate nose; rich chunky flavour, yet with a touch of piquancy.* Tasted October 1971 ★★
Chambolle, Charmes Grivelet	*Deepish, plummy; delicate yet ripe; medium weight, fine flavour and quite a bite.* Tasted at Larry Feldman's in San Francisco, May 1971 ★★★
Charmes-Chambertin Mommessin	*Bottled for the Swedish-American line and showing well in February 1971. Later in the year, I found it overblown and not very nice. The following year, fairly deep coloured; a ripe old Pinot bouquet and flavour.* Last tasted February 1972 ★★ Drink up.
Corton Calvet	*I have always been partial to Calvet burgundies and cannot recall a less-than-nice bottle: full, fine colour; calm, convex nose, with slight touch of vanilla; full bodied, rich.* Tasted December 1975 ★★★★
Corton L. Jadot	*Still deep plummy purple; fullish plummy character too. Quite nice but short.* At an after-sale supper at Dublin airport, April 1971 ★★
Corton, Bressandes L. Latour	*At lunch with Louis Latour junior, who told me that the very old vines in their portion of this vineyard produced only a small crop: some 1,800 bottles in all. Almost opaque, plummy, still youthful looking; fine but undeveloped bouquet; slightly sweet, full bodied, lots of flavour and grip, yet very soft and rich. Amazing power, beautiful balance.* Tasted September 1975 ★★★★ Drink now — 2000.
Corton, Bressandes F. Loufte	*Bottled by the English-domiciled owner of a holding of the Bressandes vineyard. Medium colour, mature; a very nice nose, slightly sweet;̈ medium-full body — a very nice soft wine, the real thing.* Tasted January and April 1970 ★★★★
Corton, Clos du Roi H. Thévenot	*Deep coloured; very fragrant; soft, good fruit, with dry end acidity.* Tasted July 1976 ★★★
Corton, Hospices, Cuvée Dr Peste	*Excellently bottled by Hedges & Butler. First tasted in February 1971: somewhat austere but good. Later served at the annual dinner at the Vintners' Hall during my chairmanship of the Institute of Masters of Wine: fine colour; very good meaty Corton bouquet and flavour. A fine, rich, well-balanced wine.* Last tasted March 1971 ★★★★
Corton, Maréchaudes Doudet-Naudin	*A decently coloured wine; rich nose; meaty, burnt character. Nice mouthful.* Tasted May 1971 ★★★
Ch. Corton-Grancey L. Latour	*Rich and stylish in October 1971. Later: a rich-looking wine; good but undeveloped bouquet; fine, nicely made and well balanced, with deep Corton smokiness and the firmness that I normally associate with a good Côte de Nuits rather than a Côte de Beaune.* Last tasted November 1972 ★★★(★) Plenty of life left.
Echézeaux Dom. de la Romanée-Conti	*Sweetish, ripe, lovely flavour at a Lebègue tasting in 1964. Thirteen years later: soft, velvety, ripe. A magnificent wine.* Last tasted at an Options Club lunch with Len Evans in Sydney, February 1977 ★★★★

Grands-Echézeaux Grivelet	*A very appealing wine: complete, gentle, rich, attractive, beetroot* Pinot *nose; very flavoury and elegant on the palate, with a singed, rich flavour. Overall very nice, with good sweetness, good acidity and a marvellous aftertaste. Tasted July 1979 ★★★★ Drink now — 1985.*
Grands-Echézeaux Dom. de la Romanée-Conti	*First noted at one of the annual Lebègue tastings in 1964: similar to the Echézeaux, perhaps richer, and very impressive. Next, at a Lebègue tasting held at Christie's in 1972: not as deep coloured as expected, but a very attractive, well-developed, sweet bouquet; fat, with dry finish on the palate. Five years later, at Len Evans's in Sydney: fine fullish colour; lovely rich* Pinot *nose; soft, very flavoury, but with marked 1957-like acidity. Most recently, at a domaine dinner: not very deep in colour; lovely, very rich bouquet and flavour; fairly full bodied, very good acidity. Outstanding.* *Last tasted March 1979 ★★★★★*
Mazis-Chambertin T. Bassot	*Fullish; delicately rich* fraise des bois *bouquet; slightly sweet, most excellent weight, character and fruit. Tasted December 1972 ★★★★*
Mazis-Chambertin J. Regnier	*Trust an Irishman to produce two '59 burgundies at a light supper before an evening flight back to London. This was a similar weight to Jadot's Corton, but livelier and more mature; stylish nose; distinguished wine, good* Pinot *fruit and finish. With Jim Fitzgerald at Dublin airport, April 1971 ★★★*
Nuits St-Georges H. Gouges	*Not very impressive: an indefinable colour; sweet, rather stewed nose; light, fluffy style. Not the usual Gouges style and character, but quite nice. Tasted July 1971 ★★*
Nuits St-Georges, 1er cru	*The only '59 at the big Leroy tasting: medium colour with a marvellous even gradation; magnificent hot-vintage bouquet; sweet wine, rich, very well put together, firm and holding well.* *Tasted at the Dom. d'Auvenay, September 1979 ★★★★ Drink now — 1990.*
Nuits St-Georges, **Ch. Gris**	*Owned and bottled by Lupé-Cholet. The real thing: rather pale and mature looking; ripe, rich, high-toned, slightly piquant* Pinot *bouquet; slightly sweet, but lightish and almost fading away for a '59. A good rich though delicate flavour and an appealing prickle of acidity. Tasted April 1970 ★★★★ Drink up.*
Richebourg C. Viénot	*Bottled in Geneva. Medium colour, very mature looking; a pleasant smoky/meaty nose; lightish for a '59, soft, nice flavour and tangy finish. Tasted June 1973 ★★★★*
Romanée-Conti Dom. de la Romanée-Conti	*First noted, and enormously impressed by it, at a big Lebègue tasting in 1964: an incredibly rich, fantastically concentrated wine. Recently, at a Romanée-Conti dinner: a fairly deep, very lively appearance; nose slightly aloof and withdrawn, excellent but still hard; a huge, dry tannic and alcoholic wine, almost Latour massiveness. Unready. Last tasted March 1979 ★★★(★★) Drink now — 2000.*
Clos St-Denis de Villamont	*Slightly youthful edge; old nose; dry and somewhat unreal flavour. Tasted June 1970 ★*
Savigny-les-Beaune Bouchard Père	*Palish, very mature in colour and on nose. A lovely little wine.* *Tasted before a big sale of Gilbey-Vintner wines at the Beaver Hall, April 1971 ★★*
Clos de Tart Mommessin	*Good colour, powdery sediment; low-keyed nose; rich, nicely balanced in February 1978. Later, from a magnum: deep coloured but, I thought, a dull and heavy wine. Last tasted in Denmark, June 1978 ★*

Volnay Bouchard Père	*A light, pretty wine; fragrant, but not for further keeping.* Tasted *May 1972* ★★
Volnay, Caillerets H. Boillot	*Rather pale in colour; good old* Pinot *nose and flavour. Sound and attractive. A relatively elegant '59.* Tasted April '59. *Tasted April 1974* ★★★
Vosne-Romanée Bouchard Père	*Nice in February 1971. Later: medium colour, mature; attractive, stylish, scented* Pinot *bouquet; dry, nice weight and quality.* Last tasted June 1971 ★★★
Vosne-Romanée P. Ponnelle	*Not very deep, maturing well; rich bouquet in July 1970. Later: I found it a suave classic wine, with a beautifully developed, classic, ripe* Pinot *bouquet, refined, fine texture and balance.* Last tasted January 1971 ★★★★
Clos Vougeot Marey & Liger-Belair	*Not very deep, overmature in colour and on palate; indifferent nose; slightly tart.* Tasted March 1970.
Clos Vougeot Patriarche	*Tasted blind: richly coloured; curious, opulent ("sweaty boots" someone said) and rather unclassic bouquet; fairly full bodied, with rich, red-earth, iron flavour, tannin and acidity. Dry finish. Barolo? Coonawarra? Rhône? Burgundy never crossed my mind.* Tasted December 1976 ★★?
Clos Vougeot *Ch. de la Tour*	*I found this most fragrant and attractive in May 1975. Later: four poor bottles all overripe and cracking up.* Last tasted April 1978.

Some good '59s tasted in the 1960s:

Chambolle-Musigny Dr Barolet	*Lovely colour, very rich; a beautiful, sweet, biscuity bouquet; soft, lightish, delicate.* At the pre-sale tasting, December 1969 ★★★
Musigny Bouchard Père	*Deep; clove-like bouquet; fine deep flavour.* Tasted April 1969 ★★★★
Musigny de Vogüé	*Lovely colour, still youthful; curiously undeveloped nose and flavour. Seemed quite unready.* Tasted June 1968 ★★(★★) *Probably excellent now.*
Pommard Dr Barolet	*Still in cask ten years after the vintage. Lovely rich colour; sweet, strawberry aroma; fine, fruity, lovely fresh acidity. Quite remarkable.* Tasted October 1969 ★★★
Clos St-Denis	*Rich, soft coloured; indeed rich and soft throughout. A most excellent wine.* Tasted July 1969 ★★★★
La Tâche Dom. de la Romanée-Conti	*Tasted only at its first appearance at one of Lebègue's spectacular cellar tastings under the arches beneath London Bridge station: ripe and remarkably luscious at five years of age.* Tasted October 1964.
Vosne-Romanée Dr Barolet	*Firm Nuits character, fine flavour and balance.* Tasted December 1969 ★★★

1960 ★

Large crop of unripe, uneven-quality grapes; and mainly poor wines. Climate: generally mild winter with some end-of-April frosts. May favourable, fine weather and beneficial rains in June. Flowering under good conditions but lack of warmth in July made the ripening irregular and early promise spoiled by a rainy August and September, which resulted in rot, inducing some growers to pick early (and unripe). Market: once again, as with the '51s, '56s, and even the less unworthy '58s, the trade did not touch this vintage. In any case, almost everyone had invested heavily, perhaps too heavily at the time, in the '59s. One cannot help wondering what happens to pools of neglected wine; a question like: "Where do flies go in the winter time?" Tasting notes: my notebooks reflect the dearth of '60s. I have notes of only one:

Volnay Ropiteau?	*I assume this was a Ropiteau wine as I drank it at dinner with one of the Gordon-Clarks, the agents. It was light but very attractive.* *Tasted April 1966* **

1961 ★★★★

A very good vintage but not in my opinion as great as the '59, and not on the same plane as '61 red Bordeaux. Firm, well-constructed, stylish wines. Climate: mild and wet winter followed by warm spring weather. By May the vines were months ahead of normal but the flowering in June was prolonged (over 20 days instead of one week) because of variable weather. The early advantage was lost during the summer months when the average temperature was comparatively low, with especially cool nights. August hotter, but variable. Fine and warm in September, harvesting from 25th under good conditions. Slightly below average crop of fairly evenly ripe grapes. Market: the comparatively small crop of good wines and a growing world demand induced growers to ask 50 per cent more for their '61s than for the '59s at the same period. Not for the first or last time did the trade press express worries: "It's not certain that the purchasers and consumers will fall in with these apparently exorbitant demands. . . ." Assessment: a distinctly attractive, flavoury vintage and for me, in retrospect, like '47s, only leaner. Probably the majority were at their best either side of 1970, the lesser wine thinning out by then. But the more solidly constructed and better balanced wines are still lovely. Tasting notes: almost as many notes on the '61s as '59s, and almost as many, to my surprise, as on claret of the same vintage. Not that it is relevant to compare them numerically as the permutations in Burgundy of grower, shipper, merchant and bottler are so much more varied and significant. Well over half were tasted in the 1960s. First, a selection of those wines tasted in the 1970s:

Aloxe-Corton L. Latour	*A pleasant but less than memorable wine at a memorable lunch at the Connaught with Pamela Vandyke Price as my guest. Afterwards I was knocked off my bicycle in the King's Road, Chelsea, through careless inattention.* *It happened to be Friday 13 August, 1971* **
Aloxe-Corton C. Viénot	*I have always found the Viénot wines very flavoury and this was no exception. Not great but authentic.* *At the Stafford Hotel, November 1970* ***
Beaune, Clos des Ursules L. Jadot	*Maturing; hard nose but showing some age; fullish, stylish wine. Dry. Could have been a hefty Côte de Nuits.* *Tasted July 1971* ***
Beaune, Vignes-Franches Pasquier-Desvignes	*Plummy in colour, smell and taste. Dry and unappealing. Tart finish.* *Tasted December 1973.*
Bonnes-Mares L. Brück	*Deep coloured; good nose; nice stylish wine, well balanced. Good, but not great.* *Tasted January 1972* ***
Bonnes-Mares de Vogüé	*Very pretty garnet red; smoky, ripe* Pinot *nose; sweet, velvety, well constructed, elegant, completely mature.* *Tasted March 1971* ****
Chambertin, Clos de Bèze Damoy	*Medium, very mature; sweet, fine, rich nose and flavour. Most attractive, well developed.* *At a Heublein tasting, June 1975* ****
Chambertin, Clos de Bèze J. Drouhin	*A gorgeous velvety wine in 1971. Two years later: medium pale and very mature looking; a lovely ripe bouquet; dry, stylish, with more power than anticipated from the colour.* *Tasted December 1973* ****

Chambertin, Clos de Bèze Drouhin-Laroze	*Medium, maturing; a lovely refined* Pinot *aroma which blossomed in the glass; dry, refined, lightish in style but quite alcoholic and with good acidity. Lovely but more of a Musigny weight and shape.* *Tasted December 1972 ★★★★*
Chambertin, Clos de Bèze Domaine unknown	*Fairly deep; very fragrant; extremely rich and tangy, opened up well.* *At a Saintsbury Club dinner, October 1978 ★★★★*
Chambolle-Musigny, 1er cru Caves Maxim, Paris	*Curious smoky/vanilla nose and taste. Rather unknit with noticeable acidity.* *At a Heublein tasting in Atlanta, June 1978 ★*
Chambolle-Musigny, *Amoureuses* Bichot	*Marvellously rich colour; very good wine, dry though a little severe.* *Tasted November 1971 ★★★★ Doubtless softened by now.*
Chambolle-Musigny, *Vignes du Château* Grivelet	*Variable notes: better flavour than nose in 1973 but quite rich and appealing in 1978. Deep; deliciously rich* Pinot *nose and flavour; ripe and attractive.* *Tasted April and November 1978 ★★★*
Chassagne-Montrachet, *Caillerets* Marc Morey	*On the palish side; a light but overripe* Pinot *nose; nice light style with meaty flavour. Pleasant aftertaste.* *Tasted October 1974 ★★★*
Corton H. Thévenot	*Very rich colour; fullish, nice wine. Harry Waugh, a friend of Jean-Pierre Bloud, the owner of the stock, had a high regard for this wine. Though good, I preferred the Clos du Roi and Bressandes (below).* *Tasted April 1972 ★★★*
Corton C. Viénot	*Deepish colour; rather stewed* Pinot *nose; quite a fine flavoury wine, though not top drawer.* *Tasted July 1972 ★★*
Le Corton Sichel	*Rich plum colour, good legs; bouquet deep, meaty, hot-vintage character; dry, fullish, rich positive flavour and nice finish. Lots of vigour.* *Tasted January 1971 ★★★*
Corton, Bressandes Mérode	*Good nose; gentle, volcanic/earthy Corton character, fairly full bodied, soft and rich, well balanced.* *Tasted December 1970 ★★★★*
Corton, Bressandes H. Thévenot	*A deep, rich, nutty wine, with plenty of life-supporting tannin and acidity. Long finish.* *Tasted April 1972 ★★★★*
Corton, Clos du Roi H. Thévenot	*Excellent colour, fine and deep; very rich, fine* Pinot *nose and flavour, a perfect copybook Corton; rich, fairly full bodied, rounded, with a certain earthiness.* *Tasted April 1972 ★★★★*
Ch. Corton-Grancey L. Latour	*A deep, rich, burnt, meaty* Pinot *bouquet and flavour. Lovely wine.* *Tasted November 1971 ★★★★*
Corton, Maréchaudes Doudet-Naudin	*Made by what they call the* méthode ancienne. *Medium colour, very mature; forthcoming but slightly astringent. Sweet, chocolaty nose and flavour; light peppery finish.* *Tasted May 1979 ★★*
Echézeaux P. Ponnelle	*Little nose; sound commercial quality, slightly short.* *Tasted December 1973 ★★*
Echézeaux Dom. de la Romanée-Conti	*First noted at a big Lebègue tasting in 1964: fairly dry (the '59 was sweet), positive and flavoury, but with a certain piquancy. Seven years later, a customer complained that this wine was corked, so I readily accepted an invitation to try it over dinner alongside his Grands-Echézeaux '64 and '66. It looked a lightweight; the nose was not bad but not quite right; the flavour was spoiled by a marked and slightly bitter end acidity. I tried another later in the month and thought it had undergone a secondary fermentation in the bottle.* *Last tasted October 1971.*

Gevrey-Chambertin, Combottes L. Jadot	*Quite a nice wine, rather chocolaty in style, firm but lacking any '61 depth.* At one of the always pleasant annual buffet luncheons at the Vintners' Hall given by the rather ineffective and now defunct Wine Merchants Union, June 1970 **
Grands-Echézeaux Dom. de la Romanée-Conti	*First noted at the big annual Lebègue tasting in London, autumn 1964: light, attractive bouquet and lovely flavour but a bit green. Next at Lebègue's in 1967: piquant. I preferred the '62. Then at the Romanée-Conti tasting at Christie's: mature looking; slightly sweet, almost soapy nose; dry, not very substantial, with a stringy, raw finish. Disappointing.* Tasted September 1972 **
Latricières-Chambertin P. Ponnelle	*A pleasant, good enough, soft and flavoury wine.* Tasted June 1973 **
Morey St-Denis Sichel	*Fair quality and condition. Quite nice but lacking real style.* Tasted January 1974 **
Musigny, Vieilles Vignes J. Drouhin	*Lovely bouquet; rich yet quite a tang. Stylish, lively.* Tasted January 1975 ****
Nuits St-Georges, Argillières	*Deeper than the '62; gentle, fragrant bouquet with touch of vanilla; medium dry, rich, complete, still firmly constructed, with tannin and acidity.* One of the top wines at the Leroy tasting, September 1979 ***(*)
Nuits St-Georges, Clos de la Maréchale J. Regnier	*At one of the "Will you dine with a Master of Wine?" series of dinners for the old* Wine *magazine: palish, mature; a rather speciously scented* Pinot; *on the light side, soft, a bit too easy. Quite nice quality. For some reason or other I had reservations — an attractive restaurant wine, but not for keeping.* At the Brompton Grill, August 1970 **
Nuits St-Georges, Hospices, Corvées Paget	*Deeper and richer looking than the Argillières but showing age; a bit mushroomy on the nose; somewhat aggressive, rough and chunky, with an uneven finish.* At the Leroy tasting, September 1979 *
Pommard, Epenots, Clos des Citeaux J. Monnier	*An authentic* 1er cru: *deep coloured; good nose, full, rich meaty flavour with lovely tang.* At Freddie Price's, of Dolamore's, July 1972 ****
Pommard, Rugiens H. Boillot	*Fairly deep; good meaty nose and flavour — more like a Corton. Marked end acidity.* Tasted November 1978 **
Pommard, Rugiens Gannoux	*Lovely* Pinot *aroma and flavour. Rich, good acidity. A charmer.* Tasted November 1974 ****
Richebourg Dom. de la Romanée-Conti	*First noted at the Lebègue tasting in 1964: lovely wine, warm, crisp. Next at Lebègue's in October 1967: paler than expected; rich, stylish, with good acidity. Later: very rich and most attractive bouquet; medium dry, medium body, soft and yielding, yet a firm supporting structure. Great style and quality. Will keep.* Last tasted August 1972 **** (*)
Clos de la Roche J. Drouhin	*Medium pale, very mature; good bouquet; slightly sweet, lightish body and style, very flavoury. Lovely but a touch of bitterness at the finish.* Tasted March 1975 ***
Romanée St-Vivant Bouchard Ainé	*A good British Transport Hotels bottling. Several notes in 1976, rich, soft and very flavoury.* Last tasted July 1977 ***
Savigny-les-Beaune, Lavières	*Very attractive, ripe* Pinot *nose and flavour. Good balance. Good example of a modest growth in a ripe year.* Tasted April 1973 ***

La Tâche Dom. de la Romanée-Conti	*A bit scrawny and green at the big Lebègue tasting in 1964. Six years later: a similar colour to the Grands-Echézeaux; sweet, rich, but a bit edgy. Much preferred the 1962. Last tasted September 1972 ★★★*
Volnay de Villamont	*Palish, very mature, light in style. Delicious. Tasted April 1974 ★★★ Probably finished now.*
Vosne-Romanée Chavot-Labaume	*A touch of overmaturity but attractive; rich, silky and ripe. Lovely wine. Tasted February and May 1974 ★★★★*
Vosne-Romanée Lupé-Cholet	*London bottled. Quite mature looking; light, pleasant, easy, fruity nose and flavour. Slightly sweet. Tasted March 1975 ★★★*
Vosne-Romanée, Beaumonts Army & Navy Stores	*A magnificent wine, perfectly bottled. Bought blind, on Raymond Harcourt's advice, for my senior partners. Two bottles, opened for lunch at my chairman's house in Wales, filled the room with perfume. The wine had a deliciously fragrant and opulent bouquet and flavour, with perfect balance. I wrote to Mr Harcourt there and then saying how reassuring it was that one could still rely on a real wine merchant who knew how to select, ship and bottle fine burgundy. He later told me that this was a Drouhin wine, the last he was able to ship in cask for bottling in the A. & N. cellars. Tasted at Colby Lodge, August 1977 ★★★★*
Clos Vougeot Bouchard Père	*Fine rich '61 colour; bouquet firm but not fully developed; slightly sweet, fine, flavoury, refreshing acidity. Tasted June 1970 ★★★*
Clos Vougeot Paul Bouchard	*Fairly deep; meaty; rich and a bit chocolaty. Tasted June 1976 ★★*
Clos Vougeot Justerini & Brooks	*A good London bottling: mature, excellent, fine rich wine. Tasted October 1977 ★★★*
Clos Vougeot, le Prieuré P. Ponnelle	*Not very deep, very mature looking; dry. Quite nice only. Tasted February 1976 ★*

Outstanding in the 1960s but not tasted since:

Bonnes-Mares J. Drouhin	*Beautifully bottled, in magnums, by the London agent Reynier (not to be confused with the Burgundian firm of Jules Regnier). Immature in colour and on palate, but lovely. Tasted September 1966 ★★★★*
Chambertin, Ruchottes T. Bassot	*A real, budding, tangy Chambertin, still with marked youthful acidity. Tasted November 1966 ★★★★*
Le Corton Bouchard Père	*Soft, meaty, rich, well balanced. Tasted November 1967, February 1968 ★★★★*

1962 ★★★★

Fragrant, flavoury and stylish wines, perhaps lacking the consistency and firmness of the best '61s. Climate: a slow start; cold spells until the end of April and low temperatures in May. June favourable for flowering; July moderate; August fine and warm, with welcome rain in September. Belated harvest, 8 October. Grapes, benefiting from the exceptional temperature, were gathered fully ripe and in absolutely sound condition. Market: shippers and merchants had been shaken by the prices of the '61s and it was thought that a reasonably good crop of good '62s would cool things down. However, growers' prices held firm and early in 1963 there was some resistance from the local merchants. Later in the summer it seemed that there were more buyers than sellers in a prosperous market, so prices, far from easing, strengthened. In retrospect, they look cheap, though 1962 never had the cachet of 1959, 1961 or 1964. Assessment:

rich and appealing, though it is noticeable that the really good wines were slow starters. The moderately good wines probably at their best around 1970, but most of the better wines have developed further and make most excitingly attractive drinking now.

Aloxe-Corton H. Thévenot	*Scented* Pinot *nose; dry, rather light style. One bottle found oxidized in April 1972. A very attractive bottle in 1973. A year later, ripe but thin and disappointing.* Last tasted February 1974. At best ★★
Aloxè-Corton, Boutières Doudet-Naudin	*Grown near the cellars. Good nose; sweet, rich, chocolaty Naudin style.* Tasted May 1971 ★★
Aloxe-Corton, Fournières H. Thévenot	*Deep-scented* Pinot *aroma; dry, lightweight style. A little tannic and noticeable acidity. But rich and flavoury.* Tasted April 1972 ★★
Beaune, Hospices, Cuvée Maurice Drouhin	*Bottled by J. Drouhin. Deepish but mature; rich, meaty bouquet; lovely full flavour, balance and acidity.* Tasted May 1977 ★★★★
Bonnes-Mares Clair-Daü	*A burgundy-lover's burgundy: lovely richness of* robe; *incredibly scented, ripe bouquet; fairly full bodied but supple, rich but delicate. Classic.* At the Peppercorn's, December 1971 ★★★★
Chambertin Bouchard Père	*One of those misleadingly unforthcoming wines which appeared better after a second careful examination. Relatively immature and raw, a trifle austere but with an excellent length and finish.* Tasted May 1970 ★★★(★) Probably better now.
Chambolle-Musigny J. Drouhin	*Palish, light rimmed; quite attractive but a stewed, high-toned nose; rather fluffy character. Appealing but not much grip or life.* Tasted July 1972 ★★
Charmes-Chambertin L. Jadot	*A good specimen: nice colour; good* Pinot *aroma; dry, medium weight, rich.* At a pre-sale tasting, March 1974 ★★★
Corton Jaboulet-Vercherre	*Fairly full flavoured and good, but not a patch on the Jadot.* Tasted at White's with Col. Johnstone, October 1972 ★★★
Corton L. Jadot	*Fine, deep-coloured wine; magnificent bouquet; fairly sweet, fairly full, soft and velvety.* Tasted October 1972 ★★★★★
Corton, Bressandes H. Thévenot	*First tasted before the Bloud sale in April 1972: fine wine but not as good as the '61. Sweet and lovely in 1974. Showing well at David Somerset's in 1975. Lastly, at the Tower Club, Fort Lauderdale: just a little disappointing on the nose, though with the deep, authentic burnt-Corton style; fullish, soft, round but still beefy on the palate.* Tasted November 1975 ★★★
Corton, Clos du Roi H. Thévenot	*Not as deep or as fine as the '61, but an excellent wine none the less.* Tasted April 1972 ★★★
Echézeaux Dom. de la Romanée-Conti	*At the Lebègue tasting in 1964: slightly sweet on nose and palate; light character, a touch of richness countered by light piquant acidity.* Last tasted October 1967 ★★
Fixin, Clos Napoléon	*What was a vineyard at the top end of the Côte de Nuits in Napoleon's time is now being encroached upon by the suburbs of Dijon. French bottled. Good nose; attractive, firm flavour, slightly hard finish.* At a Hedges & Butler dinner, April 1974 ★★
Gevrey-Chambertin Hasenklever	*Also a Nuits St-Georges, both showing quite well: very mature looking; attractive and flavoury.* At a Heublein tasting, May 1973 ★★

Grands-Echézeaux Dom. de la Romanée-Conti	*First seen at the big Lebègue tasting in October 1964: a nice wine, beginning to mature. Developed well: rich and very attractive at Lebègue's in 1967. Five years later: fine, deep, rich colour; firm, fishy Pinot bouquet; sweet like the '64, with a lovely rich flavour, perfect balance.* Last tasted at the Lebègue tasting at Christie's, September 1972 *****
Grands-Echézeaux de Villamont	*Quite the best of a variable range of '62s from de Villamont's own part of that vineyard. Rich, attractive, good aftertaste.* Tasted in Savigny-les-Beaune, September 1975 ***
Iles de Vergelesses L. Latour	*Not often seen. A plummy, chocolaty little wine, very sweet for a red, almost too glibly pleasing.* Tasted April 1971 ***
Latricières-Chambertin Bachey-Deslandes	*Rather cardboardy Pinot nose; lightish but very flavoury, noticeable but refreshing acidity.* Tasted August 1977 **
Musigny Chévillot	*The first of a trio of Musignys at a barbecue in Coconut Grove, near Miami. Our genial host was Doug Erickson, the owner of an excellent (air-conditioned, of course) cellar. This wine was stylish with rather an idiosyncratic nose: Spanish root and landladies' cats. Firm, stylish.* Tasted January 1975 ***
Musigny, *Vieilles Vignes*	*Another, also French bottled but under an I.E.C. Wine Society label: very mature looking; exceptionally ripe Pinot nose; a lovely wine, soft yet crisp, fully mature but holding well.* At the Erickson's, January 1975 ****
Nuits, Corvées Chauvenet	*Paler but brighter than the Clos St-Denis; attractive bouquet; dry, lightish, quite nice.* Tasted April 1979 **
Nuits St-Georges H. Gouges	*Characterful, with that recognizably burnt cellar dust and singed Pinot Gouges hallmark.* At the Asher Storey pre-sale tasting, January 1970 ***
Nuits St-Georges, *Argillières*	*Showing well at the Leroy tasting: pretty colour; a light, open, delicately fragrant and attractive bouquet; sweet, medium body, firm, lovely flavour, elegant.* At the Dom. d'Auvenay, September 1979 ****
Nuits St-Georges, *Vaucrains*	*Also sweet like the Argillières, rich, but more chunky and a less satisfactory, dry finish.* At the Leroy tasting, September 1979 ***
Richebourg Dom. de la Romanée-Conti	*I thought this was curiously dry, light and thin at the Lebègue tasting in 1964, but perhaps it was simply too immature and undeveloped, for three years later I found it rich and developing well.* Tasted October 1967 ***(*) Not tasted since, but now doubtless firm and in full blossom.
Clos de la Roche J. Drouhin	*Fine, elegant wine with great depth and character, but still a bit peppery.* Tasted July 1972 ***(*) Probably excellent now.
Romanée-Conti Dom. de la Romanée-Conti	*Totally undeveloped, with a parsley-like nose and dry, unripe flavour, at the Lebègue tasting in October 1964. Still a bit hard and not fully developed, but powerful and impressive in Australia.* Last tasted at Berek Segan's in Melbourne, March 1977 ***(**)? A long-haul wine.
Clos St-Denis Chauvenet	*Palish, orange tinged; unexciting but quite flavoury.* Tasted April 1979 *
La Tâche Dom. de la Romanée-Conti	*One of my favourite burgundies. Quite immature in Lebègue's cellars in October 1964, but well developed, fabulously sweet and rich by September 1972. Opulent, velvety, almost fluffy compared with Léoville-Las-Cases '62 at a dinner in 1973. The only possible wine that could have been served at a past-midnight dinner following the "20th-century Latour" tasting at Marvin Overton's. The*

	perfume exuded from the glass — intensely fragrant, strawberry-like, fullish body but a lightweight compared with the preceding Latours. Fabulously rich flavour and aftertaste. Last tasted at Dr Overton's, Fort Worth, Texas, May 1976 ★★★★
Volnay, Hospices, Général Muteau	*Brilliantly bottled by Berry Bros: not a lightweight Volnay, but rich, scented, and stylish. Lovely acidity.* Tasted July 1972 ★★★★
Vosne-Romanée Doudet-Naudin	*The best and most stylish of a range of Doudet-Naudin '62s at a pre-sale tasting in Geneva.* Tasted April 1975 ★★★
Vosne-Romanée, Grande Rue H. Lamarche	*Most attractive. Mature; soft, blancmange bouquet; elegant and firm yet lacking muscle. Nevertheless, exciting and flavoury.* Tasted May 1972 ★★★★
Vosne-Romanée, Malconsorts	*The best of three quite nice de Villamont '62s: deepish colour; rather scented nose.* At the Geneva pre-sale tasting, April 1975 ★★
Clos Vougeot Boissot-Estivant	*Rather rich medicinal nose; extremely good, full of flavour and power.* Tasted March 1976 ★★★
Clos Vougeot Bouchard Père	*Lovely deepish colour, a little weak at the rim; curious boiled-beetroot Pinot nose, just a little sickly; dry, full bodied, chunky yet soft. Frankly I preferred the Australian '54 All Saints Shiraz.* Tasted at a Wine and Food Society dinner in Melbourne, March 1977 ★★

1963 ★

A vintage that never quite made it. Mainly small, pale, acidic wines but not all bad. Climate: cold spells after a long severe winter gave way to good weather and some promise in June. Normal weather with some rain in July and a fairly wet August. Late September and October warm and sunny. An enormous crop which really started to mature after 18 September. A late and protracted harvest through October and ending, in Pommard, in sunshine on 2 November. On that date the Beaune correspondent of *The Wine and Spirit Trade Record* reported that "this late harvest . . . will not only give us substantial quantities but also a quality which will make 1963, without any manner of doubt, a good year." Market: it is impossible to glean from the trade press what went wrong in 1963. What is certain is that the English trade, knowing that the '63s in Bordeaux were not good, assumed burgundies would also be poor. After the '59s, '61s and '62s there was no great incentive to rush in and by the time they felt like buying more, the '64s had come on the scene. Assessment: unripe and lacking perhaps, but certainly not a really "off" vintage like 1965. I suspect that some of the little birds fluttered into congenial nests. If any do turn up under a '63 label, they will be genuine and could be interesting. Tasting notes: my notebooks reflect the lack of trade interest in '63s. I have tasted only six wines, two of them Beaujolais.

Beaujolais-Villages Deinhard	*Clean and fruity on the nose; dry, light, slightly acidic and bitter at the end.* Tasted February 1967.
Chambertin, Clos de Bèze Pierre Gélin	*Palish colour; not much of a nose; slightly sweet, very light, not bad middle flavour. Light acidity.* Tasted November 1971 ★
Chambolle-Musigny Grivelet	*Medium pale in colour; attractive — the usual overripe Pinot Grivelet style; touch of sweetness, lightish style and body, soft, fully mature.* In magnum, March 1968 ★★

Romanée St-Vivant *de Villamont*	*Pale, mature, weak rim; an odd, lightly scented nose; medium dry, light, rather nice little flavour and aftertaste.* Tasted June 1970 ★
St-Amour *Sichel*	*Hardly any red; stewed, old and tart.* Tasted February 1974.
La Tâche *Dom. de la Romanée-Conti*	*Medium colour, browner and deeper than the '65; quite a nice nose, balance and texture. Better than the '65, which was distinctly raw and acidic.* At the Romanée-Conti tasting at Quaglino's, April 1974 ★★

1964 ★★★★

Undoubtedly excellent: rich, meaty, soft, ripe and rounded wines. Climate: deepest snow in January for 20 years; cold March followed by frequent rains, fairly low temperature and weak sunshine. However, perfect weather in June for the flowering. July almost too hot though some rain in August. Conditions in September excellent with rain followed by sun. Fine weather for harvest, 19 September. Drought reduced an abundance to a fair-sized crop. Considered at the time to be a great year, a judgement confirmed by time. Market: well accepted from the start. But as the dismal months of 1965 progressed the prices hardened as growers and merchants sought to conserve their stocks. Popular and much traded-in wines. Assessment: a thoroughly attractive vintage, broad, open-knit style, sweet, flavoury, lasting well. But where I have been able to compare like with like, it is often not as fine as the '62, for example at the Domaine de la Romanée-Conti. Good growths are still well worth looking out for. Tasting notes: I have more notes on the '64s than on any other burgundy vintage. A representative selection follows:

Aloxe-Corton *H. Thévenot*	*This was the first of half a dozen Thévenot wines with corks branded Michel Couvreur, which I had been asked to taste and appraise in the cellars at Bouze-les-Beaune. The first wine, which was made from young vines, was palish and still quite youthful looking, with quite nice nose and flavour. The second, made from old vines (about 20 years old), was deeper and richer looking, and had a better, more complex nose and flavour.* Tasted December 1972 ★★ to ★★★
Aloxe-Corton, Fournières *H. Thévenot*	*Another Couvreur bottling: touch of rich bottle-age on the nose; characterful, but with noticeable acidity. The 1er cru Vercot was similar.* Tasted December 1972 ★★
Beaune, Clos des Mouches *J. Drouhin*	*A characterful wine, rather closed up and severe.* Tasted 1972 ★★(★) *Should be mature now.*
Beaune, Hospices, Clos des Avaux	*Well bottled by de Villamont. Excellent bouquet; lovely flavour, balance and finish.* Tasted April 1975 ★★★★
Bonnes-Mares *P. Ponnelle*	*Bottled by Forsyth's of Oldham, a reputable family firm which collapsed in one of the late-1960s credit squeezes. Rich, attractive colour; meaty nose but still a little hard; a rather dry, severe wine with a fair amount of acidity. Perhaps time would have softened the wine and healed the firm.* Tasted November 1972 ★★(★)
Bonnes-Mares *J. Regnier*	*Plummy; medicinal nose; nice weight, flavour and good end acidity.* Tasted February 1976 ★★★
Bonnes-Mares *de Vogüé*	*Lovely in July 1974. The following year: fine mature colour; slightly singed, mature Pinot bouquet; medium body, lovely flavour, perfect balance and finish. Burgundy at its well-mannered, most elegant best.* Tasted October and, last, in November 1975 ★★★★★

Chambertin A. Rousseau	*I mention a somewhat out-of-date note because it illustrates that at the time, I was, like most English merchants, influenced by the cooked-up and blended burgundies so much part of our stock-in-trade. Faced with the real thing, I found the wine lovely but a trifle light in style. I described it as a "welterweight" at the time. And the price only ten years ago retail: 52s. (£2.60) a bottle.* At a big Loeb & Co. tasting, November 1969 ★★★★
Chambertin Trapet	*A grower whose wine is not much seen in England. I drank this in a local restaurant and found it excellent: palish in colour, completely mature looking; a gentle, elegant nose; quite powerful yet curiously light in style.* Tasted in Fixin, December 1972 ★★★★
Chambertin, Clos de Bèze Damoy	*From Le Pavilion restaurant, New York: really pale and mature; rich but fading.* At a Heublein tasting, May 1973 ★★
Chambolle-Musigny J. Drouhin	*Medium pale, attractive colour; rich, meaty, high-toned nose; touch of sweetness, medium-light body, nice flavour but short. Not unlike the '62.* Tasted July 1972 ★★★
Chambolle-Musigny Harvey's	*I sometimes wonder whether some English-bottled wines had built-in obsolescence, but I doubt if this one was intended to remain unconsumed for 14 years. Rather lactic nose; tired but better on the palate.* Tasted April 1978.
Chambolle-Musigny, 1er cru de Villamont	*Palish, very mature; showing a bit of age but a nice wine.* Tasted April 1975 ★★★
Chambolle-Musigny, Amoureuses Lionel Brück Roumier	*First, Lionel Brück's: rich, forthcoming bouquet; stylish and attractive, better than his Gevrey-Chambertin and the best of a range of good but not great Brück wines tasted at Corney & Barrow.* January 1972 ★★★ *Next, a lovely Roumier wine, scented and appealing.* Tasted February 1972 ★★★★
Charmes-Chambertin Lupé-Cholet	*Deep; soft, sweet nose; dry, flavoury.* Tasted February and April 1976 ★★★
Corton Leroy	*Drunk rather casually in a small restaurant in the Hunter Valley in the middle of the vintage, with Murray Tyrrell and Len Evans. The wine was quite nice but not as characterful and colourful as the company and the occasion.* Tasted in Australia, February 1977 ★★
Corton H. Thévenot	*Bottled by Couvreur. Still with a surprising touch of pink/purple-rimmed youthfulness; meaty, but a bit disappointingly stewed — not as good as the Bressandes, noted below.* Tasted May 1977 ★★
Corton, Bressandes J. Drouhin	*Still rather youthful looking; rich, almost smelly, nose; slightly sweet, lightish for a '64 Corton, and curious.* Tasted July 1972 ★
Corton, Bressandes H. Thévenot	*A Couvreur wine. Still not fully mature; soft, clean, meaty bouquet; dry, fullish and rich. A* vin de garde. Tasted December 1972 ★★★★
Ch. Corton-Grancey L. Latour	*Rather disappointing at the shippers' offices in June 1974. Then: plum coloured; sweet, rich, some silkiness but a fraction stewed, unrefined.* Last tasted, at the Louis Latour dinner at Boodle's, October 1976 ★★
Corton, Hospices, Charlotte Dumay	*Bottled by Grivelet-Cusset. A sweet, rich, most attractive wine. Somehow mild but rich and ready.* Tasted February 1973 ★★★★
Corton, Clos du Roi Lionel Brück	*Deepish; trace of vanilla on nose; soft, meaty, quite nice.* Tasted February 1976 ★★★

Corton, Clos du Roi H. Thévenot	*Bottled by Couvreur. Fairly deep colour, rich to the rim; good ripe nose and flavour.* Tasted December 1972 ★★★
Echézeaux Gros	*Which Gros I do not recall. A most excellent wine with splendid flavour and character.* Tasted February 1972 ★★★★
Echézeaux Shipper unknown	*Memorable mainly because it was at my first (but the 400th of the chapitre) Trois Glorieuses dinner. I was the guest of Peter Reynier. Fairly deep; rich, plummy nose; a good, warming mouthful with the cheese.* At Clos Vougeot, November 1971 ★★★
Grands-Echézeaux Dom. de la Romanée-Conti	*Pale and undeveloped, pleasant but lightweight, in October 1971. Next, surprisingly pale (the '62 was much deeper); rather premature smell; sweet, piquant style. A deceptively light style of wine that could develop very well with another handful of years in the bottle. I cannot wait to try it again.* Last tasted September 1972 ★★(★★)?
Griotte-Chambertin J. Drouhin	*The only burgundy in a fascinating tasting of various '64 red wines in Florida. Compared with such clarets as Montrose and La Conseillante the colour seemed curiously limp and ill defined. The nose was a marvellous contrast — prune juice as opposed to blackcurrants. Interesting, different, but I expected more.* Tasted at Dr Wittens, March 1971 ★★(★)
Latricières-Chambertin J. Regnier	*Most stylish and attractive. Probably at its best.* Tasted September 1971 ★★★★
Mazy-Chambertin A. Rousseau	*The variations in vineyard spellings are endless. Mazy or Mazis, I found this a bit weak kneed and watery for a quality '64, with rather scented and candy-like fruitiness, and thin.* Tasted July 1972 ★
Monthélie Leroy	*Not often seen. Palish, clear-cut colour with slightly immature pink tinge; moderate, stewed* Pinot *nose; rich yet unknit, with a little raw acidity.* Tasted March 1978 ★
Nuits St-Georges, 1er cru Leroy	*The best '64 and, after the '29, equal second at the big Leroy tasting. Fairly deep coloured, but the most mature looking of the four '64s presented: an open, forthcoming, rich and ripe bouquet; magnificent flavour of Romanée-Conti standard, great length, tannic acidity and excellent aftertaste.* Tasted September 1979 ★★★★★
Nuits St-Georges, Boudots	*Also at the Leroy tasting: curious, light but complete and slightly singed nose; sweet, rich, chunky, quite a bite.* Tasted September 1979 ★★★
Nuits St-Georges, Chaboeufs de Villamont	*A good bottling. Nice* Pinot *nose and flavour.* Tasted April 1975 ★★★
Nuits St-Georges, Clos des Corvées	*Medium pale, losing its colour? Fairly rich* Pinot *nose that reminded me of mustard and cress; a most elegant and stylish wine. I liked this very much.* At the Leroy tasting, September 1979 ★★★★
Nuits St-Georges, Clos de la Maréchale J. Regnier	*Pink hued; rich nose; firm yet flowery wine, lightish style. Nicely mature.* Tasted March 1973 ★★★
Nuits St-Georges, Porets Army & Navy Stores	*Good London bottling: bouquet developed well in glass; rich, quite good, dry finish.* Tasted 1973, January 1977 ★★★
Nuits St-Georges, Poulettes	*Interesting, attractive nose, with a touch of liquorice and ginger; odd style, a bit raw, with a lightly tannic yet decidedly sweet finish.* At the Leroy tasting, September 1979 ★★

Nuits St-Georges, Pruliers H. Gouges	*A brilliantly typical Henri Gouges wine: medium-pale colour but with a feeling of depth; attractive smoky* Pinot *bouquet; slightly sweet. Flavour to match nose.* Tasted February 1974 ****
Nuits St-Georges, Vaucrains Misserey	*From the Mandel cellar: a slightly medicinal but attractive bouquet; lovely meaty flavour.* At the Heublein tasting in Atlanta, May 1978 ****
Pommard, Clos des Epeneaux Armand	*Epenot, Epenots, Epeneaux — a rosé by any other name, for it was pale in colour; the bouquet developed in the glass; delicate, refreshing, elegant but with high fixed acidity.* Tasted December 1971 ** Might have simmered down and softened by now.
Richebourg Dom. de la Romanée-Conti	*First only briefly noted, as there were so many wines to taste, at the big Lebègue tasting in October 1967. Noticeably pale coloured and sweet. More recently: maturing nicely; very rich bouquet — spicy, subtle, some age showing; distinct sweetness, fairly full-bodied, powerful, mouth-filling wine, fabulous aftertaste. Magnificent state of development.* Tasted September 1975 *****
Clos de la Roche A. Rousseau J. Drouhin	*Rousseau's rich in 1969 and perfectly lovely in 1970. J. Drouhin's also good: fine colour; firm and fine* Pinot; *medium body, most elegant, beautifully balanced.* Tasted March 1975 ****
Romanée-Conti Dom. de la Romanée-Conti	*Alas, being a professional and not a wealthy amateur, I have not tasted this since it was first shown to the trade in London by Lebègue, when it was noticeably lacking in colour; bouquet undeveloped; fairly sweet, not a heavy wine but a lot to it, and great potential.* Tasted October 1967 **(**) Probably only just approaching its best now.
Romanée St-Vivant Marey-Monge	*First noted in my wine-buying committee days at Harvey's. It was amongst a line-up of 24 cask samples tasted in Bristol remarkably soon after the vintage, in December 1964. We liked it and bought some* barriques *for bottling. Last noted as domaine bottled: rather hard, stalky, disappointing nose; touch of sweet ripeness, but austere finish. Perhaps time will soften it further.* Tasted December 1975 **(*)
Ruchottes-Chambertin Shipper unknown	*A very good copybook burgundy: palish, very mature looking; boiled-beetroot* Pinot *nose; slightly sweet, richly flavoured flesh over very firm alcoholic bone structure.* At a Masters of Wine study course tasting, January 1973 ****
La Tâche Dom. de la Romanée-Conti	*At Lebègue's in 1967: extraordinarily pale coloured; little bouquet, yet very sweet and lovely. Then, at the Romanée-Conti tasting at Christie's two variable bottles. The first: dull on the nose; raw and not very good. The second: attractive bouquet; slightly sweet, highly flavoured and loaded with acidity which will take time to shake down.* Tasted September 1972 ***(*)
Clos Vougeot J. Drouhin	*A deep-coloured heavyweight; well balanced but unready.* Tasted April 1971. Should now be at least ***
Clos Vougeot Leroy	*In June 1975, an interesting bottle which might well have suffered from a voyage to and from Australia. Then, at Christmas, another bottle had a honeyed, nutty bouquet; lightish style though alcoholic and with an interesting texture.* Last tasted December 1975. At best ***
Clos Vougeot, Ch. de la Tour	*Morin's domaine: a dull Godfrey & Duchêne bottling in 1971, and a better but not great domaine bottling at a Heublein tasting in the United States. Not a patch on the '59.* Last tasted May 1975 **

1965

A thoroughly bad year. Thin, deficient, overacid wines. Climate: crop completely ruined by the weather. Throughout the summer the temperature and hours of sunshine were well below average. In some areas the hours of sunshine recorded were the lowest since 1910. By early September the soil was waterlogged, the bunches small, many grapes had not changed colour and, jammed together, rot spread quickly. On the night of 8 September, Burgundy was struck by the most appalling storm in living memory, soil was washed down the slopes and some vineyards were swept away. The harvest, such as it was, was four weeks delayed and the belated sun at the time of the picking (starting 12 October) was simply too late. Market: quite clearly reports emanating from trade centres must be taken with a pinch of salt, more as sales propaganda than reliable judgement, for in February 1966 the Beaune correspondent of *The Wine and Spirit Trade Record* wrote: "The wines of the 1965 vintage show excellent qualities for the most part." (Presumably this was the same correspondent who reported that 1963 was "without any manner of doubt a good year"!) Clearly the readers took no notice for this vintage was avoided like the plague; and, for the *Record*, it folded soon after. Assessment: thin, meagre, overacid wines which have doubtless wasted away by now. Tasting notes: once again I find I have few notes, not because I disdain to taste wines of poor vintages — on the contrary I am always fascinated by all the variations on a theme — but because few have come my way.

Beaujolais Villages *Morgan Furze*	*A London bottling, which I report partly because it was rare to find any '65s, but mainly because my description of the wine, then 16 months old, uncannily resembles the run-of-the-mill, quickly vinified beaujolais, which are made even in good vintages nowadays: medium pale with a delicate purple tinge; ordinary, clean-scented Gamay aroma; touch of sweetness, light, an attractive fruity little flavour. Nice acidity, not too much. A bit short.* Tasted January 1967 *
Grands-Echézeaux *Dom. de la Romanée-Conti*	*First tasted at the Romanée-Conti tasting at Christie's in September 1972 when I found it palish and very mature looking, with a curious hot, piquant, fruity aroma; a touch of sweetness on the palate, quite nice flavour but rasping acidity on the teeth. It was trotted out again at the Lebègue/Romanée-Conti tasting at Quaglino's and, though flavoury, was what I call stringy — thin, raw and unbalanced.* Last tasted April 1974.
Savigny *H. Thévenot?*	*I tasted this in the Couvreur cellars in Bouze-les-Beaune and believed it to be a Thévenot wine. It was very pale, a watery orange red tailing off to nothing; high-toned, superficial, volatile nose; dry, very light and thin, but reasonably sound.* Tasted December 1972.
La Tâche *Dom. de la Romanée-Conti*	*In September 1972: similar colour to the Grands-Echézeaux; a better nose, light, attractive, piquant; distinctly sweet, with a touch of richness, but raw and short. It was then served, not inappropriately, as a light luncheon wine, at the later Quaglino's tasting: very mature looking; the nose curiously appealing, grass and mint leaf; sugar no longer masked the acidity for it was raw and clearly had no future.* Last tasted April 1974.

1966 ★★★★

A very satisfactory vintage though not, perhaps, as excellent as its counterpart in Bordeaux. Firm, stylish, middleweight wines. Climate: some hail damage in the spring; the summer not particularly good though the weather improved at the end of August. September was sunny and balmy, with a little rain to swell the grapes, and exceptionally fine conditions for the picking, which started on 28th. Market: there were worries that the quantity was going to be small but, once the crop was in, there was a pleasant surprise. There was a two-way worry in the spring of 1967: English merchants saw prices moving to levels never before attained; Burgundian merchants were wondering about the possible effect of new British labelling regulations. Burgundy at this time had regained its top position in the export league of French wines. Assessment: firmer, leaner, less relaxed than the '64s, but at their best, elegant, fragrant and flavoury. Some were noticeably pale and acidic; but fine burgundies have a knack of settling down, gaining confidence and absorbing their own acidity. Even the apparent weaklings can develop surprising stamina. Overall an attractive vintage. Near to perfect in the Côte de Nuits. The best wines are still nice. Tasting notes: the first '66 tasted was an attractive beaujolais in March 1967. That was the spring of my first full year at Christie's, the year of the huge Lichine sale (26,000 cases of vintage Bordeaux — still, in volume, an all-time record). The first Côte de Nuits '66s tasted were all, as it happens, from the Domaine de la Romanée-Conti, in the autumn of 1967. The point of mentioning this is that I was more preoccupied with organizing wine auctions than assessing young vintages. From then on, mature, old and rare wines became my speciality. Nevertheless I have many notes well spread over the past decade though only about half a dozen in the past two years. I have selected what I trust will be the most representative, with emphasis on the most recently tasted.

Beaune, Clos de la Feguine Dom. Jacques Prieur	*Owned by Calvet. An attractive raspberry-scented wine; dry, stylish, plenty of zing.* Tasted July 1972 ★★
Beaune, Grèves French bottled	*Selected by Harry Waugh for Robert Jackson's store in Piccadilly: the last flicker of light and life before that once excellent emporium declined and then closed. A warm, attractive wine, perfectly formed.* Tasted May 1977 ★★★
Beaune, Marconnets Bouchard Père	*Mature, attractive; dusty/smoky Pinot nose; positive and flavoury, still with tannin and acidity.* Tasted May 1977 ★★★(★)
Bonnes-Mares de Villamont Hasenklever P. Ponnelle	*De Villamont: very mature but rather dull.* Tasted April 1975 ★ *Hasenklever: deep, plummy; sweet oaky nose; pleasant flavour and nice finish.* Tasted February 1976 ★★★ *Ponnelle: maturing nicely in appearance; no nose; some richness, pleasant style, good flavour and finish.* Tasted May 1977 ★★★
Chambertin Bouchard Père	*Rather a rich, jammy wine, attractive, but lacking finesse.* Tasted October 1972 ★★★
Chambertin, Clos de Bèze J. Drouhin	*Medium colour; very attractive bouquet; nicely ripe, good shape, not heavy, easy and pleasing. Will keep.* Tasted November 1975 ★★★(★)
Chambolle-Musigny, 1er cru de Villamont	*Medium light, very mature looking; really lovely bouquet and flavour.* Tasted April 1974 ★★★
Chambolle-Musigny Prosper Maufoux	*Rather good Pinot nose; ripe, soft and attractive.* Tasted November 1973 ★★★
Charmes-Chambertin A. Mermès de Villamont	*A. Mermès: fairly deep and mature looking; old, meaty nose, touch of iron; stylish but drying out.* Tasted October 1978 ★★ *De Villamont: scented and very attractive.* Tasted April 1974 ★★★
Corton, Bressandes Chandon de Briailles	*Soft, supple, very attractive.* Tasted June 1973 ★★★★
Corton, Bressandes Remoissenet	*One of the best wines at a big Remoissenet tasting held by Avery's. Rich, meaty, extremely attractive (expensive at the time: nearly £4 a bottle). The Gevrey-Chambertin, Combettes also good.* Tasted October 1974 ★★★

Corton, Meix and Renardes de Villamont	Both wines medium in colour and weight; nice nose. The Renardes slightly more scented. *Tasted April 1975* ★★★
Corton, Clos du Roi Bachey-Deslandes	Quite good stewed beetroot nose; mature, fairly full bodied with a backbone of acidity. *Tasted July 1976* ★★(★)
Corton, Clos de la Vigne au Saint L. Latour	Medium colour; very good, fully mature, nose; slightly sweet, soft, lovely middleweight flavour and balance. Will keep. *Tasted October 1978* ★★★(★)
Echézeaux Dr Barolet (de Villamont)	A nice, rich, flavoury wine, quite elegant. *At Prue Leith's, February 1972* ★★★
Echézeaux Dom. de la Romanée-Conti	Tasted only once, at its début: medium colour, still some purple; very rich aroma and flavour. Slightly sweet. Zestful. *At Lebègue's big annual tasting, October 1967* (★★★)
Echézeaux H. Sichel	French bottled. Very mature looking; forthcoming, ripe Pinot aroma; some elegance, fairly high levels of alcohol and acidity. *Tasted July 1976* ★★
Gevrey-Chambertin Dzikowsky	Fairly consistent notes: very rich, fruity and attractive nose; dry, flavoury, with some bite. Better than his Mazis-Chambertin. *Tasted February 1974, November 1976* ★★★★
Gevrey-Chambertin, Estournelles St-Jacques Clair-Daü	An astonishing Clair-Daü wine. Misleadingly pale and mature for its age and vintage, for it had quite an alcoholic backbone. Stylish. *Tasted November 1971* ★★★
Grands-Echézeaux Dom. de la Romanée-Conti	Very rich as early as October 1967. Showed very well at dinner in October 1971, with beautifully developed nose and flavour. Next, at the Lebègue tasting at Christie's in September 1972, I slightly preferred it to the '62 and to La Tâche '66, which is high praise indeed. Last tasted at an Under 40s Club tasting at Lebègue's, thanks not to my age, for I was well beyond eligibility, but to a kind invitation from the then managing director. Palish, completely mature looking; nice nose; medium body, very rich with a real "domaine" peacock's tail of flavour opening up in the mouth. *Last tasted June 1977* ★★★(★★)
Latricières-Chambertin Faiveley	I have a lot of respect for Faiveley but this wine did not show well at a blind tasting of wines for a Wine and Food Society convention: curiously flat, cardboardly, with raw acidity. *Tasted August 1977* ★
Latricières-Chambertin Trapet	Pale, elegant; nose undeveloped at the time, but a light though nicely balanced and stylish wine. *Tasted December 1972* ★★(★★)
Mazis-Chambertin Dzikowsky	Flavoury in February 1974. Later: palish, mature; scented Pinot aroma and flavour; lightish, some style. *Last tasted November 1976* ★★★
Morey St-Denis J. Drouhin	A bit raw and unready in July 1971. That autumn: medium colour; scented nose; elegant, feminine. *Last tasted October 1971* ★★(★)
Nuits St-Georges, Les St-Georges H. Gouges	At a pre-sale tasting in November 1974: deep colour; rich smoky/fishy aroma; a good, confident, assertive wine. Later, from a half-bottle, Gouges at his unmistakable best: gentle smoky Pinot aroma; lovely flavour. With a wine like this one can see why Nuits St-Georges came to be in such demand, and why it is copied. Perfect weight, balance, flavour. *Last tasted in Geneva, April 1975* ★★★★
Pommard, Clos des Citeaux J. Monnier	Quite rich and characterful, but lacking the firmness and zest of some of its counterparts in the Côte de Nuits. *Tasted March 1975* ★★★

Pommard, Clos des Epeneaux Pasquier-Desvignes	*Plum coloured; rather hard, cardboardy nose, not vinous, no fruit; nice enough drink but dull and undistinguished.* Tasted February 1978 ⋆
Richebourg Dom. de la Romanée-Conti	*Time to note only its very rich nose at Lebègue's in October 1967. At the Under 40s Club: palish, very mature and most attractive looking; markedly dry, powerful flavour, very rich and excellent aftertaste.* Last tasted June 1977 ⋆⋆⋆⋆
Romanée-Conti Dom. de la Romanée-Conti	*First noted briefly at the big Lebègue tasting in October 1967: rich, more body, more completely balanced than the other Domaine '66s. Ten years later: not very deep coloured, in fact very mature looking; slightly burnt, very rich bouquet; ripe and rich on the palate, firm, even a little austere, with a dry finish. Despite its misleading and relatively pale appearance, clearly years of development ahead.* At the Under 40s Club tasting, June 1977 ⋆⋆⋆(⋆⋆)
Romanée St-Vivant Bouchard Père	*Palish, very attractive, most stylish.* Tasted May 1972 ⋆⋆⋆⋆
Romanée St-Vivant Marey-Monge	*Lovely in May 1973. Later: deep, mature; fabulously rich, high-toned, fishy Pinot nose and flavour — what James Christie would have described as "high flavour'd" in his 18th-century catalogues. Fragrant, long dry finish.* Last tasted May 1975 ⋆⋆⋆⋆(⋆)
Savigny, Dominode Chanson	*Deep; meaty nose; excellent flavour and vigour (the Marconnets tasted alongside was dry, just a little dull).* Tasted September 1975 ⋆⋆⋆
La Tâche Dom. de la Romanée-Conti	*At the Lebègue tasting in October 1967: even then it had a very rich aroma and flavour, with a touch of exciting piquancy. Next, at Christie's in September 1972: outstandingly attractive, most flavoury, velvety yet zestful. Then at lunch at Corney & Barrow's, the old-established City wine merchants: intensely deep, brown — seemed to have little red left; opulent bouquet exuberant not to say overblown. Most recently, at the Under 40s Club at Lebègue's: deeper, richer colour than the other Domaine '66s; lively, fragrant, smoky bouquet; some richness, leading to a dry finish via an excellent firm flavour. Still quite a bite. Will doubtless develop further.* Last tasted June 1977 ⋆⋆⋆⋆(⋆)
Vosne-Romanée, Beaumonts Noëllat	*This should have been excellent but it was stewed and disappointing. Not bad but no middle, and with an upturned acid end and bitter finish. To be fair, it might have been badly stored by the restaurant serving it.* Tasted August 1973.
Vosne-Romanée, Grands Suchots P. Ponnelle	*A warm, fragrant Pinot bouquet and flavour. Dry finish.* Tasted May 1977 ⋆⋆⋆
Clos Vougeot Drouhin-Laroze	*Medium; positive, elegant, tangy Pinot bouquet; a lovely wine, perfect balance, charm, excellent finish.* Tasted January 1975 ⋆⋆⋆⋆⋆
Clos Vougeot Moreau-Fontaine	*Palish but a lovely, evenly shaded, gentle colour; sweet nose; dry, medium body, elegant and refreshing.* Tasted December 1976 ⋆⋆⋆⋆
Clos Vougeot, Ch. de la Tour Morin	*Not very deep but a ripe, almost farmyard stably nose; a rich wine, better than his '64 but not as fragrant and attractive as the '59. (His Nuits, Cailles, at the same tasting was woody.)* Tasted May 1975 ⋆⋆⋆⋆

1967 ★★★

A fairly good though uneven vintage, lighter than 1966, thin compared with 1964. Not a long-distance runner but perhaps better than '67 Bordeaux. Climate: the weather was unusually favourable. The widespread frost on 4 May acted, in effect, as a supplementary pruning, the smaller amount of grapes later benefiting from a greater amount of nourishment. The ensuing summer was so warm and sunny, particularly in July and August, that some vineyard owners thought they could safely economize by cutting out the customary dusting to protect the vines against disease. In these vineyards ten days of rain in September produced some disastrous results. Good weather returned in time, however, for the vintage on 2 October. High degrees of alcohol were noted, but variations in quality ensued not only as a result of some diseased vines, but because of the increasing tendency of some wine makers to speed up the fermentation. Some wines were said, later, to lack acidity. Market: a time of credit squeezes in England but seemingly inexorable demand in Burgundy, not just from the fully reawakened United States but from the other increasingly prosperous traditional markets such as Belgium. Noticeable that more wine was shipped in bottle, less English bottled. Assessment: most were distinctly appealing in the early 1970s, just as the '67 clarets were. But as the sugar wears off, the once masked acidity takes over. Increasingly noticeable were the paler, unblended, apparent light-weights, then new to the English palate. The effect of rotten grapes is noticeable in some wines (see Nuits St-Georges, Poulettes) though the good wine makers, with *grand cru climats* on the slopes (see de Vogüé's Musigny) produced very satisfactory wines — endorsing the original trade journal report that it was an uneven vintage and one had to select carefully. The best are still extremely pleasant. Tasting notes: I have as many notes as for the '66s. A cross-section follows:

Beaune, Champimonts Chanson	*Very pale indeed and very mature looking; light, pleasing; dry, light, flavoury, attractive. For quick drinking.* Tasted May 1977 ★★
Beaune, Clos de la Feguine Dom. Jacques Prieur	*Very pleasant nose; medium light, attractive flavour, nice quality.* Tasted November and December 1976 ★★★
Beaune, Grèves Chanson C. Masson	*Chanson: pale, dry, taut and austere.* Tasted February 1974 ★★ *C. Masson: light, mature nose; dry, lightish, fragrant.* Tasted November 1976 ★★
Beaune, Theurons L. Jadot	*Good nose; dry but rich.* At a pre-sale tasting, February 1974 ★★★
Beaune, Vignes-Franches L. Latour	*Palish, mature; meaty nose; touch of sweetness, medium light in body, rich, attractive, but no depth. An acid background.* Tasted November 1976 ★★
Bonnes-Mares L. Jadot	*Fullish, ripe bouquet; distinctly sweet, nice wine.* Tasted November 1973 ★★★
Chambertin A. Rousseau	*Consistent notes. First tasted in December 1975, and a year later: not deep, but rich and very mature; fabulous bouquet, scented Pinot; low-keyed, delicate flavour. Dry, lightish in style and weight, soft yet '67 acidity edging through. A bit thin but fragrant and ethereal.* Last tasted November 1976 ★★★
Chambolle-Musigny Grivelet	*Pale, mildly plum coloured; rich, overripe wine but quite flavoury.* Tasted October 1974 ★
Chapelle-Chambertin Bouchard Aîné	*A 1974 Tastevinage wine: deep, plummy; pretty good, root-like Pinot nose; a nice, rich, hefty wine with a good aftertaste.* At a lecture tasting in Barbados, February 1978 ★★★
Charmes-Chambertin Bourrée	*Browning; boiled-beetroot Pinot aroma and taste; sweet, good commercial stuff.* At a lecture tasting for Len Evans in Sydney, February 1977 ★★

Chassagne-Montrachet Ropiteau	*At the pretentious London version of Le Grand Véfour shortly after its opening: light red; quite nice scented little bouquet; medium dry, light. A pleasing if insubstantial drink.* Tasted April 1971 *
Corton Chanson	*Excellent, ripe, fishy-Pinot nose; dry, nice vinosity.* Tasted February 1974 ***
Fixin, Les Arvelets G. Berthaud	*Very clean, straightforward little wine; no great character but its slightly sweet end flavour opened up in the mouth nicely.* At a nice little restaurant in Fixin, called Chez Jeannette, December 1972 **
Gevrey-Chambertin, Clos de la Justice Bertagna	*Fine colour; well-developed bouquet; very rich meaty wine from a leading domaine.* Tasted November 1975 ****
Musigny de Vogüé	*Palish, mature; stylish, smoky bouquet; elegant and flavoury.* Tasted April 1975 ****
Nuits St-Georges, Clos des Argillières	*The best of the three '67s at the big Leroy tasting: rather light-weight looking, weak rimmed; rather light, open-style bouquet, sugared; pleasant, flavoury, a bit facile.* Tasted September 1979 **
Nuits St-Georges, Chaboeufs	*Deep, plummy colour; smooth, rich Pinot nose, but spoilt for me by a slightly sickly overtone; slightly sweet on entry, a short dry departure.* At the Leroy tasting, September 1979 *
Nuits St-Georges, Poulettes	*Fairly similar colour to Argillières; ivy, unclean, touch of rot on the nose? — distinctly so on the taste. Short, loose, untidy finish.* At the Leroy tasting, September 1979.
Clos de la Roche Chanson	*A pretty red colour; rich rather oily nose; dry yet rich, pasty — a little raw, acidity lurking.* Tasted February 1974 *
Clos de la Roche Chauvenet	*Quite nice nose, touch of vanilla; dry, meaty.* At a pre-sale tasting, April 1979 **
La Tâche Dom. de la Romanée-Conti	*The only '67 at the Romanée-Conti tasting at Christie's: very pale, pink tinged, maturing; an instantly forthcoming and very attractive bouquet; dry, light in style, very flavoury with a touch of piquancy.* Tasted September 1972 **
Clos de Tart Mommessin	*Borderline: pale, not much red left; flavoury but overripe in October 1975. Later: light, ripe Pinot nose, held well in glass; slightly sweet, light in style, a fluffy wine with a slightly bitter acid finish. Thin. An unstable feel about it.* Last tasted December 1975 *
Vosne-Romanée J. Clerget	*Fragrant, most attractive nose; dry, light, delicious flavour but lean, not to say thin. To an Englishman weaned on bonne cuisine burgundies it appeared distinctly lightweight, but the owners considered it to have a good ten years of life ahead.* Tasted July 1972 ***
Vosne-Romanée, Suchots Bouchard Père	*Palish, mature; very assertive, ripe, jammy Pinot nose and taste. Dry.* Tasted March 1975, November 1977 ***
Clos Vougeot Faiveley	*At a memorable dinner in New Orleans. Though I was a somewhat last-minute guest of David Milligan's, Clifford Weihman, the Grand Pilier Général, dubbed me a Chevalier de Tastevin on the spur of the moment — presumably inspired by this Clos Vougeot, which coped manfully with foie gras de Strasbourg and fonds d'artichauts Bayard. All I can really remember was that it was a great occasion and that the wine was deepish and had a good flavour and balance.* Tasted November 1974 ***

Clos Vougeot Misserey	*Lightish in colour, and on nose and palate. Pleasant though; dry with surprising hardness.* Tasted November 1971 *(**)*

Some English-bottled '67s:

Chambolle-Musigny Avery	*Fat, soft, smooth.* Tasted January and February 1973 ***
Chassagne-Montrachet, *Clos St-Jean* Berry Bros	*Deepish; lovely, rich, forthcoming* Pinot *nose and flavour.* Tasted December 1976 ***
Corton, Maréchaudes Berry Bros	*Substantial colour; a bit cheesy on the nose; meaty, quite good flavour and balance in July 1976.* Last tasted March 1979 **
Richebourg British Transport Hotels	*A Paul Bouchard wine. Fairly light; stewed ripe* Pinot*; soft; quite elegant, nice acidity.* Tasted June 1976 **
Vosne-Romanée I.E.C.W.S.	*A good enough wine, well bottled by* The Wine Society. Tasted October 1972 **

1968

A poor year. Thin, unripe wines. Climate: a reasonably clear run through the spring, no frost or hail. June excessively hot, but too little sun and too much rain in July and August. September better, vintage started on 30th in reasonable conditions. Market: the vintage was considered catastrophic and, most significantly and rarely, the Hospices de Beaune auction was cancelled. A depressed but realistic Beaune correspondent reported that "in the various 1968 vats it will be a question of taking one's choice". Put another way (I quote Gerald Asher's perceptive report of May 1969), "1968: a year for the foxes" and "whatever turns you on, honey" — as Shelley Winters apparently said on a Rowan and Martin Laugh-in programme. The English trade rightly bypassed 1968, ignoring Mr Mountchesney's dictum, "I rather like bad wine, one gets so bored with good wine" (from Disraeli's *Sybil*). Assessment: genuine '68s, should any remain, will be thin and tinny. Tasting notes: only seven notes, five of them beaujolais.

Fixin, Les Arvelets G. Berthaud	*Ordered out of stinginess and curiosity: pretty pale; light, quite pleasant for quick drinking.* Tasted December 1972 *
La Romanée Dom. de la Romanée-Conti	*Surprisingly deep colour; rather overblown, meaty nose; soft, quite nice.* Tasted May 1976 *

Of the beaujolais:

Beaujolais Hellmers	*Rather artificial boiled-sweet (candy fruit drops) smell and taste, but not unattractive.* Tasted January 1971
Brouilly Marcel Amance	*Variable: one vinegary, another, with a fresh* Gamay *aroma, quite flavoury.* Tasted December 1969
Fleurie and Brouilly Bottled by Christopher's	*Both had a chaptalized, boiled-candy smell, and were rather short and tinny.* Tasted August 1972
Juliénas, Clos des Capitans	*A light, skinny, strawberry-jam flavoured wine.* Tasted January 1971

1969 ★★★★

An excellent vintage. Distinctly good, deep, rich wines, of classic elegance, not unlike 1949. And certainly far better than the '69 red Bordeaux. Climate: mild winter followed by cold, rainy spring. Late flowering counterbalanced by very fine, warm, ripening weather in July and August. Cold and wet in September but exceptionally fine weather for vintage on 5 October. Smallish vintage of high quality. Sound ripe grapes. Market: there appeared to be two classes of burgundy, the better domaines producing the first *vin de garde* vintage since 1966, and some lighter wine shipped for quick bottling and early drinking. The market was firm and prices fairly high. Assessment: the best started off with a rich and brilliant ruby-red colour, full of aroma and body, with tannin and acidity to ensure a long life. I have a feeling this vintage is now distinctly underrated, partly because the wines are not all that frequently seen, but mainly because there is an association in the mind with '69 Bordeaux, some of which are now distinctly poor. Still excellent, and the finest will be long lasting. Tasting notes: I have a fairly large number of notes ranging from beaujolais up to the best Côte de Nuits, fairly evenly spread over the decade of the 1970s, and fewer poor wines than usual. I have tried to select a representative range to illustrate style and condition.

Beaune, Grèves, Hospices d'Alléry	*On label "Bureau de Bionfaisance". Deepish, fairly red still, but maturing nicely.* At a tasting tutorial in Denmark, June 1978 **(*)
Beaune, Clos des Mouches J. Drouhin	*Lightish red; an altogether elegant wine, gently scented, nice acidity.* At the Hotel Richemond, Geneva, April 1974 ***
Chambertin Dom. Jacques Prieur	*Fairly deep, maturing; rich, stewed* Pinot *nose; good flavour, plenty of bite.* Tasted May 1977 **(*)
Chambolle-Musigny Doudet-Naudin	*Big, brown, virtually opaque; chocolate-elixir nose; a big plummy wine. A bit short.* Tasted October 1978 **
Chambolle-Musigny Lebègue-Bichot	*At my club, the Traveller's, with Colin Fenton and an American nicknamed "Phil Oxera" as guests. An elegant, attractive enough wine, slightly bitter on the finish.* Tasted February 1974 **
Chambolle-Musigny C. Viénot	*Medium colour; very flavoury with the usual Viénot stylishness, but still hard.* Tasted November 1978 **(*)
Corton Geisweiler	*Pink tinged; scented* Pinot*; lighter than expected, flavoury, tough, lightly acidic finish.* Tasted October 1978 **
Corton C. Viénot	*Deep; meaty; alcoholic yet soft. Some noticeable acidity.* Tasted October 1978 ***
Corton, Languettes Prosper Maufoux	*Very deep coloured; rich, scented* Pinot*; dry, full bodied, very alcoholic, still hard.* At a court luncheon of the Worshipful Company of Distillers, January 1979 **(*)
Fixin, Hervelets H. Clemancey	*Rather indifferent, neutral, bland nose and flavour, slightly bitter finish.* At an Oxford University Wine Circle tutorial, February 1972 *
Gevrey-Chambertin Varoilles	*Slightly immature looking in March 1972, but very flavoury. Later: fragrant, dry, but a bit tart.* Last tasted May 1977 **
Gevrey-Chambertin, Clos de la Justice Avery's	*First, at dinner with John Avery in July 1979, then presented by me two months later at a tasting tutorial: fairly deep; an extremely good, ripe beetroot aroma; rich, intense, dry finish.* Last tasted at Andrew Lloyd-Webber's Sydmonton Festival, September 1979 ***
Gevrey-Chambertin, Clos St-Jacques F. Pernet	*Incredibly deep, virtually opaque; fragrant, complex, mineral overtones; a rich wine with tremendous zest and bite.* Tasted November 1977 ***(*)
Gevrey-Chambertin, Clos St-Jacques A. Rousseau	*A marvellous wine: rich throughout in colour, on nose and on palate. Wonderful root-like/earthy* Pinot *aroma and flavour. Mouth-filling. Ten years of life ahead.* Tasted September 1977 ***(*)

Grands-Echézeaux Dr Barolet	*Tasted from the* cuve : *thick, plummy, purple coloured; very good aroma, good fruit; about maximum natural strength, 13°G.L. (13 per cent alcohol by volume) and 7° acidity. Full flavoured, still raspingly young. Some future.* Tasted October 1969 (★★★)
Grands-Echézeaux Dom. de la Romanée-Conti	*Palish and pink, not nearly as deep and purple as I expected; bouquet fresh, youthful, intensely fragrant; dry, rather light in style yet firm with quite a tang and youthful acidity.* At the Romanée-Conti tasting at Christie's, September 1972 ★★★(★)
Musigny Hudelot	*An elegant, soft, agreeable, feminine style of wine. Rather overpowered but not outclassed by a Beaulieu Vineyards Beaumont Pinot Noir.* At a comparative tasting of California v. French classic wines at Narsai's restaurant north of San Francisco Bay, May 1972 ★★★
Nuits St-Georges, Clos des Argillières Leroy Elmerich	*With Les Pruliers below, the best of six good '69 Nuits at the Leroy tasting: deep rich colour; fabulously rich, sweet, slightly singed Pinot nose; very rich, meaty, almost Corton-like in weight and style. Excellent finish and long life ahead.* Tasted September 1979 ★★★(★) *A month later I tasted Elmerich's bottling from the same vineyard but of the Domaine Guachon: still youthful looking; sweet, flavoury, with sustaining tannin and acidity.* Tasted October 1979 ★★★(★)
Nuits St-Georges, Chaignots H. Gouges Leroy	*Noticeably high acidity. Tasted on two occasions. First a Henri Gouges domaine bottling (with grouse at the Brompton Grill in August 1978): medium colour, nice gradation; piquant Pinot aroma; stylish and flavoury, very high acidity and lacking the usual Gouges smoky character. At the Leroy tasting: similar in almost every feature, positive, flavoury.* Last tasted September 1979 ★★
Nuits St-Georges, Pruliers Leroy	*Opaque in colour; incredibly rich, heavy, port-like nose, "Pinot and prunes", but very fragrant; magnificent wine, like a great Richebourg. A long future.* Tasted September 1979 ★★★(★★)
Nuits St-Georges Other vineyards	*All at the Leroy tasting. Corvées: deep coloured, lively, sweet, rich, chewy, still hard. Les Murgers: singed, alcoholic, firm, dry finish. Les Vaucrains: complex chocolaty nose, a bit lactic; sweet, flavoury, firm.* Tasted September 1979. All ★★★(★)
Richebourg Dom. de la Romanée-Conti	*In June 1977, a bottle returned from the United States: similar depth to La Tâche, perhaps slightly less brown; richer, spicier nose; distinctly dry, positive flavour, fairly high acidity but hard to justify claim of poor storage/treatment. More recently: fully mature appearance; fragrant, root-like Pinot richness; dry, contradictory light style but highish alcohol, rather hard, unmellow, powerful finish—no "peacock's tail" .* Tasted September 1977 ★★(★★)?
Santenay J. Drouhin	*The real thing: pink; jammy nose; piquant. "A suitable case for treatment" (blending).* Tasted July 1973 ★
La Tâche Dom. de la Romanée-Conti	*First noted at Lebègue's Romanée-Conti tasting at Christie's in September 1972: not very deep though slightly deeper than Grands-Echézeaux; youthful, gentle nose which developed well; dry, fuller bodied and richer than the colour led one to expect. Quite a tang and still a little raw and acidic. Next at the Romanée-Conti tasting at Quaglino's in April 1974: deeper and browner than the pale 1970 La Tâche; brown sugar nose; dry, medium body, slightly burnt flavour, but good. Most recently, a bottle returned from the United States: not very deep, but mature and attractive appearance; very fragrant, rich, perhaps a little stewed*

	(was this due to hot storage??); dry, still quite a bite, not settled down. Frankly, a puzzle. Tasted June 1977 (★★★)
Volnay, Santenots J. Drouhin	*Medium light, pretty colour; extraordinary style — high-toned, perfumed, chocolaty bouquet and flavour; lightish, elegant.* Tasted February 1973 ★★★

Some English-bottled '69s:

Gevrey-Chambertin J. Drouhin	*Beautifully bottled, as always, by the London agents, Reynier: deep, rich, excellent aroma, flavour, balance.* Tasted July 1973 ★★★★
Nuits St-Georges, Vaucrains Avery's	*Tasted with the Australian Wine and Food Society convention in mind: fairly deep garnet red; ripe, intense fishy* Pinot; *slightly sweet, full bodied, lots of grip.* Tasted September 1979 ★★★(★)
Volnay Harvey's	*Appealing, high toned, dry, light.* Tasted February 1973 ★★
Vosne-Romanée Avery's	*Firm, pleasantly balanced. (A Pommard Rugiens tasted alongside was oxidized.)* Tasted November 1979 ★★

1970 ★★★

Reasonably full, rich, rounded wines. Nice quality. Climate: bad weather in April and May but good for the flowering in June. Very sunny in July, and after a short cold spell in August, the weather was hot through September and into October. Picking began 30 September. Large crop, ripe wines. Market: in early November, Beaune joyfully celebrated a successful vintage. All price records were beaten at the Hospices de Beaune sale. It was a period of euphoria; a good vintage for the grower and merchant. Assessment: supple and reasonably well-balanced wines, appealing when young but not as firm or stylish as the 1969s or as great as the finest 1971s. Rather like a spoilt child, pretty, amusing, fussed over, but lacking depth and intellectual interest now that youth has passed. Some are crumbling, but the best are nice, soft, easy wines, and the very best will develop further.

Auxey-Duresses R. Ampeau	*Palish; quite nice, light fruity nose; dry, flavoury. A lightweight wine.* Tasted March 1979 ★★
Beaune, Bressandes A. Morot	*A good, rich wine. But Morot's Cent-Vignes so pale that it was practically fading away.* Tasted March 1975 ★★★ and ★ respectively.
Beaune, Clos de Fèves Chanson	*Palish, very mature but rich looking; sweet, ripe, almost overblown* Pinot *nose; slightly sweet, medium light, ripe, flavoury, still a little bite but lacking finish.* Tasted March 1980 ★★
Beaune, Grèves, Vigne de l'Enfant Jésus Bouchard Père	*Deepish; rich chocolaty nose; dry, quite nice, flowery wine.* Tasted September 1977 ★★
Beaune, Hospices, Cuvée H. & L. Bétault	*Very mature looking; fine, smoky* Pinot *nose; slightly sweet, very good flavour and balance.* Tasted December 1975 ★★★
Beaune, Theurons Calvet	*Singed, root-like* Pinot *nose; light style, leathery texture. Quite nice.* Tasted November 1978 ★★
Beaune, Theurons and Cent-Vignes A. Morot	*Very pale, slightly orange coloured; high-toned* Pinot *nose; dried out and tart.* Tasted May 1977. *The same grower's Beaune, Cent-Vignes, similar.* Tasted 1977.

Bonnes-Mares *Drouhin-Laroze*	*Most attractive, good nose in November 1975. Later: medium, slightly indefinable colour; scented bouquet; lightish, dry, a bit unmellow but appealing.* Last tasted July 1977 **
Bonnes-Mares *de Vogüé*	*Attractive colour, lightish; rich, classic nose, but nutty in the almond-kernelly sense; rich, medium body, soft entry, velvety yet firm middle flavour, which opened up. Some tannin and acid on the finish. Classic flavour but just lacking the trim elegance and style of Bonnes-Mares at its best.* Tasted August 1977, October 1978 ***
Chambertin *Trapet*	*Good in April 1974. Later: good colour; very stylish bouquet; very good flavour and balance. Needs time.* Last tasted April 1975 ***(*)
Chambertin, Clos de Bèze *Drouhin-Laroze*	*Not very deep but still youthful; fabulous flavour and aftertaste.* Tasted May 1974 ****
Chambertin, Griotte *T. Bassot*	*Not very deep; rich bouquet and flavour. Nice balance, dry finish.* Tasted February 1975 ***
Chambolle-Musigny, Charmes	*Calvet: perfectly straightforward. Grivelet, 1er cru: drier but richer.* Two rather uninspired pre-sale samples, both tasted November 1978 *
Chapelle-Chambertin *Bouchard Père*	*Palish, pretty colour; some richness about the nose but dry and lacking the style and flavour expected.* Tasted March 1980 **
Chassagne-Montrachet, Clos de la Chapelle *Magenta*	*Attractive colour, mature; nice nose and flavour. Perfect now.* Tasted November 1979 ***
Corton *C. Viénot*	*Deep colour; rather a stewed* Pinot *nose; quite nice, but swingeing tannin and acidity.* Tasted July 1977 *
Corton-Bressandes *Marcel Amance*	*Pleasant, firm.* Tasted December 1974 ***
Corton-Bressandes *Mérode*	*Medium. Fairly mature, plummy coloured; a good, rich, singed Corton nose; medium dry, fullish body, good rich flavour.* Tasted 1979, March 1980 ****
Ch. Corton-Grancey *L. Latour*	*Medium colour, no great depth; sweet, very attractive high-toned bouquet and flavour.* Tasted November 1977 ***
Corton, Maréchaudes *Mérode*	*Medium pale, healthy glow but less deep, more mature looking than Bressandes; sweet, ripe, fragrant bouquet; dry, surprisingly light but pronounced flavour and bite, tannin and acidity.* Tasted twice in 1979. Last tasted March 1980 ***
Corton, Pougets *L. Jadot*	*Attractive colour; rich, meaty nose; dry, powerful wine.* Tasted November 1977 **(*)
Corton, Clos du Roi *Thénard*	*A Remoissenet wine: a bit weak in appearance; good pronounced aroma; some richness but a bit skinny in the middle. Dry finish.* Tasted June 1976 **
Corton, Clos de la Vigne au Saint *L. Latour*	*Pale, very mature; rich smoky/meaty bouquet and flavour. Lovely character.* Tasted November 1977 ****
Echézeaux *Jaboulet-Vercherre*	*A British Transport Hotels wine: deepish, pink rimmed; quite nice* Pinot *nose; dry but rich, some tannin and acidity still.* Tasted June 1976 **(*)
Gevrey-Chambertin *Humbert*	*Nondescript colour; rather common nose and flavour. Dry.* Tasted November 1977.

Gevrey-Chambertin L. Latour	*Two qualities tasted: both very mature looking, the village wine being more open-knit and sweeter than the* 1er cru, *which had a rich, burnt, scented nose with lovely flavour and dry finish.* Tasted November 1977 ∗∗∗ and ∗∗∗∗
Gevrey-Chambertin, Cazetières Villerange	*Medium colour; some depth and richness. Very pleasant.* Tasted December 1974 ∗∗∗
Gevrey-Chambertin, Pruliers Clair-Daü	*Lovely smoky* Pinot *aroma; very fruity, good middle flavour. Slightly unready.* At the annual Oxford v. Cambridge tasting competition at Harvey's, February 1974 ∗∗∗
Iles de Vergelesses L. Latour	*Lively colour; quite attractive little wine, rich, positive, with twist of acidity.* Tasted 1974, twice in 1976 and November 1979 ∗∗
Latricières-Chambertin Drouhin-Laroze	*Palish; good flavour, stylish but not as impressive as the Vougeot.* Tasted November 1976 ∗∗∗
Morey St-Denis L. Latour	*Elegant, dry, good flavour, firmness and finish.* Tasted November 1977 ∗∗∗(∗)
Musigny de Vogüé	*Palish; rich, rather stewed nose; distinctly sweet, chunky, slightly unknit, rich but quite a bite. As with the Bonnes-Mares, lacking the firmness and elegance of a vintage like 1969.* Tasted January 1978 ∗∗
Nuits St-Georges Doudet-Naudin	*About the best of fifteen '70s at a Doudet-Naudin trade tasting in London, ranging from Beaujolais Villages at £58 per hogshead F.O.B. Beaune to £185 for a Charmes-Chambertin. Consistent, reliable, a trifle uninspired.* Tasted May 1971. Ranging from ∗∗ to ∗∗∗
Nuits St-Georges, Boudots	*The only '70 in the Leroy tasting of Nuits: fairly deep but more mature than the '71; a good, rather open-knit* Pinot *nose; touch of ripe sweetness, medium body, a relaxed, easy flavour, dry, slightly pasty finish.* Tasted September 1979 ∗∗∗ Nice now.
Pommard, Epenots Gouroux	*In Geneva: pretty colour; slightly sweet, rich, nice wine. The same grower's Echézeaux and Grands-Echézeaux pleasant but unremarkable.* Tasted April 1974 ∗∗
Pommard, Grand Clos des Epenots de Courcel	*A rather seedy aristocrat: bright appearance but beads at the rim; stewed, cardboardy nose; flavour not bad but prickly, with bitter finish.* Tasted twice in March, and in May 1979.
Clos de la Roche Bouchard Père	*Distinctly pale; unimpressive nose and flavour with touch of volatile acidity peeping through.* Tasted only once, March 1980. Judgement reserved.
La Romanée Paul Bouchard	*I must confess to not liking these Château de Vosne-Romanée wines. This had a nice enough colour; sweet chocolate and damp cardboard nose; quite nice flavour spoilt by a too dry, slightly bitter finish.* Tasted February 1976.
Romanée St-Vivant Noëllat	*Nice, but I expected more. First tasted in February 1975. Later the same year: palish, very mature; low-keyed rather unimpressive nose; lightish body, pleasant flavour, easy style, light dry finish.* Last tasted October 1975 ∗∗
Clos St-Denis Bouchard Père	*Palish, pink tinged; sweet, attractive light style of wine. Pleasant, straightforward.* Tasted March 1980 ∗∗
Savigny, Marconnets Chanson	*Palish, mature; rather neutral nose; dry, firm enough, but lacking flavour.* Tasted November 1979 ∗

La Tâche Dom. de la Romanée-Conti	*This appears to be the only Romanée-Conti domaine '70 I have tasted. Remarkably pale, maturing quickly (less colour than the '69 and '71); light and sugary aroma; slightly sweet, soft yet some acidity. But flavoury as always.* Tasted at Quaglino's, April 1974 ★★(★)
Clos de Tart Mommessin	*Palish, mature; nice nose, a little medicinal; dry, very flavoury but fluffy and insubstantial. Tinny Pinot on the palate but nice after-taste. I must admit to finding Clos de Tart frequently lacking in conviction and depth: a sort of blowzy blonde.* Tasted November 1976 ★★
Volnay, Bois d'Or Jaboulet-Vercherre	*Rather dull. More bois than d'or.* Tasted May 1976.
Volnay, Champans L. Latour	*Medium light, mature; very rich stable-yard nose; dry, flavoury. Style and charm.* Tasted November 1977 ★★★
Volnay, Santenots J. Clerget	*Medium pale, fully mature; fragrant, light; medium dry, flavoury, a bit short.* Tasted October 1979 ★★
Vosne-Romanée L. Latour	*Slightly insubstantial in colour and on palate, but nice nose and flavour. Dry.* Tasted November 1979 ★★
Vosne-Romanée, Chaumes de Villamont	*Medium, mature; fragrant — a little stewed; dry, nice.* In Amsterdam, November 1979 ★★
Vosne-Romanée, Suchots Remoissenet?	*Avery selection: very mature looking, little red left; gentle, ripe Pinot nose; soft, rounded but dry acid end.* Tasted February 1978 ★★
Clos Vougeot Drouhin-Laroze	*Lovely wine: still quite youthful looking; rich, scented Pinot aroma; mealy, excellent flavour.* Tasted November 1976 ★★★(★)

1971 ★★★★★

An outstanding vintage. Deep, firm, well-constituted wines. Climate: settled weather from the spring until the end of October though there was some flower failure in June. Some hail mid-August and a week of poor weather at the end of that month which was speedily corrected by a particularly warm and sunny first half of September. Picking began early, on 16th. The small crop followed some failure in flowering, hail and shot berries but the effect was that of a heavy pruning, the remaining grapes benefiting from the nourishment normally shared by many bunches. The overall quality high, with deep-coloured wines. The Côte de Nuits was less affected by hail than the Côte de Beaune, where the crop was one-third to one-fifth of 1970. Market: because of the boom time and short crop, there was a sharp price rise. By November 1971, first growths were up 25 per cent to even 50 per cent. Assessment: this has always been a favourite vintage of mine though some think the wine too substantial and untypical. The better wines are still developing well and it will undoubtedly be one of the longest lasting vintages of the past twenty years.

Auxey-Duresses Leroy	*At a blind tasting of Côte de Beaune to choose wines for a Wine and Food Society convention: attractive, mouth-watering citrus-fruit aroma and acidity. Very flavoury but not serious enough for a convention of gastronomes.* Tasted August 1977 ★★★ Drink now — 1985.
Beaune, Grèves Avery's	*At the above tasting, labelled "A.C. Bourgogne": a stunningly beautiful Pinot nose; full, smoky flavour, very good aftertaste. Selected for a convention dinner.* Tasted August 1977 ★★★(★) Drink now — 1990.
Beaune, Grèves, Vigne de l'Enfant Jésus	*A very attractive Bouchard Père domaine wine: rich mulberry bouquet; classic.* Tasted 1973, May 1977 ★★★★ Drink now — 1995.

Beaune, Hospices, *Cuvée H. & L. Bétault*	*Bottled in Beaune. Not very deep, but attractive colour; de-liciously ripe, very fragrant bouquet; intensely rich, tangy* Pinot. *Tasted May 1979 ★★(★) Drink now — 1990.*
Beaune, Hospices, *Cuvée Maurice Drouhin*	*Beautiful wine; excellent ripe* Pinot *aroma; fullish, lovely flavour and balance. Dry finish.* *Tasted July and October 1975 ★★★(★) Drink now — 1995.*
Beaune, Perrières Roland Thévinin	*Pretty colour, slightly pink; light but a bit oversweet on the nose; medium body, firm but flavoury.* *Tasted November 1976 ★★★*
Beaune, Toussaints de Villamont	*Mature looking; sweet vanilla nose; dry, quite nice.* *In Amsterdam, November 1979 ★★ Drink now.*
Beaune, Vignes-Franches L. Latour	*Maturing nicely; gentle, soft yet alcoholic backbone.* *Tasted January 1977 ★★★ Drink now — 1986.*
Chambolle-Musigny L. Latour	*At a blind tasting of Côte de Nuits: good, rich nose; flavoury, attractive citrus-fruit acidity.* *Tasted August 1977 ★★(★) Drink now — 1986.*
Chassagne-Montrachet, *Abbaye de Morgeot* P. Ponnelle	*A bit stiff nosed; soft and just a little sickly sweet. Worth keep-ing to see if it will develop.* *Tasted May 1977 ★(★) Drink now — 1985.*
Chassagne-Montrachet, *Clos St-Jean* Audiffred	*Fairly deep; lightly scented and jammy; slightly sweet, firm, nice texture, pleasant enough.* *At a junior members' Wine and Food Society tasting, December 1975 ★★ Drink now.*
Le Corton Bouchard Père	*A* tête de cuvée *wine at two Heublein tastings in the United States, first in 1973. Three years later: fairly deep; dry, full of flavour, still tannic, long finish.* *Last tasted May 1976 ★★(★★) Drink now — 1995.*
Corton, Clos Fiètres Voarick	*First tasted and quite liked in 1975. In March 1976 it had a noticeable sediment and a rich, ripe nose—but rather foolishly I did not taste it. I tried another bottle later that year: the overripe* Pinot *nose, rather like a decorative fly-catching plant, concealed a terribly tart wine.* *Tasted December 1976.*
Ch. Corton-Grancey L. Latour	*Deep, powerful '71 colour; rich meaty bouquet and flavour. Still fairly tough and noticeably high tannin and acidity.* *At Gravetye Manor, 1979 ★★★(★) Drink 1982 - 1995.*
Corton, Hospices, *Cuvée Charlotte Dumay*	*Doubtless a Bouchard Père bottling but much lighter in colour than their Le Corton; very good meaty nose; lighter in style, rich, more advanced.* *Tasted May 1976 ★★★ Drink now — 1990.*
Corton, *Clos de la Vigne au Saint* L. Latour	*Fairly deep and still youthful; rather hard, undeveloped nose; a good tough '71. Needs time.* *Tasted October 1978 ★★(★★) Drink 1982–1995.*
Echézeaux Dom. de la Romanée-Conti	*Most people do not realize the gap in stature and price between the domaine's Echézeaux and Grands-Echézeaux, not to mention La Tâche and of course Romanée-Conti itself. Price at the opening trade tasting at Quaglino's: £94 per dozen. Rather pale in colour; little nose; a light, pleasant, strawberry-like flavour. Not, in fact, very impressive.* *Tasted April 1974 ★★(★)? Not tasted since. Drink now — 1988?*
Gevrey-Chambertin L. Latour	*Noticeably deep; rich but rather stiff nose; very good in its class.* *At a blind tasting of Côte de Nuits, August 1977 ★★★(★) Drink now — 1990.*
Grands-Echézeaux Dom. de la Romanée-Conti	*In April 1974 (£140 per case to the trade): medium pale and sur-prisingly mature looking; very rich nose; slightly sweet, curiously*

rich, open fluffy texture. And at the Under 40s Club in 1977, most attractive colour but seemed exceptionally dry and immature. Most recently: medium-pale, most attractive finely gradated colour; beautiful bouquet, fruit, vinosity; medium sweet, fairly full bodied, lovely flavour and texture. Complete. Perfect. At John Holt's domaine tasting, March 1980 ★★★★★ Drink now — 1995.

Grands-Echézeaux Gouroux	*Medium, very mature appearance; stewed jammy nose, with a dollop of molasses. Curious.* Tasted March 1979. Drink up.
Mazis-Chambertin Faiveley	*Fine colour; excellent nose, ripe* Pinot *maturity; touch of richness on the palate, not heavy but substantial.* At a Solicitors' Wine Society and Wine and Food Society tasting in Manchester, April 1979 ★★★(★) Drink now — 1990.
Mazis-Chambertin Alfred Martin	*Showing well at a tasting for the Oxford University Wine Circle: lovely colour, still youthful; very good clear-cut aroma; fullish, stylish wine with flavour, balance and future. And again, for the Exeter University Wine Society: singed, brussels-sprouts nose. A fine rich wine.* Both in November 1977 ★★★(★) Drink now — 1995.
Mercurey, Clos du Roi Voarick	*Very mature looking; nice, fruity, piquant, scented nose; distinctly dry, rapier-like flavour.* Tasted July and October 1975 ★(★) Drink soon.
Meursault (rouge) Ropiteau	*One rarely comes across red Meursault and one can understand why. This should have been white: its colour was very pale, feeble, watery pink orange; very little bouquet or flavour; dry.* Tasted May 1979. Drink up.
Morey St-Denis Remoissenet	*An Avery selection, first noticed at a blind tasting of Côte de Nuits at Christie's in August 1977 and selected because of its fabulous bouquet and outstanding flavour for a Wine and Food Society convention. Next, equally impressive, in November 1978, and a year later: not quite as deep as expected; a positive and immediately attractive* Pinot nose, *which seemed to rein back and then reassert itself. A touch contrived. Slightly sweet, lightish in style with some delicacy, very flavoury but touch of end bitterness.* Last tasted November 1979 ★★★ Hard to project development, perhaps now — 1986.
Musigny de Vogüé	*Fairly deep, rich robe; wonderfully calm, harmonious, rich bouquet; fine, fairly powerful yet with great finesse, fruit and length. Made the preceding Morey St-Denis '71 look a bit flimsy.* At a Studley Priory Wine Weekend, November 1979 ★★★★(★) Drink 1982–2000.
Nuits St-Georges, **Clos des Corvées** Faiveley Elmerich	*The Faiveley wine at lunch with Robert Carrier at Hintlesham Hall: very good flavour and aftertaste.* Tasted November 1978 ★★★ *The Elmerich: medium colour, mature; a magnificent tangy* Pinot *aroma; excellent flavour and balance.* Tasted October 1979 ★★★(★) Both: drink now — 1992.
Nuits St-Georges, **Les St-Georges**	*The only '71 at the Leroy tasting and certainly in the top league: fairly deep, lively colour; rich, fragrant, similar tangy/meaty* Pinot *character to the Corvées noted above; medium dry, very rich, full, alcoholic, lots of grip, dry finish.* Tasted September 1979 ★★★(★★) Drink 1981–1995.
Pommard, Chanlains Ropiteau	*The best of four Ropiteau '71s: rich, ripe, high toned; slightly sweet, lighter style, very fruity.* Tasted May 1979 ★★★ Drink now — 1986.
Pommard, Rugiens Clerget	*Supplied by the Malmaison Club: fairly deep, still very red; very good nose; natural ripe sweetness, good but peppery and unready.* At a tasting conducted at Imperial College, London, October 1978 ★★(★) Drink now — 1988.

Richebourg *Dom. de la Romanée-Conti*	*At a Lebègue tasting in 1974 (price to the trade £220): not at all deep in colour; considerable depth on the nose, slightly roasted; rich, burnt* Pinot *flavour, tannin and acidity. Three years later, although it looked fairly advanced in maturity it packed a punch. Earthy, powerful, still with tannin and acidity.* Last tasted at the Under 40s Club, June 1977 ***(*) Drink now — 2000.*
Romanée-Conti *Dom. de la Romanée-Conti*	*These '71s caused quite a stir at the Domaine/Lebègue tasting at Quaglino's in April 1974. Mme Bize-Leroy and Aubert de Villaine extolled the virtues of their '71s; merchants bemoaned the prices. Their top wine was an unprecedented £290 per dozen, duty paid and delivered, to the trade. Paradoxically and confusingly, the wine was not deep coloured, already appearing to mature; rich nose and flavour: leather and velvet. At the Under 40s Club tasting: bouquet developing well, rich and complex; slightly sweet, not heavy but very mouth-filling.* Last tasted at Lebègue's, June 1977 ***(**)? Drink 1985–2000 plus.*
Romanée St-Vivant *Marey-Monge*	*The price of this wine has rocketed since this domaine came under the wing of Romanée-Conti. At the opening tasting it was £220, the same price as the Richebourg. Same sort of colour, too, but a gently fruity* Pinot *aroma; soft, rich, open, delightful. Not tasted since, but I am sure it will be the epitome of elegance now.* Tasted April 1974 ***(**). Drink now — 1995.*
Clos St-Denis *Dujac*	*Jacques Seysses produced this at lunch to illustrate the effect of hail damage (there had been severe hailstorms that summer, as in 1971). The wine was not as deep as expected; very advanced, with an overripe* Pinot *nose; ripe flavour and a just detectable mousy (hail effect) end taste.* Tasted September 1979 ** Drink up.*
La Tâche *Dom. de la Romanée-Conti*	*At the opening tasting in April 1974 (price £255 per case): pretty colour, slightly pink; inimitably stylish, high-toned La Tâche nose (the Château Margaux of Burgundy); richly flavoured, quite a bite. At the Under 40s Club: distinctly dry, very fine but a bit severe. Will undoubtedly open up. Most recently: deeper coloured than Grands-Echézeaux; bouquet fine but lower keyed than expected; a surprisingly powerful, assertive flavour, wonderful peacock's-tail aftertaste. Perfect.* Last tasted at John Holt's, March 1980 ****(*) Drink now — 1995.*
Volnay, Caillerets *Bouchard Père*	*Very purple and hard in May 1973. Developing well in August 1976. Then at a Heublein dinner in New Orleans with Bob Balzer, Nathan Chroman and others: an appealing wine, light, scented style, nice quality.* Last tasted May 1977 *** Drink now — 1988.*
Volnay, Clos des Chênes *de Moucheron*	*This is my idea of a Volnay: medium-light, attractive colour; fragrant, strawberry-like bouquet; dry, lightish, with elegance and charm.* Tasted February and October 1975 *** Drink now — 1988.*
Volnay, Fremiets *Cru d'Angerville*	*A Piat selection: deep colour; a massive, jammy, alcoholic nose; positively sweet, very rich and powerful. Not my idea of a Volnay, but impressive.* Tasted December 1977 **(*) Drink now — 1990.*
Clos Vougeot *Varoilles*	*Good colour; lovely flavour, depth, richness.* Tasted November 1979 **** Drink now — 1995.*
Vougeot, Clos Perrière *Bertagna*	*Lovely colour; rich, complex nose full of fruit and vinosity; dry, firm, tannic.* At Imperial College, October 1978 **(**) Drink 1982–1995.*

1972 ★★★

An unusual vintage: firm, flavoury, pretty well constituted and underrated. Climate: fairly severe winter with rain and snow in January and February. End of March warm, the vines budding in April then wet, cold weather. The summer lacked both heat and rain — most unusual to be both cold and dry. However, it was followed by marvellous sunshine in September which saved the day. Vintage late: healthy grapes picked under good if rather cold conditions. Market: a huge crop with large quantities over the permitted yield which stimulated some concern in Burgundy about the problems of excess production, its valuation and future marketing. But there was no let up in prices. The English trade, having bought the previous three vintages, were in no rush to buy and were a bit sceptical, doubtless influenced by the ridiculous prices asked for the distinctly poor '72 red Bordeaux. Noticeable that English bottlings are not much to be seen. Assessment: there is clearly some justification for the confidence of the Domaine de la Romanée-Conti in this vintage; quite a few others are impressive too: deep, firm wines with good acidity. Difficult to say whether the touch of bitterness of some will wear off. But on the whole, good flavoury burgundies worth looking out for, and relatively good value. Tasting notes: I tasted a range of '72s at Louis Latour's and de Villamont's in September 1975. Some of Latour's had marked youthful acidity which, it is to be hoped, will have worn off by now; de Villamont's were all immediately attractive. But I have noticeably fewer '72s than '71s in my tasting books which is a measure, if arbitrary, of the relative disinterest of the English trade. From the selection extracted I hope that an indication of quality and condition will be gleaned.

Beaune, Bressandes Morot	*Richly coloured; very good bouquet; highly flavoured, firm, high-ish fixed acidity.* Tasted November 1979 ★★★ *Drink now — 1988.*
Beaune, Theurons Bouchard Père	*Rather uninteresting nose but soft and pleasant.* Tasted November 1979 ★★ *Drink now — 1985.*
Beaune, Toussaints Morot	*Like the Bressandes, high toned, fragrant and attractive.* Tasted November 1979 ★★★ *Drink now — 1988.*
Beaune, Vignes-Franches L. Latour	*First tasted and showing well in Beaune in September 1975, and again a month later in London. More recently: a bit bland and unimpressive compared with the '76s (but less expensive).* At a Louis Latour tasting, October 1977 ★★ *Drink now — 1985.*
Chambolle-Musigny Barault-Lucotte	*Still youthful looking; bouquet fair to middling; surprisingly rich on the palate.* Tasted twice, in June 1976 ★★(★) *Drink now — 1990.*
Ch. Corton-Grancey L. Latour	*Deepish colour; slightly sweet, quite rich burnt/meaty Corton nose; fullish, rich, good firm flavour. Somewhat austere. Very dry finish.* Tasted September 1975 ★★(★) *Drink now — 1992.*
Corton, Renardes Voarick	*One of half a dozen interesting '72s at a pre-sale tasting: medium pale; fragrant, scented nose; lightish style — not a meaty Corton — but very flavoury.* Tasted November 1976 ★★★ *Drink now — 1988.*
Corton, Clos du Roi Thénard	*Showing well at an Avery tasting: nutty; dry, meaty, some depth.* Tasted October 1974 ★(★★) *Drink now — 1992.*
Echézeaux Dom. de la Romanée-Conti	*Positively cheap compared with the '71s: only £28 a case, in bond (London). Palish; sweet nose; dry, lightish, fairly marked acidity.* Tasted October 1975 ★(★) *Drink now — 1986.*
Echézeaux Dujac	*Fine crisp colour; aromatic Pinot—excellent bouquet; very flavoury, fine style and quality but a touch of end bitterness.* At the Waterside Inn, Bray, as the guest of Tawfig Khoury, August 1977 ★★(★)? *Drink now — 1988.*

Gevrey-Chambertin *Varoilles*	Tastevin *label. Seemed rather unknit and unsatisfactory to me.* Tasted November 1979 ★ Drink up.
Gevrey-Chambertin, Cazetières *A. Rousseau*	*Palish, pink tinged; good nose; dry, short but interesting flavour. (The same grower's Lavaux St-Jacques was woody.)* Tasted November 1976 ★★ Drink now — 1985.
Grands-Echézeaux *Dom. de la Romanée-Conti*	*First tasted at the domaine in September 1975: very rich bouquet and flavour, meaty, powerful, dry finish. And in London the following month: impressive, flavoury, long finish.* Last tasted October 1975 ★★★(★) Drink now — 1992.
Mercurey, Clos du Roi *Voarick*	*Sweet, meaty nose; nice flavoury wine.* Tasted November 1979 ★★ Drink now — 1985.
Nuits St-Georges, Chaboeufs	*Deep, immature; good, stylish fragrant nose; some richness, fullish body, lots of life.* At the big Leroy tasting, September 1979 ★★(★) Drink 1982–1995.
Nuits St-Georges, Clos des Corvées	*Rich, plum coloured; excellent bouquet: rich, forthcoming, fruity; fullish, fairly powerful wine, good fruit, well balanced, lots of life.* Also at the Leroy tasting, September 1979 ★★★(★) Drink 1982–1995.
Pernand, Ile des Vergelesses *Chandon de Briailles*	*Youthful appearance; fragrant* Pinot *aroma; dry, fullish, very flavoury, excellent grip and aftertaste.* Tasted November 1976 ★★★ Drink now — 1988.
Richebourg *Dom. de la Romanée-Conti*	*First tasted at the domaine in September 1975: medium colour; soft, very fragrant, rather blackcurrant/fruity aroma; exquisite flavour, powerful, firm, long. And as impressive in London a month later. Most recently: deepest of the '72s, richly coloured, mature; sweet rich nose; very attractive, lovely texture and consistency. Fine rich wine.* At John Holt's, March 1980 ★★★★ Drink now — 1995.
Clos de la Roche *A. Rousseau*	*At two tutored tastings in the same month: one for a* Les Amis du Vin *workshop, the other for the Cambridge Wine and Food Society: a medium weight but deep, mature red brown; good, rich root-character nose, organic, sweet almost voluptuous; slightly sweet, fullish body and flavour, well constituted but soft. Will go on developing well.* Both tasted October 1979 ★★★(★) Drink now — 1992.
Romanée-Conti *Dom. de la Romanée-Conti*	*Opening price to the trade: £152 a dozen in bond. Nose completely undeveloped; very dry, rich complex flavour, concentrated. Unready. Should be excellent in due course.* Tasted October 1975 ★★★(★★) Drink 1982–1995.
Romanée St-Vivant, *Marey Monge* *Dom. de la Romanée-Conti*	*First tasted in the domaine cellars, September 1975: palish, forward; sweet gentle nose; dry, elegant, powerful backbone but green. A month later in London: elegant, with extended flavour. Recently: gaining depth of colour; sweet, low-keyed but attractive bouquet, singed, fragrant; slightly sweet on the palate, elegant, quite rich. Developing well.* At John Holt's, March 1980 ★★★(★) Drink 1981–1992.
Clos St-Denis *Dujac*	*Fullish, fine and lively colour; fragrant, still a bit immature on the nose; lovely flavour with Morey elegance and Dujac stylishness. A little unready.* At Jacques Seysses's (Dujac is short for the Domaine du Jacques), September 1979 ★★(★★) Drink 1982–1992.
Savigny-les-Beaune *Barton & Guestier*	*I do not normally think of Barton & Guestier as burgundy people but this wine represented its type well at a Hepworth trophy tasting: mature; lovely ripe* Pinot; *slightly sweet, ready.* Tasted March 1979 ★★★ Drink now — 1986.

La Tâche Dom. de la Romanée-Conti	*In the cellars, September 1975: strangely deeper in colour than the Richebourg; sweet, rich nose; powerful, rich flavour, assertively dry finish. A month later, in London, I found the bouquet more typically delicate and scented; on the palate dry, still hard, with firm acidity. Most recently: medium weight, beautiful colour; very open, forthcoming bouquet; slightly sweet, lovely richness and texture. Perfect now.* At John Holt's, March 1980 ★★★★ Drink now — 1990.
Clos de Tart Mommessin	*Palish, pink tinged; low-keyed nose and flavour; dry, lightish, little to it. A touch of metallic acidity I associate with some '72s.* Tasted March 1980 ★★ No great future.
Volnay, Champans d'Angerville	*Palish, slightly pink; fragrant, elegant, nice dry wine.* Tasted November 1976 ★★★ Drink now — 1988.
Volany, Santenots d'Angerville	*Palish but attractive colour; quite nice nose; dry, firm, some elegance and backbone.* At the no longer rustic Hostellerie du Vieux Moulin near Savigny-les-Beaune, September 1975 ★★(★) Drink now — 1990.
Vosne-Romanée, Brulées René Engel	*Palish, touch of pink; nice nose; dry, firm, unready.* Tasted November 1976 ★★(★) Drink now — 1990.
Vosne-Romanée, Suchots Chanson	*Medium colour, bright, maturing well; good, positive nose; slightly sweet, lightish style but firm alcoholic backbone, nice finish.* At a Chaine des Rottisseurs and Dutch Institute of Directors tasting in Amsterdam, June 1978 ★★★

1973 ★★

A distinctly light, pallid and undistinguished vintage. Climate: Flowering in good conditions. Until mid-July the weather was the driest since 1945, then heavy rain on the Côtes. Rain again at the late and extended vintage, 22 September to 18 October. The third large crop in four years: an overabundance of light wines tending to lack acidity. Market: some worries again expressed about overproduction. Too much wine surplus to *rendement*, that is, over the permitted yields per acre; and too many grapes too filled out by too much rain. Prices at the Hospices de Beaune sale, a barometer of quality and demand, showed a drop of 10 per cent, which, bearing in mind inflation at the same rate, meant a real drop of 20 per cent. *Négociants* unanimously decided not to buy until 15 December at the earliest to give an opportunity for the quality of the '73s to be seen in perspective and to evade the overheated market of previous years — a not too difficult decision in the face of mounting resistance to prices, particularly from the United States. Assessment: surely the ultimate in feebleness. A damp squib of a vintage and one, even allowing for inclement weather, to make the connoisseurs of the world despair. It was not as if these insipid wines were inexpensive. At best they still retain a fleeting charm. Mainly for quick drinking.

Beaune, Cuvée Latour L. Latour	*Fragrant if chocolaty nose; dry, lightish, fruity, with a twist of acidity.* Tasted September 1975 ★
Beaune, Grèves, **Vigne de l'Enfant Jésus** Bouchard Père	*Palish, mature looking; soft, very attractive flavour. But not a stayer.* Tasted November 1979 ★★★
Beaune, Hospices, **Guigone de Salins**	*Medium-pale colour, insubstantial looking; very fragrant, if superficial, fully developed bouquet; dry, quite lovely flavour. Light style, no great length, but attractive.* At the Oxford and Cambridge tasting competition at Harvey's, March 1979 ★★★
Beaune, Toussaints Charles Deroy	*One of two attractive '73s supplied by the Malmaison Club for Dr Jenkins's tasting group: medium colour, very mature; copybook*

	boiled-beetroot Pinot *aroma, well-knit; good positive flavour, soft, nicely made for the year, but tailing off to a light, rather insubstantial finish.* At Imperial College, London, October 1978 **
Beaune, Vignes-Franches L. Latour	*Tasted in Beaune and in London, in September and October* 1975. *And, two years later: pale, quick maturing; very forward* Pinot *nose; light, soft, pleasant enough.* Last tasted October 1977 **
Chambertin, *Hérétiers Latour* L. Latour	£81 *per dozen to the trade. Palish; little nose, quite undeveloped; dry, a fair amount of body and length. Could develop nicely.* Tasted October 1975 **(*)
Chambolle-Musigny L. Latour	*Palish, peppery, dry, slightly bitter.* Tasted in Beaune, September 1975.
Chambolle-Musigny Dom. de Villamont	*Palish; rich, attractive nose but very dry and short.* Tasted September, 1975 **
Le Corton Bouchard Père	*From Bouchard Père's own domaine: palish pink, unimpressive though attractive colour; sweet nose, a trace of Corton meatiness but comparatively lightweight. Agreeable.* At several pre-sale tastings in 1979. Last tasted March 1980 **
Ch. Corton-Grancey L. Latour	*Noted in Beaune in September* 1975: *raw and thin. More recently: pale; some meaty Corton character, but elusive and spirity; some richness, some body and grip but a shade of its usual self.* Tasted October 1977 **
Corton, Renardes Blanchard de Cordambles	*Deepish colour, slightly plummy, maturing; a curious, artificial bouquet, with some fruit; assertive but short, sweet yet with a hard blunt end.* Tasted October 1978 *
Côte de Nuits Villages Bouchard Père	*Curious how so many burgundies shipped to the United States have a supplementary* tête de cuvée *or* 1ère cuvée *on the label, for extra reassurance I suppose. This was a* 1ère cuvée: *incredibly pale, almost rosé; no nose; dry, light, little to it. So what the* 2me *and other* cuvées *were like one dreads to think—a sort of Mateus rosé? And only* $100 *per case.* At a Heublein pre-sale tasting, May 1978.
Gevrey-Chambertin André Morey	*Palish, mature; little nose; sweet, flavoury.* Tasted November 1979 **
Grands-Echézeaux Dom. de la Romanée-Conti	*At the domaine in September* 1975: *palish; light, fruity, undeveloped nose; medium dry, fairly lightweight, fruity. And at the Under 40s Club: palish, pink, with weak watery rim; light, fragrant but slightly stewed nose; distinctly dry and edgy, with thin dry finish.* Last tasted June 1977 *(*) Big question: will it blossom?
Grands-Echézeaux Dom. de Villamont	*Palish, maturing; dry, not bad but not as rich as the '72.* Tasted September 1975 **
Mercurey Nicolas	*A notable, attractive little wine in the* Pinot Noir *section of Gault-Millau's notorious wine* Olympiade *in Paris. Attractive garnet red; bouquet fragrant, a little stalky, nice quality but light; some body, elegant, very flavoury, citrus-like refreshing acidity, but a bit raw.* Tasted June 1979 **
Nuits St-Georges, *Argillières*	*Pretty colour, medium, still youthful; lovely, gentle, fragrant, rooty* Pinot *nose; lovely flavour, surprisingly powerful for a '73, rich, firm, but with a dry, slightly bitter, finish.* At the Leroy tasting, September 1979 **(*)

Nuits St-Georges, Clos des Corvées	*Similar colour to the Argillières; nose rather unknit and medicinal; rich, fullish, slightly better balance.* Tasted September 1979 ★★★
Richebourg Dom. de la Romanée-Conti	*Medium pale, pink tinged; nose not special; dry, doing its best, a little flavour opening up in the mouth.* Tasted June 1977 ★★
Romanée-Conti Dom. de la Romanée-Conti	*Very pale, mature for its age; stewed Pinot aroma and flavour; some richness, lightish, making an effort to spread its flavour — a peacock's tail with quite a few feathers missing. Peaky. Being an eternal optimist, I feel that this could hold and develop with bottle-age. But. . . .* Tasted June 1977 ★(★★)?
Romanée St-Vivant L. Latour	*Some fruit; quite nice, some richness, loose-knit, dry finish.* Tasted September 1975 ★★
Romanée St-Vivant Dom. de la Romanée-Conti	*Palish, pretty colour; slightly sweet, light and fragrant bouquet supported by quite nice fruit; medium body, very flavoury, sweet overall — on entry, in middle and on finish, though some good end grip.* At John Holt's tasting of domaine wines, March 1980 ★★(★) Drink now — 1986.
Savigny-les-Beaune, Le Village Dom. de Villamont	*Palish; light, scented, chocolaty nose; dry, light, good flavour and surprising length for its class and year.* At de Villamont's, September 1975 ★★★
La Tâche Dom. de la Romanée-Conti	*First tasted in June 1977: undeveloped nose; dry, lightish and quite flavoury but overall unimpressive, the finish slightly spoiled by immature bitterness. Recently: developed more colour, deeper and browner than the Romanée St-Vivant; a very appealing bouquet, broad, open, fragrant Pinot; drier than the St-Vivant, lighter in style and very flavoury, gentle fruit and an attractive aftertaste. Extraordinary how these domaine wines can suddenly blossom.* Last tasted March 1980 ★★★ Drink now — 1988.
Volnay T. Bassot	*From the Malmaison Club: palish but pretty colour; rather gently sweet, marshmallow nose; dryish lightweight but firm and with some tannin. Stylish.* Tasted at Imperial College, October 1978 ★★
Volnay, 1er cru L. Latour	*At a trade tasting in London: palish; light and thin.* Tasted October 1975 ★
Volnay, Fremiets, Clos Rougeotte Bouchard Père	*Palish, completely mature looking but good legs; a lightly singed/charred Pinot aroma, very harmonious and attractive; medium dry, medium-light body, soft, lovely flavour.* Tasted March 1978 ★★★
Vosne-Romanée, 1er cru L. Latour	*Very pale; no nose; dry, austere.* Tasted October 1975 ★

1974 ★

Dull, ungracious wines, lacking essential balance. Climate: a mild early spring punctuated by frosts. Difficult flowering in June; warm and sunny in July and August. Intermittent rain in September with snow in the Montagnes de Beaujolais — coldest for many years. Harvest from 21 September in cold, wet, gusty weather. Market: optimistically described by one burgundy importer as "the sixth good vintage in a row ... the wines were perhaps a little tired by the rough vintage weather". He went on to say that it could be described as "a good commercial vintage, varying between good and not-so-good qualities of quick maturing wines, priced accordingly". At the Hospices auction in November, prices were 25 per cent down, with virtually no overseas purchasers. It was a gloomy time. There was no great rush to buy, for the recession was biting deep. In March 1975, Bouchard Aîné reported that "the growers of the Côtes de Beaune and Nuits have in their cellars not only the 1974, but also large amounts of the

1973s. Despite this prices remain the same, mainly because production costs and taxes are up and they have money in reserve." Surpluses have now been mopped up, but it is a poorly regarded vintage in the eyes of the fine-wine world. Assessment: a dingy, mainly depressing vintage. Probably worth shopping around, buying odd bottles and snapping them up if they are decent and inexpensive. Tasting notes: at this stage I must state quite plainly that the paucity of my notes does not indicate my lack of interest, nor is it just indicative of the lack of interest in this vintage by the trade but, as I have said before, mainly because my business lies in mature, older and rarer wines and few '74s came into the saleroom in the late 1970s.

Beaune, Grèves P-Y Masson	*Three dreary notes: pale and feeble; cheesy; raw, charmless —* *oh dear!* Tasted twice, in April and November 1978.
Corton, Maréchaudes Doudet-Naudin	*Made by their* méthode ancienne: *deepish colour; rather stalky* *nose and flavour, but not bad.* Tasted May 1975 ⋆
Echézeaux P-Y Masson	*About the best of a tinny, acidic group of depressing quality.* Tasted *at two sessions a fortnight apart in April 1978.*
Echézeaux Dom. de la Romanée-Conti	*Quite deep in colour, very brown; not much fruit but clean; unknit, touch of fleeting sweetness at first but overall dry and devoid of charm.* At John Holt's domaine tasting, March 1980. Drink up.
Gevrey-Chambertin, Combottes Dujac	*One of a range of flavoury wines that demonstrate what an alert and conscientious young wine maker can do with selected grapes from the best vineyard sites even in a severely handicapped vintage. Tasted in cask: delicious flavour and aftertaste. Highish acidity.* September 1975 (⋆⋆)
Monthélie, Duresses Ropiteau	*Very pale; no nose; insignificant.* Tasted May 1979.
Nuits St-Georges, Pruliers	*One of the tremendous benefits of a tasting like Mme Bize-Leroy's, comparing nearly 40 wines, all of similar standing and from the same district, and spanning half a century, is the way each vintage stands out clearly in perspective. This, the first of the pair of '74s, was deep coloured; a curious, light, peppery closed-up nose, with a touch of volatile acidity; some richness, but stalky and raw, with acidity confirmed on the end taste.* Tasted September 1979.
Nuits St-Georges, Richemone	*Paler colour, but also hard, closed up and peppery on the nose, though with some fragrance; dry, better balance than the Pruliers, but with a raw edge.* At the Leroy tasting, September 1979 ⋆
Nuits St-Georges, Vaucrains Blanchard de Cordambles	*Palish, very mature, little red, more of a tawny hue; sweet, plausible nose; a bit feeble on the palate.* Tasted October 1978 ⋆
Pernand-Vergelesses Doudet-Naudin	Méthode ancienne: *fairly deep coloured; very nice meaty wine.* Tasted May 1975 ⋆⋆
Pommard, Chanlains Ropiteau	*Medium pale, plum coloured; sugary, jammy, yet a touch of hardness. Unappealing.* Tasted May 1979.
Pommard, Jarollières H. Boillot	*Palish, plum coloured; stewed chaptalized nose; slightly sweet, plausible flavoury* Pinot, *unbalanced and uneven but quite attractive.* Tasted October 1978 ⋆⋆ Drink up.
Richebourg Dom. de la Romanée-Conti	*Best, pinkest of the four domaine '74s, not as deep brown; gentle, fragrant, slightly gingery nose; nice vinosity. Outstandingly the best of a poorish group.* At the domaine tasting, March 1980 ⋆⋆⋆ Drink now — 1986.

Clos de la Roche *Dujac*	*Still gassy in cask, but basically delicious and fragrant, with a good aftertaste. Interesting to see development.* Tasted September 1975 *(★★)*
Romanée St-Vivant *Dom. de la Romanée-Conti*	*Rich colour, fully mature, rather brown; overmature nose, some fruit though, developed quite well; dry and raw though with not bad consistency. Could improve slightly.* At the domaine tasting, March 1980 ★(★) Drink now — 1985.
La Tâche *Dom. de la Romanée-Conti*	*Deeper colour than the St-Vivant; curious singed nose, some fragrance, trying hard; medium dryness and body, slightly pasty/acidic texture and finish.* At the domaine tasting, March 1980 ★ Drink up.

1975 ★

The worst vintage since 1968. Poor, thin, rotten wines. Climate: marvellous weather late spring and early summer; hot at end of July, otherwise mixed conditions including hail in July/August. Stormy, wet and humid end of August to early September, followed by cooler, drier weather. Widespread rot. Picking began 25 September. The crop was two-thirds of the 1974 vintage and half the size of the 1973 vintage. Market: 1974/75 witnessed the lowest ebb of business activity for a long period. The French domestic market was depressed and exports suffered from the worldwide recession. The variability of quality seemed, in early 1976, to be irrelevant. Indeed, whilst there was some movement of stock in the lower price ranges, fine-wine sales were virtually static. In 1977 the trade press reported that "the 1975 vintage is not generally shown to visitors in Burgundy". A grim endorsement of quality. Tasting notes: the last sentence is certainly borne out by my paucity of notes. I have precisely fourteen notes, five on the Domaine de la Romanée-Conti, where they picked late, two being on beaujolais and the rest on wines of no importance.

Côte de Beaune Villages	*On this occasion I am not prepared to mention the shipper's name. To be frank, I am not overly impressed with this firm's wines at the best of times but their '75s reached rock bottom: this had a peculiar dirty-stables nose and taste, slightly oxidized. Horrid. A second bottle two weeks later was woody and overacid. Desecrates the name of burgundy.* Tasted April 1978.
Echézeaux	*The same shipper. Curious colour, both brown and purple; acetic nose; thin, tinny acidity. Another bottle later in the month not too bad.* Tasted April 1978.
Echézeaux *Dom. de la Romanée-Conti*	*Nice, clean cut, similar depth of colour to the '76 Echézeaux; sweet, slightly caramelly chaptalized nose, quick maturing; slightly sweet, hollow, loose-knit, some fragrance but dry, edgy finish.* At the domaine tasting at John Holt's, March 1980 ★★ Drink now — 1986.
Grands-Echézeaux *Dom. de la Romanée-Conti*	*Slightly deeper but more mature looking than the '76; subdued nose, some fruit; medium dry, better consistency but still an open-work style, slightly edgy acidity.* At the domaine tasting, March 1980 ★(★) Drink 1981–1986.
Richebourg *Dom. de la Romanée-Conti*	*Quite attractive colour, paler than the '76, more orange; open, mature, singed Pinot; some richness but not firm enough.* Tasted March 1980 ★★ Drink now — 1985.
Romanée-Conti *Dom. de la Romanée-Conti*	*Palish, mature, orange tinge; the most attractive nose of the group — like toasted coconut; dryish, the most full bodied and far more power and intensity than the other '75s. Good finish.* At the domaine tasting at John Holt's, March 1980 ★★(★) Drink 1982–1990.

Romanée St-Vivant *Dom. de la Romanée-Conti*	*Maturing, a touch of orange—never too healthy a sign; sweet, quite rich nose; open, loose-knit style, slightly edgy, dry finish.* Tasted March 1980 ** Drink now — 1985.
La Tâche *Dom. de la Romanée-Conti*	*The palest of the domaine '75s, mature looking; touch of rotten grapes on the nose, not too good; dryish, lacking firmness and grip. Does no credit to its name.* Tasted March 1980 * Drink up.
Volnay	*Palish, slightly purple, quite a pretty colour; light, jagged, high-toned nose with excess volatile acidity; dry, light, poor. Another bottle was acetic.* Tasted April 1978.

1976 ***(*)

A quite good classic vintage. Deep, firm: some long-lasting wines. Climate: fine, dry winter, without frost. Extreme heat and drought throughout the summer. Weather benevolent during early September vintage. Market: this good vintage coincided with the end of the recession in sight; the overall quality was heartwarming after its dreary predecessors. Nevertheless, after heavy buying in November after the vintage, there was a halt in the New Year with resistance to the price of fine wines, demand being heaviest for lower class burgundies. Another important change, following the opening of the autoroute, was, and still is, the very considerable increase of cellar-door sales, to the disadvantage of the traditional broker and local merchant. Assessment: healthy, deep-coloured wines, the best of which need time in bottle. Firm, flavoury, well-knit, the first true *vins de gardes* since 1971. Also at long last, many outstanding beaujolais with depth, consistency and balance capable of development like the best '59s, '64s and '47s. Tasting notes: one of the most interesting tastings was organized in November 1979 by the Institute of Masters of Wine for its members in the old cellars of Hedges & Butler in Regent Street. Other notes are from miscellaneous tastings and dinners.

Aloxe-Corton *L. Latour*	*Immature looking; rich, fruity aroma; slightly sweet, chunky. No length but good in its class.* Tasted November 1979 *** Drink now — 1985.
Beaune, Champimonts *Chanson*	*A bit raw and unknit at the time of tasting, as was Chanson's Clos de Fèves.* Tasted November 1979 *(**) Drink 1982–1990.
Beaune, Hospices, Dames Hospitalières	*Bottled by J. Drouhin. Dumb nose but inherent depth and fruit beneath; dry, substantial, positive, a* vin de garde. Tasted November 1979 **(**) Drink 1982–1990.
Beaune, Marconnets *Avery's*	*Palish, even gradation of colour, rather a weak rim; good, ripe, singed, earthy* Pinot *nose; slightly sweet, medium light in style but with its fair share of alcohol, good flavour, ending a bit abruptly. Already fully mature.* At Exeter University, March 1980 *** Drink now — 1986.
Beaune, Marconnets *Bouchard Père*	*Fairly deep colour; heavy style, rather stewed; fairly hefty but raw and unready.* Tasted November 1979 *(*) Drink 1982–1988.
Beaune, Clos des Mouches *J. Drouhin*	*Rich but with a touch of raw stalkiness on the nose; fullish body, fruit, tannin and acidity.* Tasted November 1979 **(*) Drink 1981–1988.
Beaune, Vignes-Franches *L. Latour*	*Medium, red, pretty colour; flowery, vanilla, depth of fruit underlying; good flavour, nice texture, reasonable finish.* Tasted November 1979 *** Drink 1981–1988.
Chambolle-Musigny *L. Latour*	*Firm, full, rich, nicely balanced.* Tasted October 1977 *** Drink now — 1988.
Le Corton *Bouchard Père*	*Fairly deep colour; very forthcoming, rather plausible but sound* Pinot *nose; sweet, full bodied, chunky, dry finish.* Tasted November 1979 **(*) Drink 1981–1990.

Ch. Corton-Grancey L. Latour	*An extrovert: deep coloured; lovely, rich fruity bouquet; dryish, deep, firm, good texture, flavour and follow-through. Classic.* *Tasted November 1979* ★★(★) *Drink 1982–1995.*
Corton, Pougets L. Jadot	*Surprisingly and deceptively pale and mature looking; delicate complex bouquet, alcohol, high extract; dry, deep wine fragrance masking considerable power. Tasted November 1979* ★★(★) *Drink 1982–1995.*
Corton, Clos de Vergennes Dom. Cachat	*A Moillard wine: chunky yet with some delicacy; sweet, soft, long dry but rather tapered finish. Tasted November 1979* ★★ *Drink now — 1990.*
Echézeaux Dom. de la Romanée-Conti	*First tasted in March 1979: immature and tannic. Recently: medium colour, maturing; very fragrant nose, ripening and forthcoming — reminded me of prunes and rhubarb; medium dryness and body, flavour made an immediate impact but lacking depth. Some tannin and acidity still. At a tasting of domaine wines at John Holt's, the importers, March 1980* ★★(★) *Drink 1982–1990.*
Fixin T. David	*Quite deep, purple; raw, fruity, some style, but faded a little; dry, fullish, firm, tannic, well-knit. Minor wine but good. Tasted October 1978* ★★(★) *Drink now — 1985.*
Grands-Echézeaux Moillard	*Lovely bouquet, rich tangy/earthy Pinot; dry, firm, rich, fullish, open-knit. More to come. Tasted November 1979* ★★★(★) *Drink now — 1995.*
Grands-Echézeaux Dom. de la Romanée-Conti	*Good colour; deep, rich, singed character; dryish, medium body, more substantial and positive than the Echézeaux, with length and acidity. At the domaine tasting, March 1980* ★★(★) *Drink 1983–1995.*
Hospices de Nuits, **Les Didiers St-Georges,** **Cuvée J. Duret**	*Deepish, very bright, light purple tinge, heavy legs; distinctly disappointing nose, a high-toned, whole-fruit, macération carbonique type of aroma; lightweight style, but fair body, green and unripe. The last wine in a mammoth lecture/tasting in Odense, Denmark, June 1978* ★(★)? *Drink now — 1985.*
Morgon Marc Doudet	*An example of a really well-constituted beaujolais, such a change from the pale, light and tinny specimens of recent years. Medium colour with strong purple rim; nose undeveloped; fullish style, good chunky flavour, excellent consistency and balance. Tasted at Corney & Barrow's, September 1977* ★★(★) *Drink 1981–1988.*
Moulin à Vent Marc Doudet	*The most powerful of a deeply impressive range of '76 beaujolais: an old-fashioned, deep-coloured, purple wine; very un-beaujolais-like on the nose, more of a deep Mâconnais; dry, full bodied, chunky, packed with fruit, tannin and acidity. Tasted at Corney & Barrow's, September 1977* ★★(★) *Drink 1981–1990.*
Le Musigny L. Jadot	*Fine, deep, firm colour; dry, powerful but elegant. Great length and aftertaste. Tasted November 1979* ★★★(★) *Drink 1981–1996.*
Nuits St-Georges, **Clos des Corvées** Dom. Général Gauchon	*A deep-coloured Moillard wine; most interesting aroma, cress-like with fruit under; rich yet dry finish, plenty of tannin and acidity. Impressive and unready. Tasted November 1979* ★★(★★) *Drink 1982–1990.*
Nuits St-Georges, Ch. Gris Lupé-Cholet	*Deepish colour, very bright and lively; intensely fragrant; youthfully refreshing style and flavour. At lunch with the inimitable — I nearly said formidable, but they are too charming — Lupé sisters, September 1979* ★★(★★) *Drink 1981–1991.*
Pernand-Vergelesses Chanson	*Pale; light style and appealing character, but I thought it tailed off. Tasted November 1979* ★★ *Drink now — 1984.*

Pernand-Vergelesses L. Jadot	*Most unusual and pronounced aroma, cats and crystallized violets; medium dry, open-knit, highly flavoured, still a bit raw. Most attractive.* Tasted November 1979 ★★(★) Drink 1981–1986.
Pernand-Vergelesses J. Drouhin	*Deepish colour; deep, rich bouquet, with similar violets overtone; a bigger wine than Jadot's, very attractive, flavoury.* Tasted November 1979 ★★★ Drink now — 1985.
Pommard J. Drouhin	*Medium-deep ruby colour; sweet nose, more meaty than the Volnay of d'Angerville; lightish, lovely* Pinot *flavour, dry finish.* Tasted November 1979 ★★★ Drink now — 1986.
Pommard, Epenots L. Latour	*One of the nicest '76s at a Louis Latour tasting in London: medium colour, immature; rich, slightly burnt* Pinot *aroma; very flavoury, packs a punch.* Tasted October 1977 ★★(★) Drink 1981–1990.
Richebourg Dom. de la Romanée-Conti	*Medium pale, the most mature looking of the domaine '76s; firm, deep, undeveloped nose; medium full-bodied, very pleasant broad flavour which fans out in the mouth.* At John Holt's domaine tasting, March 1980 ★★★(★) Drink 1982–1995.
Romanée-Conti Dom. de la Romanée-Conti	*At a small preview tasting at the Ritz Casino in London. Rather distracting surroundings and not easy to taste. Noted a medium colour, not as deep as the Echézeaux; intense, concentrated but as yet undeveloped nose and flavour; intensely rich, already with a fabulous penetrating aftertaste.* Tasted March 1979 ★★(★★★) Drink 1984–1996.
Romanée St-Vivant Dom. de la Romanée-Conti	*Similar nose to the Grands-Echézeaux, perhaps more flowery; dry, fairly austere, powerful grip.* At the domaine tasting, March 1980. Drink 1984–1998.
Savigny, Lavières Dom. de l'Ouvrée	*Alas, unimpressive and not well enough made: overhigh acidity, austere.* Tasted at the small hotel of that name, and their own wine, September 1979.
Savigny, Marconnets Chanson	*Medium colour; very appealing high-toned fragrant nose; dry, elegant, nice texture.* Tasted November 1979 ★★★ Drink now — 1985.
La Tâche Dom. de la Romanée-Conti	*Nice rich colour; good fruit; lighter style than Richebourg, elegant, flavoury but quite an end bite and good aftertaste developing.* At John Holt's domaine tasting, March 1980 ★★★(★★)
Volnay, Caillerets, Cuvée Carnot	*A pleasant Bouchard Père wine: light, immature, dry.* Tasted November 1979 ★★ Drink now — 1985.
Volnay, Champans d'Angerville	*Palish; sweet, elegant, fruity bouquet; dry, lovely Volnay lightness of style and elegance.* Tasted November 1979 ★★★ Drink now — 1986.
Volnay, Santenots du Milieu Comte Lafon	*A* tête de cuvée *wine, deep coloured; dry, very flavoury, tannic.* Tasted December 1979 ★★(★) Drink 1982–1990.
Vosne-Romanée, Malconsorts Moillard	*Deepish; rich, earthy/fruity aroma; powerful wine, nicely made.* Tasted November 1979 ★★(★★) Drink 1982–1990.

1977 ★

Better than anyone dared expect, but judgement reserved. Climate: weather conditions almost diametrically opposite to 1976: rain and still more rain; rain daily in July. But the first two weeks of August fine and hot followed by two severe thunderstorms. Sunny weather during September and through to late harvest starting 4 October. Above-average production. When first noted the wines had good colour, high acidity and satisfactory alcohol levels. Market: the growers, having sold their '76s at satisfactory prices, were in no rush to sell '77s; nor was there a rush to buy. Falling between the '76s and excellent '78s they have not been much sought after, but the better wines can be excellent value. Tasting notes: frankly I have tasted few and am in no position to advise or generalize. Once again I would remind readers that my business is with mature wines and, in any case, I feel it would be out of place to comment, however objectively, on wines forming the stock-in-trade of shippers and merchants. Two '77s noted below were tasted at the Leroy marathon and were at least in the company of Nuits St-Georges of the same class but of different vintages. They gave me the first inkling of the character and quality of this particular vintage. So, for the record:

Nuits St-Georges, Argillières	*Medium colour, very advanced for its age; very rich, ripe Pinot, a good root-like aroma; slightly sweet, medium body, leaner than the '77 Perdrix, very flavoury, rather dry, taut finish.* At the Leroy tasting, September 1979 *(**) Drink now — 1985.*
Nuits St-Georges, Perdrix	*Deeper and richer coloured than the above, and still immature looking; good rich, fresh, youthful aroma; dry, fullish, firm, good flavour and bite. Powerful. Hard finish.* At the Leroy tasting, September 1979 *(**) Drink 1982–1987.*

1978 ★ ★ ★ ★ ★

An outstanding vintage. Climate: spring and first half of summer particularly cold, retarding vegetation and flowering. The weather changed around 20 August, grapes setting at this period. The superb weather in September and October saved the vintage, the small bunches of grapes needing plenty of sunshine. The harvest started in the Côte d'Or around 11 October. A perfectly healthy crop, good alcoholic content, well coloured. Wines were aromatic from the start. Market: Edmund Penning-Rowsell's article in the January 1979 issue of *Wine and Spirit* was headed "Gold Rush on the Côte d'Or": "With fine quality but a small crop, small stocks of previous vintages and a buoyant demand, growers opening prices were about 100 per cent above 1977s at the same period. With these prices, an uncertain political and economic climate, high interest rates, it is understandable to worry about who will eventually pay the price. But if it is any consolation, there is nothing new in all this. Doubtless inflation will eventually make them seem almost cheap." Tasting notes: unusually, for I do not make a habit of touring the districts tasting young wine (the autumn is my busiest auction season), I was given several opportunities to taste a wide range of '78s in the tasting rooms of Bouchard Père et Fils and some others during a brief visit to Burgundy in September 1979. Assessment: from what I have tasted and heard, the '78s in general are immensely impressive, showing very noticeable depth of colour, richness derived from ripe grapes and the essential balance from a satisfactory blend of component parts: fruit, tannin, acidity, alcohol and minutiae which provide intense fragrance and finesse. A vintage to buy and nurse and to enjoy in five to fifteen years time.

1979 ★ ★ ★

Good, healthy, rich, prolific vintage. Climate: cold, damp and snowy winter; low temperatures in March and April delayed vegetation. Budding coincided with frosts in early May. Moderate summer with three hailstorms, one very severe in June which cut a swathe through some vineyards between Nuits St-Georges and Chambolle-Musigny. The remaining vines were healthy and the harvest was satisfactory, around the end of September. Market: an abundant harvest of good quality. Prices at the Hospices de Beaune eased an average of 18 per cent from the 1978 auction level. Assessment: at the time of writing it is too early to tell. These should be satisfactory wines.

WHITE BURGUNDY

For the purist, for the dedicated connoisseur, white burgundy is the wine that precedes and complements claret at table. I might add "for the wealthy", for the world demand for white burgundy so far exceeds its production that prices asked, and paid, are exorbitant. As with red burgundy, a hidden reason for this price surge has been the change in laws, practice and marketing: the advent of domaine bottling, the growth of cellar-door sales, the virtual cessation of shipments of quality white burgundy in cask, and the more rigorous (but by no means watertight) application of the *appellation contrôlée* laws. On the other hand it is fair to remind ourselves that wines like Montrachet have always been scarce and expensive (see vintage 1818, white burgundy).

What accounts for the demand for this dry, subtle, sometimes austere wine? First and foremost it is an excellent drink, its style, weight, lack of sweetness and refreshing acidity making it a perfect accompaniment to a fish or chicken dish. It is flavoury without being obtrusive; moreover it never pre-empts or overcomes the flavour of the red wine served after it.

White burgundy reflects the perfect union of grape variety, soil and climate and, at its best, epitomizes the summit of the wine maker's art: a dry wine that satisfies the palate with subtle flavour, gentle persistence and perfection of finish. No wine better illustrates the contrast, in intention, style, grape variety and wine making, between the French and German producers of quality white wines. Both, excellent in their own way, have a different role to play.

In the "good old days", roughly up to the mid-1950s, a great deal of white burgundy was simply called Chablis by wine merchants and in gentlemen's clubs. The demand for Chablis became so great that the genuine wine became prohibitively priced, demand faltered and the trade and consumer lost interest. True Chablis only re-established itself in the late 1960s. Since that time almost all good white burgundies have become over-priced. For example, Pouilly-Fuissé, an innocuous little wine, has been elevated well above its intrinsic worth. Other lesser dry whites have also achieved a status based more on price than real quality; districts like Montagny, for example, supplying merely nice wine at prices formerly paid for *premier cru* Meursault.

Climatic variations

As a rough and ready guide it can be fairly assumed that a good year for red burgundy was also good for white. So, for the weather conditions of any vintage quoted, please refer to the red burgundy section.

However, a good vintage for red is not necessarily a good vintage for white, and vice versa. Because of the nature of the grape, particularly in deteriorating weather situations, the *Chardonnay*, picked early, might well produce a better quality white wine in a given year than red wine made from *Pinot* grapes picked later. Conversely, excessive heat in the summer and early autumn will create an abnormally high sugar content, with a correspondingly high degree of alcohol, usually accompanied by lack of acidity. The result is an atypical white burgundy, as in 1959, 1964 and, to some extent, 1976.

Tasting notes

I have been far more selective than I was with the reds. First of all, subtle dry white wines are extremely difficult to describe and I want to avoid repetition. Secondly, the notes on wines that were impressive when tasted young and fresh 20 years ago are hardly relevant now.

That I bother to quote quite a few old vintages demonstrates how well many of the really good dry whites keep and how, like old champagne, they develop a style of their own which can delight the open minded, even if our French friends consider this yet another example of a *vice anglais*, an eccentric aberration bordering on necrophilia. Having said this, most white burgundies should be drunk whilst young and fresh. Only the Montrachet and Corton-Charlemagne consistently improve with age.

The really old vintages are listed to put the whole subject into its fullest perspective.

1770

In February, the first white burgundy to appear in a Christie's sale, Chablis catalogued as Chablet.

1775

The first mention of Montrachet and Meursault, in Christie's catalogue of the sale of the cellar of the retiring French ambassador, the Marquis de Noailles.

1794

At James Christie's biggest burgundy sale: "White Burgundy of the Great Growth of Montrachet" (32*s*. [£1.60] to 45*s*. [£2.25] a dozen).

1818

"From the M. le Marquis de Lasseny['s] celebrated estate of Montrachet which produced but two hogsheads in 1818." Fifteen dozen sold for 42*s*. (£2.10) a dozen at a Christie's sale in 1828.

1832

Montrachet "from the excellent cellar of James Watt, F.R.S., deceas'd", commanded the high price of 84*s*. (£4.20) a dozen at a Christie's sale in 1849. Half-bottles of 1804 Meursault sold for 47*s*. (£2.35).

1858–1878

These two golden pre-phylloxera decades were as good for white burgundies as they were for reds. The best vintages were: 1858, 1864, 1865, 1868, 1869, 1870, 1874, 1875.

1890–1893

The oldest white burgundy I have ever tasted was from the cellars of Château de la Fot, an imposing estate near Poitiers belonging to the Marquis de Vasselot. I turned the billiard table into a tasting bench and laid out a range of wines of this period, including Margaux 1890, Lafite 1893, a Beaune and a Corton *c*. 1890, Yquem 1890 and 1892, and Filhot and Sigalas-Rabaud 1896.
Clos de Charlemagne. Believed to be 1890 and probably bottled at Château de la Fot. Good level, original cork a bit crumbly. Excellent colour — light yellow gold, very bright; a gentle, fudge-like bouquet, smoky old *Chardonnay* aroma and flavour; medium dry, lightish, clean and sound.
Tasted September 1975 ★★★

1906 ★★★★

An outstanding vintage — the finest, if kept well, are still more than just interesting.
Le Montrachet. This was the oldest burgundy in a cellar discovered by Russell Hone near Beaune and sold at Christie's in 1978. The precise details of domaine and bottler were not known so we called it "the Quancard collection" after the name of the family firm that had bought the stock. Pure amber, deep yellow gold, bright and healthy looking; old, smoky, oak-chip, *Chardonnay*, dry leaves, nutty bouquet; a dry wine, fair body, deep meaty flavour and very long, with firm finish.
Tasted prior to cataloguing, March 1978 ★★★★

1919 ★★★★

One of the three great vintages of the decade (1911 and 1915 being the other two).
Clos Blanc de Vougeot (Jules Regnier). The first really old white burgundy I ever came across. I bought it at Berry Bros for a small dinner party at home. Amongst the six guests were Janie and Melvin Masters, a young English couple with fine palates, now well known in the United States. I decanted the wine at 5pm and served it at 9pm. It had a deepish but lively old-gold colour; great depth of bouquet, but showing some age; a big, strong, firm, dry wine. The ripeness of the grapes of that vintage was still apparent in a veiled, sweet, lightly honeyed overtone on nose and palate.
Tasted January 1969 ★★★★
Montrachet (Geisweiler). At pre-sale tastings: excellent capsules, labels and general appearance, but the wine in the first bottle had a dead brown look, an oxidized nose and was overacid in April 1972. Another, a few months later, had a deep amber-yellow colour; maderized but not bad nose; dried out and a little raw — more bones than flesh, but alive and kicking.
Last tasted July 1972 ★★

1920 ★★★

A good vintage.
Chablis, Monopole Réserve Spéciale (Guichard-Potherot). This Chablis, in a range of '18s, '19s, and '20s from a doctor's cellar in Dinard, was believed to

be 1920 and I include it to show how well an old dry white can keep. Bright but tarnished gold; nose old but with vinosity, honeyed bottle-age; very dry, lightish, a lively, piquant, refreshing but not overacid flavour.
Tasted October 1969 ★★

1921 ★★★★★

A magnificent vintage for white wines throughout France and Germany. White burgundies now getting tired and, of course, scarce.
Corton-Charlemagne (Labaume Ainé et Fils). From the original cellars, sold by the owner's widow: medium-pale amber gold; nose a bit maderized but some honeyed bottle-age; dry, fading somewhat in body but still with a good flavour and balance.
Tasted prior to cataloguing, August 1967 ★★

1923 ★★★★

Another excellent vintage in Burgundy.
Meursault, Hospices, Goureau. This was the oldest white wine in the Barolet collection, first tasted in the courtyard above the cellars in October 1969 and again just before the sale: medium pale, very bright old gold; slightly maderized and toffee-like, yet rich and not decayed; distinct touch of sweetness on the palate, rich, meaty, overmature verging on tartness at the end.
Last tasted December 1969 ★★

1928 ★★★★★

Probably the best white burgundy vintage between 1921 and 1937. Firm, nutty wines.
Chablis "Moutonne" (Long-Dépaquit). Four notes, slightly variable. All reasonably good levels despite soft crumbly corks. Pronounced yellow-gold colour, with a light, bitty sediment; nose not bad, fresh for its age, with a character that reminded me of sherry or a *vin jaune* — appley, straw-like; dry, reasonable flavour and balance. Interesting but not exciting.
From the extensive and remarkable Garvan family cellar in New York, which was shipped to London and sold in two parts. Tasted October and December 1971, April and June 1972 ★ *to* ★★
Grand Montrachet (Baron Thénard). Bottled by Berry Bros. Extremely good appearance, just one-inch ullage. Pale, excellent colour; touch of old sulphur on the nose but otherwise fine; dry, nice soft nutty flavour, dry finish.
From the Garvan cellar. Tasted November 1971 ★★★
Meursault (French bottled). "Cuvée réservée au Restaurant les Févriers." Body label, vintage neck label and cork in pristine condition. Tasted twice, first in Paris in July 1975: most characterful but I thought the nose a bit like old apples and tokay. More memorably, at lunch in the City with Peter Palumbo, who had bought some at our original sale: an amazing colour — deep, warm, almost orange-tinged amber gold; delicate, nutty, fumed-oak aroma; dry, medium body, firm, crisp, lovely old flavour and in perfect condition.
From the outstandingly good, cold, dry cellars of the Baroness Guillaume at La Bretèche. Last tasted March 1979 ★★★★

1929 ★★★★

A magnificent, soft, ripe vintage, not as crisp and firm as the 1928.
Bâtard-Montrachet. My first experience of a '29, at a

wide-ranging tasting of white burgundies in the cellars of Justerini & Brooks. Lightly honeyed bouquet; dry edged, still fresh in its way but tailed off.
Tasted August 1956 ★
Grand-Montrachet (Baron Thénard). Bottled by Berry Bros. Tasted three times, first shortly after shipment from the Garvan cellar in New York in the autumn of 1971. A long, unbranded and rather spongy cork. Beautiful colour — bright, green-tinged gold; glorious flavour spoiled by a rubbery, hen-house overtone, probably old sulphur. Better at the pre-sale tasting. But unforgettably perfect on the wine's 50th birthday: pronounced yellow colour not dissimilar to a '61 Coulée de Serrant that preceded it; exquisite bouquet, nutty, lightly honeyed, which developed in the glass — biscuits and dried mushrooms; very dry but an intrinsic ripeness, fabulous harmonious flavour, holding together well, the finish a little soft.
Last tasted at Arthur Hallé's in Memphis, Tennessee, October 1979 ★★★★★

1933 ★★★

A lovely vintage in Burgundy, still showing well in the mid-1950s. I particularly recall an attractive, crisp Chablis at tastings in 1956, and a delicious Montrachet of Lebègue.
Meursault (Labaume Ainé). The last '33 tasted. From the original Labaume family cellars: lovely bright gold colour; quite good nose; dry, light, silkily attractive but slightly unbalanced, with a slightly yeasty finish.
At the pre-sale tasting, July 1968 ★

1934 ★★★★

A very good vintage.
Meursault (Dr Barolet). One of four different '34 Meursaults in the extraordinary Barolet cellars. This one was rich and good, better than some of the individual vineyard wines.
Tasted before the sale, December 1969 ★★★
Meursault (Quancard collection). Amber; pleasant though caramelly, maderized nose; dry, very clean and attractive.
Tasted March 1978 ★★
Meursault, Charmes (Dr Barolet). I have ten notes of this wine, the first made in the courtyard of the Barolet mansion in Beaune, and showing well, a lovely wine, in October 1969. Also at the pre-sale tasting in Paris in December 1969. Then, as I bought some for office lunches, several times since, in 1973, 1974 and 1977. All fairly consistent. Most recently: deep yellow; a bland, honeyed/vanilla nose; dry, firm, not a long flavour but good acidity.
Last tasted February 1978 ★★
Meursault, Charmes, Hospices, Bahèzre de Lanlay. A Grivelet wine bought for office lunches. Half a dozen very consistent notes, mainly in 1973. The most recent: fine straw-amber colour; very sound, waxy, nutty bouquet; notably dry, more tannic than acidic, firm, clean. Preferred to the Barolet Charmes.
Last tasted July 1974 ★★★★
Meursault, Chevalières (Dr Barolet). I also bought some of this at the Barolet sale and have several notes over a period of five years from 1973: bright, attractive palish gold; good smoky nose, no decay; dry, nice body,

excellent flavour, positive and lovely.
Last tasted January 1978 ★★★★

Meursault, Goutte d'Or (Dr Barolet). I thought this was outstandingly the best of all the Barolet white burgundies of any vintage when I first tasted it in London before the sale in December 1969. Despite a wormy cork, the wine was pale, fresh and lovely. Later, at Denis Foley's in San Francisco, I thought it had aged and was more of a curiosity than a real pleasure.
Last tasted May 1975. At best ★★★★

1935 ★★★

Good vintage, better for whites than reds. Hardly ever seen now but, for the record:
Chassagne-Montrachet (Quancard collection). After the 1906, the best of the Quancard cellar white burgundies. bright yellow gold; most attractive, lightly scented oak and lemon-peel nose; dry, medium light, lovely *Chardonnay* flavour, excellent balance and acidity.
Tasted March 1978 ★★★★

Meursault, Goutte d'Or (Dr Barolet). In Paris I thought it rich and sound though showing age. The same year, in London before the sale, it was rather dull.
Last tasted December 1969 ★★

1936 ★

A minor and rarely seen vintage.
Meursault, Chevalières (Dr Barolet). Quite good colour and nose; flavoury but dry, with a slightly unclean, yeasty finish.
Tasted October 1969.

1937 ★★★★

Although this was a good white burgundy vintage little was shipped before the war. After hostilities had ceased, what little remained unconsumed was considered too old. Rather surprisingly, for I have quite a few tasting notes of '37s from other regions, I have only one on white burgundy.
Meursault (Paul Bouchard). Fairly deep coloured; some fruit; dry, quite nice but nothing special.
At a Restell pre-auction tasting, October 1955 ★

1938 ★

Average. Of little interest now.
Meursault (Viénot). First tasted in 1973: a bit beery and not too good. Showed better at a lunch at Woodrow Wyatt's in 1975: deep old gold — really looked like tea; old but sound nose; dry, nice acidity but tired. I felt that by drinking it I was putting it out of its misery. On the last occasion the cork fell in. The wine was sour.
Last tasted at an office luncheon, January 1978.

1941 ★★★

Crisp wines. Once again it was the inveterate hoarder, Dr Barolet, who provided me with the most notes.
Meursault (Dr Barolet). Straw coloured, pale for its age; good, meaty, sound nose; distinctly dry, lightish, fascinatingly youthful still — a veritable Peter Pan.
Tasted December 1971 ★★

Meursault, Charmes (Dr Barolet). Wormy cork. Palish colour; good nose — more like Chablis than Meursault; very dry, fresh but slightly astringent.
Tasted December 1969 ★★

Meursault, Charmes, Hospices, Grivault. Bottled by J. Drouhin. Remarkably youthful looking, pale straw; old but sound bouquet, developed in the glass, revealing a surprisingly fresh Meursault character; dry, very clean, good firm backbone of acidity.
From the cellars of the Restaurant Drouant-Est in Paris, April 1969 ★★★

Meursault, Goutte d'Or (Dr Barolet). One of the most outstanding Barolet white burgundies. Three notes. First tasted in the original cellar in October 1969. Next, before the big Christie's sale in December of the same year: marvellous colour, pale lemon yellow with glint of gold; lovely fresh bouquet and flavour. Dry, almost pristine condition. Most recently, under the Etienne Vergy label, also good.
Last tasted at the Heublein tasting in Chicago, May 1970 ★★★★

1942 ★★

A moderate, lightish vintage. Rarely seen.
Montrachet (Lebègue-Bichot). Unbranded, short, wartime cork. Medium-pale light gold; mature but not mellow; dry, lightish, just holding itself together. Interesting only.
Tasted June 1967 ★

1943 ★★★

The best vintage between 1937 and 1945. Well-kept wines still interesting and drinkable.
Chablis (Dr Barolet). At the original pre-sale tasting: rather deep amber; nose like cold tea; far too sweet and rich for a Chablis, and a curious flavour.
Tasted December 1969.

Chablis, Grand Cru (Dr Barolet). Despite a wormy cork and low level, far better than the ordinary Chablis. Few clients are attracted by old white burgundies so I bought some. Consequently, I have nearly a dozen happily consistent notes over a period of ten years from December 1969. Most recently, with Katie Bourke, Bill Rice of the *Washington Post* and Harry Yoxall: a pronounced yellow colour, but bitty and needed decanting; attractive, sound old smoky nose; fairly dry, rather foursquare and lacking zest, indeed a bit short, but totally reliable. More than just interesting.
Last tasted at an office luncheon, October 1979 ★★★

Meursault (Sichel). Yellow, pale for its age; rather bland nose, almond paste overtones; soft, yet lovely acidity. Very attractive in its way.
Tasted July 1970 ★★★

Meursault, Perrières (Sichel). Although I tasted quite a few '43s in the mid-1950s, I did not like them much at the time. I mention this particular wine because, at one of his own tastings in February 1955, Allan Sichel was in raptures about a wine that I merely noted as amber in colour, with a goaty nose and flavour. It was some time before I began to appreciate the qualities conferred on dry white wine by bottle-age.

Montagny (Quancard collection). Very good colour for its age, lemon tinged; clean, twist of lemon peel on nose and palate; dry, lightish, sound and refreshing.
Tasted March 1978 ★★

1944

Poor vintage. Little shipped. Not tasted.

1945 ★★★★

A hot, ripe vintage, small crop. I find it curious that only once during my days as a wine merchant did I taste a '45 white burgundy. Sir Guy Fison tells me that he managed to import three '45s in 1949, but they lasted only a couple of years on the Saccone & Speed list. The principal reason for this, he says, was government import restrictions, which were very severe up to the end of 1948. I cannot see any '45 white burgundies in my Harvey lists dating from 1955. Apart from the first mentioned, all the notes date from my post-1966 days at Christie's.

Bâtard-Montrachet Saccone & Speed	*My first '45 white: a remnant half-bottle, bottled by the firm I had just joined. I found it nutty but nearly over the hill — hard to say now whether this was due to my inexperience.* Tasted November 1953.
Meursault, Charmes French bottled	*From Claridge's, Paris, via The Wine Society: fine deep yellow gold; rich, ripe, golden, soft vanilla bouquet; dry yet rich, lovely oaky/smoky flavour, excellent finish and aftertaste.* At a pre-sale tasting, February 1978 ★★★★★
Meursault, Hospices, *Cuvée Jehan Humblot*	*A Wine Society selection, probably also from Claridge's, similar to the Charmes: a lovely fragrant wine, which opened up in the mouth.* Tasted August 1978 ★★★★★
Meursault, Hospices, *Cuvée Loppin*	*Also from Claridge's: pale, very bright, lovely colour; more honeyed than the Charmes; crisp, excellent flavour and condition.* Tasted February 1978 ★★★★
Meursault, Poruzots	*Amber gold; mild, disappointing nose, no decay but absence of honeyed bottle-age; dry, rich, tangy. Slightly drab flavour but nice acidity.* Tasted July 1973 ★★
Montrachet Grivelet	*Four notes: first at an annual Drink Tank lunch at David Somerset's in 1972. Next, at an office lunch, with Dennis Wheatley as a guest, in 1974. Again in 1976 and, most recently: deepish straw yellow, needed decanting; waxy, old oak/vanilla nose; quite rich, nutty, a bit overripe. Frankly, less than great but considerable character.* Last tasted March 1980 ★★★

1946 ★★

As with the reds, probably far better than its reputation. Rarely seen; not tasted recently.

Corton-Charlemagne Saccone & Speed	*Sir Guy Fison clearly spotted a winner here to ship and bottle. I first tasted it with him at a Saccone office lunch, entertaining customers, in March 1954, when it was 14s. 6d. (72p) a bottle. Two months later, at a tasting arranged by the department that supplied officers' messes, I noted that though it had gone up a shilling it was "most interesting and first-rate value". Full, fresh bouquet; dry, full body, nutty lingering flavour.* Last tasted May 1954 ★★★ Dead now?

1947 ★★★★

A ripe, rounded, early maturing vintage, but the very best can still be good. Tasting notes: rather predictably, most of my notes on this vintage were made in the period from 1952 to 1960. In fact the first white burgundies I ever tasted, as a professional, were '47s in my first month as a trainee with Tommy Layton: a Pouilly Fuissé and a Meursault, both Pierre Ponnelle wines, at a Circle of Wine Tasters dinner in September 1952. In 1956, I made a note of a Chablis, Vaudésir, which is of Thurber-like pretentiousness: "faint [bouquet], fine but not outspoken, dry, deceitfully good." One of the best '47s was an excellent, deep-flavoured, lovely Bâtard-Montrachet of Pierre Ponnelle that I drank at dinner with that great but modest connoisseur Leslie Haworth in Cheshire in 1957. More recent notes follow:

Bâtard-Montrachet *de Monthélie*	*Deep old gold; lovely, old smoky bouquet; bone dry, good flavour and acidity. Holding well.* At lunch at Edward Sheldon's, March 1976 ****
Meursault, 1er cru *Quancard collection*	*Good pale colour; nose a bit hard, touch of lemon; dry, rather austere, lacking* Chardonnay *character, dull finish.* Tasted June 1978 *
Montrachet *Belgian bottled*	*Bottled by J. van der Meulen. Remarkably pale and youthful for its age — bright yellow, with a hint of green; fresh, honeyed, attractive but not great; medium dry, flowery, sound as a bell.* From a good private cellar near Ostend. Tasted May 1977 ***

1948 ★★

Quite good, but virtually disregarded by the English trade. I am nevertheless surprised, in retrospect, that at no time in the 1950s did I come across one; nor have I since.

1949 ★★★★

Excellent year: supple, well-constructed wines. Tasting notes: mostly tasted and drunk in the mid-1950s. The best are still undoubtedly firm and characterful wines.

Chassagne-Montrachet *Ch. de la Maltroye*	*Deep, fine, old gold; very good bouquet, honeyed bottle-age over oak; a rich, soft wine, fine depth of flavour, very mature but charming, pleasant finish.* At lunch at Justerini & Brooks, March 1975 ****
Corton-Charlemagne *Various shippers*	*The first '49 white burgundy tasted, in October 1952, from Tommy Layton's stock, supplied by Robertson, Vilar & Watson (London shippers, long since gone): pure yellow; intense bouquet; full, gentle, nutty. Next, a rather anonymous, vanilla-flavoured specimen in 1960. Most recently, one of high quality, said to be de Moucheron's but unlabelled and with an unbranded cork: a fine gold colour; honeyed nose and fine deep flavour. A quality wine.* Last tasted February 1970. At best ****
Le Montrachet *Baron Thénard*	*Old gold; lovely, sweet, slightly caramelized nose, fading a little; medium dry, excellent warm nutty flavour, showing some age but with nice finish.* At a Heublein pre-sale tasting in Las Vegas, May 1975 ****

1950 ★★★

As in Bordeaux, a better vintage for whites than reds. General notes: a certain flabbiness and lack of length noticeable in the less fine wines. I tasted most '50s between 1953 and 1962, the most outstanding wine being a Montrachet presented at a Wine Trade Club lecture I attended in 1954 — which shows the quality the British trade took for granted in those halcyon days; also a Bâtard-Montrachet bottled by Saccone & Speed and considered "good but far too young" and "not worth 15s. [75p] now" — in 1954. I also noted the variations on the theme of Chablis: the vast difference between a *premier cru* bottled in France, and a deadly dull, London-bottled "Chablis" — both shipped by Brown, Gore & Welsh, the Bouchard Père agents. There was a pleasant, fruity, refreshing Chassagne-Montrachet from Sichel in 1955, and I noted how one year's bottle-age had turned an unsure Harvey-bottled Meursault into a very pleasant and interesting wine in May 1956. I have notes of two Montrachets tasted a decade apart:

Montrachet Laguiche	*Bright yellow gold; old, smoky* Chardonnay *nose, sweet, fragrant, with a touch of vanilla; medium-dry, assertive, almost pungent flavour leading to a powerful dry finish. Impressive.* At the Restaurant Darroze, Villeneuve-de-Marsan, July 1978 ★★★★
Montrachet, Tastevinage Dom. Jacques Prieur	*A Calvet-owned domaine. Good colour; sweet, soft, sound nose, honeyed bottle-age; medium dry, fairly full bodied, strong, rich flavour, but mellow. Just lacking the length for greatness but with a nice aftertaste.* Tasted October 1968 ★★★★

1951

Poor thin vintage. Wedged between so many good years, this was completely bypassed by the trade. None tasted.

1952 ★★★★

An extremely fine, firm vintage, widely bought by wine merchants. Tasting notes: I tasted quite a few, mainly bottled by Harvey's, for whom I was working in the period from 1955 to 1966. Most of these notes are too old and irrelevant — they range from a dull Meursault at 12s. (60p) in 1955 to a far superior Perrières at 14s. 3d. (71p), and a crisp Puligny-Montrachet at 12s. 6d. (62p). I liked neither the Avery bottling of Bâtard-Montrachet, which was fruity but acidic at 16s. 9d. (84p), nor Harvey's at 19s. 9d. (99p). After the latter I wrote: "Was it the oysters?" (What a life I led on a salary of £500 a year.) In 1957 I noted that a '52 Montrachet needed four hours to develop its nose and flavour. One of the best '52 white burgundies was a Meursault-Charmes, bottled by Berry Bros. It was turning golden and had a lovely, scented, honeyed bouquet. Dry, with good body, flavour and nice acidity, at its zenith in 1960. Somewhat more recent notes:

Chablis, Vaudésir Reynier	*From Peter Reynier's family holding in this* grand cru *vineyard. Yellow-straw colour; lovely depth and vinosity, honeyed bottle-age; dry, assertive, with marked but refreshing acidity. Perfect.* At Reynier's hospitable lunch table in London, September 1966 ★★★★
Chassagne-Montrachet, Morgeot Laguiche/Drouhin	*This was certainly not ready in 1960: a pale straw colour; somewhat restrained nose; lightish style, good but understated flavour. But two more years in bottle worked wonders: it had gained a hint of gold and the nose and flavour were well developed though still fresh.* Last tasted June 1962 ★★★
Meursault Dr Barolet	*At the original pre-sale tasting in 1969: fine, bright gold colour; age on the nose; rich flavour let down by poor finish. Eight years later, admittedly after a long journey, the colour had deepened and the nose and taste had deteriorated: an odd, stalky, woody, varnishy flavour with a poor yeasty finish.* Last tasted in Sydney, March 1977.

Le Montrachet *Laguiche*	*A group of Yorkshire's best palates, headed by David Dugdale and Anthony Hepworth, produced this at dinner, in magnum, between a century-old Sillery and a '29 Figeac. Very fine colour, golden and bright; lovely, complete, forthcoming, mature; medium dry, a touch of ripe grape sweetness, intense yet delicate, excellent acidity, length and aftertaste. Absolute perfection.* Tasted in Halifax, January 1969 ★★★★★

1953 ★★★★

Lovely wines, soft, ripe but lacking the firm backbone of the '52s. Tasting notes: this was an immensely pleasing and popular vintage both for reds and whites. A lot of bottlings (mainly English) appear in my notebooks between August 1955 and January 1961; then there is a gap. In fact, all the '53s I tasted up to July 1957 were Harvey bottled, the worst being a beery Chablis, the best a Bâtard-Montrachet, perfect in 1957, with a fragrant Beaune, Clos des Mouches, and a Meursault with a fruity, hock-like nose in between. They were, on the whole, soft, pleasant and good value, ranging from 10s. 9d. to 14s. 6d. (54p to 72p) per bottle. So cheap were they that I wondered (in 1959) whether a beautiful Montrachet of Laguiche could possibly be worth the price, then 33s. (£1.65) a bottle. What appealed to me in 1958 was a Meursault, Perrières, first tasted at the Domaine Morey, later in England: fully developed bouquet and fabulous flavour, rather a sweet wine. Also a ripe Corton-Charlemagne of Bouchard Père. But a Meursault, Chevalières of the Domaine Monnier I thought distinctly earthy, like an old German wine from the Palatinate, soapy and at death's door. In 1967 I enjoyed a Montrachet of Jaboulet-Vercherre, but I felt the quality was not as great as its name.

Meursault, Charmes *L. Latour*	*The only '53 tasted recently direct from Louis Latour's cellars: bright straw gold; a mellow, low-keyed bouquet (perhaps up-staged by the Hugel Riesling Réserve Exceptionnel '53 that preceded it); medium dry, nice weight, lovely depth of flavour — smoky Chardonnay, with positive acidity. No signs of fatigue.* At the jubilee dinner of the Masters of Wine, March 1978 ★★★★

1954 ★

Not bad, but as with the red, largely neglected as there were better vintages either side. Rarely seen. Tasting notes: I have only five notes and they are of just two wines, both Harvey bottled. In September 1956 a Chablis, which was fresh but had lack-of-sun tartness, went very yellow within a year and developed a terrible goaty nose, though the flavour was not too bad — strong, clean, with a trace of lemon (unripe grape) acidity. And, twice in 1960, a Meursault, Perrières: a plausibly attractive wine, its sugar masking its acidity. It was still positively attractive and crisp in 1962. No other '54s tasted since. I doubt if they have the balance to survive.

1955 ★★★★

A very attractive white burgundy vintage. Nice weight, well balanced, stylish. Tasting notes: I have an extensive range of notes from the summer of 1956 to the mid-1960s, many bottled by Harvey's, one or two flabby and dull, others full and flavoury, including a delicious Chassagne-Montrachet, Caillerets and some crisp Chablis. I also tasted rival merchants' wines, noting a lovely delicate Meursault, Poruzots, bottled by Avery's (and at 14s. 6d. [72p] "more expensive than ours", in October 1959). There were some beautiful French-bottled wines: a Meursault, Perrières of Morey, a delicate, beautifully balanced Bienvenus-Bâtard-Montrachet of

Prudhon, some perfect Chablis, Beugnons and Vaudésir at the domaine of the blind M. Long-Dépaquit. The following notes just recall some really outstanding wines and/or the most recently tasted. Assessment: on reflection, one of my favourite white burgundy vintages — not too heavy, not too light, more charm and less solidity than the '59s and '52s, perhaps a little firmer than the '53s. The best can still be delicious.

Chablis, Les Clos M. Febvre	*Fine colour with pale but pronounced yellow hue; mature, smoky/vanilla character. Dry. Keeping well. At a Heublein tasting, June 1979 ★★★*
Chablis, Les Preuses M. Febvre	*Pale for its age, light yellow; good nose; dryish, medium light, fresh, firm, excellent flavour and balance. The right weight, just steely enough, subtly lean but mouth-filling. An extremely attractive wine. At a Heublein pre-sale tasting in New Orleans, June 1976 ★★★★*
Chassagne-Montrachet Leflaive	*Despite the visual diversions and competition from the Oysters Rockefeller, a fine, dry, full-flavoured, stylish wine. One of my favourite growers. Dinner at Antoine's in New Orleans with David Milligan, June 1973 ★★★*
Chassagne-Montrachet Ch. de la Maltroye	*A wonderful wine: fine, bright, light gold; beautiful bouquet, wonderful fragrance; fabulous flavour — distinctly sweet, fullish. Since this tasting I have always looked out for this wine, particularly with bottle-age, which I think it needs. Tasted July 1961 ★★★★*
Chevalier-Montrachet L. Latour	*A fine wine, but so powerful that I felt it would need several years more to develop. Tasted February 1967 ★★★★*
Corton-Charlemagne Bouchard Père	*From Bouchard's own three hectares. Production in 1955: 6,000 bottles; half the normal crop. A lovely, bright, buttery yellow; tremendously rich nose but kernelly; slight touch of sweetness, full bodied (13.9° G.L. when made — an incredibly high degree of alcohol for a dry white wine), fat rich flavour, nutty. Impressive. At the jubilee dinner of the Institute of Masters of Wine, March 1980 ★★★★*
Corton-Charlemagne J. Drouhin	*Deepish yellow gold; nutty, oaky; full, ripe, soft, lovely, rounded and perfectly developed. At a Northern Wine Society dinner, April 1964 ★★★★★*
Corton-Charlemagne L. Latour	*In early 1969: still young looking; a fresh but most forthcoming bouquet — rich, nutty, honeyed; fullish, soft, rounded, plump yet with nice acidity. Three years later: deepening in colour; bouquet fully opened up, smoky; rather loose-knit but with the inimitable nutty flavour. Not as heavy as the '59, nor with the acidity of the '57. Last tasted December 1972 ★★★★★*
Meursault Dr Barolet	*Palish; pleasant smelling; medium dry, soft. Nice condition. Agreeable but lacking refinement. At the pre-sale tasting, December 1969 ★★*
Montrachet Dom. du Ch. de Beaune	*A Bouchard Père wine from an English cellar. Deepish yellow colour; completely spoiled for me by its almond-kernels smell; slightly sweet on the palate, rich, better flavour than nose but not very typical Montrachet. Like a Graves in weight and an indifferent Chablis in character. Tasted November 1979 ★*

1956

Poor thin wines, unripe, overacid. Tasting notes: only eight notes, all but two between September 1960 and December 1962, and not very encouraging: a Bâtard-Montrachet with unripe apple (malic acid) nose and a poor beery taste; a not too bad but prematurely ageing Meursault, Charmes, tasted twice, its acidity too bare and raw, and its colour swiftly deepening; and a Perrières, distinctly oxidized. The best was a Criots-Bâtard-Montrachet, which was pale, clean, with tolerable acidity but short, though only months later I noted some deterioration.

Corton-Charlemagne L. Latour	*Produced by Bruce Todd at lunch, with the '62 for comparison. Curiously, it had a similar appearance to the '62, perhaps more straw coloured; a far less pronounced bouquet; light in every way, in style and in body, but with a vestige of smoky/meaty character. Dominant but tolerable acidity. Shows what a good wine maker and a good estate can do in a poor year.* Tasted March 1971 ⋆

1957 ★★★

Quite good, firm, rather acidic but flavoury wines. Climate: although the weather was reasonably favourable for Côte de Beaune whites, it was disastrous in Chablis, the major part of the harvest, including almost all the finer growths, being wiped out by severe frosts (one of the handicaps of this northerly area) on 8 and 9 May. The vintage there, such as it was, started late, about 7 October, and ended on the 25th. Assessment: acidity either spoils or sustains. If the wines have enough fruit and a decent balance they will survive though might not develop much. Tasting notes: most of the trade, certainly Harvey's, bought '57s quite heavily, but amongst a wide variety of wines only one Chablis appears, as might be expected from the frost report above. The majority were tasted, noted, sold and drunk within five years — which is perfectly normal with dry white wines. My early notes start with tastings in cask in September 1958. Those selected were shipped in October for bottling in January 1959. The only Chablis was Long-Dépaquit's "Moutonne", a golden colour, lovely and lively in 1962. Other particularly attractive wines:

Bâtard-Montrachet Labaume Aîné	*Strong yellow colour, but pale for age; very good, ripe, smoky/oak-chip Chardonnay bouquet; medium dry, rather fat — a plump Bâtard (the wine, not the host), loose-knit, characterful. I expected more acidity.* At lunch with Len Evans in Sydney, March 1977 ★★★
Meursault, Genevrières Dolamore's	*A good London bottling: still fresh and lemon tinged; very attractive, well-developed bouquet; flavoury, noticeable '57 acidity, but good.* At a Saintsbury Club dinner, October 1975 ★★★

1958 ★

Minor wines, light, insubstantial. Tasting notes: relatively few tasted, half a dozen between the autumn of 1959 and the summer of 1961 — all innocuous wines, pleasant enough, a little acidic. A couple of nondescript Justerini & Brooks bottlings in 1968. A Bouchard Père Corton-Charlemagne (distinctly better than their '57) in 1969. All of which partially reflects, as with the reds, the fairly justified lack of interest in the vintage. Two years later, however, I tasted a wine that proves real connoisseurs have a nose for the best:

Chassagne-Montrachet, Caillerets Dolamore's	*Fine golden sheen; rich, honeyed bottle-age; a dry wine, good classic flavour and surprising length for a minor vintage.* From Sir Gerald Kelly's cellar, June 1971 ★★★

1959 ★★★

Impressively constituted wines, full, ripe, rounded, if anything lacking in acidity. Wagner rather than Mozart. As in other hot years, 1947 and 1964, for example, '59 white burgundies tended to be somewhat atypical — too sweet and too heavy — vinification being quite a problem. Louis Latour reported, however, that "our white burgundies were never better. . . . They are rich and soft, and full of what we call marrow." Who am I to argue? Assessment: not as great as one might have expected. Clearly better in those areas where the ripening sun is less often felt, which accounts for the lovely, if untypical Chablis (the sun was also unusually beneficial in the Loire and in Champagne). Tendency to flabbiness, but the few greats *are* great. Tasting notes: I have a considerable number of notes, starting with tasting from the cask in Bouchard Père et Fils cellars in June 1960, the whites all being incredibly sweet at that stage, and a large number in the tasting rooms in Bristol, where I was on Harvey's table-wine buying committee for many years. The vast majority of my notes date from the 1960s, when the wines were being bought, sold and drunk. The first broadly comprehensive tasting of Harvey-bottled '59s was in March 1961: 14 wines ranging from Mâcon Blanc to Chassagne-Montrachet, Morgeots, and varying from dry and light to rich and characterful. On the whole I felt they were uninspired. Even one of my favourite domaines, Maltroye at Chassagne-Montrachet, was (in June 1961) already rather deep coloured for its age, full, soft and a trifle flabby, and rather dull and stodgy a year later. One of the few really admiring notes in the mid-1960s was on a Bâtard-Montrachet of Louis Poirier, shipped by O. W. Loeb and drunk in January 1966 at The Wine Society Dining Club, which I was to address later the same evening: a lovely, ripe, straw-yellow colour; fine fruit, refreshing bouquet; medium dry, lovely deep flavour and satisfactory acidity. Also a couple of Hospices de Beaune, Meursault, Genevrières, a Cuvée Baudot (bottled by Bichot) and Cuvée Philippe le Bon, both good, particularly the latter (in May 1967). Quite a few were showing well in the late 1960s: a good middle-quality wine was Calvet's Meursault, tasted several times in 1967 and 1968; a Puligny-Montrachet, Clos du Cailleret of J. Drouhin (though I found the latter's Bâtard-Montrachet hollow, with no middle and not much of a finish), an excellent Meursault, Charmes (Dom. Rougeot) and a Puligny-Montrachet of L. Latour. Some '59s showing well since the late 1960s:

Bâtard-Montrachet Dolamore's	*A London-bottled 1er grand cru: very bright yellow, pale for its age; waxy and low-keyed at first, but it developed in the glass; medium-dry, straightforward flavour and condition, twist of lemon acidity.* At a Saintsbury Club dinner, October 1979 ★★★
Chablis, 1er cru French bottled	*A most attractive classic Chardonnay nose, almost like Corton-Charlemagne — I assumed this was the richness of the vintage plus bottle-age; medium dry (sweet for a Chablis), soft, smoky flavour, rich and stylish. Not a rapier-like Chablis but delicious.* At dinner with the Sichel's at Ch. d'Angludet, April 1973 ★★★
Chablis, Fourchaume A. Regnard	*Excellent: pale, still slightly green tinged; rich, scented bouquet; medium dry, rich, soft, fluffy textured, yet enough acidity. Fully mature.* Tasted April 1972 ★★★
Corton-Charlemagne J. Drouhin	*Fine yellow-gold colour; complex bouquet; medium dry, fair body and fabulous flavour — rich, nutty, oaky, ripe.* At a Heublein tasting in Las Vegas, May 1975 ★★★★
Montrachet Harvey's	*A declassified Montrachet. Straw coloured, a little cloudy; rich bouquet with a touch of vanilla (oak); dry, fullish, heavyweight in style, with a smoky/oaky flavour. Possibly a touch of oxidation.* At Harry Waugh's, June 1975 ★★
Musigny, Blanc de Vogüé	*The most outstanding '59 tasted in the 1960s. Palish, very bright, with a light golden sheen; lovely nose, rich, great style and quality;*

medium dry, fairly full bodied but neither fat nor clumsy, lovely, refined, excellent flavour and finish. Montrachet quality and consistency. At a Charrington vintage dinner at Claridge's, October 1968 ★★★★

1960

A poor vintage, not much better than 1965 or 1968, but slightly better for whites than reds. Assessment: thin, overacid wines of no interest now. Tasting notes: a couple of dozen notes only, and all made in the 1960s, from a curious Grivelet Le Montrachet in February 1962, to a woody, thin and unattractive Pierre Ponnelle/Scottish-bottled Chablis in March 1969. The most interesting wines in between:

Bâtard-Montrachet Leflaive	*Basically a good nose but sulphury; dry, lightish, not the usual firm style and quality, but nice. Leflaive's Puligny-Montrachet, Clavoillon, also pleasant, and a delicious if acidic Les Pucelles.* All tasted between February and July 1967.
Chablis "Moutonne" Long-Dépaquit	*The old wizard of Chablis managed to produce a pleasant, soft though short wine in this otherwise skinny year.* Tasted October 1968 ★
Chassagne-Montrachet, Morgeot Laguche	*Very advanced for a two-year-old: deepish gold colour; already mature nose; dry, quite good body and richness, but prematurely aged, with a dubious finish. A curiosity.* Tasted September 1962 ★

1961 ★★★★

Stylish wines, not as good as the reds, perhaps not as successful as some '62s. Market: thanks to the reputation of the '61s as a whole, to the paucity of the preceding vintage and the relatively small supply, white burgundies of this vintage were snapped up. Fewer were shipped for bottling in England. Assessment: undoubtedly attractive, and most definitely at their best in the mid- to late 1960s, but the finest and best kept can still make a rich, characterful drink. Tasting notes: as can be expected from a vintage of interest to the trade, I have quite a large number of notes, starting with shippers' and growers' samples tasted in Bristol in March 1962. Most of the wines were noted, sold and drunk in the 1960s, and I have fewer than two dozen notes since 1970. The most significant of the latter are listed first, then a summary of those tasted in the 1960s, with some notable wines singled out.

Bâtard-Montrachet Cuvée Exceptionnelle	*An Avery wine. Palish, green tinged; lovely vinosity; austere but refined, drier than and not as plump as the Ramonet-Prudhon, below.* Tasted June 1972 ★★★
Bâtard-Montrachet Ramonet-Prudhon	*First noted and admired in 1969. Three years later: deep yellow gold; rich, smoky bouquet; powerful wine, rich, well balanced.* Last tasted June 1972 ★★★★
Chablis, Beugnons Long-Dépaquit	*Attractive: pale, clean and dry when first tasted in 1965, but slightly less appealing a year later. Most recently: deepish colour; quite good nose; very dry, tangy flavour, good but age a positive disadvantage.* Last tasted March 1972 ★★
Corton-Charlemagne L. Latour	*The second best of ten wines (after Latour's own 1962): medium-pale straw yellow, not showing its nine years of age; fresh, stylish, meaty bouquet; distinctly dry, crisp and fine, preserving youthfulness.* Tasted October 1970 ★★★★

Corton-Charlemagne H. Thévenot	*At the same tasting: deep gold tinge; touch of caramel and honeyed bottle-age; medium dry, soft, rich, fully mature.* Tasted October 1970 ★★★
Meursault, Genevrières, *Hospices,* *Cuvée Philippe le Bon*	*An outstanding wine, bottled by Berry Bros, tasted twice in 1968 and later at a Saintsbury Club dinner: firm, youthful colour — palish gold with yellow sheen; excellent bouquet — charred Chardonnay, well developed yet fresh; medium dry, lovely soft smoky flavour, perfect balance.* Last tasted October 1973 ★★★★★
Montagny F. B. Bernolin	*Very yellow, attractive; extremely good smoky Chardonnay nose; dry, reasonable body, positive flavour. Easy to see why the demand has grown for this district, which was once considered to be minor.* Tasted April 1975 ★★★
Le Montrachet Laguiche	*Drunk with the '64 at a modest seafood supper of oysters, clams and stone crabs. Pale for its age, slight lemon tinge; excellent, charred Chardonnay nose, touch of vanilla, very firm; nutty flavour, long, firm and steely. Years of life ahead.* With Dr Will Dickens at the Fort Lauderdale Yacht Club, January 1975 ★★★★★
Puligny-Montrachet, *Folatières* P. Ponnelle	*Very pronounced yellow; deep, rich, honeyed (bottle-age) bouquet; medium dry, ripe, rich — a little hefty, even clumsy — with dry finish.* Tasted October 1978 ★★★
A summary of '61s tasted in the 1960s:	*In their first year the '61s showed considerable variation, some quite soft and fleshy, albeit with youthful acidity, others appley and raw. By and large they were attractive and expensive. By the autumn of 1963 the lesser wines were ripening. Pierre Ponnelle's Puligny-Montrachet exemplified the attractive fruity character, flavour and balance of the vintage. A Corton, Blanc of Avery's was light in character but full flavoured, soft and most attractive in the spring of 1964. A Corton-Charlemagne of Buisson-Larue was unready in mid-1965. Monnier's Meursault, Chevalières was perfection in the summer of 1966, and two Leflaive wines, Puligny-Montrachet, Clavoillon, and Bienvenus-Bâtard-Montrachet, were refined and elegant respectively in 1967. Also showing well, a Meursault, Genevrières of Ropiteau and, in 1969, a Puligny-Montrachet, Les Combettes of Calvet: a fine straw yellow; crisp refreshing bouquet; medium body, lovely flavour and firm crisp style, dry overall. Etienne Sauzet's Puligny-Montrachet, Les Referts was perfection in 1967: bright, palish lemon yellow; vanilla-tinged, scented Chardonnay nose; dry, clean as a whistle, positive, crisp, good aftertaste — for me a copybook Puligny.*

1962 ★★★★★

An outstanding vintage for white burgundy: wines with just the right body and acidity, flesh and crispness. A smallish crop of well-balanced wines. Tasting notes: again, mostly noted prior to 1970, and only eight notes since that date. The first '62 that made me really sit up was a Harvey-bottled Bâtard-Montrachet: brilliant yellow gold; magnificent bouquet, honey and truffles; beautiful smooth yet nutty flavour, acidity refreshing but not marked and ready for drinking in March 1965. Two wines that were perfection in 1966: a Chablis, Vaudésir, green tinged; cob-nut bouquet; very dry, clean as a whistle, perfect acidity; and Drouhin's Puligny-Montrachet, Clos du Cailleret, a most striking wine, crisp yet rather rich. Not so striking was an oily Montrachet of Comte Lafon and a surprisingly deep-coloured Chassagne-Montrachet, Ch. de la Maltroye, tasted in 1966 and 1967. Maltroye is a wine of curiously interesting character that seems to thrive on bottle-age and it was indeed much more attractive and more fully developed, soft, rich and flavoury when tasted again in 1969. A Criots-Bâtard-Montrachet of Delagrange-Bachelet, was positively opulent in 1967: deep old gold, with an intensely rich, honeyed bouquet and flavour. I wrote "full of protein . . . like a California wine" (though I had tasted few by that time). Boillot's Puligny-Montrachet, Les Pucelles, was classic, dry and austere in November 1960, and Bouchard Père's Bienvenus-Bâtard-Montrachet was lovely and perfectly balanced when tasted, from magnums, on several occasions at Christie's boardroom luncheons in 1968 and 1969. Outstanding '62s tasted in the 1970s:

Bâtard-Montrachet Delagrange	*Unusually pale for its age; excellent smoky* Chardonnay *bouquet; very dry, steely, with rapier-like elegance, lots of life.* At a Bordeaux Club dinner at Harry Waugh's, November 1974 ****
Chablis, Les Lys Calvet	*I cannot recall tasting a Calvet Chablis before, but their ordinary Chablis and Les Lys showed well.* At an extensive pre-sale tasting, April 1970 ***
Chassagne-Montrachet Delagrange	*Deepish colour, rather hazy; deep, smoky bouquet, with honeyed bottle-age; dry, medium body, attractive but showing age. Fully mature.* Tasted March 1975 ***
Corton-Charlemagne Bouchard Père	*In January 1970 I found this wine pale and bright, good, nutty, but slightly short on the finish. Only a year later; deepish yellow gold; good, rich, nutty; not too dry, medium body, an attractive wine, rich, well balanced.* Last tasted at the wine trade's annual Benevolent Banquet, June 1971 ***
Corton-Charlemagne L. Latour	*The outstanding wine at Sir Guy Fison's Corton-Charlemagne tasting, endorsing Latour's supremacy in this great white burgundy vineyard. still palish, very bright and appealing, with slight lemon tinge; a gloriously deep, nutty nose; dry, medium body, fine smoky flavour, excellent character, quality and condition.* At a III Form Club tasting, October 1970 *****
Corton-Charlemagne H. Thévenot	*At the same tasting: medium pale, straw coloured; rich, very oily nose (what Guy Fison calls "chicken"); dry but oily again on the palate. Interesting, but I did not like the style.* Tasted October 1970 **
Meursault, Perrières Renée Morey	*Deepish lemon gold; rich nose, like hot melted butter; ripeness and richness on the palate balanced by fair acidity. A lot of character but not my style of wine.* Tasted June 1971 ***
Montrachet Laguiche	*With Dr and Mrs Will Dickens in Florida: marvellous wine, seemed fully mature and at its peak in October 1975. More recently: buttery yellow; gentle, delicate smoky/vanilla, with underlying fruit; slightly sweet, medium body, lovely rich flavour with refreshing twist of acidity.* Last tasted at John Avery's, July 1979 ****

1963 **

Much better for whites than for reds; very dry and low in alcohol, but some surprises. Market: tainted with the general '63 reputation, few were bought by the trade though odd "parcels" of domaine-bottled wines of surprisingly attractive quality have been offered at give-away prices from time to time. Tasting notes: not the sort of vintage to interest Harvey's, though I have notes in 1966 and 1969 of a rather full, Bristol-bottled Meursault. The only '63s I noted at a trade tasting were a trio of attractive Meursaults of Ropiteau, in June 1966. Several more than interesting domaine wines have come my way and are still worth looking out for, if only to fool your friends at a blind tasting.

Corton-Charlemagne Bouchard Père	*From Bouchard's own domaine, first drunk with "Wog" Dela-force, at L'Ecu de France (where he was the wine buyer). He had been offered it at £1 a bottle and we both felt it was well worth buying (in December 1971). Five years later it seemed to have suffered no deterioration: fairly pronounced yellow; quite good, old smoky Chardonnay bouquet; dryish, full flavoured, rich middle, short finish.* Last tasted at a III Form Club annual dinner, January 1976 ★★
Corton-Charlemagne L. Jadot	*Deepish yellow gold; not at all bad on nose and palate; dry, nutty, but with edgy end acidity.* At Dublin airport in the company of two gourmet trenchermen, Tom Whelehan and Jim Fitzgerald, April 1971 ★★
Corton-Charlemagne L. Latour	*Palish yellow gold; open, rich, chaptalized nose; very dry (the driest of all, from 1961 to 1966), nice flavour, Latour style with added piquancy.* At the Corton-Charlemagne tasting, October 1970 ★★
Montrachet Bouchard Père	*First tasted in May 1969: fairly deep yellow; rich, vinous, surprisingly attractive nose and taste; dryish, rich and tangy. Three years later: deeper gold; nose a bit stewed; good but short.* Last tasted May 1972 ★★
Montrachet Lafon	*Very yellow; lemon-vanilla, honeyed bouquet; dry yet rich, lovely flavour and, to the surprise of my American guests, Denis Foley and Rick Sajbel, with a really lovely aftertaste.* Tasted June 1975 ★★★

1964 ★★★★

Perhaps more fair to say three or five stars, depending on your taste. Like 1959, one of those rare, rich, ripe, rather untypical white burgundy vintages, intensifying the character of the big wines like Montrachet and Corton-Charlemagne, but strangely and inappropriately filling out the leaner, steelier, Puligny-Montrachets and Chablis. Market: '64 burgundies were immensely popular and, by present-day standards, not unreasonably priced though the total raised at the annual Hospices de Beaune sale reached a new record. Assessment: although ripe, rich and attractive when young, on the whole they did seem to lack the suppleness, dryness and zest that conservative wine lovers admire. A vintage for the lusciously inclined. The best balanced and best kept are still deliciously mouth-filling.

Corton-Charlemagne L. Latour	*Although the Latour family consider this one of the best they ever made, it was way behind the '62 and even the '61 at the III Form Corton-Charlemagne tasting: still palish, very bright; the nutty nose verging on woody; dry, full bodied (a most alcoholic white burgundy), fine, but it just seemed to lack the shape and certainly the finesse of the '62.* Tasted October 1970 ★★★
Corton-Charlemagne Rapet	*First tasted in 1968: golden colour; rather opulent and overblown, and a bit too sweet. Then, at the Corton-Charlemagne tasting: similar to Thévenot's in colour; ripe, slightly oily, with a squeeze of lemon on the nose; fullish flavour but lacking zest.* Tasted twice, in October 1970 ★★
Corton-Charlemagne H. Thévenot	*Deeper coloured; attractive, deep, smoky bouquet; very dry, with an intriguing nutty/smoky Corton flavour.* At the III Form Club Corton-Charlemagne tasting, October 1970 ★★★★
Meursault L. Latour	*Consistently good. First, at Claridge's in 1969 (very yellow then), and later, in magnums, at boardroom luncheons: vanilla scented; dry, very pleasant.* Tasted throughout 1970 ★★★

Meursault, Blagny L. Latour	*Rarely are the clarets preceded by a good dry Graves at our Bordeaux Club dinners — white burgundies are the usual openers. Lord Walston hosted and produced this immediately attractive wine: yellow colour; bouquet of vanilla and honey; dry but rich, fully mature, but the flavour just tailed off, lacking end acidity.* Tasted January 1978 ★★ perhaps just ★★★
Meursault, Blagny Morin	*Tasted twice and an interesting comparison to Latour's. Pale for its age; straightforward, fresh, wet straw, charred nose; dry, smoky flavour, better acidity.* Tasted November and December 1977 ★★★
Le Montrachet Laguiche	*It is surely no coincidence that on the two occasions, far apart, that I have tasted this wine I have found it showing badly. First, at a Wine and Food Society tasting in 1968: dull yellow; partially oxidized nose; rich, but not showing well (like a wine left in a shop window, I noted). Then, from an excellent air-conditioned cellar in Florida: deeper than the '62; rather dull nose; flabby — I noted that it might have been affected by heat during shipment.* Last tasted January 1975. *Two other Montrachets, of Lafon and Fleurot-Larose, were nice but not spectacular.* Both tasted June 1968 ★★★
Morey St-Denis, Blanc, Mont Luisants Dom. Ponsot	*One rarely sees white Côte de Nuits wines and this, I think, was my first ever Morey Blanc. I cannot remember where I acquired the bottle, but I served it at dinner for Katie Bourke and Dr Louis Skinner, a leading member of The Wine and Food Society in the United States. Pale straw yellow; most excellent rich nose; medium dry, lovely flavour — with the elegance and middleweight one might expect from the area. Vinous but not nutty or fruity.* Tasted October 1970 ★★★

1965

A disastrous year. Mainly thin, meagre wines. Market: "Rot Raced Ripeness in 1965," ran a headline in the 15 April, 1966 issue of *Harpers Wine & Spirit Gazette*. No one rushed to buy. Tasting notes: I have but one note — singing, if a little out of tune.

Le Montrachet Dom. de la Romanée-Conti	*Perhaps it was the company (David Milligan, the reverse of "a Yank at Oxford", an old Etonian wine merchant, then in New Orleans, and Jackie Quillen, a highly articulate local retailer, now with Christie's in New York) and the surroundings — Brennan's, in the heart of the French quarter; perhaps it was the after-effect of my favourite aperitif, a Ramos Gin Fizz, but I found this a stylish wine, much better than expected: straw gold, lively and attractive; good, smoky Chardonnay nose that developed well in the glass; dryish, fairly light, good though short flavour, and acidity just the right side of refreshing.* Breakfast at Brennan's, January 1975 ★★★

1966 ★★★★

Dry, lean, crisp, elegant wines. Market: a keen demand resulting in unfalteringly high prices. Assessment: on reflection, one of my favourite white burgundy vintages, combining a certain austerity with fragrance, lean but not skinny — on the contrary with good, firm flesh. Just enough fat, and certainly the acidity, to keep the wine long and well. Tasting notes: I have more notes on white burgundies of this vintage than any other. Very noticeable is the high percentage of domaine, or at least French-bottled, wines, reflecting the decline of shipments in cask of the finer quality growths for English bottling and, to be fair, also reflecting the direction in which my professional interest then lay. The vast majority have been tasted within the past ten years, so I have taken a wide cross-section of notes.

Bâtard-Montrachet *J. Drouhin*	*Palish-yellow straw; a rich, intriguing, pineapple/vanilla nose; medium dry, full body and flavour, rich nutty finish.* Tasted April *1971* ****
Bâtard-Montrachet *E. Sauzet*	*A magnificent magnum to begin dinner (at midnight) following the six-hour Latour tasting. Pale and bright; excellent, smoky/oak-chip bouquet; dry, rapier-like flavour with length, firmness, and the same smoky aftertaste.* At Dr Overton's in Texas, May *1976* ****
Chablis, Les Clos	*The cellars at Ch. d'Angludet certainly contain well-selected white burgundies. A copybook Chablis: pale; crisp, smoky Chardonnay aroma; very dry, steely, delicious, subtle but penetrating smoky flavour, crisp finish.* At dinner with the Sichels, September *1973* ****
Chablis, Fourchaume *Various shippers/growers*	*Chauvenet's: steely, good and dry. Another, firm, subtle, finely scented. Both tasted in January* 1969. *And from La Chapelle-Vaupelteigne, a wine not as exciting as its name.* Tasted May *1971* **
Chassagne-Montrachet *Ch. de la Maltroye*	*Fine colour; remarkably good, almost Le Montrachet-quality bouquet; fine firm flavour and balance.* Tasted April and June *1970* ****
Chassagne-Montrachet *H. Thévenot*	*A Couvreur selection, tasted in his cellars: pale yellow; pleasant smoky nose and flavour; dry, lightish. Nice quality.* Tasted on the spot in Aloxe-Corton, December *1972* ***
Chevalier-Montrachet *Bouchard Père*	*Not very exciting in May 1971. Some nuttiness but not as good as the '67 in May 1972, though later that month I tasted it against, and preferred it to, the '64.* Last tasted May *1972* ***
Chevalier-Montrachet *Leflaive*	*Yellow-straw colour; hard, dry yet spicy bouquet with good Chardonnay aroma; dry, heavily scented, spicy flavour, yet light and elegant. A copybook example.* Tasted February *1971* ****
Corton-Charlemagne *L. Latour*	*Two excellent bottles in April 1970. Good but capable of more development in October 1970. Fine, heavyweight, in July 1971. Most recently, an outstanding opening to a tasting for college lecturers: some yellow but pale for age; magnificent nutty bouquet and flavour; deep, meaty/oaky Corton character, perfect balance and finish.* Last tasted at The Wine Trade Education Trust, July *1975* ****
Corton-Charlemagne *H. Thévenot*	*A Couvreur selection: fine yellow colour shot with gold; wonderfully perfumed bouquet with characteristic cob-nuts smell; dry, excellent nutty flavour and balance. Good acidity, lovely aftertaste.* Tasted in Couvreur's cellars, December *1972* *****
Corton-Charlemagne *Other shippers*	*Pierre Olivier's in May 1972: deep coloured; oily nose; nutty but lacking finish. Bouchard Père's in May 1971 and 1972: sulphury, sharp and dull. Later, R. d'Herville's: good character.* Tasted November *1972.*
Criots-Bâtard-Montrachet *Delagrange-Bachelet*	*Lovely lemon gold; good nutty bouquet and flavour, though too much sulphur; very dry, fine finish.* Tasted October *1969* ****
Meursault, Charmes *Calvet*	*Calvet's Domaine Poupon: very good.* Tasted December *1969* *** *Avery's: very pleasant in December 1970, but a tired bottle later.*

Avery's *J. Drouhin*	*Last tasted September 1971. At best ★★★ J. Drouhin's: pleasant, mouth-filling, but a little superficial. Tasted April 1971 ★★*
Meursault, Hospices, *Goureau*	*A Drouhin bottling shipped by his London agent for an Essex wine merchant, and consumed at lunch in Florida. Most elegant — still fresh, youthful and fruity; dryish, stylish, Chardonnay smokiness, lovely balance, nice dry finish. Travels well. Tasted January 1975 ★★★★*
Meursault, Perrières *Ropiteau* *Lafon* *Matrot*	*Ropiteau's: rather acidic. Tasted March 1971. Comte Lafon's: extremely good. Tasted June 1970 ★★★ Pierre Matrot's: lemon sheen; lovely smoky bouquet; dry, but firm flavour. Nice wine. Served with shad roe, at Denis Foley's in San Francisco, May 1975 ★★★*
Le Montrachet *Dom. de la Romanée-Conti*	*Fine colour; rich, singed oak-chip Chardonnay bouquet; dry, rapier-like, fresh, firm — but, after warming in glass and mouth, opened up full throttle with fabulous power and fragrance. Years of life ahead. Preceding a range of the finest claret at a Bordeaux Club dinner hosted by Michael Behrens, January 1976 ★★★★★*
Montrachet *Bouchard Père* *Laguiche*	*Bouchard Père's: lovely. Tasted May 1969 ★★★★ Drouhin's Laguiche: medium dry, good but not great in November 1971. Four years later: pale for its age; gentle bouquet; fairly dry, delicate, not at all assertive but with delicious smoky flavour and nice acidity. Last tasted July 1975 ★★★★*
Puligny-Montrachet *Boillot* *Ch. de Verneuil* *Albert Morey* *J. Drouhin*	*A Clos de la Mouchère of Boillot's: a straight classic style. Tasted May 1969 ★★★ Ch. de Verneuil: quite nice. Tasted May 1970 ★★ Albert Morey's: fine, classic, firm, crisp, lovely balance. Tasted January 1971 ★★★★ A Tastvine of J. Drouhin's: light style, firm enough, a little undeveloped. Tasted April 1971 ★★★ Liger-Belair's: stewed and uninteresting. Tasted April 1972.*
Puligny-Montrachet, *Cailleret* *J. Drouhin*	*Most elegant: deeper and richer than his Folatières; beautiful balance. Tasted April 1971 ★★★★*
Puligny-Montrachet, *Champ Canet* *E. Sauzet* *Piat*	*Perhaps I was expecting too much of Sauzet. Good, firm but not outstanding. Tasted April 1971 ★★★ A Piat selection: nice but a little lack-lustre. Tasted June 1972 ★★*
Puligny-Montrachet, *Combettes* *Shipper unknown*	*Conducting a comparative tasting in California, in front of a distinguished audience of Napa growers and Bay area connoisseurs. My first experience of comparing a Chardonnay from California with a French classic. It was good, but just seemed limp and impotent after the '66 Chardonnay of Charles Krug: a magnificent statuesque wine. Tasted at Narsai's, July 1971 ★★★*
Puligny-Montrachet, *Les Referts* *de Villamont*	*Lightly honeyed, nicely balanced in June 1971. Five years later: medium pale but pronounced yellow; good nose, slightly lemon tinged; very dry, lightish, clean but short, with a twist of fruit acidity. Last tasted May 1976 ★★*

An outstanding English bottling:

Bâtard-Montrachet *Bourée/I.E.C.W.S.*	*Shipped by Bourée and skilfully bottled by the I.E.C. Wine Society: marvellous colour; magnificent nose, nutty Chardonnay; some richness on the palate balanced by crisp acidity, and powerful meaty flavour and body. At Wootton, the home of Edmund Penning-Rowsell, the chairman of The Wine Society, July 1971 ★★★★*

1967 ★★★★

Better year for whites than reds. Dry, refreshing, flavoury wines. Market and notes: once again, the trade seemed more willing to pursue the fashionable '66s than the indisputably good '67s. Taking my records as the most arbitrary barometer of interest, I see I have fewer notes on the '67s than the '66s, and none since the end of 1975. Assessment: I found them distinctly appealing — much more to my taste than the fuller, rounder '59s and '64s. If I saw any good domaine-bottled '67s coming up for sale, I would not hesitate to give them a try.

Bâtard-Montrachet L. Latour	*Wonderful wine: deep; richly vinous aroma; dry, fine, full character and quality. I felt it had a five- to ten-year life ahead.* Tasted February 1972 ★★★★
Beaune, Clos des Mouches J. Drouhin	*The opening wine at a tasting of Drouhin whites given in April 1971 by Miami's principal Drouhin protagonist, Jim Redford: pale; very characterful and attractive; good fruit and finish. Later, another stylish bottle.* Last tasted May 1972 ★★★★
Chablis, Valmur A. Pic	*Pale; clean; very dry, lightish and attractive.* Tasted May 1969 ★★★
Chassagne-Montrachet Ch. de la Maltroye	*Magnificent, out of magnums, many times at boardroom lunches from 1970 to 1972. Also firm and fine in 1974. Probably at its best the following year: fine yellow colour; well-developed bouquet, a cool, elegant, steely Chardonnay; dry, fine flavour.* Last tasted February 1975 ★★★★
Corton-Charlemagne Bouchard Père	*Lemon yellow; rich bouquet — highly scented, spicy; medium dryness and body. Very nice flavour.* Tasted November 1971 ★★★★
Corton-Charlemagne Bonneau de Martray	*First tasted in October 1970. Next, as an Avery selection bottled by Remoissenet: lemon yellow with gold highlights; good nose, low keyed though rich, with vanilla; medium dryness and body, with a nutty flavour that expanded in the mouth. A bit short, but good acidity.* Tasted March 1973 ★★★
Corton-Charlemagne Chanson	*Palish; good smoky Chardonnay nose, not as nutty as Latour's; dry, reasonable body, fine flavour and acidity.* Tasted August 1975 ★★★
Corton-Charlemagne J. Drouhin	*Slightly sweet, rich, bottle-age nose; medium dry, rich, a good foursquare wine, not nutty enough and rather too light.* Tasted April 1971 ★★★
Corton-Charlemagne L. Latour	*Excellent in November 1971. Later: full coloured but still appealingly fresh and youthful; characteristic rich smoky/nutty bouquet; dry, even, austere but lovely flavour. Stylish but just a bit short and blunt ended.* Last tasted November 1972 ★★★★
Meursault Ropiteau	*Ropiteau is a respected firm in Meursault. The first time I encountered this particular wine, at the Brompton Grill in August 1970, it was pleasant and in a soberly dressed bottle. A year later it had assumed a title with a ring of confidence: "Le Meursault de Ropiteau," and a new uniform, a rather fancy bottle. The wine inside remained diffident, pleasant enough.* Last tasted April 1971 ★★
Meursault, Blagny R. Cavin	*Yellow; rich bottle-age; attractive. Cavin's Meursault Clos de la Barre also good: very yellow, stylish and flavoury.* Both tasted October 1974 ★★★

Meursault, Blagny L. Latour Lupé-Cholet	*Louis Latour's: excellent and stylish.* Tasted March 1972 **** *Lupé-Cholet's: a lovely deepish yellow gold; good nose; extremely attractive flavour and acidity.* Tasted December 1975 ****
Meursault, Charmes Chanson	*Deepish; showing some age, austere but attractive.* Tasted April 1974 ***
Meursault, Chevalières R. Monnier	*Good yellow colour; clean but undeveloped nose; very dry, nicely made and flavoury but a little short.* Tasted December 1972 **
Le Montrachet Laguiche	*Two bottles at Dr Skinner's in Miami. The first: palish, a poor bottle. A much better one followed: the nose developed in the glass amazingly over an hour or more; medium dry, fine flavour.* Tasted November 1972. At best ****
Puligny-Montrachet, Champs Canet E. Sauzet	*Sweet, rich, appealing bouquet; dry, lightish, lovely flavour and zest, much better than the 1966. Sauzet at his best.* Tasted November 1971 ****
Puligny-Montrachet, Les Combettes Ampeau Prieur	*Robert Ampeau's: most attractive, fresh, flavoury, with refreshing acidity.* Tasted December 1971 *** *Jacques Prieur's (Calvet): nice wine, dry, nutty, good balance.* Tasted June 1972 ***

1968

A bad vintage with generally thin, unripe, overacid wines. Tasting notes and assessment: fewer than 20 wines tasted; yet, as in 1963, a surprise or two. By dint of skilful chaptalization and a bit of patient nursing, one or two good growers made palatable wines. A matter of "don't shoot the pianist, he's doing his best": the notes speak for themselves. Unless you have an insatiable appetite for curiosities (as I have), they can be forgotten.

Chablis Grivelet, Laroche	*Only two tasted. Grivelet: tinny.* Tasted July 1970. *Dom. Laroche: very dry, light but quite nice.* Tasted February 1971 *
Chassagne-Montrachet Ch. de la Maltroye	*My co-directors being rather partial to Maltroye, I bought this, as with the 1966 and 1967, in magnums because it was both agreeable and excellent value. I have several consistent notes: pale colour; light but quite characterful nose; dry, stylish, a bit thin, but a pleasant, light luncheon wine.* Tasted March — October 1971 **
Meursault Michelot de Moucheron	*Bernard Michelot's: I am afraid I described the nose as "old socks". Not too good.* Tasted February 1971. *Comte de Moucheron's: not at all bad — fairly deep yellow; nose not bad, vanilla; medium dry, fairly light, quite nice but faded in the mouth.* At a III Form Club dinner, February 1971 **
Meursault, Genevrières Michelot-Garnier	*Palish; quite good nose, with a whiff of Chardonnay; dry, flavoury, not thin but a bit short. Some character.* Tasted March 1976 **
Meursault, Tillets J. Germain	*Jean Germain's selections are usually very good and it was interesting to taste this wine: a fine straw gold; very good Meursault nose; dry, reasonable body, excellent depth of flavour and, even more surprisingly, a good finish.* At Justerini's, 1971, July 1972 ***
Le Montrachet Leroy	*Another surprising example of an interesting, if not fine, wine made in a vintage of ill repute (see also 1963): a positive, clean-cut, palish yellow-straw colour, with none of the orange-brown tinges of*

a rotten wine; an agreeable oaky Chardonnay *aroma but with a touch of oiliness, doubtless sugared; dryish, lightish, quite attractive flavour. Lacking nuttiness and finish but more than interesting.* Tasted August 1978 ★★

1969 ★★★★

Firm, well-constituted, classic whites of even quality. Assessment: I had not realized until I started extracting my notes in vintage order how highly satisfactory the whites of this vintage were, and still can be. Overall impression is of firm, dry wines, lean but with flesh, perfection for everyone except those who prefer sugar and water. And so well constructed that the *grand crus* will last for years. Tasting notes: rather more notes on '69s than '67s and spread fairly evenly across the decade of the 1970s. Not a single bad wine, at worst a merely less than inspired commercial one. A cross-section follows:

Bâtard-Montrachet Clerc Henri	*A Remoissenet wine: very yellow; good nutty* Chardonnay *bouquet; good entry and "shape" in the mouth. Full, firm flavour. Fragrant end taste.* Tasted May 1972 ★★★★
Bâtard-Montrachet Jaboulet-Vercherre	*Palish; excellent, crisp, nutty* Chardonnay *bouquet; very dry, firm and steely. If anything, not yet fully mature. Should be perfect now.* With Robert Sakowitz at Tony's in Houston, October 1974 ★★★★
Bâtard-Montrachet L. Latour	*Perhaps I was being overcritical, expecting something greater. I just thought the wine quite good, with a nice smoky/oaky aftertaste.* At a III Form Club dinner, January 1978 ★★★
Bienvenus-Bâtard-Montrachet Claude Ramonet	*Deep yellow; curious bouquet, waxy — like a recently snuffed candle — and old apples; medium dry, fine rich flavour, high acidity (similar to the '73 Bienvenus). Perhaps just immature, but risky.* Tasted November 1972 ★★★?
Chablis, Clos des Hospices	*One of a hundred wines, ranging from nice to outstanding, tasted at a wine week that I conducted in Florida. The enthusiasm of the local wine lovers did not surprise me, but the condition of the wines in that hot spot did. None, thanks to air-conditioning, was less than perfect for its class. This Chablis was a good example, positive, clean, dry, with steely acidity.* Tasted March 1971 ★★★★
Chablis, Les Clos Long-Dépaquit	*A copybook Chablis: very pale, greenish tinge; gentle but refreshing nose, vanilla, refined; very dry, lightish, fine, firm, steely, subtle flavour and good finish. Following a '62 Dom Pérignon, it occurred to me how similar it was, minus bubbles.* Tasted April 1971 ★★★★
Chablis, Mont de Milieu L. Pinson	*Good colour; fresh, clean, dry, hard end. Unready, as was a Chablis, Grenouilles.* Both tasted November 1971 ★(★★)
Chassagne-Montrachet A. Morey	*Medium pale, fine colour; attractive vanilla* Chardonnay *nose; dry, crisp, lovely oaky varietal flavour* Tasted October 1973 ★★★★
Chassagne-Montrachet Liger-Belair	*Palish; good bouquet; dry, firm, classic shape and quality.* Tasted October 1973 ★★★★
Corton-Charlemagne Bonneau de Martray	*A Remoissenet wine: palish; pleasant nose and flavour, but short and no persistence.* Tasted May 1976 ★★

Corton-Charlemagne Bouchard Père	*Even in its youth, a golden yellow; rich almost fat, but without Latour's nuttiness in November 1971. More recently: very yellow, deeper than the 1970; rich, interesting bouquet and flavour; smoky Chardonnay character, touch of vanilla.* Last tasted November 1977 ★★★★
Corton-Charlemagne J. Drouhin	*Palish; slightly sweet nose; medium dry, a rich, foursquare wine but not very nutty, with a 1967 lightness of touch.* Tasted April 1971 ★★★
Meursault G. Roullot Remoissenet de Villamont	*Guy Roullot's: fine classic nose; excellent firm flavour and finish. Outstanding.* Tasted January 1972 ★★★★ *Remoissenet's Goutte d'Or: rather neutral.* Tasted May 1971 ★ *De Villamont's: sulphury on the nose; dry and nice enough.* Tasted June 1971 ★
"Le Meursault de Ropiteau"	*Distinctly better than the 1967 that I was lukewarm about: palish straw; slightly vanilla bouquet; full, dry, lightish, good, positive, buttery flavour and finish.* Tasted May 1976 ★★★
Meursault, Charmes Abel Garnier	*An outstanding Loeb selection: medium pale; bouquet almost too good to be true — fabulous rich Chardonnay; dry, nice body, broad, rich, smoky flavour and good acidity.* At the 154th dinner of the Aquitaine Society, July 1972 ★★★★
Meursault, Charmes Leroy	*Palish, star bright; very good honeyed nose; dry, fullish body and flavour, quite a bite — will keep.* The opening wine at a tasting tutorial I gave for Len Evans in Sydney, February 1977 ★★★
Meursault, Charmes G. Roullot L. Jadot	*Guy Roullot's: soft and characterful.* Tasted November 1971 ★★★ *Louis Jadot's: good colour; attractive, fragrant, high-toned nose, with a touch of vanilla, dry, medium weight, lovely flavour. Slight lemon-tinged acidity, smoky dry finish.* Tasted April 1971 ★★★★
Meursault, Perrières J. Drouhin	*Stained-glass yellow; straw nose; medium dry, fullish body and flavour. Quite zestful.* At the Tate Gallery restaurant, much frequented by wine lovers because of the enlightened pricing policy and the "no smoking" zones, January 1978 ★★★
Morey St-Denis, Blanc Dujac	*Only the second time I have had a Morey Blanc. The grower, Jacques Seysses, told me that he made it in the old-fashioned way with an old press. It was not chaptalized or racked, nor was sulphur-dioxide used. The wine had a pronounced yellow colour; extremely good nose, low-keyed, honeyed, harmonious; medium dry, medium body, quite a fat, rich wine, counterbalanced with excellent acidity.* Lunch at the Domaine Dujac, September 1979 ★★★★
Pouilly-Fuissé Ch. Pouilly	*At the Florida wine week already mentioned. Fresh, youthful, dry, light and rather ordinary, but included just to demonstrate how this perfectly nice but innocuous type of wine has, on the demand of name alone, transcended all reasonable price barriers. At the time it was overpriced at $5 retail.* Tasted March 1971 ★
Puligny-Montrachet, Clavoillon Leflaive	*A masterly producer of stylish wines — dry, lean, sinewy, with great finesse.* Tasted September 1972 ★★★★
Puligny-Montrachet, Combettes Jacques Prieur Dom. de Leflaive	*Jacques Prieur's: a straightforward Calvet wine, good flavour and balance.* Tasted September 1971 ★★★ *And an outstanding Leflaive: lemon gold, rich "legs"; great vinosity, smoky, elegant, crisply dry.* Several consistent notes in 1972 ★★★★★
Puligny-Montrachet, Pucelles Leflaive	*Absolutely my idea of a fine, dry, steely yet palate-satisfying Puligny: pale, stylish, excellent.* Tasted February 1973 ★★★★★

1970 ★★★

Variable: from dull to extremely distinguished. A tendency to softness and overrichness, some lacking acidity. Market: big production, popular vintage, high prices. Assessment: really it amounts to a matter of taste and pocket. Uneven. All but the very best now showing tiredness. Tasting notes: quite a large number of notes, revealing a far more uneven style, quality and condition than the '69. The great growers stand out like Mount Everest in a vintage like this, whereas the decent commercial wines are a little dull and some, omitted from this record, unmentionably bad.

Bâtard and Chassagne-Montrachet Remoissenet	*At an Avery tasting for the trade, a very good nutty Bâtard being offered at £279 per hogshead, twice the price of an extremely flavoury Chassagne.* Both tasted May 1971 ★★(★★)
Bienvenus-Bâtard-Montrachet Leflaive	*Medium pale, fine bright appearance; magnificently scented bouquet; very dry, combining fragrance and floweriness with a steely core.* Tasted August 1974 ★★★★
Chablis G. F. Grant Pinson A. Pic	*A Chablis Montmains bottled in France for G. F. Grant: pale, dry, fairly marked acidity.* Tasted August 1974 ★ *Pinson's Les Clos: dry, quite good.* Tasted October 1974 ★★ *Pinson's Mont de Milieu: a bit medicinal, light.* Tasted October 1974. *Pic's Bougros: pale, dry and straightforward.* Tasted February 1975 ★★
Chassagne-Montrachet J. Drouhin	*Pale, dry, excellent — less steely than a good Puligny, not as buttery and broad as a Meursault.* Tasted July 1973 ★★★
Chassagne-Montrachet, Caillerets Delagrange-Bachelet	*Very pleasant, fragrant bouquet; dry, vanilla, good flavour and acidity.* Tasted February 1975 ★★★
Chassagne-Montrachet, Morgeot Delagrange-Bachelet	*Yellow; lovely, smoky* Chardonnay *bouquet; dry, fairly full body and flavour, long dry finish.* Tasted August 1975 ★★★★
Chassagne-Montrachet Ch. de la Maltroye	*In magnum: palish; very hard and immature on nose and palate; very dry, austere. Too young; the wines of this property really do need bottle-age.* Tasted June 1972. *Probably excellent now.*
Chevalier-Montrachet Leflaive	*Good yellow colour; excellent bouquet, pure, refined* Chardonnay*; dry, magnificent flavour, elegance, subtle penetration.* Tasted February 1975 ★★★★
Corton-Charlemagne Mignon Bouchard Père	*Mignon's: pale, deep, very scented.* Tasted November 1974 ★★ *Bouchard Père's: a bit stewed in 1974. Later: fresh, green tinged, paler than the '69; hard and sulphury nose; dry, lightish, unimpressive. Their '69 far better.* Last tasted April 1977 ★
Meursault L. Jadot Avery Moreau-Fontaine Doudet-Naudin Grivelet	*Jadot's: very good.* Tasted twice, in January 1973 ★★★ *Avery's Charmes: scented, rather short, clipped, acid finish.* Tasted February 1974 ★★ *Moreau-Fontaine's Charmes, "Special Reserve", bottled by Hatch, Mansfield: unworthy.* Tasted October 1974. *Doudet-Naudin's: alas, just dull and dry.* Tasted May 1975 ★ *Grivelet's Charmes: charmless.* Tasted October 1974.
Meursault, Tillets Javillier	*Palish; good sweet nose; slightly sweet (for a white burgundy) on the palate, medium body, broad rich flavour. Attractive.* Tasted February 1973 ★★★

Montagny *P. Ponnelle* *L. Latour*	*Because of the price of classic white burgundies, Montagny has become a well-established favourite particularly in the restaurant trade. Ponnelle's: dry, pleasant.* Tasted May 1977 ** *Latour's: virtually identical — good bright colour; attractive, true* Chardonnay *aroma; very dry, straightforward, pleasant but lacking finish.* Tasted November 1977 **
Le Montrachet *Dom. de la Romanée-Conti*	*First tasted at Berek Segan's in Melbourne, March 1977. Next, curiously, preceding a Laville-Haut-Brion: very pronounced yellow, star bright; an opulently lovely bouquet, soft, smoky, snuffed-candle* Chardonnay *that gradually opened up, finally blossoming fully in the glass; dry but rich, powerful yet supple, good acidity.* At a Bordeaux Club dinner at Culham Court, hosted by Michael Behrens, May 1978 *****
Nuits St-Georges, Clos de L'Arlot *Jules Bélin*	*A rare tête de cuvée white Nuits. Very pleasant yellow colour; scented oaky/vanilla nose that developed well; distinctly dry, in fact rather swingeingly austere.* Tasted December 1977 ***
Puligny-Montrachet *L. Latour*	*Les Folatières: crisp, youthful but stylish.* Tasted April 1973 *(**) *The straight Puligny very good: palish; good nose with slight vanilla overtone; dry, medium body, firm, pleasant smoky flavour, twist of lemon acidity. Holding well.* Tasted May 1979 ***
Puligny-Montrachet, Clos du Cailleret *J. Drouhin*	*When young it seemed rather "cold", undeveloped and sulphury, though with a good long flavour.* Tasted July 1973 *(**) *Drouhin's Les Folatières: pale; ripe yet mouth watering; medium dry, medium body. Attractive, dry, pleasantly lemon-acid finish. At peak.* Tasted August 1975 ***
Puligny-Montrachet, Clavoillon *Leflaive*	*Yet another magnificent Leflaive wine: yellowish, bright and appealing; fine, rich, smoky* Chardonnay; *medium dry, full fine flavour, mouth-filling fragrance and aftertaste.* Tasted January 1974 *****
Puligny-Montrachet, Combettes *L. Jadot*	*Palish; good nose and flavour; dry, nice quality and balance.* Tasted August 1973 ***

1971 *****

Outstanding: firm, vigorous, long-lasting wines. Market: overheated and overpriced but one must relate world demand to distinctly limited production. The real thing is genuinely scarce and, naturally enough, expensive. Assessment: before I came to extract these notes and assemble them in vintage order, I was firmly convinced in my own mind that this was the most outstanding white burgundy vintage of the past two decades, certainly since 1966. Now, however, I am not altogether sure. The '69s seemed to have greater style and, certainly from my own experience, more consistency. But the better wines are really good and the best are dry, firm, with marvellous backbone and subtle penetration of flavour which will develop further. Tasting notes: a large number, arising fortuitously and not as a result of critical comparative tastings. The following are a varied selection:

Bâtard-Montrachet *Delagrange-Bachelet*	*Very appealing, golden; lovely nose, slightly vanilla; dry, refined, deep flavoured, lovely aftertaste.* Tasted October 1975 ****
Bâtard-Montrachet *Jaboulet-Vercherre* *Ramonet-Prudhon*	*An excellent Jaboulet-Vercherre Bâtard: crisp, nutty, very dry, firm.* Tasted October 1974 **** *Two disappointing Ramonet-Prudhon's: bright lemon yellow; acidic* Chardonnay *on nose and palate. Also short.* Tasted April 1978 *

Chablis, Clos des Hospices Moreau	Dans les Clos, grand premier cru. *The wine, fortunately, lived up to its rather elaborate title and pretentiously numbered bottles. Bright and appealing colour, palish, with slight green tinge; very scented, very fruity and refreshing nose, reminiscent of Sancerre; a touch of ripe sweetness, excellent flavour, good acidity, intensity and persistence. Tasted January 1974 *****
Chablis, Côte de Lechet J. Defaix	*Magnificent: deep coloured for its age — green gold; very positive cress and mint-leaf aroma; dryish, fine body, wonderful flavour and exquisite blossoming aftertaste. Tasted May 1976 *****
Chablis Simonet-Febvre Harvey's	*Simonet-Febvre's Les Clos: pale, good, straightforward, dry but with a certain softness. Tasted February 1975 *** Harvey's selection Mont de Milieu: palish yellow; remarkably rich and meaty nose; medium dry, ripe, almost fat for a Chablis. Tasted September 1978 ****
Chassagne-Montrachet Delagrange-Bachelet	*Yellow; lovely smoky aroma; dry, fine, full flavoured, long finish. Tasted August 1978 *****
Chassagne-Montrachet, Boudriotte Gagnard-Delagrange	*Very yellow; lovely Chardonnay nose; medium dry, beautiful consistency and flavour. Tasted December 1975 *****
Chassagne-Montrachet, Ruchottes Ramonet-Prudhon	*Rich, scented bouquet; dry, good flavour. Tasted July 1977 *** Morgeot: very fragrant. Tasted July 1977 ***
Chevalier-Montrachet L. Latour	*Fine rich yellow; excellent oak and fruit on the nose; dryish, fairly full bodied, fine, rich, crisp, good length and finish. Outstanding. Tasted September 1975 *****
Chevalier-Montrachet Leflaive	*Similar to Latour's but less developed, drier and more steely. I felt it needed more time. Tasted November 1975 ***(**)
Corton-Charlemagne, Ancien Domaine des Comtes de Grancey L. Latour	*Fabulous, rich, forthcoming, nutty yet refreshing bouquet; medium dry, fairly full bodied, excellent flavour, rich and extended aftertaste, in October 1976. And more recently: slightly lemon-tinged nose and flavour, developing sweet nuttiness in glass. Last tasted at Louis Latour's dinner at Boodle's, May 1978 ****(*)
Corton-Charlemagne Avery's Prosper Maufoux Bouchard Père	*Avery's: positive, fresh, with some weight. Tasted August 1973 *** Prosper Maufoux's: palish; mild, rather milky Chardonnay; medium dry, excellent firm flavour but nearer a Puligny in style than a meaty/nutty Corton. Tasted February 1977 ** Bouchard Père's: good colour; nutty nose; dry, firm and fine. Tasted May 1977 ***
Mâcon-Lugny L. Latour	*Another modest substitute for the expensive Côte de Beaune whites, from even farther south than Montagny: very pale; scented but rather ordinary; dryish, lightish, pleasant enough but hollow. Tasted February 1978 *
Mâcon-Lugny, Genevrières L. Latour	*Palish, attractive; positive nose, but with a slightly sickly sweet overtone; medium dry, medium light, very flavoury but short. Tasted December 1977 *
Meursault Michelot-Buisson	*Good colour; broad and attractive oaky nose, flavour and aftertaste. Tasted July 1977 ***
Meursault Avery's Dolamore's Justerini & Brooks	*Avery's Genevrières: attractive, soft yet nice acidity. Tasted July 1977 *** Dolamore's: attractive enough, fleshy, sound, with backbone and acidity. Tasted 1976, January 1977 ** Justerini's: very stylish. Tasted October 1974 *** Louis Latour's: extremely good in all respects.

L. Latour Mommessin	*Tasted October 1975 **** Mommessin's Les Bouchères: dry and ordinary. Tasted October 1974 **
Ch. de Meursault de Moucheron	*Copybook: attractive yellow; curiously soft buttery nose with twist of refreshing acidity; dry yet rich and elegant. Lovely wine. Tasted February 1975 *****
Meursault, Clos Cromins Javillier B. Morey	*A very dry, almond-nosed Javillier Selection. Tasted February 1975 ** Bernard Morey's: lovely deepish yellow; extremely good smoky/oaky aroma, well-developed bouquet; dry, firm, crisp. Long finish. Tasted twice, in March 1976 *****
Meursault, Genevrières, Hospices, Cuvée Philippe le Bon	*Palish; vanilla, some bottle-age but not great; dry, good nutty/smoky flavour but on a gently inclined plateau — going down. Tasted October 1977 ***
Meursault, Hospices, Cuvée Loppin	*Bottled by Caves des Batistines: rather unknit bouquet; dry, positive, lemon tinged. Nice, crisp, flavoury. Tasted December 1979 ****
Meursault Perrières Léon Oszga	*First tasted at lunch with Nigel Broackes: amazingly rich wine (in December 1976). Then at Michael Hague's after my lecture to the combined wine societies in Manchester. Remarkable colour — buttery yellow gold; strange, rich, honeyed bouquet; marvellously rich and ripe but firm, with excellent honeyed bottle-age, slightly vanilla flavour, refreshing acidity, fabulously fragrant, charred-oak aftertaste. Not everyone's cup of tea, but certainly mine. Last tasted April 1979 ******
Meursault, Tillets J. Germain	*Jean Germain's selection: yellow with gold highlights; excellent, very rich charred-oak bouquet; dryish, fine, rich, full, firm flavour. Still a bit hard. Tasted August 1976 ***(*)*
Montagny L. Latour	*Pleasant, innocuous in 1974. More recently: clean cut, quite good Chardonnay (much better than the rather neutral nose of the Mâcon-Lugny); dry, lightish, pleasant, short. Last tasted January 1978 ***
Le Montrachet Dom. de la Romanée-Conti	*Very positive yellow; nose as yet undeveloped; medium dry, fairly full bodied, incredibly rich yet austere and immature. Flavour of mint leaf and gun flint. Powerful, long, lingering. The opening wine at the Domaine tasting at Quaglino's, August 1974 ***(**) Drink now — 1990.*
Pouilly-Fuissé L. Latour	*Agreeable and unexceptional. Once (rightly) modestly priced, now less frequently seen in England due to the inordinate demand from the United States which has elevated Pouilly-Fuissé well above its true station. Tasted November 1975 ***
Puligny-Montrachet Leflaive	*In fine form: pale; very positive and attractive fresh aroma; dry and clean as a whistle. Rapier-like. Intense. Tasted October 1977 *****
Puligny-Montrachet B. Morey Berry Bros	*Bernard Morey's: pale; fragrant; dry, rapier-like, excellent. Tasted February and June 1975 **** Berry Bros: pale, crisp, very dry. Tasted several times, in 1976 ***
Puligny-Montrachet, Combettes Remoissenet Dom. Jacques Prieur	*Remoissenet's: tasted undeveloped, dry, steely. At an Avery tasting, October 1974 **(*) Prieur's: good colour; fresh, characterful nose; dry, excellent, firm, attractive smoky flavour and good acidity. Tasted with M. Poupon of Calvet at the domaine, September 1975 *****
Savigny-les-Beaune, Le Reduscal Berry Bros bottling	*Very yellow; quite nice, undemonstrative nose; medium dry, mild oaky flavour swelling in mouth. Good acidity. Tasted October 1977 ****

1972 **

Quality of the whites more even than the reds, some lacking intensity and finesse, some very stylish, some a little overacid. Assessment: an unimportant vintage though some pleasant enough wines to be found.

Bâtard-Montrachet Avery's	Palish; good clean nose; dry but still a little hard and stalky. Time might ameliorate. Tasted August 1977 **(*)
Chablis, Les Lys Testut	Pale, lemon tinged; very forthcoming nose; lightish, quite good steely dryness and persistence. Tasted March 1975 ***
Corton-Charlemagne Bouchard Père	I think this was a Bouchard wine: very pale; youthful nose; dry, crisp acidity. Performed adequately in a rarified atmosphere. At the Waterloo dinner at Christie's, September 1976 ***
Mâcon Blanc J. Drouhin L. Latour	Drouhin's Mâcon-Lugny: dry, clean and pleasant enough. Tasted November 1974 * Latour's Mâcon-Villages: a minor wine, far from home. A somewhat strained and tired rince-bouche at the Colony House in my favourite American town, Charleston. Tasted May 1978.
Meursault, Casses-Têtes J. Germain	One of several good Jean Germain selections. Casses-Têtes: good colour, lemon tinged; smoky vanilla nose; excellent flavour, nice light acidity. Tasted July 1979 *** Meursault, Tillets: zestful acidity. Tasted 1976 ** Meix-Chavaux: stylish. Tasted 1977 ** Charmes: very good Meursault nose — "like asparagus", to borrow Dr Taams' description; distinctly dry, flavoury, nice acidity. At big Christie's pre-sale tasting in Amsterdam, December 1979 ***
Meursault, Charmes L. Jadot	Good yellow hue; nose undeveloped in 1977. More recently: the nose still seemed youthful; very dry, lightish, a little austere. Last tasted January 1979 ***
Meursault, Genevrières Michelot-Garnier	First tasted in December 1975 at Harvey's. Little change after four years: distinctive Meursault yellow; rich, some oak, slightly oily nose; medium dry, lovely broad expansive flavour, rich middle, twist of lemon acidity. At Ann and Edward Hale's, July 1979 ***
Meursault, Poruzots J. Germain	Label almost as explicit as on a German bottle: Selection Jean Germain S.A.R.L. L'élevage et le conditionnement des vins fins, Négociants à Meursault. Monsieur Germain sounds rather like a trainer at the Spanish Riding School in Vienna. But I think he does select and nurse his wines very well. (English merchants were good at selecting but less good at élevage.) The wine: still palish but intrinsically richly coloured with a faint green tinge; very fresh, stylish nose; dryish on entry, crisp, elegant, smoky flavour, dry finish. Tasted September 1979 ****
Montagny d'Esgrigny	Accustomed as we are in England to Louis Latour's Montagny, it was interesting to see what is shipped to Holland. Embellished with elaborate subtitles, "le vieux château", "Domaine Laboulaye", etc., the wine was dryish, soft, pleasant. Nice but nothing more. Tasted December 1979 **
Le Montrachet Dom. de la Romanée-Conti	First noted at a trade tasting in October 1975 and struck by its style and character, with a twist of lemon in the colour, on nose and

on palate. Next, the opening white and youngest vintage served at a 20-wine dinner given by Len Evans. Although completely out-classed by over half the other wines, mainly old rarities, it showed well: palish, very bright and appealing; smoky Chardonnay aroma, nutty, with a touch of vanilla; rich flavour and firm, dryish, light end acidity. Stood up to sand crabs (and the illus-trious company) pretty well. *Last tasted at Bulletin Place in Sydney, February 1977* ★★★

Puligny-Montrachet Paul Deloux	*It is salutory to taste a wine of such ineffable dullness. It throws into perspective those with finesse and character. Tasted May 1976.*
Puligny-Montrachets, Combettes Avery's	*Palish; rich stylish nose; dry, more positive and powerful than the Folatières alongside. Tasted August 1977* ★★★
Puligny-Montrachet, Pucelles Leflaive	*Fine bright yellow-straw colour; beautifully fragrant smoky bou-quet; touch of richness, lovely flavour and weight, good dry finish. Tasted August 1977* ★★★★
Rully-Varot J-F. Delorme	*Typical of many south Burgundy whites moving up to replace the expensive Côte de Beaune wines: bright yellow-straw colour; good clean nose — vinous not varietal; dryish, light, quite a pleasant style but tailed off. Tasted December 1976* ★
St-Véran G. Duboeuf	*Deservedly famous for his beaujolais selections, Georges Duboeuf also picked a winner here from Burgundy's newest* appellation contrôlée *district, near Pouilly-Fuissé. Pale straw yellow; fra-grant, almost scented; dry, light, crisp, flavoury. Not a classic, but satisfactory and good value. Tasted November 1978* ★★★ *in its class.*

1973 ★★★★

Wines of delicacy and finesse. Assessment: Louis Latour, at his London presentation in the autumn of 1975, considered his '73s better than the '70s but not as good as the '71s. His white wines were bottled after about 15 months in wood. 1973 is certainly one of my favourite white burgundy vintages, infinitely superior to the reds, lacking perhaps the firmness of the '69s and '71s but, at its best, with an irresistible charm and fragrance. Probably best to drink up rather than keep. Tasting notes: a surprising number of notes, far more than for 1972, and almost as many as for 1971. A cross-section follows:

Bâtard-Montrachet L. Latour	*First tasted at a '45 Club dinner at Christie's in January 1978. Later the same year: very fragrant nose, some oak; medium dry, medium weight, a charming wine that opened up in the mouth. Dry finish. Last tasted at a Louis Latour lunch at The Vintners' Hall, October 1978* ★★★★
Bienvenus-Bâtard-Montrachet Thévenin	*This was a wine I bought with a III Form Club annual dinner as its first destination, in January 1979: half the members thought it was going over the hill, the other half that it needed more bottle-age. I am now inclined to the former opinion but am keeping a little back to see if the acidity will ameliorate. Tasted again in July 1979. Most recently: a fine yellow colour with faint green tinge; sweetish, vanilla and oak nose, touch of aniseed; searingly dry, good, steely, but lacking flesh and length. Last tasted October 1979* ★★
Chablis, Fourchaume A. Regnard Laroche	*A. Regnard's: pleasing. Tasted May 1976* ★★ *Laroche's: palish; good nose and flavour; dry, reasonably firm and steely. Tasted December 1977* ★★

Chablis, Montmains Bouchard Ainé	*Pleasant yellow straw; mellow vanilla nose; very dry, firm, smooth, good flavour and attractive smoky aftertaste.* At a tasting tutorial in Barbados for fellow Master of Wine George Dowglass, February 1978 ***
Chablis, Les Preuses Maladière Moillard	*From the Domaine de la Maladière: a bit yeasty in 1976. Later: a hard, but clean-cut, classic Chablis, very dry and crisp.* Last tasted September 1977 *** *Moillard's: pale; curious nose, wet grass and almond kernels; dry, light, acidic.* Tasted November 1978 *
Chablis Moreau Laroche	*Chablis-Moreau: rather ordinary and Sancerre-like.* Tasted November 1974 * *Laroche's Blanchots: attractive.* Tasted July 1976 ** *Moreau's Clos des Hospices: dry, light and crisp.* Tasted May 1976 **
Chassagne-Montrachet Delagrange-Bachelet	*A rather unknit, two-part nose, meaty, vanilla; dry, raw, less flavour than a '72 Leflaive Pucelles tasted alongside, but with a firm, nicely acid finish.* Tasted August 1977 **(*)?
Chevalier-Montrachet L. Latour	*Les Demoiselles: unbelievably beautiful at the first Latour tasting of '73s in London.* Tasted September 1975 ***** *The Chevalier, paired with the Bâtard at one of David Allan's '45 Club dinners in January 1978, was also an exquisitely fragrant wine. Later: palish yet positive yellow, still with a youthful greenish tinge; served too cold, it took time for the bouquet to develop in the glass; dryish, medium-light body and style, excellent nutty/smoky flavour, balance, acidity and length.* Last tasted November 1979 ****
Corton-Charlemagne Bonneau de Martray	*Showed well at a trade tasting in September 1975. More recently: gold tinged; rather hard and alcoholic nose, which did not develop; dry, some body, better flavour than bouquet, opened up a little. Bottle-age would improve it.* Last tasted November 1978 **(*)
Corton-Charlemagne L. Latour	*Smoky, nutty, fairly dominating a Louis Latour tasting in October 1975. More recently: straw yellow; excellent and characteristic nutty, smoky aroma which developed a delicate honeyed overtone; dryish, medium body (not a hefty wine like the '70 or '64), lovely flavour, rich yet crisp and elegant.* Tasted February and October 1978 ****
Criots-Bâtard-Montrachet Delagrange	*An outstanding copybook white burgundy of the highest quality: very good colour, slightly buttery yellow; lovely, smoky, perfectly developed bouquet; medium dry on entry, very good charred oak-chips middle flavour, dry finish and fragrant aftertaste. Like an elegant, svelte, slender but curvacious, well-bred young lady.* Tasted at the Benedict's dinner, as guest of Michel Roux of La Gavroche, November 1979 *****
Mâcon-Lugny L. Latour	*Fragrant, flavoury.* Tasted September 1975 ** *Genevrières: a thoroughly pleasant if minor wine, easy and dryish. Though less distinctive and firm, I preferred it to the '71.* Tasted December 1977 **
Montagny L. Latour	*A good clean firm statement, somewhat broader in style than the Mâcon-Lugny, but rather short.* Tasted September 1975, December 1977 *
Meursault, Clos de la Barre Lafon	*Appealingly star-bright, slightly yellow hue; delicate, fragrant nose; dry, nice weight, austere at first sip but opened up, with a nice oaky flavour.* Tasted at Saling Hall, April 1979 ***
Meursault, Casses-Têtes Ch. de Puligny-Montrachet	*A Heymann Brothers' selection: very appealing and pronounced buttery yellow colour; good nutty nose and flavour; dry, but also a little fatness, fine constitution and finish.* Tasted September 1977 ****

Meursault, Charmes P-Y. Masson A. Morey	*Masson's: yellow; straw nose; dry, flat, just not interesting.* Tasted *July 1977, November 1978. Auguste Morey's: similar colour; waxy, kernelly nose; dry, rather disappointing.* Tasted July 1977, November 1978.
Meursault, Genevrières L. Latour J. Germain Ropiteau	*Latour's: outstanding, soft, scented, nutty.* Tasted October 1975 **** *Jean Germain's: very characteristic and stylish.* Tasted October 1977 *** *Ropiteau's: yellow colour; musty/dusty nose, which I thought was the glass at first, some nuttiness; very, dry, light, fragrant, with slightly tinny end acidity.* Tasted October 1979 **
Meursault, Hospices, *Cuvée Loppin*	*"Raised" by Ropiteau and sent out into the world in numbered bottles: lovely, bright buttercup yellow; excellent nose, lovely scented vanilla; dry, lightish, delicately smoky, lemon-tinged flavour that seemed to sweeten in the mouth.* Tasted April 1978 **** At peak.
Meursault, Meix-Chavaux J. Germain	*Consistent notes in 1977. Tasted twice in 1978. Most recently: pale, bright; pleasant delicate nose and flavour, dry, lightish.* Tasted March 1979 *** Drink up.
Meursault, Perrières J. Germain	*Notable because of its fresh and curiously spicy bouquet and flavour, dry, faintly clove-like.* Tasted March 1977 ***
Meursault, Clos Richemont Durnat	*Trust Hugh Johnson, with his innate taste and enquiring mind, to come out with a stunning little wine from, for me, a rarely seen vineyard and an unknown grower: dry, charred-oak character. Very pleasant.* Tasted at Saling Hall, August 1976 ***
Montrachet L. Latour	*At a '45 Club dinner: forthcoming, fresh, fragrant bouquet; ripe, really very rich yet with lovely acidity, charred-oak flavour and aftertaste.* Tasted March 1979 ****
Le Montrachet Thénard	*First noted at an Avery tasting: far too immature and undeveloped, rather loose-knit and not particularly striking in October 1974. But the sleeping beauty was fully aroused after five further years in bottle: very bright and appealing, distinctly yellow with lemon tinge; a bit dumb at first but opened up as the chill wore off, first stage vanilla and oak, then a lovely warm bouquet, which reminded me of madeira cake; touch of sweetness, lightish in body and style, a much more immediately forthcoming flavour — smoky/oaky, mouth-filling, with good persistence and aftertaste.* At the opening dinner of a wine weekend at Studley Priory, November 1979 ****
Musigny, Blanc de Vogüé	*A problem wine: the nose more woody than oaky, not as distinguished or as distinctive as anticipated though the flavour was better. Dry, refined, but at £23 a bottle an expensive and not wholly rewarding experience.* Tasted at the Waterside Inn, Bray, August 1977 **
Puligny-Montrachet L. Latour	*Very bright; good nose; dry, steely, tingly texture.* Tasted October 1975 *** *Latour's Puligny, Les Referts: showing well, a dry stylish wine.* At a trade tasting, September 1975 ****
Puligny-Montrachet E. Sauzet	*Disappointing, and not a patch on his '76. A bit stewed on the nose; dry, medium body, a little lacking.* Tasted October 1979 *

1974 *

Thin wines, lacking body. Assessment and tasting notes: not a popular vintage, in any case it appeared on the market in a period of severe recession. Significantly, I have fewer than 20 notes, ranging from a source-withheld Petit-Chablis that smelled of glue, to the brazen charms of Le

Montrachet, with a pleasant, dry, smoky Chassagne-Montrachet, Morgeot, in between (at the quietly elegant Le Taillevent — I was too overawed to note the domaine). Unlike that three-star restaurant, '74 white burgundy definitely does not *mérite un détour*.

Chablis, Montée de Tonnerre Maladière	*Bright, crisp looking, pale yellow; scented but unharmonious, vanilla plus a trace of bitter almonds; very dry, steely, altogether too austere with its slightly bitter finish. Tasted February 1978.*
Le Montrachet Dom. de la Romanée-Conti	*A substantial proportion of the tiny production of this vineyard was liberally poured into the glasses of a host of fellow tasters, including Odette Kahn, Jeannette Yasseen, Georges Prade, Georges Duboeuf, the brothers Troisgros and other great French restaurateurs, as we waited in the balmy early autumn sunshine for the Leroy tasting of "50 years of Nuits St-Georges" to begin. The wine was easy to drink but harder to evaluate in a pre-prandial context. Its colour was a positive buttery yellow; rich yet not immediately striking bouquet, but an amazingly powerful scent hung around in the empty glass; fairly full, rich, with marked acidity but good length and aftertaste. Tasted September 1979 ∗∗∗∗*
Puligny-Montrachet L. Jadot	*Medium pale; singed oak and vanilla; dry, lightish, fairly firm, good flavour and nice quality. Tasted January 1978 ∗∗∗*
Puligny-Montrachet Leflaive	*If anyone can make a good Puligny in an indifferent year, it is Leflaive: good bright colour; good clear fresh nose; dry, lightish, nicely put together, steely, refreshing — but not a '71 or a '73. At Marti's in New Orleans, October 1976 ∗∗∗*
Puligny-Montrachet Lupé-Cholet	*Lunch at the "Côte d'Or" in Nuits St-Georges, with the Lupé sisters. Very yellow; oaky vanilla nose; surprisingly rich but a twist of overacidity. Tasted September 1979 ∗∗*
Puligny-Montrachet, Folatières J. Drouhin	*At a comparative tasting conducted for Chip Cassidy's chapter of Les Amis du Vin. More of a Meursault yellow; low-keyed at first, but developed; dry, subtle flavour (compared with the riper, more open flavour of a '75 Chardonnay of Freemark Abbey), with pasty, palate-cleaning acidity. Not the best vintage to represent burgundy. Tasted in South Miami, February 1978 ∗∗*

1975 ∗

A totally lack-lustre vintage. Short, deprived wines. Assessment and tasting notes: a couple of dozen notes from which I have extracted a representative dozen. These were all arbitrary, the wines merely noted as I came across them at table or in the tasting room. They will perhaps give an indication of the inadequacy of the vintage.

Chablis, Les Forêts Vacoret	*An unfamiliar, to me, premier cru vineyard and grower: palish; full, rather clumsy vanilla nose; dry, lightish, very crisp, slight vanilla flavour. Moderate only and short. Tasted October 1979 ∗*
Chablis, Vaillon Moreau	*Pale; good, clean but indefinable nose; distinctly dry, lightish, zestful. Tasted December 1977 ∗∗*
Chablis Various shippers	*A Montée de Tonnerre: rather undistinguished, little to it. Tasted March 1978 ∗ A Grenouilles of Loeb's: no character on nose and*

	palate, but dry and drinkable. Knowing how good Loeb's selections are, this was plainly the best they could find in a dreary vintage. Tasted July 1979 ⋆
Corton-Charlemagne L. Jadot	*One respects Jadot, one venerates Corton-Charlemagne, but in 1975 the relationship was strained: rather common nose; dry, austere, lacking style, fruit or flavour. Very disappointing.* Tasted April 1977.
Meursault Faiveley	*Palish, bright; clean but not much bouquet or flavour; dry, light-ish, fresh but a bit short.* Tasted November 1979 ⋆
Meursault, Casses-Têtes Dom. de Puligny-Montrachet	*Surprisingly agreeable: palish, yellow tinged; root-like vanilla aroma; dry, quite refined flavour that opened up in the mouth. Tolerable acidity.* Tasted August 1977 ⋆⋆⋆
Meursault, Genevrières Ropiteau	*Remarkably deep golden colour; soft, honeyed nose but trace of overacidity confirmed on the palate. Very dry, rather abrasive.* Tasted October 1979.
Pouilly-Vinzelles Charpenay	*In the Mâcon-Lugny category, an agreeable enough substitute for the more expensive white burgundies. Clean, fresh, neutral, dry, well made but minor.* Several notes in 1979 ⋆
Puligny-Montrachet Bouchard Père	*Very yellow; medium dry, full flavoured and really very pleasant if not great.* Tasted January 1979 ⋆⋆⋆
Puligny-Montrachet Eschenauer	*How a Bordeaux shipper's Puligny found its way to the Scilly Isles, I do not know. One of the many shipwrecks? Bright yellow green; some quality and firmness, but spoiled by a tainted, kernelly nose and taste.* Tasted at the Star Castle Hotel, April 1979.
Puligny-Montrachet Leflaive	*Well, not even Leflaive could do much with the '75: disappointing nose; dry, light, pleasant enough flavour but flabby, lacking essential Puligny crispness.* Tasted May 1978 ⋆

1976 ⋆⋆⋆

Pleasant, variable, some a bit soft and lacking acidity, nothing like the quality of the reds. Climate: the reason for a certain lack of success was the excessive heat and drought which force-ripened the grapes. For reds, full ripeness is highly desirable, but for whites it is a handicap. The heat creates too much sugar and reduces the acidity, the first resulting in an overhigh alcoholic content and clumsiness, and the second depriving the wine of its fresh crispness. The same problems occurred in 1959 and 1964. Judging by some of the notes that follow I suspect that some grapes were picked hastily before they became too ripe; and green unripe grapes were pulled in as well. The vintage in Chablis started on 15 September, an almost unprecedented early date in an area which is generally considered northerly, over-prone to frosts, and producing grapes that, in most years, tend to fall short of ripeness. Market: demand and prices keen. First of all the recession had ended and demand had revived; second, there had been two bad vintages and there was a general shortage of stocks; third, the '76 white burgundy reputation basked in the reflected glory of the reds. Assessment: some nice wines made, but on the whole lacking essential firmness and zest.

Bâtard-Montrachet L. Jadot	*Attractive yellow colour, green tinged; lovely, fragrant, complex nose; medium dry, nice weight, exquisite flavour, refined, fragrant aftertaste.* Tasted July 1979 ⋆⋆⋆⋆
Bâtard-Montrachet L. Latour	*Rich yellow colour; hard, youthful aroma; rich, smoky flavour, twist of (immature) lemon acidity.* Tasted November 1979 ⋆⋆(⋆)

Beaune, Clos des Mouches *J. Drouhin*	*Positive yellow green; sweet, subdued nose; dryish, medium light, lovely open smoky/oaky flavour, crisp finish.* Tasted July 1979 ★★★
Bienvenus-Bâtard- Montrachet *Leflaive*	*Pale, very bright and appealing; curious rich cheesy nose; fullish, really rather hefty wine, rich, nutty, excellent aftertaste.* Tasted October 1979 ★★★
Bienvenus-Bâtard- Montrachet *Maroslavic-Tremeau*	*Fine colour, green tinge; vanilla and lemon; dryish, very flavoury but a bit raw and unknit. Needs time.* Tasted November 1978 ★★(★)
Chablis, Grenouilles *L. Michel*	*Pale; delicate, pleasant but indeterminate bouquet; dry, lightish, firm, clean.* Tasted January 1979 ★★★
Chablis, Montmains *A. Pic*	*Palish; a bit almond kernelly; dry, quite nice, reasonable acidity.* Tasted March 1980 ★★
Chablis, Montée de Tonnerre *A. Pic*	*Pale, rather dull. My reaction was that English wine growers can do far better than this.* Tasted July 1978.
Chablis, Valmur *Vacoret*	*Fine positive yellow; refreshing vanilla aroma; very dry, not all that impressive.* Tasted October 1979 ★
Chablis *Bouchard Père* *Coron*	*Bouchard Père's: rather yellow; straightforward, ripe, a little too fat.* Tasted November 1978 ★★ *Coron's: a bit too yellow for Chablis; nose and flavour not too good. Tailed off.* Tasted May 1979.
Chassagne-Montrachet *L. Jadot* *Moillard*	*Jadot's: paraffin-wax nose; dryish.* Tasted July 1979 ★ *Moillard's: rich but unknit nose, vanilla, meaty — possibly too much cask age; slightly sweet, broad, open, lacking finish.* Tasted July 1979 ★
Chassagne-Montrachet, Les Embrazées *Albert Morey*	*Palish yellow; good, open, oak-chip aroma — reminding me of the smell of an old-fashioned grocer's shop; ripe, excellent flavour, length, finish and aftertaste.* Tasted January and April 1979 ★★★★
Chassagne-Montrachet *Ch. de la Maltroye*	*Pale; very fragrant, youthful; dry, crisp, immature. Will improve with age.* Tasted September 1978 ★(★★)
Chevalier-Montrachet *L. Jadot*	*Yellow; fragrant but still unknit; alcoholic, dryish, firm, somewhat austere and immature but good.* Tasted July 1979 ★★(★)
Chevalier-Montrachet, Les Demoiselles *L. Latour*	*Yellow; bouquet lacked harmony; dryish, steely, good flavour but curious acidity. Dubious future.* Tasted July 1979 ★★
Corton, Vergennes *Chanson*	*A Hospices wine: very attractive, high-toned, appealing Chardonnay nose with twist of lemon; dry, medium body, excellent balance, lovely smoky flavour and aftertaste.* Tasted July 1979 ★★★★
Corton-Charlemagne *Bonneau de Martray*	*Positive yellow, touch of straw gold; broad, sweet, meaty, vanilla; nutty, nice acidity, but neither fat nor long.* Tasted July 1979 ★★
Corton-Charlemagne *L. Latour*	*Appealing when young (October 1977). More recently: bright yellow green; rich, vinous, touch of overacidity on the nose; medium dry, fairly full, very positive nutty flavour and aftertaste. Still youthful. Needs more time.* Last tasted July and November 1979 ★★(★)
Mâcon-Lugny, Charmes *Cave de Lugny*	*Labelled* Pinot Chardonnay *for the varietal-conscious American market: good lemon-yellow colour; fresh, crisp; dryish, lightish, very positive flavour, but short.* In Florida, February 1978 ★★
Meursault *L. Latour*	*L. Latour's: pleasant and positive.* Tasted October 1977, March 1978 ★★ *Palish yellow; clean, pleasant; dry, medium light, attractive oaky*

R. Verdot J. Drouhin	*tang, nice acidity. Only £15 a bottle!* At the Savoy, February 1980 ★★★ *Renée Verdot's: rather immature, dry, steely.* Tasted November 1978 ★ *Drouhin's: star bright; disappointing nose, kernelly, little character; very dry, crisp but a bit meagre.* Tasted October 1979 ★
Meursault, Blagny L. Latour	*When tasted young, a bit sulphury though flavoury (October 1977). Developed well: fruity fragrant nose; broad smoky/oaky, good middle flavour, overdry finish.* Last tasted November 1979 ★★
Meursault, Charmes Guijon J. Drouhin	*Guijon's: waxy, cheesy nose; dry, flat and dull.* Tasted June 1978. *Drouhin's: medium pale, bright, appealing; rich, open, fruit-salad nose; nice acidity, stalky and kernelly.* Tasted July 1979 ★★
Meursault, Genevrières Avery	*A tête de cuvée, bottled in Bristol. Deepish colour; lovely nutty flavour.* Tasted August 1979 ★★★
Meursault, Perrières Chanson	*Straw colour; curious unknit nose — vanilla and pineapple husks; dry, high acidity, raw verging on tart.* Tasted July 1979.
Montrachet Laguiche	*Paler than expected; high toned and immature, lemon/pineapple husks; medium dry, fullish body, potentially rich but undeveloped. Good acidity.* Tasted July 1979 ★★(★★)?
Montrachet Dom. de la Romanée-Conti	*Palish, lemon yellow, very bright; touch of vanilla, fragrant but still hard and youthful; dry, firm, flavoury.* Tasted March 1979 ★★(★★)?
Pernand-Vergelesses Chanson	*Pale; light nose, touch of vanilla and refreshing acidity; dry, light, crisp, attractive.* Tasted July 1979 ★★
Puligny-Montrachet Mommessin L. Latour	*Mommessin's: very dry, slightly woody, unimpressive.* Tasted November 1978. *Louis Latour's: bright, yellowish; still undeveloped but with interesting cream-cheese nose; dryish, lightish, good crisp varietal flavour but a bit short and perhaps lacking acidity. Preferred it when young, in October 1977.* Last tasted November 1979 ★
Puligny-Montrachet, Cailleret J. Drouhin	*Lemon-tinged colour; rather curious, high-toned, fruit-acid aroma; dry, steely, a bit austere. Immature and no finish.* Tasted July 1979 ★
Puligny-Montrachet, Combettes Avery's Leflaive	*Avery's selection: rather low-keyed, good but undemonstrative.* Tasted September 1979 ★★(★) *Leflaive's: perfect appearance; deep, rich nose — more vinous than varietal; dryish, medium body, rich, positive flavour, curious light, loose end acidity.* Tasted October 1979 ★★
Puligny-Montrachet, Folatières L. Latour E. Sauzet	*Latour's: fine potential.* Tasted October 1977 ★(★★) *Sauzet's: lovely palish yellow gold; bouquet dumb at first but emerged diffidently — youthful, mouthwatering; touch of richness, smoky, long flavour, dry finish.* Tasted December 1978 ★★(★★)
Puligny-Montrachet, Pucelles Leflaive	*Palish, green tinged; undeveloped nose; lovely soft* Chardonnay *flavour, long lasting, mouth-filling.* Tasted December 1978 ★★(★★)
Puligny-Montrachet, Referts Bouchard Père	*Good colour; forthcoming, warm, open nose; dryish, positive flavour, some fragrance.* Tasted September 1979 ★★
St-Véran G. Duboeuf	*Bright; fresh, dry, lightish, agreeable wine.* Tasted January 1979 ★★
"Dom. Baron Thénard" Avery's	*Shipped by Avery's and said to be a declassified Montrachet: fragrant aroma, fresh mint leaves and cress; some richness and nuttiness. Good but curious.* Tasted September 1978 ★★(★)

1977 ⋆

Damp, dismal vintage. Pick and choose carefully. Market: despite the appalling summer and poor reports there was speculative buying on account of the small crop and the lack of stocks. Prices, striving to meet an insatiable demand, rose out of all proportion to quality. Tasting notes and assessment: as I have written more than once, I am not in the young-wine business and it would be grossly unfair to praise or condemn a vintage like this on the strength of so few notes. But there is no hiding the fact that conditions were well below ideal, and there are many other areas producing dry wines of nice quality at a price well below what is asked for white burgundy.

Chablis Moreau A. Regnard Bouchard Père	*Moreau's: yellow; very odd meaty nose; dry, assertive but short.* Tasted January 1979 ⋆ *Regnard's: dry, clean and straightforward.* Tasted March 1979 ⋆⋆ *Bouchard Père's: raw on the nose; light, acid.* Tasted November 1979 ⋆
Chablis, Montée de *Tonnerre* Regnier	*Good nose; dryish, pleasant, straightforward wine with nice acidity.* Tasted February 1978 ⋆⋆
Chablis, Montmains A. Regnard	*Pale, bright, greenish tinge; fresh and appealing nose but no special character; dry, lean, rapier-like not to say thin, but nice quality.* At the Decanter Magazine Dining Club dinner at Harvey's restaurant, Bristol, July 1979 ⋆⋆
Chassagne-Montrachet, *Les Embrazées* Albert Morey	*Supplied by Dolamore's for a Cambridge Wine and Food Society tasting: bright and appealing; light, slightly buttery nose, oak-chips; dryish, medium body, better flavour than nose, nice quality.* Tasted October 1979 ⋆⋆
Meursault, Charmes Michelot-Buisson	*Yellow; lovely oaky* Chardonnay *nose; fairly dry, nice nutty flavour, slightly overacid and unknit. Might be better with a year or so more in bottle.* At the Oxford v. Cambridge tasting competition at Harvey's, March 1980 ⋆⋆
Meursault, Clos Mazeray Jacques Prieur	*Palish yellow; a certain intensity and butteriness, but an overtone that I did not like; dry, lightish. So-so.* Tasted July 1979 ⋆

1978 ⋆⋆⋆

At last, a good vintage, the best for white burgundy since 1973. Supple, well constituted. A promising and interesting vintage for the near future and middle distance. Assessment and tasting notes: whilst in Burgundy for the big Leroy tasting, I snatched the opportunity to taste one or two '78s, the most extensive range being kindly provided by Claude Bouchard in the tasting room of the Château de Beaune. The impression I got was of good, dry, stylish wines, well balanced, with length and finish. Of the Bouchard Père range, I liked best the Meursault, Genevrières and, particularly, an outstanding Chevalier-Montrachet: star bright, rich yellow tinge; soft, gentle, peach-like nose; very good finish. Tasted September 1979 ⋆⋆⋆ to ⋆⋆⋆⋆

1979 ⋆⋆⋆?

Probably quite good. Certainly conditions looked promising, with healthy vines and good vintage weather. Time will tell.

GERMAN WINES

Although fine German wines have always had a following, appreciation of them has never been widespread in England or, as far as can be seen, in the United States. This was not always so. In the Middle Ages "Rhenish" was as popular as claret in London taverns; in the 18th and early 19th centuries "old hock" was highly fashionable and much sought after. It was a genteel drink in Victorian times, and hock and seltzer became a fashionable thirst-quencher — doubtless the influence of royal cousins.

World War I made all things German unpopular, and the growing awareness of wine seemed to exclude hock, mainly because wine became almost wholly associated with food, and fine German wines are best drunk by themselves.

Paradoxically, therefore, German wines, though the easiest in the world for a beginner to enjoy, are ignored by many connoisseurs of wine. They fail to appreciate the aims of the German wine maker and, if English, prefer sackcloth-and-ashes claret to the sensual opulence of rich ripe hock.

The German style

In contrast to the French, German wine makers not only have as their basic material a different range of grape types, grown in a different geographical situation, but their aim is different also.

For the *Riesling*, and other more or less related grapes, the grower and maker in the Rhine and along the banks of the Moselle seeks as his ideal a ripe but fresh wine with a perfect balance of fruit and acidity. This goes for every wine of quality, even up to the majestic *Trockenbeerenauslesen*.

I have one major criticism: it is that wine making has become so skilful, that it seems to dominate: grape rules over soil, science over nature. The new German wine laws and the rationalization of vineyard names has endorsed this trend. So what used to be kaleidoscopic is in danger of being reduced to a simple pattern.

Increasingly, since World War II, German wines have been made for quick bottling, "to capture the freshness", quick sale and quick consumption. No harm in this, but it has some of the built-in obsolescence of a mass-produced car. Those who prefer a custom-built limousine must stick to the best vintages of leading growers and pay that little bit extra. For those who like real character, old vintages — collectors' pieces — are to be found and can give immense delight. A word of warning: German corks are not always of the quality to withstand the rigours of time.

The German quality range

Without wishing to repeat what can be read in any book on German wines, let me just say that the terms *Spätlese* and *Auslese* do not refer to sweetness but to ripeness and richness. It is quite possible to have a medium-sweet *Spätlese* and a medium-dry, even a

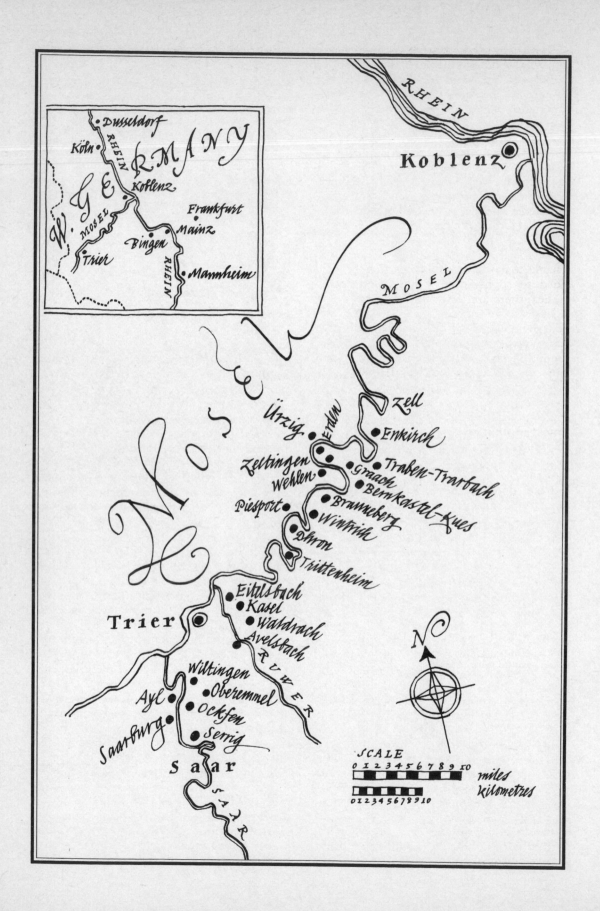

dry, *Auslese* though the latter is rare.

Beerenauslese wines are always sweet, like Sauternes. *Eiswein* is also sweet but, in my experience, rarely has the intensity of bouquet or length of flavour.

Trockenbeerenauslese wines are from the truly overripe, raisiny grapes reduced in water content by *Edelfäule*, or noble rot, the equivalent to *pourriture noble* of Sauternes. They tend to have a far more grapy, raisin-like aroma than Sauternes, and a most delectable and felicitous counterbalancing acidity.

Vintages

Thanks to pesticides and other vineyard aids allied to sophisticated wine-making techniques, there are fewer hopelessly bad vintages in this erratic northern climatic area than there were before the 1960s. Nevertheless, vintages are important. Naturally ripened, fully ripe grapes produce a wine that is noticeably fatter, softer, yet firmer on the palate than an indifferent vintage that has been sweetened and improved. To demonstrate, try almost any 1971 Rhine wine against almost any more recent vintage, for example, a 1975. The 1971s have an extra dimension.

Tasting Notes

I have divided these into ancient and modern. The former are included out of curiosity, to demonstrate the antique style and some miraculous keeping qualities; the latter to exhibit, in so far as any mere words can, the range and style of district and vintage, and their drinkability and condition.

1653 ★★★

Rüdesheimer, Rheingau. Tasted from the cask in the historic vaulted cellars beneath the town hall, Bremen, with the director, Heinz ten Doornkaat. The large casks in the Rose Cellar and in the Cellar of the Twelve Apostles are kept bung full. Very little is drawn off as the casks are only broached on special occasions. The slight ullages are topped up with *Spätlese* or higher quality Rhine wine of a recent good vintage. The old wine "feeds" on the young wine, enjoying the refreshment and quickly absorbing it. This particular wine, the oldest in the cellar, has an alcoholic content of 15 per cent and 19.6 grams per litre of acidity, which accounts for its stability and longevity. *Tasting note:* deep, rich, amber, star bright; aromatic, pungent, madeira-like but not maderized; dry, intense, powerful, with acidity only matched by very old madeiras.
Tasted September 1977. Ten stars for a rare experience.

1673 ★★★

Not tasted, but to demonstrate the high fashion and saleability of old hock, wine of this vintage "Preserved in the Cellars of a Family Mansion in Westphalia" sold at Christie's for a substantial price on 15 July 1815 — only a week or so after the battle of Waterloo.

1719 ★★★

"Excellent Genuine Old Hock" of this vintage "being the remainder of a large quantity purchased in Mayntz in Germany and imported in the year 1775" — extract from Christie's sale catalogue, 15 May 1777.

1723 ★★★

A good vintage: price 41s. (£2.05) per dozen at Christie's in April 1778.

1726 ★★★

"Hock Hochheim 1726 imported from the Reduced Convents in Germany" and auctioned by James Christie on 1 August 1792 at 42s. (£2.10) per dozen.

1727 ★★★★

Rüdesheimer Apostelwein, Rheingau. Perhaps the most venerated old hock in the Bremen cellar. First encountered at a tasting of Wines of the World at Schloss Vollrads in May 1973, to celebrate the 80th birthday of Graf Matuschka-Greiffenklau. The first and oldest of the German classics at the tasting, it was presented by Herr Basting, the *Ratskeller* director at that time. I next tasted the 1727 at Len Evans's monumental old-wine dinner in Sydney in February 1977, from a half-bottle purchased at Christie's two years previously. As it happens, the wine was no stranger to the Great Rooms in St James's, a quantity of the 1727 Rüdesheim being sold at Christie's in 1829 for 105s. (£5.25) a dozen, a high price in those days. From the cask in Bremen: intense yellow-amber colour; waxy, gently maderized, reminiscent of a nutty old sherry, with the old-apple smell of tokay; distinctly dry, powerful nutty flavour, remarkably good.
Last tasted September 1977 ★★★★

1739 ★★★

An abundant vintage, reputed to be of good quality, sold at Christie's in 1792.

1748 ★★★★★

A great vintage and, as it happens, the *first vintage* of any wine sold by James Christie (in July 1772). The vintage appeared again in 1817 and fetched a high price.

1752 ★★★

Good and prolific. A "Red Hock, Asmanshausen" [*sic*] sold for 54s. (£2.70) in 1829.

1753 ★★★★

Very hot summer; small, high-quality crop. "Gogel's Hock" of this vintage fetched 86s. (£4.30) in 1843.

1767

A poor vintage, but the first *year* in which German wine appeared in a Christie's wine catalogue — "Hock (fine old)" — on 16 February, 1767, just two months after James Christie's opening sale.

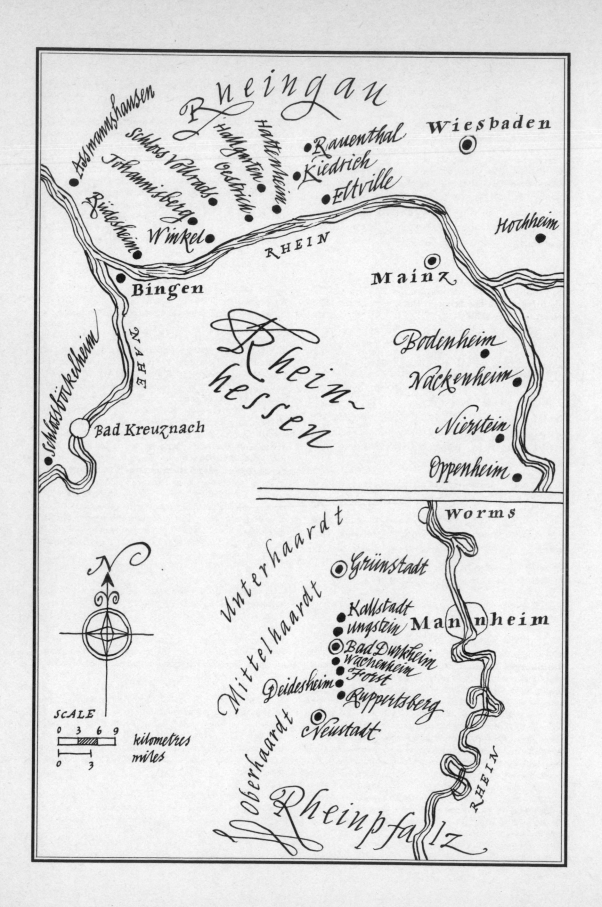

Rheingau

Assmannshausen
Schloss Vollrads
Johannisberg
Hallgarten
Rüdesheim
Oestrich
Hattenheim
Rauenthal
Kiedrich
Eltville
Winkel

Wiesbaden

Hochheim

RHEIN

Bingen

Mainz

NAHE

Rhein-
hessen

Bodenheim
Wackenheim

Niersteen

Schlossböckelheim

Bad Kreuznach

Oppenheim

Worms

Unterhaardt

Grünstadt

Mittelhaardt

Kallstadt
Ungstein
Bad Durkheim
Wachenheim
Forst
Ruppertsberg

Mannheim

Deidesheim

Oberhaardt

Neustadt

N

RHEIN

SCALE

0 3 6 9 kilometres
miles
0 3

Rheinpfalz

1794 ***, 1800 ***

Both good vintages.

1802 ****

A very hot summer.

1808 *

A moderate vintage, but the year in which "Very Old Hock" was sold at Christie's for £10 2s. 6d. a dozen, the highest price paid for any wine at auction between 1766 and the late 19th century.

1811 *****

The renowned "Comet" vintage, reputed to be the greatest vintage of the 19th century.

1815 ***

A good vintage. Rare evidence of early bottling: "Hock, 1815, bottled 1816" mentioned in the catalogue of the sale in 1827 of a fine cellar in Putney, property of "a gentleman deceas'd".

1818 ****

Massively constituted wines. "Very fine Johannisberger" of this vintage "procured directly from the Castle" by Lord Seaford, and sold at Christie's in 1832.

1819 *****

An outstanding vintage.

1822 ****

Excellent.

1834 ****

Very good. Deinhard's 1834 Steinberger sold at Christie's in 1865.

1846 ****

Excellent; smaller quantity than 1822.

1857 ***

Abundant and exceptionally fine.

1862 **

Very big vintage shipped on a large scale to England.

1865 *****

Probably the greatest vintage after 1811; certainly one of best of century. Small production, high priced.
Steinberger Cabinet, Rheingau (Adolf Rau, Frankfurt). Of 40 bottles remaining in Lady Younger's cellars in Alloa, Scotland, and sold at Christie's in 1973, one sample bottle was opened to see if it was drinkable, and another at the pre-sale tasting. The labels and capsules were remarkably good, the corks soft but in one piece. The first bottle was best: not as deep as expected, a sort of weak-tea amber, remarkably bright though with a few bits of sediment; nose sound as a bell, still holding some fruit, a waxy old age though no sourness or mustiness; dry, faded but some body, clean, a bit short, with some acidity yet not old and edgy. Quite remarkable for a white wine over a century in bottle. The second was a bit duller in colour and on the nose, but a lively enough centenarian.
*Tasted August and December 1973 **** for perseverance.*

1868 ***

A moderately good vintage, exceptionally abundant yet high priced, a reflection of prosperity and heavy demand.
Marcobrunn, Rheingau (Masbach Bros, Mayence). The oldest and best of a trio of pre-phylloxera Rhine wines at a memorable old-wine dinner at Christie's given in conjunction with an American collector, Kerry Payne. Guests included Hermann Segnitz, a most respected wine merchant from Bremen. These old German wines were an unprecedented eye-opener for him. Lovely old-gold colour, with a bright and healthy glow; just like an old Sauternes, deep, honeyed crème-brûlée bottle-age; yet quite dry, medium and firm bodied, lovely acidity. In excellent condition, no decay and an immensely enjoyable drink.
*Tasted in the Christie boardroom, November 1976 *****

1870 ***

A good vintage, well constituted.
Castle Johannisberg, "Prince Metternich's first growth", Rheingau. Shipped by Manskopf & Sons, Frankfurt, and clearly destined, by the anglicizing of the German names, for the English quality market of the period. This, the above 1868 and the following wine, all had excellent labels, wax seals, high levels and sound enough original corks, having spent most of their lives in a cold, dry, English country-house cellar. First tasted in July 1976. Next, at the Christie's dinner mentioned above: colour of old gold; nose seemed strange at first — slightly resiny, with a squeeze of lemon; medium dry, lightish, with charm. Remarkably sound
*Last tasted November 1976 ***
Marcobrunner Cabinet, unusually but appropriately labelled "First growth". Another Manskopf wine: slightly paler and brighter; fragrant, lightly spicy bouquet — sage and mint; dry, a slightly resinous and spicy flavour, balanced and very complete. Excellent finish.
*Tasted at the same dinner, November 1976 ****

1874 ****

Small yield, great wines.

1884 ***

Brauneberger Goldtröpfchen, Moselle. Shipped by "Gustav Weigand, Hamburg les Bains"! From the cellars of Hopetoun House, near Edinburgh, and auctioned at the great Rosebery and Linlithgow sale of "Finest and Rarest Wines". Colour of a palish oloroso; old, sherry-like nose; dry, assertive flavour, nice acidity. A curiosity.
*At Christie's pre-sale tasting, May 1967 **

1886 ****

Marcobrunner Auslese, Rheingau (v. Schönborn). Shipped by Gebrüder Drexel. From Lord Rosebery's cellars at Dalmeny House, near Edinburgh. A cloudy sample, palish oloroso colour; lovely rich nose, with fine honeyed bottle-age; dry, lightish, good nutty flavour.
*Tasted before the sale, April 1967 ***

1889 **

Good but small crop, half the normal yield.

1892 ***

Very good quality, similar yield.

1893 ★★★★★

A great year. After 1811 and 1865 probably the best vintage of the 19th century. Small production, very rich wines, the apotheosis of German wine at that time.

Rauenthaler, Rheingau (Wagemann). The first old hock I ever tasted: deepish yellow amber; rather syrupy bottle-age, but still fruity; remarkably dry, quite a tang, drinkable, but the acid that had preserved the wine made it rather rasping on the teeth.
Tasted at Hallgarten's in London, May 1958 ★★

Wiltinger Kupp, Saar (Deinhard). From the cellars of Dalmeny House. Good level and general appearance. The cork broke; otherwise fine. Deepish orange amber; honeyed old nose, but sound and held a long time in the glass; decidedly dry, yet with a softness and delicacy, still very much alive, but with a slightly peaty aftertaste. Remarkable for a 74-year-old Saar wine.
At the great Rosebery pre-sale tasting, May 1967 ★★★

Schloss Vollrads Kabinet, Rheingau. Warm, palish amber gold; a benign old gentleman on the nose, but a touch of asperity on the palate.
At Graf Matuschka-Greiffenklau's tasting, May 1973 ★★

1895 ★★

Moderately good.

Brauneberger Auslese, Moselle (Feldheim). From Lord Rosebery's cellar. High fill. Lovely, bright medium-sherry colour; deep, rich old nose; dryish, nutty. A distinctly curious but fascinating drink. Brauneberg produces some of the richest wines in the middle Moselle, which probably accounts — with the cold, slightly damp cellar conditions — for its survival.
Tasted at Christie's, April 1967 ★★

1900 ★★★★

Excellent vintage, considered better balanced than 1893.

1906 ★

Not a particularly notable vintage.

Berncasteler Superior, Moselle (Gebrüder Stein). To demonstrate that minor wines of less than good vintages are unlikely to survive. Brown gold; rich but maderized nose; not bad flavour but too tart. Unsaleable.
In Christie's tasting room, May 1967.

1911 ★★★★★

Excellent vintage (as in Burgundy and Champagne) and considered at the time almost a repetition of the legendary 1811. Rheingaus particularly fine.

1915 ★★★

Good, abundant.

1920 ★★★

Variable: basically good, some outstanding late-vintage wines made.

Schloss Johannisberg, Rheingau (v. Metternich). From Lord Rosebery's cellar at Mentmore: medium old-gold colour; lovely rich bouquet, ripe peaches; very dry, good body, assertive and piquant.
Tasted at Christie's, April 1967 ★★

1921 ★★★★★

One of the most renowned vintages of the century. Full, ripe, soft wines. *Climate:* spring frosts and drought during the summer reduced the crop. Grapes, free from disease and fully ripe, picked in warm vintage weather. High sugar, low acidity. *Market:* Deinhards reported from Coblenz that "there is hardly any doubt that the 1921s, both on the Moselle and on the Rhine, will rank amongst the finest wines made during the last 50 years". High priced. Though now rare, rich and interesting, of the seven '21s to come my way the most fascinating have been the minor wines, including a stunning half-bottle of a Nassauer Bros' Liebfraumilch "Extra Superior" from Gorhambury House, St Albans.

Eitelsbacher Karthauserhofberg feinste Auslese (Ruwer). From the Rautenstrauch estate and the oldest wine at Hallgarten's Third Quadrennial Tasting: very bright, palish amber; lovely honeyed bouquet; medium dry, nice body, excellent crisp/rich flavour, remarkably fresh and attractive acidity.
Tasted February 1968 ★★★★★

Niersteiner Oelberg Orleans Spätlese, Rheinhessen (P. Finck'sches). Made from the rare *Orleans* grape, which Dr Fritz Hallgarten thought was probably *Chenin blanc* from the Loire. Pronounced yellow amber; not a sign of age on nose or palate; dry, rich but austere, slightly smoky finish. Fascinating and characterful.
At a Hallgarten tasting in London, August 1970 ★★★★

Oppenheimer Goldberg Riesling Trockenbeerenauslese, Rheinhessen. Deeper, more orange tinged than the above *Spätlese*; touch of old age on nose, but it cleared and held well; once intensely sweet, now drying out, but still rich, tangy, good finish.
Tasted at Hallgarten's, August 1970 ★★★★

Schloss Johannisberg, Rheingau (H. Sichel). After some less than overwhelming '21s, a delightful surprise: warm orange-amber colour; lovely bouquet, no decay, developed aroma of ripe peaches; medium sweetness and body, rich, liquid gold, just a little short.
At lunch at Berry Bros, December 1972 ★★★★

Siefersheim Hollberg Trockenbeerenauslese, Rheinhessen (Jean Schneider). From the Alzay. Beautiful yellow, but not very bright; deep, rich, old, overripe grapes/bottle-age; dried out but still fat and rich.
Tasted October 1971 ★★★

1925 ★★★

The first decent vintage after 1921. Rich wines; rare.

Forster Kirchenstück Riesling Trockenbeerenauslese, Pfalz (Bürklin-Wolf). A three-quarters full bottle opened out of curiosity. Deep old amber; fabulously rich bouquet, very fine, great depth; still sweet, fat, very rich, just a twist of end acidity. Remarkable.
An unsaleable sample at Christie's, tasted March 1974 ★★★★

1929 ★★★★

1929 was the first vintage of real renown after the 1921. For, unlike Bordeaux (still less like Burgundy), which enjoyed no fewer than seven good vintages, Germany had a thin time in the 1920s. *Climate:* the almost inevitable spring frosts followed by an exceptionally hot, dry summer, all through July and well into September. Like 1921, grapes free of disease and fully ripe. Reduced crop. After a rather ordinary Rüdesheimer Rosengarten tasted in 1969, I noted no fewer than six '29s in a tasting of old hocks collected by vinous squirrel Archie Ling.

Ranging up to *Auslese* quality, few were more than interesting, three had the pungent rubbery smell of broken-down old sulphur, and most were overacid. But they were a pretty motley collection from a variety of sources. I have no doubt that the finest wines from good cold cellars can still be excellent.

1931

The second of three poor vintages.

Hochheimer Daubhaus, Rheingau (A. Hallgarten). Lovely colour, a very pronounced yellow; an initial twitch of life, but rather dull nose and palate. Dry.
A surprising survival, tasted February 1968.

1933 ***

An abundant crop of soft and gentle wines.

Niersteiner Rehbach Spätlese, Rheinhessen (Langenbach). Remarkably pale and youthful looking for its age, lemon yellow; delicate, honeyed (ripe grapes and bottle-age) nose; soft, gentle, deep, attractive. A second bottle seemed slightly sweeter, with crisper acidity.
*Both tasted at Col. Norman Johnstone's, March 1967 ****

Niersteiner Pettenthal feine Spätlese, Rheinhessen (Balbach Erben). Lovely bright gold; ripe bouquet but a bit oily and reminiscent of Colman's mustard; medium dry, lovely rich flavour and tang.
*At an Avery tasting of prewar German wines, October 1969 ***

Erbacher Honigberg, Rheingau (Block, Fearon). Demonstrating how a decently made, natural, unsugared wine, bottled by a good London wine merchant and stored in a cold, damp, Cambridge college cellar can give the purest delight after 45 years. Not a single bad bottle. Bright palish gold; beautiful, gentle, honeyed bouquet, fresh as a daisy, rather like a ripe Barsac; medium dry, perfect balance, perfect acidity, not great but unobtrusively delightful.
*Nearly a dozen notes, April–July 1978 ****

1934 ****

Niersteiner Hipping Edelbeerauslese [*sic*], Rheinhessen (Senfter). Lovely golden sheen; excellent nose, rich, ripe; medium sweet, lovely, soft, sound as a bell.
*Tasted February 1971 ****

Berncasteler Doktor Auslese, Moselle (Dr Thanisch). A half-bottle: unhealthily orange coloured; dry, alive, but short and dull.
The least good '34 at Avery's tasting, October 1969.

Deidesheimer Langenböhl Riesling, Pfalz (v. Bühl). Very bright lemon gold; lovely ripe nose, old honeyed bottle-age with a touch of liquorice; medium dry, rich and ripe. Nice wine. Von Bühl's Forster Ungeheuer a deeper orange gold with a lovely tang.
*One of the best at the Avery's, October 1969 ***

Kiedricher Gräfenberg feinste Auslese, Rheingau (Dr Weil). Fine golden colour; an opulent bouquet of honey, fruit and flowers; fairly sweet, lovely flavour, balance. Perfect harmony, length and finish.
*Tasted October 1969 *****

1935 *

Niersteiner Pettenthal feine Spätlese, Rheinhessen (F. K. Schmitt). Bright yellow; rather oily nose; dry, sound enough, but lacking real quality and interest.
*The only '35 tasted, February 1968 **

1937 *****

Outstanding vintage, the best since 1921 and, in my opinion, the finest of all the post World War I vintages. *Climate:* fine spring, quick and early flowering in good conditions (always a good omen); hot and dry summer, some rain in September to swell the berries, but small crop of fully ripe grapes harvested early. *Assessment:* excellent quality, still magnificent.

Forster Ungeheuer Riesling Auslese, Pfalz (v. Bühl). A beautiful wine from a great estate: deep orange amber; exquisitely honeyed bouquet; fairly sweet, fullish, very rich, fine flavour and acidity.
*Tasted October 1969 *****

Johannisberger Kochsberg Trockenbeerenauslese, Rheingau (v. Mumm). Incredibly deep oloroso-orange colour with intense yellow rim; concentrated, raisiny nose; one of the sweetest wines I have ever tasted, incredibly rich — an almost syrup of figs concentration, fabulous long flavour with burnt raisin aftertaste. Decades of life ahead.
*The oldest and greatest at a Hallgarten tasting in Mittelheim during a visit of the Masters of Wine to Germany, June 1969 *****

Lorcher Bodenthal Riesling Auslese, Bacharach (v. Kanitz). One does not often see wines from the stretch of the Rhine below Bingen. Remarkably pale; gentle mint-leaf Riesling nose; dryish, lightish, soft and attractive.
*Tasted May 1973 ***

Marcobrunner Trockenbeerenauslese, Rheingau (v. Schönborn). Old-gold colour; beautiful, perfectly aged *Edelfäule*, concentrated grape-essence bouquet; still sweet and intensely rich, with flavour of marvellous complexity and perfect acidity which both preserves the wine and cleans the palate to prepare for another sip. Without acidity these sweet wines would pall.
*At a Hallgarten tasting, February 1968 *****

Niersteiner Pettenthal Riesling Beerenauslese, Rheinhessen (F. K. Schmitt). Deepish old gold; opulent, raisiny smell; sweet, fairly full, very rich yet refined. Exquisite aftertaste.
*Tasted October 1961 *****

Rüdesheimer Berg Rottland Riesling Trockenbeerenauslese Cabinet Rheingau (v. Ritter). Rather astonishing: the bottle had been opened some years previously, the wine tasted, and the bottle recorked. Yet there were no signs of decay or fatigue. Fairly deep amber; gentle, harmonious, honeyed; intensely sweet, rich, fat yet with beautiful counterbalancing acidity.
*From one of the royal cellars, January 1974 ****

1941

For obvious reasons, few vintages between 1938 and 1944 were drunk outside Germany. Unlike the situation in the French districts, there were no labour shortages, prisoners of war being employed in the vineyards.

Rauenthaler Gehrn, Rheingau (Schloss Eltz). Very pale lemon; very dry, thin and decidedly sour.
At the birthday tasting at Schloss Vollrads, May 1973.

1943 **

The best of the wartime vintages.

Kiedricher Gräfenberg Riesling Beerenauslese, Rheingau (v. Ritter zu Groensteyn). Deep coloured, with tartaric acid crystals; heavy, somewhat maderized — dull, brown treacle; a bit appley, old and acidic.
At the Schloss Vollrads tasting, May 1973.

1945 ★★★★★

Fairly concentrated, flavour-packed wines. Climate: a hot dry year, the quality and quantity being influenced more by end-of-war problems than climate. Some war damage. Growers not only deprived of POW labour but suffered much looting by released Polish and Russian prisoners. Vine diseases could not be held in check. As a result the harvest was one of the smallest in living memory, some districts of the Moselle producing nothing at all. But the little that was made reached the quality of 1893, 1911, 1921 and 1937. Tasting notes: half a dozen notes, four of the most interesting and characteristic follow. Scarce. The finest will still be good.

Deidesheimer Herrgottsacker Riesling Auslese *Pfalz (Langenbach)*	*Fairly deep amber, an even gradation of colour; fabulous bouquet, peachy, slightly vanilla; medium sweet, good body and flavour, ripe fatness. Almost of* Beerenauslese *quality except for a some-what blunt, dry finish.* Tasted August 1973 ★★★★
Deidesheimer Maushöhle Auslese *Pfalz (v. Bühl)*	*Lovely medium yellow gold; beautiful nose, honeyed; fairly sweet, firm and attractive.* Tasted February 1968 ★★★★
Hochheimer Domdechaney Riesling Spätlese *Rheingau (Dom. Werner)*	*Lovely deep old gold; magnificent bouquet; medium dry, fine, packed with flavour, fragrant aftertaste.* At a Heublein tasting in San Francisco, May 1971 ★★★★
Schloss Johannisberg Himmelblaulack Auslese *Rheingau* *(v. Metternich)*	*The wine did its best to emulate its "heavenly blue" seal: fairly deep old amber; rich honeyed nose; moderately full, intense flavour and tang. Really a bit too old and dried out.* At a tasting in the Rheingau on the Masters of Wine tour, September 1969 ★★

1946 ★★

A surprisingly adequate vintage but lacking sustaining quality. Totally bypassed by the trade and wrongly considered an "off" vintage like 1951. I have tasted only one.

Niersteiner Auflangen Riesling Spätlese *Rheinhessen* *(R. Senfter)*	*Bright lemon yellow; low-keyed but nice nose; very dry, light, not much flavour and curious acidity. The paleness of colour, due to lack of extract, and the raw acidity, were the result of unripe grapes.* At Hallgarten's Third Quadrennial Tasting, February 1968 ★

1947 ★★★

A good generous vintage. Climate: extraordinary conditions. Long weeks of severe frost in the winter prevented water penetrating the soil. Spring and summer exceedingly warm and dry. Healthy grapes but not enough moisture to develop them fully. Medium-sized crop. Assessment: abundant, rich, soft wines, some lacking acidity and short lived. A vintage I saw something of in my mid-1950s wine-trade days. They varied. Of the few tasted since 1970:

Hochheimer Rauchloch Riesling Spätlese *Rheingau (Dom. Werner)*	*Attractive lemon gold; bouquet ripe, with sweet bottle-age, still lovely and fresh; distinctly dry, good fresh fruity flavour but lacking the finish and aftertaste of the 1945.* Tasted May 1971 ★★★

Schloss Vollrads **Trockenbeerenauslese** *Rheingau*	*The climax of Graf Matuschka-Greiffenklau's 80th birthday Wines of the World tasting, a marathon two-part session, 50 wines in all. This wine was boldly paired with a '37 Yquem. I gave both a fairly even rating. Each had a similar bright amber-gold colour; Yquem more honeyed on the nose, Vollrads far richer, but a touch of old apples lurking in the background; far sweeter and softer than Yquem. Gentle, rich, harmonious. At Schloss Vollrads, May 1973 ★★★★*

1948 ★★

Moderately good. Little seen. It is extraordinary how even contrasting wine areas, producing differing types of wine, are affected in similar ways not only by the same weather but by similar market conditions. Coming between the ripe '47s and the stylish '49s, they were ignored by the trade. I have only tasted a few but the following two give some indication of style:

Geisenheimer Rothenberg **Riesling Spätlese** *Rheingau*	*Pronounced yellow, gold tinged; fabulous nose, fragrant; decidedly dry and austere on the palate. Extraordinary flavour, with good acidity and finish. Tasted at Schöll & Hillebrand's, June 1969 ★★*
Niersteiner Hipping Riesling **Goldbeerenauslese** *Rheinhessen (Heyl)*	*Tasted twice, when comparatively young: rather bleak, not as enticing as its name. Quite deep coloured; little nose; rich, earthy/meaty flavour, blunt dry finish. Tasted 1954, October 1955 ★*

1949 ★★★★★

A great classic vintage. Excellent, harmonious, supremely elegant wines with firmness and staying power. The best Moselles since 1921. Climate: a very fine summer with a well-timed amount of beneficial rain. Crop size reduced by early spring frosts which affected districts in varying degrees. Market: the vintage also coincided with the recovery of the market; still a period of general austerity. 1947s awakened interest, '49s were well timed and of a quality to rise to the renewed market demand. Tasting notes: the first German vintage of which I have a substantial number of notes, starting with a fat rich Pfalz (Palatinate) wine in the autumn of 1954. Exactly half were noted prior to 1960, but none, I regret, tasted since May 1973. The following are descriptions of some outstanding and characteristic wines tasted:

Dürkheimer Spielberg **Scheurebe Auslese** *Pfalz (Deinhard)*	*Unusually interesting, as this must have been one of the earliest wines from a classic district and vineyard, and certainly the first vintage I have tasted, in which the Scheurebe grape (a new cross of the classic Riesling and the softer, quicker ripening Müller-Thurgau vine varieties) was used. First noted at a Deinhard tasting in London in August 1966. Seven years later the pronounced yellow gold had deepened, displaying a lovely richness and sheen; fabulous bouquet and flavour, the opulent grapiness of the Scheurebe enriched by ripeness and bottle-age; sweet, beautiful weight and balance. At the III Form Club annual dinner, January 1973 ★★★★*
Erbacher Marcobrunn **Beerenauslese** *Rheingau (Schloss Rheinharthausen)*	*Palish; deep, rich, ripe, honeyed bouquet; sweet, perfectly lovely flavour, rich yet with finesse, and exactly the right amount of acidity. Tasted May 1973 ★★★★*
Hattenheimer Hassel **Riesling feine Auslese** *Rheingau (Adam Albert)*	*Surprisingly pale lemon yellow; delicious bouquet, fresh pineapples and honeyed bottle-age; medium sweet, rich yet crisp, beautiful flavour, weight and balance. At Schloss Vollands, May 1973 ★★★★*

Hattenheimer Wisselbrunn Beerenauslese Rheingau (Schloss Rheinharthausen)	*The colour of ginger ale; lovely, rich, raisiny nose and taste; fairly sweet, good, crisp, dry finish. Beginning to show its age after 20 years. Tasted December 1969* ★★★
Niersteiner Pettenthal Trockenbeerenauslese Rheinhessen (Anton Balbach)	*Very bright, more yellow than gold; delicate, scented; sweet, rich, yet gentle, soft and ripe. Beautiful, elegant but overpowered by a great 1959 Trockenbeerenauslese. Tasted February 1968* ★★★★
Niersteiner Pettenthal 1. Terrasse Riesling allerfeinste Goldbeerenauslese	*The "rationalization" and simplification of German names and the 1971 wine laws have made the marvellous tongue-twisting and mind-boggling names like this a thing of the past. A pity. At six years of age, in June 1955, this wine was most extraordinary, with a highly flavoured fruity intensity that I had never before encountered. Six years later: a 2. Terrasse feine Auslese (of Anton Balbach) was delicate, grapy, dry and delicious. Last tasted May 1961* ★★★★
Rauenthaler Baiken Trockenbeerenauslese Rheingau (Staatsweingut)	*Deep, slightly orange tinged, with slight sediment; excellent, ripe, raisiny TBA nose; sweet, full flavoured, richness and intensity perfectly countered by lovely acidity. At a "Drink Tank" lunch at Lord Rothschild's, with David Somerset and Michael Tree, July 1970* ★★★★★
Steinberger Auslese Kabinett Rheingau (Staatsdomänen)	*Excellent in 1961 (but nothing like as delicate or fine as the above Niersteiner Pettenthal 2. Terrasse feine Auslese). More recently: medium-pale yellow straw; very good nose and flavour; medium sweet, firm, supple, good aftertaste. Last tasted February 1968* ★★★
Wehlener Sonnenuhr Riesling feine Auslese Moselle (J. J. Prüm)	*Beautiful colour, intense lemon yellow; unbelievably rich yet refreshing bouquet; remarkably sweet, incredible richness and power for a Moselle, but with tangy acidity. Perhaps just thinning a little at 20 years of age. At first Heublein tasting in Chicago, May 1969* ★★★★★
Wehlener Sonnenuhr feinste Beerenauslese Moselle (J. J. Prüm)	*A perfect wine. First noted in 1968 at a dinner party given at Laurie Strangman's Harcourt Rooms by those great American connoisseurs Dr and Mrs Bernard (Barnie) Rhodes. Two years later: as a little light refresher after a 1906 Tokay Essence: fine, bright, medium-pale yellow gold; remarkably fresh, fragrant, mouth-watering nose; sweetish, appeared to be drying out slightly, doubtless overpowered by the tokay. Lovely crisp flavour, with beautiful finish combining inimitably (as only the finest estates can, in a great year) fragrance, elegance, richness, refreshing acidity. Last tasted at Harry Waugh's, April 1970* ★★★★★

1950 ★★

Moderate, variable. Tasting notes: coming after the brilliant 1949 almost any vintage would be an anticlimax. Judging from the paucity of my notes — just a dozen, all but one tasted between the autumn of 1954 and (a couple of Harvey-bottled Hochheimers) February 1957 — of modest commercial quality. However, a Rüdesheimer Berg Spätlese of Deinhard's was very pleasantly grapy and fresh. Just one freak TBA:

Schloss Böckelheimer Trockenbeerenauslese Nahe	*A small pocket of grapes left to absorb the late autumn sun in a sheltered corner of the valley. Palish; intense fruit-salad Nahe aroma; not as sweet as expected but very rich, flavoury and with refreshing acidity. At Archie Ling's tasting of old hocks, October 1971* ★★★

1951

As poor and thin as everywhere else in Europe.

1952 ★★★

A firmly constituted and underrated vintage. Climate: a capricious year: a good opening lead-ing to an exceptionally hot and dry July and August. The boiling sun raised hopes of another 1921. By the end of August grapes were ten days ahead, but cold wet weather in September and October prevented them from achieving the state of ripeness necessary for a really outstanding vintage. Tasting notes: starting with a modest, light, dry Dhroner Hofberg of Deinhard's, 125s. (£6.25) per dozen, in November 1954, my eyes were really opened the following year by a magnificently flowery Schloss Johannisberg and a stunning Wachenheimer Gerümpel Riesling Auslese standing out at a wide-ranging Hellmer tasting of '50s, '52s and '53s, in May 1956. Ten Harvey-bottled '52s also showed well at a tasting in February 1957, an excellent Forster Ungeheuer Riesling Auslese — full, rich, with staying power — being the most expensive at 31s. 6d. (£1.57) per bottle. To give some idea of the wide range of German wines listed by Harvey's in those days, on the same day I tasted nearly 60, representing all the main districts, vintages ranging from 1949 to 1953, prices starting at under 10s. (50p) a bottle.

1953 ★★★★ *to* ★★★★★

Beautiful, ripe, fruity wines, with variations between districts. Climate: the late autumn of 1952 enabled the wood to ripen. Some severe frosts in May affected mainly the lower grade areas. Thereafter favourable weather, vines free from disease, fine and dry with sunshine in all districts prior to, and during, the harvest. Great wines predicted. Tasting notes: it is some reflection of the popularity of this vintage that I have about five times as many notes on German wines of the 1953 vintage than the 1952, and many more — much to my surprise — than on 1953 red burgundies. First, a brief summary by district: Moselle: nearly all my notes on 1953 Moselles were made between 1955 and 1958, and the majority were soft, easy, pleasant enough commercial wines, not meant to last. The best were undoubtedly the few high-quality wines from the Saar and Ruwer districts. Nahe: it was the 1953 vintage that first opened my eyes to the crisp and lovely Nahe wines, three of which are described below. Rheingau: perfection in this district, where the most elegant, firm yet supple, of Germany's classic fine wines are produced. Rheinhessen: generally more open-knit and softer wines, in 1953 they varied from blowzy blondes to rather luscious lovelies, but the *Sylvaner* grape and the *Scheurebe* (the equivalent of a dyed blonde, plausibly attractive at first but eventually the dark roots show through) were less satisfactory. Pfalz: from the warm earth of the Palatinate, rather overpowering wines, lacking the finesse of the Rheingaus in this vintage. Notes on some leading '53s:

Annaberg Riesling Auslese
Pfalz
(Stumpf-Fitz)

Going back a bit, but included to demonstrate the quality of Ger-man wine bottled, and bottled well, by Harvey's and one or two other English wine merchants up to the mid-1950s: rich, grapy yet earthy aroma; medium dry, a fullish, fattish, ripe, warm Pala-tinate wine, with a splendid dry finish. First tasted in 1960, 24s. (£1.20) a bottle — I noted "a bit expensive". In 1962 of five-star quality. The Scheurebe Auslese more grapy, rich and earthy. Last tasted February 1968 ★★★★

Annaberg Scheurebe Trockenbeerenauslese *Pfalz* *(Stumpf-Fitz)*	*First noted, enthusiastically, in the Harvey tasting room in Octo-ber 1961. More than £6 a bottle even in those days. Next, a luscious half-bottle: golden; fabulous* Scheurebe *grapiness and* TBA *concentration; remarkably soft and fat, but the magnificent finish noted in its youth had faded. I am sure a pure* Riesling *grape would not have lost its grip in this way.* Last tasted April 1971 ✶✶✶✶
Bretzenheimer Kronenberg Riesling Trockenbeerenauslese *Nahe (v. Plettenberg)*	*Undoubtedly the most magnificent Nahe I have had of this vin-tage: deep, rich old gold; concentrated bouquet; sweet, of course, with the golden botrytis taste counterbalanced with superb, crisp, fruity acidity.* Tasted June 1966 ✶✶✶✶✶
Eltviller Kalbespflicht Riesling feine Auslese Kabinett *Rheingau (Jakob Fischer)*	*First tasted in Wiesbaden in April 1969 and in Chicago just two months later. Most recently: fine yellow gold; magnificent bou-quet, high toned, very grapy; medium sweet, concentrated fruit flavour, balance and life.* Last noted at a Heublein pre-sale tasting, May 1971 ✶✶✶✶
Forster Freundstück Riesling Trockenbeerenauslese	*German bottled, it cost Harvey's 1,000s. (£50) per dozen, a fairly substantial price in those days, for what I noted as "superfine essence of raisin wine".* Tasted February 1957 ✶✶✶✶✶
Geisenheimer Kirchgrube Spätlese *Rheingau* *(Schloss Waldeck)*	*This was one of my favourite '53s. Most recently, at 16 years of age: lovely colour, gold tinged, bright; ripe, rich, honey and fruit bouquet in perfect condition despite a slightly loose and grubby cork; dry throughout, a gently swelling flavour but now lacking final end acidity. Several notes.* Last tasted New Year 1979 ✶✶✶✶
Hochheimer Domdechaney Riesling Beerenauslese Kabinett *Reingau* *(Staatsweingut)*	*A gold medal winner, and certainly one of the most fabulous wines I have ever tasted: a fine yellow gold (the colour of pure gold in fact); perfect bouquet, quintessence of grapes, ripe, rich; sweet, luscious, soft yet not cloying, concentrated but fully ready. Adjec-tives fail.* At a Heublein tasting prior to the auction in Chicago, May 1970 ✶✶✶✶✶
Hochheimer Domdechaney Riesling Trockenbeerenauslese *Rheingau* *(Staatsweingut)*	*Deeper colour than the* Beerenauslese*; highly concentrated on nose and palate; intensely sweet, magnificent but not as opulently mature. I noted it had another 10 to 20 years.* Only at an annual Heublein auction, in between other great wines, can one sample, one after the other, a pair of closely related "pearls" like these Hochheimers. Tasted May 1970 ✶✶✶✶(✶)
Hochheimer Steinern Kreuz Naturrein *Rheingau* *(Domdechant Werner)*	Naturrein *from ripe grapes with no sugar added, officially rated just below* Spätlese *(late-picked ripe grapes). Unsugared wines that have the best capability of developing and longevity. The bottles had good levels but the corks were a bit ropy. Very pro-nounced yellow; soft, sweet, waxy/honeyed nose (rather like the smell of a honeycomb); soft, with gentle but distinctly dry finish.* Tasted December 1978, January 1979 ✶✶✶
Johannisberg Klaus *Rheingau* *(Schöll & Hillebrand)*	*Not an estate-bottled wine and, frankly, the least satisfactory of my recently bought '53s. Pale for its age (probably the result of a hefty dose of sulphur dioxide before bottling), lemon yellow, watery rim; nose reasonably sound but not as rich and honeyed as some of the others; dry, lightish, higher acidity giving it freshness, but short. Deteriorated in the glass.* Tasted several times in 1979 ✶✶
Kinheimer Rosenberg feine Auslese *Moselle* *(Kies-Kieren)*	*Bright yellow with a light golden sheen; rather Graves-like on the nose, gently sweet, ripe and waxy; drying out and losing fruit, but sound. End acidity a little marked, but refreshing.* Tasted October 1975, November 1979 ✶✶✶

Kreuznacher Kahlenberg Riesling feine Spätlese Nahe *(Ludwig Herf)*	*One of my favourites: beautiful nose, quite overpowering in 1955 and 1956. Lovely the following year. Perfection in 1959: palish; beautiful pineapple-husk/fruit-salad nose; dry, crisp fruit, lightish but firm, seemed to blossom in the glass. A year later: age and acidity pushing through.* Last tasted March 1960. At its peak ★★★★
Kreuznacher St. Martin Riesling Edelbeerenauslese Nahe (Ludwig Herf)	*Because of the Kahlenberg noted above, I determined to call on the grower and did so on my first visit to Germany. I drank this wine, a luscious gold and silver medal prize winner, at Freiherr Ludwig Herf's home in June 1956 ★★★★*
Piesporter Goldtröpfchen Auslese Moselle (v. Kesselstatt)	*Variable: one with a loose cork was spoiled, another was buttery yellow; at best, a gentle, sound, waxy/honeyed bouquet; distinctly dry, firm, nice acidity.* Several notes, New Year 1979 ★★★
Rauenthaler Baiken Spätlese Rheingau *(Schloss Eltz)*	*Palish, very bright straw yellow; good nose; dry (unlike the uniformly medium-sweet wines that have become such a feature of latter-day hocks), nice medium weight, straightforward, firm, undemonstrative, well-balanced wine.* Tasted February 1968 ★★★
Rauenthaler Langenstuck Beerenauslese (Max Wagner)	*A wonderful wine, with that extra dimension of richness that the Rauenthal soil must provide.* Tasted twice in 1957, January 1962 ★★★★
Rüdesheimer Klosterkiesel Naturrein Kabinettwein Rheingau *(Staatsweingut, Eltville)*	*Lovely bright gold; very attractive, very sound, honeyed, ripe Riesling bouquet; medium dry, rich but a pleasant lightweight style, good acidity. Bought at a Christie's sale, autumn 1978.* Last tasted December 1978 ★★★
Steinberger Kabinett Auslese (Staatdomänen)	*Lovely, good, crisp, almost Moselle-like delicacy and aftertaste.* Four admiring notes in 1956, 1961, 1963, February 1968 ★★★
Steinberger Kabinettwein Naturrein Rheingau *(Staatsweingut)*	*Very bright and positive buttery amber gold; complex, honeyed, a trace of vanilla, even pineapple; medium dry, flavour to match the nose, soft yet firm, dry finish. A delightful drink but lacking the length and persistence of the Auslese quality wine.* From a private cellar. Five consistently good bottles, tasted December 1978–February 1980 ★★★
Wachenheimer Fuchsmantel Scheurebe Pfalz	*The Auslese quality first tasted at Harvey's: golden, even in January 1961; grapy rich; medium sweet yet cleanly refreshing, lovely, broad, open flavour. Then, the straight Scheurebe: at 7 years of age a fairly prominent yellow; lovely deep grapy muscatel aroma, smothered in honeyed bottle-age; dry, medium body, fine, stylish and still fresh.* Last tasted at Hellmer's, February 1970 ★★★
Wallufer Walkenberg Spätburgunder Rotweiss Edelauslese Rheingau *(Josef Becker)*	*A double rarity — a white wine made from overripe red grapes: amber colour slightly stained by the red grape skins; a rather clumsy heavyweight on the nose; sweetish, assertive flavour but rather flat. Frankly a "bastard brew": I doubt if it would have made a fine red wine (the Spätburgunder grape is the same as Pinot) or an elegant white. At any rate, it was interesting.* At the Schloss Vollrads tasting, May 1973 ★★
Wiltinger Kupp Saar *(Bischöfliches Priesterseminar)*	*At "sweet 17", in a remarkable state of preservation: delicious bouquet, high toned, fruity; bone dry, light, crisp and fresh.* Six consistently good notes, July 1969 — February 1970 ★★★★
Winkeler Hasensprung Jesuitengarten Riesling Trockenbeerenauslese Rheingau *(Karl Hamm)*	*Lovely bright amber gold; exquisite bouquet and flavour, Edelfäule (botrytis) richness and concentration, a sort of extract of grape, though not overpoweringly sweet. Marvellous balance, acidity. With a grace and delicacy that makes even the finest Sauternes look clumsy.* At the Schloss Vollrads tasting, May 1973 ★★★★★

1954

Very poor year, the worst since 1927. <small>Climate:</small> disastrous. Frost damage, followed by a prolonged wet summer.

Wachenheimer Schlossberg *Pfalz (H. Sichel)*	*The only '54 hock tasted: grapy nose; a heavily sugared wine, too sweet yet insubstantial.* <small>At Sichel's in London, January 1955.</small>

1955 ★★

Moderate, variable. <small>Climate:</small> cold, unsettled weather delayed budding, but no frost damage. Conflicting reports about flowering, but it was late. From mid-July eight weeks of favourable weather encouraged development. Severe frost on 18 and 19 October. Harvest the following week. Crop 50 per cent of normal. Quality uneven. <small>Assessment:</small> a vintage to forget. <small>Tasting notes:</small> only about a couple of dozen notes, all prior to 1970, and very few Moselles, though they were reputed to be excellent. Most were relatively inexpensive commercial wines, hardly any even of *Spätlese* quality, some distinctly poor. One particularly attractive wine was an Alsheimer Goldberg made from the *Siegerrebe* grape, a relatively new vine crossing and the first I had tasted: a very grapy, exotically flavoured little wine, in November 1959.

1956

A complete disaster, the worst year of this century, both for quality and quantity. <small>Climate:</small> cold winter, cold spring, with frost damage; rainy summer and a premature autumn in which the early morning mists, normally so useful in the final stages of ripening, induced rot. Many growers just abandoned their vineyards after the frosts. At harvest time fewer grapes were gathered than are usually left behind by pickers in a normal vintage. <small>Postscript:</small> my wife and I spent a busman's holiday, mainly in the Moselle, in June. We were on a motor scooter and it rained every day. A very damp introduction to the German wine districts.

1957 ★★

Moderate. Particularly good in the Moselle. <small>Climate:</small> who would be a vine grower? Mild early spring advanced growth but heavy frosts on 5 and 6 May inflicted great damage. The growth of undamaged vines caught up again during a warm, sunny June, the fine weather continuing until early August. Then almost continuous rain until the end of September, rot setting in. The weather improved in October, the later-ripening *Riesling* benefiting considerably. Picking took place late. <small>Tasting notes:</small> just 20 notes, all but two made between July 1958 and October 1967, and none of the earlier tasted wines of above *Kabinett* quality yet most must have been late picked, though not in the *Spätlesen* sense.

Annaberg Scheurebe Auslese *Pfalz* *(Stumpf-Fitz)*	*Lovely, palish old gold; rich peaches and honey bouquet; medium sweet, nice weight, lovely tangy flavour and acidity.* <small>At lunch at Deinhard's, July 1975 ★★★</small>

Johannisberger Schlossberg
Riesling
Rheingau
(Langenbach)

Clearly the cold, dank cellars of the Factory House, Oporto, had preserved the wine well: unexpectedly pale for its age; very sound attractive bouquet, nice fruit; dryish, firm, pleasant flavour, good acidity. Holding well, but I advised the members to finish it up! The surprise opening wine at the annual Treasurer's dinner, Oporto, November 1979 **

1958 **

A huge crop of moderate and variable wines. Climate: despite unsatisfactory weather during the flowering period, by July the vines were in good shape and developed well in the fine August and early September weather. Variable from then to the vintage time, mid-October. Because of the size of the crop, the biggest for 20 years, harvesting took over five weeks. Market: after two disasters and two indifferent vintages, the abundance was welcome even if few quality wines were made. Tasting notes: under a dozen notes. Wines all rather dull and some overacid. Only one tasted since early 1967:

Erbacher Hohenrain
Riesling Naturrein
Rheingau
(v. Oetinger)

A rather freak wine from the estate of the Freiherr *who conducted the marathon auction in Wiesbaden in April 1969. Pale, still green tinged; nice if undemonstrative nose and flavour. Dry, light little wine.* At a Christie's pre-sale tasting, November 1978 *

1959 *****

Excellent. Full-bodied and fully ripe, naturally sweet wines. Arguably the greatest since the war and certainly one of the outstanding German vintages this century. Climate: conditions almost too perfect. Rapid and even blossoming; a prolonged hot and sunny summer, rather too hot and dry in September and October. Vines virtually free from pests and diseases. With the exception of a few of the larger estates, where the picking did not end until mid-November, all the grapes were safely gathered by the end of October. Wine making: one factor stressed by all the serious reports emanating from the vineyard areas was the problem of wine making in such a hot year. Few German estates had recent practical experience of coping with grapes of such high sugar content. Dr. Otto Loeb reported, in May 1960, that "never before had so many *Beeren-* and *Trockenbeerenauslesen* been made in the Moselle district ... they have record 'must' weights — some estates with over 250° Oechsle, and the records of 1921 will be broken by the 312° of Dr. Thanisch's Berncasteler Doktor". There was worry about possible lack of acidity, as in 1921, and arguments about the virtues of early and late bottling cropped up again. It would seem that those vines grown on lighter soil were more affected by the lack of moisture in the ripening months; and "those growers", to quote Dr. Fritz Hallgarten, "who were negligent during the first hours of the wine's life ... and allowed the must to ferment too quickly" made less superior wine. Any bad wines in 1959 were due to human failure and not to nature. Market: the quantity even more prolific than in 1958. And high quality seemed nature's way of putting things right. As Ronald Avery said, "it balanced the account". But the tremendous publicity given to the vintage augmented the already fully awakened trade interest, so prices were high. Selection was crucial. By 1959, the trade had become accustomed to buying early for early bottling, early sale and early consumption, but the wines of this vintage confounded the inexperienced. The '59s were old-fashioned, slow-developing heavyweights which could not be effectively judged — on taste — until well into 1960; but customers could not wait and merchants were fearful of missing out. A great vintage is not necessarily problem free. Assessment: just as I feel that 1959 was the last big, heavyweight classic vintage in Bordeaux and indeed particularly in Burgundy, so does Fritz Hallgarten describe 1959 as "the last of the three great natural vintages". (He was referring, in June 1979, to the vintages of 1952, which he considered underrated, 1953 and 1959.) Despite some clumsy, flabby wines, the result of wine-making problems referred to above, one thing is certain: the best are amongst the greatest ever produced in Germany. And the finest are still excellent. Tasting notes: I had no idea I had so many notes on '59 German wines — twice as many as red and white burgundy put together. Never in one vintage have I noted so many high-quality wines, the vast majority being *Spätlesen* and *Auslesen*, with all the variations tolerated before the 1971 wine laws put a stop, very shortsightedly, to the subtle if unquantifiable *feine, feinste, edel* and *hochfeine* qualifications. I have been fortunate enough to taste around three dozen *Beeren-* and *Trockenbeerenauslesen*. Notes of some of these and other selected '59s tasted in recent years:

Berncasteler Doktor Beerenauslese Moselle (Deinhard)	*First tasted in June 1969 at Deinhard's estate on the Moselle: a medium yellow gold; wonderful concentration and length. Eight years later: fairly deep gold; rich, sweet, marvellous fruit and acidity, still with years of life ahead.* Last tasted May 1977 ★★★(★) *And I might as well just mention a* Badstube Trockenbeerenauslese *(Pfarrkirche St. Michael — nothing to do with Marks & Spencer) which was very like the Dhronhofberger below.* Tasted October 1975 ★★★★★
Berncasteler Schwanen Auslese Naturrein Moselle (Meyer-Horne)	*Palish, still with a fresh green tinge; very ripe, sweet, honeyed bouquet and flavour. Lovely wine.* At a III Form Club tasting at Christie's, December 1977 ★★★★
Canzemer Altenberg feinste Auslese Saar (Bischöfliches Priesterseminar)	*1959 was a perfect and rare year for Saar and Ruwer wines. This was from Fuder (cask) No. 590, and was a gold medal winner: deep yellow gold; unusually ripe and full bodied, grapy, honeyed, almost overrich.* At Larry Seibel's in San Francisco, May 1972 ★★★★★
Dhronhofberger Trockenbeerenauslese Moselle (Bischöfliches Priesterseminar)	*Intense amber-orange gold; incredibly rich honeyed/grapy bouquet; one of the sweetest wines I can recall, fabulous concentrated flavour yet enlivened and uplifted with a touch of Moselle acidity. Worthy of six stars!* First noted at the pre-sale tasting of Christie's only wine sale in Germany, in June 1973. Immensely impressive. We must have bought a bottle or two for I see I later served it at three office lunches. Twice in 1974, and October 1975 ★★★★★ Drink now — 2000 plus.
Dom Scharzhofberger (Hohe Domkirche)	*The* feine Auslese *was crisp yet soft and earthy in June 1963 and surprisingly dry but beautiful in June 1965. Seven years later, but without* Prädikat *(that is, not* Spätlese *or* Auslese*), it had a deepish gold colour; a slight oiliness on the nose; very dry with prickly end acidity, on the verge of cracking up, I thought.* Last tasted February 1972.
Hattenheimer Wisselbrunn Edelbeerenauslese Rheingau (Dr Markus Giffl)	*Yellow gold; lovely nose, the honey smell of bottle-age and ripe grapes; fairly sweet — drying out a little; fullish fruity flavour, beautiful balance, perfect acidity.* At Henry Askew's, August 1978 ★★★★
Horsteiner Abtsberg Reuschberg Riesling Trockenbeerenauslese Franconia	*One normally associates* Steinwein *in* Bocksbeutels *(flat-sided flagons) with rather dry, steely and austere wines. This was the opposite: a deep coloured, yellow amber; a fabulous bouquet, fragrant, ripe, almost singed; sweet, intensely concentrated flavour and perfect acidity. Like a tightly grasped bouquet of alpine flowers.* At a Whitwham tasting in Altrincham, November 1975 ★★★★★
Johannisberger Hölle Riesling feinste Auslese Rheingau (Anton Eser)	*A similar colour to the Canzemer '59 and a not dissimilar ripe nose though more scented; great depth of flavour, but a slightly hard bitter finish.* Tasted May 1972 ★ *I preferred another of Eser's '59s, the* Vogelsang feine Spätlese: *soft and ripe.* At the pre-sale tasting, February 1972 ★★★

Johannisberger Kahlenberg Auslese *Rheingau* *(v. Mumm)*	*Showing well at our pre-sale tasting in Düsseldorf in June 1973. Later, in London, rather goaty farmyard smell — a bit too heavy and rubbery; medium dry, a fat, rich wine though pendulous and showing its age.* Last tasted May 1975 ★★
Kaseler Kernagel Trockenbeerenauslese *Ruwer (Bisch. Konvikt)*	*An Oechsle reading of 230°, the second highest sugar content I have come across, and high acidity: 15°. Its bouquet was surprisingly delicate, rich and raisiny, but that level of acidity gave it an incredibly rich, prolonged flavour, almost syrupy. Frankly this class of wine makes Sauternes look feeble, but one must remember that the production of these great German wines is tiny, and only the tip of the iceberg. This wine will see the century out.* The climax of an outstanding tasting in historic but uncomfortable conditions, in the huge, vaulted, dark and extremely damp cellars in Trier shared by the great domaines: the Bischofliches Konvikt, Priesterseminar and Hohe Domkirche, during a visit of the Institute of Masters of Wine, June 1969 ★★★★★
Kreuznacher Bruckes Riesling Trockenbeerenauslese *Nahe* *(Anheuser)*	*Deep coloured, looked like an oloroso sherry; intoxicatingly rich (but not alcoholic), flowers and superfine raisins; intensely sweet but exquisite. Made a 1955 vintage port taste like dill-water.* This, a Hallgarten selection, was rightly drooled over (though some guests affected not to like sweet wine) at a Stourbridge Wine Society dinner, March 1975 ★★★★★
Liebfrauenstift Kreuzgang und Kapitelhaus Riesling hochfeine Spätlese Kabinett *Rheinhessen (P. J. Valckenberg)*	*Despite the label, which reads like the cast list of Wagner's Tristan, a too soft, flabby wine, with a bouquet like a vanilla meringue.* At Dr Witten's, Coral Gables, Florida, March 1971 ★
Maximin Grünhäuser Herrenberg feinste Auslese *Ruwer (v. Schubert)*	*Great estate, great year. A perfect combination. First tasted in 1963: beautiful, crisp, delicate. Eight years later: fabulous peach-like flavour; medium dry, extraordinarily lively yet delicate style — a crystal clear bubbling mountain stream — exquisite finish.* From Dr Witten's cellar in Florida, March 1971 ★★★★★ It slightly upstaged an excellent Scharzhofberger Auslese of Egon Müller and outclassed a good Rheingau and a flabby Rheinhessen (see the Liebfrauenstift) at the same tasting.
Maximin Grünhäuser Herrenberg hochfeine Beerenauslese und Trockenbeerenauslese *Ruwer* *(v. Schubert)*	*First noted in June 1963 at a tasting of 18 Moselles from the Harvey list. By this time, most Harvey hocks and Moselles, except for the cheaper generics, were bottled by the German shipper or at the estates. When young the bouquet was heavier, lusciously full on the palate, with a tingling almost spritz acidity. Nine years later: still pale; softer and more peach-like bouquet; still marvellously sweet, ripe, grapy, combining richness and delicacy.* At the Erichson's in Coconut Grove, Florida, November 1972 ★★★★★ The Trockenbeerenauslese, as can be imagined, was truly magnificent, the bouquet being distinguished by the extra dimension of Edelfäule — an intensely honeyed smell. Tasted April 1971 ★★★★★
Niersteiner Pettenthal Rehbach Beerenauslese *Rheinhessen* *(G. A. Schmitt)*	*Although I noted an Orbel Trockenbeerenauslese as rather disappointing in 1971, the Pettenthal has been consistently lovely: fine bright yellow; very good bouquet and flavour; sweet, rich, clean cut, lovely weight, mature and soft.* Tasted 1972, 1974, March 1975 ★★★★★
Oestricher Eiserberg Riesling Trockenbeerenauslese *Rheingau (Deinhard)*	*More like a '49 in colour; fabulous essence-of-grape richness; intensely sweet, full, fat, marvellous balance of natural sugar and acidity.* At Peter Hasslacher's, October 1973 ★★★★★
Rauenthaler Baiken Spätlese, Fass 601 *Rheingau (Staatsweingut)*	*The first of three '59 Rheingaus. A perfect wine — pale, delicate, well mannered, refined.* With the great collector and enthusiast Ben Ichinose ★★★★ *An Erbacher Kahlig Spätlese of Schloss Rheinharthausen: fuller*

	and richer ✶✶✶✶ And the third, a Rauenthaler Rothenberg Beeren-auslese of von Simmern: *drying out a bit though very rich and slightly raisiny* ✶✶✶ *All tasted in San Francisco, May 1972.*
Schloss Vollrads Riesling Kabinett Blue Label Rheingau	*From the "cellars" of the* Queen Mary: *fresh looking; fine, fruity,* Riesling *nose; dryish, middleweight, good fruit.* At Heublein's in Atlanta, May 1973 ✶✶✶
Schloss Vollrads Trockenbeerenauslese Rheingau	*Tasted in its youth at Hallgarten's, in London in 1962: marvellous, but cradle-snatching. Next, seven years later: deep amber gold; incredibly sweet, full bodied, concentrated, raisiny, with excellent acidity. A great classic.* At Hallgarten's in the Rheingau, June 1969 ✶✶✶✶✶
Uerziger Würzgarten Moselle (Various shippers)	*A* feine Auslese *(of the Bischofliches Priesterseminar) was outstandingly good in February 1970: fine, deep, grapy nose, excellent fruit and acidity. But elderly gentlemen seem fatally attracted to this lady of faded charms for, on 18 October 1976, I shared a bottle (grower Peter Nicolay) with Mr Hartung, a delightful Dutch connoisseur, at his hotel in Vreeland, and the following night in London drank an* Auslese *of the same wine at the 89th meeting of the Saintsbury Club. Three years later: still a healthy bright mid-yellow; gentle, lightly grapy, very sound bouquet; dryish, pleasantly rich middle flavour but showing tiredness on the finish.* At the 94th meeting, April 1979 ✶✶
Wehlener Sonnenuhr Abtei Trockenbeerenauslese	*I did not note the grower's name, but I did note that the wine had an* Oechsle *reading of 165° and, very surprisingly, for Trocks are often of very low strength, an alcohol content of 20 per cent. It had won a gold medal and the "Great Silver States Honour" prize in 1961.* The members of the Northern Wine Society quite liked it too, in March 1965 ✶✶✶✶✶
Wehlener Sonnenuhr Riesling Beeren und Trockenbeerenauslese Moselle (St-Johannishof)	*The only occasion I can recall tasting a wine made of both individually selected and dry, overripe berries. Lovely richness and grapiness though not very sweet and slightly lacking finish.* Tasted May 1970 ✶✶✶
Winkeler Hasensprung Riesling feine Spätlese Rheingau (C. Petri)	*Typical of the fine, soft, stylish Rheingaus of this vintage. Perfect ripeness and balance.* Tasted April 1972 ✶✶✶✶

1960 ✶

Not a quality year. An abundance of short-lived wines, ranging from poor to pleasant enough. Climate: poor weather with wet summer delayed development, but a large crop. Assessment: judging by the admittedly limited number of notes, the '60s seemed to be too light, exposing raw, unripe acidity, or too soft. Clearly the most southerly classic region, the Palatinate, did best but it is a vintage no longer of interest. Tasting notes: just a dozen, ranging from a couple of exceedingly dry Steinweins at Fritz Hallgarten's tasting of noble vines and crossings in April 1962: a crisp, light, steely Würzburger Stein Riesling of the Staatlicher Hofkeller, and a grapy nosed Ippesheimer Herrschaftsberg made from the *Perle* variety; a Niersteiner Rehbach Riesling feine Spätlese, smelling of cats, dry and certainly not fine in 1963; a couple of Domtals, one dull, the other, bottled by Justerini's, soft and spicy in 1968; a minor Oppenheimer and a horrible Liebfraumilch St-Katherine; an acidic Johannisberger Erntebringer — a *naturrein* that, for a change, really needed sugar; and three soft, earthy Palatinates: a Wachenheimer Mandelgarten in 1967, to a Dürkheimer Spielberg, one of two '60s tasted since 1970. The other:

Ruppertsberger Hohenberg *Riesling Kabinett* Pfalz *(Bürklin-Wolf)*	*To show what a top grower in the more southerly Palatinate can do* *in a modest year: very bright and appealing yellow with slight* *green tinge; attractive, soft, honeyed (bottle-age rather than ripe* *grapes); dry, reasonably firm. No length or complexity, but pleas-* *ant.* Tasted November 1978 ⋆

1961 ⋆⋆

Medium-quality wines. Climate: early hopes following a good spring were dashed by bad summer weather. Vintage prospects took an astonishing turn for the better with uninterrupted hot sunshine (on several occasions up to 85°F) from the beginning of September. Acidity a bit high, considerable crop variations from vineyard to vineyard, but overall a small production and high prices, roughly double those of the 1960s. No great *Beeren-* and *Trockenbeerenauslese* wines made, but quite a few *Spätlesen* and some *Eiswein*. Assessment: not remotely in the same class as the 1961 vintage in France. Uneven, middling, and only the best and best kept likely to be of more than passing interest now, except for those who like a challenge. Tasting notes: only 60 or so notes, not more than a dozen of *Spätlese* quality, and only two since 1970. My first encounter was at a big tasting of '61 white wines in Harvey's tasting room in June 1962. It included 27 German wines from Loeb, Langenbach, H. Sichel, Hallgarten, Walter Siegel, Carl Jos Hoch and Huesgen. None were of *Prädikat* quality, but all were of good districts and vineyards. A few samples were cloudy and fermenting, few had anything on the nose except sulphur dioxide, one or two were appley unripe. On the palate they ranged from bone dry to dryish, most were light, dry and frankly unappealing. The following spring, a further range of 20-odd '61s was tasted, from a light Deinhard's London-bottled Berncasteler Riesling at 103s. (£5.15) per dozen (price to Harvey's) to a nice Dürkheimer Hochbenn Riesling Spätlese at 218s. (£10.90). Of the Moselles, a Brauneberger Juffer (bottled by Deinhard's in Germany) showed best: delicate, fruity, with a crisp finish. There were one or two nice Rheingaus but by and large they were dwarfed by some 1959s, at admittedly higher prices, then priced from 173s. (£8.65) to 454s. (£22.70) per dozen for a *Beerenauslese*. There were 60 wines in that morning's tasting. In the evening I conducted a white wine tasting for a group of Harvey customers. I had no need of antacid tablets in those days.

One of the nicest Moselles I came across was Uerziger Würzgarten feine Spätlese of Peter Loosen Erben, refreshing in 1965 but taking on a gold colour and turning from a frisky youth into a more sedate fellow in a matter of a year; and in 1967 an Eltviller Rheinberg of von Simmern, excellent but lightweight, and a well-made Forster Langenmorgen of von Bühl.

Dürkheimer Schenkenböhl *Sylvaner Spätlese* *Naturrein* Pfalz *(Karst)*	*An interesting combination of district and grape: a lovely nose,* *deep, soft, broad fruitiness (I thought it was* Traminer*); medium* *dry, fairly full and fat, soft, with the* Sylvaner's *main drawback,* *lack of acidity. Yet with a finish and really very attractive.* At dinner at David Peppercorn's, October 1965 ⋆⋆⋆
Merler Königslay *Klosterberg Spätlese* *Eiswein* Moselle *(M. Schneider)*	*Made from grapes picked on 25 November 1961, 125° Oechsle.* *Won a "Golden State Honour Prize" in 1964. It did not* *quite live up to expectations: hardly any bouquet, but plenty of* *sulphur on the nose; medium sweet, an attractive crisp flavour but* *lacking real richness.* At a Northern Wine Society tasting in March 1965 ⋆⋆ (*Not the* *only disappointing Eiswein: Anheuser's Kreuznacher St-Martin feine Spätlese Eiswein had a* *similarly dull sulphury nose; intensely dry, thin and acidic, in July 1967.*)
Mettenheimer Goldberg *Scheurebe Spätlese* Rheinhessen *(Langenbach)*	*Just to demonstrate the immediate appeal of a young wine made* *from the* Scheurebe *grape: palish; pronounced muscatel-like* *aroma, fresh and scented; dryish, fairly light, soft delicate grapy* *flavour.* Probably at its best (*at Percy Fox's, the Langenbach's agent*) in July 1963 ⋆⋆⋆
Niersteiner Oelberg	*One of the only pair of '61s tasted since 1970: pale; uninteresting*

Terrassen Riesling **feine Spätlese** *Rheinhessen (F. J. Sander)*	*nose; medium dry; rich but not well-knit and not living up to its name. Tasted June 1971* ★
Rauenthaler Wieshell **Kabinett** *Rheingau (Staatsdomänen, Eltville)*	*Medium pale; pleasant, rich, well-developed nose and flavour though a basically dry wine with nice acidity. Tasted June 1971* ★★★

1962 ★★

A reasonably good "bread and butter" vintage in all areas except the Moselle; acidity higher than in 1961. A large number of ice wines made. Climate: a long cold spell, lasting far into April, retarded growth; uneven and late blossoming; uncertain weather — in fact a year of extremes, with a long period of dryness. Towards the autumn, growers throughout Germany had lost hope but just hung on in case. A dramatic change in the weather occurred at the beginning of October and grapes were left as long as possible, harvesting continuing on the Rhine into late November and in the Rheingau, Rheinhessen, Palatinate and Nahe the last grapes were picked early December, in temperatures of minus 12° to 13°C. The ice wines, because of their late gathering, were known as Nikolausweine. Assessment: by and large, pleasant enough wines though with little depth or staying power in the lower rungs of quality, and none sporting anything worthy enough to be called a bouquet. Clearly the ice wines were, and probably still remain, the stars. Tasting notes: almost an identical number of notes to 1961, all but three prior to 1970 and fewer than a dozen of *Spätlese* quality, not including some *Eiswein* (descriptions of one or two follow). My first exposure to '62s was at a big Deinhard tasting in March 1963, which opened with twenty 1962 Rhine and Moselle cask samples all, or certainly 15 of them, distinctly dry wines (a stark contrast to the almost uniformly sweetened wines of more recent years). As with all wines tasted young, from sample bottles, there were one or two out of condition. Prices (to the trade) ranged from 86*s*. 9*d*. per dozen, duty paid (just over 35p per bottle, in our currently devalued money), for a Zeltinger Schwarzlay to 125*s*. 6*d*. (£6.27) per dozen for Niersteiner Findling Spätlese. Once again, as with the previous two vintages, I rather preferred the Palatinate wines, though an intriguing Justerini & Brooks-bottled Erbacher Herrenberg Riesling Spätlese, with a nose that reminded me of cold tea and syrup, and a nice, rich but piquant flavour, cropped up once or twice in the late 1960s.

Eltviller Rheinberg Riesling *Rheingau* *(v. Simmern)*	*In a good year, a most appealing style of wine. Even von Simmern could not do much with it in 1962: pale, over-sulphured — a trait of the vintage, presumably a fearful dose to keep the wine stable; dry, light, quite nice but little to it. Tasted April 1970* ★
Niersteiner Auflangen **Eiswein Christwein** *Rheinhessen*	*Pale; a fresh but not very forthcoming bouquet, with noticeable sulphur; sweet, fullish, rich yet a light touch. Frankly, the extra dimensions are not there to back up the sweetness. I described it as a "quite nicewein", but no more. At the Peppercorn's, March 1969* ★★
Niersteiner Kehr Riesling **Sylvesterwein und Eiswein** *Rheinhessen* *(H. Seip)*	*Another '62 ice wine: surprisingly pale coloured; a deep, cheesy nose; sweet, medium body, fruity, a most attractive wine, opulent, flagrantly exposing its charms, yet without the ripe honeyed bouquet of a* Beerenauslese *or the concentration of a* Trock. *One of 61 wines at a Christie's pre-sale tasting of burgundy and hock. Vendors were clearly much more willing to let us extract a bottle from their stocks in those days. This sold for 300s. (£15) per dozen at auction. Tasted May 1969* ★★★★
Oestricher Doosberg **Scheurebe** *Rheingau* *(Deinhard)*	*The most recently tasted '62. Nose not bad but not even the rather assertively grapy Scheurebe could break through the '62 barrier; medium dry, quite pleasant and flavoury, with refreshing acidity. Tasted February 1971* ★★

Rüdesheimer Bischofsberg Spätlese *Rheingau* *(v. Ritter)*	*Colour pale lemon; old sulphur on the nose but some underlying fruit; dry, little flavour, short, with marked acidity. An example of the lack of quality and staying power of the '62s.* Tasted April 1970.

1963 **

Better than 1960: useful quantities of light wines, though not much exported probably because English and American customers associated the year with the thin and deficient '63 Bordeaux. Climate: I quote Dr. S. F. Hallgarten's succinct summary in the *Wine & Spirit Trade Record*: "cold winter, frozen Rhine, frozen vines, cold spring, late blossoming — end of June, beginning of July — a splendid July but rain in August, rain in September, rain in October, with an Indian summer towards the end of October." Assessment: variable, an equal amount above and below average, and up to a fifth of the crop of low quality, with sugar content too low and acidity too high. "Clearly only the top wines in the above-average section will be worth drinking. No district better favoured than another, virtually all producing quantity rather than quality. Moselles, in my experience, the weakest." Tasting notes: around twenty '63s tasted, only two being Moselles, and all but three prior to 1970. The first were noted at a big Matthew Clark tasting in June 1966, which included two of von Plettenberg's Nahe wines, a very dry, thin Kreuznacher Riesling and an extremely attractive Kreuznacher Brückes Auslese Kabinett (a gold medal winner) with a rich, deep, fruit-salad nose; medium sweet, fullish lovely grapy flavour, light but clean finish. At the same tasting a Schloss Vollrads Kabinett, Blue and Gold Seal, had a nice flavour but very marked acidity. The last two wines were tasted again in February 1967, the former still most attractive and the latter, the Vollrads, seemed to have "swallowed" some of its acidity: I liked the wine. One of the best '63s to come my way was before a major sale of wines from the Kesselstaat estate in the Moselle, a Piesporter Goldtröpfchen Auslese, a silver medal winner from Fuder 3122: a dryish, light, delicate wine to tickle the palate and refresh — three stars in October 1967. Another attractive wine was a Niersteiner Auflangen und Oelberg Riesling und Traminer Auslese of Johannes Volkner — after I had noted its excessively elaborate and informative name all I had room for was "light, pleasant acid finish" — two stars in June 1969. Four of the most interesting are noted below:

Alsheimer Rheinblick Riesling Siegerrebe Auslese *Rheinhessen* *(Arno Balz)*	*A most appealing wine: very fruity* Siegerrebe *aroma, rather like the* Scheurebe *only lighter and somehow higher keyed, with richness of selected ripe grapes on nose and palate; medium sweet, good balance.* At the Gilbey Vintner pre-sale tasting, April 1971 ***
Casteller Trautberg Perle Beerenauslese *Franconia* *(Fürstlich Castell'schesweingut)*	*An extraordinary double prize-winning wine: deepish yellow colour; beautifully fine, rich bouquet; sweet, combining the richness of ripe berries with the light steeliness of a Steinwein.* Tasted at the fine wine auction in Wiesbaden, April 1969 ****
Deidesheimer Letten Scheubeerenauslese *Pfalz (Thoman selection)*	*A silver medal winner: pale for its age, with a light, grapy* (Scheurebe) *scent, grass-like, attractive; fairly sweet but light style, fragrant.* Tasted at dinner with the shipper, Dora Thoman, November 1974 ***
Ruppertsberger Reiterpfad Riesling Kabinett *Pfalz (Estate bottled)*	*Bright; nose tinged with almond-kernel overtones; medium dry, with rich, "goaty", earthy, Palatinate style, lacking any elegance or finish.* Tasted October 1971 *

1964 ****

The best vintage between 1959 and 1971. A generous abundance of soft ripe wines, the Mosel-Saar-Ruwer wines being outstanding. Climate: the weather did its best, perhaps tried even too hard. From the spring on, growth was ahead of time and fine weather in May, July and August pleased the growers. Worries began to be expressed in early September: there had been no rain worth mentioning for months. No doubt about it, 1964 had been the hottest and sunniest year ever, the hours of sunshine exceeding even 1959. But the equally essential rainfall was low, one-third of average, and even one-third less than in 1959. The wines had a high sugar content and low acidity. In the end, it was a huge harvest which took a long time to pick, some of the larger estates harvesting up to the end of November. Market: headlines in *Harpers Wine and Spirit Gazette* on 30 October, 1964: "Sun no guarantee of quality, but Riesling Year in Germany," and on 20 November: "Cornucopia Year for Germany." Worries were expressed about the great increases in production due to extensions of vineyard areas (30 per cent increase in the Moselle in ten years) and overcropping, resulting in some poor-quality wines. Nevertheless it was a welcome and popular vintage. Assessment: undoubtedly Moselle's year, and superb in the Saar and Ruwer, the two remote tributaries in which grapes so rarely reach their full natural ripeness: there, in 1964, acidity and ripe fruit were, for once, in perfect harmony. The vintage was also successful in the Nahe valley and, happily, in the seat of the noble *Riesling* grape, the Rheingau. Less successful in Rheinhessen and Rheinfalz where a huge crop of the softer, less firm, *Sylvaner* and *Müller-Thurgau* grapes was harvested. In Franconia, the unusually low-acid content of the grapes deprived all but the finest of their characteristic dry, steely style. The best now are probably those Rheingaus and Moselles of *Spätlese* quality from good estates. Lesser wines are soft and lacking. Tasting notes: my tasting books reflect the popularity and abundance of the vintage: hundreds of notes, almost as many as on the 1959s. They took a long time to sift in order to present a balanced picture. A large number were tasted in their formative years, when they were being selected for purchase, and 90 per cent were tasted/drunk and noted within five years of the vintage. In fact, I have only about 30 notes made since 1970. The first extensive tasting of '64s was in February 1966 when I was with Harvey's. Samples of over sixty '64s from several shippers, representing all the main districts, were tasted in one morning. There were considerable variations but, rather like correcting examination papers, the exceptionally good and the bad stand out. Price, as always in trade, was a factor: value for money as well as pure quality. George McWatters, my chairman, was keen on German wines and Harvey's list at that time was one of the best in the country. I am sure I am not letting out trade secrets if I say that Harvey's orders for the '64s varied from 75 cases of Dr. Thanisch's excellent Berncasteler Doktor to 1,200 cases of a Johannisberger Erntebringer. The overall tasting impressions, then and since, confirm the predictions in the postvintage reports. A selection of the more interesting and more recent individual notes follows:

Assmanshauser Höllenburger Spätburgunder Rotweiss Beerenauslese Kabinett Mid-Rhine (*Staatsweingut*)	*One of the most unusual German wines I have ever tasted and an eye-opener. Winner of a gold medal and the* Grosser Preis D.L.G. *in 1968, a half-white wine made from red (*Pinot*) grapes: colour basically straw, but tinged with a warm red brown due to colour being extracted from the skins before the overripe grapes got to the fermenting cellars; a curious sweet, heavy nose; sweet and rich on the palate, with a piquant acidity. A few half-bottles fetched a high price.* At the big Wiesbaden tasting and auction, April 1969 ***
Deidesheimer Hofstück Riesling Pfalz (*Langenbach*)	*I am sure the shippers never intended this wine to survive years at sea and a final landfall in America: it was curious, with a touch of sweet bottle-age but little to sustain the flavour. At the same tasting a Dorf Johannisberger had given up the ghost.* Both from the Queen Mary stocks, at a Heublein tasting in Atlanta, May 1973.
Deidesheimer Langenmorgen Riesling und Traminer Spätlese Pfalz (*H. Sichel*)	*Probably a von Bühl wine. The* Traminer *grape, normally soft and less acidic than the* Riesling, *would have made a totally flat and flabby wine alone in 1964, so a fifty-fifty blend was made. Full yellow colour; lovely, soft ripe nose, honeyed overtone; dryish, fairly full bodied for a German wine, the* Traminer *aroma (deep grapy) and taste (rich, earthy) dominating.* At a most informative lecture-tasting given to visiting Masters of Wine by Herr Meyer of Sichel's in Mainz, June 1969 **

Geisenheimer Altbaum Rheingau	*A modest, pallid and weary wine, with a modicum of flavour and just enough acidity to sustain it.* Not unlike some of the gentlemen in whose company I drank it, in April 1977 ★
Graacher Domprobst Moselle (Fried. Wilh. Gymnasium)	*A perfect example, at seven years of age, of the purity and balance of an unsugared middle Moselle: lovely, bright, light golden sheen; bouquet with a 1953 Rheingau-type delicacy and charm, a pure clean statement, ageing gracefully; dryish, lovely flavour, light but clean finish. Not the length or richness of a* Prädikat *wine but good.* Tasted at lunch at Walter Sichel's, June 1971 ★★★
Hattenheimer Hassel Riesling Spätlese Rheingau (v. Schönborn)	*Lovely wine: rich, well-developed bouquet yet very dry with* Rheingau *Riesling firmness, almost steeliness. Time in hand.* Tasted July 1970 ★★★★
Hattenheimer Nussbrunnen Riesling Kabinett Edelbeerenauslese Rheingau (v. Simmern)	*A* Grosser Preis *winner in 1966. Pale lemon straw; good classic* Rheingau *nose; medium sweet, rich yet with charming, light, piquant touch.* Tasted at the Wiesbaden auction, April 1969 ★★★★
Hochheimer Domdechaney Riesling feine Spätlese Rheingau	*Hochheimer is really off the beaten track, at the Frankfurt end of the Rheingau. The wines have some of the broad earthiness of Bodenheim in the Rheinhessen opposite. This one combined depth with delicate flavour and balance.* Perfect in June 1969 ★★★★
Marcobrunner Riesling Auslese Rheingau (v. Simmern)	*Lovely lemon-gold colour; rich ripe* Riesling, *slightly grapy, slightly honeyed bouquet; medium sweet, fine ripe flavour with body and elegance. A classic, excellent in 1970.* At its peak when last tasted, July 1972 ★★★★
Marcobrunner Riesling, feine Spätlese Kabinett Rheingau (v. Schönborn)	*Despite its* Goldener Kammerpreismünze *und* Grosser Preis *in 1966, I found it dull but just adequate on the nose; dry and lacking acidity. It rightly fetched only a relatively modest price at the Wiesbaden auction.* Tasted April 1969 ★
Maximin Grünhäuser Herrenberg Ruwer (v. Schubert)	*Tasted several times. Charming but correctly classed — not of* Spätlese *quality. Most recently: palish but pronounced yellow; bouquet fruity, gently ripe, lightly honeyed; fairly dry, light but not lacking, holding its flavour and interest, mellow rather than acidic. My host, Hugh Johnson, had been a keen member of the Cambridge Wine & Food Society and recalled a formal candle-light dinner at Trinity College given in honour of Herr von Schubert, who had been deeply moved by the occasion. We toasted the owner of this great wine estate standing in leaky punts on the moat at Saling Hall.* Before lunch one Sunday in July 1979 ★★★
Mulheimer Helenenkloster Riesling Baden	*Considering the size and commercial importance of the Baden district, on the edge of the Black Forest and across the Rhine from the Palatinate, it never fails to surprise me that we see so few of these wines in England. Probably mere convention. For centuries — yes, back to the Middle Ages — we have imported Rhine or "Rhenish" wines, and most connoisseurs think only of the three or four classic districts. Well, here was an outsider, imported by the British Transport Hotels, and very nice too: bright; grapy nose; medium dry, light and agreeable.* Tasted October 1971 ★★
Münsterer Kapellenberg Riesling und Ruländer Auslese Nahe (Staatsdomänen)	*Pale; light, delicate yet intense fruity bouquet (a Nahe characteristic, often like pineapple or fruit salad) with flavour to match. The* Ruländer *grape (a* Pinot gris*) adds body, is comparatively neutral and good for blending. The wine had Moselle character but was softer.* Herr Meyers's tasting at Sichel's in Mainz, June 1969 ★★★

Niersteiner Brudersberg Riesling Beerenauslese Rheinhessen (Heyl zu Herrnsheim)	*Described in the auction catalogue as "Lage im Alleinbesitz" . . . "Goldener Kammerpreis" and "Grosser Preis D.L.G." in 1967, with a gold medal in Ljubljana thrown in. A pale wine; still young and peppery on the nose, unready but rarin' to go; fairly sweet and full flavoured, rich, curious flavour. But fine.* Tasted in April 1969 ★★★★
Niersteiner Schnappenberg feinste Spätlese Rheinhessen (G. A. Schmitt)	*A more recently tasted wine, noted here because it exemplifies the rather vapid character and tiredness of a wine with some pretence to quality, from a good estate, but probably not made from the Riesling grape. Medium-pale lemon straw; ripeness and slightly honeyed bottle-age but somehow empty on the nose; dry, quite nice but light on the finish. Needed an ice bucket.* Tasted November 1978 ★
Oberremeler Karlsberg feine Auslese Saar (v. Kesselstatt)	*The most attractive of the Kesselstatt '64s. A silver medal winner, and deservedly, from first glance to end taste: lovely, with that rare Saar uplift, deftness of touch and balance.* Tasted July 1971 ★★★★
Piesporter Goldtröpfchen feine Auslese Moselle (v. Kesselstatt)	*At Christie's first major sale of wine from the cellars of one German estate. A most interesting range including six '64s, four from Kesselstatt's Piesporter vineyards, and from different casks, one of fruity, rich feine Auslese quality, all balancing slight sweetness with adequate middle-Moselle acidity.* Tasted July 1971 ★★★
Rüdesheimer Berg Frenz Ruländer feine Auslese Rheingau (v. Mumm)	*Medium pale; attractive grass-like nose; very much a medium wine, the sort the English complain about because it is not dry enough to sip as an aperitif and too sweet to drink with a meal. To the Germans it is predominantly a sociable drink. They mainly drink beer with their food. But it is interesting on several counts, a Rheingau made from the Ruländer grape (then fairly rare), from a noted estate, and holding well. Perhaps lighter in body, less firm and steely than a Riesling, more open and mild, though this wine had a nice tingling flavour.* Tasted December 1972 ★★★
Schloss Johannisberg Rotlack Rheingau (v. Metternich)	*Pale for its age; more fragrant than the Niersteiner Schnappenberg; dry, nice weight, good Riesling flavour, sustained by a light acid backbone and fresh clean finish.* Tasted November 1978 ★★★

1965

Poor. Surely eligible for the title "worst of the century". Climate: very changeable weather conditions. Development of vines uneven and retarded. Heavy rot-inducing rain in the summer, the soil in the Palatinate being saturated by the end of August. The coolest summer for a decade. Picking delayed until November, but to no avail. Who would be a wine farmer? Assessment: thin, poor wines although some attractive minor wines could be found. Also some ice wines, though really of little interest. Tasting notes: under 20 notes, including three ice wines made right at the end of the autumn. The first '65 tasted was at Hellmers in July 1966, remarkably attractive and excellent value at 112s. (£5.60) per dozen from Mr Scott's favourite Oberhaart district. It was a Nussdorfer Kirchenstück: soft, delicate, grapy. Three others showing well in 1969:

Ingelheimer Spätburgunder Rheinhessen	*A bit unfair, but a caricature of a German red wine: light rose with a dash of plum red; totally indifferent sugared nose; not dry enough, dull, soft, harmless. Really more of a heavy rosé, lacking fresh youthful acidity.* At lunch somewhere near Heidelberg, April 1970.
Johannisberger Vogelsang Riesling Naturrein Eiswein	*First tasted in 1972: pale; uninteresting nose; sweet with some crispness. Two years later: very yellow; deep fruit, rather creamy*

Auslese Rheingau (v. Mumm)	*nose; fairly sweet, rather heavy and sugary style, flat and cumbersome. An apology for the* Beerenauslesen, *which could never be made in a year like 1965.* Tasted December 1974 ★
Zeltinger Schlossberg-Sonnenuhr Eiswein Moselle (St. Studert)	*Picked from 1 to 3 November in 7 degrees of frost. The bunches were frozen, the water content of the grapes being solid ice, so when pressed, all that flowed was a sort of concentrated fruit juice of high sugar and acid content. After all that effort: an oily rich nose; sweet, nice grapy rich flavour but short. One felt for the pickers. At a tasting for Masters of Wine at the Bischoflischen Weingut, June 1969 ★★*

1966 ★★★

Reasonably well-balanced, stylish and useful wines. Smallish crop. Few dessert wines. Climate: good, well-balanced weather conditions ending with rain and cold in early November, which both delayed harvesting of grapes not already in and limited further ripening. Thanks to the cold snap, however, some (apparently popular and profitable) ice wines were made. Assessment: "stylish" is an adjective that seems to apply to all '66s, no matter where made: vintage port, Bordeaux, burgundy, and German wines. Equally the cry from all districts was: quality up, quantity down. Nicely balanced lady-like wines, with good acidity but lacking the extra dimensions of a riper year. Tasting notes: a moderate number of notes, some 120 in all. I had left Harvey's in 1966 and, by vintage time that year, the newly re-formed wine department was just starting at Christie's. I no longer tasted big ranges of young vintages as I had done on Harvey's wine-buying committee, notes being made at more evenly spread pre-sale tastings, and through the generosity of shippers who invited me to their tastings. The first comprehensive tasting of '66s was at Deinhard's in June 1967, a nice range of 30 wines from the major districts. I found them far better balanced and more even in style than at many big tastings of previous vintages (except for the uniformly excellent '59s) and noted particularly several excellent Nahe wines and a trio of Dom Avelsbacher Altenbergs (from their own little corner of the Ruwer district), of which the *Spätlese* was exquisite, lovely, crisp. Later, before one of our own sales, I tasted a range of excellent Hochheimers of *Spätlese* quality from the Geheimrat Aschrott'sche Erben estate, all remarkably pale in colour, fragrant, with a touch of earthiness but light in style. Out of the 87 lots tasted at the big fine-wine auction in Wiesbaden in 1969, 17 were '66s, though from my notes I see that they were eclipsed by the 1964s and older wines. A Bodenheimer from this tasting is noted separately. The best range of all, over forty '66s, was tasted two months later, during the first official visit of the Institute of Masters of Wine to the German wine-growing regions. One or two of the most interesting tasted are noted:

Berncasteler Badstube Eiswein Moselle (Deinhard)	*Oechsle reading 98°, higher than their 1966* Spätlesen *but lower than their 1959* Auslesen. *High acidity: 9.6 grammes per litre. Typical ice wine lack of colour, very pale, watery; unripe, high-toned nose; medium sweet, long, pronounced fruity flavour with fresh delicacy — much finer on the palate than the Geisenheimer below.* Tasted in Deinhard's cellars on the Moselle, June 1969 ★★★
Bodenheimer Hoch Riesling feinste Auslese Rheinhessen (Oberst Liebrecht)	*A double prize-winning wine in 1968. Pale; very rich, spicy bouquet; combining dryness on the palate with an intense richness and extraordinary fragrance.* Tasted April 1969 ★★★★
Geisenheimer Fuchsberg Eiswein Auslese Rheingau (Basting-Gimbel)	*As if to demonstrate the severity of the cold snap mentioned under "climate", these grapes were picked on 2 November, in 7 degrees of frost: pale; gentle, rich, almost sickly nose; medium sweet, lightish, soft, flavoury but short.* At the Schloss Vollrads birthday tasting, May 1973 ★★
Hattenheimer Hinterhaus Riesling Beerenauslese Rheingau (Winz. Hattenheim)	*Remarkably fresh colour for its age with a lemon tinge to its yellow; good fruit, sweet, straightforward, sound as a bell. Attractive but unspectacular; good but not great.* Tasted March 1980 ★★★

Hattenheimer Rothenberg Beerenauslese *Rheingau* *(H. Sichel)*	*Tasted twice in 1974 with almost identical notes the following year: yellow-gold colour, rich when young, deepening with age; ripe, soft, almost creamy nose; medium-sweet, rich, attractive ripe-grape flavour.* Probably at its best when tasted in July 1975 ***
Horsteiner Abtsberg Rieslaner·Beerenauslese *Franconia* *(Staatl. Hofkellerei)*	*I do not see many Steinweins, let alone from the Rieslaner grape and of this calibre, but by an extraordinary coincidence I have tasted this wine twice: first during the big fine-wine auction in Wiesbaden and just a month later at a Heublein pre-sale tasting in Chicago. Notes happily consistent: rich yellow colour; fabulous bouquet, sweet yet refreshing with a minty overtone; medium sweet, lovely spicy flavour, very rich but with a crisp, firm, quite pronounced acidity.* Tasted April and May 1969 ****
Mettenheimer Goldberg Riesling und Sylvaner hochfeine Auslese *Rheinhessen (P. Witsmann)*	*Much preferred this to the Eisweins: ripe, yellow-gold colour; honeyed nose; medium sweetness and body, lovely rich flavour and finish.* Tasted December 1971 ****
Niersteiner Rosenberg Scheurebe feine Spätlese *Rheinhessen* *(Estate bottled)*	*An outstanding wine shown by Langenbach's in a range of '66s, certainly one of the best I have ever tasted made from this grape: very fine, delicately grapy Scheurebe aroma and flavour; medium dryness and body, perfect balance.* At Schloss Dalberg, June 1969 ****
Oppenheimer Herrenweiher Schloss Spätlese *Rheinhessen (Senfter)*	*Not holding its ten years well: yellow; oily on nose and palate; dryish, soft, flabby.* Tasted June 1976.
Schloss Vollrads Riesling Kabinett *Rheingau*	*A pair at a Heublein tasting. The blau-gold seal: pale, still with a greenish tinge; broad, open bouquet; dryish, light, crisp, dry finish.* Tasted May 1975 ** *The blau seal: deeper coloured, very bright, with a lemon tinge; full, fragrant, fruity bouquet; a little more body but still light and elegant with a pleasing finish.* Tasted May 1975 ***
Wormser Liebfrauenstift Kirchenstück Riesling Auslese Naturrein *Rheinhessen* *(Langenbach)*	*From the best vineyard, by the big church near the heart of the city: medium yellow; very little nose but a warm, earthy, tangy flavour, with a distinct and curious smoky end taste — I can only in all innocence assume this is the smoke of the town absorbed by the top soil over the years — unless ashes are scattered by funeral parties leaving the porch.* Tasted June 1969 ***

1967 ** to ****

Distinctly uneven, mostly average to good, some lesser wines poor and thin, but some excellent dessert wines made. Climate: a comparatively mild winter followed by an extraordinary spring; April and May witnessing sunshine, rain, blasting cold winds and some thunderstorms, retarding growth; early June cold and wet, but blue skies and sun from 21 June (the date summer officially begins) through August. But high hopes were dashed by heavy rains in September. The harvest was a wash-out in some districts but, in others, great estates were able to capture some late autumn sun to produce high-quality dessert wines. Assessment: really already summarized. The best dessert wines still good. Tasting notes: although I tasted fractionally fewer '67s than '66s, I am surprised, having sifted through the notes, at the high quality of the vintage and the number of *Beeren-* and *Trockenbeerenauslese* wines. My first main exposure to '67s was eight Hochheimers from various Aschrott vineyards, many of *Spätlese* quality, and noted for their uniformly rich aroma, in December 1968. A large number, nearly 60, were tasted in all districts during the Masters of Wine visit to Germany in 1969, the most notable being at von Buhl's estate, with an excellent *Beerenauslese* at Schloss Eltz and a deliciously racy Saar wine noted below. The highest number of fine '67s were tasted in Wiesbaden in April 1969, no fewer than 46 of the 97 lots sold (and tasted) over an eight-hour session being of this vintage. Of these, 11 were *Beeren-* and six were *Trockenbeerenauslesen*, the best of the entire marathon session being Bürklin-Wolf's, described below. The dessert wines from the Nahe were also most notable. Fred May had an excellent soft and grapy Dhronhofberger Auslese, in his September 1970 tasting, followed by a lovely Forster Kirchenstück Auslese, with a mustard-and-cress aroma, deservedly almost as expensive as a Niersteiner Orbel Beerenauslese at 605*s*. and 625*s*. (£30.25 and £31.25) per dozen respectively. Loeb had three excellent '67s in their tasting in 1971, a Ruppertsberger Reiterpfad Riesling Spätlese with a nose reminiscent of egg and cress and a dry, rich flavour; an Eltviller Kalbspflicht Riesling Auslese — whether it was the name having a subliminal influence or not, I thought the nose smelled of calf's-foot jelly; and an outstanding Nahe wine. Hellmers had some good Wachenheimers at their July 1972 tasting.

Deidesheimer Leinhölle **Riesling** **Trockenbeerenauslese** *Pfalz* *(v. Buhl)*	*Slightly the better of an excellent pair of TBAs that I bought at Christie's only wine auction in Germany. First noted at the pre-sale tasting in June 1973. Later: medium-pale lemon gold; very good, rich yet delicate, grapy Palatinate nose — somehow riper, more open, a different "shape" to Rheingau; very sweet, rich of course but not a heavy wine, fine flavour and lovely aftertaste. At office luncheons, July 1974, October 1975* ★★★★
Eltviller Sonnenberg **Riesling Auslese** *Rheingau (Egon Mauer)*	*Just to show that elegant wines were made between washed-out minor wines and the great TBAs. Light, delicate, attractive aroma; dry, lightish, refined, fresh and complete. Tasted April 1969* ★★★
Erbacher Siegelsberg **Riesling Beerenauslese** *Rheingau* *(Schloss Rheinhartshausen)*	*Fairly deep gold colour; very rich* Edelfäule *nose — honey gold, overripe grapes; sweet, excellent richness, less hefty and more lively acidity than the Palatinate TBAs. At the Heublein tasting in Las Vegas, May 1975* ★★★★
Forster Kirchenstück **Riesling** **Trockenbeerenauslese** *Pfalz (v. Buhl)*	*The twin of the Deidesheimer noted above and tasted three times. Paler than expected; incredibly rich, honeyed but fresh bouquet; a good, plump, sweet Palatinate TBA with excellent flavour and finish. At Wine department luncheons, twice in 1974 and September 1975* ★★★★
Kallstadter Kobnert **Riesling Auslese** *Pfalz* *(Gerhard Schuster)*	*A beauty: pronounced overripe grapy bouquet; sweet, medium body, rich, lovely, spicy flavour, balance and finish. Of Beerenauslese standard. The only '67 Rhine wine at Graf Matuschka-Greiffenklau's 80th birthday tasting. Perfect in May 1973* ★★★★
Rauenthaler Herberg **Auslese Kabinett** *Rheingau (v. Simmern)*	*Glorious colour, bright yellow gold; lovely ripe, honeyed bouquet, perfect fruity Rauenthal richness; fairly sweet but not heavy, fat yet beautifully balanced. At a pre-sale tasting, March 1980* ★★★★
Ungsteiner Herrenberg **Sylvaner und Riesling** **Auslese** *Pfalz (Karl Schaefer)*	*Slightly deeper coloured than the Rauenthaler; clean, ripe, sweet bottle-age bouquet; medium sweetness and body, good, broad, rich flavour and balance — holding well and a bargain at under £50 a dozen. At a pre-sale tasting, March 1980* ★★★
Wachenheimer Gerümpel **Riesling** **Trockenbeerenauslese** *Pfalz* *(Bürklin-Wolf)*	*"Grosser Rheinpfalzischer Weinpreis 1969" and a silver medal. Deep golden yellow; strong, raw, concentrated nose, quite undeveloped; incredibly sweet, it is hard to imagine such sweetness, its fatness rolled around the mouth, fabulously intense quintessence of grapes flavour, with a powerful, immature tang. The last of 87 wines (offered in 87 lots, the quantity varying in each lot) tasted and auctioned in Wiesbaden in April 1969. I entered the Kurhaus with my hosts, the Kendermanns, after a light lunch (with Apollinaris) at 1pm in spring sunshine. When I left the hall at 7.45pm, having missed my plane back to London, it was snowing. After a very German supper with lots of beer, I departed the next morning with a light foot, a surprisingly clear head and a full notebook. Next, sipped at lunch at H. Sichel's in London. Perfect. Last tasted June 1971* ★★★★★

Wachenheimer Rechbächel **Riesling** **Trockenbeerenauslese** *Pfalz* *(Bürklin-Wolf)*	*Just after extracting the above note I spotted two more recent notes of its twin brother, same grower, different vineyard: first at H. Sichel's "Tasting of the Century" in March 1975. Notes told us that the grapes were picked on 12 November, Oechsle reading 184°, acidity 9.3 grammes per litre: deep gold; deep, rich, raisiny; incredibly sweet and fat. Two years later: very deep orange amber; highly concentrated but fragrant bouquet; very sweet, mouth-filling, very rich and, I found, really too fat and cloying.* At the second of David Allan's '45 Club dinners, June 1977 ****
Wiltinger Braunfels **feine Auslese** *Saar* *(Wwe van Volxem)*	*Pale; surprisingly deep, earthy bouquet with the honeyed richness of fully ripe grapes — I thought it was of* Beerenauslese *quality; medium sweet, with a light fragrant style, crisp acidity and Saar raciness and zing.* At a tasting given by Michael Weber in Trier, June 1969 ****
Winzenheimer Rosenheck **Riesling feinste Auslese** *Nahe (v. Plettenberg)*	*Lovely fruit-salad nose; medium sweetness and body, rich, concentrated, grapy flavour and excellent aftertaste. (£3.20 a bottle.)* At a Loeb tasting, November 1971 ****

1968

Poor. A large quantity of inferior wines useful for quick selling and quick drinking. No high-quality wines possible. Climate: late flowering due to cold, rainy weather end of June/early July; development and ripening hampered by dull, damp and dismal weather in August and September. The wrong sort of botrytis (rot) set in, grapes dropped, the remaining grapes swelled by the rain but picked late and unripe. In earlier times this would have been a ruinous wash-out. As it was, the chemist and wine maker were able to produce a patched-up job, compensating for the natural lack of sugar and overhigh acidity, so that a mass of saleable wines could be made. Assessment: the lesser quality wines simply not worth remembering but, as so often in a really no-go year, one or two pleasant surprises. Tasting notes: just two dozen. First tasted at Hellmers in February 1970: two Palatinate wines including a very attractive Huxel-rebe noted below. Later in the year two small batches of very raw, dull, indifferent, generic hocks and Moselles put into end-of-bin sales; a surprisingly attractive batch at another Hellmers tasting in August and four more, two Moselles and two Badens, one of which is noted below, at the Asher Storey pre-sale tasting in November 1970. Lastly, a rather overblown, short of breath Niersteiner Heiligenbaum at a trade disposal in November 1978.

Durbacher Grillenhalde **Clevner Traminer Natur** *Baden* *(v. Neven)*	*It took the taste and enterprise of someone like Gerald Asher to spot this, an apparently unsugared wine from two types of grape grown in the vineyards of Baron von Neven, and marketed by the huge, competent Zentralkellerei. Pronounced yellow colour; lovely soft grapy/spicy* Traminer *aroma; medium dry, lightish but very flavoury — not for keeping, of course.* Tasted November 1970 **
Dürkheimer Spielberg **Scheurebe Auslese** *Pfalz* *(Schaeffer)*	*Roughly the same latitude as the Baden vineyard, but across the Rhine to the west. Already stained deep yellow gold; really lovely sweet ripeness on bouquet and in taste. Full, sweet, grapy flavour, for a change the high acidity of the unripe vintage giving the often drooping* Scheurebe *an uplift.* Tasted August and December 1970 ***
Niersteiner Burgweg **Traminer** *Rheinhessen* *(Wehrheim)*	*Another example of how the overacidity of a poor year can crisp up a soft grape, this time a* Traminer*: very good nose; medium dry and quite excellent for the vintage. Also reminds me what quiet imagination and enterprise my old friend Mr Scott hid behind his phlegmatic façade.* At Hellmers, August 1970, February 1971 ***

Rohrbacher Mandelpfad *Huxelrebe* Pfalz (Hellmers)	*Just to show what can be made with a fancy grape and the judicious use of sugar in an "off" year. A flagrantly exotic aroma compounded of blackberry-flavoured boiled sweets, muscatel and landladies' cats; medium sweet, light, with a seductively deep, grapy flavour that tailed off and left one stranded. Tasted February 1970 ★★ for trying.*

1969 ★★★

Variable. Firm wines not unlike '66s. Moselles best since 1964. Climate: reasonably good weather conditions with hopes for a great vintage. There was not enough rain in September to swell the berries, however; worse, a dense fog enshrouded the vineyards for a full three weeks, the sun not being strong enough to penetrate to ripen the grapes. Those who did not have to pick early benefited from late October/early November sun. The Palatinate and Rheinhessen in particular, with the earlier ripening varieties, fared worst but the Rheingau and the Moselle, with the late-ripening *Riesling*, took advantage of a late burst of sunny weather and made good wines. Assessment: still well worth looking out for: both the better-quality wines and cheap bin ends. Tasting notes: my first '69s were noted on a trip to the Moselle with Katie Bourke and Mr Scott of Hellmers in early April 1970. What with the cold, raw weather, flurries of snow, a quite indigestible supper, an early morning tasting of 40 young wines (at Dr. Rudolf Müller's in Reil) followed by a tasting standing in inches-deep water in Dr. Thanisch's cellars, I was feeling distinctly liverish and, I am ashamed to say, it showed. Despite the discomfort, I noted a wide spread of good, dry, crisp wines. I retasted several at Hellmers in August and December 1970. Hallgarten in August 1970 showed an admirable range of seventeen '69s, the seven Moselles being uniformly better than the rest, growers like von Volxem, Ehses-Berres, von Nell and Egon Müller showing well; there was also a delicious Mittelheimer Edelmann Kabinett. Next a brilliant sextet of Mosel-Saar-Ruwer wines at a Loeb tasting in November 1971, from a delicate Oberemmeler Hütte with a scent like cut daisies, to the Graacher described below; the Rhine wines, even two Nahes, were not as good. Most recently we opened a range of six '69s at a pre-sale tasting. They came from a private English cellar: the tasting was a revelation.

Berncasteler Doktor und *Graben* *Spätlese and Auslese* Moselle (Dr Thanisch)	*(Thanisch's Doktor always marketed as "Doktor und Graben".) From the cask, two Spätlesen, one "cold", curiously scented and piquant, the other with a lovely young Riesling aroma; slightly drier, lightish, good fruit/acidity. And an Auslese with an undeveloped nose; medium sweet, fuller bodied, lovely crisp fruit. Tasted in the Thanisch cellar, April 1970 ★ to ★★★*
Eltviller Sonnenberg *Riesling Kabinett* *and Auslese* Rheingau (Schloss Eltz)	*The Kabinett wine shown at two tasting tutorials in 1973: very flavoury nose, almost exotically grapy and light in style like a Moselle. The Auslese, more recently, had a bright gold colour; nose in perfect condition, fine, honeyed; medium sweet, soft, rich, nice balance. At the pre-sale tasting, March 1980 ★★★★*
Graacher Himmelreich *feine Auslese* Moselle (J.J. Prüm)	*Presumably pale (I did not note the colour); a lovely bouquet which, in a rare fit of poetic licence, I described as being like Blue Grass perfume; medium dry, lightish in style and weight though with a rich, crisp, most refined flavour. At Loeb's, November 1971 ★★★★*
Hattenheimer Nussbrunnen *Riesling Auslese* Rheingau (v. Simmern)	*Quite yellow in colour; honeyed bottle-age on the nose; medium sweetness and body, quite rich and holding well. The oldest of a group of von Simmern's wines at a Heublein tasting in New Orleans, May 1977 ★★★*
Hochheimer Königin *Victoria Berg* *Riesling Auslese* Rheingau (Deinhard)	*Curious: much lighter than expected and the least impressive of the six '69s recently tasted, though still good: palish yellow; light, fresh crisp nose and flavour but lacking length. Tasted March 1980 ★★*

Kallstadter Saumagen Scheurebe Beerenauslese *Pfalz* *(F. Ruprecht Erben)*	*The only '69 Beerenauslese tasted: surprisingly colourless, like water; fragrant, high-toned Scheurebe aroma, reminding me of lychees; sweet, light for a Palatinate, charming, lovely grapy flavour and surprisingly crisp acidity.* Tasted, February 1973 ★★★
Kallstadter Steinacker Gewürztraminer Auslese *Pfalz* *(F. Ruprecht Erben)*	*Good pronounced yellow; heavenly aroma: ripe, rich, spicy* Traminer; *slightly sweet, spicy yet earthy Palatinate character. Like all* Traminers, *pulled a little — but a luscious mouthful.* Tasted March 1980 ★★★★
Maximin Grünhäuser Herrenberg *Ruwer (v. Schubert)*	*A Loeb selection: pale; delicately scented; dryish, gentle, feminine yet firm and crisp. Wonderfully fresh character. Perfection of fruity acidity.* Tasted for Wine magazine at Thornbury Castle, August 1971 ★★★
Niersteiner Pettenthal Terrassen Riesling Auslese Kabinett *Rheingau (F. K. Schmitt)*	*Palish; lightish fruity bouquet; medium sweet, elegant, attractive — and demonstrates how appealing and well preserved are wines of this quality from the major districts.* Tasted March 1980 ★★★
Niersteiner Rehbach Steig Veltliner *Rheinhessen* *(Hellmers)*	*Although a lot of new (to the Rhine) grape varieties had been planted and were coming into fruition in the late 1960s, this is the first and one of the few* Veltliners *I have ever noted, a grape more associated with the soft, gentle, fruity Austrian wines — a description that fitted this wine: fairly dry, light and charming.* Tasted August and December 1970, February 1971 ★★★
Rüdesheimer Rottland Riesling feine Auslese *Rheingau (Deinhard)*	*Buttery yellow; good bouquet; medium (neither dry nor sweet), soft, grapy flavour, very attractive.* At a pre-sale tasting, March 1980 ★★★
Schloss Böckelheimer Kupfergrube Riesling Auslese *Nahe (Deinhard)*	*The palest of the group; very light, delicate fruit-salad nose; dryish, lightish, fresh flavour, just a little short.* Tasted March 1980 ★★★
Schloss Vollrads Adventswein *Rheingau*	*The lower quality '69 Vollrads were rather dull. This was rather special: from grapes picked on 23 December. Fairly yellow; curious rich creamy mint nose; rich but short. Like most ice wines, saints' wines and sex, mainly in the mind but fascinating.* Tasted May 1975 ★★

1970 ★★

An average year, with an abundance of light easy wines. Totally eclipsed by the 1971s. Climate: blossomed too late for a great year, a dry summer, moderate autumn with a burst of Indian summer. In those districts where the grapes were picked early, average wines were made. In the Palatinate, late pickers were rewarded with high-quality wines. Picking continued right through November in mild weather and even in December. According to Dr. Hallgarten, the 1970 harvest in fact ended on 6 January 1971: growers who had left a few grapes on the vines were, after the previous night's sharp frost, able to make a *"Drei Königs"* day ice wine. Production: not only was the vintage itself bountiful but it is well to note that the vineyard area in production had been increased 50 per cent in 20 years, from the low of 1950 to an area equal to the 1938 level though still not as high as before World War I. Of the 1970 production, roughly 80 per cent was average to good, 10 per cent was classified "inferior" and just under 10 per cent of high quality. Assessment: minor wines of little stature but few giving offence. Tasting notes: half as many as 1969, a mere 10 per cent of my 1959 total, and only about a dozen of Spätlese or Auslese quality. The first '70 I tasted was an *Eiswein*, followed by two batches of ordinary, innocuous wines in June and July 1971. Loeb had a couple of pleasant but insubstantial '70s from great estates in the Saar and Ruwer, and a self-assured Wachenheimer of Bürklin-Wolf, but lacking length in November 1971; a sugar and water Moselle of Deinhard's in March, and a couple of attractive Palatinates at the Hellmers tasting in July 1972. And so they continued, ranging from pallid to quite charming; two Rheingaus from well-respected estates, both with poor noses and pasty raw acidity (October 1973) and a very minor Uerziger Würzgarten in July 1975.

Annaberg Scheurebe Spätlese Pfalz (Stumpf-Fitz)	*A nice example of a successful, ripe, 1970 Palatinate: pale; very attractive, grapy bouquet; medium dry, soft, gently mouth-filling, lovely flavour and balance.* Tasted July 1973 ★★★
Dorsheimer Burgberg Riesling Auslese Nahe (Staatsdomänen)	*One of the few '70s of Auslese quality tasted, and from a little-seen wine village, but exhibiting the deliciously characteristic Nahe fruit-salad nose; medium dry, with good fruit, consistency and acidity.* At a Fred May tasting, July 1974 ★★★
Leiwener Klostergarten Auslese Weihnachts-Eiswein Moselle (Josefinengrand)	*A Christmas ice wine shown in London within five months of the grapes being picked: very pale; dumb, neutral nose; fairly sweet, a very fat glyceriny wine, some richness and a dry tang but — not my style of wine. These ice wines seem gimmicky to me. Give me a wine made from beautifully sun-ripened grapes any day.* At a Franz Reh tasting, May 1971 ★★
Maximin Grünhäuser Herrenberg Ruwer (v. Schubert)	*A Schubert quartet: the ordinary quality, delicate and charming in November 1972, with an aroma that reminded me of* Sauvignon-Blanc *(crisp, fruit-bush acidity), and pleasant in June 1974. The* Kabinett *wine showing well: a very nice aroma, refined, crisp and attractive when it was one year old (at Loeb's tasting, November 1971). A* feine Spätlese *pale, with a hard, immature nose; dryish, light, with a peach-like flavour but a bit too hard and undeveloped in February 1973. Finally the* Auslese: *displaying a good colour; a ripe, peachy bouquet; touch of sweetness but with wonderful Ruwer acidity and a most attractive grapy flavour.* Last tasted at my club, the Traveller's, in July 1975 ★★ to ★★★

1971 ★★★★★

An excellent vintage. Ripe, beautifully constituted wines, certainly one of the most delicious and elegant vintages of the postwar years. Climate: all the hallmarks of a top-quality year: early, well-developed flowering, an extraordinarily fine summer, constant sunshine from early July to a long almost summer-like autumn. The grapes were free of rot and ripened to full maturity, the lack of rain kept the berries (and subsequent production) small and concentrated. The autumn in the Moselle was particularly perfect, with grapes absorbing the moisture from the early morning fog called the *Traubendrucker* (grapepresser) which was then dispersed by the sun and the ripening process continued. Market: growers and merchants are rarely satisfied. Despite a superabundance of 1970s of commercial standard, there were soon complaints about the dearth of wine for the lower end of the trade. The overall quality in 1971 was simply too high. Assessment: there is a world of difference between a German wine made from ripe grapes, and the contrived and sugared wines of lesser years. 1971s have softness and ripeness without the broad, sometimes flaccid character of the '64s or the statuesque almost intrusive richness of the '59s. They have more of a '53 or '49 weight and charm. The top-quality wines have only just started to blossom, and will continue in full bloom for years to come, whilst the great dessert wines will go on developing right to the end of the century. To sum up: '71s have balance: ripe sweetness and perfect fruit acidity. Tasting notes: the only vintage I can recall where I have tasted more *Beeren-* and *Trockenbeerenauslesen* than wines below *Spätlese* level, and of the couple of hundred wines in between, more of *Auslese* than *Spätlese* quality. A plethora of notes, starting with a good Deinhard tasting in June 1972. Twenty-three wines ranging from a pleasant light Wiltinger of `Kabinett quality at £8.20 per dozen ex-cellars Koblenz to an

Oestricher Trockenbeerenauslese at £117.10. An even bigger tasting three months later, from a range of top-class estates, at F. & E. May's, and over a dozen beauties shown by Loeb two months later. The main lessons of these early tastings were that the quality was transparently fine and there was an even spread of lovely wines across the main districts. Outstandingly the best, indeed one of the most memorable, was the H. Sichel's "Tasting of the Century": 24 of the most magnificent '71s, fine wines all, including six of the greatest *Trockenbeerenauslesen* ever to be shown at one tasting. Individual notes below. But unlike earlier vintages such as 1966 and 1969, which seemed to disappear below the horizon after a relatively short time on the market, '71s go on. Yet, like all mature German wines, they are underappreciated and undervalued. I would not be thanked by the publisher or the reader if I wrote 250 notes glowing with admiration, so I have attempted the impossible: to put the greatest '71s into words and to describe some of the attractive but less grand wines most recently tasted.

Ayler Herrenberger Auslese Saar (Bischöfliche Konvikt)	*Medium pale, very bright and appealing in November 1977 and 1978. A year later: deep fruit, wonderfully ripe well-knit bouquet, yet a hard Saar undertow — will keep; medium dry, soft, ripe yet firm. Lovely tingling end acidity.* Last tasted November 1979 ****
Canzemer Altenberg Auslese Saar Bischöfliche Priesterseminar)	*Palish; open, delicate, crisper than the Ayler, firmer acidity; medium-dry, lightish, excellent attenuated flavour and finish.* Tasted November 1979 ****
Erdener Treppchen Auslese Moselle (Bischöfliche Priesterseminar)	*Three notes, twice in the autumn of 1978 and a year later: pale; the least assertive nose of the group of '71 Auslesen, yet subtle, creamy, and flowery; medium dry, distinctly heavier than the Saar wines, flowery, nice dry finish.* Last tasted November 1979 ***
Graacher Himmelreich Trockenbeerenauslese Moselle (Fried-Wilh. Gymnasium)	*Only 214 bottles were made of this wine, from overripe "noble rot" grapes individually picked from seven and a half acres on the steep slopes of the Himmelreich vineyard. Oechsle reading 153°, acidity 13° reduced to 9.7°. Kept in oak and bottled on 3 May, 1972. Bouquet intensely rich but buttoned up; fabulous flavour, amazing powerhouse of fruit, natural residual sugar, acidity and sustaining alcohol — but unready.* The first of five TBAs at Sichel's "Tasting of the Century" at the London Hilton, March 1975. Then ***(**) Drink 1985 — around 2010.
Hattenheimer Engelsmannsberg Beerenauslese Rheingau (B. Ress)	*Amber gold, tinge of orange; overripe botrytis bouquet of soft, creamy, honeyed grapes; sweet, medium body, excellent flavour and balance — light but firm end acidity. Tasted blind: deduced a Rheingau Beerenauslese but thought it was older than '71, perhaps a '67.* At Robert Sakowitz's in Houston, October 1978 ****
Hattenheimer Pfaffenberg Riesling Trockenbeerenauslese Rheingau (v. Schönborn)	*Sichel's noted: one of the greatest Rheingaus ever made, with extract an incredible 245.2 grams per litre. A deep amber gold, with a slight flaky sediment; the bouquet was incredible, combining, as only the greatest German wines can, intense richness with delicacy; an overpowering wine, chewable, a concentrated richness that defies description. Sheer nectar.* Sipped (no spitting out that day), March 1975. Ten stars. Drink 1990–2030.
Hochheimer Hölle Riesling Auslese Rheingau (Aschrott)	*Fairly pronounced yellow; good rich nose, ripe grapes and bottle-age; medium sweet but totally inadequate as a semi-dessert wine, medium body, fairly fat and a touch of Hochheim earthiness, good balance.* At the Waterside Inn with Len Evans, October 1974 ****
Kiedricher Gräfenberg Riesling Beerenauslese Rheingau (Probably Dr. Weil)	*Very pronounced yellow; almost overpoweringly rich bouquet; fairly sweet, fullish, a perfectly lovely wine but seemed to me to have a hard, immature finish.* The only non-1953 wine at the Masters of Wine Jubilee Dinner at Vintners' Hall, March 1978 ****(*) Drink now — 2000.

Leinsweiler Herrlich
various grapes, Auslese
(Hallgarten selection)

Included to demonstrate the revolutionary changes in the formerly plodding Palatinate, with its stern Rieslings *and fat earthy* Traminers. *This was made from a mixture of* Müller-Thurgau, Sylvaner *and* Morio-Muscat *(a highly spicy, muscatel-like grape) grapes: deliciously fragrant, delicate — a real bouquet of flowers — on nose and palate. Contradicts the Englishman's view of the rather serious Germanic approach: a dancing wine, more blue Danube than Rhine in character.* Tasted November 1977 ★★★

Niersteiner Klostergarten
Silvaner und Huxelrebe
Trockenbeerenauslese
Rheinhessen
(Berzirks-Winzergenoschenschaft)

I associate wine cooperatives with competent wine making and rational marketing. But nature and genius consorted here, and the 250 bottles squeezed out of the vineyard could scarcely be considered an economic proposition. The use of the relatively new Huxel *grape gave the wine the colour and light of a great Impressionist painting: Oechsle reading 235°, acidity 12.5° to 10.9°. Deep rich colour; perfect, harmonious, flowery bouquet holding back a little, like a racehorse at the starting gate; a most extraordinary flavour, unbelievable richness and fatness yet with a deft touch of delicate floweriness. But the rewarding thing about these unmatchable German wines is that one does not have to have great knowledge to appreciate them; they are not an acquired taste. They are just beautiful to look at, to smell, to savour, to linger over.* At the Sichel tasting, March 1975. Ten stars. Drink now — 2010.

Niersteiner Kranzberg
Riesling Spatlese
Rheinhessen
(G. A. Schmitt)

Yellow colour; rich nose and ripe flavour; a good example of a classic, relaxed open-knit Hesse wine — the sort the English do not know what to do with if they insist on drinking wine only with food. Tasted November 1978 ★★★

Niersteiner Orbel
Trockenbeerenauslese
Rheinhessen
(Dr A. Senfter)

Wonderfully bright old gold; intensely rich, honeyed nose, good fruit, quite complex and clearly made of other grapes besides Riesling; *sweet, luscious, beautiful complex grapy flavour and acidity.* Tasted at a Studley Priory wine weekend, November 1979 ★★★★★

Niersteiner Spielberg
Silvaner
Trockenbeerenauslese
Rheinhessen
(Bezirks-Winzergenossenschaft)

Oechsle 175°, acidity 10.5° reduced to 8.7°. Deep coloured; quite different from the Graacher and Wachenheimer, the Sylvaner *grape being somehow broader spanning, more open, seductive; softer, yet with beautiful acidity balancing the sweetness. A lovely, luscious wine.* At Sichel's great tasting, March 1975 ★★★★★ Drink now — 2000.

Piesporter Goldtröpfchen
Auslese
Moselle
(Vereinigte Hospitien)

After Berncastel, perhaps one of the most popular Moselle wine names. What's in a name? A great deal, particularly in a year like '71. This was the real thing: nice, plump, ripe nose; medium sweet, rich, good acidity. Tasted November 1979 ★★★★

Schloss Böckelheimer
Riesling Auslese
Nahe
(v. Plettenberg)

Another Nahe, an Edesheimer Ordensgut Kabinett tasted in May lacked acidity, so I was interested to see how this was shaping: rich, positive yellow; rich yet delicate fruit-salad/pineapple nose, gaining deep honeyed bottle-age; medium sweet, distinctly rich, soft, flavoury, perfectly mature — if anything losing its teeth. At Robin Don's, August 1979 ★★★

Trittenheimer Apoteke
Auslese
Moselle
(Bischöfliches Priesterseminar)

At the upper end of the Moselle it has always seemed to me that Trittenheim wines fall a little feebly between two stools, having neither the peachiness plus acidic zest of the Saar/Ruwer wines nor the slight fleshiness, lightness and charm of the middle Moselles. But this is about as good as they get. Now medium-pale yellow; consistently the least interesting, low-keyed, light, honeyed, ripe Riesling *bouquet; reasonably dry, light, firm, straightforward.* Tasted three times, the last in November 1979 ★★★

Wachenheimer Rechbächel Riesling Trockenbeerenauslese *Pfalz (Bürklin-Wolf)*	*A bigger contrast between this and the* Leinsweiler Herrlich, *a comparative flibbertigibbet, can scarcely be imagined. The whole of* Wagner's *Ring rolled into one. Picked 12 November, Oechsle 184°, acidity 9.3°. Deep golden colour; no description of the nose can convey the sense of depth, of layers of richness, of complexity — ambrosial raisins not earthly grapes. As sweet as a wine can be, fat, concentrated, yet a sheer and incredible delight to sip. At Sichel's great tasting, March 1975 ★★★★★ Drink now until beyond 2000.*
Wehlener Sonnenuhr Auslese *Moselle* *(J. J. Prüm)*	*One expects perfection from "J.J." in a perfect year. This was what all ripe middle-Moselle wines aspire to be: slightly sweet yet delicate with lively but unobtrusive acidity, unassertive, fruity, delightful. Perfect in Florida at Dr Louis Skinner's, March 1978 ★★★★*
Wiltinger Kupp Auslese *Saar* *(Vereinigte Hospitien)*	*Tasted twice in autumn 1978. A year later: the deepest yellow of the group; gentle, ripe, rich, complex, peachy bouquet; one of the driest of the* Auslesen, *delicate but firm with lovely acidity. Last tasted November 1979 ★★★★*
Winkeler Hasensprung Riesling Auslese *Rheingau* *(Wegeler)*	*A Deinhard wine. Ripe and attractive in November 1978. Palish, bright; very good fruit; medium, neither dry nor sweet — yet stood up to some raspberries well, thanks to its completeness and perfect acidity. Last tasted and probably at its best, July 1979 ★★★*
Winkeler Jesuitengarten Riesling Spätlese *Rheingau* *(v. Hessen)*	*Very positive yellow, really buttery gold, star bright and very slightly* spritzig; *the smell of perfectly ripe Riesling, fruity but not grapy, the overriding honey element resulting from its ripeness and the development in bottle; medium dry, on the light and elegant side but complete in all respects. Perfect balance and condition. At a workshop conducted for Les Amis du Vin and a week later at a tutorial for the Cambridge Wine and Food Society, October 1979 ★★★*
Wormser Liebfrauenstift Kirchenstück Riesling Trockenbeerenauslese *Rheinhessen* *(Valkenberg)*	*Old gold, with a staining of yellow due to the colouring matter from grapes starting to ferment on the vine; intensely sweet on nose and palate, concentrated sugar grapes, yet with crisp dry finish. At Studley Priory, February 1978 ★★★★★*
Zeltinger Himmelreich Auslese *Moselle (Vereinigte Hospitien)*	*Very bright; gentle low-keyed nose, I thought I detected a whiff of sulphur; medium sweet, pronounced flavour, rich, ripe and lovely. Tasted September 1978, November 1979 ★★★★*

1972 ★

Dull and of modest quality. A useful stopgap vintage providing the trade with lesser wines denied to them by the extravagantly great '71s. Climate: mild winter, insufficient rain; early spring but too short. Late budding (beginning of May). Cold weather in June and cool nights in July retarded blossoming. Then very hot. By early September vines 18 days behind. Cold weather, late ripening, mid-October harvest. Assessment: after the low expectations at the time of picking, a London shipper reported in the New Year of 1973 that "Quality wines . . . after the permitted treatment combined with German scientific thoroughness . . . were a pleasant surprise". After scientific treatment, "surprise" is hardly the operative word. But growers and merchants have to live. Hopefully all '72s have been drunk. Tasting notes: only 20 or so notes, only one of *Spätlese* nomenclature, a Niersteiner of a good grower (Dr. Senfter), but lacking quality and length in April 1974. Anheuser's Schloss Böckelheimer Königfels at the same tasting was austere and dull, with an identical note three months later, which was an indication that '72 Nahe wines were equally uninspired; and one of Deinhard's, nice but neutral in March 1976. The best were a range of eight Moselles from various good estates shown by F. & E. May in July 1974, but my notes were peppered with "austere", "short", "tails off", "fair finish". One of the nicest noted was a Brauneberger Juffer Sonnenuhr Riesling Kabinett of von Schorlemer in November 1976 and, lastly, a Hattenheimer Nussbrunnen Kabinett from von Simmern's estate was milky nosed, dry, lightish and short at a Heublein tasting in New Orleans in May 1977.

1973 ★★

Some charming wines of nice quality. The most abundant vintage ever, but not for long keeping. Climate: late spring followed by late flowering — a discouraging omen in these northerly climes. One of the hottest summers in living memory righted the situation: July, August — September almost tropical — with little rain. Happily the near-drought conditions were redressed by several days of grape-swelling rain in late September. Then sun and a huge crop of ripe, healthy grapes. Moreover, the weather turned cool in November enabling the newly made wines to fall bright. Assessment: despite the happy prognostications, the wines varied from rather insipid to superficially plausible, mainly because of low extract (some lack of concentration undoubtedly due to overproduction) and low acidity. Charming though hollow. Not worthy of deep friendship, but pleasant enough casual acquaintances. Tasting notes: quite a few notes, for someone not specializing in German wines. A group of '73 Moselles led off the F. & E. May tasting in July 1974 and they were distinctly more appealing than the '72s. Dolamore's presented seven quite nice '73s at a tasting in April 1974, Huesgen's Ayler Kupp Spätlese being delicious. A couple of Baden wines (one from an estate with an unfortunate name, Otto Sick) produced at Sunday lunch by Edmund Penning-Rowsell were, in March 1975, with due respect, indifferent — I felt that many English wine growers could do much better. Seven Heymann Bros '73s from different estates ranged from a dry and cardboardy Brauneberger to a pair of pleasantly flavoury Rheingaus of *Kabinett* quality: a Winkeler Hasensprung of Jakob Hamm and a very pale but rich, grapy Oestricher Doosberg from Schloss Schönborn in November 1976.

Avelsbacher Altenberg Riesling Ruwer (*Hohe Domkirche*)	*Palish, slightly* spritzig; *an enchanting bouquet, youthful, gentle fruit; dryish, fairly light, delicate and delightful, with nice* pétillant *end acidity (but with a rapier-like middle)*. Tasted January and February 1976 ★★★
Kiedricher Sandgrub Riesling Kabinett Rheingau (*Dr Weil*)	*A Berry Bros selection. Palish, slightly* spritzig; *fragrant, some depth; medium dry leading to a dry, tingling finish. Some Rheingau firmness and steeliness with fruit in the middle.* Notes made at a Spastics Society tasting. What is particularly interesting is not only the pleasing style but the sheer value for money, £2.32 per bottle retail in 1976, only a fraction of the price of white burgundy of similar quality or the much traded-in red Bordeaux. Tasted September 1976 ★★★
Lieserer Schlossberg Riesling Spätlese Moselle (*v. Schorlemer*)	*Palish, very bright; an appealing, light, slightly grapy nose; medium dry, light body and style, just sufficient fruit/acidity. Superficial but with winning ways. A Hicks & Don wine noted for a recent Spastics Society tasting list and perhaps typifying the lightness and charm of the better '73s.* Tasted October 1979 ★★
Maximin Grünhäuser Abtsberg Kabinett Ruwer	*Delicate peach-like aroma; dry, lightish and rather lacking — hollow, short, slightly* spritzig. *Refreshing but fleeting.* Tasted June 1979 ★
Ruppertsberger Reiterpfad Kabinett Pfalz (*Bürklin-Wolf*)	*Tasted twice, once to select (from Loeb's list) and once to present at a tasting. If genius is the art of taking pains, Dr Bürklin-Wolf qualifies: a calm, delicately fruity bouquet; medium dry, more body — of course, being a Palatinate — than the Avelsbacher noted above — beautifully made.* Tasted January and, in Oxford, February 1976 ★★★

1974 *

Variable, mainly poor wines. Climate: a fairly dismal year with one of the wettest autumns in memory, continual periods of heavy rain of an unusual intensity throughout the harvesting period. A wash-out. Market: the economic situation as gloomy as the vintage. Roughly two-thirds of the prolific 1973 production, and very few wines of more than ordinary quality. Assessment: not a year to seek out, even out of interest. Spend your money and time on the underappreciated and still undervalued fine vintages. Tasting notes: just under a dozen notes which, if arbitrary, is some indication of the lack of interest in this vintage and the few that were shipped. Mostly Moselles, mainly of totally uninteresting style and quality. The first tasted was, in fact, a rather flowery Serriger Antoniusberg of Steinback Rohmann in September 1975; the last being a totally dry, dull and flat Steinwein drunk without enthusiasm at Kettner's (alas now closed) in June 1978.

1975 **

Quite a good vintage, particularly in the Moselle. Climate: warm winter; cold and wet April checked advanced growth. Very warm from mid-June, speeding flowering. Tropical heat in August, heavy rain at the beginning of September succeeded by a mild autumn with misty mornings followed by ripening sun, a total contrast to 1974. Picking from 17 October. Market: a big battle between the purists and the sweeteners, between fully fermented-out dry men and the induced residual-sugar boys. It seems curious to an Englishman that a choice is allowed purely on popular taste and marketing grounds, for there is no doubt in my mind that the plethora of uniformly slightly-too-sweet light German wines is blurring their image and certainly reducing their character. It is more and more difficult to tell the difference between one district and vineyard and another; the soil and the microclimates counting for nothing, blotted out by the bland impartiality of grape taste and sugar. I have a feeling that there will be a reaction. Assessment: frankly, in retrospect, light, pleasant enough. Better than 1974 but largely uninspiring. Tasting notes: quite a large number, more than I realized before they were plucked from my last seven notebooks, and ranging from cheap wines, which tempt me to think that German prices have been stable because the price of sugar and water has not kept up with inflation, to pleasing middle-quality wines, a small cross-section of which is noted below, including part of a group of *Spätlese* and *Auslese* wines of good pedigree tasted in March 1979, nothing like the similar class 1971s, distinctly less substantial.

Berncasteler Doktor Auslese Moselle (*Zach. Bergweiler-Prüm*)	*Bouquet like rather luscious grass, plus fruit; medium, fruity, crisp and very pleasant.* At a Sakowitz pre-sale tasting in Houston, November 1978 **
Johannisberger Hölle Riesling Kabinett Rheingau (*A. Zerbe*)	*Very pale; a sweet, quite ripe, honeyed and delicate nose; medium dry, lightish, pleasant easy fruitiness and nice balance.* At the opening tasting tutorial of a Masters of Wine study course, January 1979 **
Kreuznacher Hinkelstein Nahe (*v. Plettenberg*)	*Fairly pale, unspectacular; light bouquet, body and style; dryish, pleasant enough but not very exciting.* Tasted March 1980 *
Niersteiner Gütes Domtal Beerenauslese Rheinhessen (*M. Weber*)	*Very yellow; a golden honeyed, overripe-grapes aroma; sweet and lovely. Better than morning coffee.* A surprise "package" emanating from Michael Weber's, the big wholesale wine merchants in Trier, and drunk with a noted Danish connoisseur, Holger Ewald, in the well-stocked cellar-cum-bar of his home in Jutland, June 1978 ***
Niersteiner Oelberg Riesling Kabinett Rheinhessen (*Dr Senfter*)	*The only '75 hock at a Rudolf Müller tasting. Only slightly less expensive than a '76 Erbacher and nowhere near the quality: oily nosed and too soft.* Tasted February 1978 *

Scharzberger *Spätlese and Auslese* Saar *(v. Hövel)*	*The* Spätlese *very pale, practically colourless; rather ordinary young nose; dry, light, little to it. The* Auslese *nose not very clean but more fruit; medium dry, light, pleasant fruit and tingling acidity.* Both tasted March 1979 ∗ and ∗∗
Serriger Vogelsang *Spätlese and Auslese* Saar *(Vereinigte Hospitien)*	*First tasted in March 1979. Both pale in colour, the* Spätlese, *surprisingly, more peach-like on the nose, but distinctly piquant and mouth-watering; drier, light, rather almond-kernelly flavour. very light dry finish. The* Auslese *nose rather raw and youthful, medium dry, with a touch of sugar to mask the lightness of body and high acidity. But tasted alongside the 1969s noted earlier, they paled into total insignificance demonstrating, a little unfairly — for Saar and Ruwer wines tend to be particularly feeble in an indifferent year — the chasm in quality between vintages in Germany, and also that youthfulness without character and quality is no match for age with depth and style.* Last tasted March 1980 ∗
Trierer St. Maximer *Kreuzberg Riesling Kabinett* Upper Moselle *(Benedikterinnen Kloster)*	*Palish; neutral nose; the usual medium dryness, very light, refreshing,* spritzig *wine.* Pleasant out of doors on a hot August day in Vreeland, a pretty Dutch village on the banks of a canal, August 1979 ∗∗
Wehlener Sonnenuhr *Spätlese* Moselle (Zach. Bergweiler-Prüm)	*A pleasant, light wine with reasonable fruit and nice enough balance, drunk in balmy Charleston, South Carolina.* Tasted May 1978 ∗∗ *A J. J. Prüm Kabinett wine fairly similar in quality and weight, pale and* spritzig, *no length.* Tasted January 1979 ∗

1976 ∗∗∗∗

Outstandingly good if not great vintage, certainly the best since 1971. Climate: 1976 was a year of exceptional heat and drought in northern Europe, the temperature in the growing areas from May being far above average. Blossoming was encouragingly early, between the end of May and mid-June. By the end of August the grapes along the banks of both the Rhine and Moselle were about three weeks ahead of normal. The long-awaited rain to swell the grapes came at the very end of August. From mid-September to early October the weather was warm and pleasant, and warm, damp weather then encouraged noble rot in the late-ripening varieties. Crop yield varied: 50 per cent normal in the Moselle, 10 or 20 per cent lower than 1975 in the Rheingau. Assessment: delightful, fruity, well-balanced wines, less obviously ripe than '71s, not remotely fat or hefty like some '64s and the '59s, but full of charm. Perhaps not for long keeping. Tasting notes: first tasted in New Orleans of all places — three very good Rheingaus at a Heublein black-tie tasting in May 1977, and spasmodically since. The following notes are intended to give an indication of weight and style.

Bergzaberner Altenberg *Gewürztraminer* *Beerenauslese* Pfalz *(Lorch)*	*Something of a novelty, a* Beerenauslese *from the upper Haart area of the Palatinate domestically known, if at all, for volume not quality production: pale yellow; pleasant, fresh and grapy on nose and palate; fairly sweet, balancing acidity.* Tasted November 1978 ∗∗
Eltviller Sonnenberg *Riesling Spätlese* Rheingau *(H. Lang)*	*One of my favourite styles of hock: bright, palish yellow; most harmonious bouquet, fruit brushed with honey; flavour to match, medium dry, balanced in an effortless sort of way.* Presented at a Les Amis du Vin workshop, March 1978 ∗∗∗∗
Erbacher Honigberg *Riesling Kabinett* Rheingau *(Wagner-Weritz)*	*Firm but delicately ripe nose and taste, the standard medium dryness still with a touch of hardness.* One of a pair of extremely attractive Rhine wines at a Rudolf Müller tasting in London (the other was a Kiedricher Sandgrube Spätlese). Tasted February 1978 ∗∗∗

Forster Ungeheuer Riesling Auslese *Pfalz*	*Good colour; really lovely bouquet; fairly sweet, rich but almost a Rheingau weight.* A stunning wine at the annual Oxford v. Cambridge tasting competition at Harvey's, March 1979 ★★★★
Josephshöfer *Moselle* *(v. Kesselstatt)*	*A wholly-owned Kesselstatt vineyard. Delightful bouquet — spicy, fragrant, overripe peaches; on the light and dry side, excellent fruity acidity, balance and great charm.* Tasted January 1979 ★★★★
Kiedricher Heiligenstock Riesling Kabinett *Rheingau (Schloss Groenesteyn)*	*Palish, good colour; youthful, rather piquant nose, fruity; medium sweet, medium light, attractive fruit/acid interplay.* At a Hepworth trophy tasting, March 1979 ★★★
Niersteiner Rosenberg Gewürztraminer Auslese *Rheinhessen* *(A. Balbach)*	*Normally Gewürz is associated with Alsace. The German version is different: a ripe almost Beerenauslese/dessert wine yellow; exquisite bouquet, not at all like the spicy, grapy, earthier Alsatian counterpart; medium sweet, ripe, fairly rich, delicate fruit acidity — the characteristic that marks a German Rhine wine from the French Rhine style in Alsace. Plenty of development ahead.* At a Hepworth Trophy competition, March 1978 ★★★★
Ruppertsberger Giesböhl Spätlese *Pfalz* *(Bürklin-Wolf)*	*Typical of the lighter, charming Palatinate wines, from a consistently excellent estate: yellow gold; less a bouquet, more a posy — pretty, flowery, sweet; medium sweetness and lightish body, very easy attractive wine, nicely balanced.* Tasted September 1979 ★★★★
Scharzberger Riesling Spätlese *Ruwer (v. Hövel)*	*A delightful wine. Three notes, twice in July 1977: pale; fresh, fruity and attractive; medium dry, charming, light but with some ripe flesh, delicate refreshing acidity.* Last tasted August 1979 ★★★★
Serriger Vogelsang Riesling Auslese *Saar* *(v. Kesselstatt)*	*The bird* (Vogel) *did sing a little in this vintage (see the 1975 notes of the same wine): pale in colour,* spritzig; *attractive in a minor, low-keyed way. But overshadowed by some mature '69s.* Tasted March 1980 ★★
Steinberger Riesling Auslese *Rheingau* *(Staatsweingut)*	*Tasted the summer after the vintage: rich yellow colour; interesting nose with a young, pear-like fragrance; medium sweetness, medium light in weight. Fresh fruity style, ripe-peach flavour.* Tasted May 1977 ★★(★★)?

1977 ★★

Light, mainly ordinary-quality wines for quick drinking. Climate: growth started early but delayed by cold April and May, deferring flowering, 20 June to 10 July. Rainy August. Very changeable weather in September, with some thunderstorms and heavy rain delaying progress; yet in early October some of the warmest weather for years, with cold nights and warm winds from the south blowing the fog away. The early-ripening grapes picked during this period: *Müller-Thurgaus* around 8 October, *Sylvaner* next, late-ripening *Rieslings* last with conditions ideal for noble rot and, towards the end of November, for a small quantity of ice wine. Assessment: do you take sugar in your wine? This vintage presents a choice. I have not tasted enough to see the vintage in full perspective, but from the few I have seen, I am not overimpressed. Tasting notes: as explained in the previous sections of this book, my main business lies with mature wines; nor have I force-fed myself on young vintages for the sake of filling out my notes. Although I tasted a small group of '77s at a trade tasting as early as February 1978 — rather hard raw little wines of no great quality — subsequent notes have been spasmodic, just as they have cropped up. My relatively few notes to date have included half a dozen *Trocken* (dry) wines. Some noted, without enthusiasm, below. For any Englishman blasé enough to be in the habit of familiarly referring to Germany's great dessert wines as "trocks", the new *Trocken* wines are confusingly, if correctly, named. *Trocken* wines are the wine-makers' answer to one side of the sweet-versus-dry controversy. Having myself complained, mainly privately, of the increasingly boring medium-sweet wines that have been churned out by the hectolitre over the past few years. I confess that I find the absence of sugar in the new *Trocken* wines leaves something to be desired. Remove the sugar from modern lower-middle-class hock and one is left with a dry and empty shell. Perhaps there is something, after all, in wine made in a homespun, ingenuous way, with well-pruned grapes grown on underfertilized soil — weather permitting. And I suppose the answer to this is that it doesn't pay.

Erbacher Rheinhell *Weissburgunder Trocken*	*This smelt of cats and tasted of nothing: dry, dull and flat (see also Wachenheimer).* Tasted November 1978.
Schloss Vollrads *Trocken* Rheingau	*The first* Trocken *wine I ever tasted and it came as a bit of a shock. Very pale; light, fruity, youthfully acidic nose; bone dry, light, clean, straightforward but lacking any charm or finesse. At last, after the recent sugared years, a dry hock. Perhaps it should have been tried out in a riper vintage.* It was the first wine I had to speak about at a tasting arranged by the director of the Wine School at the invitation of the V.S.O.D. (The Danish Wine and Spirit Association). For once I was stuck for words, in Copenhagen, June 1978 *
Wachenheimer *Mandelgarten* *Weissburgunder Trocken* Pfalz (Siegel)	*I suppose this was an attempt to make a German white burgundy: pale; nondescript but vinous nose; dry, austere and simply lacking interest.* Tasted November 1978.
Wiltinger Scharzberg *Halbtrocken* Saar (Huesgen)	*Some more German marketing ingenuity — a "half-dry" wine. Palish; I did not notice any bouquet. If there was any it was swamped by the scent and smoke of a coach trip to a Scotch whisky launch at Leeds Castle. On the palate — surprise, surprise — medium dry, like all the other German wines of this class for the past 15 or so years, very light, inoffensive. I think I would have preferred tea.* Tasted August 1979

1978 ★★

Moderate vintage, better quality than the previous two but far short of 1976. Climate: a poor start: inclement spring and dismal summer — but, as in France, a sudden about turn in September with an extended period of balmy autumn weather, warm, sunny and rainless, reducing the size of the crop, particularly small on the Moselle. Late harvest.

1979 ★★★

Light, easy wines. Climate: adverse winter conditions and very severe frosts in January damaged the dormant vines, the extent of the damage only apparent in May. The Moselle-Saar-Ruwer and parts of Rheinhessen most badly hit, but the hardy, late-ripening *Rieslings* least affected, particularly on the steep classic vineyard sites.

VINTAGE

CHAMPAGNE

Champagne is special: it has allure, it has panache. It has been the fashionable wine *par excellence* for three centuries. Indeed, it has never been out of fashion. But the big brands, *les grandes marques*, ebb and flow with the tides of taste, as much a result of image and good salesmanship as of quality.

Some of the differences are more in the name and in the mind than on the nose and palate. By and large, only those who foolishly treat bar ladies in the Place Pigalle to champagne will come across the raw, appley bubbly of the worst sort. Most of the non-vintage of reputable champagne houses and the sort supplied to good wine merchants as a B.O.B. (buyer's own brand) are refreshingly respectable and respectably refreshing. Few sparkling wines from without the demarcated Champagne region have the style and quality of the prototype.

Style and quality
What is it that a good vintage champagne has that lesser wines have not? An appealing colour, a steady stream of fine bubbles — a gentle but persistent *mousse*; next, a purity of bouquet, a distinctive, refreshing scent, perhaps with the smoky aroma of the blended *Pinot* and *Chardonnay* grapes; a dryness without austerity, a cleanness and crispness of flavour, a subtle yet discernible character and, above all, length — an extended flavour, a crisply refreshing finish. And with the greatest, an aftertaste, by which I mean a flavour that lingers, and an internal bouquet that ascends after the wine has been swallowed.

What's in a name?
Sometimes a great deal. In my early days in the trade, a colleague at Saccone & Speed was the first person who effectively explained the differences between the various brands that we handled; and in 1957, a two-week Champagne Academy course in Reims and Epernay helped put the *grande marque* houses into perspective. But fashion and prejudice ride high: people like what they think they ought to like.

From my study of Christie's sale catalogues one thing is apparent: the names fashionable in the past are not necessarily top of the heap today. The greatest era for champagne was from mid-Victorian to Edwardian times. The fashionable brands then were Ayala, Delbeck, Giesler, Irroy, Moët, Pommery and, above all, Perrier-Jouët. Krug and Bollinger simply did not appear in the cellars of the nobility during that period, but they certainly do now.

To aid and abet fashion there has always been the salesman. Examples of this are Pommery & Greno, represented in England by no less a figure than André Simon, from the turn of the century until the early 1930s; and more recently, Taittinger, a brand that joined the fashionable élite in the 1950s thanks to an active agent and the support of the sales-minded Taittinger family.

Vintages

Champagne vintages are in effect "declared", like port vintages. They can, or at least should, reasonably be regarded as *la crème de la crème*.

As in other sections I have quoted examples from past vintages, creeping up towards the present day. However, the purpose of this book is to praise and explain and not wantonly to criticize, so my comments on recent vintages are somewhat circumspect. Apart from not wishing to offend old friends in the trade, I must confess that I am less consciously critical of young champagne. After all, one mainly drinks it at parties or before meals, and even an obsessive note maker like me finds these situations quite the least conducive for making sensible judgements. But quality will out.

Age

I am an incurable romantic: I love the taste and the challenge of an older wine. But a word of advice about age, corks and ullage. The life and strength of the cork are all important. No matter how old the champagne, if the cork appears tightly swelled and sound, it can be drinkable.

Sometimes an older wine will look ullaged, with its level below the neck foil or even lower. Its condition and drinkability will then depend on the cork. If it is firm then the odds are that the ullage is not bad air but carbon dioxide out of solution: the bubbles are in the neck. The champagne will no longer be lively and effervescent; it will be like an old dry white wine with a slight prickle. The pedants might argue that this is not champagne.

Perhaps this is the moment to mention the still champagnes, particularly Sillery and Ay, which were highly prized by the English and Scottish aristocracy from the late 18th to mid-19th century. They were extremely dry and nutty, bearing some relation to sherry or to old hock and a complete contrast to the heavy, sweet, muscat-flavoured wines that dominated the popular taste of the time. Still champagnes on the market today bear no resemblance to the old Sillery. As for Bouzy Rouge, it is fun on the Montagne de Reims at vintage time but almost as scouring as a red Vinho Verde in an everyday English context. It is all a matter of taste.

1728

28 May: following the accession of King George II, a Bill was passed to prohibit the importation of wine in bottles (and not repealed until 1800). This affected sales of champagne though some shipments continued to be made.

1743 ★★★

A good vintage.

1753 ★★★

Another good vintage.

1766

Wines from Sillery became renowned. One of the best-known makers: Marquis de Paisieux.

1768

8 February: first appearance of Champaigne [*sic*] in a Christie's sale, on behalf of "A Gentleman of Distinction leaving off Housekeeping".

1769

25 October: Christie's first sale entirely devoted to wine included 12 lots of "Champaigne" in three dozen lots, which sold for 30s. (£1.50) a dozen.

1771

A shipment of 400 bottles of "M. de. Puissieux's [*sic*] champaigne the finest available. Price with all charges en route 4s. 6d. [22p] per bottle." (André Simon, *Bottle-Screw Days*.)

1779

28 June: a sale at Christie's for the "Marquis de Almadovar". "Red Champagne" up to 91s. (£4.55) per dozen — a phenomenal price in those days, well over double that of the best claret.

1783 ★★★★

1788 ★★★

1790

"Almost everywhere [the English] ask for a dry wine; but they want a wine so vinous and so strong, that there is hardly anything but Sillery will satisfy them." (André Simon, *Bottle-Screw Days*.) See vintage 1857.

1794

5 August: "White Sillery Champagne" realized 75s. (£3.75) per dozen, Lafite only 40s. (£2) and Ch. Margeau [*sic*] 39s. (£1.95) per dozen.

1797

Trade stocks of champagne ran out.

1802

The first year that champagne was officially permitted to be imported direct from France in bottles, but quantity restrictions imposed.

1812

10 June: sale of the Duke of Roxburghe's cellars at

Christie's, including Thackeray's champagne — first mention of a merchant's own blend now known as B.O.B. 10 July: "Sweet Champagne d'Aye" and "Dry Sillery" both 84s. (£4.20). Compare Warre's port at 56s. (£2.80).

1815 ★★★★

The "Waterloo" vintage. Moët's Sillery 1815, the first vintage champagne to appear in a Christie catalogue, in January 1835.

1822 ★★

1825 ★★★

1829

17 November: first mention of a champagne house by name in a Christie catalogue — "Moët's Sillery Champagne", six dozen at 100s. (£5) a dozen compared with 90s. (£4.50) for Lafitte [*sic*], vintage 1819 in same sale.

1837 ★★

1842 ★★★

1846 ★★★★★

A great champagne vintage.

1857 ★★★★★

"The great vintage of '57." (George Saintsbury, *Notes on a Cellar Book.*)
Sillery. A great curiosity from Lord Rosebery's cellars. In heavy old champagne bottles, seals heavily rewaxed in the 1920s. First noted at the sale preview tasting in April 1967: dry, nutty, with a bouquet like an old Château-Chalon. Tasted again ten years later, almost identical notes: pale yellow amber; nutty, smoky bouquet, reminiscent of old, rich stables and oilcloth; dry, not a heavyweight, assertive flavour yet delicate, excellent acidity, slightly yeasty finish.
At an old-wine dinner co-hosted with Denis Foley at the Traveller's Club, September 1977 ★★★

1858 ★★★

1864 ★★

1865 ★★★★★

Excellent wines, fruity, full colour.

1868 ★★★★

A great vintage.

1870 ★★★★

A great vintage.
Sillery. A magnum, "believed to be 1870", from Lord Rosebery's cellar at Mentmore and purchased at Christie's sale of "Finest and Rarest Wines" in May 1967: pale for a century-old white wine, bright but very bitty — a *Goldwasser* of thread-like floaters; rich, stably nose, nutty, old but still somehow fresh; a bone dry wine, fairly full bodied, firm as a rock, fine flavour. Made a good aperitif — a cross between a mature *vin jaune*

from the Jura and Montilla with a dash of Sancerre.
Before dinner with a group of Yorkshire connoisseurs: David Dugdale (one of the best palates in England), Anthony Hepworth, Gordon Cran and others, in Halifax, January 1969.

1874 ★★★★★

The most renowned vintage of the period: "Excellent wines, fruity, full colour . . . a grand wine, full-bodied". (Charles Walter Berry, *In Search of Wine.*) Climate: early frosts but not as severe as the year before which almost completely destroyed the harvest. Fine warm weather for harvest. Moderate-sized crop. 1874 was in fact a landmark. It was the vintage that finally established champagne as the most fashionable, most socially acceptable, most desirable (it had almost always been the most expensive) wine of the high Victorian period, eclipsing fine claret. The subsequent disastrous string of vintages then gave '74s an additional value — scarcity: '74s were the darlings of the salerooms (rather like 1961 claret today), much sought after and fetching extremely high prices at Christie's in the 1880s and 1890s. Judging by their appearance and price, the most fashionable *grandes marques* were in roughly this order: Perrier-Jouët (the '74 fetched up to 780s. [£39] per dozen magnums at Christie's in 1887, an unprecedented price, many times that of a first-growth claret and a level not exceeded at auction for any wine until 1967); Irroy; Veuve-Clicquot; and Moët. Fashion, scarcity and price succeeded in establishing unprecedented levels of prosperity for the champagne houses in Reims and Epernay and the champagne trade in England.
Sillery (Payne's). The third of a trio of old Sillerys from Lord Rosebery's cellars at Mentmore and Dalmeny. This one was supplied by Randolph Payne, one of the best of the many excellent London "carriage trade" wine merchants of the Victorian period. Medium-straw colour, older looking than the '57 and slightly cloudy; nose rather gnarled and twisted; dry, body fading though clearly once a powerful wine, spoilt by a beery finish. Interesting only as a memento of a great vintage.
At the sale preview tasting at Christie's, April 1967.

1875 – 1879

A string of poor vintages. 1875, ordinary. 1876 and 1877, both spoiled by wet Septembers. 1878, a glut of common, unsaleable champagne. 1879, contemptible yield, quality the worst on record. "The result surpasses the worst expectations. The disaster is complete; never in memory of man has it been paralleled in this district." (*Ridley's Journal,* November 1879.) These poor vintages boosted demand and prices for the remaining 1874s.

1880 ★★★

Big wines of good quality. *Climate:* severe frosts; dry May; good flowering; August to mid-September fine.

1881 – 1886

1881, abundant, quite good. 1882, moderate weather and wines. 1883, mediocre. 1884, better quantity and quality good following fine hot summer. 1885, all perfect up to the eve of picking. Then rain and cold. Quality hopes dashed. 1886, bright prospects, but mildew and poor weather reduced crop to 45 per cent of the ten-year average.

1887 ★★

Moderately good vintage. *Climate:* bad start, wet all May; June to August favourable, hot and dry; September cold with frosts after rain.

Pol Roger. Extra Sec, Cuvée de Réserve. Lovely colour: pale old gold, very little sparkle, just a light gentle *mousse*; curious old nose, fungi, not very good; not *sec* at all but medium sweet, nice lightish body, fresh enough to make an interesting drink but passé.

This was the opening aperitif at a dinner party given by André Simon, on his 90th birthday, prior to leaving London to retire to the country. It was followed by a non-vintage Pommery & Greno (André was the London agent from the turn of the century until the early 1930s), which some of us added to the '87 to give the latter a shot of life — a practice recommended by George Saintsbury and André Simon, and one that I still follow at office lunches when my old vintages of champagne are a little too tired. Tasted March 1967.

1888

Poor. Vines weakened by frosts. Mildew spoiled quality and quantity.

1889 ★★★

Good year. Splendid harvest.

Vin d'Ay. Sec (Payne's). Level three inches below the cork (very good for its age), good wax seal and hard cork. A yellow-amber colour, still a fair sparkle; good honeyed bouquet, not showing age; dry, fullish body, straightforward flavour, remarkably sound and attractive but not great.

From Lord Rosebery's cellar at the pre-sale tasting, May 1967 ★★★

1890

Unsettled weather, variable wines.

1891

Wretched end of summer, phylloxera makes its appearance. Small crop, poor wines.

1892 ★★★★★

Exceptionally fine though quantity reduced 25 per cent by spring frosts. Harvest in superb weather.

1893 ★★★★

"Very good but too ripe." (Charles Walter Berry of Berry Bros.) George Saintsbury's favourite vintage. *Climate:* a precocious year: fine spring, growth advanced; hot June through to unprecedently early harvest late August. Ripe and bountiful crop.

1894 – 1897

Variable: 1894, small, moderate. 1895, hot summer, quality not bad, small yield. 1896, poor summer, rotten grapes. 1897, poor August, incessant rain in September caused widespread rot. Yield half that of 1896. Commercial quality.

1898 ★★★

"Hard in its early stages but developed very well." (Charles Walter Berry.) *Climate:* successively cold, warm and wet; tropical heat and drought in August and September.

1899 ★★★★★

A great vintage.

1900 ★★★★

An abundance of very good wines. *Climate:* hard spring; June fine for flowering; July intensely hot; welcome rain storms in August; September hot, vintage started on 20th in ideal conditions. (Phylloxera was progressing through vineyards.)

Duc de Choiseuil. "Grand Cabinet de l'Empéreur, Cuvée de Choix." From the cellars at Glamis Castle: pale straw, lively; clean, nutty (old *Pinot*) bouquet; rich, still some life and a very good flavour.

At the pre-sale tasting, June 1971 ★★★

1901 – 1903

Variable: 1901, incessant rain dashed hopes. 1902, little better, thin wines. 1903, rain ruined crop.

1904 ★★★★★

Very good wines following almost ideal weather conditions, right balance of sun and rain.

Koch. Carte Dorée, Extra Dry. From the Glamis Castle cellars. A magnum, level one inch below foil. Remarkably pale, very slightly cloudy; very mild, old cellar-age nose; dry, lightish, surprisingly nice flavour and balance, held together by beautiful fresh acidity.

The opening wine at the pre-sale dinner at Christie's, June 1971.

Moët & Chandon. Freshly disgorged. Remarkably pale for its age; fine bouquet, damp straw smell the only indication of age; medium dry, excellent flavour and life, good finish. Still a lovely wine.

The oldest wine tasted during the Champagne Academy course, September 1957 ★★★★

1905

Poor, uneven, small yield. Weather (torrents and a cyclone) causing *coulure* then mildew.

1906 ★★★★

Very good. Nearly as great as the 1904. *Climate:* summer favourable but August drought reduced crop.

Pommery & Greno. Old-straw colour, slight sediment; meaty, maderized nose, like a rather drab amontillado sherry; dry, similar meaty flavour but interesting. The finish clean — not beery as expected.

A half-bottle from a cellar in Northumberland, November 1970.

1907 – 1910

As variable as the weather: 1907, changeable. Hot September but part of crop left to rot through shortage of labour. 1908, the worst year in living memory: wet summer — mildew attacked both leaves and grapes simultaneously. 1909, very small yield due to fruit loss and damage. Harvest picked late in rain. 1910, an unprecedented disaster. Floods. Mildew destroyed entire crop. So much for idyllic Edwardian summers.

1911 ★★★★★

Excellent, probably the finest wines since 1874. Troubles in the industry, riots at Easter. Early flowering, dry hot summer, vintage in early September.

Ayala. It looked like draught cider — deep straw, faint sparkle; tired but clean nose; medium dry, slightly spicy.

A half-bottle aperitif before lunch, after inspecting an old cellar in Scotland, August 1973 ★★

Moët & Chandon. First noted at a strange tasting of old

champagnes in May 1958, the place and host not re-corded: quite lively, dry, a bit short but interesting. Next, a fairly recently disgorged bottle shipped to and drunk in Florida of all places. Excellent labels and foils. Very lively and pale for age; old-straw bouquet, oaky old *Pinot*; dry, nutty, like a gently effervescent old white burgundy, good refreshing acidity, very dry finish.
Lunch at Will Dickens's in Fort Lauderdale, January 1975 ★★★★
Perrier-Jouët. Original cork. Deepish straw gold, showing age but still sparkling; bottle-age bouquet, meaty yet still fresh; a lovely wine, still very much alive with quite a tang.
At a memorable dinner given by Ted Hale in my early Harvey days, March 1956 ★★★
Wallace. (B.O.B.) A rare old "buyer's own brand" — a champagne shipped and labelled for a wine merchant, "A. F. Wallace & Co., by appointment to His Majesty": deep *oeil de perdrix* colour, possibly an old pink cham-pagne; musty; refreshing prickle. An acquired taste.
From the Bastard family cellar, July 1968.

1912

Changeable weather, mainly sunless. Ordinary wines.

1913

Poor summer, late harvest, low quality and quantity.

1914 ★★★★

Very good. Vintage similar to the 1904. *Climate:* good flowering; variable summer; by August vines excellent, but much of the locality occupied by German soldiers.
Bollinger. An astonishing wine believed to have been disgorged in 1955: palish, gold sheen, some sparkle; lovely smoky *Pinot/Chardonnay* bouquet and flavour; dry, very good.
The highlight of a Bollinger tasting at the III Form Club, December 1975 ★★★★★
And another, with a haze of bubbles; creamy old cob-nut bouquet; wonderful.
Tasted October 1976 ★★★★★
Delbeck. Good cork and level. Amber colour, faint signs of life, a bit cloudy; caramelly (maderized) but clean; surprisingly sweet, good positive flavour, crisp *spritzig* finish.
An odd half-bottle sample from an old cellar, August 1969 ★★
Giesler. Avize. Amber gold, no life; gentle old nose; nice rich flavour, slight carbon dioxide uplift, clean, crisp acid finish.
Tasted February 1971 ★
Moët & Chandon. Lively and youthful; excellent bouquet; well preserved.
Tasted May 1958 ★★★

1915 ★★★

Good vintage; fine and well-balanced wines. Early flowering. Early picking (from 6 September) by pris-oners of war and soldiers on leave.
Moët & Chandon. Dry Imperial. Level two and a half inches below sound cork which, for its age, emerged with a good healthy pop. Palish gold, fine *mousse* of steady small bubbles; clean bouquet, dry, sound and balanced. Nice old-wine flavour. Lacking length.
From the Bastard family cellars and drunk with my chairman, a lover of old champagne, at his house in Wales in July 1968 ★★★

1916 – 1918

Variable: 1916, changeable, small crop of unequal ripe-ness. 1917, small quantity of good, fragrant wines. 1918, moderate amount, quality irregular.

1919 ★★★

A fine, elegant vintage following April snow and a scorching August.

1920 ★★★★

Very good quality. Weather the opposite of 1919 — mild winter and spring, cold August — but harvest in glori-ous sunshine.

1921 ★★★★★

Wines of exceptionally fine quality despite trying con-ditions. *Climate:* spring frosts damaged two generations of buds. Long, very hot and dry summer. Small crop, high quality.
Veuve Clicquot. Seemed to be one of the high-water eras for Clicquot. Very good hard cork, excellent level. Excellent colour, bright old gold, lively; most attractive and sound bouquet, with smoky (nutty) character; dry, fairly mouth-filling body, firm crisp flavour and finish.
Served on the lawn before a "Drink Tank" lunch at Woodrow Wyatt's, June 1975 ★★★★★
Pol Roger. Tasted twice within a month of being dis-gorged. Rather too pale; very indifferent and disappoint-ing nose and flavour; dry, light, short — on balance I prefer a real "oldie" with the original cork.
At "Concorde to Christie's" reception, September 1978 ★

1922

Not a vintage year owing to poor summer, rotten grapes; also shortage of labour, casks and even baskets.

1923 ★★★★

Good quality but small crop: one-third destroyed by frosts in April, May. Late flowering. Late harvest.
Veuve Clicquot. "Dry England". Old stock in pristine condition thanks to the cold dry cellar below the court-yard at Glamis Castle. Level of wine just below foil, indicating carbon dioxide in neck, but nice life when poured — a steady *mousse* and lovely colour; touch of decay on nose but rich and nutty; medium dry, excellent body, balance and acidity.
At a pre-sale dinner, June 1971 ★★★★★
Two years later, the same vintage disgorged in Clicquot's cellars in 1972: similar colour to Glamis bottle but high fill and more lively; good, deep, smoky old *Pinot* nose and taste; dry, similar weight, good finish.
At lunch with Peter Palumbo, January 1973 ★★★★★

1924

Promising crop ruined by rain, hail and disease.

1925

Bad weather in August and September brought on dis-eases and pests.

1926 ★★★

Below average crop; good quality wines.
Moët & Chandon. Good nose; light and still pleasant.
Tasted May 1958 ★★★
Pol Roger. Several consistently good bottles: wonder-

ful deep, warm, amber colour, bright, gentle prickle of bubbles; lovely, mellow, smoky *Pinot* bouquet, sound as a bell; slightly sweet, indeed almost fat and rich but not at all heavy. Long honeyed aftertaste.
Last tasted at a '45 Club dinner, October 1977 ★★★★★

Pommery & Greno. One of the last vintages shipped by André Simon before he lost the Pommery agency — an occurrence which resulted in his foundation of The Wine and Food Society in the early 1930s. Deep, lively; sweet old nose; rich, just a bit cidery but attractive.
Tasted August 1955 ★★

1927

Deplorable: rain, hail, thunderstorms from early July to a late washed-out harvest.

1928 ★★★★★

Excellent. Firm, well-constituted wines following weather conditions the reverse of 1927: rough winter, damp until mid-May, fine July, August, September. *Tasting notes:* nearly 20 notes of ten different *marques*, including my first taste of an old champagne, a rather maderized half-bottle at a tasting of Roederers in October 1954, a magnum of the same being rich and meaty in 1972. Amongst the freshest and best were Mumm and Charles Heidsieck, both rich; Ayala from Glamis Castle, drier; another Roederer, this time disgorged in 1950 and very dry and rich in 1973; a Veuve Clicquot rosé, like a pale Tavel, with just a prickle of life in April 1978. Other wines:

G. H. Mumm's Cramant. A rare and unusual wine from the cellar of a great connoisseur, Sir Gerald Kelly. Firm branded cork. Good pale colour; light, clean, slightly vanilla nose; distinctly dry and light though steely flavour, *spritz* but not sparkling, long dry finish. Good acidity.
At a pre-sale tasting, November 1968 ★★★★

Krug. I thought this was perfection: an appealing pale-gold colour with an indolent stream of surprisingly large bubbles; delicately scented yet rich bouquet; the slight sweetness of a wine of a thoroughly ripe old vintage, just enough sparkle to give one an uplift, and simply beautiful flavour, balance and acidity.
Before lunch at the Krug's house in Reims, October 1957 ★★★★★

Moët & Chandon. A perfect opening to one of the most memorable lunches ever, at which Lafite and Yquem, both 1869, were drunk exactly a century after they were made. The Moët was remarkably pale for its age but was less than half sparkling; light, scented, nutty *Pinot* bouquet; dryish, really like a fine Montrachet with a touch of *pétillance*. Beautifully balanced, gentle refreshing acidity.
At the Coq Hardy, Bougival, November 1969 ★★★★★

Our host, Peter Palumbo, also produced a magnum of '28 Moët a year later: distinctly deeper, amber gold; more meaty on nose and palate.
At lunch at Buckhurst Park, December 1970 ★★★★

And yet another: rich yet steely, perfect with poached turbot.
Preceding an 1874 Lafite at another memorable centenary lunch at the Coq Hardy, May 1974 ★★★★★

Roederer. The last tasted and best of the Roederers, in one of the most civilized of bottle sizes, the Imperial pint — just right for a single gentleman of temperate

habits. Palish yellow, faint sparkle; excellent bouquet; dryish, reasonable body still, positive flavour and finish.
Last tasted September 1978 ★★★★

Veuve Clicquot. Lovely pale gold, light *mousse*; very attractive bouquet, rich, nutty/old straw; distinctly dry, nice weight, very firm and fresh, crisp finish. A beauty.
The oldest wine at Parrot & Co.'s Clicquot tasting at Claridge's, September 1978 ★★★★★

1929 ★★★★

Fine summer, interrupted only by hail and wind from end July to early August. Abundant yield of exceptionally attractive wines, softer, less firm and long lasting than the 1928s. Only two tasted. A soft Pommery & Greno lacked finish in September 1978. Also:

Veuve Clicquot. Clearly Clicquot's decade: amber gold, very light sparkle; deep, honeyed bottle-age, harmonious, rich bouquet; rich on the palate, too, though not sweet, fine depth of flavour, rather short but with good, very dry finish. Deeper coloured, riper and rounder than the '28.
In magnums at the Mirabelle, December 1969 ★★★★

1930 – 1932

As everywhere in France, dismal years. 1930 set the pattern with frosts, persistent rain, hail in July, a spell of grape-scorching heat, and storms for the harvest. 1931, unremittingly wet, grapes did not ripen. 1932, rain, scorching sun, and rain again.

1933 ★★★★

Wonderful summer, quality very good, optimistic report after harvest: "May rank as top year of the century." But the trade waited for the 1934s. I have not tasted any.

1934 ★★★★

An abundance of very good wines, complete, balanced, following exceptionally fine weather conditions. Early ripening, disease-free grapes. *Tasting notes:* six notes, from a Pol Roger tasted at its opulent, rounded best in 1954 (it was on Saccone & Speed's list at 34s. 6d. [£1.72] per bottle). Twenty-two years later, in June 1976, it was drying out but characterful.

Veuve Clicquot. Golden; ripe; vinous and good.
Tasted 1967 ★★★★

Bollinger. Rich creamy nose; lovely flavour and balance.
Recently disgorged before tasting November 1976 ★★★★

Heidsieck Monopole. Pale gold and very lively; dry, good.
Tasted September 1978 ★★★

1935

Cold, rainy and misty weather in September prejudiced quality. Not a vintage year.

1936

Very wet summer, diseased vines, uneven ripening. Generally unsatisfactory quality and quantity.

1937 ★★★★★

An excellent vintage, the best of the 1930s. Rich, complete wines. The best of those kept in good cold cellars can still be drinkable though the wines show age and '37 acidity. *Climate:* spring and summer favourable; August hot and dry; rain and chilly weather in September induced some rot and necessitated selective picking from 20th. Quality and quantity good. *Tasting notes:* just ten notes, from a very dry Veuve Clicquot and a soft round Charles Heidsieck in 1954. Both wines were in Saccone's list at 33*s.* and 34*s.* 6*d.* (£1.65 and £1.72) a bottle respectively — Château Margaux 1939 was 23*s.* (£1.15) and Yquem 1947 was 35*s.* (£1.75). Bollinger was showing well in 1960, but another bottle flabby and maderized in 1975; de Venoge lifeless and appley the same year. More recently:

Heidsieck Monopole. Medium-yellow straw gold, still lively; nutty old *Chardonnay*-type bouquet; very flavoury, fuller than the 1934, with '37 piquant acidity. *At a pre-sale tasting, September 1978* ★★★

Salon Le Mesnil. Disgorged April 1978. Good colour, not too deep, lively; very unusual bouquet of walnuts (Colin Fenton's description) and freshly picked mushrooms; very dry, rich but showing a touch of old age and overripeness. Fascinating and characterful. *At a pre-sale tasting, June 1978* ★★

Veuve Clicquot. A bottle disgorged in 1976 was very dry and very fresh, with a buttery/smoky old *Pinot* nose in October 1976. Later, and probably the same year of disgorgement: a faintly mushroomy old nose and flavour, less dry but with nice acidity. *At the Clicquot tasting at Claridge's, September 1978* ★★ *to* ★★★

1938 ★★

A vintage of uneven quality not shipped because of the war and rarely come across. *Climate:* good flowering; fine warm weather to midsummer, thereafter unsettled. Rain at vintage necessitated much "picking over". Plentiful crop. Only one wine tasted:

Krug. First tasted in magnum at a post-harvest dinner in 1957, with Paul Krug and Victor Lanson at the latter's press house in Verzenay: remarkably frothy and light. Five years later: deepish gold but bright and lively; lovely bottle-age bouquet with richness and depth; dry, fullish, meaty Krug style, just a bit light on the finish but keeping well. *Last tasted September 1962* ★★★

1939

Late (mid-October) protracted vintage. Inexperienced female and child labour brought in uneven, unripe grapes.

1940

Not a vintage year.

1941 ★★

A moderately good but little-seen wartime vintage. Nice quality, lacking length and finish. *Tasting notes:* just four notes but all good: a lively, firm and flavoury "praise all round" Roederer at a tasting in 1954. A palish and very lively Heidsieck Monopole, very sound but a bit short in 1975. And the two noted below:

Ayala. Extra Dry. Disgorged at the Château d'Ay in February 1972. Palish gold, good colour for age, lively enough; deep mature old champagne nose — reminiscent of apples maturing in a loft; dryish, medium body,

soft, agreeable, slightly short on the finish. In excellent condition. *An aperitif preceding 13 vintages of Haut-Brion (1962–1906) at a Berkmann dinner at Lockett's, November 1972* ★★★

Bollinger. Surprisingly good: deep old-gold colour with some life; showing age on the nose but an appealing delicacy and richness; medium-dry, rich, meaty old-vintage character. *At a III Form Club tasting at Mentzendorff's (the Bollinger agents), December 1975* ★★★

1942 ★★★

A good but little-known wartime vintage. Just two notes:

Veuve Clicquot. Shipped immediately after the war and listed by Saccone & Speed: very dry, disappointing, with acidic finish. *Tasted at Saccone's, 1954.*

Charles Heidsieck. Palish; a mature meaty bouquet; slight, rounded but quite attractive. *In the firm's tasting room in Reims, September 1957* ★★★

1943 ★★★★

A very good year, probably more successful than in any other classic district, and the first major vintage to find its way into export markets after World War II. The best kept are still most attractive. *Tasting notes:* with one exception, good. Quite a few tasted in the mid-1950s: Roederer, very pale, dry, with plenty of life and quality in 1954; Georges Goulet, ageing gracefully if not great, and Krug, dry and firm, both in 1955; Perrier-Jouët, very refined and elegant in 1957. More recently:

Veuve Clicquot. An excellent bottle before a Justerini & Brooks luncheon in 1975: colour of old straw, very lively for its age; nose aged but supported by lively fruit; dry, very flavoury with high but refreshing acidity. Later, a Coronation Cuvée jeroboam, not very lively, with a strained damp-straw nose — dull. The wine had not been aged in the jeroboam but was probably decanted from bottles just before shipment in 1953. Doubtless it was good at the time of Queen Elizabeth's coronation but had lost its freshness and grip in the large bottle over the succeeding 14 years. *A disappointing start to "A dinner to honour 1929 Mouton-Rothschild" at Brooks's, June 1967. At best* ★★★★

Pol Roger. Palish and practically no bouquet in 1957. Later: deeper; richly developed smoky *Pinot* bouquet; the same medium dryness, fine rich flavour and very dry finish. *Last tasted August 1973* ★★★

1944

Not a vintage year.

1945 ★★★★★

Exceptional: big, rather hard, long-lasting but vinous and elegant wines. Tasting notes: these range from 1954, though I have not tasted any '45s since 1977. Krug, tasted in Reims in 1957 was, I thought, distinctly tinny on nose and palate; Louis Menon turned out to be a deservedly unknown *marque* in 1969; Charles Heidsieck was excellent, rich, soft yet firm in 1971, and Lanson was tired, flat but vinous in 1974. The following notes on a trio of *grandes marques* trace their development.

Heidsieck *Dry Monopole*	*Pale gold; rather chocolaty nose, lacking firmness in the Heidsieck tasting room in 1957. Eleven years later: a far more attractive bottle, still palish gold and with moderate sparkle; a good, honeyed, but not over-aged bouquet; touch of sweetness, attractive and lively.* At an Aquitaine Society dinner at Tony Alment's, May 1968. At best ★★★
Pommery & Greno	*Full, fruity and deliciously smooth in 1955. Next, a couple from stately homes in the late 1960s. The first was lively, good, pale straw gold; sound, deep, meaty nose; dry, most attractive and sound as a bell, from Clandeboye in Northern Ireland in 1968. Later, a bottle just on the brink, with sauntering bubbles, a wonderfully rich tangy flavour masking a touch of sourness.* From a ducal cellar in Scotland, July 1969. At best ★★★★
Roederer	*First noted at a comparative tasting of Roederers in 1954: richly coloured, on the sweet side and, I felt, a little overrated for a '45 grand vin. A deep, lively, ageing but nice half-bottle in 1960. Most recently: holding its colour and condition magnificently at over 30 years of age; fine and rich.* Last tasted May 1977 ★★★★

1946 ★

Useful wines for blends but not a vintage year.

1947 ★★★★

Soft, fruity, broad, open, generous wines. Climate: a wonderful summer, similar to 1898, with record hours of sunshine in August. Clean and perfect grapes picked in excellent harvest conditions. Quantity below average because of lack of rain, but quality at the time of the vintage reported as one of the half-dozen really great years since the mid-19th century, combining the finesse and bouquet of 1884 and the body and richness of 1893. Tasting notes: one of my favourite vintages. Once again Roederer the first tasted: touch of sweetness and soft but needing bottle-age in 1954. Heidsieck Monopole undemonstrative in 1957. Charles Heidsieck with Bollinger-like richness the same year and Bollinger itself beautiful, rich and meaty in 1958. Pol Roger full flavoured though short, and Mumm lovely, both in 1959. A poor lifeless Ruinart in 1971.

Veuve Clicquot	*Medium dry, good, but needing more age in 1955. Marvellous out of magnums the evening I shattered the music stand of the de Vogüé family's Pleyel grand piano in October 1957 (a silly accident that haunted me for years). Excellent again in 1970, and also a recently disgorged bottle in 1976. Smoky, rich and refreshing in March*

	1978. Six months later: lively; outstanding ripe Pinot bouquet; an easy, medium-dry and most attractive wine. At the Clicquot tasting at Claridge's, September 1978 ★★★★
Krug	*Pale, nice, young and lively, needing far more age in 1955. Rich, yet with some delicacy in 1957 (but considered too old by Paul Krug — which effectively demonstrates the difference between French and English tastes in champagne: the French like it young and frothy; the English, or at least some of us, prefer it less gaseous and more deep and winy). Five years later beautifully developed: dry, remarkably youthful, a fine deep draught.* Last tasted July 1962 ★★★★
Lanson	*A beauty — with richness preceded by dryness and with lively acidity in 1969. Three variable bottles in 1970. The most recent and best bottle: deep, winy, lovely finish.* Last tasted 1972. At best ★★★★
Salon Le Mesnil	*First noted at Colin Fenton's opening tasting in May 1978. Again, a month later: a characteristic walnut bouquet; dry but rich and nutty.* At the pre-sale promotional tasting, June 1978.

1948 ★

Not a vintage year. Climate: early prospects good but cold and wet until end of July, then a short heatwave followed by storms — damaging hail and rain — in August. Sun before harvest prevented disaster.

1949 ★★★★

A very good vintage. Firmer than 1947, fruity, elegant. Climate: exceptionally warm and dry summer, with occasional rain and some hail, made up for difficult and prolonged flowering. Not a very big crop and reports at the time cautious: "first class, maybe a vintage year". Tasting notes: 50 notes spanning a period of 21 years — a sort of 1949 Rake's Progress from pale, frothy and dry to mellow old gold, gaining depth and richness, and strewed with a few premature deaths *en route*. Starting with Charles Heidsieck in 1957: dry, light and clean in London, positively frothy in Reims. Perrier-Jouët, dry, surprisingly ripe and rounded in the late 1950s and then considered at its peak by M. Budin, the president of the company. Veuve Clicquot: dryish, light and elegant in 1957, developing colour and a rich bottle-age bouquet by 1959. Lanson, also in 1959: palish, lively, a good clean wine showing no age. Mumm: dry, short and rather weak in 1957 — not tasted since. Roederer: pure gold and dryish in 1957; very lively old gold, medium dry, meaty flavoured but fresh finish in 1968. Also, a bevy of beauties all of which seemed to me to benefit enormously by at least ten years' bottle-age and most of which, as recounted below, gained extra dimensions, richness, nuttiness with 20 or more years' maturation. The only real dud was an Ayala, flat and oxidized in 1977. In short, the '49s have turned out to be winners, and can still be delicious — if you like the style of old champagne.

Bollinger	*When first tasted, in 1955, I thought it was remarkably thin and unmeaty for Bollinger. Pale, good, though low-keyed in 1957. In magnums, preceding one of Berkmann's great dinners in June 1971: deepish colour; a faintly corrupt nose; rich and flavoury. Then, in 1975, a beautiful bottle: fine gold colour and lazy sparkle; smoky/peaty bouquet and flavour; lovely, rich yet dry — my idea of fine old champagne. Lovely again in 1976; and six bottles all good in 1977, the last with a hard, tight cork, good colour for its age,*

	a lively mousse *and steady sparkling stream; a rich well-preserved smoky bouquet; medium dryness and body, lovely flavour and persistence.* At home before a Bordeaux Club dinner, June 1977 ★★★★★
Krug	*A great wine. The deepest coloured of a range at the Krug tasting in 1957: dry but meaty with intense, pervasive flavour. Just as good in 1961. More recently: deep yellow, faint sparkle; nose souring a little; hefty but too old.* Last tasted in 1975 ★ But if in good condition should still rate ★★★★
Moët & Chandon	*First tasted in 1957. Two years later: a lively pale gold; deeper more honeyed nose. In 1970, at the age of 21: still lively but with a touch of old gold; deep nose and flavour; dry, fullish, good balance and life-preserving acidity. The following year: a rather dry, austere bottle.* Last tasted 1971.
Pol Roger	*Perfect in 1968: lovely appearance, lightish straw gold; very good nose; dryish, fine, delicate but rich flavour. Seven mainly excellent bottles at office lunches in 1974: bright, lively straw gold; deep smoky bouquet; dryish, meaty. Five lively, nutty-flavoured bottles in 1977 and three the following year.* Last tasted in February 1978 ★★★★
Pommery & Greno	*Pale; dry, very light and fresh but with a rather weak finish in 1957. Deeper coloured, with large loose bubbles; attractive, winy, but an old and over-the-top bottle in 1965. Ten years later, an amazingly well-preserved example: pale; sound nose; dryish, healthy and youthful, with refreshing dry finish. Most recently: still pale for a champagne nearly 30 years old, but semi-sparkling; rich* Pinot *bouquet, fragrant and still fresh; dryish, medium body, perfect balance, attractive delicacy.* At an office lunch, February 1978 ★★★★

1950 ★

Wines suitable for non-vintage blends.

1951

Appalling summer. Thin acid wines.

1952 ★★★

A firm, well-balanced, elegant vintage. Climate: extremely healthy grapes, rain at the right time to swell berries. Quality expectations at the time "the same as 1893". Tasting notes: quite an extensive range, notable for the fragrance of bouquet, firmness and balance. Krug: outstanding, probably the best since 1928. Bollinger: interesting, but not its usual meaty style. Mumm: deeper in colour than other '52s and meaty. Perrier Jouët: fresh, very dry and a bit appley. Pommery & Greno: scented, rich middle, flavoury but immature. Charles Heidsieck: very pale, fresh but also unripe. All tasted in 1957. Dry Monopole: pale, scented, immature cooking-apples smell, thrice in 1957 (though at that time considered by Heidsieck the best for years) and still maintaining youthfulness though a bit dull in 1968. Major wines tasted several times, and a faded rosé, are noted below:

Bollinger	*A five years old: pale, lively; fresh, most pronounced bouquet; not very dry nor the usual meaty style, but elegant. The* brut *a bit austere in 1960. A magnum in 1962 confirmed its unmeaty and more Perrier-Jouët style. In 1965 I felt it was passing its best, but in 1968 I enjoyed a lively bottle, developing at last a deep, rich meatiness with bottle-age. Most recently: broadening out (middle-age spread?) and flavoury.* At a 111 Form Club tasting, December 1975 ★★★
Krug	*In 1957: pale; deep and meaty nose; dry, fuller bodied than the 1953 Krug, lovely flavour. Magnificent as an aperitif in 1960. At peak in December 1966: its sparkle simmering down; a refined gentle bouquet; on the palate softening, but with good long flavour. Eleven years later, still perfection: lively, pale for its age, even sporting a youthful lemon tinge; perfect soft, nutty bouquet; medium dry, neither too full nor too light, lovely rich flavour.* Last tasted with a group of wine trade contemporaries at a lunch at Christie's to celebrate my 50th birthday and my 25 years in the trade, May 1977 ★★★★★
Pol Roger	*Lively; meaty, vinous, and at its peak in September 1966. Yet at the age of 27, a beautiful wine: an appealing yellow gold with fine but few bubbles; lovely mature smoky bouquet and flavour; dry, firm, excellent balance, and long finish with refreshing prickle.* At Hugh Johnson's, July 1979 ★★★★
Roederer Rosé	*Why is it that rosés are so lacklustre, no matter whether still or sparkling? This wine was a deepish pink, had an uninteresting nose, and was dry, firm, a bit austere, yet neither vinous nor lively. Clean but too old.* Tasted March 1964.

1953 ★★★★

Excellent: full, fruity, harmonious wines following an equable, well-balanced summer and fairly early harvest starting 14 September. Tasting notes: several dozen notes of just a dozen *marques*, from the autumn of 1957 to 1979. Generally attractive wines: rounder, less firm and perhaps less elegant than the best 1952s. An early beauty was Roederer Cristal Brut: very pale, delicate, dry and refined in 1959. An appealing, not too dry but short-lived Mumm in 1960. A most attractive Perrier-Jouët: rich yet light and dry, fresh with good finish, tasted twice in 1961. Pommery & Greno: soft in 1961, at best in 1962 and dull old straw by 1978. Lanson: rich and good in 1967. A plausibly attractive Irroy on the decline in 1974.

Bollinger	*First tasted in 1959: a good, full, meaty Bollinger, reverting to type after the lighter '52. Excellent at a Champagne Academy dinner in 1960, and most recently, a curiosity, disgorged in 1964.* Last tasted at the Masters of Wine Silver Jubilee dinner, 1978.
Veuve Clicquot	*First tasted in 1959: pale; slightly sweet, with soft approach but a very refreshing dry finish. A good dry mouthful, twice in 1961. Fully ripe in 1967. Most recently: lively; most forthcoming on the nose; shapely in the mouth.* Last tasted September 1978 ★★★★
Charles Heidsieck	*First tasted in 1960. I have always liked the style: a meaty* Pinot *character, perhaps lacking the final polish of Bollinger or Krug but always less expensive. Deepening in colour, very dry in 1961. Rich and crisp in 1967. Developing rich nuttiness in 1978. Excellent.* Last tasted at office lunches, October — December 1979 ★★★★
Krug	*At four years old: pale; similar nose to the '55 but richer and*

more meaty; round, refreshing, lovely flavour (considered by Paul Krug to be the best balanced of his vintages from 1945–1955). A perfect magnum in 1977: fine continuous mousse; harmonious nose with no signs of old age; not crisp or nutty like the '52 but excellent. Good in 1978. Well-knit, well preserved in April 1979, with oaky, charred, bottle-age bouquet; bone dry, lovely flavour and finish. Last tasted at office lunch, October 1979 *****

Roederer	One of the palest '53s and, in 1961, still with rather tinny youthful acidity. More recently, variable half-bottles with variable corks — moral, do not keep half-bottles of champagne too long. Last tasted 1968.

1954 **

Very acceptable for blending but not vintage quality.

1955 *****

Extremely good, underrated vintage. Climate: cold and wet early spring; excellent April; hot second half of June; good flowering 2 July. Picking started 29 September. Large crop. Reports at the time ranked '55s "amongst the highest vintages"; very rarely had there been such quality of juice in such a quantity of grapes. Tasting notes: I have more individual tasting notes on the 1955 vintage than on any other except the 1961. There were few failures — notably two Dom Pérignons in poor condition, whose corks had not survived 22 years, though also in 1977 Laurent Perrier was showing well. In its youth Pol Roger was dryish with a fairly full soft flavour, the best of a group of six '55s tasted in 1961; good notes in 1962, too. Mumm: attractive, fruity, with hock-like aroma in 1961. A lovely Roederer: ripe in every way in 1965. Ayala, not often seen in England today, a rich wine at its peak in 1966. The following notes trace the adolescence and maturity of an eminently satisfactory vintage:

Bollinger	First noted at a Bollinger lunch in London in 1962: a broad mellow style, sweeter and more meaty on nose and palate than the '52 tasted alongside. By 1966 almost "chewably" meaty on the nose, mature and flavoury. A year later: still with a very lovely mousse; soft earthy nose; lovely meaty flavour and in perfect condition. Most recently: amber gold; old smoky bouquet; dry, rich, ageing gracefully. Last tasted at a Bollinger tasting, December 1975 *****
Bollinger R. D.	The first fully marketed vintage of the "retarded" or "recently disgorged" Bollingers: certainly impressive, rich and crisp when first tasted in April 1969. And a bottle that had been disgorged in 1968, tasted nine years later: rich but austere, with an extended dry/acid finish. Last tasted in 1977 ****
Veuve Clicquot	Not tasted until it was 12 years old: though nice I thought it a bit short (in magnums, 1967). Deep and attractive in 1971. Recently: gentle, civilized and delightful. At the 200th dinner and the 21st anniversary of the Aquitaine Society at the Northampton and Country Club, January 1977 ****
Charles Heidsieck	Pale, drier than the '53 and a bit piquant in 1961. Full of flavour in 1962. Sixteen years later: still lively, smoky, dry and nutty at the "Concorde to Christie's" reception in 1978. Most recently: rich and characterful, but better for being refreshed with Berry Bros non-vintage. Last tasted January 1979 *** On the decline.

Heidsieck **Dry Monopole**	*The deepest (dull gold) and least lively at a tasting of six '55s in 1961; very dry with light tinny end. Greatly improved with bottle-age.* Last tasted in magnums, December 1970 ⋆⋆
Krug	*Henri Krug tells me that the '55 Krug was a blend of 23 different growths (individual wines of varying styles from different vineyards). Fifty-nine per cent were made from the* Pinot Noir *grape, 26 per cent from the* Chardonnay *and 15 per cent from the* Pinot Meunier. *First tasted, newly disgorged, in the tasting room at Krug's in October 1957: very pale with a creamy froth; light bouquet, clean and scented; very dry yet excellent full flavour, but "green" and quite unready. Next, 12 years later, in magnum: classic, a masterly understatement and perfect at a "No Name Society" dinner at Lord Crawshaw's in 1969. Singed, smoky and rich in 1976, and as good at the "The Krug Award for Excellence" judges' dinner in Hedges & Butler's cellars in 1978. Also perfection when last tasted (disgorged December 1963 with a dosage of 0.75 per cent): a most attractive buttercup yellow, gentle mousse; lovely rich, smoky, ripe* Chardonnay *bouquet; touch of ripe sweetness on the palate, fullish body, deep meaty flavour, perfect balance. A hint of end acidity.* At the Jubilee Dinner of the Institute of Masters of Wine, March 1980 ⋆⋆⋆⋆⋆
Lanson	*Dry, light, feminine and frothy in 1961 — tailor made for a French actress's slipper. In 1967, crisp, drier than the '53, fresh but deeply satisfying. Equal top at a blind tasting of 12 champagnes in May 1971, for although it was losing its sparkle the bouquet and flavour had developed. A dry wine with powerful tang and fine finish. Two years later: calming down and putting on a little weight (blonde flibbertigibbet becomes mature young matron); dull flavoured with refreshing acidity. Most recently; an attractive magnum, though showing age.* Last tasted March 1974 ⋆⋆⋆ But now on the decline.
Moët & Chandon *Brut Imperial*	*First tasted whilst young and fresh (both the wine and I) at Château Saran, twice in June 1960: very pale; bouquet, as with the young Krug, light, fresh, scented; very dry, light and still youthfully acidic. A pleasant middle-of-the-road champagne at a comparative tasting in 1961, and showing no great development by 1966. Hard-corked magnums, one lively and sound if unexciting in 1967, and another at its peak a year later.* Last tasted 1968 ⋆⋆
Perrier-Jouët	*I have always liked the style of Perrier-Jouët, once (in the 1880s) the star of the salerooms. The '55 was typical, even at 13 years of age: palish, very lively; distinctly dry, with a clean, light style and dry, crisply acidic finish.* Tasted only once, in 1968 ⋆⋆⋆⋆
Pommery & Greno	*In 1962: sweet on nose and palate, and full flavoured. Deepening to a yellow gold, very nice quality in 1965. Two years later from a jeroboam: appropriately soft, ripe and very attractive wine, clearly happy to exchange its comfortably commodious vessel for relaxed and convivial company.* An impressive opening to the first meeting of the Jeroboam Club (the brainchild of Melvyn Master and Jeremy Palmer) in 1967 ⋆⋆⋆⋆
Ruinart Brut *Selection Philippe de Rothschild*	*An all too rare appearance of Ruinart, the oldest established Champagne house (now playing a secondary role in the Moët-Hennessy empire): seemed to have rather loose meandering bubbles; not much evidence of bottle-age; very dry, lightish and rather austere, some end acidity.* At the Westbury Hotel, July 1969 ⋆⋆

1956 ★

Acceptable quality but not a vintage year. Climate: frosts until the end of March; cold and wet spring; poor weather through summer — rain and hail, except for two or three weeks in September. Quality and quantity below average.

1957 ★

Poor. Not a vintage year. Climate: variable, then almost completely washed out by incessant rain through harvest, from 23 September to 6 October. Small, low-quality crop.

1958 ★

A third non-vintage vintage. Climate: wet winter delayed pruning; improvement in March but still cold in April; first half of June stormy — poor flowering conditions; bad weather in August, with mildew, but fine September and late picking from 6 October.

1959 ★★★★

As if to make up for three dismal years, a great vintage: very good, well-constituted, ripe but rather massive wines. Climate: from May, a long hot summer with little rain; flowering in excellent conditions; harvest excellent. First-class wines, thought at the time to be the best for decades — one had to go back to 1893 for a comparison. Tasting notes: the trade went nap on this vintage. Not only was it highly acclaimed but it came just in time, for stocks of the '52s, '53s, and even the prolific '55s, were running out. André Simon said he drank champagne every day of his life. Certainly something kept him sparkling well into his 93rd year. Alas this will be just another thing I will never have in common with that great man. I am surprised how relatively few '59 champagnes I have noted, only a few dozen, of a dozen different *marques*, from 1962 to 1976. But the general style and weight of the vintage comes through. The 1959 heaviness did not seem to suit some wines. Lanson, for example, usually a fresh, light "French" style, wore its 1959 ripeness and weight with ill grace — I thought it was a bit flabby at the Champagne Academy dinner in 1966, and ripe but short of breath later the same year though it seemed to have regained its balance in 1968. But Pol Roger, Churchill's favourite champagne, carried its big 1959 frame easily, like the great man himself. Tasted in 1967, it was pale, with a spray of finely divided bubbles; a good nose; dry, crisp and lively. Perrier-Jouët was flavoury and well balanced in 1966. Giesler, another famous old brand not much seen today, was a bit unbalanced, with tinny acidity in 1968. Irroy "Extra Dry" was not at all dry, nor lively, in 1969, but Moët & Chandon retained both colour and vigour at the same age.

Bollinger	*One might have expected Bollinger to be rather heavy in a vintage like 1959. Not so. Although it had the characteristic "meaty" style, it was fine in every respect: fine palish colour; fine delicate but ripe bouquet; surprisingly dry, medium full bodied, fruity, rich but refined.* Tasted 1965, 1966 ★★★★★ *Should still be excellent.*
Dom Pérignon	*It must have been in the late 1950s when this* de luxe *brand started to top the charts. I first had the '59, in magnums, in Florida in 1972: I found it very dry, full bodied but somehow not to my taste.*

Perhaps it needed age, because four years later, whilst maintaining its lively sparkle, the bouquet had taken on a deep, mature, smoky character and did not seem as austere. Indeed it was rich and very good indeed, though how I managed to make a note of it at 3 am after a marathon six-hour evening tasting of 40 vintages of Latour and a superb midnight dinner, I do not know. Last tasted at Dr Overton's in Fort Worth, May 1976 ★★★★

Charles Heidsieck

I cannot think why this brand features so frequently in my notebooks. It used to be known as "the tarts' champagne", through the activities of a charming and energetic West End representative who made sure that it was stocked and drunk in all the London night clubs. Vintage Charles Heidsieck has a certain mildly opulent style and the '59 is a good example: a bit frothy in May 1965, but rich and fullish in body. Nubile and refreshing later in the same year. Deepening in colour and with a richer bouquet, three times in 1966. An excellent magnum in Dublin in 1971. Also excellent a couple of years later: a good colour, bright, light gold; a good rich meaty nose; dryish, fairly substantial flavour, well preserved with a refreshing twist of end acidity. Last tasted September and November 1973 ★★★★ Probably still good.

Krug

Dry, but rich and meaty, ripening nicely in 1960. By 1971 it had broadened out: fairly deep straw colour; a really deep and meaty bouquet; dry, fairly full bodied, lots of "beef" and character but not refined, and perhaps lacking the style and balance of the '55. Very good mouthful though. Last tasted June 1972 ★★★★

Taittinger
Cuvée Comtes de Champagne
Blanc de blancs

It is interesting to observe how brands come and go. Several of the most fashionable marques of the "Champagne Charlie" period had dropped out by the 1920s. Krug and Bollinger have gained their reputation since those days, Taittinger is one of the most recent fashionable brands, stemming from the 1950s. First tasted in January 1964, I found it clean, light and dry but a bit too young and frothy. By 1966 it had put on a bit of weight; and it was distinctly riper and more to my taste a year later. (The "extra dry rosé" tasted in 1969 was a rather grubby pink and not very attractive.) The brand has been successful (in England at any rate) for several reasons: a touch of showmanship, the Taittinger family making many publicized visits. In the mid-1950s they had a dynamic agent, then a fairly precocious young man, who became a politician. Moreover, their top blend, "Cuvée Comtes de Champagne", which struck a note just the right side of pretentiousness and "blanc de blancs", when it first came out, was in the advance guard of fashion. As it happened, 1959 was a heavyweight vintage so it was a plump "blanc de blancs", not the crisp, light, dry style one expects today. Last tasted 1967 ★★★★

1960 ★★

Abundant but not of vintage quality. Climate: heavy winter frosts; February mild and wet; May dry and sunny but July rainy and cold; a little sun, rain and hail in August. Fairly early harvest from 14 September. Large crop. Market: the 1959 vintage had assuaged the trade's thirst for vintage champagne, and after the really poor trio of years, 1956, 1957 and 1958, the champagne houses needed supplies to top up their non-vintage stocks. The 1960 vintage was timely.

1961 ★★★

Firm, fine, fragrant and flavoury wines. Climate: first three months fine, mild with some rain; stormy in April, cold in May; warm and sunny in June for the vital flowering; July cold, dry and windy after a warm start; fine and warm, with a little welcome rain in September — harvest in brilliant sunshine. Tasting notes: many more notes on the '61s than on the '59s, with a fascinating comparative blind tasting of the major brands in the offices of Pol Roger's London agents in February 1967. Out of nine different brands, outstandingly the most attractive was Roederer; Krug came out sixth on the panel's average though I placed it fourth — it was clearly immature, a wine needing much more time in bottle. Pol Roger averaged second though I placed it eighth. Pommery & Greno, a lively, meaty but dry wine, was a unanimous third and Veuve Clicquot and Bollinger tied for fourth place. Around this time Dom Ruinart started to appear in the ranks of the *de luxe* champagnes: a pale, certainly fine, dry, crisp, well-balanced wine (at three Bass Charrington Vintage Dinners in 1967, 1968 and 1969). Another, with aristocratic pretensions, Prince A. de Bourbon Parme Brut, was as grand as its title in 1969, but I have never seen it since. Piper Heidsieck's Florent Louis, yet another *de luxe* brand, followed the stylistic footsteps of Dom Pérignon: pale, very bright, with a fine stream of small bubbles; a nose of refined straw; bone dry, steely, rather austere, tasted in 1971. And a fourth, de Castellane's *de luxe*: palish, not very lively; good nose; dry, steely but flavoury in 1973. The standard '61 vintage de Castellane was showing well at a Wine and Food Society wine committee meeting in 1969: a nice quality, individual wine with an attractive flavoury *Pinot* character and good finish. Other wines tasted only once include Giesler, a lively, dry, meaty style of wine in 1970; a Perrier-Jouët with a remarkably rich and attractive bouquet, a dryish, medium-light, nice flavour but short — not as good a nose in 1970; and a Taittinger Comtes de Champagne, gaining colour but holding its *mousse* with good rich bottle-age on the nose, fine flavour, texture and length, and richness balanced by good crisp acidity in 1974.

Bollinger	*First tasted at Mentzendorff's, Bollinger's London agents, in 1966: pale, dry, medium light — much lighter than the '59 — a little austere but good. Pale but soft and meaty in 1967. A most refreshing, lovely and enticing wine in 1968. Excellent in 1971: fully developed, much better than the '62. Tasted several times since. At 14 years of age it was just taking on a gold sheen, but still lively; fully developed bouquet — lovely smoky Pinot, deep, attractive and in perfect condition; some body, firm rich flavour, perfect balance, dry finish with excellent acidity.* Last tasted at a Bordeaux Club Dinner at Christ's College, Cambridge, October 1975 ★★★★★
Veuve Clicquot	*Surprisingly little mousse in 1967, though a nice wine with rather a sweet finish. The same year the "Brut" was fullish, certainly not brut, rather rich, very attractive. Eleven years later: still pale and lively; nose deepening and straw-like; dryish, nice flavour, retaining a slightly sweet finish, though lacking a little persistence.* Last tasted at the Clicquot tasting, September 1978 ★★★
Dom Pérignon	*Only tasted once, when the wine was ten years old: very pale straw colour with very steady spray of fine bubbles; classic bouquet; very dry. Overall the impression was of great refinement, yet austere. Admirable, but I personally prefer a meatier style of champagne.* Last tasted at the Alment's, July 1971 ★★★★
Heidsieck Dry Monopole	*A curious wine, lively but rather deep; oddly attractive nose — a sort of fishy Pinot aroma; dryish, light in style, not too good a finish.* Tasted twice, in 1967 ★

Krug	*Bouquet undeveloped, distinctly immature but good length and potential in 1967. As mentioned earlier it was well down the list at the comparative tasting of '61s but I felt it merely needed time. Indeed it was better four years later, but by 1978 I found it rather disappointing: fleshy, but not as deep and meaty as I had expected. A year later it was a medium-pale straw colour with little* mousse *— indeed there was little sign of life after a short while in the glass; a bouquet like damp straw, neither fruity nor nutty; on the palate medium dry, medium body, positive flavour but lacking zest and a touch overacid. On this showing, a relatively short-lived and rather disappointing Krug.* Last tasted at Studley Priory, November 1979 ★★
Moët & Chandon	*In 1966 it seemed very dry but this was probably youthful acidity. At the blind tasting in 1967 it had a piquant, slightly grapy nose, and seemed the sweetest of the nine brands. Later the same year I noticed its flowery and very attractive bouquet, and its acidity once again gave it a dry feel. At 15 years of age it opened with a burst of exuberance, large bubbles being superseded by a small steady stream; rich fragrant bouquet; dryish, flavoury but a bit short.* In the French style, at the end of dinner, at Robert Sakowitz's in Houston, October 1976 ★★★
Pol Roger	*A rather poor start — a corky, stalky-nosed bottle, rather hard in 1967. A good mature bottle in 1974, gaining colour and simmering down; dry but deep and rich. Most recently: old straw colour but lively, steadily streaming bubbles; good, deep, straw-like, slightly charred* Pinot *bouquet and taste; dry, nice acidity.* At La Mission Haut-Brion, April 1978 ★★★★
Pommery & Greno	*Very lively; good rich nose, but dry and austere in 1967. Later the same year: very scented nose; dry, odd meaty flavour, still a little acid. Two years later: still pale lemon; good nose; good flavour, balance and finish.* Last tasted 1969 ★★★
Roederer	*A beautifully balanced wine, the apotheosis of elegance — rich but well mannered and voted top of the nine* grandes marques *at the blind tasting in 1967. Its quality was endorsed at a dinner at the Harcourt Rooms in 1968: palish; excellent bouquet; dry but rich, medium weight, lovely vinosity, perfect balance. Later the same year an extraordinary "cream of mushroom soup" bouquet; rich refined flavour, with a wonderful follow-through and finish. I bought some at auction in the autumn of 1974 and consumed it at dinner parties over a couple of years. Some of the corks were failing and I had one or two tired bottles, but at its best it had a medium-pale yellow colour, a nice spurt of sparkle which quickly settled down to a gentle* mousse; *a rich yet cracklingly dry, smoky* Chardonnay *bouquet and flavour, with a lovely finish.* Last tasted June 1976. At best ★★★★
Roederer Cristal Brut	*In short supply, expensive and not easy to obtain, Cristal Brut deserves its reputation as perhaps the most refined of the de luxe champagnes: a slender stream, almost a haze, of fine bubbles; fragrant yet understated bouquet; beautiful texture in the mouth.* Enjoyed with George Rezek, so long the head of the North American branches of the International Wine and Food Society, at the Café Royal, April 1969 ★★★★★
Salon Le Mesnil	*Supplied by Berry Bros to the Traveller's Club, where I drank it in the early 1970s: a dry, fine, thoroughly elegant wine with a long finish.* Last tasted July 1972 ★★★★★

1962 ★★★★

A good vintage. Dry, fruity, elegant wines. At best, refined. Climate: cold spring; dry June with vines in healthy condition; mild July but not enough summer sun; a fine hot September enabled the grapes to catch up with their ripening, and the harvest took place in early October in good conditions. Tasting notes: I have tasted far fewer '62s than '55s, '59s or '61s — merely a couple of dozen notes of eight *marques*. With the exception of the first tasted (a rather uninteresting Mumm in 1967), I found them consistently good and noteworthy.

Bollinger	*Not the usual meaty style, perhaps drier and more refined. Nicely balanced in 1969. Rather immature and frothy in magnums in 1971. Two years later, approaching its best: good colour and life; richly developing bouquet; dry, steely, fine.* Last tasted in February and March 1973 ★★★★ *Doubtless excellently mature now.*
Dom Pérignon	*First tasted in the spring of 1971: a most elegant, understated wine, bone dry. More recently, in tandem with Cristal Brut: very pale — a lemon-green tinge, remarkably youthful looking for a 15 year old; a hard crisp Chardonnay nose, showing no signs of age; very dry, lightish, ultra refined, fine dry finish. A little too austere and still not to my taste, but impressive.* At the opening of Len Evans's great dinner in Sydney, February 1977 ★★★★★
Charles Heidsieck	*Good, clean, medium-dry wine in 1969. Later, two flavoury attractive magnums.* Tasted June and December 1972 ★★★★
Heidsieck Diamant Bleu	*The* de luxe *blend of Heidsieck Monopole and the first vintage I noted in trend-setting, skittle-shaped bottle. Happily the contents were good, though a touch too sweet for me.* Tasted May 1971 ★★★★
Krug	*As with Bollinger, the Krug '62 did not at first have the usual beefiness and weight, though excellently balanced in 1969. (I noted at the time that the relationship of the '61s to the '62s was not dissimilar to the Bordeaux wines of the same vintages. The '62 champagnes lacked flesh but were supple and easy.) Palish, though deeper coloured than the Krug '64; sturdy yet refined, with a powerful flavour, but not fully mature in May 1970. Bouquet developing in 1971, and beginning to show some age eight years later: dry, rich, refined. Probably at its peak of development in mid-1970s.* Last tasted April 1979 ★★★★
Philipponat Clos des Goisses	*I had not come across this* marque *before and am told that the Clos des Goisses is a genuine* clos, *not just a fancy name. It was another worthy* de luxe *of Dom Pérignon style: pale for its 15 years; an extremely characterful nose with that curious tangy, fishy Pinot aroma that I associate with Chambertin; on the palate distinctly dry, fine, a trifle austere.* With Berek Segan, Philipponat's Australian protagonist, in Melbourne, March 1977 ★★★★
Pommery & Greno Avize	*A bit immature and raw in 1968. Still pale with a nice steady mousse; very clean refreshing nose which had developed a little bottle-age; very dry, lightish in style, good acidity and finish.* Last tasted October 1971 ★★★★
Roederer Cristal Brut	*A lovely golden colour, quite a contrast to the Dom Pérignon; rich, slightly yeasty nose; medium body, lovely broad style, yet refined. Extremely attractive. I preferred the style of the Cristal Brut, but*

the Dom Pérignon was fresher, indeed in superlative condition. The opening champagne at Len Evans's great wine dinner, with a formidable array of noses and palates headed by the Australian prime minister, in Sydney, February 1977 ★★★★

1963

A poor year, for which the weather was entirely to blame. Climate: still cold in May after a long period of frost; then promising weather, hot but humid in June; totally unsuitable weather at the crucial late summer period — cold and wet throughout August and September. Some rot. Picking started 30 September in rain, though the sun did finally appear.

1964 ★★★★★

Full-bodied, ripe and fruity wines. Climate: cold winter followed by warm spring and early flowering — always a good omen; hot dry summer favoured ripening; showery weather at the end of August swelled the grapes and brought them to perfection for an early harvest. Characteristics: totally different in style to '61 and '62. Broader, softer, riper, more rounded, but lacking the dry refinement of '62 and, perhaps, the finesse of '61. Tasting notes: quite a number of notes from January 1970 to November 1979, spanning a range of 16 *marques* and spelling out for me a lesson loud and clear: top quality champagne of a big vintage needs time in bottle. It is such a waste to drink it too young, before it has matured and developed its true character. Eight to fifteen years seem to be the optimum — but they last far longer. Of course, this is commercially unappealing, but if you can afford to keep vintage champagne in your own cellar, I think it is worthwhile.

Bollinger	*When first tasted in 1971 I thought the nose "green" and immature, like raw pea-pods; on the palate it was dry, meaty and a bit short. In a matter of a year it had deepened in colour and character, becoming almost a fat wine that appeared to lack acidity, though this might have been because it was not served cold enough. Two years later, seven notes: consistently meaty, good — distinctly more substantial than the '62, developing the smoky* Pinot *character that I personally like. Around that time I found some half-bottles variable and others reaching the end of their tether. It was much better in magnums.* Last tasted 1973 ★★★★
Bollinger R. D.	*I am never quite sure about Bollinger's late-disgorged wines. I think I prefer original bottlings that have been aged without interruption. But this was good: pale for its age, lively though not skittish; good nutty nose; dry, rich, good flavour and balance.* Tasted November 1979 ★★★★
Deutz & Geldermann	*I have a feeling this was one of the German-sounding brands that lost its popularity in World War I. Thanks largely to one ubiquitous Master of Wine, it began to regain lost ground in the 1970s. The '64 was a good, rich, fine wine, holding well.* At Peter Morrell's in New York, May 1977 ★★★★
Dom Pérignon	*Here is an example of the characteristics of a vintage impressing themselves on the wine. Though still dry and austere, much less so than usual in 1973 and 1976. Most recently: very pale for its age; not much bouquet; bone dry, refined though somehow a bit blunt. I feel that 1964 and Dom Pérignon were not exactly compatible.* Last tasted January 1977 ★★★

Dom Ruinart	*Pale, lively enough; good nose; dryish, excellent flavour and balance. Keeping up a good* de luxe *standard.* Tasted December 1972 ★★★★
Heidsieck Diamant Bleu	*If it were called Dom Heidsieck it would fetch a higher price at auction. A magnum in 1976: dry, Dom Pérignon-like and really rather good. Also good in 1977. A year later: pale and lively, very fine mousse; "cold steel" nose, not showing its 14 years; dry, crisp, steely, good flavour, long finish.* Last tasted February 1978 ★★★★★
Krug	*Despite the reputation of the '64 vintage, I did not find this the heavyweight I had expected. In February 1971: fragrant bouquet; dryish, attractive, well balanced, fruity with good acidity, By May, a particularly good bouquet developing and a powerful flavour — as if it were in full thrust. Later the same month, at a blind tasting of a dozen champagnes, seven of which were non-vintage, I thought it excellent but unready, and second to the Krug Brut Réserve (non-vintage), which was rich and perfectly developed. The trouble about a non-vintage champagne is that one cannot tell before opening it whether it will be young and frisky or has ameliorating bottle-age. A magnum in 1973 confirmed my original impression that it was less beefy than one might have predicted (just as in a rather hard vintage such as '52 one would expect a big masculine wine like Château Latour to be even more tough and stern than usual. In fact it is not). In 1974 I noted a tinny element, but in 1977 it — or my palate — was back on form: the wine, like me, was putting on weight with age. Then in October 1977 we had a complaint. A customer brought in a bottle for us to taste, which we did in the company of a former Krug agent. As so often happens, the sample turned out to be perfect: still palish for a 13 year old, fine bubbles, good life; good rich and subtle smoky nose; fullish, rich, yet with counterbalancing acidity and a flavour that opened up like a great burgundy.* Last tasted August 1978 ★★★★★
Lanson	*A cultural shock at the launching party in London: here was vintage Lanson in a trendy, skittle-shaped, red-labelled bottle. I cannot say I was bowled over, though fortunately the wine inside tasted like champagne: dry, rather more substantial than usual (doubtless the '64 weight), and agreeable.* Tasted January 1970 ★★★
Moët & Chandon	*The annual dinner of the Champagne Academy is an opportunity, despite the pleasing distractions of old friends, to taste new vintages. In May 1970 I thought the '64 Moët was a lively wine and surprisingly dry — a bit too raw and immature at this stage. After a further year of bottle-age the nose had developed and flavour ripened, and at a blind tasting in May it showed well, one of the best vintage Moët's I can recall. My opinion was confirmed later that year.* Last tasted May 1978 ★★★★
Mumm	*At the blind tasting in May 1971 it was pale and sparsely sparkling; the bouquet was its best feature, ripe, rich, vinous; on the palate it had no middle and tailed off. A year later it was nice enough in magnums.* Last tasted May 1972 ★
Perrier-Jouët	*Dry, stylish and refreshing.* Tasted twice, in 1972 ★★★
Pol Roger	*A good wine: pale, clean, stylish, refreshing and refined in 1970. Still lively and youthful in 1975. Blossoming in magnums in 1976: developing a gold sheen; a rich, ripe wine, drier than the '66. At 14 years of age in outstanding condition: palish, lively; lovely nose, flavour, balance and finish.* Last tasted February 1978 ★★★★★

Roederer Cristal Brut	*Clearly a bottle prematurely aged by warm storage conditions, rather deep in colour, showing age on the nose and not helped by the accompanying bacon and eggs (in Florida in 1975). Later, an exemplary bottle: very attractive, medium pale gold; clean nutty bouquet; dry, fairly austere but refined.* With George Rainbird at Whitchford, December 1976 ★★★★★
Roederer	*First tasted in 1971: stylish, refreshing. Four years later: straw coloured, lively enough; very flavoury with fine tanginess, noticeably more acidic than the 1961.* Last tasted March 1975 ★★★
Roederer Rosé	*I suppose there must be a demand or they would not make a rosé. This was a palish orange-rose colour, almost onion skin; light, stalky indifferent nose; medium dry, medium body, rather dull, flat and flabby.* At the 16th annual dinner of the Champagne Academy, May 1973.
Taittinger Brut	*Pale and lively, fat and short. I felt this was not really top class in 1971, lacking the style of the Comtes de Champagne, though I thought it good a year later.* Last tasted April 1972 ★★

1965

Poor year. Climate: gloomy summer; severe storms at the end of June followed by cold and hail; dry and warm September, but the damage had been done.

1966 ★★★★

A fine vintage: firm, elegant, perfect balance and finesse. Climate: frosts bad enough to damage vines in January; very hot days in June which led to early blossoming though some flowers were killed by a sudden cold spell; much rain and little sun in August, some mildew; fine weather before the vintage. Tasting notes: a large number and broad in range. I included a fairly wide selection because I think that, in a copybook vintage like this, there are quite a few lessons to be learned: that pink champagne and any less than brilliant *blanc de blancs* should be drunk young; that the well-constructed classics benefit enormously from bottle-age, and that even the middling quality wines can blossom in bottle.

Billecart-Salmon Blanc de blancs	*Pale, still lively and frothy; unexceptional nose; not really dry enough for a "blanc de blancs", light, insubstantial and not very harmonious. Should have been drunk when five to eight years old.* Tasted February 1980 ★
Billecart-Salmon Brut	*Far more satisfactory: good richness, quality and character on the nose; dryish, firm, good flavour and balance.* Tasted February 1980 ★★★
Billecart-Salmon Rosé	*Poor colour: faded,* pelure d'oignon, *like a stained white wine; dull nose and flavour. Short, uninteresting. As with the "blanc de blancs", should have been drunk young.* Tasted February 1980.
Bollinger	*The first '66 tasted, in the London agents' offices in September 1971. Even at that age a positive straw colour; fresh but meaty nose; dryish, medium body, classic Bollinger style, reasonably rounded and nice acidity. In 1972 it was served at the third convention of the International Wine and Food Society in Paris,*

preceding the banquet at the Hôtel George V: I found it stylish. Several good bottles and half-bottles in 1974. An interesting contrast in styles: against the '66 Schramsberg Brut, Bollinger was more mouth-filling, with a better finish (at Denis Foley's in San Francisco in 1975). Developing lovely meatiness throughout 1975 and 1976. *Last tasted at the Waterloo dinner at Christie's, September 1976* ★★★★

Deutz & Geldermann	The first of a veritable spate of Deutz bottles. Medium dry and very agreeable. *Tasted in the spring and summer of 1974* ★★★
Deutz Blanc de blancs	In clear glass bottles: palish; very clean fresh nose; dry, lightish, slim and fairly steely, well made and refreshing in March 1974. Later, a good last-minute substitute for a maderized 1943 Clicquot: very dry, still very fresh. *Last tasted at Brooks's, June 1977* ★★★★
Deutz Cuvée William Deutz	The Deutz de luxe, in an elegant Dom Pérignon-reminiscent bottle: pale, fine mousse; good, rich, smoky Pinot aroma; dryish, gentle but fine rapier-like flavour cutting across the palate, firm, refined. *Tasted from March to July 1974* ★★★★★
Dom Pérignon	The de luxe marque that so many others seek to emulate. Palish in colour, refined mousse — that is to say, a steady unwavering spray of tiny bubbles; clean, refined, refreshing nose; dry but seemed not as bleakly austere as some earlier vintages. *Tasted only once, in May 1974* ★★★★★
Charles Heidsieck	Already by 1972 its characteristic rich Pinot nose well developed. Good, fullish, meaty magnums in 1973. Three years later, tasted twice: developing a good colour, lively; very fragrant nose — like a sea breeze; slightly sweet but with a dry finish, very flavoury. Twice in 1978: very attractive with good fruit. Most recently, lively but drying out. *Last tasted December 1979* ★★★★
Charles Heidsieck Royal	The one and only time I have tasted this de luxe blend: drier than the standard vintage, stylish. *Tasted May 1976* ★★★★
Heidsieck Dry Monopole	Frankly not impressed when I first tasted it in 1975, but developing a good smoky bouquet, dry, firm and very good in 1978. Again quite recently, first to liven up an ullaged 1923 Monopole, then as an agreeable pre-lunch aperitif: lively, nutty, dry — just a little short. *Last tasted March 1980* ★★★
Jamin Théophile Roederer	I am not sure where this came from, but I drank it with enjoyment twice: dry, firm and good. *Tasted June and July 1972* ★★★
Krug	I did not taste this until it was already ten years old: a relatively heavy, meaty style, though dry in June 1976. Immensely impressive a few months later and better still the following year. *Last tasted February 1977* ★★★★★
Lanson Red Label	Fine colour, lively; very pleasant bouquet; dry, medium body, firm on the palate, extended flavour. *Tasted twice, in May and June 1979* ★★★★★
Laurent-Perrier	Palish and lively; indifferent nose; slightly too sweet, lightish and no finish. Singularly unimpressed. The Cuvée Grand Siècle, a fine non-vintage blend, was infinitely more stylish. *Both tasted April 1972* ★★★
Mumm Cordon Rouge	Medium-pale straw colour, lively enough; some age on the nose; dryish, sound, lively but lacking flavour and finesse. Assez bon in 1977. Tasted three times the following year, and the next: distinctly tired, old-straw colour and nose. *Last tasted June 1979* ★

G. H. Mumm **Cordon Rosé**	*Clearly intended to be drunk when young and rosy cheeked. No pink left — rather drab onion-skin colour; dry, positive flavour but old and a bit maderized.* Tasted July 1979.
Perrier-Jouët	*Tasted only once, out of jeroboams, and very good too: pale, lively; very attractive nose and flavour; dry light style.* At the 16th annual reunion dinner of the Champagne Academy, at the Savoy, May 1973 ****
Joseph Perrier	*Fairly pale, bright and lively; attractive, clean, refreshing nose and flavour, holding very well.* Tasted July 1979 ***
Piper Heidsieck Extra Dry	*I do not often come across Piper. Although also labelled "Brut" it was only dryish. Some colour and lively; deep, rich, smoky Pinot aroma and flavour, with good finish. I thought it remarkably attractive and stylish.* At an end-of-seminar dinner at Sakowitz's, Houston, November 1974 ****
Pol Roger	*A most reliable and attractive brand. Pale, lively; good nose; dry, straightforward in 1972. Very good in magnums in 1974, ripening in 1976 (though curiously firmer and more lively in Florida than at Hugh Johnson's later in the year).* Last tasted August 1976 ****
Pommery & Greno	*André Simon was the Pommery agent from the turn of the century to the early 1930s, so this was the most appropriate aperitif to drink at the centenary celebrations. All I had time to note (as I had a speech to worry about) was "good colour, nose and flavour".* At the South Australian Wine and Food Society's Centenary Dinner in Adelaide, on what would have been André Simon's 100th birthday, 28 February 1977 ***
Roederer	*Dryish, elegant and stylish in 1976. A loose cork and rather lifeless bottle in May 1977, but another, a splendidly ripe wine, two months later.* Last tasted July 1977 ****
Roederer **Cristal Brut**	*Top wine in a tasting of champagnes in California: pale; low-keyed, gentle, subtle but highly refined bouquet; dryish, long, persistent and firm flavour, lovely aftertaste.* Tasted May 1972 *****
Taittinger **Comtes de Champagne** Blanc de blancs	*Pale and dry: good nose, lightish, clean as a whistle. A total contrast in style to a ripe Krug or Bollinger and probably best drunk fairly young between five and eight years after the vintage.* Tasted May and June 1972 ****
Veuve Clicquot **Brut**	*Fine sparkle, dry and elegant in 1975. Colour deepening but firm and flavoury at Dennis Wheatley's 80th birthday party in 1977. Firm and elegant in 1978.* Last tasted May 1979 ****

1967

Not a vintage year. Climate: good weather conditions in the early spring and for flowering; summer months hot, with storms; August dry, but the harvest spoiled by heavy rain in September, which not only hampered ripening but caused intense and widespread rot.

1968

A disastrous year. Climate: cold weather prolonged flowering; rain almost every day from May to September except during the second half of August; irregular ripening; late harvest; crop 20 per cent below average.

1969

Flavoury wines, *bouqueté* — fragrant, acidity higher than usual. Climate: poor spring, late flowering; cold and grey until mid-July, then a hot summer and autumn broken only by some cool spells in August. Grapes ripened fully for a late vintage in October. Tasting notes: a moderate number of notes from which I have made a selection to indicate style and maturity.

Ayala	*Ayala, once popular and fashionable in Victorian times, is not much seen in England today and I have only tasted this particular vintage in America: a pleasant fresh colour and lively* mousse; *clean attractive bouquet, "dry" and smoky; on the palate dryish, on the light side, with nice balance and flavour.* At a Chaîne de Rôtisseurs' dinner in Burlinghame, San Francisco, May 1975 ✴✴✴ Drink now — mid-1980s.
Bollinger	*First tasted before a Bordeaux Club dinner at Harry Waugh's in 1974: very pale, not particularly bubbly and lively despite its youthfulness; very clean cut, positive, with stylish nose and taste; dry, medium body. Next, in 1975, with Jan Hein Verlinden, Bollinger's agent in southern Holland: developing nicely on the nose; dry fine flavour, soft but firm. Again with Harry Waugh, in 1976 — a magnum: slightly sweet, flavoury but with somewhat tinny acidic finish. I thought it unlikely to make a great old bottle. Perhaps the most memorable, and certainly the most welcome bottle was drunk in 1977, on Kangaroo Island, with freshly caught whiting cooked by Len Evans after a day bobbing about in a boat. Several excellent half-bottles in 1977, but I found it austere for Bollinger at the Champagne Academy dinner that year. Most recently: dry, refined, excellent finish.* Last tasted with the Ichinose family at Kee Joon's, Burlinghame, May 1979 ✴✴✴✴ Drink now — mid-1980s.
Veuve Clicquot	*Extremely good in magnums at Louis Latour's dinner at Boodle's in 1976. The following year: dry, very pleasant and stylish.* Last tasted April 1977 ✴✴✴✴ Drink now — well into the 1980s.
Collery Brut	*A distinctive individual grower's wine from Ay. At ten years of age still quite youthfully frothy; good nose; medium dry — not brut at all — rich firm fruit, surprisingly attractive (I had expected a thinner, more acidic wine).* Tasted March 1979 ✴✴✴ Drink now — mid-1980s.
Charles Heidsieck	*First made its appearance at a Champagne Academy dinner in 1974: noticeably deep for such a young wine, with a distinct yellow tinge; nice nose and flavour, medium dryness. Fairly full bodied, rich. Next, at lunch with Raymond Harcourt, the retired wine buyer of the Army & Navy Stores. My note might apply equally to the wine and to Mr Harcourt: fine appearance; stylish nose; meaty, flavoury and quite a lively tang. Also good several times in 1977.* Last tasted October 1977 ✴✴✴ Drink now — well into the 1980s.
Krug	*Tasted not very critically but enjoyed considerably with Michel Roux, to celebrate his award. It seemed a fine, dry, less meaty, less hefty style of Krug.* At the presentation of the Krug Award for Excellence, at the Gavroche, January 1979 ✴✴✴✴ Drink now — 1990.
Moët & Chandon	*Tasted only once: good lively appearance and an attractive wine. Nothing more to be said except that the largest champagne house turns out, as it should, a consistent and reliable non-vintage and*

> good if not ecstatic vintage champagne (not forgetting that they are also responsible for making the most prestigious Dom Pérignon).
> Tasted May 1975 ⋆⋆⋆ Drink now — early 1980s.

Mumm	*An end-of-season celebratory magnum: palish, nice life but, at ten years of age, no longer frothy; very good bouquet, creamy, fragrant; dry, lightish, firm, excellent flavour and condition. Good dry finish. One of the best vintages of Mumm that I can recall.* Tasted at Christie's, August 1979 ⋆⋆⋆⋆⋆ Drink now — 1990.
Perrier-Jouët Belle Epoque	*As elegant and evocative as the name and bottle: a fine dry wine.* At Holger Ewald's in Hobro, Denmark, June 1978 ⋆⋆⋆⋆
Pommery & Greno	*The vast turn-of-the-century edifice on the hill to the east of Reims is a monument to Pommery's golden years. The company's reputation and sales were high in the late-Victorian period and, in England, André Simon carried the Pommery torch from the high Edwardian era through to the early 1930s. Today, an open-knit style of wine, consistent and of nice quality. The 1969 sampled only once: lively and attractive.* Tasted May 1978 ⋆⋆⋆ Drink now.
Salon Le Mesnil	*Salon was in effect relaunched in England in 1978, and I first noted the '69 vintage at Colin Fenton's opening tasting at the Traveller's Club. Next, in jeroboams at Dr Overton's reception in Fort Worth: pale; good clean nose and palate; dry, medium light, a firm, elegant wine. Most recently, in magnums: a positive yellow colour, gentle* mousse; *fine vinosity, a singularly noteworthy bouquet (so often at a pre-dinner reception a fine champagne can go unnoticed); dryish, that is to say a touch of maturity and not too dry, just the right supporting weight, most attractive flavour and finish.* Last tasted at the 95th meeting of the Saintsbury Club, October 1979 ⋆⋆⋆⋆ Drink now — 1990.

1970 ⋆⋆⋆⋆

Some champagne houses claimed that their '70s were lighter than the '69s, but most of the wines I have had seemed to be fuller and more fruity. Climate: cold spring and late blossoming in good weather; heavy rainfall in June, but from then on appropriate weather conditions — warm, sunny, periods of dryness, welcome showers — through to the vintage. Tasting notes: I have tasted only a limited range of '70s, but they are good, with natural ripeness and body not seen since 1959. They should develop further and keep well.

Bollinger *Brut*	*Pale and lively, nice quality in 1977. The following year: fairly pale; bouquet and flavour refined but somewhat hard and undeveloped; dry, still a little austere, good nutty finish. Needed more bottle-age.* Tasted November 1978 ⋆⋆(⋆⋆) Drink 1982–1995.
Bollinger Tradition R. D.	*Outstanding. In magnums: very appealing, crisp, lively appearance; rather low-keyed straw/*Pinot *nose, bouquet undeveloped; dry, medium body, lovely meaty* Pinot/Chardonnay *flavour, fine, dry finish.* At the reception to celebrate the 100th anniversary of Harpers Wine and Spirit Gazette, July 1979 ⋆⋆⋆⋆(⋆) Drink 1981–1990.
Bollinger Vieilles Vignes	*Pretty well unique in Champagne: a wine made from a five-acre vineyard of ungrafted pre-phylloxera vines. Lively* mousse *settling down to a steady stream of fine bubbles; lovely nose; dryish, lightish, I thought it needed crisping up at the end. In fact*

not my idea of Bollinger at all, but interesting, rare and expensive. Will probably develop well but I would prefer not to base my judgement on this one tasting. Tasted March 1979 *(★★★★)?*

Veuve Clicquot Brut	*Medium straw colour; excellent smoky* Pinot/Chardonnay *aroma and flavour; a ripe-vintage touch of sweetness, good finish.* Tasted November 1978 ★★★(★) *Drink now — 1995.*
Deutz **Cuvée William Deutz**	*In magnum: dry, elegant, stylish.* Tasted May 1978 ★★★★★ *Drink now — 1990.*
Charles Heidsieck Brut	*Similar colour to Clicquot; pleasing, straightforward nose and taste; medium dry, good smoky character.* Tasted November 1978 ★★★ *Drink now — 1992.*
Philipponat **Clos des Goisses**	*Pale, fine appearance; attractive fresh, medium dry nose; medium dry body, rich, meaty, nicely developed flavour which opened up well in the glass.* At an Amitiés Gastronomiques Internationales dinner in Melbourne, March 1977 ★★★★ *Drink now — late 1980s.*
Taittinger Blanc de blancs	*A most attractive, very stylish wine. I think that these "blanc de blancs" champagnes are best in a good ripe vintage, though it could be argued that the extra substance and weight spoil the light fresh "blanc de blancs" character. A matter of taste.* Tasted in Houston, October 1976 ★★★★ *Drink now — 1985.*

1971 ★★★★

Fine crisp wines. Climate: far less settled than 1970; storms in May, June cold, humid, flowering in indifferent conditions; storms again in August but September hot and dry. Tasting notes: a rather arbitrary and unbalanced selection but, comparing like with like, vintage against vintage, the '71s seem a complete contrast to the '70s. Leaner, drier, at best stylish and tinglingly refreshing. Improvement potential in the medium term.

Deutz **Cuvée William Deutz**	*Fine yellow-gold colour, very lively; curious, creamy musk-scented bouquet; dry, lightish, firm and fine, good crisp finish.* Tasted February 1978 ★★★(★) *Drink now — 1992.*
Charles Heidsieck	*A corky, end-of-dinner magnum in January 1978. Later: hard, lacking fruit, dry, austere — not the style of Charles Heidsieck that has appealed to me so much in past vintages. Needed lots more bottle-age.* Last tasted May 1978 ★(★★)? *Drink 1982–1992.*
Charles Heidsieck **Rosé**	*Very lively, palish orange pink; nose and taste hardly noteworthy; dry, some body, just managed a finish. After making such an effort to be pink, it seems to say "enough is enough". Perhaps those who make pink champagne think that the people who buy it have no taste anyway. They are probably right.* Looked at, sniffed and swallowed, February 1978 ★
Krug	*Palish, lively; excellent nose; dry, medium-full body — not as full as it can be — excellent flavour and finish. An impressive wine. Will keep and develop further.* Tasted June 1978 ★★★★(★) *Drink 1982–1995.*
Lanson **Red Label**	*First noted at a Champagne Academy dinner in 1977: very pale; dry, a lightish, very French, Lanson style. A year later, the bouquet had developed nicely but I still found it dry, a bit austere and immature.* Last tasted May 1978 ★★(★)? *Drink 1982–1990.*

Mumm	*Palish; lively; dry, unspectacular. Frankly I thought both it and the Lanson a bit characterless but perhaps bottle-age will do'them both good.* Tasted May 1977 ** Drink 1982–1990.
Perrier-Jouët Belle Epoque	*In rather attractive art deco bottles. First tasted in February 1978: fine colour; fragrant charming bouquet; medium dry, light style but good quality and consistency on the palate. Then, most memorably, in March, out of a jeroboam at Dr Skinner's Café Louis in Florida.* Last tasted May 1978 **** Drink now — 1990.
Philipponat Clos de Goisses	*Palish, good* mousse; *an attractive, smoky* Chardonnay *type of aroma; dry, nice weight, refined, good length and finish.* Tasted several times in 1978 ***(*) Drink now — 1988.
Roederer Cristal Brut	*Pale, lively; a dry, firm-flavoured wine with extended finish. The ultimate in refinement.* At the Capital Hotel, June 1979 ***** Drink now — 1990.
Salon Le Mesnil	*Tasted and enthusiastically noted at its first presentation: pale, elegant, and — I must use the word again — refined. Needed a little time in bottle.* At Colin Fenton's introductory tasting, May 1978 ****(*) Drink now — 1990.
Taittinger Rosé	*Unimpressive colour — a sort of blue-rinsed pink; dry, not particularly noteworthy and totally unsuitable with a beautiful* délices de framboises. *Like drinking champagne after a mouthful of wedding cake covered with marzipan and icing: it just tasted tinny.* At a gourmet dinner at the Dorchester, November 1979 * Drink up.

1972 ★

Not declared a vintage. Climate: early spring warmer than usual; April cold — vine growth arrested until early May; fine weather reported in August and September; late harvest, 12 October, in good weather.

1973 ★★★

A vintage of some quality and charm. Climate: hot dry summer; heavy rain in September. Tasting notes: not at all representative, but those tasted, including a lightish, pleasant Pommery and a Ruinart not noted separately, are on the light side, lacking the body and flesh of the '70s and the lean firm style of the '71s. But agreeable wines, a nice bit of bubbly now, and will possibly broaden with a little bottle-age.

Bollinger Tradition R. D.	*First bottle opened was corky and tasted woody. The next: pale; crisp, rather austere on nose and palate; very dry and refined but for me lacked a bit of flavour. Needed bottle-age.* Tasted January 1979 **(**) Drink 1983–1995.
Veuve Clicquot	*The youngest of six vintages of Clicquot shown at Claridge's in 1978: very lovely to look at, a palish yellow-green, lively; most attractive nose and taste; medium dryness and body, elegant, well balanced. The best of four '73s the following year.* Last tasted July 1979 ***(*) Drink now — 1992.
Charles Heidsieck Rosé	*Pale pink; somewhat dry and hard on the palate.* Tasted July 1979 *(*)

Moët & Chandon *Rosé* Dry Imperial	*A curious colour — quite a deep mauve pink. Perfectly straight-forward but better with a* vedette *at the Cannes film festival than with cheese and fruit.* At lunch at Moët's in London, February 1979 ★★
Perrier-Jouët	*First tasted at a Champagne Academy dinner in 1978. Fine colour and sparkle; fragrant and charming aroma and flavour; medium dry, lightish. Copybook Perrier-Jouët. Also showing well in mag-nums.* Last tasted July 1979 ★★★(★) Drink now — 1992.

1974 ★★

Not widely shipped. Climate: poor weather conditions overall. Good fruit set but inclement weather just after flowering had begun, then dry and excessively hot; beneficial rain in August. Picking began 28 September in the middle of an unforseen and prolonged period of rain beginning on 23rd. Average quantity, disappointing quality. Assessment: variable wines, some reputed to be good and worth looking out for.

1975 ★★★★

Reputed to be very good. Just coming on the market at the time of writing. Climate: wet winter; snow in March; end of April hot and sunny. Average temperature higher than usual, but lack of sun and a wet second half of September delayed picking to around the beginning of October. Production 10 per cent below 1974. Assessment: officially reported to be "round and harmonious and of very good quality".

1976

Excessive heat and drought; rain in the autumn.

1977

Complete reverse of 1976. Damp and dismal with improvement in September.

1978

Not dissimilar to 1977. Inclement weather retarded growth; poor flowering; from September, an extended period of sun, though without great heat, forestalled complete disaster. Crop of inadequate size. "Musts" sweet but of high acidity.

1979

Possible vintage year. Climate: very severe winter cold through to end of April; heavy frosts in May delayed growth; reasonable summer conditions. Late harvest in October. Bountiful crop. Quality high.

Postscript: as this is a book about vintages, ordinary blended wines do not qualify. But it can be argued that standard blends of non-vintage champagne, particularly those from the quality houses, are not ordinary wines at all: they are costly to produce and they maintain, or certainly should maintain, a level of quality distinctly higher than lesser sparkling wines from other regions. So a word about the types.

Non-vintage champagne. A remarkable number of wines, of the main grape varieties and from different districts, go into every *grande marque* blend, the object of which is to maintain a house style of recognizable character and quality. They range from a light style, such as Lanson and Perrier-Jouët, to the slightly heavier and meatier ones, such as Krug and Bollinger. Krug is the highest priced. The company does not like it to be referred to as non-vintage — they prefer to call their standard blend *Brut Réserve*. The quality is high and consistent. A serious wine. Bollinger is another wine liked by the English *amateur*. I like it too. And one non-vintage champagne I have always found consistently satisfactory is Roederer.

Pink champagne. I have already made several unkind remarks about pink champagne. Rosés are notoriously difficult to produce in the traditional way, which is to extract just so much colour from the skins before removing them during fermentation. But why it is that rosé wines, not just champagne , have so little character — usually little if any varietal aroma and often only a neutral taste — I do not know. Pink champagne is associated with Rule's, Maxim's, stage door Johnnies and chorus girls. Fun and froth. Let us leave it at that.

Vintage champagne and its sub-varieties. By now you might think that I have said all that I have to say on this subject. It may not, however, be fully realized that, as with port, vintages of champagne are in effect "declared" — that is to say, only following years of exceptional quality will some of the best wines be earmarked for a high-quality vintage blend. This is how it should be. I have a sneaking feeling that in recent years the finest wine is selected for, and the greatest trouble taken over, the highly profitable *de luxe* vintage blends and that standard vintage champagne is a little too standard. Not that it is a bad thing to have three grades — it is just confusing. Moreover, as with German wines, there has been a lot of commercial pressure to market these wines for immediate drinking whereas, as I have tried to demonstrate in my notes, the best certainly improve enormously with age. R.D. (recently disgorged) champagnes were introduced — or reintroduced, for it was an old tradition — by Bollinger. The wine is left on the lees, with the yeasts, which cause the secondary fermentation, for much longer than the customary period, until it is disgorged and recorked before shipment. In my experience it is best to drink R.D. wines within a year or so of them coming on to the market. Bollinger's first R.D. was the 1952, but the quantity was tiny. The first more generally available was the 1955.

There have been whispers that vintage champagne is becoming a costly anachronism and, as with port, the same specious argument is being produced: that the finest wine would be better used to maintain the quality of the standard bread-and-butter non-vintage blends. I personally would like to see less scrambling to outdo the opposition with *de luxe* and fancy blends and more concentration on two old-fashioned types: a straightforward, good non-vintage bubbly, and a vintage wine of greater depth, elegance and style, capable of further development in bottle. The non-vintage to provide the commercial foundation of the market; the second to build up a quality superstructure. Vintage champagne should satisfy the most discerning buyer, and, like vintage port, act as both standard bearer and standard setter.

VINTAGE
PORT

Port vintages are much easier to understand and predict in terms of development and life expectancy than, for example, Bordeaux. The prime reason is that although grapes are grown, harvested and made into wine every year, a "vintage" is declared only when, generally through a consensus of the leading shippers, the wine is agreed to be of unusually high quality, and then only if the market can absorb a new vintage.

Moreover, the life span of vintage port is more uniform than that of other wines, due to the comparative consistency of quality between shippers and to the robust constitution of this essentially sweet and fortified wine. Vintage port takes a longer time to mature than almost all of the classic wines and its intrinsic sturdiness holds it in better shape.

There are, however, variations of style and weight, both between shippers and vintages. The following notes attempt to describe these styles and the state of development of all the major vintages.

The number of port firms declaring a vintage is indicative of the importance of that vintage and the state of the market. Port was usually shipped in "pipes" of approximately 115 gallons (roughly 56 dozen bottles) two to five years after the vintage. From the turn of this century, two years became the norm.

1734 ★★★★★

One of the great vintage years of the 18th century.

1755 ★★★

An abundant vintage, but slump conditions. Shippers refused to pay the farmers more than £3 per pipe.

1765 ★

The first vintage year quoted in an auction catalogue (Christie's, April 1773).

1767 ★

Red port of this vintage offered in cask and bottle at a Christie's wine auction in September 1773. Thirteen pipes commanded £35 each; the 1767 port, "bottled 18 months", sold at £4. 13s. 0d. (£4.65), per five dozen lot.

1771–1774 ★★★ to ★★★★

All shipped as individual vintage years.

1775 ★★★★★

A very fine vintage as regards both quality and quantity. According to Warner Allen: "the first wine which could worthily claim the title of vintage port."

1779, 1788, 1790 ★★

All offered as vintages on the London market.

1792 ★★★

Fifty-five thousand pipes of this vintage shipped to England; the greatest quantity ever imported up to this date.

1797 ★★★★★

"The best port vintage ever known." (George Sandeman, writing in 1809.)

1799 ★★★

A vintage year.

1802 ★★★

"Curious old port of the vintage 1802 of high Burgundy flavour and rare quality, termed the droppings of the grape." (From a Christie's catalogue of August 1829.)

1804 ★★★

A vintage year.

1805 ★★

A moderately good vintage. "Warre's Port 1805, Laid in 1808" sold at Christie's in July 1813.

1806 ★★★

Fine.

1807, 1809 ★★

Both moderate.

1811 ★★★★★

The famous "Comet" vintage.

1815 ★★★★

The renowned "Waterloo" vintage.

Wenceslaus de Souza Guimaraes. Probably bottled mid- to late 19th century. Ullaged mid-shoulder. Very old amber-tawny colour; bottle stink at first, then cleared, turning sweet and rich on the nose; medium dry — either an old sweet wine that had dried out with age or, more likely, an old white port. Very good flavour, curious old nutty character. Holding well. A rare experience.

Tasted at the Waterloo dinner, September 1976 ★★★

Quinta do Vesúvio, Garrafeira Ferreira. Probably bottled late 19th century. Good level. Beautiful warm amber colour, ruddy, with golden sheen; very old nose, high acidity; still quite sweet, faded but fascinating.

At a Heublein tasting, May 1978 ★★

1816–1819

A string of wretched vintages.

1820 ★★★

A vintage year, widely shipped, which "owed much of its éclat to the circumstances of the four previous vintages". (T. G. Shaw.)

Shipper unknown. "R. D. Blackmore, port, 1820" on label. Cork branded "Vintage 1820, London". Ullaged mid- to low shoulder. Old amber colour with lemon edge; light, old, a bit uneven on the nose but held well; still quite sweet, nice, delicate old flavour with tingling end acidity.

Tasted July 1974 ★★

1834 ★★★★

A great classic vintage. Kopke's Roriz: a giant wine. Taylor's 1834 sold for a high price at Christie's in 1862 and was "beautiful and brilliant" when tasted by a wine merchant in 1949.

Garrafeira 1834. Cask aged, or what I call a vintage tawny, of Fernando Porto Soares Franco, tasted at two Heublein pre-sale tastings, first in 1977: old amber tawny; high toned, madeira-like acidity; medium sweet, a bit maderized but clean aftertaste. Interesting.

Last tasted May 1979 ★★

1837 ★★★

A good vintage.

Shipper unknown. A bottle from a famous Scottish cellar. Bottled by Divie Robertson. Pale in colour, little red left; bouquet just holding, reminiscent of Spanish root; dried out on the palate, with little fruit or sugar, though no decay (no mustiness or sourness).

Tasted May 1972 ★

1844 ★★

Moderately good vintage.

J. and C. White & Co. Very pale amber, no vestiges of red — probably a white port originally; old, madeira-like nose; still medium sweet but very light and faded, though clinging to life.

At a Heublein tasting, May 1972 ★

1847 ★★★★★

The great classic vintage of the mid-19th century. Shipments in the 1840s averaged 30,000 pipes per annum.

"Hibernia". Bottled by Green & Co. Quite attractive, warm, tawny (like a deep Anjou rosé); ancient and spirity on the nose, sometimes volatile; old, faded, some richness but ethereal, sometimes overacid.

Tasted 1967, 1968, 1970, August 1973. At best ★★

Sandeman. Very pale but still with a tinge of pink — a beautiful autumnal colour; unbelievable on the palate — still sweet though faded, no hardness, little fruit but still a fine delicate drink.

Tasted April 1956 ★★★

Shipper unknown. From Sherborne Castle: pale and faded with a touch of volatile acidity.

Tasted November 1974.

1851 ★★★★

Known as the "Great Exhibition" vintage. Mildew slightly tainted nine out of ten wines, otherwise a good year: hard, long-lasting wines. George Saintsbury's "finest year for port" — as recalled in 1920.

Stibbart's. From the Gladstone cellars at Fasque. Incredibly deep coloured for its age — like a 1948; amazingly sound, firm, fruity nose; still retaining sweetness and body, rich, powerful flavour, excellent acidity. The most magnificent old port I have ever drunk.

Tasted May 1972, October 1975 ★★★★★

1853 ★★★

A fine vintage year.

1854 ★★★

Another "Comet" vintage. Four shippers.

1858 ★★★

A good vintage, particularly Sandeman's.

Shipper unknown. Bottled by Chillingworth & Son. Remarkably good, old tawny colour; old, light, but still a little fruit on the nose, and sound; retaining some sweetness with interesting flavour and finish.

Tasted May and June 1969 ★★

1859 ★★★★

A very fine vintage.

1863 ★★★★★

A vintage of universally proclaimed excellence.

Shipper unknown. Bottled by Johnstone & Sadler.

From a Norfolk cellar: original cork and wax seal. Very pale but bright and attractive; light, high toned and spirity; drying out, light, ethereal, faded and spirity, but clean and with a nice finish.
Tasted January 1977 ★★

1865 ★

"A vintage of no general repute . . . but Rebello excellent," according to George Saintsbury.

1867 ★★

Some good wines made. Rarely if ever seen.

1868 ★★★★

A great vintage. All except Croft shipped; Fonseca, the biggest wine ever; Sandeman very dry, considered the finest wine of the year.
Martinez. From the Sherborne Castle cellars. Wonderful old amber colour; crisp, positive though volatile bouquet, vanilla scented; drying out and faded but with great power. Very dry, powerful and acidic finish.
Tasted September 1976 ★★★

1869 ★

Shipped only by Croft.

1870 ★★★★★

Nineteen shippers. A superlative vintage.
Cockburn. Old tawny colour; probably open for some time — rather medicinal nose and dried out flavour with flat finish.
Tasted October 1976.
Roriz. Bottled by J. Barrow & Sons. Good colour for age, healthy glow; light, pleasant bouquet showing no decay; drying out but lively. Still slightly peppery, with nice finish. Fascinating and attractive.
Tasted March 1972 ★★★★

1872 ★★★

Sixteen shippers. A good vintage. Rarely seen and not tasted.

1873 ★★★

Sixteen shippers again. Slightly more highly regarded by the trade at the time.
Meyer. Probably the name of a merchant, not a port shipper. Good colour for age — medium-light tawny with healthy red tinge; no decay but a curious, slightly soapy nose and flavour; medium dry, medium-light body, still good to drink, dry finish.
Tasted March 1972 ★★

1874 ★

Three shippers only. Rarely seen.

1875 ★★★★

Eighteen shippers. "Fine, elegant quality but not very big, and matured early . . . owing to phylloxera the yield was not very large." (F. A. Cockburn.)
Shipper unknown. Bottled by Bell, Rannie of Perth. From the Fasque cellars. Though not deep, a beautiful ruddy colour, and very bright; slightly musty at first, old, faintly sour but rich and still in its way refined; medium sweet, medium light, gentle, faded but complete. Strange but good flavour and variable acidity.
Tasted several times, May to August 1972 ★★★

1878 ★★★★★

Twenty shippers. "With 1870, the very best. The last of the great phylloxera-free ports. Dow one of the best ports of the century." (George Saintsbury, writing in 1920.)
Cockburn. Recorked 1920. No ullage. Medium light, good but very mature colour; lovely bouquet, fruity, very sound; medium sweet, nutty, Spanish-root/cinnamon flavour, lovely finish. Holding well.
Tasted March 1972 ★★★★
Dow. Medium light — but better colour than Graham 1908; medium dry with a long powerful flavour and punch. Still very sound. Dry finish.
Tasted July 1967 ★★★
Shipper unknown. Bottled by Harvey's. "Port, 1878, Rich" on seal. Medium deep, lovely warm amber colour, rich and lively; deep powerful bouquet with a touch of decay, gradually soured in the glass; still remarkably sweet, warm, alcoholic, powerful. Excellent flavour and a lovely drink — but not to linger too long over.
Tasted at Harvey's, September 1978 ★★★★

1880 ★

Six shippers. Moderately poor vintage. Rarely seen. Probably finished.

1881 ★★

Declared a vintage by 20 shippers but its "promise never fulfilled though Cockburn best rich port ever". (George Saintsbury.)
Thompson & Croft. Medium pale; mushrooms and old lace; medium sweet, lightish, ethereal, fragrant, aged but charming.
Tasted June 1977 ★★★

1884 ★★★★★

Twenty-one shippers. A great year. "The last of the classic vintages." (C. W. Berry.)
Cockburn. Medium pale, very mature amber tawny but with a healthy touch of red; sweet, soft, forthcoming, no signs of decay on the nose; sweet, soft, light but complete, with long finish.
Tasted April 1972 ★★★★
Shipper unknown. Remarkably good colour, slightly hazy sediment; little nose; sweet, excellent flavour and balance, fruity, not too spirity. Very good.
Tasted March 1967 ★★★★

1885 ★

Five shippers. Moderate only. Not tasted.

1887 ★★★

Queen Victoria's "Golden Jubilee" vintage: 20 loyal shippers.
Cockburn. Lightish, fully mature tawny; nutty, dried-out bouquet; still fairly sweet with good backbone and sustaining acidity.
Tasted April 1972 ★★
Graham. Richer, ruddier colour; rich complex old nose, which developed nicely; medium sweet, fuller than Cockburn, lovely flavour though "hot" and spirity.
Tasted December 1972 ★★★★

Shipper unknown. Varying from medium to pale tawny; very fragrant, waxy, good though showing age; medium sweet, flavoury, soft, delicate, dry finish — in June and November 1978. Later: two bottles from my own cellar for the last dinner of David Allan's '45 Club at Gravetye Manor — with brie fritters! Pale, like a really old tawny, only ruddier; old, spiry Spanish-root nose; medium — drying out and faded, remnants of fruit but good mellow brandy left, rare and clean. *Last tasted November 1979* ★★★

1890 ★★★

Twenty shippers. A good vintage, tough when young.
Cockburn. Palish; rich but slightly scented and volatile; still quite sweet, medium light, attractive flavour and balance. One bottle slightly spoilt by volatile acidity. *Tasted April 1972, March 1974* ★★
Dow. Bottled by Schofield Bros, Manchester. Medium pale old tawny shading off to a weak watery rim, but with a healthy glow of life; still sweet on the nose with remains of fruit and richness, attractively complex and fragrant; medium sweet — drying out a little, lightish, somewhat faded with a refined and ethereal flavour. *Tasted March 1979* ★★★★

1892 ★

Ten shippers. Moderate vintage. Rarely seen.

1894 ★★

Thirteen shippers. Moderate to good.
Sandeman. An even, light-brown colour; light, liquorice-like nose, very good and holding remarkably well; sweet, light in body but lovely, rounded, well-balanced flavour. Very lively and firm for age. *Tasted January and March 1966* ★★★

1896 ★•★★

Twenty-four shippers. A great classic vintage. Now variable.
Cockburn. Some depth and redness; old, spiry, but some fruit; medium sweet, spiry, holding fairly well. *Last tasted March 1972* ★★
Dow. Light, mature but healthy; still some fruit but brandy obtrusive; drying out but still fruity and in good condition. Spiry finish. *Tasted January 1970* ★★
Fonseca. Very mature; sound for age, Spanish root; drying out but powerful. *Tasted November 1975* ★★★
Martinez. Very pale, mature colour; slightly woody and severe at first but nose developed raisin-like fruitiness; sweet, lightish, firm, nice flavour, holding well. *Tasted January and March 1972* ★★★
Sandeman. A Harvey bottling had a mushroomy nose and musty flavour. Past it. *Tasted February 1967*
Tuke Holdsworth. The first disappointment of my career: a thin, passé, drinkable but not unforgettable magnum (November 1952). A better bottle: amber; old, rich, sound; medium sweet, austere but holding well. *Tasted in magnum, March 1967* ★★

1897 ★★★★

"Royal Diamond Jubilee" vintage. Another good year,

but only seven shippers including "Sandeman's, fortified with Scotch whisky, because all the stocks of brandy had been used up for the '96s". (Maurice Healy.)
Sandeman. A three-bottle magnum from Tim Sandeman's cellars. Fine, medium-deep colour; spicy, fragrant bouquet — remarkably good; drying out a little, fine cob-nut flavour, very rich. Fabulous, perfect condition — one of the finest ports ever drunk. No flavour of whisky noticed. *Tasted at the Waterloo dinner, September 1976* ★★★★★

1899 ★

One shipper only. Rarely seen.

1900 ★★★★

Twenty-two shippers. The first of four great classic years prior to World War I. Exceptionally fine quality.
Croft. Pale oloroso sherry colour, though with a healthy ruddy glow; deep, nutty, old but sound; still sweet though light, silky, excellent flavour. *Tasted February 1973* ★★★★
Rebello Valente. Medium pale, very mature; old, dry and spiry but sound; drying out, becoming light and thin, with a fairly long dry finish. Very good in its way. *Tasted February 1971* ★★★
Smith Woodhouse. Palish old amber tinged with rose; rich old tawny character, brandy showing on nose; medium sweet, light, fading gently, but soft, complete and very attractive. *Tasted May 1968, January 1969* ★★★
Shipper unknown. Bottled by W. Smith of Bishop's Stortford, noted merchants. Light, lively, touch of ruby; excellent gentle bouquet; drying out but rich, stylish, elegant. Quite a tang. Perfect drink. *Tasted March 1971, July 1972* ★★★★★

1904 ★★★★

Twenty-five shippers. A lighter but classic vintage.
Cockburn. Fortified with brandy from the Azores. A gentle old man on the nose; medium sweet, lightish, firm dry finish. *Tasted March 1972* ★★★
Dow. Variable: one fruity and rich still; another, with shrunken cork, sour. *Tasted March 1973. At best* ★★★
Sandeman. A Harvey bottling; also a magnum of Averys. Medium pale, mature colour; sweet, fruity bouquet — lovely, hint of vanilla; still quite sweet, medium light and fading but very flavoury. Very good. *Tasted Harvey's, January 1967, Avery's, July 1978. Both* ★★★★
Taylor. Medium light but lively attractive colour; light but rich nose with trace of acidity; medium sweet, lightish, gentle and attractive. *Tasted March 1974* ★★★
Tuke Holdsworth. Pale but evenly graded; straightforward bouquet; sweet, light, nice, soft, gentle, but thin. *Tasted July 1967* ★★

1908 ★★★★★

Twenty-six shippers. A great vintage. Initially darker and more full bodied than 1900 and 1904, it maintained colour and body throughout its span of maturity.
Cockburn. One of the great classic wines of the 20th century. I was privileged to taste it on half a dozen

occasions between 1962 and 1972: a palish though rich tawny; fragrant, gentle, attractive bouquet with overtones reminding me of melon and liquorice; still retaining some sweetness, lightish, but some fatness and fruit, silky, lovely balance and finish.
Last tasted April 1972 ★★★★★

Croft. Fine old tawny colour; peppery and dry, yet with a rich coffee liqueur-like nose; still quite sweet, rich and fruity. Slightly spirity, astringent finish.
Tasted 1972, December 1973 ★★★

Dow. Tawny — no red left; sweet, rich, waxy mulberry bouquet; still quite sweet but with dry finish. Good remnants of fruit and flesh.
Tasted May 1978 ★★★

Fonseca. Fairly full coloured; musty old nose masking fruit; lovely, big-hearted flavour but declining.
Tasted June 1967 ★★★

Graham. Fairly light; nice nose; still sweet, rich, fading honourably.
Tasted July 1967 ★★★★

Taylor. Bottled by W. Smith of Bishop's Stortford. Good but very mature colour; gentle bouquet; still quite sweet with fine flavour, well balanced and with Taylor firmness and backbone.
Tasted October 1970.

Shipper unknown. "Finest reserve 1908." Very mature; rich, attractive bouquet, medium sweet, lightish though rich, with end acidity.
Tasted March 1974 ★★

1911 ★★★

"Coronation" vintage, shipped only by Sandeman.
Sandeman. Pale tawny with amber rim, and beeswing; beautiful bouquet though brandy showing through; quite sweet still, lightish body and style though firm. Lovely flavour reminiscent of crystallized violets. Tasted several times in the 1960s.
Last tasted November 1964 ★★★★

1912 ★★★★

Twenty-five shippers. A great classic vintage now fading, but rich as well as ethereal. *Climate:* wet winter, warm spring, midsummer cool, flanked by hot May and August. Hot also in September but slight rain at time of gathering delayed picking. Result: good colour, body and flavour.

Cockburn. Retaining colour reasonably well; rich and fruity although brandy showing through; still remarkably sweet and rich though losing body. Refined, lovely, fine finish. Tasted on several occasions.
Last tasted April 1970 ★★★

Dow. Pale tawny colour with pink tinge; spirity almost spicy bouquet; surprisingly sweet, lightish in body, lovely flavour and very sound. (Several "shippers unknown" with similar characteristics.)

Taylor. Lighter than Cockburn: beautiful old tawny with hint of red; marvellous, ethereal bouquet; drying out but with delicate, fragrant fruit. Fading but delectable. Tasted eight times since 1968. Good in halves.
Last tasted March 1979 ★★★★

1913

Not declared. Uneven weather with four months' drought reduced quantity, but quality not bad.

1914 ★★

Hopes of abundant vintage destroyed by mildew. Small yield, quality good. World War I curtailed shipments.

1915 ★★

Intense heat before vintage, quality and quantity good, but not declared.

1916 ★★

Favourable weather, considerable production of good wine, but not declared.

1917 ★★★

Fifteen shippers. A light, elegant vintage. Attractive wines but not considered a great classic. Fading but holding reasonably well. Never a beefy port, now recognizable by its light colour and style, yet smooth, silky and beguiling. *Climate:* snow late April, excessively dry summer. Picking began first week of October. By the very nature of the vintage, its age and scarcity, '17s are not seen much these days. I have tasted the vintage on 20 occasions, mainly in the 1960s and early 1970s, but as port declines as slowly as it matures, even the older notes can be relevant.

Croft. Medium light, very pretty colour with nice amount of ruby; light, delicate, trace of liquorice; medium sweet, lightish, charming small flavour, high toned. Attractive
Tasted 1962, March 1970 ★★★

Delaforce. An excellent bottle drunk at David Delaforce's home near Oporto: medium colour, certainly deeper than expected; very attractive bouquet, sound and rich — prune-like — developed well; drying out on the palate but still with good flesh, fruit and balance. Firm and fine.
Tasted November 1979 ★★★

Graham. A bottle with a crumbly cork tasted in 1971 was old, thin and faded. More recently: very pale tawny, hardly any red left but a healthy glow; light bouquet with a touch of cinnamon; very sweet, remnants of richness but light and faded, though with a long finish. A fading beauty.
Last tasted June 1974 ★★★

Quinta do Noval. Lovely and lively.
Tasted 1964.

Rebello Valente. Very fragrant, silky and attractive when first tasted in 1968. My most recent note less enthusiastic: medium pale, old and rather dull plummy brown; very light, faded, old and creaking bouquet; still sweet, gently rich, light and fading, though with a nice grapy flavour and spirity finish.
Last tasted January 1977 ★

Sandeman. Tasted in mid-1960s and in 1973. The first: lovely amber red; beautiful bouquet; sweet, smooth and silky. The more recent, bottled by Locketts of Liverpool in 1919: lighter, more mature; touch of Spanish root (liquorice) on the nose — this is normal and attractive, not a fault, just the nearest evocative smell for me; still sweet, lightish, piquant and attractive.
Last tasted March 1973 ★★

Taylor's Vargellas. Bottled in 1919. Extremely pale, ethereal, a faded old lady.
Tasted 1973.

Shipper unknown. Bottled by Schofields. Lovely colour — palish to rich old mahogany; bouquet dried out

but fragrant with a touch of my favourite Spanish root (liquorice), a little hard and spirity; some sweetness, lightish, delicate yet firm, in excellent condition.
From an old Cheshire cellar. Tasted June 1979 ★★★

Shippers unknown. Various bottlings: fairly consistently soft, silky, faded but appealing.
Tasted 1966–1969.

1918 ★

Not declared. Small quantity due to scorching summer. Average quality.

1919 ★★

Not generally declared, though quantity abundant, quality good. Offley's Boa Vista said to be very good.

1920 ★★★★

Twenty-three shippers. The first major vintage after the famous 1912. Small quantity, good quality. Good, ripe, fairly robust wines, the best still very good. *Climate:* spring favourable, May cold, intense heat in July with some scorching, August warm with rain, glorious late September harvest conditions.

Croft. Full, fragrant, superb when first tasted in 1952. Bottles tasted later in 1952 and in 1953 were thin, spirity and disappointing. Tasted most recently from a magnum, ullaged low shoulder: medium-light tawny; trace of volatile acidity but fruit under; still sweet, old but very flavoury. Acid taking over.
Last tasted November 1978.

Gould Campbell. "Kennaway's Reserve 1920." Deep and healthy; sweet; flavoury. Unusual style.
Tasted 1973.

Graham. One of my favourites, tasted three times. 1968 to 1970. All were excellent but the best was bottled in 1922 by Skinner & Rook, Nottingham: fairly deep, a good colour for a 50-year-old wine; most attractive rich bouquet; remarkably sweet, hardly dried out at all, fullish, ripe, fine. Well-nigh perfect.
Tasted January 1970 ★★★★

Taylor. First tasted at Mentmore in 1967. It was then Lord Rosebery's everyday port: full, fruity, vigorous. More recently, bottled by Justerini & Brooks: lost a little colour but nicely aged; very positive and attractive bouquet though slightly peppery and spirity; still fairly sweet, the usual Taylor body, yet soft, almost sultana-like flavour, with a deep fruity finish.
Last tasted September 1971 ★★★

Warre. Not showing too well.
Tasted 1967.

1921

Not a declared vintage. Grapes not fully mature.

Rebello Valente. Rather a freak wine tasted 40 years after the vintage: very light red brown, almost rosé in colour; light, though balanced; old liquorice-like flavour, no brandy showing through, delicate and delicious.
Tasted May 1961 ★★

1922 ★★★

Eighteen shippers. Quantity short, quality good though not great. Surely one of the most neglected vintages of the 1920s. Not a light and elegant vintage like 1917, but beefier; the best wines are still full of colour and charac-

ter. *Climate:* a bad start after heavy winter rains and poor spring. Much rot. Sound grapes matured rapidly in August and September.

Bom Retiro. Rare single-quinta wine. Surprisingly good, glycerine and blackcurrants.
Tasted 1955.

Croft. Fairly pale, very mature old tawny, very little red; slightly dusty, nutty bouquet, complete and sweet; medium sweet, good rich flavour though light, complete and sound, spirity finish.
Tasted 1968, 1971, May 1975 ★★

Gould Campbell. Magnificent colour; powerful nose but spirity and high acidity like madeira.
Tasted 1972.

Taylor. Bottled in Oporto in 1924. Pale, dried out, old and woody.
Tasted 1973.

Tuke Holdsworth. Bottled by W. Smith, Bishop's Stortford. Surprisingly deep, with heavy crust; sound, deep, positive, healthy nose; drying out but very full for its age and vintage, fine flavour and good dry finish.
Tasted twice, April 1970 ★★★

Shipper unknown. Bottled by Schofield's, Manchester. The same weight and shade as the 1917 but with more of an orange tinge; attractive but slightly less fruit than the 1917; drying out noticeably, a sweet austerity and leanness, a light, dry, peppery finish.
At a pre-sale tasting, June 1979 ★★

1923 ★★

Not declared, though yield better than 1922 and quality good. *Climate:* cold and dry winter and spring; many grapes perished in intense August heat. Useful rain, then unsettled, heat again and late harvest at the beginning of October.

Quinta Boa Vista. As customary, Offley's marketed an "off" or rather "non" vintage Boa Vista. In the mid-1950s it was sweet and soft, with a raisiny bouquet, by no means going down hill. Tasted twice recently, good, long, branded corks: light in colour, like a true pale tawny, healthy; dusty and varnishy on the nose, some fruit but showing age; still quite sweet, light, ethereal, very pleasant. Better taste than most.
Last tasted November 1979 ★★

1924 ★★★

Eighteen shippers. Quality considered good, quantity reduced. *Climate:* strange weather — summer remarkably cool, heavy rainfall in early September after four months of total drought.

Croft. A poor bottle, bitter in 1954, but later, bottled by W. Smith of Bishop's Stortford: fine deep, rich colour, bouquet and flavour.
Last tasted 1970. At best ★★★

Dow. Tasted 14 times since 1955. Variable, mainly good, fruity, rich, but sometimes a little acidity showing.
Last tasted 1967. At best ★★★

Gould Campbell. Peppery, rich, Spanish root; nice.
Tasted 1968 ★★

Graham. All but once sweet, soft, rich and fruity.
Tasted five times, 1953–1967. At best ★★★★

Rebello Valente. Pleasant enough.
Tasted 1955 ★★

Taylor. Tasted on no fewer than ten occasions since

1953 and consistently good: very lively colour, full, redder than 1927, similar weight to 1935; remarkably youthful, peppery bouquet, brandy showing bare; still quite sweet, fine deep flavour, usual Taylor backbone, slightly short compared with 1912, 1927 or 1935, dry finish. Holding well.
Last tasted March 1969 ★★★★

Warre. Fine colour; lovely ageing bouquet; quite sweet, not heavy, excellent flavour, well constructed, elegant.
Tasted March 1972 ★★★

1925 ★

Not declared. Quality and quantity reduced. *Climate:* thoroughly unsettled year, particularly poor summer, endless pests and diseases but late harvest conditions very good.

Boa Vista. The irrepressible quinta: pale, pretty but weak colour; faded, spirity but sound bouquet; sweet, lightish but surprisingly rich. Spirity but attractive.
Tasted 1972 ★★

1926 ★

Small yield, some good wine made. *Climate:* hottest summer for years. Very little rain. Grapes dried up. Remainder picked under favourable conditions.

Kopke. Pale, fully mature — a peculiar pink-orange tinge, fruity, piquant, nice bouquet: light, curious, sweet stalky flavour, fading.
Tasted 1967, 1972.

Quinta-Lages. A Graham's single-quinta wine. Most distinctive flavour, dry edge, spirity, aftertaste of olives.
Tasted 1964 ★

Taylor. Rare. A quarter-cask was specially shipped for a Lancashire wine merchant for one of his customers whose son was born in 1926. The family sold the remaining few dozen at Christie's and this note was made at the pre-sale tasting: medium pale, fully mature colour; very faint, spirity and slightly sickly nose; sweet with dry finish, spirity, interesting.
Tasted February 1976 ★

1927 ★★★★★

Thirty shippers. A great classic vintage, one of the best ever, "declared" and heavily bought at the height of the port market. *Climate:* contemporary weather reports did not anticipate the quality of the vintage. In the summer, rain was followed by fine, hot weather which burnt some grapes. But hardly any heat or sun at the beginning of a late harvest in October. Ten days of fine weather transformed the situation.

Cockburn. Considered a great classic. Subtle and delicate, not a beefy wine. First tasted in 1959 and consistent — never deep. The last tasted (a Harvey bottling): lightweight tawny in colour; intriguing, ethereal, high-toned bouquet; medium sweet, lightish in weight and style, attractive but with a dry, severe finish.
Last tasted January 1979 ★★★★

Croft. Distinctly light but flavoury.
Many notes, last tasted June 1980 ★★★

Delaforce. Consistently good notes.
Tasted 1955–1965 ★★★

Dow. Since 1955 consistently soft, full and attractive, losing colour but lovely, gentle fruit and Spanish-root bouquet; losing sweetness and weight but with appeal-

ing flavour and long warm finish.
Last tasted August 1976 ★★★★

Fonseca. Surely one of the best. First tasted in 1955: deep and good. One rather "hollow" and bitter bottle in 1971. And recently: classic old tawny colour; bouquet nutty, a little spirity and old but not a trace of decay; drying out and thinning a little but still fleshy, with lovely flavour, finish and nutty aftertaste.
Last tasted December 1976 ★★★★

Graham. Very rich, almost chocolaty in 1955–1967. Fully mature, spirity though very rich still.
Last tasted 1971 ★★★★

Martinez. Slight variations since mid-1960s but mainly good. Most recently: good colour, firm, fully mature; lovely nose, soft, rich with a touch of cinnamon; sweet, medium light, soft, flavoury, perfect balance.
Last tasted January 1979 ★★★★

Noval. Oporto bottled and recorked by the shippers: fine, ripe, delicate in 1972. And, bottled by the I.E.C. Wine Society: still fairly deep coloured; a lovely harmonious waxy bouquet; medium sweet — drying out a little, lightish body, excellent even-tempered wine, beautifully balanced.
Tasted November 1979 ★★★★

Offley. Full and sweet.
Tasted 1957–1959 ★★★

Sandeman. A thick, dull and lifeless bottle in 1955, followed by four good examples. The best from a "cooh" — a three-bottle magnum — lovely and fragrant in 1976. And from a magnum: medium-deep colour; gentle spirity bouquet; still quite sweet, very flavoury but fading a little.
Last tasted May 1977 ★★★

Stormont Tait. A winner from a little-known shipper: medium, lovely colour; gentle, sound bouquet, not too spirity; still sweet, medium body, lovely flavour, fruity, fairly high acidity but attractive.
Tasted June 1977 ★★★

Taylor. Tasted 13 times since 1954. Its condition now depends on the bottler and how it has been kept. Initially very deep, now medium; basically a very rich fruity aroma which varies between perfect full bloom, subdued and dusty and even spirity and ethereal. A Justerini & Brooks bottling in 1973 was almost perfect — fat, waxy, smooth. A more recent and different bottling surprisingly sweet, exciting on the palate, the flavour opening like a peacock's tail, but a bit stringy and bitter on the finish.
Tasted March 1979 ★★★ to ★★★★

Warre. A gentle, attractive, charming wine. The best I have noted were bottled by H. & E. Selby and that fine old firm, Stallard's of Worcester.
Tasted 1966–1970. At best ★★★★

1928 ★★

Not declared. Quantity small, late harvest; quality good.

1929 ★★

Not declared. Dry year. Small quantity, good quality.

Offley's Boa Vista. In magnum: medium pale, very mature looking; bouquet neither good nor bad; rather dry, lightish, quite flavoury, slightly raisiny, pungent, austere. Not good vintage port but quite a good drink.
Tasted 1967 ★

1930

Not declared. Here was a bad year: weather unsettled throughout. Intense heat damaged grapes. Quantity small, quality mediocre.

Taylor's Vargellas. From a single quarter-cask shipped in May 1932 by Taylor's, from their best quinta, bottled by the Lancashire wine merchant who bought the '26 and "laid down" by the same customer for his second son born in 1930. The family's sale of the remaining bottles of this wine gave me a possibly unique opportunity to taste a '30: medium, mature "off-vintage" colour — lacking depth; light, slightly dusty nose, with some sweetness and brandy; still sweet, lightish, slightly spirity but very pleasant.
At a pre-sale tasting, March 1977 ★

1931 ★★★★★

Not generally declared but a great vintage year made famous by just one wine, Noval. The market was dead: in Britain (the main outlet for vintage port) the economy was at a low ebb and cellars, both private and trade, were still full of '27s. *Climate:* little rainfall in winter but copious in March; cool weather for flowering continued through to the end of August. September really hot, lacking a little beneficial rain, but vintage under splendid conditions. Above-average yield.

Quinta do Noval. Tasted on nine occasions since 1972. Consistently magnificent: incredibly deep, plummy colour, still quite pronounced ruby red; very distinctive aroma like glycerine and blackcurrant pastilles, great depth of fruit; sweet, full bodied, powerful yet soft — iron fist in velvet glove — very attractive flavour and wonderful aftertaste.
Last tasted January 1979 ★★★★★ Drink now—2020.

Several other '31s, mainly single-quinta wines, tasted:
Boa Vista. Lightish; unusual honeyed nose; sweet, attractive, tangy.
Tasted 1970 ★★★

Burmester. Tasted blind recently in ripe company at "The Great Port Controversy" lunch, host John Davy, guest of honour Charles Dickens's grandson, Cedric. Suffice to say that out of a dozen noted wine men, four got the vintage (including, happily, myself), one even recognized the extremely rarely seen shipper — which, in my experience, is good going. The wine was deep coloured, rich to the rim, mature; a surprisingly gentle, delicate bouquet and light pepperiness; still fairly sweet and full bodied. The flavour was extraordinary, from recollection: prunes and whiff of cloves, very unfamiliar style, a hot-vintage warmth, and very alcoholic with lots of grip and good persistence.
Tasted at Mother Bunch's, February 1980 ★★★★

Pinhão. Attractive, dry crisp finish.
Tasted 1967 ★★★

Rebello Valente. (Capsule embossed "Robertson's", the owner of the Rebello brand.) Similar to Roncão, possibly the same wine, sweet, rich yet refined.
Tasted 1971, January 1978 ★★★★

Roncão. Lovely colour, powerful bouquet and flavour, unusual style.
Tasted 1970 ★★★★

Sandeman's Quinta do Bragão. Fairly deep, mature; very rich, sort of mulberry-like fruitiness; sweet, fruity, lovely flavour, tannic finish.
Tasted 1971, 1975 ★★★★

Warre. Not outstanding but classic balance.
Tasted 1960 ★★★

1932

Poor year. Cold and wet May, good summer weather but late harvest washed out.

1933 ★★

Not declared. Curious weather: good, flowering one month early, heatwave of remarkable intensity from end July. Very early vintage.

Cedovim. Single-quinta wine bottled by The Wine Society. Pale, pink; sweet, light, complete and charming.
Tasted 1965, 1969, 1970, 1972 ★★

Quinta do Noval. Small stocks held for special occasions. Fairly full colour, bouquet and flavour. Soft, spirit showing, light character, good long dry finish.
Tasted 1967, and at the quinta 1970 ★★

1934 ★★★★

Twelve shippers. The first properly declared vintage after 1927. Once a great favourite of mine but very few to be seen today. Most of my notes are therefore old. All the makings of a well-balanced classic year. Seemed to be at peak in 1960s. On decline now but worth watching out for. *Climate:* hot dry summer. Satisfactory quantity of well-ripened grapes harvested from 24 September.

Dow. Rich in 1960. Lighter but nicely balanced in 1968. More recently, drying out (half-bottle) and losing fruit.
Last tasted 1976 ★★★

Fonseca. Certainly one of my favourites, consistently lovely, an outstandingly sweet, rich, soft, rounded wine.
Tasted 1953–1968 ★★★★★

Gould Campbell. Still young and vigorous.
Tasted 1955 ★★★

Martinez. Very deep coloured but supple and fruity.
Tasted 1957–1965 ★★★

Noval. Most attractive in 1961. Later, lovely but on gentle decline.
Last tasted 1973 ★★★

Sandeman. Full, fat and chocolaty in 1955, sweet and absolute perfection in 1967. More recently, still fat but getting a little dull.
Last tasted 1971 ★★★

Taylor. Rich, beautifully balanced.
Tasted 1966 ★★★★

Tuke Holdsworth. My favourite, big, soft and velvety.
Tasted 1955–1969 ★★★★

Warre. A bit hot and spirity, good but not outstanding.
Tasted twice, in 1955 ★★★

1935 ★★★★★

Fifteen shippers. Picking began 23 September. A very successful vintage. High quality. *Climate:* healthy growing season. Harvesting in perfect weather. Quantity smaller than 1934.

Calem. Soft, gentle, not big but pleasant.
Tasted 1974 ★★★

Cockburn. Rather spirity even in 1953. Now medium pale and very mature in colour; attractive, slightly ethereal bouquet, old cob nuts; medium sweet, medium body, rich, soft and with lovely long flavour.
Last tasted November 1978 ★★★★

Croft. Tasted only three times. In 1975, the wine was austere with a dry, rasping finish. A second much better. Most recently: a lovely mature colour; delicate, fruity, plus Spanish-root bouquet; fairly sweet, medium light, delicious flavour.
Last tasted November 1977 ★★★★

Graham. First tasted in 1955. Perfection in the late 1960s. Still fairly deep in colour, rich and mature; lovely bouquet, calm, candle-wax, intriguing citrus-like overtone, a little brandy showing; still very sweet, medium body, very rich yet delicate, ripe and flavoury. Absolute perfection.
Last tasted July 1979 ★★★★★ *Drink now—1990.*

Hooper. Bottled in Oporto and of a Portuguese aged-in-the-wood style. Drying out, quite nice but not a true vintage port style or character.
Tasted 1970, 1971 ★★

Martinez. Rather light and thin.
Tasted 1966 ★★

Offley. Very agreeable.
Tasted 1955 ★★★

Rebello Valente. Slightly bitter.
Tasted 1952, 1955 ★

Sandeman. Last tasted from a "tregnum" or "cock" (three-bottle magnum): medium colour; excellent, gentle candle-wax bouquet; sweet, soft, perfect flavour and condition.
Last tasted January 1977 ★★★★

Taylor. I put this top. It is a most magnificent wine, which I have been privileged to drink and/or taste on more than a dozen occasions, since the autumn of 1953. Now it is medium full with a fine, even gradation of colour, perfectly mature; the most even, harmonious bouquet, gently uplifting, subtle fruit, delicate vinosity — totally different in character from Taylor 1912, 1945 or 1948 — complete, perfect — that was just the nose; on the palate, sweet, medium body — unobtrusive weight, elegant, fragrant in the mouth, beautiful texture and a lovely extended flavour and finish.
Last tasted March 1979 ★★★★★ *Perfect now—1990.*

1936 ★★

Not declared. Not a bad year; indeed quality fairly good but not of "vintage" standard, and too soon after the 1934s and 1935s.

1937 ★★

The same applies. Sound crop, quite good quality.
C. da Silva. "Reserva 1937." Pale old tawny colour; very good wood-aged bouquet; medium sweet, medium body but assertive flavour. Excellent acidity and finish. The style of what I call a true "vintage tawny" — not bottled after the conventional two years but matured in cask.
Tasted October 1976 ★

1938 ★★

Not generally declared, though quite good wines made. *Climate:* warm dry spring; increasingly hot and dry. No rain for eight weeks — grapes hardened. Some rain mid-September improved the situation and a good harvest began on 26th.
Noval. Tawny, good nose but slightly unbalanced.
Tasted 1970 ★

Taylor. Light, delicate, soft.
Tasted 1956 ★★

1939

Deficient in quantity and quality.

1940 ★★

Better, smallish crop but quite good quality. Not declared.

1941 ★

Quality not as good as 1940 due to poor spring and damp August. Harvest fine. Not declared.
Quinta do Noval. Bottled in 1944. Rich and luscious.
Tasted 1954.

1942 ★★★

Ten shippers. A good year which suffered from wartime interruption. All bottled in Oporto. Rarely seen. *Climate:* favourable spring, stormy June, July better, August good. Good harvest conditions around the end of September. Quality considered first class.
Croft. Lightish colour; sweet from start to finish. Best '42 I have had.
Tasted 1956, 1958 ★★★

Gonzalez Byass. Curious nose and flavour. Unattractive.
Tasted 1969.

Graham. Full ruby in 1955. Well matured, stylish but lacking Graham plumpness.
Last tasted 1971 ★★

Morgan. Big, strong, tangy wine.
Tasted 1965, 1968 ★★

Noval. Bottled in 1945. Fat, full flavoured.
Tasted 1955 ★★★

Rebello Valente. Very fruity bouquet and flavour. Lovely.
Tasted March 1960 ★★★

1943 ★★

Not declared but not a bad wine. *Climate:* early flowering and grape set; great heat in summer; early gathering — mid-September. More plentiful than expected. Satisfactory quality.
Sandeman. Pale tawny colour; deep liquorice nose; sweet, nice, some fruit but thinning.
Tasted 1964 ★★

1944 ★★★★

Not properly declared though wines of excellent quality. *Climate:* hot dry spring and summer; rain May and August. Early harvest in fine weather.
Delaforce. Deepish and rich looking; sweet, nice fruit; fat, full flavour.
Tasted 1964 ★★★★

Dow. Fairly deep colour; lively bouquet; fullish, long liquorice flavour. Dry finish.
Tasted 1959, 1961 ★★★★

Quinta do Milieu. Oporto bottled in 1948. Curiously red and immature; nice, rather youthful, peppery.
Tasted 1969 ★★★

1945 ★★★★★

Twenty-two shippers. The first really great vintage since 1935, and singularly well timed, though of insufficient quantity to replenish war-drained cellars. Mostly bottled in Oporto. Characteristics: magnificent, firm, taut, fruity, concentrated, long-distance runners. Climate: inclement spring. Small crop ripened in perfect weather for very early September harvest. I am informed by Michael Symington of Dow's that the grapes were gathered under conditions of exceptional heat and many shippers were worried at the time about possible instability. In fact, it turned out to be one of the best vintages of the century though quantity well below average.

Barros	*I must confess to being a bit snooty and uninterested in "Portuguese" ports as opposed to the good old British shippers, but I have two very consistent and good notes against Barros '45, probably bottled in 1948: first in February 1978 and, at a recent Studley Priory wine weekend: fairly deep coloured and impressive; good classic plummy/fruity, well-developed bouquet; still sweet, fairly full bodied, almost Fonseca-like fruit and character, well balanced, lively.* Last tasted November 1979 ★★★ Drink now — 1995.
Croft	*Tasted over a dozen times since 1966. Consistently good but drying out a little now: medium deep, lovely colour; soft, sweet, fruity, excellent bouquet; medium sweet (as ports go), medium body, elegant, flavoury, good balance. Although drying out, an extended finish.* Last tasted November 1977 ★★★★ Drink now — 1995.
Delaforce	*Not ready in 1961. Later, ripening and velvety.* Last tasted 1968 ★★★★ Drink now — 1990.
Dow	*First tasted in 1959. Now a lovely, evenly graded colour, medium deep, warm and ruddy; lovely, complete bouquet, reminds me of Spanish root; still quite sweet, attractive flavour and perfect balance.* Last tasted March 1979 ★★★★ At peak now — 1990.
Ferreira	*Not ready in 1966. Later: lovely, rich, ripe bouquet, sweet, soft, lovely wine with perfect balance.* Last tasted 1972 ★★★★ Drink now — 1990.
Graham	*Five notes from 1960. Fine colour; soft, rich, gentle bouquet, lovely fruit; fairly sweet, soft yet crisp, very good fruit and flavour. Excellent condition.* Last tasted November 1978 ★★★★★ Drink now — 2010.
Martinez	*Some bottled in Britain in 1948: fruity nose, sweet, fat but with austere finish. Probably perfect now.* Tasted 1966 ★★★? Drink now — 1990.
Niepoort	*Bottled March 1948: very deep colour, sweet, chunky, powerful, attractive in a non-classic way.* Tasted 1966–1969 ★★★ Drink now — 1995.
Quinta do Noval	*Although deep in colour, comparatively light in style even when first tasted in 1956. Most recent note: still fairly full coloured; very fat, rich, waxy nose, with flavour to match. Charming.* Last tasted October 1974 ★★★★ Drink now — 1990.
Quarles Harris	*Attractive colour; stylish; sweet, soft, good backbone, exceptionally nice wine.* Tasted 1968–1974 ★★★★ Drink now — 1990.
Rebello Valente	*Deep and overpowering in 1958. Later, simmering down and lovely.* Last tasted 1964 ★★★★ Probably now — 1990.

Sandeman	*Both Oporto and London bottled: fullish; chocolaty sweet nose and flavour; fine, chunky wine, ten years before reaching mature plateau.* Noted in 1970 ★★★★ Probably now — 1990.
Taylor	*A magnificent wine, described by a rival Oporto shipper in 1966 as "head and shoulders the best '45". When I first tasted it in 1967 it was enormous. I thought it the equivalent of Noval '31 (or Mouton '45). Several bottles and a dozen years later: fine, rich colour, still holding its youthful ruby hue — a sleeping giant; gentle, low-keyed bouquet, slow to develop, but lovely; not very sweet or fat, but magnificent depth and concentration, firm end acidity.* Last tasted March 1979 ★★★★★ Drink 1990–2020.
Warre	*Said to be one of the best '45s. I found it curious, framboise-scented in 1964. More recently, woody — a poor bottle.* Last tasted 1973 ★★★? Drink now — 1990.

1946 ★

Not "declared". Uneven quality followed uneven weather pattern: April, May wet; June hot but mildew problems. Mid-August very hot; by mid-September cool and grapes backward.

Sandeman	*Depth of colour similar to the Warre; gentle, old, spicy bouquet; same sweetness and weight, very flavoury and pleasant.* Tasted June 1977 ★★ Drink up.
Warre	*Bottled in Oporto, 1949: lightish, mature colour; curious and very mature nose; lightish but attractive.* Tasted 1967 ★ Drink up.

1947 ★★★★

Eleven shippers. A very good vintage. Happily supplying still depleted cellars with both quality and quantity. Climate: heavy spring rains; summer reports of the Oporto correspondent were more concerned with cricket matches in the "colony" than with weather, but on 17 August he reported "no rain since May, and great heat". Some welcome showers in September, the harvest starting on 22nd in perfect conditions. Quality reported good. Although I have tasted many '47s, few have been tasted in recent years.

Butler Nephew	*Fully mature; spirity; lightweight, somewhat astringent but flavoury.* Tasted twice, in 1967 ★ Drink up.
Cockburn	*Medium, mature; good but losing fruit; attractive, overall dry in style. Five notes.* Tasted 1964 — September 1971 ★★★ Drink up.
Constantino	*Oporto bottled, 1949: opaque, with very brown rim; curious aroma, like mustard and cress; full, tough and uninteresting. Not in the true British tradition.* Tasted 1968, 1971 ★★★ Drink now — 1995.
Delaforce	*Mature looking; good, brandy showing; medium sweet, nice but unready.* Tasted in 1965, 1967. Should be excellent now ★★★? Drink up.
Dow	*Deepish colour; very fine bouquet; sweet, medium body, very attractive. A lovely wine in splendid form when last sampled.* Tasted 1958–1972 ★★★★ Drink now — 1990.

Koppenhagen	*Like Constantino, huge, opaque but still with a purple rim; sweet, fruity and rich aroma and flavour. Not a "true" vintage port, but quite a good warming mouthful of wine.* Tasted 1971 ★★★ *Drink now — 1990.*
Quinta do Noval	*Tasted a dozen times since 1958. Most recently: medium colour, mature; excellent bouquet, fruity, mature; still quite sweet, rich, rounded, excellent flavour and condition. One of the best '47s.* Last tasted 1971 ★★★★★ *Drink now — 1990.*
Quinta do Noval Nacional Ungrafted vines	*From ungrafted vines. Deeper, rich and heavy looking; rich, intensely fruity, Spanish-root aroma; sweet, more full bodied, lovely flavour, dry finish. Remarkably good and youthful for its age.* Tasted 1970 ★★★★★ *Drink now — 2000.*
Quarles Harris	*Medium pale, mature, but very healthy glow; good nose; medium sweet, medium light, good flavour, very nice texture.* Last Tasted October 1977 ★★★ *Drink now — 1985.*
Rebello Valente	*Medium pale, very mature, quite a lot of colour lost, but rich; spirit showing in 1970 and very noticeable now; drying out (medium sweet for port), flavoury and attractive.* Last tasted March 1978 ★★★ *Drink now — 1985.*
Sandeman	*Variable. A Harvey bottling: light, fair, fruity in 1958. Another (unknown) bottler: fullish ruby colour; dull nose; sweet, fullish, some softness — but a good "officers' mess" port.* Last tasted 1961 ★★★ *Probably completely ready.*
Smith Woodhouse	*Pale coloured; fruity nose and flavour. Ready early.* Tasted 1955–1961 ★★ *Probably over the hill by now, so drink up.*
Taylor's "Special Quinta"	*Bottled 1949 (Taylor's did not ship '47 as a "vintage"). Medium, fully mature; curious nose, both bland and citrus fruit; drying out, rich, fruity but not a classic Taylor.* Tasted 1970–1972 ★★ *Drink up.*
Tuke Holdsworth	*When last tasted: medium colour, still slightly pink tinged and youthful; tiny, gentle and pleasant bouquet; fairly sweet, soft, lightweight and flavoury. Not a great deal to it, but very enjoyable.* Tasted 1969–1971 ★★ *Drink up.*
Warre	*Surprisingly light; quite nice bouquet and flavour, twist of end acidity.* Tasted 1958–1972 ★★ *Drink up.*

1948 ★★★★

Nine shippers. An extremely good year, which tends to be underestimated, possibly because of the association with '48s in Bordeaux and elsewhere. The major trio: Taylor, Graham and Fonseca. Characteristics: deep, hefty, masculine wines; alcoholic and long lasting. Beefy, but less concentrated than the '45s. Climate: early budding, prolific flowering. Great heat from mid-August right through harvest time. The lack of rain and burning of the grapes reduced yield: thickening skins, concentrated and raised sugar levels, resulting in deep, high strength port.

Dow	*Oporto bottled. Not seen in England but shipped to Denmark: less deep than the Fonseca, mature; hard nose; good chunky wine and fine finish. From a merchant's cellar in Copenhagen.* Tasted 1970 ★★★ *Drink now — 1990.*

Fonseca	*Tasted nearly a dozen times since 1958. Consistently good, plummy colour, "big vintage" depth and richness but maturing; hot alcoholic nose; losing some of its pristine sweetness, still fairly hefty in style and certainly very alcoholic, fruity, long, slightly tough, dry finish. Most recently: a fine, spicy-flavoured wine bottled by Justerini & Brooks. Last tasted November 1979 **** Drink now — 2000.*
Graham	*One of my favourite ports, tasted on more than a dozen occasions between 1958 and 1976. Still holding its immense depth of colour; magnificent bouquet, broad, sweet, fruity, a great classic; Graham sweetness, not as full bodied or alcoholic as Taylor but a big, rich, fruity flavour, soft yet plenty of grip. The perfect full wine. Last tasted March 1976 ***** Drink now — 2000.*
Mackenzie	*Good nose and flavour. Tasted 1958, 1970 ** Drink up.*
Smith Woodhouse	*Peppery nose; attractive. Tasted 1965 ** Drink up.*
Taylor	*Very dark, opaque even, when first tasted in 1958; certainly the fullest '48. Consistently good on the 13 occasions tasted since, but I notice that at two recent comparative tastings it was less deep than I expected: medium-deep colour — not as deep as the 1945 — plummy and browning; lovely, calm, candle-wax bouquet, fruit with alcohol under; sweeter than the 1945, full bodied, very rich, fruity and firm. Years of life. Last tasted March 1979 **** Drink now — 2000.*

1949

Not declared. Climate: critical: exceptional drought from end of previous season through to June. From end of June unprecedented heatwave, 148°F and upwards in the sun; a little rain, an early harvest, cooler with much rain. Reduced quantity.

1950 ★★

Thirteen shippers. A good but by no means great year. Climate: dry spring, rain in May and June; harvest 25 September in ideal conditions. Excellent quality reported at the time.

Cockburn	*Tasted a dozen times since 1959 but never found it inspiring. Medium colour, mature; sound, undemonstrative, spirity nose; fairly sweet, medium body, quite nice positive flavour. Last tasted June 1976 ** Drink now — 1990.*
Croft	*Harvey and British Transport Hotels bottlings good in 1962 and 1970. Oporto bottled; light, very mature; spirity on nose; very sweet, fruity and ready. Tasted 1970 *** Drink now — 1985.*
Delaforce	*Sweet nose; fruity — a good "mess" wine in 1961. Later, pleasant, perhaps a little astringent. Last tasted 1966, 1968 ** Drink up.*
Dow	*One of the fullest '50s, rich, slightly severe. Tasted 1966, 1970 *** Drink now — 1990.*

Graham	*Medium, plummy colour; smoky, old sealing-wax; drying out, slight liquorice taste (which I happen to like), dry finish. The least interesting vintage of Graham that I know. Tasted May 1978 ★ Drink now.*
Morgan	*Lightish, very mature in colour and on palate; sweet but showing age. Completely mature. Tasted 1976 ★ Drink up.*
Quinta do Noval	*Tasted several times but not recently. Corney & Barrow bottling excellent: medium, fairly mature; very pleasant bouquet; sweet, lovely, forthcoming, almost grapy flavour. Last tasted 1970 ★★★ Drink up.*
Quinta do Noval Nacional Ungrafted vines	*The deepest colour of all the '50s; very good fruity bouquet; fruity, soft, delicious. The best of the vintage tasted to date. Last tasted 1969 ★★★★ Drink now — 1995.*
Quárles Harris	*Plummy; slightly raw peppery nose and palate. Quite nice. Tasted 1958–1969 ★★ Drink up.*
Sandeman	*Tasted five times since 1962. Medium, plummy, mature colour; distinctly sweet nose with a sort of pasty vanilla character; still quite sweet on the palate, lightish style, pleasant, flavoury, with a very slightly bitter finish. Last tasted May 1978 ★★★ Drink now — 1985.*
Smith Woodhouse	*Old looking in the mid-1950s. Later: nice but slightly astringent. Last tasted 1968 ★ Drink up.*
Tuke Holdsworth	*Medium; tough, unyielding bouquet; severe, long finish. Tasted 1969, 1970 ★ Drink now — 1985.*
Warre	*A Harvey bottling: aroma and taste of filter pads, otherwise nice and fruity. Tasted 1962 ★★? Drink now — 1985.*

1951 ★

Not declared. Not a washout as in France, but a late harvest lacking the quality required for a vintage wine.

1952 ★★

Not declared. Climate: most disturbed. Unusually wet spring, early and late summer damp, close and oppressive. Late harvest. Small yield.

Dow	*Oporto bottled, 1954: light colour; raw nose; palate also raw but sweet and quite a nice flavour. Tasted 1967 ★ Drink up.*
Ramos Pinto	*Oporto bottled: fairly deep ruby still, though maturing; excellent, very fruity aroma, still a bit hard and peppery; sweet, full bodied, rich and alcoholic. Hint of cloves and liquorice. Not a wine for the lily livered. Tasted August 1979 ★★★ Drink now — 1995.*

1953 ★

Not declared. Climate: not the best of conditions, mainly too dry with a sudden bout of excessive heat in August. Harvest conditions better than expected. But. . . .

Sandeman	*Oporto bottled: medium, mature colour; lightish, delicate high-toned bouquet — attractive; very sweet but lacking body, gentle, very flavoury.* Tasted June 1977 ★★ Drink up.

1954 ★★★

Not really declared, mainly because 1955 turned out to be more generally satisfactory. But some very good wines made. Worth looking out for. Characteristics: fairly deep, nicely constituted and distinctly sweet wines. Climate: arctic winter and spring throughout Europe; unexpected frost in April reduced crop; June cool, July fine but grapes backward; August coolish and little rain; September saved the year — excellent weather, harvest about 24th in good conditions. Small yield; good quality. Not many '54s to be seen and few tasted recently.

Boa Vista	*Extremely deep colour when cask sample tasted in 1956. Later: medium deep; nice fruity bouquet and flavour. Six notes from 1956.* Last tasted May 1971 ★★★ Drink up.
Dow	*Oporto bottled and shipped to Denmark: attractive colour; light nose; very sweet nice wine.* Tasted 1970 ★★★ Drink up.
Quinta da Foz	*Surprisingly deep colour; good, rich, still slightly immature nose; full, fruity and characterful.* Tasted April 1975 ★★ Drink now — 1990.
Graham	*Almost certainly the best. First tasted in 1972: fairly deep, maturing; good nose; distinctly sweet, fullish, fat and attractive. More recently, at lunch with the Symington family in Oporto: medium colour, nicely mature; still sweet, soft, delightful and perfect now.* Last tasted November 1979 ★★★★ Drink now — 1985.
Harvey's	*Said to be Graham's. Very deep when young; nose almost too sweet; rich, soft yet firm, lovely wine.* Tasted 1956–1968 ★★★★

1955 ★★★★

Twenty-six shippers. The most highly regarded and the most widely shipped vintage of the period from the immediate postwar years to 1963. The market was considered "ripe" by all the leading shippers and the vintage readily taken up by the British trade. I have quoted below some of the opening prices to the trade per pipe (F.O.B. Oporto). Most extraordinarily, at auction, these wines are now commanding per dozen what they originally sold for per pipe. Also where known I have quoted the degree of sugar to compare the original sweetness of the major wines. Climate: a bundle of Portuguese excesses: heatwave in April and first half of May. Vines flowered well and benefited from rain at the end of May and in June. July satisfactory. August hot. Grapes in good condition. The correspondent in Ridley's trade journal reported "quality not equal to 1954" — beware of contemporary assessments!

Cockburn	*Residual sugar 3.4°. Price £170 per pipe. Tasted in cask: very deep colour, lilac edged; fresh, pungent blackcurrants aroma. Progressed to: medium colour; plummy/fruity nose, a little peppery and spirity; medium sweet, medium body, peppery wine, still a bit raw and with quite an end bite.* Last tasted November 1978 ★★(★) Drink 1985–1995?
Croft	*Residual sugar 3.0°. Price £170 per pipe. Variable notes on nine occasions since 1966. Colour consistent — medium and now*

mature; bouquet sometimes nicely developed, most recently power-ful; basically a very sweet wine but not heavy, although I have had one which seemed very alcoholic. Bottlings do vary: I have had several English bottlings (one in a half-bottle which was beautiful) and Oporto bottlings (shipped to Denmark). Last tasted September 1978 **(*) Drink now — 1990?

Delaforce	*Deep and dense in 1961. Later, medium full, fragrant, fruity and developing well.* Last tasted 1969 ***? Drink now — 1990.
Dow	*First tasted, bottled by Harvey's, in 1966: sweet, soft, very positive dry finish. Five consistently good notes since. Most recently, at lunch at Silva & Cosens in Vila Nova de Gaia: still quite deep in colour but maturing nicely; very fragrant bouquet; still fairly sweet, a crisp, extremely pleasant wine.* Last tasted November 1979 **** Drink now — 2000.
Ferreira	*Full colour and body; nice nose and flavour. Sweet, but raw and unready in late 1960s.* Tasted 1967, 1969 *** Drink now — 1990.
Fonseca	*Residual sugar 3.0°. Very full and sweet when first tasted in 1958. Consistently good. Still fairly deep; fine rich bouquet; still sweet, fairly full, lovely flavour, balance and condition. Perfect and will improve.* Last tasted January 1978 **** Drink now — 1995.
Gould Campbell	*Beautiful wine in 1967. A Smallwood bottling: nice flavour spoilt by searing end acidity in 1969. Most recently: very fine deep plummy colour; a good fruity peppery nose; soft, flavour reminded me a little of syrup of figs but more agreeable.* Last tasted June 1979 *** Drink now — 1985.
Graham	*Residual sugar 3.8°. Price £170 per pipe. Tasted on a dozen occasions, always good. Fat chocolaty nose, very big and sweet in 1958. Still a fairly deep, fine colour; excellent, rich peppery (alcohol, life) bouquet; quite sweet still but not overpoweringly so, fullish, soft, velvety, magnificent. Perfect now.* Last tasted May 1980 ***** Drink now — 1995.
Mackenzie	*Bottled by Harvey's: full coloured; nice, rather bland nose; sweet, good fruit, very attractive but raw. Needed time.* Tasted 1958, 1967 *** Drink now — 1985.
Martinez	*Several bottlings tasted from 1958. Edward Sheldon's: very full and purple; hard, alcoholic; fruity but unready in 1971. Winterschladen's: fullish plummy purple; sweet, full bodied, powerful end, very good indeed.* Last tasted June 1977 **** Drink now — 1995.
Niepoort	*Oporto bottled, 1958: medium, plummy colour, mature; nice rich plummy nose and flavour. Sweet, full, rich, nice balance.* Tasted twice, in 1969 *** Drink now — 1990.
Quinta do Noval	*Tasted nine times since 1966. Lighter from the outset, medium colour; the nose a bit hard and spirity; medium sweet, agreeable. A pleasant, rather feminine style of wine, unassertive but lively.* Last tasted October 1977 *** Drink now — 1990.
Rebello Valente	*Almost opaque; immature nose though developing well; sweet, soft but dry edged. Needed time.* Tasted 1969 ***? Drink now — 1990.
Sandeman	*Residual sugar 2.9°. Price £150 per pipe. Tasted and enjoyed a*

dozen times since 1958 (when it was very deep in colour, though displaying signs of early maturing), not counting a bad bottle affected by cork weevil in 1969. Sandeman's own bottling (in Oporto) seems lighter and more mature in colour, perhaps softer (in 1977) than a more recently tasted English bottling: medium-deep colour; soft, sweet bouquet with some depth; very good flavour, firm, well balanced. Tasted October 1978 ✱✱✱✱ *Drink now — 1990.*

Quinta de Sibio	*Medium full; medium sweet, dull, unready.* Tasted 1966 ✱ *Drink up.*
Smith Woodhouse	*Medium pale, mature; pleasant, sweet, open bouquet; sweet, fat little wine, light style, flavoury.* Tasted March 1980 ✱✱✱ *Drink now — 1988.*
Taylor	*Fifteen notes, starting in November 1958. An enormously powerful wine that I found unpleasantly raw and spirity up to the early 1970s. Some variations due to bottlings. Berry Bros: much less deep, more mature looking, fine fruit and very strong flavour in 1975. Most recent (bottler unknown): medium-full colour, mahogany rim, showing considerable maturity; a calm, harmonious, evenly distributed, vinous bouquet, sweet, rich, tobacco-like; fairly sweet, fairly full, lovely flavour supported by the characteristic Taylor backbone, good balance.* Tasted March 1979 ✱✱✱✱✱ *Drink now — 2010.*

1956

An appalling vintage worth reporting just to be aware of the weather conditions that caused it. Climate: unprecedented cold and heavy snowfalls in February, coldest and wettest on record. Wolves entered villages to eat domestic animals. Heavy rain and floods in March. April unpleasantly cold and wet. End of May irregular, hot then heavy rain. Summer abnormally cool and wet. Slight respite early September, then thunder — and more rain. Washed-out harvest early October.

1957 ✱

Not declared. Irregular weather but some good wines made.

Cockburn	*Late bottled: light tawny colour; green, stalky and not very attractive nose; sweet, raisiny flavour, soft, rather dull.* Tasted 1965–1969. *Drink up.*
Taylor's Vargellas	*Bottled 1960: medium colour; lovely, rich fruity nose, rather claret-like; fairly sweet, a bit "skinny" but flavoury.* Tasted 1973 ✱ *Drink up.*

1958 ✱✱✱

Twelve shippers. A good but generally light vintage. Climate: mixed. March sunny then gales; April cold; June hot, but with highest rainfall since 1896. July to mid-August sunny, thereafter cold and wet. September first unsettled then hot. Harvest, starting around 25th, was interrupted by a week of torrential rain in early October. Thereafter hot and sunny. Assessment: a soft, holding-the-fort sort of wine to drink while the big battalions are being deployed. Easy, variable. Martinez the most unusual.

Delaforce	*Tasted on eight occasions since 1966, but not recently. Medium, a light vintage colour; pleasant bouquet, nothing special; medium sweet, lightish in body and style, pleasant, straightforward and neat.* Last tasted June 1976 ** Drink now.
Dow	*Only tasted once. Full coloured; a big, very fruity, severe wine.* Tasted 1969 **? Must retaste.
Feuerheerd	*Little colour or bouquet yet curiously sweet, fat, rich.* Tasted 1974 *
Guimaraens	*Sturdy and slow maturing, quite nice, a little ungenerous.* Tasted 1966–1971 ** Drink now — 1985.
Martinez	*Tasted seven times since 1968. Something of a freak. Possibly the best '58, certainly far deeper and fuller than other '58s and a bigger wine than the 1955 and 1960 Martinez; very good fruity bouquet; sweet 1963-like body, attractive flavour and good balance.* Last tasted January 1978 **** Drink now — 1990.
Quinta do Noval	*Tasted a dozen times since January 1966. Consistently pleasant, agreeable, palish in colour — in fact rather weak, mature; little to the nose; sweet, very agreeable with a light, refreshing, peppery end.* Last tasted November 1976 ** Drink now.
Quarles Harris	*Good colour and lovely positive flavour.* Tasted 1966–1969 ** Drink up.
Royal Oporto	*Light, very mature tawny; good nose and flavour but of Portuguese style: raisiny, sweet. Not classic.* Tasted 1972 ** Drink up.
Sandeman	*Sweet, soft and flavoury from first tasting in 1966. A good colour; complete, fruity, slightly peppery nose; sweet, gentle, attractive and nearing peak.* Last tasted June 1978 *** Drink now — 1985.
Taylor's Vargellas	*Lightish, nice wine.* Tasted 1971, 1973 ** Drink up.
Warre	*Consistently pleasing: good rich nose; sweet, soft, nice easy wine. Eleven notes from 1966.* Last tasted March 1980 *** Drink now — 1985.

1959

Not declared. The vintage of the century everywhere except in Portugal. Climate: variable, wet spring. Thunder, hail, rain and intense heat in June — confusing for the vines, difficult for the farmer. July extremely hot. August normal, but harvest disappointing.

1960 ★★★★

Twenty-four shippers. The opposite to 1960 in France: a good vintage. Climate: January cold but dry; then continual rain for two months. April perfect, May variable. June and July very hot — prospects good. August and September ideal, fine, enough rain to swell the grapes. Harvest began in a heatwave, ended in rain — difficult weather in which to control fermentation. Assessment: a satisfactory, middle-of-the-road vintage, generally well balanced and developing well. Drink before the 1963 vintage.

Cockburn	*Nearly a dozen notes from 1966. Surprisingly deep colour every time; dull raw nose when young but has developed nicely; fairly sweet, fullish, flavour of Pontefract cakes (liquorice).* Last tasted October 1979 **(*) Drink now — 1995.

Croft	*Took 15 years to develop, now medium deep in colour, maturing well; sweet, open, rich bouquet but some of the initial raw brandy still showing; sweet, fairly full, pleasant though still a little hard.* Last tasted November 1977 ★★(★) Drink 1983–1995.
Dow	*Tasted on 17 occasions since 1966, various bottlings. The best note is against a Corney & Barrow bottling in 1976. Later, a bottle at a Dow tasting had a distinct touch of excess volatile acidity due — Michael Symington said — to the heat during the vintage. Most recently: completely mature looking; high-toned bouquet; sweet, some fatness.* Last tasted March 1980 ★★★ Drink now–1990.
Feuerheerd	*A Harvey bottling: sweet, fruity, slightly raw edge.* Tasted 1967, 1972 ★★ Drink now — 1990.
Fonseca	*Various English bottlings tasted between 1966 and 1977 all good, noticeably by Corney & Barrow, Thompson's of Leith and Winterschladen's. The Swedish State Monopoly bottling tasted in June 1978 unrecognizable: still purple in colour; raw stalky nose; very alcoholic and citrus-like flavour. Very odd. A good recent Christopher's bottling had a medium-full plummy colour (not fully mature); good rich fruity nose; distinctly sweet, fullish, fat, fruity and packed with flavour.* Tasted March 1980 ★★★(★) Drink now — 1992.
Gonzalez Byass	*Curious cheesy bouquet and flavour.* Tasted 1972★? Probably needs drinking.
Graham	*Consistently fine. So attractive that it was very pleasant to drink after ten years, but still deepish coloured; lovely, fresh, fruity bouquet and flavour — with a fruity and refreshing acidity all of its own.* Tasted June 1978 ★★★★ Drink now — 1985.
Martinez	*One of the best of the '60s. First tasted in 1974. All bottlings I have come across have been good except a bottle of Winterschladen's, 1977, which had a rubbery nose, clove-like, but better flavour. Summing up earlier notes: medium colour, maturing nicely; rich, fruity, exciting high-toned bouquet, a whiff of madeira-like acidity; sweet, fullish body and very flavoury. Lots of fruit, rich, quite a bite.* Last tasted February 1980 ★★★★ Drink now — 1985.
Morgan	*Plummy colour; Spanish-root nose and palate, quite nice.* Tasted only once, in 1976 ★★ Drink up.
Quinta do Noval	*Medium colour, mature appearance; pleasant, fragrant, gentle, fruity bouquet; sweet, soft, charming. Ready. Seven notes.* Last tasted March 1980 ★★★★ Drink now — 1988.
Quinta do Noval Nacional Ungrafted vines	*Fabulous colour, nearly opaque; rich, concentrated bouquet and flavour; sweet, full bodied, magnificent but unready when last tasted.* Tasted 1969, 1970 ★★★(★) Drink now — 2000.
Quarles Harris	*A Harvey bottling: attractive, a bit short.* Tasted 1972 ★ Drink up.
Rebello Valente	*Deep coloured; sweet, very fruity, hard dry finish.* Tasted 1967, 1968. Probably ★★(★) Drink now — 1990.
Sandeman	*Consistently good with steady progress from first tasting in 1966. Now a very fine colour, medium deep, maturing; sweet, well-developed bouquet; distinctly sweet, soft, fleshy. Very agreeable mouthful in November 1977, though I confess that the last time I drank it I was nervous and preoccupied. It was at the factory*

	house and I had the honour of being the guest speaker at the treasurer's annual dinner. Last tasted November 1979 ★★★ Drink now — 1988.
Quinta de Sibio	*Very sweet but hard.* Tasted 1974 ★(★) Drink now — 1985.
Taylor	*Fairly deep colour; exceptionally rich nose, like meat extract; very rich, rather odd in 1975. A Hedges & Butler bottling: much more developed in colour than the '63; still hard, spirity, low-keyed; not very sweet, otherwise straightforward. It will be interesting to see how this wine develops.* Last tasted March 1979 ★★(★) Drink 1985–1995?
Tuke Holdsworth	*Only tasted once: fairly deep, good colour, maturing; sweet, creamy bouquet; sweet, medium body, crisp and very flavoury, lovely flinty dry finish.* Tasted November 1978 ★★★ Drink now — 1990.
Warre	*A very good wine, tasted more than any other '60. Several bottlings sampled, of which Stowell's, in 1971, was not true to form, and a recent one from Corney & Barrow was overmature and grubby tasting. Probably bad bottles or poor storage as a Corney & Barrow bottling tasted in 1971 was excellent. So, if I can generalize: medium colour, maturing well; good fruity nose; sweet, soft yet quite a bit to it.* Last tasted June 1979 ★★★(★) Drink now — 1985.

1961 ★★

Good wine made but vintage not declared, not just because of overall quality, but too hard on the heels of the 1958 and 1960, and with 1963 in the offing. Some single-quinta wines and the newly developed (useful commercially) late-bottled vintages put on the market. Climate: a switchback of sun, heat, storms, cold. Manageable but intense heat and no rain in August. Very early vintage, 4 September, in cool conditions.

Croft	*Late bottled in 1965. Difficult to place stylistically, but sweet, soft, yet not rounded.* Last tasted 1971 ★★ Drink up.
Dow	*Late bottled in Oporto, 1965; plummy and pleasant.* Tasted 1965 ★★ Drink up.
Graham's Malvedos	*Single quinta, Oporto bottled, 1963: little nose; very good fruity wine, full, peppery end.* Tasted 1971 ★★ Drink up.
Noval Crusted	*Nutty bouquet; sweet, fruity, charming.* Tasted 1976 ★★ Drink up.
Taylor's Vargellas	*Single quinta, bottled 1964: interesting; rich; recognizable Taylor backbone.* Tasted 1973 ★★ Drink up.

1962 ★★

More or less the same thing: some good wine, but vintage not declared. A further issue of single-quinta and late-bottled port. Climate: disastrous floods in January. Moderate spring; good midsummer; hot and dry August/early September. End of month rain and late harvest in warm weather.

Dow	*Bottled 1966: mature colour; low-keyed; attractive.* Tasted March 1979 ★★ Drink up.

Quinta do Noval *Nacional* Ungrafted vines	*Magnificent, a collector's piece: big blackstrap wine, deep coloured; incredibly rich nose, like black treacle; sweet, full bodied, rich and concentrated.* Tasted 1969 ★★★(★★) Drink now — 2000.
Offley's Boa Vista	*Deep coloured; remarkable fruit and attractive bouquet and flavour.* Tasted 1973, 1976 ★★★ Drink now — 1986.
Sandeman	*Pleasant colour; self-assured nose; nice wine, lacking a bit of flesh.* Tasted 1974, 1976 ★★ Drink up.

1963 ★★★★★

Twenty-five shippers. Undoubtedly one of the finest vintages in recent times. Like the 1927, widely shipped, widely purchased. Although there are trade secrets, undoubtedly much wine of vintage *lotes* was made, enough to keep all the London clubs and regimental messes going for several decades. Characteristics: well constituted, deep and stylish with some long-distance runners, in particular Taylor, Dow, Fonseca and Warre. Climate: by Douro standards an uneventful growing season: snow and rain dying out by the end of April; high hopes then cold and wet to mid-June. July and August fine and dry. Some rain to swell grapes in September. Picking started on 23rd in perfect weather.

Avery's	*Very sweet, fruity, dry finish.* Tasted 1973.
Borges Roncão	*Single-vineyard wine: good colour; good fruity aroma; very sweet, fat, rich. Quite a surprise.* Tasted March 1979 ★★★★ Drink now — 1990.
Burmester	*Medium pale but not impressive; open; a bit feeble.* Tasted June 1979 ★ Drink now — 1986.
Cockburn	*Opaque; liquorice and raw brandy in June 1965. More recently, a Peatling & Cawdron bottling: medium-full colour, beginning to show maturity; a spicy, peppery and rather hard nose; sweet, rich, some fat (recent impressions of the Cockburn style have been consistently lean and a little ungracious), nice flavour and dry finish.* Tasted November 1977 ★★★(★) Drink 1983–1995.
Croft	*Tasted frequently since 1965. Consistently good, though my notes on colour vary from the deepest of a group of '63s in 1975, to a Corney & Barrow bottling tasted recently: medium pale, showing quite a bit of development (maturity); very attractive bouquet, hefty but forthcoming; sweet, rich, soft, lovely flavour and balance. Classic.* Tasted March 1979 ★★★★ Drink now — 1995.
Delaforce	*Only tasted when very young: sweet, full, nice wine.* Tasted 1965.
Dow	*Many tastings since 1965. Consistent notes following the wine's development. Very often impossible to know the name of the bottler but Avery, Harvey, Edward Sheldon all good. Two Oporto-bottled wines (by Dow, of course) were noticeably deeper and less mature in colour; powerful and hard (both tasted in 1976). Another Oporto-bottled wine was highly preferred by a professional panel. My notes at this tasting: medium-full colour, firm, maturing; crisp, fruity bouquet; fairly sweet, rich, fullish body.* Last tasted March 1980 ★★★★ Drink now — 1990.
Feuerheerd	*Quick maturing, rich.* Tasted 1974 ★★★

Fonseca	*Highly successful: sweet and fruity in 1965, sweet and fruity now. Fine deep colour; magnificent bouquet; fairly full bodied, lovely flavour, great style, excellent finish.* Last tasted June 1978 ★★★★(★) Drink now — 2000.
Graham	*Fullish colour; deep fruity nose, still a little hard and spirity; sweet, full bodied, huge and alcoholic. Impressive.* Last tasted December 1978 ★★★★(★) Drink 1982–2010.
Mackenzie	*Sweet, fullish, nice.* Tasted 1965.
Martinez	*Tasted different bottlings on several occasions since 1965. Not inspired — not as good or as interesting as the '58 or '60. Surprisingly light and forward in appearance, for a '63, a bit feeble in colour and on the nose; medium-sweet flavour, lightish, pleasant enough but not impressive.* Tasted March 1979 ★★ Drink now — 1983.
Quinta do Noval	*Sweet and soft in 1965; sweet and soft now. One of the best Noval vintages, exuding feminine charm and style: medium colour, fairly mature now; soft sweet bouquet and flavour. Forward, easy, elegant.* Tasted June 1976 ★★★★ Drink now — 1990.
Offley's Boa Vista	*Attractive, flavoury, fruity wine.* Tasted 1965–1967.
Quarles Harris	*Full, good wine — a little too early to judge.* Tasted 1965.
Rebello Valente	*Conflicting notes, too early to be significant.* Tasted 1965, 1967.
Sandeman	*One of the deeper-coloured '63s: full, plummy colour; good nose, fruity but still peppery immaturity; very sweet when young, still sweet, full bodied, lots of grip, good flavour and balance. Probably the best postwar Sandeman. Needs time.* Last tasted July 1978 ★★★(★) Drink 1982–1995.
Quinta de Sibio	*Opaque; fruity nose and Spanish-root flavour.* Tasted 1974.
Taylor	*Fairly·deep but maturing; fine bouquet; fine, markedly sweet, full bodied, rich, with firm backbone. Taylor at its impressive near-to-best — perhaps not up to the '55 or '45. Time will tell.* Last tasted June 1978 ★★★★(★)? Drink 1985–2000?

1964

Not declared. Climate: difficult: severe winter, late start; early drought, spring rains; caught up by August. Very hot mid-September. Rain too late. Varied weather affected picking — and vineyard labour affected by illegal emigration of workers to France. Only one '64 tasted.

Guimaraens	*Full, purple and lots of fruit.* Tasted 1966 ★★ Probably needs drinking now.

1965

Not declared, but some nice wines made following moderate weather conditions, no difficulties and good sugar readings.

Taylor's Vargellas	*Fairly deep; sweet, rich, maturing well.* Tasted 1973.

1966 ★★★★

Twenty shippers. An attractive, underrated and undervalued vintage. Characteristics: firm, well-constituted wines, slight variations in character and weight but overall good. Climate: wet winter; storms and low temperatures in May, with sun at end of month. Hot in July, but more leaf than usual prevented grapes burning. Vintage interrupted by rain.

Croft	*Medium deep, plummy; harmonious, deep but fragrant nose; medium rich, elegant, but still a bit severe.* Last tasted March 1980 ★★★(★) *Drink 1982–1992.*
Delaforce	*Deep, plummy, immature; sultana-like; medium sweet, full bodied, rich powerful wine, quite an end tang.* Tasted September 1978 ★★★ *Drink 1982–1992.*
Dow	*Quite deep, plummy, immature; good bouquet: sweet, firm, crisp; flavour to match. Elegant. Good end grip.* Last tasted March 1980 ★★(★★) *Drink 1982–1992.*
Ferreira	*Deep, maturing; hard, severe bouquet, some fruit under; pleasant, straightforward, good middle fruit but tails off a little.* Tasted only once, in September 1978 ★★ *Drink now — 1985.*
Fonseca	*Very deep colour but maturing; very fine, slightly spicy, classic bouquet; sweet, full, soft, lovely wine, fruity with good grip at the finish. Magnificent.* Last tasted January 1980 ★★★★(★) *Drink now — 1990.*
Graham	*Two hundred and sixty pipes shipped for English bottling. Lovely wine. Fairly deep, plummy but maturing; interesting aroma, deep and rich, reminiscent of celery, muscatels; sweet, medium, full bodied, rich, fruity, dry finish. Nine consistently good notes from 1968.* Last tasted September 1978 ★★★★(★)
Quinta do Noval	*First tasted January 1968. Slightly variable notes. At last tasting: fairly deep (for Noval of a lightish vintage) but maturing; sweet, unsettled nose; fairly sweet, firmer than expected, fruity, end a bit severe. Not the usual charm.* Tasted September 1979 ★★ *Drink 1982–1990.*
Offley's Boa Vista	*Medium deep, maturing; rich, very spirity nose; sweet, full, fat and attractive, peppery dry finish.* Last tasted January 1980 ★★★ *Drink now — 1990.*
Sandeman	*Medium, very mature looking; rather hard nose; rich enough, nice shape, leanish, a pleasant familiar style.* Tasted September 1978 ★★ *Drink now — 1989.*
Taylor	*Two hundred and fifty pipes shipped for English bottling; also Oporto bottlings. Fine, deep-coloured wine, Oporto bottlings appear to be slightly less mature looking; fine, fruity nose; still not settled down; sweet, fairly full bodied, typical Taylor firmness, length and powerful end flavour. Seven notes from 1968.* Last tasted January 1980 ★★(★★) *Drink 1986–2000.*
Warre	*Fairly deep, maturing slowly; broad, pleasant raisiny aroma; sweet, medium body, soft but still peppery. Very good potential.* Last tasted March 1980 ★★★(★) *Drink now — 1992.*

1967 ★★★

Four shippers. A confusing situation. Cockburn and Martinez each regarded their '67 as better than their '66 and stuck to their guns. Climate: dry winter, May wet and cold, but long hot summer, some rain in September to swell the grapes. Conditions good throughout vintage.

Cockburn	*At the time the '67 was declared, Cockburn's considered their wine had "breed and stamina . . . another '27". Certainly fine, deep and very rich when I first tasted it in 1972, now less deep than most '66s; nose undeveloped and spirity but basically good; medium sweet, dry finish, not a big or fat wine. Possibly a lean long-distance runner. Time will tell. Eight notes.* Last tasted March 1980 ★★(★) Drink now — 1990 plus.
Croft's Roeda	*Single quinta wine. Medium deep, clear cut, good colour; curious, hard and undeveloped nose; yet sweet, soft and flavoury on the palate.* Tasted November 1977 ★★ Drink now — 1985.
Martinez	*Oporto bottled. Medium colour, beginning to mature; nose a bit dull and spirity; better on palate: sweet, soft and rich.* Last tasted January 1980 ★★(★) Drink now — 1990.
Sandeman	*Very deep colour but maturing; sweet, soft and forthcoming bouquet; sweet, medium full, attractive, developing nicely.* Tasted November 1976 ★★★ Drink now — 1989.
Taylor's Vargellas	*Both English and Oporto bottled opaque in 1973. Medium colour now, maturing; sweet broad nose; sweet, medium-light body, positive flavour, long hard dry finish.* Tasted March 1978 ★★ Drink now — 1990.

1968

Not declared. Climate: uneven and unsatisfactory. Late flowering; very dry, exceptionally hot summer, then weather unsettled, grapes backward at vintage time though weather good during picking.

1969

A poor vintage due to rain and cold from January to end of June, hot July and August, then rain again. Unripe grapes leading to tart, overacid wines.

1970 ★★★★

Twenty-three shippers. A good, widely declared vintage. The first vintage almost entirely bottled by the shippers themselves; none shipped in cask for British merchants to bottle. Croft opening price to the trade: £9.25 a dozen bottles F.O.B. (in January 1972). Characteristics: sound, healthy, nicely constituted and straightforward. An entirely satisfactory, if not inspired, vintage. My ratings are deliberately loose and imprecise as the true qualities will take time to show up clearly. Climate: rare copybook weather pattern — cold and dry in March; after warm April, weather ideal. Some rain in September to swell the grapes, which were in perfect condition when picked from 21 September.

Cabral	*Bottled 1973: fully mature looking; raisiny aroma; quite pleasant but little to it.* Tasted July 1979 ** Drink now — 1985.
Cockburn	*Opaque in April 1972. Still fairly deep coloured, rich and plummy; nose peppery and undeveloped; fairly sweet, medium full, still a bit spirity, very dry finish.* Last tasted March 1979 **(**)? Drink 1985–2000.
Croft	*Very deep coloured; sweet, fruity, still a little raw on the nose; very sweet wine, full, fruity, long finish. Impressive.* Tasted September 1979 **(*) Drink 1985–2010.
Delaforce	*Deep coloured but developing nicely; rich plummy bouquet; full bodied, nice rich wine. Dry finish.* Tasted October 1977 **(*) Drink 1984–1995.
Dow	*Deep coloured, still youthful looking; dumb at first but slowly developing fine, rich, fruity bouquet; sweet, fleshy, fairly concentrated. Very good wine. Four notes.* Last tasted September 1979 **(**) Drink 1985–2010.
Ferreira	*Medium full, plummy colour, not very positive; broad fruity aroma; medium sweet, medium, moderate quality. Quick developing?* Tasted October 1977 *(*) Drink 1982–1990.
Feuerheerd	*Tasted only once, when young. Seemed a good rich wine.* Tasted 1974.
Fonseca	*Incredible colour, still opaque; sweet, mulberry-like aroma, spirity; very sweet, full bodied, very rich long finish. Fonseca have been making outstanding wines in recent years and this is in the top flight.* Last tasted October 1977 **(***) Drink 1985–2010.
Gould Campbell	*Deep, fine; touch of vanilla on nose and woody on one occasion; rich and pleasant.* Tasted 1973, 1975.
Graham	*The last vintage before the Grahams sold out to the ubiquitous Symington family. Very deep, purple, virtually opaque; bouquet immature but not raw, crisp, fruity; fairly sweet, full bodied. Rich, fine classic wine.* Tasted October 1977 ***(**)? Drink 1984–2010.
Krohn	*Medium plummy purple; fruity but hard; medium sweet, peppery. Quite nice.* Tasted March 1979 *(*) Drink 1983–1993.
Martinez	*Very deep plummy purple; sweet, slightly raisiny aroma, spirity still but good; very sweet, full, very rich, long warm flavour.* Tasted only once, in October 1977 **(**) Drink 1985–2000.
Quinta do Noval	*Distinctly on the light side, soft and destined for early development when first tasted in 1972. Most recently: medium full, plummy, still looks like an early ripener; nose spirity and hard to pin down; very sweet, medium body, rich, nice flavour and balance. Still a bit peppery.* Last tasted October 1977 **(*) Drink 1982–1995.
Offley's Boa Vista	*Fairly deep, plummy; sweet, broad bouquet, still hard but good; very sweet, full bodied, long flavour, rapier-like finish. Shapely and interesting.* Last tasted March 1980 **(**) Drink 1982–1995.

Rebello Valente	*Medium colour, forward; hard spirity nose; very sweet, full, rich, nice wine.* Tasted October 1977 ⋆⋆(⋆) Drink 1984–1995.
Royal Oporto, Quinta dos Carvalhas	*Lightish colour with weak purple rim; not bad nose, a bit thin; pleasant but insubstantial.* Tasted June 1977 ⋆ Drink now.
Sandeman	*Tasted on six occasions since early 1975. Consistently deep coloured, an immature plummy purple; nose sweet but hard still; sweet, full, rich, crisp, tannic.* Last tasted March 1979 ⋆(⋆⋆⋆) Drink 1985–2000.
Smith Woodhouse	*Full, good colour; hard undeveloped nose; very sweet, medium body, rich but rather short.* Tasted October 1977 ⋆⋆(⋆) Drink 1983–1993.
Taylor	*When first tasted, the next deepest in colour to Graham; fine, "black" and peppery in 1972. Still fairly deep, a lovely plummy purple; deep, hard and powerful nose; fairly sweet, very full bodied, massive, alcoholic, long tannic finish. A long wait for a long future.* Last tasted September 1979 ⋆(⋆⋆⋆⋆) Drink 1990–2020.
Warre	*Fine deep purple colour; spicy, spirity bouquet, not settled down but fine potential; sweet, fullish, fruity and good vinosity.* Tasted March 1978 ⋆⋆(⋆⋆) Drink 1985–2010.

1971 ⋆

Not declared. Late flowering, late vintage but some nice wine made.

Taylor's Crusted	*Fairly deep, sweet and attractive.* Tasted May 1977 ⋆⋆ Drink now.

1972 ⋆⋆

Not generally declared. Indeed the weather seems to have been tricky: heavy rain from January through May; heat and drought; rain returned in September and stayed. Average wines produced.

Dow	*Managed to make a nice wine, which they solitarily and belatedly declared. Fullish, forward, sweet and pleasant.* Tasted March 1979 ⋆⋆⋆ Drink now — 1985?

1973

Not declared a vintage year. Climate: heavy rainfall in first half of year followed by hot summer. Welcome rain in September which unhappily continued on and off. Consequently above-average wines were made only in isolated instances.

1974

Not declared. Climate: vintage later than usual under good conditions. Wet spring, dry summer, vintage marred by heavy rain early October. Large "authorization", mediocre quality.

1975 ★★★★

Seventeen shippers. A good vintage generally welcomed by the Oporto and British trade. Climate: average wet winter followed by a long hot summer. Welcome rain, quite heavy, in early September, swelled the grapes and improved prospects, further endorsed by three weeks of fine weather. Heavy rain over the last weekend in September caused some damage, but it cleared and remained fine and dry for the picking, which started on 1 October. Uniformly good wines were made in perfect conditions. Market: in Oporto the scene was dominated by the revolutionary crisis. As Michael Symington observed: it was "a long hot summer", politically as well as climatically. There was considerable enthusiasm for the quality of this well-timed vintage, the wines being offered in 1977 to the British trade at around £27 to £30 per dozen F.O.B. (There was mandatory bottling in Oporto.) 1975s are clearly good value but in some danger of being bypassed for a time, as the '66s were (and still are). Characteristics and assessment: young port is notoriously difficult to judge. Happily, the English merchant knows he can rely on the quality and style of a given shipper. My first comprehensive look at the '75s was at a blind tasting organized by the Masters of Wine in October 1977, though I had tasted some of the wines before and have since. In general it is a good classic vintage, well balanced and destined for a longish life.

Calem	*Massive, opaque in appearance; sweet, spirity, baked sultanas aroma; very sweet and full bodied, rich and spirity.* Tasted October 1977 ★★(★) Drink 1985–2000.
Cockburn	*Opaque in 1977. Now ruby; sweet but unknit nose; sweet on the palate yet with a dry, astringent finish, the component parts of fruit, alcohol, tannin and acidity nowhere near assembled. Harmony a long way ahead.* Last tasted March 1979 ★(★★)? Drink 1990–2000 plus.
Delaforce	*Deep; plummy nose; sweet, rich, still raw, of course.* Tasted October 1977 ★(★★)? Drink 1988–2000 plus.
Dow	*Intensely deep and purple; a big peppery aroma, good fruit; sweet, very peppery in June 1977, showing richness and fruit on palate in October 1977. An impressive, stylish wine.* Last tasted March 1979 ★★(★★) Drink 1987–2000 plus.
Ferreira	*Opaque; raw, stalky, undeveloped; very sweet, full bodied, rich, powerful, tannic.* Tasted October 1977 ★(★★) Drink 1990–2000 plus.
Fonseca	*Huge opaque wine; potentially rich, Spanish-root aroma, full of fruit; very sweet, full bodied, a powerful, rich wine with tannic finish. Characterful, stylish, will keep long and well.* Tasted October 1977 ★★(★★) Drink 1990–2010.
Gould Campbell	*One of the "second-growth" brands of Silva & Cosens. Deep purple; nice, gentle, fruity; sweet, medium body, rich. Nice balance, good value.* Tasted October 1977 ★★(★) Drink 1985–1995.
Graham	*One of my favourite shipper's styles: opaque and purple; sweeter and softer on the nose than Cockburn, Dow and Warre; as always very sweet, fairly full bodied, with pronounced flavour and after-taste. Should develop beautifully.* Tasted June and October 1977 ★★★(★) Drink 1987–2010.
Martinez	*Opaque, immature purple — as it should be; dumb, hard nose but great depth, slightly raisiny; sweet, complete, dry finish. Although from the same stable, prefer it to Cockburn's.* Tasted October 1977 ★★(★★) Drink 1987–2000 plus.

Quinta do Noval	*The most famous single-quinta wine. A beautiful property owned by the van Zeller family, where they tend to produce (except for the massive 1931) rather quick-maturing, feminine, graceful, vintage port. Very deep coloured; the nose rather similar to Martinez, still a bit spirity; medium sweet, medium body, stylish, nice flavour, leathery texture.* Tasted October 1977 ★★(★) Drink 1985–2000.
Offley's Boa Vista	*Very deep, plummy; hard spirity nose; very sweet, full, fat and rich.* Tasted October 1977 ★★(★) Drink 1984–1995.
Quarles Harris	*Another secondary brand owned by the Symington family trading as Silva & Cosens. Very deep purple; medium sweet, medium body, lighter style. Very dry end.* Tasted October 1977 ★(★★) Drink 1984–1995.
Rebello Valente	*Deep plummy purple; dumb, hard, stalky, spirity nose; medium sweet, medium full but basically a lighter style.* Tasted October 1977 ★(★★) Drink 1984–1995.
Sandeman	*Very deep plummy purple; delicate, a bit spirity; very sweet, full, soft and rich. I thought it had a good long flavour, though a respected fellow taster thought it lacked weight and tannin on finish. I personally like Sandeman's vintage port, a sort of lighter (and always less expensive) version of Graham.* Tasted October 1979 ★★(★) Drink 1985–1995 plus.
Smith Woodhouse	*Yet another Symington-owned brand. Very deep, similar to Quarles Harris, perhaps slightly less sweet.* Tasted October 1977 ★(★★) Drink 1984–1995.
Taylor	*Four notes. Huge, opaque, purple and almost overpoweringly sweet aroma in October 1977. Still deep and immature; a rich but hard, tight-knit, sweet, prune-like aroma, both broad in character and concentrated; on the palate, sweet, fairly full bodied, intense and fruity. One of the best '75s, a very good but perhaps not great Taylor. We shall see.* Tasted November 1979 ★★(★★)? Drink 1990–2010 plus.
Warre	*Opaque in 1977. Now: plummy; stalky/spirity but fruit under; distinctly sweet, full rich wine with good finish. One of the best '75s.* Tasted June and October 1977, March 1980 ★★(★★) Drink 1990–2010.

1976 ★

Not declared. Climate: driest winter on record with drought through to the last days of August. Heavy rain 25/26 September and unsettled weather throughout vintage. Low production but good average wines made.

1977 ★★★★★

Twenty shippers. Generally considered outstanding despite some reservations about declaring a vintage so soon after the last (1975), and thoughts that its entitlement to a "silver jubilee" tag might have been uppermost in loyal shippers' minds. Climate: very wet winter; cold spring with some exceptional frost. Cool unsettled summer held back development of vines but a heatwave starting early September transformed the situation. When picking started, on 28 September, the grapes (to quote Michael Symington) were in a "text book condition of perfection". The fine hot weather lasted until 7 October, by which time most of the best quintas had finished picking. After two days of heavy rain, sunshine returned, but it was much cooler, reducing the quality of the late-picked grapes — which would not be used for the vintage port *lotes* anyway. Quality assessment: even at the time of the vintage, many shippers considered their wine "vintage worthy", an opinion usually reserved until the following spring or later. Certainly the wines were immediately outstanding for the freshness of their bouquet. Shippers and their agents cooperated to hold a comparative tasting of their '77s at Christie's in November 1979. They were generally found impressively deep, of consistent quality, with the usual shippers' variations of style. Market: although port shippers are coy about the quantity of vintage wine made, I believe that the total put on the market has been cautiously small — a trickle compared with the flood of '63s. Another important factor is price. Labour and other costs in Portugal escalated between the political upheaval in 1975 and the late spring of 1979 when most shippers declared the '77. Opening prices to the trade are $33\frac{1}{3}$ per cent to 50 per cent up on the 1975 vintage, despite the devaluations of the escudo. Tasting notes: all young ports tend to be big, "black" and purple; on the nose they are invariably peppery and difficult to analyse — some seem more open and fruity than others — at any given moment. They are all sweet, with slight variations of sugar content, and are mainly raw and alcoholic — indeed positively palate-numbing. Time will tell.

First the big classic wines:	*Croft; Dow, for me a copybook wine; Fonseca, powerful; Graham, very sweet and rich; Taylor, concentrated; Warre.*
Good wines of different style:	*Delaforce; Ferreira; Gould Campbell, a soft, easy wine, very well liked at the Christie's tasting; Offley; Quarles Harris; Rebello Valente; Sandeman, Smith Woodhouse*
Other shippers/brands not yet tasted:	*Cabral; Calem; Messias; Pocas Junior; Royal Oporto.*
Not declaring the 1977 vintage:	*Cockburn; Martinez; Quinta do Noval.*

1978

Unlikely to be declared. Climate: wet winter; cold and wet spring and early summer reducing yield, drought from 25 June to 8 October. Lack of rain and great heat in September (picking began on 28th) resulted in very heavy, coarse, full-bodied wines.

1979 ★★

Abundant and above-average quality, but hardly likely to be declared so soon after 1977 and in current economic conditions. Climate: very wet vintage with heavy flooding; wet, unsettled spring; summer generally fine with another long drought from June until broken by heavy rain, 17/18 September, which greatly benefited the grapes picked from 24 September.

Postscript: the future of vintage port. Vintage port is the tip of the port-market iceberg. It may not be an important money spinner for the big port houses, but it is in fact profitable for the shipper because, of all the classic wine markets, this is the most controllable. It is slow to mature but, to offset this, it is certainly the most dependable of all vintage wines. Above all, its status and publicity value is incalculable. Vintage port is not only the standard setter but also the standard bearer.

MADEIRA
and
TOKAY

Madeira, endearing and enduring, is almost certainly the longest living of all wines; the only exception is tokay essence, which appears to have immortal qualities. It also happens to be one of my favourite wines. The trade in madeira wines, like port, was fostered, developed and dominated by British merchants. It was enormously popular in the 18th century, not only in England but in our American colonies. Although the blight oidium severely crippled production in the 1850s, and the dread phylloxera gave the trade a *coup de grâce*, outstanding quality wine was produced throughout the 19th century and it is principally these vintages and soleras I have noted.

Vintage and solera

A true vintage madeira is a wine from a cask, made from a named grape and bottled directly, or after a spell in demijohns, from the original cask. A solera is bottled from a cask that has been topped up and refreshed by wine of the same grape and quality but of younger vintages, the date on the bottle being the year of the original vintage of that blend. In practice, however, the dividing line is not quite as clear cut. A cask of vintage madeira may have been refreshed — hard to tell. Labels are not always explicit: a date on its own might imply either vintage or solera.

Vintage madeira has always been scarce and is highly prized by the connoisseur, though, in my experience, for sheer richness and pleasure in drinking, the finest soleras are hard to equal. An old vintage can be dried out; a fairly recently bottled old solera often has more flesh and life.

I think I ought to mention at this stage that many bottles of old madeira found in the cellars of country houses are rarely of the quality of the true vintage and old solera wines that emanate from the island itself. I well remember coming across an enormous stock, all about a century old and all (after random sampling) thin and acetic, dead and gone.

Grapes and districts

In addition to the four basic grapes — in ascending order of sweetness and richness: Sercial, Verdelho, Bual (or Boal) and Malmsey — other varieties also crop up from time to time, Moscatel, Bastardo and Terrantez (reputedly not replanted after phylloxera). District names sometimes appear: Cama do Lobos being the best known.

Shippers

The shippers' or merchants' names are important, and, in the case of the oldest and rarest, the full provenance. Leading British houses in Madeira are Cossart (Cossart, Gordon & Manners; Cossart, Gordon & Co), Blandy, Leacock, Tarquinio Lomelino, and Rutherford & Miles. The ubiquitous M.W.A. (Madeira Wine Association) is a consortium comprising all five.

1789 ★★★★★

Very good, particularly in the Cama do Lobos district.

1792 ★★★★

Generally good.

Malmsey, Solera 1792 (Blandy). Bottled 1957: beautiful mature amber; sweet, complete, gentle bouquet; medium sweet, soft yet intense, lovely balance, length, exquisite aftertaste.

At a Madeira Club dinner, Savannah, Georgia, April 1980 ★★★★

1795 ★★★★

Terrantez (Vinhos Barbeito). Probably a solera wine. Medium deep but very pronounced amber colour; pungent, powerful nose; drying out though extremely rich, with a lovely fragrant flavour and fine lingering finish.

Tasted March 1969 ★★★★★

1803 ★★★★

Generally very good.

1805 ★★★

Good, particularly Cama do Lobos and São Martinho.

"Trafalgar" Madeira. Recorked by the Army & Navy Stores, *c.* 1870. An unfortunate example of a true vintage madeira wine that did not survive rebottling. Its colour had gone, amber faded to a washed-out, stained, watery colour; nose old and ropy. I did not consider it fit to drink

Noted in October 1969.

1806 ★★★

Also good, particularly in the same districts as in 1805.

1808 ★★★★★

Excellent vintage, Malmsey the best ever — followed by 1822 and 1880. Noël Cossart says that Malmseys made after the late 1880s were never as robust as pre-phylloxera wines due to the "infiltration" of French *Malvoisie* vine stock.

Bual, Solera 1808 (Cossart, Gordon). Fairly deep old amber; a bouquet and flavour that resembled a very rich oloroso sherry; medium-sweet, burnt-Bual tang.

Tasted May 1976 ★★★★

Malmsey, Solera 1808 (Cossart, Gordon). First noted in 1977 at a III Form Club tasting of old madeira, sherry and port at Ellis, Son & Vidler's: clearly a great wine. More recently it was the outstanding wine in an outstanding tasting: a medium-deep amber shading off to a most pronounced yellow colour, through to a yellow-green rim; exquisite bouquet — sweet, intensely rich yet ethereal; still sweet on the palate, rich and fat but not remotely heavy, indeed the opposite. Wonderful length and persistence of flavour, the sure sign of quality in any wine. And of course with the inimitable madeira tanginess.

At a Cossart, Gordon tasting of vintage and solera madeiras, October 1979 ★★★★★

1810 ★★

"Bin 110", Vintage 1810. Shipped 1815 and bottled 1910. Americans regard madeira as their very own classic wine, and this was an interesting example of a true vintage madeira, imported and matured in cask, and bottled when a century old. A lovely colour, pale, very bright amber yellow with a green rim — for me the hallmark of a truly old madeira; bouquet very sound but lacking purity and high quality; dry, fairly light, a good flavour but tailed off and lacked follow through. It should have been drunk soon after bottling.

At a Heublein tasting, May 1976 ★★

1814 ★★★

Bual, Solera 1814 (Rutherford & Miles). Fairly deep, very rich amber; deep, rich, intense and concentrated bouquet; fairly sweet still, full bodied, lovely, fine, deep flavour. Beautiful wine.

Tasted March 1966 ★★★★★

1815 ★★★★

A good vintage made even more marketable by the "Waterloo" tag, and famous for its Bual. I have not tasted any straight vintage 1815s but several soleras, the first at Harvey's in 1961 — I notice it had a price tag of £350 per pipe, about £80 per dozen, duty paid, before adding any selling margin. There was no indication of the grape but it was probably Bual.

Solera 1815. Golden amber colour; rich bouquet with twist of lemon; rich tangy flavour with good finish.

Tasted November 1966 ★★★

Bual, Solera 1815 (Cossart, Gordon). Bottled c. 1960. Medium pale, fine amber with lemon rim; delicate flowery bouquet; medium dry, medium light, excellent firm flavour with good acidity. An extremely fine, stylish wine.

Tasted 1972 and, last, in Savannah, April 1980 ★★★★

1820 ★★★

I have tasted two authentic 1820 soleras, also one reputed to be 1820, recorked by a Sheffield merchant in 1900:

Reserve Verdelho. Deep amber tawny; rich, bottle-age, overtone of violets; a dry wine with fabulous flavour but very austere almost bitter finish.

Tasted May 1961 ★★★

Believed 1820. Recorked 1900. Pale with lemon-amber rim; very old nose, but sound; drying out, light, slightly astringent but holding well.

Tasted June 1976 ★★

1822 ★★★★★

A generally excellent vintage, better than 1815, especially good for Bual and Malmsey.

Bual, Solera 1822 (Cossart, Gordon). The 1822 vintage, which was the basis for this solera, was one of the best of the century for Bual. Tasted twice, the first time in 1961 when I thought it was spoiled a little by an unclean finish. Most recently: pale, amber rimmed; sweet, rich but delicate bouquet; fairly sweet, not a heavy wine, elegant, tangy, dry acidic finish.

At the Cossart, Gordon tasting, October 1979 ★★★

"Old Madeira" (Cossart, Gordon). Lovely wine with medium-pale amber colour; very rich good bouquet and flavour, medium dry with a lovely tang.

Tasted March 1971 ★★★★

1824 ★★★★

Bual, Solera 1824 (Rutherford & Miles). Medium-

light oloroso colour with pronounced amber rim; very rich, mouth-watering bouquet reminiscent of old stables; medium sweet, medium body, full meaty flavour, high alcohol and acidity — very refreshing bite. Good but a bit sharp.
Tasted February 1965 ★★

Bual (Newton Gordon). Shipped to the United States in the mid-19th century. Original corks. Fabulous colour — filled with golden light; medium sweet, medium-light body, outstanding bouquet and flavour. Rich yet delicate, meaty yet ethereal. What old madeira is all about.
At a Heublein pre-sale tasting, May 1976 ★★★★★

1826 ★★★★

Boal, Solera 1826 (Blandy). Fabulous colour: medium-deep amber, with lovely, strong yellow rim; exceedingly rich, fine bouquet, fragrant and ethereal; medium sweet, medium body, magnificent, powerful yet exquisite flavour, lovely acidity.
Tasted May 1974, January 1976 ★★★★★

1830 ★★★★★

Malmsey Reserve, Solera. Bottled by Harvey's. Fabulous rich, orange amber with lemon-amber rim; high-toned, rich bouquet and flavour reminiscent of cob nuts; medium sweet, highly concentrated, beautiful balance and acidity. One of the finest Malmseys ever tasted.
Tasted November 1971 ★★★★★

1834 ★★★★

Bual. Bottled by Geo. Ballantine & Son, Glasgow, around late 1890s: lovely amber colour; very rich high-toned bouquet and flavour; old but silky and rich.
Tasted November 1972 ★★★★

1835 ★★

Sercial (Blandy). Fairly deep coloured for a Sercial; nose strong, almost pungent; a full-flavoured but dry-edged wine — the only concession to the Sercial style.
Tasted 1959, January 1960 ★★★

"Old Reserve 1835" (Adega Export). Very deep; rich, meaty — quite a bit of spirit showing through; lovely flavour, great length.
From a cask sample at Harvey's, May 1961 ★★★★

1836 ★★★

Considered a good vintage, especially for Sercial.
Sercial Reserve. Bottled in the United States around 1875. Ullaged mid-shoulder, hard but crumbling cork: pale amber; good, lively and tangy nose and flavour; fairly dry, faded, high acidity.
At a Heublein tasting, May 1972 ★

Solera 1836. Bottled by Harvey's. Curious nose, old, with twist of lemon; medium dry, rich but not heavy.
Tasted November 1966 ★

1837 ★★★

Sercial, Vintage 1837 (T. T. de Camara Lomelino). Island bottled. Fine amber yellow; very rich piquant bouquet, flowery like a fine vintage cognac and scented straw; medium dry, lightish weight and style but fine long flavour and tangy, slightly astringent finish.
Tasted December 1966 ★★★

1838 ★★★★

High reputation, especially Verdelho. Not tasted.

1839 ★★★★

Malvasia, Vintage 1839. "Faja dos Padres": medium-light colour with intense amber rim; pungent, stably aroma; sweet, full, very assertive flavour, fine, concentrated, lovely balance and acidity.
Tasted July 1967 ★★★★

1840 ★★★

Bual, Finest Old (Rutherford & Miles). Palish, amber rim; good, old stably nose; medium sweet, excellent flavour and quality but appeared to be fading a little.
Tasted March 1968 ★★

1841 ★★

Malvasia (Fernando Porto, Soares-Franco). Loose cork and loss during recent shipment — level below shoulder. However, it appeared little affected: beautiful pale-amber gold; lovely rich, high-toned nose and flavour, sweet, refined, high acidity.
From a Portuguese cellar, at the Heublein tasting, May 1978 ★★

1844 ★★★★

A very good vintage, particularly for Bual.
Bual, Solera 1844 (Cossart, Gordon, imported by Evans Marshall). Tasted twice from cask samples before purchase — £220 per pipe F.O.B. in 1961. Brown-amber colour, not unlike an oloroso sherry; rich, high-toned bouquet with a hint of violets; medium dryness and body, lovely warm rich flavour, dry finish. It was bottled by Harvey's in 1962. I next tasted it in 1966 and, most recently: lovely golden colour; rich, old stably bouquet; dry overall, lightish but rich.
Last tasted March 1978 ★★★

1845

Bual, "Centenary Solera" 1845 (Cossart, Gordon). The mother solera was the 1844 vintage, but it was initiated in the firm's centenary year (1845). Bottled from the wood in 1975: fairly deep old amber; nose rather like an old oloroso, a little sickly; medium-sweet, plump, very rich, burnt-Bual flavour and tang.
Tasted 1977, October 1979 ★★

1846 ★★★★★

A great vintage: Bual, Terrantez and Verdelho particularly fine.
Terrantez, Vintage 1846 (Borges). Bottled 1900. Medium, rich amber, sight orange tinge; fabulous, intense bouquet and flavour. Rich, tangy, attenuated flavour, dry finish, excellent aftertaste.
Consistent notes in 1973 and at the Madeira Club, Savannah, April 1980 ★★★★★

Campanario (Lomelino). Fairly deep colour, viscous; exceptionally rich and fine bouquet and flavour; fairly sweet, full, powerful.
Tasted March 1967 ★★★★★

1847 ★★

Bual (Shortridge, Lawton). Lovely colour; rich, high volatile acidity; fairly sweet. Good in its way, but almost an acquired taste.
Tasted May 1972 ★★

1848 ★★

Bual, Vintage 1848 (Henriques). Bottled 1927, re-bottled 1957. Pure amber; beautiful bouquet: spirity, honeyed, crystallized melon; ethereal. Perfection.
Tasted October 1978 ★★★★★
"Old Pale East India Madeira". Bottled 1848. Re-bottled by David Sandeman & Co in 1932. Pale yellow amber, with weak watery rim; old stably nose and flavour; dry, interesting, but weak finish.
Tasted July 1970 ★

1850 ★★★

Bual, Solera 1850 (Cossart, Gordon). Bottled September 1961. Medium pale, good; high toned, pasty, high volatile acidity on nose and palate, sweetish, rich.
Tasted July 1972 ★
Sercial, Reserve 1850 (Adega Exportadora dos Vinhos de Madeira). The youngest of four cask samples: colour like Golden Syrup; not as dry as expected but a fine, rich, tangy wine.
Tasted May 1961 ★★★

1851 ★★★★

A good vintage, the last before the onset of *Oidium tuckeri*. Particularly good for Malmsey.

1853 ★★

In this year Christie's sold a quantity of madeira from the private cellar of the late James Rutherford, of Madeira and London. The 1814 fetched 42s. (£2.10) per dozen, and some 1810s fetched 68s. (£3.40).
Malmsey, Old Solera 1853 (Lomelino). Island bottled. Deep, rich, mahogany tinged; rich, heavy, slightly hard nose; very sweet, full, alcoholic, soft and rich with fine balance and finish.
Tasted March 1979 ★★★

1858 ★★★

Verdelho "VL", Vintage 1858 (Henriques). Bottled 1927, rebottled 1957. Deposit on sides of the bottle, tea-leaf-like bitty sediment. Palish straw-amber colour; extremely rich, high-toned, stably bouquet and flavour; medium dry, not heavy. Lovely wine.
Tasted March 1971 ★★★★

1860 ★★★★

Bual (Blandy). Stencilled lettering on bottle. Brown-amber colour; very good, meaty, rich nose and palate; drying out a little. Excellent flavour and quality.
Tasted March 1971 ★★★★
Sercial, Solera 1860 (Blandy). Pure amber; very good, mouth-watering aroma — earthy, volcanic, burnt character; very dry, fine intense flavour, good backbone, long, attenuated rather swingeing finish.
Tasted October 1973 ★★★★

1861 ★

"Old Sercial", Solera 1861 (Lomelino). Island bottled. Imported by Simon the Cellarer, specialist in fine madeira: medium pale old-amber colour; medium sweetness and body, curious tartness about the nose and palate. Not very clear cut.
Tasted January and December 1967 ★

1862 ★★★★★

The Terrantez of this year was the best ever vintaged. Sold at Christie's on several occasions but never tasted.

1863 ★★★

Malmsey, "Finest Old Solera" (Blandy). Lovely bright amber; rich, tangy; medium sweet, powerful yet soft, nice quality, good acidity. Less character and less definitive than 1860 Bual.
Tasted 1971, 1974 ★★★

1864 ★★★

Another madeira wine shipper deceased, this time Russell Manners Gordon. In 1864, Christie's disposed of his vintage madeira, almost 800 dozen, realizing over £2,000.
Bual, Vintage 1864 (Blandy). This was a late-bottled vintage of fine quality: strong colour, the shade of a deep oloroso sherry, with a pure amber rim; incredibly deep and intense nose that threw three solera madeiras (1815, 1822 and 1844) into the shade; medium sweetness and body, delicious, lingering, extended-with-age flavour, not heavy but fat, and exquisite finish.
At Harvey's, November 1961 ★★★★★
Gran Cama do Lobos, Solera 1864. Great classic style: palish, extremely beautiful amber colour with yellow-green rim; pronounced yet refined, stably, rich straw bouquet; medium, dried out a little, but rich, not heavy, powerful yet elegant, long finish.
Tasted January 1978 ★★★★★
Sercial, Vintage 1864 (Blandy). Lovely, pale, warmly glowing amber; exquisite, intense yet delicate, crystallized violets; dry but rich, elegant, subtle, great length and finesse.
Opening the Madeira Club tasting, Savannah, April 1980 ★★★★★

1865 ★★★★

A small but excellent vintage.
Malmsey, Solera 1865 (Rutherford). Bottled by Harvey's in 1963: palish; little nose; sweet, strong pungent flavour and tang.
Tasted March 1967 ★★
Old Verdelho, Solera 1865 (Lomelino). Island bottled. Listed by Simon the Cellarer in 1969 at 360s. (£18) per dozen! Deepish amber, green tinge; stably, rich, slight vanilla overtone; medium sweetness and body, usual tangy acidity. Not great but good value.
Tasted January 1969 ★★

1868 ★★★

Good vintage. Bual noted for its excellence.
Bual, Vintage 1868 (Blandy). Bottled by Feuerheerd Wearne, Blandy's English agents, in 1962. Price in 1967, 850s. (£42.50) per dozen. Deep coloured, slightly cloudy; rich and deep, very powerful bouquet and flavour; sweet, a huge yet soft wine.
Tasted January 1967 ★★★
"Rex", Vintage 1868 "Brussels Restaurant Reserve" (New York): pure, bright, yellow amber; rich, tangy, spirity and spirited aroma; dry — almost certainly a Sercial — yet rich, with good tangy finish. Most attractive.
At Heublein pre-sale tastings, 1976, May 1977 ★★★

1870 ★★★★

A small but good vintage, especially for Sercial.

Terrantez, Vintage 1870 (Blandy). Bottled by Feuerheerd's in 1962. Price in 1967, 1,050s. (£52.50) per dozen — the most expensive in the range. Fairly deep Bual-like colour with an intense amber-yellow rim; rich, intense yet fragrant bouquet; medium sweet but fairly full bodied. Extraordinary flavour: strong, rich, nutty, reminded me of a "fat" old cognac, with wonderfully fragrant dry finish.
Tasted 1966, January 1967 ★★★★★

Bastardo, Vintage 1870 (Blandy). Island bottled. Stencilled lettering. Very rare grape not replanted after phylloxera. Very bright amber with a golden hue, unusually tinged with red; outstanding bouquet — intense yet extremely fragrant and ethereal; medium sweet, full flavoured yet delicate, rich, many layered, with a long dry finish. One of the most magnificent madeiras ever tasted.
At a Saintsbury Club dinner in 1977 and at Dr Skinner's in Florida, February 1978 ★★★★★

1871 ★

Malmsey, Vintage 1871 (Blandy). Bottled by Harvey's in 1962. Rather pale coloured for Malmsey; curious nose — Bovril and wet straw; sweet, fullish, soft, rich, lovely flavour. Dry finish.
Tasted 1966, 1967 ★★★

1872 ★★★

Generally good. The last before phylloxera struck.

1874 ★★

Boal 1874 (probably M.W.A.). Stencilled lettering. Lovely medium amber, warm glow, yellow-gold rim; very pungent nose, smoky, high acidity; medium sweet, powerful flavour yet soft and meaty. Fabulous.
Several notes, March 1980 ★★★★

1878 ★

Sercial, Special Reserve, Solera 1878 (Henriques). Island bottled. Rich tawny colour; rich, tangy, high acidity, "volcanic"; rich but dried out a little.
Tasted 1972 and 1976 ★★

Bual, Old Solera 1878 (Rutherford). Recent island bottling by Rutherford & Miles. Curious, warm, slightly orange-tinged amber brown, not very bright; a not very appealing meat-extract smell and taste; medium sweet, disappointing.
Tasted March 1979 ★

1880 ★★★

Quite a good vintage. The Malmsey reputed to be the best since 1808.

Malvasia "F.C.", Vintage 1880 (M.W.A.). Deep amber; extremely rich bouquet with slight almond overtones; sweet, exceptionally rich flavour and lovely acidic tang. A fine classic wine.
At a Saintsbury Club dinner in 1974, also at a Heublein pre-sale tasting in May 1976 ★★★★

1882 ★★

Verdelho, Vintage 1882 (Blandy). Bottled by Harvey's in 1962. Deepish amber; old-farmyard smell and tangy flavour; medium sweetness and body, fresh clean finish.
Tasted January 1967 ★★★

1883 ★★★

A small but excellent vintage, especially for Sercial.

1893 ★★★★

A small vintage, but the first of note after phylloxera.

Fine Bual, Vintage 1893 (Rutherford & Miles). Beautiful colour; fine, pronounced bouquet and flavour; sweet, excellent long refined finish.
Tasted November 1967 ★★★★

Malmsey, Vintage 1893 (Cossart, Gordon). This came from the Campanario district. Very richly coloured — in fact rich is the operative word throughout; a most pronounced bouquet; sweet, fullish, fabulous tang, flavour and length.
At the Cossart tasting, October 1979 ★★★★

1895 ★★★

The first really good vintage for Bual after oidium.

Bual, Vintage 1895 (Cossart, Gordon). From the renowned Cama do Lobos district. Not very deep coloured; high-toned, tangy bouquet; medium sweet, lightish in style and body, elegant, great persistence of flavour.
At the Cossart tasting, October 1979 ★★★★

1897 ★

São Martinho, Vintage 1897 (Blandy). Fine, rich autumnal colour; meaty; intense but volatile acidity too high for my liking.
Tasted March 1974 ★

1898 ★★★★

Generally very good. Considered the first completely normal vintage after phylloxera. Not tasted.

1900 ★★★★★

Outstanding vintage, especially for Sercial and Verdelho.

Verdelho, Vintage 1900 (Cossart, Gordon). Stencilled label. Palish limpid amber; firm, fine, meaty nose and flavour; medium sweet, great quality and length.
Tasted October 1966 ★★★★

Moscatel, Reserva 1900 (Pereira de Oliveira). Matured in oak casks. Good, deep, rich colour, green-amber rim; rich, high-toned, burnt, slightly raisiny aroma; very sweet, concentrated wine with high acidity.
At pre-sale tastings, March 1980 ★★★

1902 ★★★

A good vintage, particularly for Verdelho.

Verdelho, Vintage 1902 (Cossart, Gordon). Island bottled. Pale amber; old stably, high acidity on nose and palate; medium dry, piquant, high flavoured.
Tasted January 1977 ★★

Malmsey (Blandy). Deep, rich, viscous; rich, pungent nose and flavour; sweet, full, lovely acidity.
Tasted December 1967 ★★★

1904 ★★

Malmsey (M.W.A.). Very deep colour; rich smoky/meaty bouquet; lovely wine, not too sweet, rich, tangy, long flavour.
Tasted in the samples room of the Madeira Wine Association, Funchal, February 1972 ★★★

1905 ★★★

A good but very small vintage.

Verdelho, Reserva 1905 (Oliveira). Similar colour to the 1900 Moscatel; rich tangy nose; medium sweetness and body, extremely good rich flavour and finish.
At pre-sale tastings, March 1980 ★★★★

1906 ★★

Another small crop, Malmsey especially good.

1907 ★★★

Bual, Solera 1907. (Bottled in Madeira by Antonio Eduardo Henriques.) Not a very intense colour for its age, but good nose, very rich fine flavour.
Tasted March 1969 ★★★

Malvasia, Reserva 1907 (Oliveira). Deep; cask-aged bouquet; fairly sweet, rich, characterful.
At a pre-sale tasting, March 1980 ★★★★

1910 ★★★★★

An outstanding vintage for all wines.

Sercial (Barbeito). A pale amber brown; good nose; dryish and on the light side, lovely flavour, fine quality, refreshing.
With the soup at The Wine Trade Benevolent Banquet, May 1965 ★★★★

Sercial, Reserva 1910 (Oliveira). Slightly paler and a harder nose than the older Oliveira madeiras, less fruit; dry but distinctly tangy and zestful. Lacking the length and intensity of the older and richer wines.
At pre-sale tastings, March 1980 ★★★

1914 ★★★

Small crop, Bual particularly good.

1915 ★★★

Generally good.

1916 ★★★

Malmsey, Vintage 1916 (Cossart, Gordon). An excellent year for Malmsey, stocks of which had been largely reserved for the Imperial Russian court, the largest market for madeira until the revolution in 1917 removed it overnight. Warm-amber colour; good bouquet; sweet, soft, rich and tangy.
At the Cossart tasting, October 1979 ★★★★

1918 ★★★★

Generally very good.

1920 ★★★★

Generally very good vintage.

Malmsey, Vintage 1920 (Cossart, Gordon). From the Faja dos Padres area. Stencilled label. Very rich, bright amber brown, finely graded to yellow-gold edge; outstanding bouquet — high toned, ethereal, tangy; sweet, fullish, rich, powerful yet refined, fabulous length and exquisite aftertaste.
Tasted March and October 1979 ★★★★★

1926 ★★★★

Bual (Cossart). Called "Solar do Val Formoso", the name of the Cossart family house. Pressed personally by Noël Cossart from specially selected Bual grapes, the fermentation arrested to retain natural sugar. No sweetening wine added, no *estufa*. Kept in cask until transferred to demijohns in 1966, and finally bottled in April 1976: a lovely warm amber colour, with green rim; most attractive rich, complex, tangy nose and flavour; medium sweet — drying a little — clove-like overtone, lovely acidity.
Tasted May 1976 ★★★★★

1934 ★★★

Verdelho, Vintage 1934 (Cossart, Gordon). A particularly good year for this grape though the only sample tasted was cloudy, with a lactic smell and taste.
At the Cossart tasting, October 1979.

1940 ★★★

Sercial, Vintage 1940 (Cossart, Gordon). From the Jardin da Serra district, 1,500 feet above sea level, the highest level at which vines will grow on the island and considered the best for Sercial. Palish yellow-amber colour; bouquet little and hard; dry, slender, yet with madeira tanginess, very dry and not too clean finish. Overwhelmed by the older and richer classics.
At the Cossart tasting, October 1979 ★

1941 ★★★

Good vintage for Bual and Malmsey.

1944 ★★★

Good for all grapes.

1951 ★★★★

1954 ★★★

Malmsey, Vintage 1954 (Cossart, Gordon). Considered still relatively immature by Noël Cossart (who reminded tasters that the 1792 vintage, bought in 1815 by Napoleon *en route* for St Helena, was not considered nearly ready for drinking when he died in 1821). Medium colour; rich but rather milky nose; sweet, soft, yet time in hand.
Tasted October 1979 ★★ (★)

TOKAY

Perhaps the most remote and strange of all the great classic wines, tokay comes from a small district in Hungary which is little more than a perfectly formed vine-clad hill about 30 miles from the Russian border — surely conceived by the romantic imagination of some Transylvanian god. Many great wine districts slope down to a river and in this case it is the placid but ugly-sounding Bodrog.

Here the finest dessert wines, with the always rare essence, essencia or eszencia at the pinnacle, were made by aristocratic landowners for their peers and neighbouring royalty. Exports were largely northwards and eastwards, to the Polish and Russian courts.

World War I destroyed the power of the Austro-Hungarian nobility. Afterwards, in the early 1920s, a quantity of the finest essences from princely domaines were imported by those distinguished wine merchants of St James's, Berry Bros, and sold at exorbitant prices, around five guineas for a standard half-litre bottle. The wine was recommended for invalids and said to be an unequalled restorative.

If Berry Bros introduced tokay essence to the British carriage trade in the 1920s, their neighbours, Christie's, can claim to have rediscovered old tokay in the late 1960s. Odd half-litres still trickle on to the market, 19th-century vintages of essence now commanding up to £200. Tokay aszú-eszencia of more recent vintages is now imported in small quantities — again by Berry's.

General characteristics
Tokay is a curious wine that shares with Château-Chalon the distinction of being the most idiosyncratic of all the "classic" wines. The area produces a full octave of wines of recognizably similar character derived from the *Furmint* grape and volcanic soil, ranging from bone dry to the most intensely sweet and concentrated.

Only wines from the top end of the quality scale have been reported in the notes that follow and if they seem fairly similar it is simply because the nuances are prescribed.

Aszús are dessert wines. The rare essence is to be sipped in thimblefuls, for the benefit of the body and the delectation of the soul. Essence usually has an off-putting muddy sediment that takes months, if not years, to settle, and is one reason why the bottle should be stored upright. True essence is the world's longest-living wine. It is possibly the highest in extract, in phosphates and other minerals derived from the soil and, happily, once opened will remain in excellent drinking condition almost indefinitely.

1811 ★★★★★
The "Comet" vintage, probably the most perfect ever recorded in Europe.
Essence. Bottled about 1840. "Formerly the property of the Princely Family of Bretzenheim which became extinct in 1863." This wine was walled in during the Hungarian revolution of 1849, rediscovered in 1925 and shipped by Berry Bros in that year. As with most old essences, the appearance of the wine was somewhat murky, old amber coloured; the bouquet was exquisite, intensely rich, piquant, reminiscent of crushed raisins, powerful and lingering; on the palate, sweet, indescribably luscious, concentrated, with wonderful binding acidity, long tenacious flavour and fabulous finish.
Bought at Christie's and tasted between December 1972 and May 1973 ★★★★★

1834 ★★★★★
Aszú. 5 putts. Also from "the Princely House of Bretzenheim", imported by Berry Bros. Medium-pale lemon-amber colour; high-toned raisiny bouquet; sweet, very rich, very like the essence but not as concentrated, with high acidity like an old Sercial madeira. Very good indeed.
Tasted June and October 1972 ★★★★

1866 ★★★
Ausbruch. Imported by Lorenz Reich, New York. Lovely medium-pale old tawny colour, rich, high viscosity; outstanding, concentrated, madeira-like bouquet and flavour; medium sweet, not intense like essence, but excellent.
At Heublein tastings, May 1975, May 1976 ★★★★

1883 ★★★★
Essence. From the estate of the Baron Maillot of Tallya-Hegyalya (the main tokay region), imported by Berry Bros in 1932. Warm amber colour, with lemon rim; very rich, concentrated yet ethereal, raisiny bouquet and flavour; sweet but not intensely so, rather light and refined in style, with lovely acidity. Fabulous.
First tasted December 1971, and another bottle similar in February 1972. Last tasted March 1976 ★★★★★

1889 ★★★★★
Essencia. Zimmermann Lipot és Fini. Deep, prune-coloured wine — not unlike an old oloroso sherry, with a rich amber rim; rich, powerful bouquet, with a Bual madeira-like tang, but more raisiny; sweet, fairly full

bodied, wonderfully rich flavour with excellent acidity. Something akin to a thick, concentrated *Beerenauslese* from the Palatinate.
Tasted February 1972 ★★★★★ *Another bottle, curiously with no sediment, had a strong, ripe, farmyard bouquet — probably an aszu-eszencia of high quality, in March 1974* ★★★★

Essenz. From the "Bekény Wineyards", Tolesvanj, Tokay. Intense but palish amber; lovely concentrated bouquet; sweet, very rich and with very high acidity.
From a private American cellar. Tasted May 1972 ★★★

1906 ★★★★

The last of the great vintages prior to the fall of the Austro-Hungarian Empire.
Essenz. K. und K. Hofkellerei, Vien. Imported by Justerini, Brooks & Bailey prior to 1930. From the late Dennis Wheatley's cellar. Brown amber, madeira-like but with typically muddy sediment; very rich bouquet, raisins and honey; fairly sweet, rich syrupy/grapy flavour, pungent, high acidity.
Tasted September 1968 ★★★★
Essence. From the Hegyalya district, imported by Berry Bros. Burnt umber colour, heavy sediment; intense, rich tangy nose; sweet, highly concentrated grapy flavour, a cross between a fine mature German *Beerenauslese* and old madeira. Lovely tingling acidity.
Tasted April 1970 ★★★★★ *Another bottle was a sandy brown, almost opaque colour, with similar smell and taste in December 1970, June 1971* ★★★★★

1922 ★★★

Essence. From the Hungarian Wine Trust museum. Deepish colour; soft, excellent bouquet, a cross between an old oloroso sherry and Verdelho madeira; fairly sweet, very rich, tangy, good acidity.
At a pre-sale tasting, January 1974 ★★★

1934 ★★

Essencia. Sarospatak Merhegy Dulo. Yellow brown; deep, grapy, rich barnyard aroma, slightly spoiled by too much volatile acidity; sweet, rich and fruity but more than a twist of end acidity, rather tart.
From one of two demijohns from a private cellar, tasted in the office of the director of the Hungarian Wine Trust, Budapest, August 1972 ★★ *Another bottle in London was the palest of the group, had the least good nose — raw apple-core aroma — and was rich but raw and unbalanced at a pre-sale tasting in January 1974.*

1937 ★★★★★

An outstanding vintage.
Essence. From the Hungarian Wine Trust museum. Medium amber colour, natural and normal cloudy sediment; fabulous bouquet, very rich indeed, like a great *Trockenbeerenauslese*; intensely sweet, high extract, most distinctive and distinguished.
Tasted January 1974 ★★★★★

1943 ★★★

Aszú. 3 putts. Flegmann s.v. és Fia, Abaujszántó. Medium amber, beautiful colour intense to rim; lovely, gentle, rich, grapy, honeyed bouquet; medium sweet, full flavoured but delicate, nice weight, fair finish.
Tasted March and April 1980 ★★★

1946 ★★★

Edes Szamorodni. Good fresh-looking amber colour; very intense bouquet; medium sweet, highly flavoured and fine.
Tasted January 1973 ★★★

1947 ★★★★★

One of the best postwar vintages.
Essence. From the Hungarian Wine Trust. Palish amber gold, still cloudy — it had not had time to settle; heavy, pungent, sherry-like aroma; fairly sweet yet extremely rich, a fat ripe wine with high acidity.
Tasted January 1974 ★★★

1951 ★★★★★

A great vintage in Hungary, particularly in Tokay.
Essence. From the Hungarian Wine Trust. Lovely colour — pure amber gold; most attractive bouquet — very fine, elegant, fresh, honeyed; sweet, not very full bodied but elegant and refined, rich yet rapier-like, with attenuated flavour.
Tasted January 1974 ★★★★

1957 ★★★★

Aszú-Essencia. Medium-pale orange amber, very bright; good, rich, straw-like nose; sweet, refined flavour, excellent long finish.
Tasted January and February 1973 ★★★★

1959 ★★★★

Aszú. 5 putts. Lovely warm amber gold; characteristic apple-like aroma of young tokay; medium sweet, fairly full bodied, soft, fat, rich but not at all heavy. Fine flavour and finish.
Tasted July 1967 ★★★★

1961 ★★★★

Aszú. 5 putts. Further described as "Ausbruch Trockenbeerenauslese Cabinet". Deepish amber gold; rich old-apples aroma; fairly sweet, fine flavour, good acidity and excellent aftertaste.
Tasted May 1971 ★★★★

1963 ★★★

Aszú-Essencia. Very sweet, richer than the '57 or '64 in January 1973: bright straw-amber colour; characteristic rich old apples; similar taste and character to the 1961. Attractive.
Last tasted February 1973 ★★★★
Edes Szamorodni. Lovely pure amber colour; medium sweet, long finish.
Tasted January 1973 ★★★

1964 ★★★★

Aszú-Eszencia. Imported from the Hungarian Wine Trust through the export monopoly, Monimpex, and first tasted at the Berry Bros "launching" in 1972: for sale by the half-litre at £11. Fine amber colour shot with gold; deep rich bouquet, reminiscent of raisins and stewed apples; sweet, refined, crisp, rich, concentrated but not heavy. Lovely acidity. And another bottle, very sweet and silky.
Last tasted January 1973 ★★★★

SHERRY
and other fortified
WINES

The vast majority of the world's fortified wines, that is to say wines with brandy added at some stage of the wine-making process, are blended. Sometimes the blends are of different grapes, more often of different qualities tailor-made, as it were, to make up standard brands. And most are blends of wines of different years.

This book is less about cause than effect, but it is perhaps worth noting that fortified wines are made almost exclusively in hot, vine-growing areas, from grapes of fairly high sugar content. The combination of natural body, sweetness and added spirit gives the wine the stability and stamina to survive blending and sometimes quite lengthy ageing in casks.

With fortified wines, it is the time factor, the length of maturation, rather than the actual vintage that counts. A year rarely appears on the label, the most notable exceptions being vintage port and vintage madeira (already dealt with), soleras of madeira and sherry started in a given year and, rather different, old-bottled sherry, the year of bottling being significant.

Sherry

Strictly speaking, sherry has no place in a book about vintages. However, like all wine, it is born at vintage time; and, if the overall subject is fine classic wine, sherry qualifies.

What I have done in this very short section on a very important wine is to describe briefly the main styles and to say something about an interesting offshoot, old-bottled sherry.

Fino. One of the basic styles and at its best one of the most perfect aperitifs, mouth-wateringly fresh and appealing in colour, smell and taste: pale yellow shading off to a colourless rim; a zestful, tangy nose almost impossible to describe — a smell resulting from, and unique to, *flor*, a special mould that lives on the surface of the wine in the cask; the palate ranges from bone dry to dryish, light in style and the lowest in alcohol of just about any fortified wine, with a taste which matches the smell, leaving the mouth with a crisp dry finish. Finos, like most dry white wines, are best drunk young and fresh and do not improve in bottle.

Manzanilla. This is a fino in all but name. The above description applies, though the wine keeps, conventionally, to the very dry end of the taste spectrum. Whether the sea air of Sanlucar really does give it a salty tang, I do not know. Taste is so often influenced by expectation.

Amontillado. Also of the fino family. The finest develop and improve in cask. A genuine old amontillado is a joy: deeper colour, more amber; distinctly richer, deeper and nuttier bouquet; from quite dry to medium dry, more body, a meatier character. But nutty is the key word — that, and length of flavour and finish, is the hallmark of quality. *Oloroso*. The second basic sherry style and quite different in smell and taste because *flor* does not grow on the surface of the wine. What many people do not realize is that all olorosos begin life dry — the wine is fully fermented out — but the slightly weightier style makes it an ideal vehicle for sweetening. A copybook oloroso will vary from medium to quite deep amber; on nose and palate it is sweeter, softer, fatter and more full bodied — a higher alcoholic content. The better qualities also age well, in cask and bottle.

For a special treat, look out for dry olorosos. They are in small demand and tend to be of high quality.

Palo Cortado and *Dos Cortados*. Fairly rare sub-varieties, nearer to a fine amontillado than an oloroso, usually amber, nutty, rich yet refined.

Brown sherry. A style once beloved of our Victorian ancestors. Deep, rich and brown coloured, as its name implies, the best having a marked amber rim; an altogether different type of bouquet — rich, singed, meaty, sometimes a little raisiny from the use of PX grapes; very sweet, intense, thicker in texture.

Pedro Ximenez. PX for short. An expatriate *Riesling* grape that becomes virtually a raisin before being vinified, with all the depth of colour, sweetness and concentration that this implies. Something of an acquired taste if drunk "neat".

Old-bottled sherries. Sherry, like port and madeira, was a British invention. The United Kingdom was historically the biggest market and old-bottled sherries are, to the best of my knowledge, a solely British innovation and confined mainly to merchants in Bristol, a traditional centre of the sherry trade. They are something of a sideline, more prestigious than profitable and well worth looking out for.

In essence an old-bottled sherry is an oloroso or amontillado of substance and quality, well matured in cask and then, at its optimum, bottled and allowed to mature further. Bottle-age gives the sherry extra dimensions. I tasted many in my Harvey days and quite a few in the 1970s when, because they were simply not selling, I was asked to thin out their stocks at auction. We managed to stimulate interest — and lost the business back to Bristol!

The following are all Harvey bottlings:

El Abuelo. Bottled 1947. Bright gold in colour; rich madeira-like nose; dry and extremely fine.

Adorno. Bottled 1947. Deeper, more amber gold; rich, scented; medium dry. Lovely flavour and finish.

Amoroso. Bottled 1948. Amoroso is a type of sherry, a soft oloroso. This had a deeper amber-brown colour; intensely rich, Bual-like nose; sweet, fairly full bodied, soft and fat. A most attractive wine.
These three tasted in early 1970s. All ★★★★

The oldest Harvey-bottled sherry I noted, in 1971, was just called "Superior" and bottled in 1937: amber gold, but the finish too acid and spirity. The 1951 bottling of Very Old Amontillado was very dry with a nutty elegance, in 1971. And the most recently tasted:

Oloroso. Bottled by Harvey's in 1954. Very rich amber colour with an amber-green rim; pungent madeira-like nose; medium sweet, very assertive tangy flavour, high acidity and a good finish. Like madeira but not madeira; not quite the same burnt toffee smell and lacking madeira's marked volatile acidity.
Last tasted March 1980 ★★★★

Portugal and its Moscatel

Port has completely stolen the limelight; yet the type of wine I am about to describe was highly fashionable and popular in the 17th and 18th centuries. The trade in these wines, which are mainly rich and deeply grapy, centred around Lisbon. The most famous was, and still is, the Moscatel de Setúbal. I have tasted many, but the following notes were all made at Heublein tastings:

Moscatel, Vintage 1900 (José Maria da Fonseca, Setúbal). Deep amber brown like an old PX sherry, with pronounced yellow-amber rim; deep, meaty, raisiny nose; sweet, extremely rich, fabulous deep liquorice flavour and character.
Tasted May 1969 ★★★★

Apoteca, 1902 (Fonseca). Medium old amber; rich, pungent, madeira-like bouquet and flavour; sweet.
Tasted May 1974 ★★★

Apoteca, 1908 (Soares-Franco). Fabulous colour — bright amber gold, warm tawny middle, green rim; gentle, fragrant, old grapy nose, nothing like as pungent as madeira; sweet, smooth, silky, yet marked acidity.
Last tasted May 1979.

Superior, 1910 (Fernando Soares-Franco). Pale amber; rich, refined on nose and palate. Sweet. Lovely texture.
Tasted May 1974 ★★★★

Roxo, 1911 (Soares-Franco). Originally red, now faded — after 50 years in cask — to old tawny with ruddy glow; powerful nose; extremely sweet, rich, excellent.
Tasted May 1974 ★★★★

Apoteca, 1912 (Fonseca). Fairly deep amber brown with fine yellow rim; high-toned, madeira-like nose; sweet, very rich, high acidity.
Tasted May 1977 ★★

Apoteca, 1914 (Soares-Franco). Wonderful old amber-gold colour; pungent yet with delicate *Muscat*-grape overtone; medium sweet, fullish, assertive but exquisite flavour and fine long finish.
Tasted April 1978 ★★★★★

Apoteca, 1917 (Soares-Franco). Purest amber colour; rich, honeyed, tangy bouquet; sweet, very rich, soft, lovely texture and long finish.
Tasted May 1978 ★★★★

Australian Muscats and "Ports"

Undoubtedly the greatest unsung heroes of that remarkable wine continent, with strong claim to being the best muscats in the world. Cradled in, if not indigenous to, the old classic area of north-east Victoria, I suspect that the quality would rapidly drop if the demand for this old-fashioned wine suddenly burgeoned. So seek out discreetly.

Morris's Liqueur Muscat. Made from the rare *Aucerot* grape. My first experience of a great Australian muscat, after dinner at Hugh Johnson's in 1976: deep, very rich oloroso colour; intensely rich, meaty bouquet with deep singed grapiness reminiscent of a Pedro Ximenez; very sweet, full bodied, rich and magnificent — perfect flavour and balance.
Last tasted at the Rutherglen Winery, March 1977 ★★★★★

Morris's Muscat. Made from pre-phylloxera grapes. From the cask: opaque; very rich and spirity; immensely concentrated, powerful wine. Almost too rich to drink.
Tasted March 1977 ★★★★★

Chambers' Rosewood Muscat. Medium, pure amber colour with the yellow-green rim that I associate with age and quality; delicate, ethereal muscat bouquet; sweet, not too full, fat yet delicate, rich grapy flavour.
With Bill Chambers at Rosewood, March 1977 ★★★★★

All Saints' Muscat. From Rutherglen *Brown Muscat* grapes. Twenty-five to thirty years old, matured in small casks. Lovely medium amber; rich, very fine — a pure off-the-stem muscatel/raisin smell; sweet, soft, lovely.
Tasted December 1977 ★★★★★

Bailey's Bundarra Prize Muscat Liqueur. First tasted at the Winery in 1977. Very deep amber; excellent nose; sweeter and fuller than Morris's Liqueur Muscat, soft, smooth, round.
Last tasted March 1980 ★★★★★

Lindeman's Reserve Tokay No. WH2. From Corowa: lovely, refined.
Tasted March 1977 ★★★★

Seppeltsfield, Vintage 1878. Very rare indeed. Deep brown; rich black-treacle bouquet, very sound but — as with old vintage port — brandy showing through; intensely sweet, very luscious, rather malmsey-madeira-like, excellent, and in remarkable condition.
Drunk, after Noval '31, at Len Evans's, February 1977 ★★★★★

Chambers' Rosewood, Vintage 1970. A "Vintage Port". Made from *Shiraz* and *Touriga* grapes. Deep, fine colour, maturing nicely; an interesting, earthy character and still youthful spirity nose; sweet, fairly full bodied, very fine rich flavour and balance.
One of the best Australian ports ever tasted, March 1977 ★★★(★)

Hardy's, Vintage 1956. Very deep colour; rich, "packed" bouquet; very sweet, crammed with fruit and flavour, fine, slightly peppery finish. Extremely good and very near a true port style. The 1976, bottled after a year in cask, was also excellent: opaque; very port-like; intense.
Tasted at Hardy's, near Adelaide, February 1977 ★★★★

Yalumba Shiraz, Vintage 1923. In bottle about 20 years. Medium light, true old tawny colour, intense; powerful, sweet, slightly pungent bouquet; still very sweet, not heavy in style, with high Verdelho-like acidity, touch of cloves. Very good, a most attractive wine.
At the Hill-Smiths', Yalumba, February 1977 ★★★★

South African Dessert Wines

Cape Wine, 1801. From the cellars of the Duke of Atholl. In a half-bottle, wax sealed, quite good level: like a medium amontillado in colour, old amber rim; rather dull nose, but sound; medium sweet, fine, firm, slightly smoky flavour and in remarkable condition.
At the pre-sale tasting, October 1969 ★★

Constantia Berg Liqueur Wine, Vintage 1922. A "pure natural wine" produced on the famous Groot Constantia estate. Bottled late 1920s? Surprisingly pale in colour — positive amber tailing off rather weakly; curious spicy nose, traces of *Muscat* and grape spirit; medium sweet, medium-light body. First impression one of *Muscat* grapiness with twist-of-lemon acidity and brandy. Warm spirity end. Interesting.
Tasted April 1977 ★★

Paarl "Port", Vintage 1945. Fine deep colour, showing maturity but not age; rich, heavy, chocolaty bouquet, curious but good; very sweet, fairly full bodied and extremely rich. Elderberry fruit on nose and palate. Lovely balance. Almost port, but not quite. Very good.
At lunch at W. H. Bauly's, January 1968 ★★★★

Rare Russian Dessert Wine

Massandra No. 81, Vintage 1909. "Fine Luscious old Maccohopa," a "Russian Crown Estates Wine". A real curiosity, presumably bought very cheaply as a nice sweet wine for the old ladies' trade, 6d. (2½p.) a glass. The cork was branded "Yates Bros. Wine Lodge, W.C.2". The wine had an incredible crust like old port, and a lovely warm amber colour with pronounced yellow rim; rich, deep old *Muscat* bouquet, very clean and sound; fairly sweet, fullish, very rich with a peppery/gingery finish. Good acidity.
Tasted December 1972 ★★★★

American Dessert Wines

Ficklin's, Vintage 1953. Madera County. Bottled from puncheons in 1957. Strength 20°. Medium colour, lighter than expected, neither ruby nor tawny but plummy; rich, slightly fig-like aroma; sweet, fairly full bodied, with a most excellent, rich, fruity flavour and finish. Well made. Not port, but excellent.
Tasted February 1978 ★★★★

Angelica, 1875. From the Cucamonga Vineyard in San Bernardino County, bottled from the wood in 1921, re-corked 1960. First tasted in 1978. A beautiful amber colour shot with gold, yellow rim; bouquet pungent — high volatile acidity — but good; medium dry, rich, very pronounced and appealing character, the high acidity carried by the body of the wine. Perfect aftertaste.
Last tasted at Heublein's in Chicago, May 1979 ★★★★

New Jersey Currant Wine, 1873. A curiosity from Governor Ward's homestead: lovely amber colour; sweetish, raisiny aroma and flavour. Most attractive.
At the Heublein pre-sale tasting, May 1977 ★★

CALIFORNIA

WINES

If asked where the greatest and most exciting developments are taking place in the world of fine wine, I would say, without hesitation — California.

But for me the excitement lies as much in attitude as in innovation. Quality does not arise of its own volition, it is stimulated by appreciation and encouragement. Quality, for the wine maker, involves extra care, experimentation, more selective vine strains, better equipment. Quality costs time and money. To warrant this necessitates not just an appreciative consumer, but one willing and able to pay.

Just as the arts flourished in Florence under the Medicis (the finest talents being attracted to that city, inspired by the level of culture and suitably rewarded not only by critical appreciation but by cash created by a wealthy society), so the wine scene in California has been aptly described as a latter-day "quattrocento".

In Europe, particularly in respect of Bordeaux, vine growers and wine makers are usually thought of not as individuals, but in terms of great estates with great traditions being handed down. In California the wine makers are the stars: André Tchelistcheff, the late Fred McCrea, Joe Heitz, Robert Mondavi and a host of others. The wine team has had great coaches such as Maynard Amerine, and a campus to train in: Davis (the famed enology faculty of the University of California). But as important have been the

"cheer leaders", aficionados and buyers: connoisseurs — mainly medical men (the latter-day Medicis of American society) such as the Doctors Rhodes, Adamson and Knudson. To change the metaphor, these men, and their equally well-informed wives, have for some 20 years flitted round the Napa Valley wineries like bees, pollinating ideas, encouraging, constructively criticizing. In their wake have followed wealthy collectors, able wine writers and professional critics. The scene is vibrant, and it is scarcely surprising to English visitors and professional observers such as Harry Waugh, Hugh Johnson and myself, that the net result of all their efforts is making the old world, particularly Burgundy and Bordeaux, look dangerously complacent — and overpriced.

The variety of wines in California is enormous. My experience is that the cheapest can be pleasant — often much more agreeable than their counterparts in France and Italy — and good value. There is a welter of commercial middle-class wine, much of little interest, and a host of small to middle-sized wineries making outstanding wines. Production of some of these is small and availability limited. Summing up, if I may perpetrate a pun: from the lowly in jug, rising to great Heitz.

Vintages
Let me dispose of a myth: that the weather is so consistently benign that vintages

do not vary. Although blessed with a better, at any rate a sunnier climate than northern Europe, like everywhere else on this planet California experiences weather variations, frequently unpredictable and often problematical: excess heat, frosts, floods, storms — not to mention pests and diseases.

Tasting notes

To my surprise I find I have tasted Napa Valley wines of every vintage since 1945 and quite a few prior to that year. For the sake of consistency I have adopted the five-star rating used throughout the book but I am, of course, open to challenge. In any case, it is one thing to indicate the overall quality of a vintage in a small district like Sauternes, quite another in a more widespread area like northern California. But some guide is better than no guide.

The notes are arranged in vintage order and, frankly, the brief selections made represent the best I have tasted and serve to illustrate, as far as I am able, the character, style, weight and condition of the finer wines of a given vintage, winery and grape.

The first California wine I ever tasted was an Inglenook Charbono in 1956; then, in 1963, I was introduced to some highly idiosyncratic Martin Ray wines with a level of acidity normally tolerable only in old madeiras. My first visit to the Napa Valley was in 1970, escorted by Dr Robert Adamson. Where else in the world would a busy, hard-working doctor take a whole day off to escort a friend of a friend round the vineyards, and then provide a dinner-tasting of great rarities? It was also my first encounter with the deep knowledge of vine growing and wine making of these American "amateurs". I have been back several times and have tasted many California wines in London; also at much publicized comparative tastings in Paris and elsewhere at which the French have been taught one or two salutary lessons.

Most of the Beaulieu Vineyards and Inglenook wines have, of course, been noted at the tastings before the big annual wine auctions that I conduct for Heublein's. I am greatly indebted to them and to their wine director, Sandy McNally, some of whose climatic notes I have quoted.

Varietals. Americans think of wine first and foremost in varietal terms, for, as in Alsace, it is under the name of the grape variety that the fine wines are marketed. A word about the principal varieties might be helpful, particularly for European readers.

Chardonnay. I put this first as I believe that, to date, it has been the most spectacularly successful California varietal, at first emulating the classic white burgundy style, but now, like a rising young actor, sometimes thoroughly upstaging the old hams.

Chardonnays can be light, heavy, fruity, buttery or oaky. Some Chardonnays are not recognizably varietal at all. Though I find many California reds too heavy, too overpowering, I do like Chardonnays with a good positive flavour, the "buttery" ones and those with a *soupçon* of oak.

Cabernet-Sauvignon. Another European vine transplant that has taken well to northern California. But because of soil differences, and the warmer climate, it makes a wine of different weight and style to Bordeaux, and I firmly believe that many of the "taste-offs" of California Cabernets versus claret verge on the fatuous: like trying to say which is the best cheese, brie or stilton. Like men and women, they are different, thank goodness.

Nevertheless, I do believe that it is absolutely right to compare intrinsic quality and relative value, though even here a note of realism must creep in. If a high quality wine is in short supply its distribution can be by way of patronage and privilege, or it can be put on the open market, the price being finally established by weight of demand. In the days when the European aristocracy or Church owned the best vineyards, distribution was limited to fellow peers and prelates, who were wealthy anyway. In California, until recently, the small production of quality wines has been distributed amongst friendly — and privileged — customers. At Stonyhill, after each vintage, Fred McCrea would telephone his regulars and tell them their allocation and the price. All very charming and medieval. Equally quaint is the Napa Valley character who said, not all that long ago, that any wine maker who demanded more than $10 for a bottle of his wine was indulging in an ego-trip. On my last visit to Heitz I noticed that his 1970 Martha's Vineyard Cabernet-Sauvignon was on offer at the cellar door for $40 a bottle: the price of a first-growth claret.

Undoubtedly wines of first-growth quality, by any yardstick, are made, but as elsewhere they tend to be the tip of the iceberg. Because great Cabernet-Sauvignons are made, it does not mean that all California Cabernets are great. Far from it. Moreover, because of climate and soil the wines tend to be deeper, heavier, distinctly more alcoholic. They often seem to me like men who have, through body building exercises, a magnificent physique: impressive, but not something one associates with finesse and intellectual stature. But overall the standard of wine making is high, ability matches enthusiasm and some splendid wines are being produced. What is more, they keep well and definitely improve with bottle-age.

Pinot Noir. Frankly the least successful of the major vine transplants, certainly as far as recognizable burgundy Pinot characteristics are concerned. There are exceptions though.

Zinfandel. If not indigenous then certainly a variety peculiar to California and making excellent red wines, like Cabernet but not Cabernet — rather hard to describe.

I have tasted Zinfandels of just over 20 wineries and of many vintages. In the following text I have noted some old vintages unlikely to be seen again and experienced by only a few tasters in recent years, and some extraordinary late-harvest developments.

Johannisberg Riesling. Until quite recently one of the least inspiring varietals in California and even now some of the commercial brands I have tasted have been lack-lustre, devoid of bouquet and the fruity acidity of the German Rieslings.

Up until the mid-1960s some of the best Rieslings were made not in California but in New York State, particularly by one vinous genius, Dr Konstantin Frank. However, all of a sudden, some small quantities of exceptionally fine wines of *Beerenauslese* quality are being made. California Rieslings have taken on a new lease of life.

Other varieties. Many other less noble varieties are cultivated, including the rare Charbono (exclusive to Inglenook, I believe), Chenin Blanc, Petit Sirah, Gamay Beaujolais — generally bearing little or no resemblance to Gamay or beaujolais, Gewürztraminer (noble in Alsace, less so elsewhere) and so forth. Few make wines of more than perfectly nice drinkable quality.

1875 ★★★★★

Cucamonga, Angelica. Bottled from the wood in 1921. From the Cucamonga vineyard of Isias W. Hellman, in San Bernardino County. Recorked by Louis Petri for the Hellman descendants in 1960. In unusual, deep-punted, litre bottles: a lovely rich glowing amber, madeira-like; magnificent bouquet, touch of muscat, lovely, intense, rich; sweet, rich, fat, powerful flavour, a cross between a Bual madeira and the finest Australian muscats. Great length, perfect condition.
Outstanding at Heublein pre-sale tastings in 1978 and May 1979 ★★★★★

Cucamonga, "Port Wine". Same provenance as the Angelica. A rich tawny colour with an intense amber-green rim more like an old madeira; pungent nose; amazing power and richness, madeira-like acidity, slightly resinous. In excellent condition.
At Heublein tastings in 1978, May 1979 ★★★★

1891 ★★★

Inglenook, Zinfandel. From the cellars of Karl Gustav Niebaum, the owner of Inglenook at this period. Short corks had survived and came out cleanly. Good levels. One bottle encouragingly bright, garnet red, the other a bit cloudy. The first very fragrant, smoky, with a touch of decay; dry, excellent flavour and life-preserving acidity. The second bottle a bit tired.
At Heublein pre-sale tastings, Chicago, May 1979 ★★★

1892 ★★★★

Inglenook, Pinot Noir. From the Niebaum cellars. Noted several times at Heublein pre-sale tastings from 1971. Very slight variations due to corks and levels but mainly good. Three bottles were opened at the most recent Heublein tastings: good wax capsules, corks soft but firm enough. Beautiful colour, like old port, faded mahogany with amber brown rim; each had a lovely nose distinctly old *Pinot*, smoky, slightly resinous; dry yet with delicate richness, complete and beautifully balanced, crisp but not a trace of overacidity, very sound. The best of all the old Inglenooks and a great tribute to the ability of the wine maker and proving, if it were necessary, that California wines can keep.
Last tasted in Chicago, May 1979 ★★★★

1897 ★★

Inglenook, Cabernet-Sauvignon. Also from the Niebaum cellars. The oldest California Cabernet I have tasted: colour still deepish; nose old but holding well; dry, somewhat astringent — no better, no worse than many a Bordeaux of this age. A curiosity.
At Heublein tastings in 1971, May 1979 ★★

1934 ★★★★

Inglenook, Cabernet-Sauvignon. Fine mature colour; good bouquet, very mature, meaty; lightish on the palate, thinning out but excellent flavour and still beautifully balanced. Unexpectedly good for an immediate post-prohibition period wine.
At a Heublein tasting, May 1971 ★★★★

1935 ★★★

Inglenook, Pinot Noir. Medium pale; delicate and faded but reasonably good for its age.
Tasted 1971 ★★

Simi, Zinfandel. Very good cork and level. Medium red, bright and mature; nose slightly cardboardy at first, alcoholic, but sound and developed well; rich, ripe, soft warm wine with just a touch of end acidity. An astonishing 42 year old from Sonoma that baffled even Len Evans's wide-ranging palate, though he got very close. *At dinner at home, December 1977* ★★★

1939★★

Beaulieu Vineyards, Cabernet-Sauvignon. The oldest B.V. tasted. Drying out but still a good drink. *Tasted May 1970* ★★

1941 ★★★★

Heavy spring rain, ten cold days, bloom delayed. Very warm summer. Dry autumn, late October harvest.
Beaulieu Vineyards, Cabernet-Sauvignon. Sugar 23.5° Balling. Still a very fine deep colour; fine rich bouquet; medium dry and fullish body. An extremely rich wine with extended finish.
At Heublein tastings in San Francisco and New York, May 1972 ★★★★
Inglenook, Cabernet-Sauvignon. First tasted in 1970: a bit austere. Again in 1972 and 1974: still surprisingly deep coloured; fine bouquet, a bit unforthcoming; slightly sweet, good flavour. Later: medium colour, orange mahogany rim; excellent nose, rich, cheesy, holding well; distinct ripe sweetness on palate. *Last tasted at Heublein's in Chicago, May 1979* ★★★★
Louis Martini, Zinfandel. Palish, very mature, rich though faded nose and flavour, bouquet developed a wonderful gingery fragrance in glass. Rare and great. *At the Adamson's after my first visit to Louis Martini's, May 1970* ★★★★

1944 ★★★

Very dry early season, 24 cold spring nights with several April frosts. Summer temperature well below normal. Harvest first week of October.
Beaulieu Vineyards, Cabernet-Sauvignon. Sugar 22°. Colour deep, impressive; rich, burnt, intriguing nose; medium dry — that is, a touch of residual sweetness on entry, medium body, silky, rich, lovely balance and still preserved by tannin and acidity.
At a Heublein tasting, May 1972 ★★★★

1946★★★★★

The weather pattern is significant: a warm and pleasant spring, moderate and well-balanced day and night temperatures in the summer and an unusually early harvest the third week of August.
Beaulieu Vineyards, Pinot Noir. B.V. was one of the first stops on my first trip to the Napa Valley in May 1970. The great wine maker André Tchelistcheff was still in charge and after a tour of the winery there was a tasting. I realized later that the wines opened were his greatest treasures — the equivalent of being given a '29 at Romanée-Conti. In fact, we tasted the Pinot Noir '45, '46, '47 and '48. The last was old and strained, the '45 soft and attractive, but the '46 . . . this was a great wine by any standards, perhaps Tchelistcheff's supreme masterpiece. From the No 1 vineyard. Sugar 24° Balling. A magnificent colour, fine, still quite deep, mature; wonderful, ripe, old, distinct Pinot nose; quite remarkably

rich and beautiful on the palate, too. Slightly sweet in fact, good body, silky yet with life-sustaining tannin and acidity. Perfection. Seven years later I tasted a bottle from the private cellar of the Marquis de Pins. It still had a fine deep "robe"; magnificent bouquet, rich, smoky old Pinot, fragrant, with flavour to match. Perfect balance and finish.
Last tasted at Heublein's in San Francisco, May 1977 ★★★★★

1947★★★★

Spring similar to 1944. Dry and amazingly warm during summer and early autumn. Vintage mid-September.
Beaulieu Vineyards, Cabernet-Sauvignon (Georges de Latour Private Reserve). Sugar 25°. Perfect balance. This was in fact the first really top class Napa Valley Cabernet I ever tasted: enormously deep, rich and full flavoured in May 1967. Next tasted in 1972: nose holding back a little; still loads of tannin. Then, a bottle from the collection of the Marquis de Pins, the son-in-law of Georges de Latour, the founder of B.V. Still incredibly deep for its age; very rich, very fine bouquet with the Napa burnt character and marvellous fruit; rich, drying a little but still full bodied with excellent flavour and texture, tannin and acidity. Will last for years.
Last tasted at Heublein's, May 1977 ★★★★(★)
Louis Martini, Cabernet-Sauvignon. Ploughing a steady furrow, this middle-sized, old-established Napa winery produces a wide range and quite a few classics, of which this was one: enormously deep; well developed, rich, earthy iron nose; rich, opulent, loads of tannin and acidity still.
At the Adamson's in Berkeley, May 1970 ★★★★★

1948★

Very wet spring, 13 very cold nights in March and April; continuously cold summer and autumn. Harvest late October.
Beaulieu Vineyards, Cabernet-Sauvignon. Sugar 21°. First tasted in 1970. Two years later: palish and very mature looking; nose that reminded me of cold tea, some richness; medium dryness and body, gentle, *à point* — quite ready.
Last tasted at Heublein's, May 1972 ★★

1949★

1950★

1951★★★★★

For those brought up on Bordeaux, 1951 spells death. In the Napa Valley the weather was different. It was a great vintage.
Beaulieu Vineyards, Cabernet-Sauvignon. First tasted in 1971 and again in 1973. I next noted it at a Heublein pre-sale tasting in May 1975: very fine colour; extremely good bouquet — a sort of volcanic/earthy Haut-Brion — with that mulberry aroma of ripe grapes; dry but a touch of richness on the palate, lovely flavour, length and aftertaste. Close to a fine Bordeaux in weight and style — indeed Marvin Overton craftily slipped this wine into the middle of his great Latour tasting: it was noticeably out of place yet ranked highly.
Last tasted May 1978 ★★★★

1952★★

Moderate.

Louis Martini, Cabernet-Sauvignon. One of the few '52s tasted, and the best. Deep; rich; lovely flavour.
At the Adamson's, May 1970 ★★★

1953★★

Moderate.

Martin Ray, Cabernet-Sauvignon. The only '53 tasted and an example of this wine maker at his most opulently perverse: deep coloured; an attractive rich nose like Fonseca port; packed with flavour but far too acidic — a level acceptable in old madeira or 1727 hock but not in a fine table wine.
Tasted with Dr and Mrs Rhodes in London, March 1967.

1954★★

Inglenook, Cabernet-Sauvignon (Cask Reserve J-3). Similar depth and hue to the 1941; gentle bouquet, touch of vanilla; slightly sweet, medium body, lovely flavour and texture. Some tannin still, but at peak of maturity.
At Heublein tastings in 1978, May 1979 ★★★

1955★★★

Inglenook, Charbono. One of the few '55s tasted. A Bordeaux-type grape unique, I believe, to Inglenook. This was a deeply vinous and attractive wine.
Tasted only once, in May 1969 ★★★

Inglenook, Cabernet-Sauvignon. Very attractive in mid-1960s: deep red brown; fragrant nose; dry, tannic. But very mature, woody on the nose and a bit leathery when last tasted.
At a Heublein tasting, May 1979 ★

1956★★

Another confusing year, one of the worst ever in Europe, quite good in California.

Beaulieu Vineyards, Cabernet-Sauvignon. Deep coloured; a pronounced Cabernet aroma with the burnt, earthy character I associate with the Napa; on the palate almost Burgundy-like in weight and character.
Tasted February 1970 ★★★

1957★★

Stonyhill, Chardonnay. I have a particularly soft spot for this winery. Fred McCrea was perhaps the prototype of the visionaries who gave up the lush pastures of business in the eastern states to create vineyards and devote the rest of their lives to making good wine. He was one of the earliest and most successful makers of Chardonnays. His widow, Eleanor, continues the good work. It was one of the first wineries in the Napa that Bob Adamson took me to in 1970, but I had previously tasted his wine in London with the Rhodes's and Adamsons who had brought over the 1963 and 1964 vintages for Harry Waugh and me to taste. The '57 was an amazing wine: golden hued; rich, honeyed bottle-age bouquet; magnificent flavour, rich, characterful, Montrachet-like.
Dining with the Adamsons after my first Napa tour, May 1970 ★★★★★

1958★★★★

An extremely good vintage for Cabernet-Sauvignon.

Beaulieu Vineyards, Cabernet-Sauvignon (Georges de Latour). First noted in 1975. Once quite deep, now settling down to a fine, mature, medium colour; bouquet sweet, complete and contented; medium dry, a touch of ripe mellow sweetness, ideal weight, lovely flavour and balance. Perfect now.
Last tasted at a remarkable dinner given by Denman Moody at Tony's in Houston, April 1980 ★★★★★

Inglenook, Cabernet-Sauvignon. Tasted several times since the late 1960s. Notable for its spicy, piny, aromatic bouquet and marvellous Cabernet flavour. Dry, crisp tannic finish.
Last tasted May 1979 ★★★★

1959★★★★

Hanzell, Chardonnay. Very yellow but pale for its age, with a slight tartrate deposit; very good nose — became sweeter in glass, honeyed, slightly nutty; medium-dry, in fact a sort of ripe sweetness, fair body, rich, buttery, high fixed acidity. An eye-opener for my Australian guests.
At dinner at home, July 1980 ★★★★

Heitz, Pinot Noir. A beautiful wine, but not burgundy. Even its appearance was rich and velvety; nose a bit unforthcoming — it was then still quite young; slightly sweet, a rich and powerful wine. Excellent, but no resemblance to any *Pinot* grown on the Côte d'Or.
Tasted March 1967 ★★★

Inglenook, Cabernet-Sauvignon. First tasted in 1970 and several times since. Most recently: the standard blend was opaque; nose concentrated and alcoholic, "intensely herbaceous" was Sandy McNally's description; dry, rich, meaty. The selected Cask Reserve J-6 was a beautiful deep garnet red; the nose more fragrant; sweeter on the palate, very fruity. Another 10 to 15 years of development ahead.
Both last tasted May 1979 ★★★(★)

Charles Krug, Cabernet-Sauvignon. Relatively few older Krug Cabernets tasted. Of the 1956, 1957 and 1959, I think the last was the most perfect: fine deep colour, mature rim; a beautiful bouquet, rich, earthy, Graves-like; medium dry, pleasantly full bodied, a really lovely rich wine. Even the highly critically tuned palate of Edmund Penning-Rowsell could not fault it.
At a rather casual Wine Publications working lunch at Christie's, July 1977 ★★★★★

1960★★★

Inglenook, Cabernet-Sauvignon. Opaque; rich; tough, and a bit rough.
Last tasted May 1979 ★(★)

1961★★★

In the Napa: dryish spring with 17 dramatically cold nights from March to May. Heavy frost damage (European vine growers will note with sympathy) critically delayed bloom. Rather cold summer; late maturing grapes, small harvest in last part of October.

Beaulieu Vineyards, Cabernet-Sauvignon (Private Reserve). Sugar 21.5°. Medium colour, mature; very fragrant high-toned bouquet; richer than expected and fine flavour. Long hot tannic/acid finish.
Tasted May 1972 ★★★(★)

Heitz, Chardonnay. The first vintage of a Heitz Chardonnay that I ever tasted. Surprisingly pale after three years in wood; the nose of the first bottle I thought a little oily, but another, later, had a distinct Meursault-like character. To continue the analogy, on the palate it reminded me of a Corton-Charlemagne, dryish, nutty. *Both bottles tasted in 1967* ★★★

Inglenook, Cabernet-Sauvignon. Dry, elegant, very nice.
Tasted May 1979 ★★★

1962★★

Beaulieu Vineyards, Beaumont, Pinot Noir. I have tasted several vintages of B.V. Pinot Noir. Many were attractive but none matched the '46. The '62, however, was a typically good one: medium colour; gentle, sweet, roasted nose; medium dryness and fullness of body, soft, rich, lovely flavour. Real burgundy character.
Tasted March 1967 ★★★★

Dr Konstantin Frank, Johannisberg Riesling, Natur Spatlese. (New York State). Of late the wines of California have enjoyed almost all the limelight, throwing New York State wines into the shade. As it happens the first wholly successful Rieslings were made in the east, by Dr Konstantin Frank, a pioneer of true *vitis vinifera* varietals in an area largely dominated by the coarser native American vine species and hybrids. This particular wine was in its way a rare classic. At seven years of age a bright lemon gold; nose slightly too sweet but with a Riesling steeliness of character; distinctly dry, light, very clean and attractive. Excellent quality and style. Tasted with Kathleen Bourke. Next, in 1970, a three star nose and palate, with a lovely nutty finish. Then, after eight years it had deepened to a most attractive buttery yellow; the bouquet had broadened and it opened up in the mouth. A marvellous wine.
Last tasted June 1978 ★★★★★

1963★★

Inglenook, Cabernet-Sauvignon. First tasted in the mid-1970s. Recently I found the regular blend far superior to the Cask Reserve. Deep; intense and fragrant with a touch of iron on nose and palate. Most attractive.
Last tasted May 1979 ★★★★

1964★★★★

In the Napa: frost damage followed by warm summer and beautiful early autumn. Harvest late September, early October.
Beaulieu Vineyards, Cabernet-Sauvignon. Sugar 23.5°. First tasted in 1970: a strapping wine, austere and quite unready. The Private Reserve not very deep, but plummy; nose undeveloped; dry yet rich, with tannin and acidity in 1972. Seven years later the bouquet had developed — rather sweet and jammy; dry and crisp on palate.
Last tasted at Heublein's, May 1979 ★★★

Charles Krug, Cabernet-Sauvignon. Fine deep colour; lovely rich nose; a very fine wine by any standards, rich but dry.
At Larry Feldman's, Belvedere, May 1979 ★★★★

1965★★★

Yet another example of a good vintage in California, bad in Northern Europe.
Beaulieu Vineyards, Cabernet-Sauvignon. Lovely in 1970, maturing nicely in 1976. Most recently: deep rich colour; excellent fruit, beautifully developed bouquet; perfect flavour, fruit and balance.
Last tasted May 1979 ★★★★(★)

Heitz, Cabernet-Sauvignon. First tasted when it was just under three years old: powerful aroma of raw blackcurrants; the most Bordeaux-like of California Cabernets, still youthfully acidic. Developing in mid-1970s. At 12 years of age the colour was less deep but very lovely; the nose had developed a recognizably earthy Napa Cabernet character; medium dryness and body, silky, elegant. This is, I feel, the weight and style the best California Cabernets should aim for.
Last tasted dining with Peter Morrell in New York, May 1977 ★★★★

1966★★★★

One of the best dry springs in two decades — total rainfall in the Napa one inch; mellow nights, sunny days. Early October harvest, small crop.
Beaulieu Vineyards, Cabernet-Sauvignon. Sugar 23°, perfectly balanced. At six years of age: medium colour, still immature; muted, earthy, volcanic, Napa Cabernet-Sauvignon aroma; dryish, gentle, nicely balanced wine. Dry finish.
Tasted twice, in 1972 ★★★★

David Bruce, Chardonnay. A buttery yellow colour, bright and appealing; most excellent smoky/oaky Chardonnay nose and flavour — more pronounced, more varietal, than any but the biggest Montrachet or Corton-Charlemagne; medium dryness and body, soft, buttery but firm, with an excellent finish. One of the greatest Chardonnays ever tasted.
On board the Flying Lady *cruising down the Wilmington, a branch of the Savannah River, Georgia, with Mills B. Lane, May 1979* ★★★★★

Heitz, Cabernet-Sauvignon. First tasted in 1970. His Cabernet from Martha's Vineyard was showing well two years later: fairly deep colour, beginning to display a little maturity; magnificent bouquet, rich, good fruit, developed that warm wholemeal biscuit bouquet in the glass as fine claret does; dry, fullish body, fine classic flavour, richness, well sustained by tannin and acidity.
Showing well at the Montgomery-Scott's (Bob was then special assistant to the American ambassador in London) tasting, June 1972. Then ★★★(★★) *Probably beautifully mature now.*

Charles Krug, Cabernet-Sauvignon. Fine deep colour, still with an immature purple rim; fragrant, attractive but distinctly Napa Cabernet character (to me a sort of warm volcanic ash earthiness); medium body for a Napa wine, excellent acidity, most attractive flavour and balance.
At lunch with Arthur Formicelli, May 1972. At least ★★★★ *now.*

Schramsberg, Blanc de Blancs. The vast majority of sparkling wines made in California and New York State are just that: sparkling wines. The exception is Schramsberg. Of the several vintages tasted this was the most classic: medium-pale straw yellow, fine even flow of bubbles; excellent bouquet, fresh Pinot; very dry, some body but crisp and with a finish vouchsafed to few wines not, strictly speaking, entitled to be called

champagne. Like the finest vintage champagne I think it is best with a little bottle-age.
Before dinner at home, April 1971 ★★★★

1967★★

Heitz, Cabernet-Sauvignon. From Martha's Vineyard grapes: full, lively, youthful; exciting, rich, peppery, blackcurranty Napa Cabernet aroma; almost raspingly dry, fullish body, raw fruity flavour. Most attractive but needed a further ten years bottle-age.
At Tom and Martha May's, Martha's Vineyard, Napa, May 1972 ★★(★★)

Inglenook, Cabernet-Sauvignon. Cask Reserve better than the regular blend as one might expect. Fragrant, dry, elegant.
At Heublein's, May 1979 ★★

Boordy Vineyards, Maryland. Again just to remind readers of some eastern pioneers. I have had one or two attractive Boordy wines though I have not tasted any recently. This was a Phil Wagner wine. It was made from a white hybrid and was very dry, Chablis-like, with a good finish.
Tasted February 1969 ★★

1968★★★★★

A great vintage.

Beaulieu Vineyards, Cabernet-Sauvignon. Still very deep coloured; magnificent ripe mulberry nose; rich, soft, perfect balance but years of development ahead. Napa at its best.
Last tasted May 1979 ★★★★(★)

Buena Vista, Zinfandel. First tasted in 1970. Eight years later: deepish, maturing; slightly peppery on the nose with a jammy aroma reminding me of a South African Pinotage; dry, with firm acid backbone.
Last tasted at an office lunch at Christie's, February 1978 ★★

Freemark Abbey, Cabernet-Sauvignon. Although outclassed by the 1966 Heitz Martha's Vineyard, it had a good old-fashioned Napa character: plummy purple; rich, strawberry-jam Cabernet nose; dry, fullish, good rich flavour and lots of acidity. Still young at that time.
At the Montgomery-Scott's, June 1972 ★★(★★)

Freemark Abbey, Chardonnay. Rather deep coloured and a bit toffee-like on the nose — possibly a touch oxidized, though with an attractive flavour and good aftertaste.
Tasted June 1972 ★★

Heitz, Cabernet-Sauvignon. Possibly the greatest California Cabernet I have ever tasted. From Martha's Vineyard, a vineyard in the heart of the Napa planted by Dr Bernard Rhodes, mentioned in the introduction. It was bought by Tom May who built a house on a knoll next to it. The grapes are sold to Joe Heitz, whose winery is the other side of the valley. This wine first tasted in 1974. Most recently: impressively deep coloured and still not fully mature; fabulous spicy bouquet, eucalyptus they say, from the trees around the vineyard, most beautiful, most fragrant; a big dry wine, magnificent, intense. A cross between Pétrus and Mouton. Years of life and development ahead.
Dining with the Mays at Martha's Vineyard, May 1979 ★★★★★

Inglenook, Cabernet-Sauvignon. Very deep; concentrated, oaky; sweet.
Tasted at Heublein's, May 1979 ★★★

Inglenook, Zinfandel. Extremely youthful appearance; subdued nose; very dry, powerful wine — marvellous value at $1.79.
Tasted May 1971 ★★★

Mayacamas, Late Harvest Zinfandel. I think this was the first vintage I tasted of this most extraordinary wine, grown at an altitude of 2,000 feet to the west of the Napa. Intensely deep — like a big young Latour in cask; nose quite dumb; touch of sweetness, incredibly full bodied (17% alcohol), powerful, port-like.
At Robert Montgomery-Scott's, June 1972 ★(★★★)

Mirassou, Zinfandel. Not from Napa but Monterey. Pure cassis on the nose, very exciting and flavoury but did not hold as well as the Sutter Home. Palled a little.
At Narsai's, May 1972 ★★

Sutter Home, Zinfandel. From Deaver Ranch, Amador County. Very deep, youthful; minty/peppery nose that held well; dry and still raw with a touch of tannic bitterness. The best of a range of Zinfandels.
At Narsai's, May 1972 ★(★★)

1969★★

Beaulieu Vineyards, Beaufort, Chardonnay. Strangely enough, although I have tasted just about every postwar vintage of B.V. Cabernet-Sauvignon, I have had relatively few of their Chardonnays. This one was at a comparative tasting in London. It showed well, second only to the Chalone: very yellow in colour; good nose; dry, elegant, well made.
At Robert Montgomery-Scott's, June 1972 ★★★★

Chalone, Chardonnay. The outstanding wine at a tasting of a dozen top California reds and whites, five being Chardonnays. Yellowish colour; beautiful, nutty, smoky Pinot Chardonnay nose and taste. Dry, magnificent.
At the Montgomery-Scott's, June 1972 ★★★★★

Freemark Abbey, Chardonnay. Yellow, rather heavy looking but with a very positive Chardonnay nose; fine and firm.
At Peter Morrell's, New York, May 1977 ★★★

Inglenook, Cabernet-Sauvignon. Several notes from 1974. Most recently I found the regular blend better balanced than the Cask Reserve G-22, which was rich but short. Very "volcanic" earthy character — no mistaking this for Bordeaux.
Last tasted May 1979 ★★★

Robert Mondavi, Johannisberg Riesling. An early example of Robert Mondavi striving for perfection, with every variety and style. A deliciously grapy aroma and taste; dryish, light, lovely fruit and good aftertaste. Better, I thought, than his '68, and it compared interestingly to a good German estate wine.
Tasted at the winery, May 1970 ★★★

1970★★★★

Severe spring frosts and excessive summer heat reduced crop to 30 per cent of average. Early harvest.

Beaulieu Vineyards, Cabernet-Sauvignon (Private Reserve). Sugar 24°. First tasted from cask samples in 1972: deep, richly coloured, immature purple; nose very fragrant but unknit — both fruity and stalky; fullish, rich, very flavoury. The standard blend was less deep, less assertive on the nose, lighter, with delightful high-toned, rather piquant, Gamay-like flavour. When last

tasted the Private Reserve was still deep coloured; harmonious nose; rich yet dry.
At Heublein's in Chicago, May 1979 ***(*)

1971**

Charles Krug, Cabernet-Sauvignon. The only wine of this vintage tasted. Well made but not spectacular.
Tasted October 1974 **

1972**

Mayacamas, Late Harvest Zinfandel. Small production: only 800 cases in 1972. First drunk in March 1978, most appropriately with Stilton cheese, as the guest of Joe Schagrin at the Down Under Restaurant in Fort Lauderdale. The wine was opaque, purple rimmed, with tremendous weight (17½% alcohol) and swingeing tannin and acidity. Half a glass was enough to send me reeling in the Florida sun. A year later, at the winery, it had softened a little: still very deep; the nose had opened up, high toned, a little stalky, with a blackberry-jam sweetness and fruitiness; slightly sweet on the palate, full bodied and richly flavoured. Again with cheese. Decades of life ahead.
With Bob and Noni Travers at Mayacamas, May 1979 ***(**)

1973****

Heitz, Chardonnay. Tasted first in a Japanese restaurant in San Francisco in 1978, and rather wasted on tempura. It showed its paces better a year later: a lovely bright buttery yellow; bouquet soft and complete but not an obviously oaky style; dry, finely balanced.
At an alfresco lunch with Joe Heitz, May 1979 ****

Robert Mondavi, Chardonnay. One of the most assiduous, articulate and enthusiastic innovators in the Napa Valley. His aim is to make the best possible wine at prices people can afford. This wine had a smoky/oaky classic Chardonnay nose and flavour, neatly combining dryness with body and a touch of opulence.
Tasted January 1979 ***

Chateau Montelena, Chardonnay. This is the wine that swept aside all burgundian competitors at a blind tasting in Paris, and it is certainly my idea of a fine California Chardonnay: lovely, yellow, but not an exaggerated colour; broad, slightly sweet, fully developed Chardonnay character, positive but not excessive; dryish, more body than a Sauzet Puligny-Montrachet, but not heavy. Fine, rich, a touch of meatiness, very good acidity. Perfect.
At Denman Moody's dinner in Houston, April 1980 *****

1974*****

An extremely good vintage, the best reds still holding plenty in reserve.

Beaulieu Vineyards, Cabernet-Sauvignon (Private Reserve). Deep, plum coloured; very good nose, intense, good Cabernet aroma, touch of iron; full bodied, concentrated, plenty of tannin. Great potential.
Tasted June 1979 ***(**)

David Bruce, Chardonnay. This outstanding winery demonstrates quite dramatically that vintages really are significant in northern California. The '74s have an extra richness, extra dimensions. Rich colour, positive yellow with gold tinge; a bouquet of butter and honey;

dry but rich, fairly full bodied, pleasantly acidic finish.
At Dr Louis Skinner's in Coral Gables, March 1978 *****

Freemark Abbey, Cabernet-Sauvignon. Like Stag's Leap a year or so previously, the '74 Freemark Abbey shattered some French illusions by coming second in the major Cabernet-Sauvignon class (the '61 Ch. Trotanoy came first; the '67 Latour was tenth). Lovely colour, fairly deep, rich to the rim, showing some maturity; very good fruit on the nose, sweet, fine, Pomerol-like, fragrant — held well in the glass; dry, medium body — not the usual Napa Valley knock-out drops, beautiful flavour and balance, soft, youthful, but a lovely drink.
At the Gault-Millau "Olympiade" in Paris, June 1979 *****

Heitz, Cabernet-Sauvignon. Beautiful colour; pronounced spicy nose; slightly sweet, full bodied, exceedingly rich and intense. Massive and magnificent.
Tasted at the winery, May 1979 ***(**)

Heitz, Chardonnay. Deeper and more golden than the '76; an extraordinary nose, incredibly rich and persistent; medium dry — the least austerely dry of any of Heitz's Chardonnays that I have tasted — fairly full bodied, high vinosity, buttery yet with high acidity.
Tasted at the winery, May 1979 ****(*)

Mayacamas, Noble Semillon. Although I doubt if Yquem need worry, this new venture is more than interesting: lovely amber gold; sweet honeyed nose; medium sweet on the palate, same sort of weight as a heavy Sauternes (14½% alcohol), fruity and crisp. End acidity a little high.
At the winery, May 1979 **

Mount Eden, Cabernet-Sauvignon. Perhaps the most astonishing wine (and price: £175 per dozen) at a recent London tasting: opaque; nose extremely rich; a huge dry wine, intense, tannic. Immensely impressive but surely undrinkable for 20 years. For those with strong teeth, an iron constitution and a sincere admiration for well-developed biceps. I nearly said not for me; but perhaps the 1870 Lafite was like this at six years of age.
At Geoffrey Roberts's tasting, March 1980 (*****)

Ridge, Chardonnay. I have had several good Ridge Chardonnays. This is the most recent note: fairly deep straw yellow; good but expected a stronger varietal flavour; medium dry, fairly full bodied and rather fat. Seemed to me to lack length and finesse — reminded me of a Châteauneuf-du-Pape blanc.
The opening wine of a dinner at Brooks's, June 1977 ***

Stag's Leap Wine Cellars, Cabernet-Sauvignon. This is the winery that caused the first great stir at a most heavily reported comparative tasting in Paris, their 1973 beating even top growths from Bordeaux. All France trembled. The '74 is even better. First tasted by me in 1976. Next, one of five '74 California Cabernets unfairly pitched against five '74 classed-growth clarets. (Unfair because '74 was a great vintage in the Napa but indifferent and uneven in Bordeaux.) However, by any yardstick it was excellent, coming out top: 19½ points out of 20; opaque, deep coloured to rim; a most attractive bouquet, peppery (alcohol) raspberry, Napa earthiness; touch of sweetness, full bodied, rich, velvety, perfectly balanced. Years of life ahead.
At the Elsevier-Bouquet tasting, October 1979 ****(*)

1975 ***

Firestone, Pinot Noir. A relatively new vineyard. This vintage was from the first crop of Pinot Noir and struck me as having a recognizably good burgundy style, a good nose, soft, pleasant weight and flavour and excellent value at £38 per dozen.
*At Geoffrey Roberts's tasting in London, March 1980 **(*)*

Freemark Abbey, Cabernet-Sauvignon. For me, the best Cabernet at a big range of recent vintages tasted in London: very deep; nose minty, fine, but still dormant; lovely weight in the mouth, delicious flavour and aftertaste. A bargain at £52 a dozen.
*At Geoffrey Roberts's tasting, March 1980 ***(*)*

Freemark Abbey, Chardonnay. Nice bright straw yellow; fruity nose laced with lemon and vanilla; dryish, ripe, refreshing acidity, lovely aftertaste.
*At a Les Amis du Vin tasting tutorial, Miami, March 1978 ***

Hoffman Ranch, Mountain Range, Pinot Noir. A very fine deep colour with rich legs; deep, fine, fruity nose, excellent, clearly Californian; very sweet and soft. Luscious and caressing. Far more successful than the '75 Cabernet-Sauvignon which lacked finish.
*At Denman Moody's dinner, April 1980 ***(*)*

Stonyhill, Semillon de Soleil. A development of Eleanor McRae, more akin to a Coteaux du Layon than Sauternes: good, sweet, waxy Semillon nose; sweet, soft, likable. Not long but complete.
*At the May's, Napa, May 1979 ***

1976 **

Beaulieu Vineyards, Beaumont, Pinot Noir. To demonstrate how enormous these wines are when young: very deep colour, a powerful-looking wine; deep, rich ripe Pinot aroma; a big wine, packed with flavour and component parts. Quite unready. This is the sort of wine that makes recent vintages of even the finest burgundy look pale and puny. But comparisons are dangerous and it is easy to overlook the delicacy, finesse and subtlety of the old-world wines. Like saying Wagner is better than Mozart. There is another important point: availability and price. This '76 B.V. Pinot Noir sold for up to $240 a dozen ex-cellars in 1978. Virtually unobtainable now.
*At Heublein tastings in 1978, May 1979 *(***)*

Freemark Abbey, Edelwein (Sweet Johannisberg Riesling). Not the first vintage of this highly successful new type of wine, but the most recently tasted: full golden colour, viscous/heavy legs; sweet botrytis nose; seemed a trifle fatter than the Phelps wine, good acidity and length. Stunning wine. It put a quite good German *Beerenauslese* (at the same price) into the shade.
*At a Wine and Food Society tasting, April 1980 *****

Heitz, Chardonnay. Three months in large oak casks, one year in small oak barrels, bottled January 1978. A pronounced yellow colour though not deep, yet already with a lovely golden sheen — perhaps it was the shaft of Californian sunshine through the winery window; nose at first seemed gentle yet rich, like wind-blown grass, but underneath, bursting to get out, was deep Chardonnay fruit and great vinosity; dry, lighter than the '74, firm, lovely texture, slightly short on the finish.
*Tasted at the winery, May 1979 ***

Joseph Phelps, Late Harvest Johannisberg Riesling. Another example of these excellent new "botrytised" Rieslings: bright yellow gold; very rich, honey sweet botrytis nose and flavour; intense, lovely.
*At Geoffrey Roberts's tasting, March 1980 *****

Mayacamas, Late Harvest Zinfandel. The latest and most recently tasted vintage of this wine: opaque, mulberry rim; incredibly rich nose, ripe, almost cheesy; dry, high in alcohol, concentrated and immensely impressive. One bottle enough for a dinner party of 12, with cheese.
*At Geoffrey Roberts's tasting in London, March 1980 *(***)*

Stag's Leap Wine Cellars, Cabernet-Sauvignon. A deeply impressive wine, drier and more severe than the '74. Came out top again, fractionally ahead of Ch. Mouton-Rothschild.
*At the Elsevier-Bouquet Cabernet tasting, October 1979 **(**)*

1977 **

Carneros Creek, Pinot Noir. Grown in one of the cooler areas, clearly right for this grape. A medium plummy red, not yet mature; at first sniff I thought it was one of those chocolaty burgundies, but it had more of a citrus fruit character, very fresh; slightly sweet, very flavoury with good acidity and aftertaste.
*At Denman Moody's dinner in Houston, April 1980 **(**)*

Chateau St-Jean, Gewürztraminer. I have never been much struck by the California Gewürztraminers. They seem to lack the true character and spiciness of the French or German original. This is one of the exceptions: bright straw yellow; really deliciously spicy aroma; medium dry, lovely flavour and length — rather a better finish than many Alsatian Gewürztraminers.
*At Geoffrey Roberts's tasting at Christie's, November 1978 ***

Freemark Abbey, Chardonnay. A nice style: good colour; nice oak on the nose; dry, good quality, persistence and finish.
*One of the four best of a number of Chardonnays at Geoffrey Roberts's tasting, March 1980 ***

Joseph Phelps, Chardonnay. Good oaky classic nose; nice flavour.
*At Geoffrey Roberts's tasting, March 1980 ***

Spring Mountain, Chardonnay. Positive colour; good nose; buttery style.
*At Geoffrey Roberts's tasting, March 1980 ***

1978 ****

Chalone, Chardonnay. Good yellow colour; high-toned waxy nose; soft, nutty finish.
*At Geoffrey Roberts's tasting, March 1980 ***(*)*

Heitz, Cabernet-Sauvignon. Deep and very purple; aromatic, crystallized violets, great depth of fruit; slightly sweet, fullish, rather jammy.
*Tasted from the cask at the winery, May 1979 *(***)*

Heitz, Chardonnay. Pale; high-toned vanilla nose; dry, very flavoury but still young and raw.
*Tasted from the cask, May 1979 **(**)*

Inglenook, Cabernet-Sauvignon (Cask Reserve). Characteristic Napa depth of colour, plummy purple; still dumb but good fruit; dry, full bodied, slight iron tang, rich.
*Tasted May 1980 *(**) Possibly a future ****

Stag's Leap Wine Cellars, Chardonnay. Lemon yellow colour; a more fruity, less oaky style of wine; dryish, good middle flavour and lovely smoky Chardonnay character on the palate.
*At lunch with the owner, Warren Winiarski, May 1979 ****

AUSTRALIAN

W I N E S

Australia — in its entirety — is surely the most wholly wine-conscious country in the world.

The industry is old, dating from early 19th-century penal-colony times; it is also extensive. But over the past 15 years the scene has been totally transformed. If California's new-found eminence has been due to the personality and effort of wine makers, technicians and connoisseurs, it can be fairly said that in Australia the wine renaissance has been to an extraordinary extent due to one larger-than-life personality, Len Evans: chairman of wineries, wine merchant, the most senior of all the wine judges, prolific writer — you name it, if it is to do with wine, he has, or has had, a hand in it. Other outsize characters include Max Lake, a doctor, vineyard owner and wine scholar; great born-to-the-job wine makers such as Murray Tyrrell in the Hunter Valley; sixth-generation aristocrats of the Barossa such as the Hill Smiths, and a great mixture of old-timers and newcomers.

Every daily and weekly newspaper has its regular wine column; each of the many local radio stations broadcasts regular wine programmes, and there are even wine chat shows on television (compèred, of course, by Len Evans). Moreover, the many wine and food societies of Australia are, in my experience, the keenest and most knowledgeable. In short, I am enthusiastic about Australia and its wines.

Vintages
Strangely, the word "vintage" does not appear in the index of *The Great Book of Australian and New Zealand Wine*, and I suppose it is well-nigh impossible to summarize the vintages in districts so widely dispersed across a great continent. So, far be it from me to rush in where even the ubiquitous Evans fears to tread.

Tasting notes
To many Englishmen of my generation, Australian wine used to have a medicinal, iron-tonic-in-a-screw-top-flagon connotation. A few interesting wines cropped up at tastings in the 1960s, but it was Hugh Johnson who first introduced me to Grange Hermitage, the great Coonawarras and to the old muscats. Then in 1978 I visited Australia and, in six weeks, visited most of the major wine areas mainly with, or with introductions from, Len Evans.

I have noted just a few of the most interesting wines tasted and have tried to describe the various styles. It is impossible in a paragraph or two to do justice to the immense range of types and qualities produced in Australia. One class of wine stands out on its own: the muscats, and these are dealt with separately in the sherry and miscellaneous fortified wines section.

For the sake of consistency, the following notes are arranged in vintage order, but therein the selections are arbitrary.

1872

Sunbury Hermitage. From an old wine district near Melbourne. Bottle ullaged, low shoulder. Colour medium, old tawny red; very deep and rich bouquet, touch of muscatel (I was told it might have been Lambrusca); dryish — still enough body, lovely flavour — more burgundy than Bordeaux in style. Considering its age and ullage, very attractive.
Just before the 1825 Gruaud-Larose at Len Evans's great old-wine dinner at Bulletin Place, Sydney, February 1977.

1946

Mount Pleasant Florence Riesling. The wine was from Pokolbin in the Hunter Valley. Though called Riesling it was made from Semillon grapes (pronounced SEM-1-LON) and smelled and tasted like an old Chardonnay — which just shows how complicated Australian wines can be. Made by the great Maurice O'Shea: deep, old-gold colour; subdued but deep and rich fumed-oak bouquet; dry, lovely — a great unsung hero from the less wine, conscious past.
Just one of a range of great classics served at a poolside lunch given by the late Victor Gibson, Melbourne, March 1977 *****

1954

All Saints' Shiraz. Deep mature red; wonderfully rich fruit; slightly sweet, full bodied, very rich, alcoholic, Rhône-like character. Marvellously warm and soft. Excellent finish.
At a Wine and Food Society of Victoria dinner at the Melbourne Club, March 1977 *****
Chateau Tahbilk Shiraz. Fairly deep; wonderfully rich Shiraz "sweaty saddle" nose; rich, soft, slight tannic iron finish. Like a husky farmer from the outback in retirement.
At a Primary Club tasting, Sydney, March 1977 ****
Tulloch's Pokolbin Private Bin. I think this was a Shiraz: very deep plummy-brown colour; fine classic nose; slightly sweet, ripe, rich, slight iron taste, excellent aftertaste.
At a Viticultural Society of Victoria lunch, March 1977 ****

1956

Hardy's "Vintage Port". Although out of place in this section I thought Hardy's port-style wines excellent and this one outstanding: very deep red; nose and palate packed with fruit and flavour; very sweet, fine peppery finish.
Tasted at the winery near Adelaide, February 1977 ***(*)
Saltram's Cabernet. Possibly with some Shiraz in it. Deep, fine, mature mahogany red; a bit closed up on the nose, alcoholic; medium dry, full bodied, packed with flavour, extract. A magnificent wine.
Lunch with Mary and Peter Lehmann at the winery, Angaston, February 1977 ***(*)
Seppelt's Great Western Chasselas M.14. A classic, made by one of Australia's great wine makers, Colin Preece, in Victoria. Still pale in colour, slightly lemon tinged; smoky/oaky bouquet, almost Chardonnay-like; bone dry, crisp, very attractive white burgundy flavour. Very fresh for its age but a bit short.
At an Amitié Gastronomique dinner, Melbourne, 1977 ***

1959

Lindeman's Hunter Red, Bin 1590. A classic:

medium, mature; earthy, slightly volcanic nose; dry, medium body. Very flavoury, elegant, lovely finish and aftertaste.
At Len Evans's, February 1977 ****
McWilliams Shiraz. From late-picked grapes at the Rosehill vineyard. Fine deep mature red; nose toasted, Rhône-like, developed beautifully in the glass; similar flavour, tangy but soft. Dry finish.
Tasted at the Mount Pleasant Winery in the Hunter Valley, February 1977 ****

1962

McWilliams Show Sauternes. Made of Semillon grapes plus a touch of old Muscat. Rich yellow, slightly green tinged; incredibly rich mint-leaf bouquet; medium sweet, fat, fragrant, more like Coteaux du Layon than Sauternes. Very complex. Lovely finish.
At the Royal Agricultural Society of N.S.W. annual competition, February 1977 *****
Penfold's Grange Hermitage. Hugh Johnson brought a bottle to taste in 1972. This opened my eyes to the great Australian classics. Still deep, with an opaque centre, mature rim; a marvellous scent — gentle, earthy, most beautiful; dry, fairly full bodied, yet exquisite flavour, balance, finish and aftertaste.
Last tasted at Grange, Adelaide, February 1977 *****
Chateau Tahbilk, Cabernet-Sauvignon. Amazingly deep, practically opaque, still purple; after the colour, strangely delicate bouquet, complete, scented, harmonious; slightly sweet on the palate, full, rich, dry finish.
At the Amitié Gastronomique dinner in Melbourne, March 1977 ****

1966

Penfold's Grange Hermitage, Bin 95. Bottled in 1967. One of Australia's great classics, equivalent to a Heitz Cabernet or Château Latour: enormously deep red, opaque in fact; nose packed and peppery; rich entry, dry finish, full bodied — a huge velvety wine with a touch of iron in the taste.
Dining with Len Evans, February 1977 ***(**)

1967

Leo Buring's Shiraz, Cabernet Res., OR.Bin 225. From South Australia: deep, fine coloured, lovely mature rim; bouquet complete, beautiful, slightly peppery; very rich, lovely flavour, crisp, excellent finish.
At a Viticultural Society lunch, Melbourne, March 1977 ***
Penfold's Coonawarra, Kalimna Shiraz, Bin 7. Aged in small oak, bottled January 1969. Deep, plummy nose and flavour. Soft, yet high acidity. Very dry finish.
Lunch at Rothbury, February 1977 **(**)

1968

Lindeman's Hunter River White Burgundy, Bin 3470 — these bin numbers add to the complication of names. Roughly speaking, the more numerals the more special the wine. Positive buttery yellow; smoky/oaky vanilla nose — from oak not from any Chardonnay: the wine was made wholly from Semillon grapes. Dry, austere, a good white burgundy style. Excellent quality.
Tasted February 1977 ****
Lindeman's Burgundy, Bin 3700. Made by Carl

Stockhausen at Ben Ean. Deep but mature; an incredibly rich, leathery/iron bouquet — the real Hunter Valley Shiraz "sweaty saddle" smell, which takes some getting used to. Flavour to match. Full of fruit. Wonderful wine.
At a Primary Club tasting held in Sydney, March 1977 ★★★★★

1969

All Saints', Cabernet-Shiraz. A gold medal winner: lovely plummy-red colour; attractive but curious nose, mulberry-ripe, slightly pungent "thoroughbred-stables" smell and taste — presumably the acidity.
At the attractive old winery in N.E. Victoria, March 1977 ★★★

1970

Brown's Milawa, Late harvest Rhine Riesling. Made from ripe botrytis-affected grapes. The most attractive of a wide range of very good wines: a pronounced yellow colour; distinctly flowery bouquet and flavour; medium sweet, rich but lightish and fresh. (The 1962 was sweeter, more powerful.)
Tasted at dinner and then at the winery, March 1977 ★★★★

1971

Gramp's Orlando Rhine Riesling Auslese. Gramp's started making *Ausleses* in 1964. This was the finest of an excellent range of vintages: deep buttery yellow; lovely fruit, honeyed ripeness and bottle-age; medium sweet, rich, lovely flavour and balance.
At the winery in the Barossa Valley, February 1977 ★★★★★

1972

Leasingham, Cabernet-Sauvignon, Bin 49. From the Clare district of South Australia: deep, purple edged; wonderfully rich, scented, Cabernet-Sauvignon bouquet; medium dry, fullish, great depth of fruit. Excellent.
At a Primary Club tasting, Sydney, March 1977 ★★★★(★)

Rothbury Estate Hunter Valley Red. The best liked of a range tasted at the winery: very mature looking; fabulous bouquet and flavour; Cabernet character, fruit and body. Yet soft.
Tasted February 1977 ★★★

Wynn's Coonawarra Cabernet-Sauvignon. A Wynn's estate wine, 100 per cent pure Cabernet. Lovely deep mature colour; very fine rich nose and flavour, full bodied. A tangy taste that reminded me of seaweed.
Tasted February 1977 ★★★★

1976

Brand's Laira, Cabernet-Sauvignon. Intensely deep and purple; concentrated and peppery Cabernet aroma and flavour. Very dry, very full bodied, firm. A great future.
Tasted at the winery, February 1977 ★★(★★)

Lake's Folly, Chardonnay. First tasted in Max Lake's surgery, then at his winery in the Hunter: lovely yellow colour; fine bouquet; medium dryness and body, fabulously expanding rich flavour, smoky, arguably the best Australian Chardonnay — a wholly recent development.
Tasted February 1977 ★★★★★

Gramp's Orlando Steingarten, Rhine Riesling. Pale and bright; delicate, peach-like, ripe bouquet; dryish, light, delicate, lovely flavour and end acidity. Quite delicious.
At the winery in the Barossa, February 1977 ★★★★

Tyrrell's Chardonnay. First tasted at the André Simon Centenary Dinner of the New South Wales chapter of the Wine and Food Society. Next, at the winery. Later, a great success at the International Wine and Food Society convention in London: pale at first, deepening a little; a clean, nutty, pure Chardonnay aroma, scented, light honey; dry, nice weight, most excellent flavour and finish.
Last tasted October 1977 ★★★★

A P P E N D I X

Aquitaine Society. A very active dining club based in Northampton. Established in the 1950s. Sir Anthony Alment, a noted gynaecologist, has been my host on a number of occasions.

Barolet. There were several tastings before the precedent-creating Barolet sale in the autumn of 1969. The first, in the courtyard above the cellars, was with Harry Waugh in October, followed by pre-sale tastings for buyers in Paris, Geneva and London.

Berkmann dinners. A series of excellent wine dinners given by Joseph Berkmann, a notable London restaurateur, the first being "an English Dinner with a selection of 1945 clarets" including all the first growths, followed by several at which a wide range of vintages of one first growth were served. I think I attended the entire series, which consisted of Latour, 14 vintages from 1917 to 1962 (in 1973); Margaux, 13 vintages from 1807 (in 1971); Mouton-Rothschild, 12 vintages from 1893 to 1955 (in 1972); Haut-Brion and La Mission-Haut-Brion. Each was attended by the owner of the château in question. Fellow guests included Harry Waugh, Edmund Penning-Rowsell, Quentin Crewe and other leading English writers and tasters.

Blayney's. This was the swan-song of a fine old North Country wine merchant. A group of us gathered in Newcastle upon Tyne for one of the most notable dinners ever. We drank Mumm '28, Montrachet '53, Pichon '34, Calon-Ségur '29, '28 and '23, Pétrus '07, Langoa-Barton 1878, Filhot '29, Yquem '21 and ended up with some port: Boa Vista '29, Graham '08, Tuke '04 and Dow 1878. As a nightcap we had an 1839 Malvasia. Our host, Bob Blayney, now growing vines in the Channel Islands, did us proud in July 1967.

Bordeaux Club. There are six members. We meet four times a year. The club was founded in 1949 and current members are: Michael Behrens, Professor Neil McKendrick, Professor Jack Plumb, Lord Walston, Harry Waugh and myself.

Bremen tasting of Pauillacs. Two old-established wine merchants in Bremen, A. Segnitz & Co. and Reidermeister & Ulrichs, decided to put on a tasting consisting entirely of Pauillacs as they felt that the Gault-Millau tastings, where wines of different districts and different classes were mixed at random, were unfair. The tasting, in September 1977, was very well organized and highly instructive.

Cambridge University Wine and Food Society. Regular tastings and dinners organized by undergraduates. I have given a number of tasting tutorials for this society over the past few years.

Charrington vintage dinners. Stylish and spectacular occasions with great wines and notable speeches, at Claridge's in October 1968, Café Royal in 1969 and elsewhere.

Châteaux sales. A series of spectacular sales for various Bordeaux estates in the mid- to late 1970s gave Christie's clients the opportunity not only to buy vintages unobtainable under normal circumstances but, at the pre-auction tastings, to compare unrivalled ranges of vintages. The Rothschild sale in June 1975, for example, enabled us to taste Lafite *and* Mouton of every good vintage from 1945. There was the huge Cordier sale in September 1976, at which 56 vintages of Gruaud-Larose from 1825 were sold, also Talbot from 1924 and 38 vintages of the Sauternes, Lafaurie-Peyraguey. Château Latour followed in June 1977 with a prestige sale of 81 vintages from 1863. The largest range was from the private cellar of the Woltner family at Château La Mission-Haut-Brion, in December 1978. Other smaller but interesting sales — and tastings — consisting of many vintages from the Châteaux Magdelaine, Trotanoy, Pontet-Canet, Lafon-Rochet, Ducru-Beaucaillou, Haut-Batailley and Grand-Puy-Lacoste.

Coq Hardy. I have had several memorable meals at this renowned restaurant at Bougival: the most quietly sumptuous being two luncheons hosted by Peter Palumbo: the first in November 1969 to taste Lafite (*en magnum*) and Yquem a century after each had been made; the second in 1974 to drink the 1874 Lafite. Most recently, with Steven Spurrier, at a tasting lunch of Romanée-Conti wines.

Decanter tastings. Organized jointly by *Decanter Magazine* and Christie's to promote, illustrate and inform. The subjects being individual châteaux, of which a range of vintages are tasted and commented upon.

"Drink Tank". A facetious title for a no name luncheon group — fellow regulars include Lord Rothschild, Michael Tree, David Somerset and Woodrow Wyatt.

'45 Club. A relatively short-lived enterprise started by David Allan, a London wine merchant, with some well-planned dinners and excellent wines at places such as Gravetye Manor.

Gault-Millau. A successful monthly wine and food journal, published in Paris and noted for its highly critical reviews of restaurants, food and wine. M. Gault and M. Millau have held two major tastings with international panels: one on red Bordeaux, in October 1976, and the other, "The Olympiad of Wine", in May 1979.

Hepworth trophy. Presented by Anthony Hepworth to the winner of the annual competition organized by the junior branch of the International Wine and Food Society, whose team engages in blind tastings against Oxford, Cambridge and other universities.

Heublein pre-sale tastings. Wide-ranging tastings held since 1969 in various cities throughout the United States prior to the annual auction of fine and rare wines. These are extremely well organized by the Wine Companies of Heublein Inc., and are conducted by the auction director Alexander C. (Sandy) McNally, and myself, the auctioneer.

Lebègue tastings. Organized by Guy Prince, these were the most notable annual events in the British wine-trade calendar in the 1950s: mammoth in size, magnificent in quality and spectacular in setting — candlelit, in Lebègue's cavernous London cellars.

Leroy tastings in Burgundy. The dynamic Mme Bize-Leroy organizes annual tastings in September to which leading French restaurateurs, wine journalists and other wine professionals are invited. A large number of notes on the tasting of Nuits St-Georges spanning 50 years, which I attended in September 1979, appear in the text.

Masters of Wine. The most highly qualified wine professionals in the United Kingdom who are formed into an institute which runs occasional comparative tastings.

Northern Wine Society. A tasting and dining group founded in 1961 by young Manchester and Liverpool wine merchants. I was invited to be its president and attended functions for a number of years.

The Overton tastings. Two of the most ambitious and successful tastings I have ever taken part in were organized by Dr Marvin C. Overton, a neurologist and dedicated wine buff from Fort Worth, Texas. The first was a tasting of 47 vintages of Ch. Latour from the period 1899 to 1972, held in May 1976; and the greatest, in May 1979, consisted of 36 vintages of Ch. Lafite representing every decade from the 1790s to the 1970s. I was privileged to conduct both tastings, the first with Henri Martin, director of Ch. Latour, and the second in the company of Baron Elie de Rothschild, Cyril Ray, Hugh Johnson and other distinguished amateurs and professionals.

Oxford and Cambridge wine-tasting competition. An annual match of palates organized by Harveys of Bristol, which I have helped umpire for a number of years.

Oxford University Wine Circle. Members are undergraduates who organize frequent tastings and dinners. Notes have been extracted from tasting tutorials that I have conducted for the Circle roughly once a year since the early 1960s.

Saintsbury Club. Undoubtedly the most prestigious dining club in the United Kingdom, founded in 1931 by a small group headed by André Simon in honour of Professor George Saintsbury. The membership consists of 25 men of wine and 25 men of letters. The club, which has a notable cellar, meets twice a year at Vintners' Hall.

Schloss Vollrads. A tasting of wines of the world to celebrate the 80th birthday of Graf Matuschka-Greiffenklau, held in the orangery of the estate in April 1973.

Studley Priory. A hotel in Oxfordshire that organizes wine weekends.

Taams tasting of 1961s. Twenty great growths of the 1961 vintage, all from the cellars of Dr John Taams, a Dutch connoisseur, were tasted by an international panel in May 1978.

III Form Club. The senior wine-trade tasting club founded in 1948. Four tastings and a dinner each year. I joined in 1968.

Vintners' Club, San Francisco. A club founded by Jerome C. Draper, with premises in the centre of San Francisco. A very active group of amateurs and professionals meet every week at the club to taste blind a wide range of European and California wines.

Waterloo dinner — September 1976. A dinner arranged at Christie's on the eve of the sale of the cellar of the United Service Club, of which the first Duke of Wellington was a founder member. The present Duke was my guest of honour. Co-host was one of my senior partners, the Hon. Patrick Lindsay. Other guests were Timothy Sandeman, whose ancestor, George Sandeman, dined with Sir Arthur Wellesley (later the Iron Duke) in 1809, Dennis Wheatley, the novelist (an ex-wine merchant and collector of Napoleonic mementoes), Peter Palumbo, Colonel Norman Johnstone and Hugh Johnson, who came dressed in an ancestor's red officer's jacket of the period. The wines: Bollinger '66 and '49; Corton Charlemagne '72 and Ch. La Tour Martillac (blanc) '29; Ch. Cantemerle '53 and Ch. L'Evangile '28; a "cock" of Sandeman 1897 — the star of the evening; Wenceslaus de Souza Guimaraes 1815 port and an 1809 Cognac.

Wiesbaden "Versteigerung Deutscher Spitzenweine". Every ten years there is an outstanding auction of the finest German wines. Each wine is tasted before the lot is sold. Notes extracted from the tasting in the Kurhaus, Wiesbaden, in April 1969 appear in the text.

Wine and Food Society. Founded by André Simon in 1933, now known as the International Wine and Food Society, with branches across the world. Any Wine and Food Society tastings mentioned in the text were conducted by myself on behalf of the society, or as a member of the Wine Committee, which I joined in 1968, taking over the chairmanship from Harry Waugh in 1979.

Wine magazine dinner tastings. *Wine* magazine was founded after the war, edited in the mid-1950s by Tommy Layton and reached its height of popularity and success under Kathleen Bourke's ownership. I was closely connected with the magazine from the mid-1960s, particularly with a regular series called "Will you dine with a Master of Wine?"

INDEX